NILE

LAURIE DEVINE

SIMON AND SCHUSTER · *New York*

Copyright © 1983 by Laurie Devine
All rights reserved
including the right of reproduction
in whole or in part in any form
Published by Simon and Schuster
A Division of Gulf & Western Corporation
Simon & Schuster Building
Rockefeller Center
1230 Avenue of the Americas
New York, New York 10020
SIMON AND SCHUSTER and colophon are registered trademarks of
Simon & Schuster.
Designed by Irving Perkins Associates

Maufactured in the United States of America

10 9 8 7 6 5 4 3 2 1

Library of Congress Cataloging in Publication Data
Devine, Laurie.
    Nile.
    I. Title.
PS3554.E92817N5   1983   813'.54   82-16960
ISBN 0-671-45170-7

Grateful acknowledgment is made of permission to include the following copyrighted material:

"People in My Country" by Salah 'Abd al-Sabur as published in *Modern Arab Poets*. Copyright © 1950, 1975 by Three Continents Press and Issa Boullata, Washington, D.C., Three Continents Press, Washington, D.C., 1976. Used by permission.

For my mother and my father

People in my country are ferocious like falcons
Their singing is like a winter tremor in the top of trees
Their laughing sizzles like fire in the wood
Their footsteps want to sink in the earth
They kill, steal, drink and belch
But they are men
And are good-hearted when they have a handful of coins
And they are believers in Destiny. . . .
—SALAH 'ABD AL-SABUR

1 ~~~~~

KOM OMBO, EGYPT / September 1945

The day Um Mona dreaded dawned clear.

Huddled on her haunches, she waited for them to come for her child.

The sun had not yet climbed over the rough red hills to the right of the river, but already it was hot, humid, heavy, so that even the birds were too tired to sing.

Um Mona, the mother of Mona, had not slept that night. Wearily she had watched for a sign that either everything was right or all was lost. But she had seen no scorpions walking backward, no fire leaping from cold stones, no bare-breasted spirits of the river gliding past her door.

Her tar-black eyes flicked over the bleak bareness around her and came to rest on nothing. Everything, including herself, was black or brown. Her robe was black. Her vast quantities of skin were muddy brown, nearly the same color as the hard earth under her dirty brown toes. The walls of her house and courtyard were the same soily brown. The iron bars on the open windows were black. The thick wooden door that sealed house from lane was weathered to the color of mud. In a corner rested a brown short-handled broom made of the dried tan tufts of date palm. Beside it sat a brown water jug baked of mud. Nearby lay an iron cooking pot encrusted to a burned black-brown. Under it were ashes of black.

Um Mona blinked as a big black fly landed on her eyelid. She brushed it away and sighed. The flies were up. The village must be stirring. She bent to the pot, stirred the ashes, lit the fire. It was almost time to wake her husband and her daughter.

Her legs were unsteady as she wobbled to her feet. She had been squatting for hours. Dawn sweat had already plastered her clothes to her body. *Malesh*, she said automatically to herself—"Never mind." It was always "never mind." And yet always she minded. Impatiently she pulled her red pantaloons away from her doughy thighs. She peeled her purple cotton housedress off her pendulous breasts. She smoothed her long black outer robe over her flabby belly. She was dressed in her best for this worst of days.

Maybe, she thought as she went inside, maybe it wasn't too late. Maybe there was still time to persuade her husband to cancel it.

Um Mona looked contemptuously down at Hassan snoring on the date-palm mat. Some women might envy her his tall good looks. But Um Mona knew Hassan was weak and unmanly. The only thing he had ever been good for was fathering her child. And now because he was the *Nubian* father of her child, they were going to maim Mona according to his tribe's primitive custom. Um Mona would have liked to kick Hassan very hard, but instead she nudged him with her bare foot. Like it or not, she might need him today. He moved away but did not wake, and so she hissed at him, "Hassan! Wake up, Hassan!" She stared at his half-open eyes. She knew how powerful he always found her eyes. It had been established on their wedding night that she could do almost anything with him when she held him with her eyes. "Hassan!" When he blinked dumbly up at her, she hissed again, "Get up!" His eyes were glued to hers, but he shook his head. "Hassan! They'll be here for Mona any minute. Get up!"

"*Malesh*," he muttered. "Never mind." He tried to turn away from her.

Um Mona crouched down and dug her fingers into his shoulder. She whispered so she wouldn't wake Mona. "I can't let this happen to her. They *can't* do it. They *can't*."

He squinted sleepily up at her. She was still carping about the circumcision. If it wasn't one thing, it was another. He thanked Allah that most mornings he didn't open his eyes to his wife. Most mornings he was away from the village, wending his way up and down the river on the barge. It was because he was home for a visit that his mother, who was even bossier than his wife, had decided they would perform Mona's ritual today.

"What you should be doing is thanking Allah you have a wife who cares about her child as much as I do!"

The whites of his open eyes were as round as eggs. She had always told him she could read his mind. "*Allahu akbar*," he mumbled—"God is most great"—invoking a perhaps greater power as counterweight to his wife's. Yet his thoughts trailed to the flesh. What eyes she had. He wondered if there was time, before the others arrived, to pull up her robes and—

"I told you, we must not do it."

Hassan sighed. Clearly there wasn't time. Even more clearly, she wouldn't allow it.

"Hassan!"

He wished it were possible to do as she asked so she would let him go back to sleep. Besides, he, too, would have liked to spare Mona the pain of the ritual. But it would have to happen sometime. The midwife had already been hired. His mother and sisters were doubtless about to arrive. Some of the food for the feast was already prepared. "No. I told you last night. We do it today."

"But *why?* Why do it at all?"

Preparing himself to repeat what he was sure she already knew, Hassan wondered if any other man in the village would have long ago beaten his nagging wife into submission. Maybe they would have . . . or maybe not. She was a powerful woman. He tried to be persuasive. "Mona's a girl. It's the custom. It will make her clean. It is what it is. *Tahara*—purification." More logic eluded him, for he could think of only one thing when she stared at him. Well, *that* had some bearing on *this*. "You don't want her to be wanton. To dishonor us. One day she'll thank us. Every girl is purified. It would be shameful not to. Even *you* had *tahara*. Even in your precious Karnak, they did it to you."

Her black eyes were scornful. "In my village they were *civilized*." Her black eyes were pleading. "But here they're going to *hurt* her. They'll take out too much. She could bleed to death. I heard about one little girl—"

"*Kefaya*," he grunted. "Enough."

"But Hassan, she's too young. She's only four and a half." Um Mona was wheedling. "Maybe we should wait. We can do it next year."

"We do it today." His tone was as final as the weight of seven thousand years of tradition. They had purified girls like this even in the time of the pharaohs. From Africa to Arabia they still did it to little girls who were Muslim and Christian and even pagan. Secure in the belief that what was to be done *had* to be done, Hassan pretended to drift back to sleep.

She curled her lip. She would pay him back for this. She would make him grovel for her. When it was just the two of them on their sleeping pallet, she would make this black-skinned, black-hearted husk of a man sorry. Her billowing black robe brushed dirt on his face as she swept by him.

Um Mona's anger turned to pity when she stood over her sleeping daughter. The frail little thing looked so vulnerable, curled up in a tight ball with her fingers in her mouth. The gutted remains of a candle lay in a puddle of wax next to her. Um Mona hadn't had the heart to blow it out last night. Mona was afraid even of the dark.

As she stared at her only child, Um Mona wished the little girl had never been born so that she could have been spared what was to happen today.

Mona's eyes fluttered open. Today as every day, she had eyes only for her mother. The first clear memory of Mona's life was her mother's ebony eyes upon her. Her mother's eyes missed nothing and judged everything. Sometimes it was hard not to burn up under their fire. Sometimes Mona saw those expectant, demanding eyes even in her dreams, and those were the nights that Mona woke up screaming. Especially she feared how her mother's eyes would drill into hers when they would watch a moth do its dance of death around the flame of a candle. Her mother always would say it was better for a bad woman to perish like that moth than to bring shame on her family. "Fire is better than shame," the mother and the daughter would nightly chant together. "Fire is better than shame." Mona had learned to fear the sight of a candle, the dying flutter of a moth's wings, the fierceness of her mother's eyes when she sang that song of shame. Mona had become adept at taking cues from even a flicker of those eyes. She would whimper when her mother's eyes narrowed with hate for her father's family. Mona would sigh sadly when they turned wistful for the village of her youth. And most of all, night and day, Mona would float with rapture when her mother's eyes radiated confirmation that she loved her. But now, looking up at the odd green flecks in her mother's mysteriously shadowed eyes, Mona could only be afraid. "Ummie!" Mona hurled herself at her mother and sank into the soft flesh of the breasts that had nursed her. "Ummie."

Um Mona bit her lip and held her child tight. Then, resolutely, she put the child at arm's length. It was better not to frighten her. "Today's your day. Are you ready?"

Her mother's eyes were smiling. Like a *gekko* lizard changing color as it creeps over a red flower, Mona smiled. Ummie's lightning mood change seemed to require enthusiasm, and so Mona recited what she had been told would happen today. "I get to wear my robe. And my veil. And eat sweets. Will we have dates?"

"Of course. And I'll put kohl on your eyes and more henna on your skin. You'll be a beautiful bride."

"Beautiful!" Mona laughed and clapped her hands.

Um Mona traced her daughter's dimples with a fingertip. Mona was already beautiful. Her father had given her high cheekbones, full lips, a straight nose. But instead of his kinky hair, hers was very dark and wavy and full of reddish luster. Too, in her his coloring had muted to dusk. She was the shade of almonds, of honey, of *café au lait*—of rich, ripened wheat, ready for the harvest. But the best of Mona was her eyes. And, Um Mona thought with a great rush of possession, *I* gave her those. It was true that Mona's eyes were not black but amber. And that they were fringed with furry smudges of lashes. But otherwise their eyes were alike: just as lively, certainly as arresting, surely the identical catty shape that brought to mind tomb paintings of slave girls dancing for Pharaoh. Total strangers, as they looked Mona over, said the girl was too pretty for her own good. They told Um Mona to dress her daughter in rags and smear dirt on her face so that the envious Evil Eye would be tricked into passing over the child. But Um Mona had been too proud of her daughter's beauty to heed those warnings.

When an imperious knock sounded on the courtyard door, Um Mona gave the child a final desperate hug. "Just remember. You are my *habibti,* my love. Mine. All mine. No matter what you—"

Again the knock. Um Mona wished she could hold her daughter forever. She wished she could always and evermore protect her from danger. She wished her a lifetime without tears. She wished . . . The heavy knocking rattled the door.

"Wait here." Um Mona kissed her once and then padded out to the courtyard. That would be Hassan's womenfolk cackling away in that curious Kenuz dialect of the Nubians. So what if they didn't think she rushed out to them fast enough? Worse was going to happen this morning. Um Mona prayed a quick "Allah!" under her breath as she flung open the door.

The four women stood swathed in filmy, ghostlike white robes and mantles. Um Mona despised the way Nubians draped themselves in white for feast days. It was just one more of their affectations. Nubians, Um Mona was always the first to insist, were at least technically Egyptian. So their skins were a little darker and their builds a little leaner? So they claimed to be cleaner and more honest? So they came from the southernmost, most barren outreaches of Egypt? Did that give them the right to look so peculiar? In Um Mona's home village, women were always more modestly and most appropriately covered from hair to toe in black. Defiantly, Um Mona still flaunted the Karnak fashion.

Hassan's mother and sisters sneered at Um Mona's black robe, yet inside the courtyard everyone observed at least minimal social niceties. In a tone that was not quite sincere, Um Hassan, the mother of Hassan, inquired after her daughter-in-law's health. Um Mona blandly praised Allah. Um Hassan praised Him, too, and went on to complain about the continuing aches in her legs, her arms, her back. Um Mona nodded as if in sympathy. Her eyes, however, were full of malice. She could think of no one who deserved to suffer more than her mother-in-law.

Hassan's sisters were abustle. Suffra was taking inside the cakes and sesame paste and flat loaves of wheat bread she had brought for the feast. Wahiba was brewing a huge vat of tea. Naima had seized the broom and was raising clouds of dirt from the dirt floor. As usual, the in-laws had taken over.

When Um Hassan called loudly for her son, he came trotting like a well-trained dog to its master. The two embraced, Um Hassan cooed, and Hassan was flushed when he peeled himself from his mother's embrace. He rearranged the soft folds of his new white robe. All the men—Nubians as well as Egyptians—wore these *gallabeiyas* that fit snugly through the chest and shoulders and then belled out becomingly to the ground. Hassan preened for his mother.

To Um Hassan, her only son looked as grand and graceful as one of those rare ancient Nubians who had ruled all Egypt as Pharaoh. Or a warrior. Her son was as straight and tall as the fiercest Nubian fighter waging war from time immemorial, for and against the Egyptians, the Romans, the Arabs, the French, the Turks, the British. But then, remembering today's mission, she turned gaily to Um Mona. "The bride. Where's the little bride?"

Um Mona sullenly inclined her head toward the house.

"Asleep? At this hour?" Um Hassan shook her head. "You spoil the child."

"So you've so often said." Um Mona led them grimly inside to Mona.

The child moved as if to embrace her grandmother. But when Um Hassan did not respond, Mona bent and touched her forehead to the old lady's fingers.

Um Hassan nodded regally down at her. "I suppose you know why we've come."

"For me!"

Everyone but Um Mona laughed, and then there was another knock at the door. Before they could answer it, in strode the *daya,* the midwife who ushered every woman through each of life's traumas. Today, as always, Shaykha Sameera made an entrance, taking possession of the compound as surely as a blue-eyed river *dogri* could take over the spirit of an unwary sailor. Everything about the *shaykha* was striking. She had blue tattoos on her cheeks, an old-fashioned silver ring through her nose, and sheep's fat smeared on her hair. Shorter and fatter than any other woman in the village, the *shaykha* resembled no one—or nothing—so much as the ferocious imp-dwarfs that decorated the Temple of Love down the river, to the north, in Dendera. Small wonder that she was the most popular *daya* in Kom Ombo. Her daily bread depended precisely on the awe, respect, and fear of women who sought her at their births and at their deaths, women who in between asked her not only for charms to ward off the Evil Eye but also talismans to make their men touch them more—or sometimes less. She nursed the women when they were sick and reaped the rewards of their well-being when they were not. For Shaykha Sameera was aware her power rested not so much in her medicine as in the women's belief in it. And since she more often than not delivered what she promised, their belief and her power had swelled from year to year. If Shaykha Sameera was a witch, she most assuredly was not a wicked one.

The *shaykha* firmly refused Um Mona's repeated offers of tea and breakfast. What she had to do today was not to her liking. She would do it not only because it had to be done but also because someone else would do it if she didn't. At least she would do it well, and quickly, so that it didn't hurt the child as much. She gave Hassan a look of dismissal, for what was to happen was not the business of men. When he scooted off for the village coffeehouse, the *shaykha* patted Mona's head. "You can paint and dress her now."

Suffra handed her mother the green henna that would turn a rosy orange when applied to the skin.

"I've painted her," Um Mona said. Mona's face, hands, and feet glowed with the burnished gleam of henna.

As if she had neither seen nor heard, Um Hassan proceeded to dab the childish toes and heels and the squat fingers and palms. She rubbed a thinner coat on Mona's thin face, torso, and limbs. Mona wriggled with delight, tingling not only to the pleasant slide of the dye but also to the unusual caress of her grandmother.

Um Mona applied the gritty black kohl with a finely pointed stick. Artfully she outlined her daughter's eyes, making the upper lines thick and voluptuous, the lower lines seductively thinner.

"Ah!" Hassan's sisters exclaimed.

Um Mona smiled. Even the in-laws had to admire her daughter. Mona, painted to resemble a bride, undeniably would someday outshine every woman in this village. It was a mystery to Um Mona how such a one could have come from her and Hassan—or, for that matter, from anyone mortal.

The *shaykha* cut off such ruminations with a series of quick commands to the three sisters. "Suffra, you bring the egg. More henna. The bowl. The thorns. The hollow reed. And the ropes." Um Mona started to sweat. "Wahiba, you heat the incense." The sweat sapped under Um Mona's arms and breasts. "Naima, you heat the knife." The sweat was rolling down Um Mona's body and clinging to her clothes. "Um Mona, you cover the child." The mother's skin was all sweat.

Woodenly she lowered the bright-red robe over Mona's glowing golden body. Slowly she arranged the sheer white veil and shawl over her face and hair. Tenderly she touched Mona's cheek.

Mona pirouetted in front of her mother. "Ummie! Ummie! Look, Ummie! Am I a beautiful bride?"

Wisely, Um Mona avoided her daughter's eyes. When the heavy sweet smell of incense began to pervade the room, Um Mona caught Hassan's mother looking at her with genuine sympathy. For once the daughter-in-law and the mother-in-law were not at odds. Of course, Um Mona thought. Of course. Um Hassan, herself the mother of three daughters, must have endured this ritual three times over. When Um Hassan put her arm around her, Um Mona did not resist.

As the curling clouds of incense swirled, the *shaykha* told the women to pray the opening chapter of the Koran. The red of Mona's robe gashed and glared against the aunts and the grandmother in white, the midwife and the mother in black, all chorusing the familiar words:

> "In the name of God, the Merciful, the Compassionate
> Praise be to God, the Lord of the Universe,
> the Merciful, the Compassionate,
> the Authority on Judgment Day.
> It is You whom we worship
> And You whom we ask for help.
> Show us the upright way:
> the way of those You have favored,
> not of those with whom You have been angry
> and those who have gone astray."

Mona tugged at her mother's robe for recognition that she had remembered most of the words. When her mother stared back without blinking, Mona shrank away from her aunts and grandmother and that ugly dwarf doctor. Ummie's eyes had signaled danger.

At an impatient jerk of the *shaykha*'s hand, the aunts removed the child's robe and veil. For the last time in her life Mona stood free, unfettered, whole, and somehow pagan-proud. But as one of her aunts seized her arms and the other two her legs, Mona screamed. "Ummie! Ummie! What are they doing!"

Um Mona took one rushed step but was held back by the iron grip of Hassan's mother.

"Ummie! Ummie! Ummie!"

The aunts eased the child flat on the floor. Um Mona mutely clenched and unclenched her fists while the aunts pulled Mona's legs wide apart until they had her trussed like a chicken.

"Ummie!"

Kneeling between the girl's legs, the midwife was a grim caricature of an eager lover of the too-far future. With a callused finger the *shaykha* probed Mona's soft cleft, finding first the deep furrow, then the flowery bud, finally its sweet center that was smaller than a drop of water, larger than a grain of sand. The *shaykha* gave the tip of the clitoris a final twitch of a caress. "Hold her very still."

Um Mona tried to look away.

The next movements were as quick as they were irrevocable. The knife gleamed for an instant, then descended. The first cut neatly severed the tip of the clitoris.

"No!" The scream was Um Mona's.

Before Mona's surprised, agonized wails could fill the room, the *shaykha* neatly rooted out the pink membrane that had nestled the clitoris. She dug out all of it she could find, for the raw wound was already slippery with blood. She cut out a bit more here and there, slicing blindly now, bloody up to her knuckles. She caught the severed sexual tissue in a bowl.

Um Mona sank to the floor by her child. Frantically she stroked her hair and wiped the sweat from her brow. But she could not blot Mona's pain.

Hassan's sisters tried to drown out the shrieks of the mutilated little girl by letting loose with the shrill, unearthly trill of the *zaghareit*—"*Ayyouy! Ayyouy! Ayyouy!*" Wise men say this is the most joyful sound that can issue from the throat of woman, yet there is wild outrage in *zaghareit*. "*Ayyouy! Ayyouy! Ayouououya!*" Still Mona's wails, as they continued to hold her splayed open, were louder than the ritual cries. "Come, you are a woman now," chanted Suffra. "Bring on the groom," sang Wahiba. "Bring her a penis," whispered Naima. "You become a bride. You become a woman," sighed Um Hassan. "*El-hamdulillah!*" Hassan's mother and sisters shrieked—"Thanks be to God!" Shaking as if convulsed, Mona screamed on and on while her mother tried to soothe her with a rhythmless melody that was both lullaby and curse.

The *shaykha* continued to work. She dribbled the wound with a raw egg to speed the healing and smoothed on green henna to ease the hurting. Mona writhed more at the touch of the yolk and the dye than she had at the stab of the knife. She tried to touch herself, to touch what had been herself. But her arms were still pinned back. "Hold her," the *shaykha* ordered. "It is not finished." She drew together the remaining skin between the child's legs, took a handful of well-washed thorns, and sutured expertly. She inserted a hollow reed between the stitches so that, for now, the child would be able to pass water. Later the opening left by the reed would drip her menstrual blood. In less than a minute the *shaykha* had not only excised every trace of the dangerous membranes but also had sealed up the path to the womb. It would take another incision by another midwife before any man could penetrate Mona. "Now the ropes." Of necessity, the *shaykha* tied them cruelly tight at Mona's thighs, knees, and ankles. The ropes would have to remain for forty days and forty nights, so that what was left between Mona's legs would become safe as safe could be: a chastity belt of blood, skin, and shame. Sighing as she went to wash in the courtyard, the *shaykha* prayed to Allah to heal the child.

Um Mona rocked her daughter as the aunts and the grandmother shrieked over them like a Greek chorus. Finally Hassan, who had been unable to stop himself from running to answer Mona's cries, slipped into the room. His wife and daughter looked miserably up at him. Mona was still sobbing under the smudges of henna, kohl, and tears. She reached for her father but then hesitated, shuddered, and tunneled into her mother's body as if she wished she had never left it. Um Mona held her fiercely. "*Emshee!*" she snarled. "Get out of here! All of you! Out! Leave us be!" At a quick nod from Um Hassan, the Nubians scurried from the room.

Um Mona sat staring into space as she gingerly cradled her child. She wondered, and not for the first time, how she could have endured these four long years so far from home, alone with these strange dark people. Although Hassan had been her only chance for a husband, she regretted marrying a Nubian. It wasn't fair that the men in Karnak had refused to marry her. It wasn't fair that Hassan had done so only to repay a debt to her brother. So *much* wasn't fair. It wasn't fair that after she had traveled the one hundred and fifty kilometers southward up the Nile to Kom Ombo, her husband's family had bullied her. It wasn't fair that they ignored her daughter. It most of all wasn't fair that she had to follow these outlandish Nubian customs. None of it was fair. Um Mona's heart was as heavy as the incense-laden air. She remembered a time, not so long ago, when life had not been so difficult. She could remember when she herself had been held by her own mother —Mona was her namesake—just as she was holding Mona now. That was before everything went wrong. That was before her own mother had met her own savage woman's end. Um Mona looked down at her daughter, naked and slick with sweat and pain. This wasn't the time to mourn the Mona she had lost. She should be comforting the one she still held. Gently she folded Mona up in the fabric of her own robe, black over gold, mother one with daughter.

"Ummie," Mona whispered. "Ummie, Ummie, Ummie."

"I'm here, daughter. I'm here."

"I hurt, Ummie. I hurt."

"So do I. So do I."

They sighed closer to one another, but then Mona pulled away.

"Ummie?"

"Yes."

"Why did you let them hurt me?"

"I tried to stop it. But I couldn't."

"You could have. You could have. You can do anything."

"Your father wouldn't let me stop them."

"Baba? He wasn't even here. But *you* were. Aren't I a good girl, Ummie? Don't you love me?"

Um Mona answered with a kiss on her lips.

Mona cringed. "It hurts, Ummie! Stop it!"

"What happened today, Mona, was the will of Allah." As always when she repeated that commonplace, Um Mona thought not of Allah but of the Nile, the mysterious, powerful, inevitable river. Like the will of Allah, the river rose and fell. Neither responded much to human prayers. But when Mona whimpered again, Um Mona forgot what she had been about to explain about the will of Allah and the sweep of the river. Instead she sought to reassure Mona with the power of her own love. "Do you remember what I told you, Mona? Before they all came today?"

The girl seemed to brighten. "About the dates?"

"No, silly. About us. About your being my little girl." Um Mona tightened her hold. "You will always be my little girl. We will always be together. And I will always take care of you so that no one hurts you."

Mona's eyes strayed down to the wound between her legs. She looked back up at her mother.

That reproach slashed Um Mona. She tried to think of words to restore what might have been forever cut. But Mona was crying again in sobs as regular and as rhythmic as breathing. Holding her, Um Mona decided it was better not even to try to explain the inexplicable to so young a child. Perhaps all Mona would understand was her touch. She stroked Mona's hair very gently. "There, now. Do you feel better?"

"No. Yes."

"The others are waiting to form the procession."

"For me?"

"For you."

"Will they hurt me again?"

"No. Not ever. Never again. I promise."

Mona stared doubtfully at her mother. Ummie had let them hurt her today. She veered away from scary thoughts about what else Ummie might let them do to her if she wasn't good. Mona licked her lips. Ummie always smiled when she fed her. "Can I have dates?"

It was easy to grant that. *"Habibti,* my love, a little later you can have as many dates as you want." When the child's tears were dry, Um Mona dipped a clean cloth in the jug of water and wiped away Mona's blood, sweat, dye, and kohl. Ever so carefully she slid on the red robe so that there was no sign of the thin shackled legs. Um Mona frowned at the contrast of that sad face above the scarlet robe. Um Mona re-applied the kohl, but this time under the cosmetic Mona's eyes were dead. To warm the ghastly pallor of Mona's cheeks, Um Mona hastily smeared on more henna. Now Mona looked like a pitifully painted old woman. *Malesh,* Um Mona muttered to herself. Never mind. It would have to do. There remained only the laying on of the extra veils: a bright-blue one over Mona's head, a sheer gold one over her face, the final heavy white one shrouding all. Before she summoned the others, Um Mona's eyes sought to penetrate the bundle of swaddled cloth. Her voice was low. "I know you hurt, *habibti.* But you must not cry. Not now. Not later. Never. Never cry, Mona. Don't let them know how you hurt! Don't say a word to them! Now and always, you must be strong for me, brave for me. *I* didn't want this to happen today. *I* was against it. *I* didn't want them to hurt you. You're safe with me. Safe only with me. Remember that. And remember something else. Try,

Mona, try! The pain you feel now will go away. But the reason for it won't. They hurt you so you won't ever bring shame to your family. As if you could! As if *you* could shame *me!* We aren't like them. We aren't Nubians. We are Saidi, Upper Egyptians. We will deny them our tears. *Saidi!* We have the blood of the pharaohs!"

"Saidi!" Mona sat as tall as she could.

Um Mona hugged her one last time, then called to the others. "Come. The bride is ready."

Hassan's three sisters fluttered in and continued their rapid-fire gossip over Mona's head.

"Did you see Aisha moping? She's still not pregnant."

"Poor thing. She's been sailing back and forth, from one bank of the Nile to the other, every day for a month, trying to start something in her belly. It's a wonder she hasn't worn out the river."

"Worn out her husband is more likely."

"Maybe *she's* not the problem. Maybe it's Gemal's fault. Maybe he can't *do* it."

"Or maybe he likes donkeys better."

"Aisha looks part donkey."

"They say that's why he married her."

Like very small girls, they held their fingers across their mouths as they giggled.

Um Mona regarded them as if they came from a different and lower species. Sex and babies, sex and babies. There had to be more to life than just sex and babies.

As the sisters began fussing over Mona, Um Mona wandered outside into the broiling late-morning sun. The courtyard was chockablock with knots of Nubian women and children who had gathered to celebrate Mona's circumcision. Some, like Hassan's mother and sisters, had yard after yard of white sheeting draped over all but their faces. Others had merely topped their brightly patterned housedresses with their best sheer navy-blue street robes. Children clothed in reds and purples and very bright greens toddled from cousin to aunt to grandmother. Infants suckled at breasts. Sweat coursed down shining faces. As the flies buzzed about in clouds, the women bragged about their triumphs and joked about their woes. A daughter had—*el-hamdulillah!*—found a husband. A son was still looking for a wife. The cataracts on this one's eyes were worse. But that one's sore joints miraculously—*el-hamdulillah!*—hurt no more. This one, that one, and *that* one over there were once again pregnant. But Aisha, the skinny one over in the corner, was still barren. Voices dropped to a whispering hiss. It was said her husband was threatening to take a second wife. Heads shook and tongues clucked in dismay. Fingers touched blue beads to ward off the Evil Eye. But then frowns turned up in grins. The story was repeated about Gemal and the donkey. As they talked with their hands and threw back their heads in coarse brays of laughter, Um Mona studied the flash of white teeth against dark skin.

That novelty—those very white teeth and that very dark skin—still fascinated Um Mona. Skin color was, after all, the most obvious difference between herself and these Nubians in her courtyard. Um Mona's people, the farmer-peasant *fellahin* of southern Egypt, were seldom darker than the light-brown mud along the banks of their Nile. Nubians, however, had skin as brown as chocolate and as black as pitch. But the distinction between Nubian and Saidi cut deeper than skin. In her own village, Um Mona had known little about the Nubians except that she was better than they could ever hope to be. Since long before the beginning of recorded time, Egyptians had overshadowed their nearest neighbors on the Nile. Nubians served in the armies of Egypt and under Egypt's changing masters. They worshiped the varying Egyptian gods, from the pharaonic Amun to the Christian Jesus to the Muslim Allah. Yet the Nubians were still faithful to many of their old ways.

As Um Mona sourly surveyed her unwelcome guests, all that mattered to her was the brutal way these Nubians had maimed her daughter. It wasn't that Um Mona was against female circumcision. She had to admit that some sort of *tahara* was necessary. Otherwise Mona might end up floating in one of the green Nile canals with her throat slit from ear to ear. Um Mona shuddered. It seemed it was either cut the girl a little now or maybe much more later. A girl had to be protected against the dangers of her own wild sexual nature. If a girl wasn't tamed by circumcision, someday—maybe inevitably—she could be compromised by a man who wasn't her husband. And then her father or brother or son would be forced to avenge family honor by killing the wayward woman. No, Um Mona thought, *tahara* was for Mona's own good. What she couldn't accept was how far the Nubians went to assure female virtue. She hated how they had sewn and bound Mona so that a midwife would have to slice her open again on her wedding night. In Karnak they simply scissored off the tip of a girl's clitoris so that she would be *nuss wi nuss,* half and half—just a little bit sexy. That way Mona maybe could have more than endured the endless hot summer nights of her married years. Um Mona would have liked her daughter to have the chance for wild wedded ecstasies. Even with simpleminded Hassan, there had sometimes been midnight passion. Um Mona sighed. She wished she could go and rock Mona to sleep. But the circumcision rites would drag on for hours.

Um Mona looked around the courtyard. As usual, Hassan had his head together with his mother, carefully watching the Koran teacher record the circumcision gifts being dropped off by kinfolk and neighbors. Perspiring in the growing heat, they followed every tight squiggle of the old man's hand: dates from this one, wheat bread from that one, tomatoes from another. Um Mona watched the pair nodding as sagely as if they could understand what the scribe was writing. Tch! The document was a travesty. Hassan's mother would never forget who brought what, and Allah help anyone who hadn't contributed her share! Um Hassan looked up as her cousin's wife sauntered past their open door as if there were no party within. Um Mona saw her mother-in-law dig her fingernails sharply into Hassan's arm. The old lady would be wracking her brain for ways to repay her cousin's wife for the insult.

Um Mona snapped to attention. In the hot blur of the sun she had almost forgotten she had come outside to ask the *shaykha* about Mona's wound. What if she hemorrhaged or burned with fever? As Um Mona edged toward the circle of women surrounding the *shaykha,* she recalled what was whispered about the old *daya.* Many, many years ago, when the *shaykha* had been simply Sameera, she had been accosted at the river by a band of soldiers bound for the Sudan front. They had been Delta men, unused to dark Nubian skin. So they had stripped her to get a better look, and then one of them had raped her to get a better feel. While the rest of them were lining up politely for their turn, Sameera had seized the soldier's spear and run it through his neck. Then she had aimed that spear at the other men so that their courage fell along with their desire. But what was bewitching about Sameera was what had happened next. Armed with the gore-soaked spear, she had told the village women she had been possessed not only by the soldier but also by the spirit of the Nile king, who had given her the strength to avenge her honor. The price of the royal intervention was that she become the Nile king's bride and nevermore be touched by mortal men. Sameera was later seen diving deep in the river, presumably to visit her spirit husband. And it was whispered that she emerged from the depths of the Nile as dry as dust.

Shortly thereafter the women began coming to "Shaykha" Sameera with wishes and fears and leaving with dreams and hopes. Um Mona didn't know how much—if any—of the story she *should* believe. She did know that, this time, she was no different from any of the other women in Kom Ombo. Um Mona *wanted* to believe—and therefore mostly *did* believe—every word of Shaykha Sameera's wondrous transformation of shame into glory.

Um Mona was near enough now to overhear the women besieging the *shaykha.* Nezla, that eccentric Nubian who always wore those clanking silver ankle bracelets, was beginning a story: "I dreamed, may God render it good and blissful . . ." Um Mona was annoyed. If the woman was going to relate one of her endless dreams, Um Mona might have a long wait for her turn. "I was walking down by the river," Nezla continued, "with my water jug—that big brown one that's so heavy . . ." Um Mona folded her arms against her chest and tried to be patient. ". . . when all of a sudden I felt a fresh, hot wind coming from the leaves of that giant sycamore tree. You know the one? The one near where we always wash our clothes? I thought you'd know the one. It was when I was there, in my dream, that it happened. Out of the burning wind that came from the leaves of that big tree walked a young handsome man. He was wearing a green silk—I think it was silk, yes, a green silk—robe and turban. He took my hand, set down my water jug, and spoke to me gently by name. He stroked back my hair. And then—so soft, so soft!—he touched my breasts. It was then that my eyes opened. Shaykha Sameera, I beg you. What does all this mean?"

By chance Um Mona met the *shaykha*'s eyes. It wasn't so very difficult to read what was in them. Nezla was lonely. Her husband, like most Nubian husbands and sons, lived and worked far from home. Since the Ottoman Empire's Turkish overlords had seized the best of the meager Nubian lands hundreds of years before, Nubia's men had been forced to feed their families by living apart from them. The pattern held in Kom Ombo, even though these Nubians had been forced to resettle on this richer land after the British raising of the Aswan Dam flooded their ancestral lands. In this courtyard today, there were at least seven women for every one man. Um Mona didn't have to know Nezla to know her story. Her husband was probably a servant up in Cairo. He probably sent her money every month and came to visit maybe every year. Nezla probably had many dreams like this one. She, like her sisters in the village, was part of a frustrated women's culture that revolved around absent men. Um Mona wondered how much of this the *shaykha* would say.

"No doubt you were visited by the spirit of a man who once loved you—and still does love you." Shaykha Sameera ignored Um Mona's smirk and made her voice as sonorous as a seer's. "He comes to you from Allah Himself, for he wears the green silk of Paradise. Visit me later. Perhaps, with the help of Allah, we can summon back the man of your dreams."

Um Mona had to admire the way the old witch got what she wanted from all of them. Perhaps that had always been the *shaykha*'s secret. Maybe all she did was twist superstition to her own advantage. There might be some way she could use the same technique to help Mona.

But as the women were gasping and Nezla was nearly swooning with pleasure, Um Mona snorted to herself. Nezla was a fool for such dreams. But Nezla was a fool anyway. They were all fools. And they all got just what they deserved. Um Mona couldn't understand why they all made do with so much less than they wanted. How could they laugh as they did, when inside there was so much deep sadness and so many broken dreams? Often Um Mona tried to puzzle out the riddle not only of their lives but her own. Everyone worked and worked and worked, and yet it never made any difference. No matter what anyone did, no matter how good anyone was, it never counted. The remaining men of the village could work and worry over their crops from sunup to sundown, and still all that mattered was whether the river happened to rise or fall. Some of the best of the men had given up caring long ago. Instead they simply planted their crops, settled under a palm tree, and waited for their seeds either to sprout or to wither. Always they greeted either result with the same "thanks be to God" on their lips. For them, maybe, it was either be passive or go crazy. Um Mona wondered if she was crazy—if she was the real fool—for not giving up like the rest. Yet she couldn't *not* care. She might go mad, but she would keep on trying. She opened her mouth to ask the *shaykha* what she could do for her Mona. But then she heard the sounds of the drum, the lute, the flute. Mona's procession was forming.

First came the two strapping cousins of Hassan who would carry Mona on a cotton sling balanced on their shoulders. The two of them clowned to the beat of the music, tossing the empty litter this way and that, as if today's business were not tragedy but comedy. The three musicians, too, looked farcical in their high red turbans and their brilliantly striped blue and green and brown *gallabeiyas*. In the lead the drummer set the processional pace by slapping the *darabukkeh* tied around his neck. Stepping smartly behind him was the lute player. As he strummed the large, shapely *oud* held against his chest, the man's bloodshot eyes roamed the crowd as if he wished he were strumming some of the women instead. Bringing up the rear was the *mizmir* man, his double-reed flute screeching like the harsh whine of a bagpipe.

Silencing them all with an imperious sweep of her hand, Hassan's mother appeared to be about to orchestrate the remainder of the ritual. If, Um Mona thought, there were any sensational circumcision rites in the depths of the Nubian past, Um Hassan would be sure to resurrect every single one of them today. Um Hassan barked out commands to her daughters. "You, Suffra, go put the bride on her throne. And make sure she's covered up so she won't humiliate us. Wahiba, you'll carry the water pitcher. Take enough this time. It's a long walk, and we don't want the bride fainting on the way. Naima, get the incense. And try to heat it up right for once." Hassan's mother turned to Um Mona. "You're supposed to carry the bowl of the bride's blood. But we all know what a delicate *fellaha* you are. So," Um Hassan's voice rang out, "*I'll* carry the blood. You stay in the back with the other women."

Um Mona's own blood rushed to her head. There was no limit to the woman's insults. Um Mona's black eyes burned. But she wouldn't provide these Nubians with an open fight that would keep their tongues wagging over endless glasses of tea. Without Hassan's support, Um Mona could never win against her mother-in-law. Yet Um Mona stared at Um Hassan as though the hot lids of her eyes were nailed to her brows.

The *mizmir* man sounded a flourish, and Hassan's cousins carried out the clump of cloth that was Mona. On the stretcher the child sat tall and proud as if, Um Mona thought, angels just above her head drew her up by invisible strings. The sun caught the gleam of her veils and sparked the scarlet of her robe, so that the blue-gold veil was like a flame above the blood-red wick of the robe. At once the assembled women broke out into trilling *zaghareit,* their ululations carrying over the courtyard wall and all through the village—*"Ayyouy! Ayyouy! Ayyouy! Ayouououououya!"* Their hair-raising shrieks rose and fell as the sun bore down without mercy.

Hassan's mother stepped to the head of the procession and held the bowl of Mona's sexblood so high that it seemed she wanted to boil it. The cousins followed, jiggling Mona's litter painfully with their every lurching step. Wahiba carried the water jug as though it, too, were a primitive offering to the gods. Naima waved her brass pot of incense so that its heavy clouds would waft around Mona and chase away any evil spirits attracted by the blood of sex. The musicians banged, strummed, and whined. The *shaykha* headed up the herd of shrieking women, a silent Um Mona trailing among them. Out of the courtyard and into the sun, they marched toward the river.

Instead of taking the usual short steep path down to the Nile, Um Hassan marched them the entire winding length of the village so that no one would miss her parade. As the procession twisted and turned through the village lanes, its numbers swelled as women and children ran to join the fun. Under the Hagg's walls painted crudely with camels and boats and the mountains of Mecca, women and children linked hands and danced around Mona's litter. Very young girls gazed up at Mona with greedy envy, while older sisters who had already had their day on the litter flinched and looked away. "Speak to us, talk to us, sing to us, O bride!" chanted the crowd. But Mona, like her mother, was mute.

"Ayyouy! Ayyouy! Ayouououououya!" shrieked the women as they passed by the lacy spindle of the minaret. Inside the open doors of the whitewashed mosque old men lay sound asleep on date-palm mats. *"Ayyouy! Ayyouy! Ayouououououya!"*

Merchants waved and smiled as the procession wove past the single-story metal-and-mud storefronts of the souk. The women were always howling up and down the village. If it wasn't a birth, death, or marriage, it was a visit to a saint's tomb or a circumcision. Aware that business was always brisk when the fever of a procession finally broke, the storekeepers did their best to coax stray piasters from the women. The spiceman leaned out over his open gunnysacks of saffron and henna, cumin and coriander. The metalsmith raised a pot he was mending. The barber brandished his razor. The tailor frantically unfurled bolts of patterned cotton. The Greek grocer held up packets of wartime's rationed sugar. Yet despite these temptations to tarry and buy, Um Hassan kept her women marching, shrieking, dancing to the Nile.

On the final wide dusty approach to the river, the women radiated their own heat. They danced harder, they screamed louder, they pranced from side to side like demons possessed of the sun. They snaked past a skinny palm tree, a snoring old man, a braying tethered donkey, seedy dogs curled in wakeful balls, fields of baking clover and corn and wheat, water buffalo turning wheels that brought Nile drops from canals to ditches to fields. The cries of the animals mixed with the trilling of the women and the zigzag quartertone moan of the music.

They stopped once under the spreading shade of a lone sycamore to give Mona water and again to refire the incense and rub the sweat into their bodies. Mona's body drooped in the heat, but the little girl was as silent as she had been told to be.

As Um Mona trudged along, the sticky rubbing of her sagging breasts made raw meat of the skin over her heart. Once she stumbled, and the *shaykha* caught her before she could fall into the dust. After that the *shaykha* supported Um Mona in the crook of her arm, crooning to her under her breath like the mythical mother she tried to be.

At last, as they reached the Nile, the musicians sounded a crescendo. Sometimes the Nile was green and clear, sometimes black and swift, sometimes gray and still, sometimes blue and gleaming. Today it brimmed brown with the remains of its yearly flood. The harvest of sludgy soil from Africa's heartland made the current sluggish, as if the Nile were burdened with all the tears and lamentations of tribes long lost in slavery. The wide Nile—too wide here for a woman ever to swim—crept over the land in one last rush before curving far to the right and then to the left around the ancient dusty pillars of a temple to the crocodile and hawk gods.

At high noon the river swarmed with more activity than a souk. On the far bank, under the stark silhouette of date palms, a line of women balanced water jugs gracefully on their heads. Heavily weighted with the three fat wives of a merchant, a felucca tacked as its single sail billowed to catch the slightest hint of a breeze. In midstream on the deck of a barge sailors smoked lazily as they huddled in the folds of their robes. Skimming the crest of the water were watermelon rinds, discarded cartons, and, near the shore, rivulets of human feces. But the shallows up and down the banks were bunched with workers oblivious to the debris. Boys washed down a camel. Girls rinsed glasses and pots. Women spread laundry on rocks. Mona's parade seemed to sigh in satisfied unison. This bustling waterway that Egyptians called *el-bahr,* "the sea," was far more than a river. Without the Nile these fertile fields would be desert wasteland. For Egypt the Nile was bread and milk, mother and father, life and death. And so Mona's sexblood would be offered to this primeval force.

As the musicians settled back under a palm tree, the women fanned in a circle around Um Hassan and Mona's litter. There was a silence as Hassan's mother raised the bowl of blood to the sky and began to chant. "We offer to you, O Nile, the blood of this daughter of the Nile. Take and drink it, as we drink you. Our blood is yours, for you bring us life." She added an Islamic seal to this pagan prayer: *"El-hamdulillah, el-hamdulillah,* thanks be to God, thanks be to God." She paused for one dramatic moment and then threw the blood and the sexual tissue. A little stained a rock brownish red, but most floated in a scum atop the water.

There was a sudden flash of white as one of the women—Aisha it was—jumped into the water. This barren woman, terrified her husband would take another wife if she did not conceive, smeared what she could see of Mona's blood on her head, arms, and torso. Sure that now she could make her own baby, Aisha grinned and licked the watery drops of Mona's blood from her face.

As one, the watching women drew in their breaths. Sacrilege! Bad luck! This might even be an omen! The little girl's sexblood was being denied the river!

Um Mona waded furiously into the water. "Stop it! I curse you and all your family!" Um Mona knocked Aisha off her feet and held her head under the swirling water. "I'll show you what Saidi do to women like you!" Slipping and sliding on the muddy bottom, the two women grappled and thrashed. Aisha kicked Um Mona's legs out from under her. Um Mona pulled hard on Aisha's hair. Finally they were pulled roughly apart by a brace of women who had jumped to the rescue. All of them stood thigh-deep in the spreading current of Mona's blood.

On the bank, Shaykha Sameera slowly shook her head from side to side. This was a bad omen for Mona. Her sexblood should be shared only by the river spirits. It was dangerous to tamper with what belonged to the river. She looked over at little Mona, abandoned on the bank with her bound legs. The *shaykha* wondered about Mona's fate, about the fate of her children and her children's children. Shaykha Sameera was glad, suddenly, that she was old and would die soon. Life was hard, hard and cruel, and it was the hardest and the cruelest when you least expected it. It was as if you were given a beautiful sweet cake and then, just as you lifted it to your lips, dust came from nowhere and made it so bitter you had to spit it out in disgust. The *shaykha* sighed. Who was she to question the workings of Allah? She walked over and spoke softly to Mona. *"Malesh*—never mind, dear."

Still true to her vow of silence, Mona did not answer. She watched her mother being held under the water by her aunts. She saw her mother kick off the three of them and struggle toward Aisha. She watched Aisha wade clumsily out of the water and up the riverbank. She saw the swirl of sandy dust as Aisha retreated toward the village. Mona's eyes went back to her mother.

Um Mona raised a fist and shouted after Aisha. But then she remembered Mona. She staggered over and folded the girl in her wet arms. "Don't worry, *habibti,* don't worry. All this means nothing. Nothing at all." As Mona whimpered like a puppy that can't find its bitch's tit, Um Mona met Um Hassan's eyes. *"Khelas,"* she said. "It is finished."

Aware that her theatrical performance had aborted, Um Hassan shouted to the women still splashing about in the Nile, "Get out of the water, all of you! You look like *gamusa*—like big fat water buffalo! Have you forgotten why we're here?" With shamed faces the women paddled to shore, showing flashes of dark thighs as they wrung out their robes on the bank. Um Hassan had the blood bowl refilled with sweet water from midstream and then handed it over to Um Mona.

Carefully she lifted Mona's veils. Although the child's face was unblemished by tears, Um Mona dipped a cloth in the water. "With the Nile I wash away your woman's tears. With the Nile I purify you." Um Mona mopped the perspiration from Mona's face and neck, then patted her moist skin dry. "Now, you are a woman."

The cousins arranged Mona back on the litter, and this time, with somber haste, they took the short uphill route home. As Um Mona intertwined her sweaty hands with Mona's, the mother and daughter nearly gagged from the excess of incense in the air. The crowd of women grumbled that even so much incense was still not enough protection, for they knew that every *jinn,* every *dogri,* every river spirit from Aswan to Luxor was already out to get Mona. Fear made the women march faster. The musicians tried once to resume their beat, but Um Hassan stopped them with a hiss and a wave of her hand. Before the men left the procession, the drummer rapped out an ominous farewell, thump-thump, *thump-thump.* As they rustled along, their robes drying stiff and rough in the sun, the women were hushed. Behind high walls other women watched at peepholes, curious at the grim silence of this parade. Not so very much later they would learn the reason why this was, for what had happened to Mona at the Nile was to become the talk of the village. It would be debated—in long animated conversations over tiny cups of sweet black coffee and larger glasses of sweeter blacker tea—why Allah had allowed that sacrilege to occur. Some would say it was a judgment against Hassan for marrying a woman from outside the village. Others would blame Um Mona for tempting fate by spoiling her child. It was Halima, the spiceman's wife, who had the most fanciful of theories. Aisha must have been bewitched long ago, she said, by river spirits who had taken her for their own. Now, Halima said, the Nile spirits would take Mona, too, as a judgment against her wayward parents. Someday, Halima concluded as she helped herself to more tea, a *dogri* would swoop down and carry both Aisha and Mona home to their silver palace at the bottom of the river. Yes, as the *muezzin* prayer call echoed at sundown through the village— *"Allahu akbar,* God is most great!"—Kom Ombo agreed that what had happened in the river had cursed that poor little Mona.

Um Mona firmly shut the door on all this speculation. Tenderly she carried Mona to her sleeping mat and removed the child's veils and robe. "You can cry now. You're with me." Um Mona kissed away the tears that overflowed Mona's cheeks and checked what she could see of her wounds. There was no blood, but already the ropes had raised welts.

Mona avoided her mother's eyes. Whatever the reason for Ummie's letting them hurt her today, Mona didn't want to know it. Whatever the reason for Ummie's fighting in the river today, Mona didn't want to understand it. But she burned so between her legs. And those ropes . . . "I hurt, Ummie. The ropes. Untie me."

"I can't, *habibti.*"

"Please?"

"I'll get you some dates."

In her search for the sweet fruit, she found Hassan as near to white of face as he would ever be. "Wife! Is it true? Tell me what they say is a lie!"

She was in no mood for Hassan. "What happened, happened. It was the will of Allah."

"She is cursed. Mona is cursed. And so are we." Hassan was near tears. "What will I do? What will I say? Everyone is talking behind our backs. It's your fault. You should have stopped it. Aisha would never have done that to any child but yours."

"And yours." Critically she eyed his dirty robe. This was supposed to be her husband, her man, her protector. She turned away from him. She wasn't sorry he couldn't touch her for forty days for fear of evil *jinn* lurking near Mona's sexblood. It had been years since she had enjoyed him. The more she aged, the less he filled her up. She bent over a crock and grabbed a sticky handful of dates.

"What will I do? Mother will never forgive me."

That was the last straw. She turned on him. "Your mother, your mother," she mocked. "Forget her for once. Try acting like a man. If you can."

He hit her once in the face, again in the belly.

She never backed down when he hit her. "Is that the best you can do?" She laughed and clenched her hands so that the dates turned to mush.

He crumpled to the floor. "You don't understand. You *never* understand." He was sobbing. "Everyone will laugh at me. Laugh at us. I am shamed. I never should have married you."

"Then divorce me."

"No! No." He looked at her longingly. Even when she acted like this—maybe *especially* when she acted like this—she thrilled him. He could never give her up.

"Enough tears!"

He blew his nose on the wide sleeve of his *gallabeiya*. Surely she would have a plan. She always had a plan. He awaited her whiplike commands.

"We'll cancel the feast and keep Mona in the house. They're all probably too frightened to come here anyway. Give the circumcision food to the *shaykha* as alms for the poor. Then go sit in the mosque and act pious. They'll all think you've been touched by Allah." As Hassan brightened, she reminded him that soon he would be returning to his barge. "By the time you come back, they'll have forgotten this ever happened." She cut off his whining that his mother would *never* forget. But she allowed him one kiss on her cheek.

Back in the sleeping room she caught Mona trying to loosen the knots in her ropes. Pull and tug as she might, however, the bonds only tightened. Um Mona held out the handful of dates.

Mona pushed them away. "Dates are for babies. You said I'm a woman now. You said so."

"And so you are." Um Mona absently ate the dates, worrying all the while about what Hassan had said. What if Mona really *was* cursed? What if Aisha's jumping into her sexblood had put a terrible spell on Mona? It was possible. It was more than possible. Um Mona decided to work some magic of her own.

She dug with her fingers in the spot of loose dirt in the floor where she hid her meager treasures. In a moment she was opening the mother-of-pearl box that had been her mother's. In the palm of her hand she held the hollow turquoise wooden bead her mother had given her. It was a mystic bead. The mother of her mother of her mother had fished it out of the Nile. Her own mother had warned her this bead should be worn only in times of great danger, for the power of the bead was too strong for daily use. But *malesh*. After that scene at the river, Mona would be in eternal peril. Um Mona threaded the bead on a length of string and tied it around Mona's neck. *"Habibti,* listen to me. You must wear this always. Forever, Mona. Never take it off. Promise me, Mona."

Mona sighed at this latest demand. But the blue bead was pretty. "Always. I will wear it always."

"Now then," Um Mona said, "now we can sleep."

Obediently Mona tried to nestle by her mother. But she couldn't get close enough because she couldn't bend her legs.

Um Mona cushioned the child's head on the fat of her arm. Rigid with outrage that her child had to suffer so, Um Mona stared at the mudbrick wall. She wanted to make balm of her body. She longed to untie Mona's legs and fold her up close and safe. But how? How could she violate the custom? Her thoughts drifted to Nezla's dream. What did *that* have to do with *this?* A dream—yes, that was it. She would have a dream. She would say that someone—maybe the Prophet or Allah Himself?—had come to her in a dream and ordered her to untie

Mona's legs. Or should she say the Nile king visited her in a dream? No. That would be bad luck. And the others might question that the Prophet or Allah Himself would come to her in a Kom Ombo vision. She would have to make do with a saint, yes, a saint who had watched the scene at the river and had come to her in a dream. She would say this saint promised to rescue Mona from the river spirits if she untied the girl's legs and took the thorns from her skin. But why would the saint tell her to do that? To pray, of course. He would have told her to unbind Mona's legs so the child could salaam for Allah's mercy. Um Mona smiled at the wall and reached for the knife. But then she hesitated. Could there someday be a great price to be paid for the lie she would be making before Allah?

Mona groaned.

Whatever the consequences, Um Mona grabbed the knife and made three short cuts in the ropes. Ah, that was it. She had freed her baby.

Mona threw her arms around her mother's neck and sighed close to her. "Ummie! Ummie, you *do* love me! Ummie!"

Later Um Mona would remove those thorns so that Mona wouldn't have to be cut open by a midwife on her wedding night. But for now she was content to hold Mona tight and make a vow:

It will be different for Mona. It will be better for her than it was for me, and my mother, and my mother's mother. As God is my witness, *I*, Um Mona, will make it so!

2

ALEXANDRIA, EGYPT / *September 1946*

On this day, as on any other, the Pearl of the Mediterranean shimmered. The sun picked out the domes of the mosques and the peaks of the minarets. It glinted off the fairy-tale roofs of the king's summer palaces silhouetted against the sky at the water's edge. Alexandria sparkled in the sun, the soft blue sea washing up in its lap, the wind rushing through its alleys and its boulevards. Is-kan-*dree*-a, the Egyptians call it, the Arabic beginning soft and sibilant and ending in a lilt, as soft as the breeze wafting in always from the sea, not so much cutting the air as singing to it: *Iskandria.*

On a day meant for dalliance, on an afternoon meant for gossip and white wine and naps on the beach, Mona and her mother hunted without success for the Villa al-Masri and the Rue Fouad. They had sat up all night on the gritty Saidi train and then had nearly missed their Cairo connection. Disoriented from their eighteen hours of travel, they had stumbled off from the station in the wrong direction. They had wandered to the city's rowdy port to stare in wonder and fear at giant cranes backed up beside monster ships. Sweaty stevedores and crisp soldiers had howled curses in Arabic, English, French, Italian, and Greek. Um Mona and the little girl had hastily backed away from the piers only to find themselves amid banks of rubble left by the recent world war's German bombardment. They skirted the shameful sailors darting into the busy brothels and ambled past the sleepy Minet el-Bassal shacks where merchants graded fluffy cotton. Soon, amid the moldering Arab slum of Anfushi, the alleys bustled and seethed, the people jostled, the dust spun and danced, the colors clashed in a mix spicy enough to tear the eyes. Breathing to the beat of the raggedy rhythms, peeking down sooty dark cul-de-sacs, Mona searched under turbans for her father. Back in Kom Ombo last winter, she had heard the mourning shrieks when her father was lost in a freak storm on the river. But Mona had not quite understood. If she was alert, she thought, someday she would find her father, maybe even having coffee on this very street. But one man was too short, another too fat, yet another too light of skin. None of them was her Baba.

In downtown Alexandria, Mona clung more tightly to her mother's hand as clanging double-decker electric trolleys swung past on shiny steel rails. Well-dressed businessmen hurried by as though it mattered when they arrived. Street signs were lettered in the alphabets of the Arabs, the Greeks, the Latins, and the Hebrews. Gibberish rose from hundreds of throats. Fat white children clutched the spotless gloved hands of slim white women. On every corner sun-wrinkled men and smooth-skinned girls bargained, flirted, and cracked clever jokes. Inside Italian espresso bars old men who were the lonely dregs of the Mediterranean propped their elbows on pink Formica tables as they sipped cappuccino. Shopkeepers displayed fabulous goods behind unsmeared glass. Delicacies that had never passed the lips of Mona or her mother—rosy shellfish, brandied fruits, layered cakes—lay waiting on bone china in the sidewalk cafés.

Mona's eyes were so sore from rubbing and staring that she no longer looked to the right or the left. Intent only on holding tight to her mother, Mona cared only that she was exhausted and cold. It was midafternoon in the rump of summer, but still Mona was cold. Born and bred in the stifling Saidi heat, she shivered in the gusty Mediterranean sea breeze.

That same windy caress, however, was intoxicating her mother. Despite her weariness, despite her confusion, Um Mona began to prance the sidewalk, propelled by the fancy that there was magic in this giddy Alexandrian air. She found herself smiling as she passed soldiers on leave from their barracks, sailors on shore from their ships, families on holiday from the heat of the South. Cheap children's toys—balls and balloons and little wooden dolls—dangled in open stalls. Alexandria was so pretty and gay and frivolous that Um Mona started swinging her hips in time to music drifting from open windows. Seized by the need to cut to the heart of this city, she steered her daughter toward the salt smell of the sea. She pulled Mona across the Corniche and put down their parcels as though their journey were at its end. From where they stood along a curve in the serpentine coastline, they saw the sea as inviting as tepid water in a porcelain bathtub. That narrow promontory encircled snug Alexandria, Um Mona thought, as a mother holds her firstborn. Not to be outdone by nature, she swung her child up in her arms: presenting the sea to her daughter, offering Mona to the Mediterranean.

Um Mona took a deep breath. *Henna,* here! They were here. They were in vibrant, alive, heady Alexandria. It would be a good place, this Alexandria. Here there would be enough—no, more than enough. Back in the villages, back in Kom Ombo and all the rest of those dots along the Nile, the most a man or woman could dream of was enough water to survive. The rest of Egypt was parched for water. With an unquenchable thirst, the rest of Egypt gulps every drop it can swallow of its Nile. The rest of Egypt, swept by hot sandy desert winds, swelters in the sun. The rest of Egypt is a sickly losing struggle. But *here,* Um Mona thought as she looked out to the wide sea, Alexandria must be cleansed and transformed and redeemed by so much water. Even when no man casts a shadow on the hottest summer day, still here was the breeze and the sea. Um Mona had a thought. Maybe life might not actually be less cruel here than elsewhere in Egypt, but perhaps even the illusion was enough to make it so. It would have to be enough to save Mona.

Back in that hateful Nubian village, she had come close to losing her precious daughter. First that barbaric circumcision, then malaria, finally pneumonia. Um Mona had brushed aside Shaykha Sameera's advice to tattoo the child in lucky blue. Instead she had carried her wasted little girl to the new government clinic and listened to the doctor's cruel verdict. Mona, he had said, was simply too delicate for harsh village life. Her life would be sapped by the summer heat, the winter cold, and all that came in between. His advice had been to forget this child, marry again, and pray that the next time Allah would grant her a stronger one. At that memory, Um Mona leaned down and kissed Mona softly where her hair curled at her temples.

That doctor had not known how it was with her and Mona. They were not two but one. Mona was not replaceable. Her destiny, Mona's destiny, was one and the same. As a sacred relic, Um Mona still kept the bloodstained robe she had worn in blessed labor for Mona. No, that doctor had not known how it was. Finally, however, after much prodding, the doctor had admitted there was a possibility Mona might thrive if she was taken away from the village and given proper food and care in an abundant, temperate place like, say, Alexandria. No sooner said than done. Um Mona had two distant cousins who were maids in a rich Jewish Alexandrian household. It wasn't hard to pry what was left of Um Mona's brideprice from Hassan's grieving family, for they all believed Mona's curse had jinxed her father. Soon—today!—they would achieve Mona's salvation at the Villa al-Masri. Um Mona hugged the little girl. "*Henna!* Oh, Mona, we're here!"

Mona glanced obediently but uncertainly up at her mother. She moved her head slightly as if searching the sidewalk for a bed. With the unconscious calculation that a smile is more cunning than a scream, Mona aimed a pathetic little grin at her mother.

Um Mona sheepishly picked up their basket of clothes and food and once more balanced the weight of their world on her head. What if Khadiga and Fatima were no longer here? What if no one offered her work? What if she and Mona starved to death in this breeze that would soon turn to a frosty winter wind? Her step, as she led Mona past the graceful villas of salmon and peach and sun-colored stone, lost its bounce. Wearily, finally, they rounded the right corner. Above them, behind the lacy iron balustrades of the mansions of the very rich, came the murmur of well-bred foreign voices in well-versed foreign tongues.

On one such balcony, two boys sat trying to smoke their first cigarettes. Blond, brown-eyed Youssef al-Masri was pretending to dark-haired Hamid el-Husseini that this particular diversion was nothing new. The slim, filterless Soussa cigarette and the gold-plated lighter fit easily into Youssef's hand. Feet propped languidly up on the banister, face set in slightly bored and petulant lines, Youssef hoped he was the very picture of sophistication. "You should give it a go," he said in English. "Makes a man feel good after a meal." Youssef cocked his head and blew a creditable smoke ring into the clear air.

Hamid nursed his misgivings. He was always eager to mimic Youssef, but he feared he would disgrace himself for lack of practice. Hesitantly Hamid took a cigarette from Youssef's proffered pack, fumbled with the lighter, and then doubled over in a coughing fit.

"*Malesh,*" Youssef consoled him in Arabic. "Never mind. It is," he continued in English, "nothing more than smoker's cough. We all have it. *C'est la vie.*" Pleased that he had managed to pepper three languages into that one trite observation, he searched for an Italian phrase to round it out. Instead he contented himself with more Arabic: "*Khelas*—it is finished." With the drama of an eleven-year-old trying very hard to be weary of the world, Youssef rose and flung his cigarette over the railing.

The butt hit Um Mona smack on her hunched nose. She steadied her basket with one hand, rubbed her nose with the other, and raised black angry eyes to the boys staring down at her with all the inborn arrogance of elevated class. She felt the old familiar tug of rage. Always she was the despised outsider. Always she was the object of contempt. It wasn't going to be any different here than it had been in the Said. Not yet realizing this was the young master of the household where she hoped to work, Um Mona shook her fist at the blond boy.

Mona's head followed her mother's fist. Her eyes met Youssef's. She saw strange light hair and a smile that made her want to smile back. She couldn't stop from turning up the corners of her mouth.

"Pretty child." Youssef regretted his careless gesture with the cigarette and was glad it hadn't hit the little girl. "Some of them are so pretty when they're young."

"And some of them aren't so bad when they get older." Hamid laughed racily. Even at this tender age, Hamid was already training for a lifetime of the ladies.

Ever the prince, ever the master of the princely gesture, Youssef dug in his pocket for a coin. The glint of gold arced in the sun and fell where he wanted it to fall, at the feet of the little Arab girl. Youssef threw the child one more gracious smile before he realized he was late. He did not wait to see Um Mona scoop up the coin, bite it to see if it was real, then tuck it inside her black robe. *"Yalla,"* Youssef was saying to Hamid in Arabic. "Let's go." They were already late for the rowing club as well as the beach. They were always late. Everybody was always late. Alexandria was, after all, still Egypt.

Um Mona put her free hand on her hip and looked from that balcony to the street. They were where they were supposed to be: on the Rue Fouad, with gardens across the street and a busy traffic circle just ahead. Those boys must have been sitting on a balcony of the Villa al-Masri. Appraising what she hoped would be her new home, Um Mona decided this villa was a shade grander than its neighbors. Carved at intervals in the Villa al-Masri's stark white stucco facade were designs of grape leaves and garlands. Ribbons of intricate, shining grillwork wrapped around each balcony. Inside the first-floor windows she glimpsed the sparkle of crystal, the sheen of marble, the sweep of velvet. Um Mona sighed with anticipation and led the girl around to the back door. "Now stand up straight, Mona. Smooth down your dress. *Mabsoota*, Mona, *mabsoota!* Look happy! And don't talk in there! Say nothing! But smile, Mona, smile." She tucked Mona's unraveling braids back into place and then, for luck, touched the blue bead around her daughter's neck.

An old woman in a long black robe answered her knock with a *sabah el-khair,* good morning on this day of light.

"*Sabah el-ful.* It is the morning of jasmine." As Um Mona insinuated them inside the kitchen, she used similarly flowery phrases to wish Allah's blessings on the doorkeeper, on the walls of the villa, on all who lived within. She had come, she said, to see her cousins Khadiga and Fatima. The old woman called out the names.

"It's me!" Um Mona added. "Samahe. Abdullah's daughter. From Karnak."

The two maids stared from over their piles of dishes, then ran and embraced the newcomers. Khadiga was Um Mona's second cousin. Fatima was Um Mona's aunt's stepsister's niece. There was the quick, ritualistic exchange of Arab greetings, more kisses, and then Um Mona sank down on a stool to spin out her stories of the Said. Her plan was to spellbind her cousins with flattery and remembrances. Only later would she enlist them to help get her work in this villa.

As her mother gestured and laughed, Mona examined the largest and cleanest room she had ever seen. Shiny brass and copper pots hung neatly on whitewashed brick walls. Utensils lined up with intimidating precision on the tables and in the cupboards. The old doorkeeper put a bucket under a pipe, turned a knob, and—magically—water gushed into the pail. A door swung open, and an austere, alert Nubian swept into the kitchen balancing a silver tray on his fingertips. Like Mona's father's, his skin was very black. Like Mona's father's, his turban and teeth and robe were very white. She smiled up at him and forgot her mother's command to stay silent. "Hello," Mona said in her father's family's language. "My name is Mona. You look just like my Baba. He went away."

The Nubian's mustache twitched almost in a smile. "Where did a little girl like you learn Kenuz?"

"In Kom Ombo. With my father and grandmother and aunts and everybody. My mother likes Arabic better. But my father is Nubian. Are you?"

He nodded gravely and this time addressed her in Arabic. "I'm Abbas. I live here."

"Yes? Ummie says we're going to live here, too." Talking to this man was almost like talking to her father. "Baba's in Paradise. I was sick after Baba went away. Ummie says I would have died if we hadn't come here. But it's cold here. So cold."

Abbas took a shawl from a hook on the wall and wrapped it around her shoulders. "Are you hungry, child?"

"Yes. And tired. Very tired."

As Abbas led Mona to a table in the corner, Fatima shushed Um Mona before she could call back her child. Abbas, Fatima whispered, was the *suffragi*, their boss. It was best not to interfere.

He called out orders, and the old woman brought over leftovers from the al-Masri luncheon. Mona traced her finger on the pink and purple flowers painted on the china plate.

Abbas smiled. *"Bon appetit."*

"What?"

"French. It means to eat and enjoy."

"Bon abbeti." She had tried her best to parrot him, but there was no "p" sound in Arabic. Abbas laughed, Mona giggled, and then she turned to the sliced beef, the whole new potatoes, and the buttered carrots. She asked for bread so she could politely convey this feast to her mouth. Instead of the familiar, flat, hollow-cored *aish baladi,* Abbas gave her a tall loaf of bread shaped like a donut with a hole in the middle. It was clumsy scooping up the meat and vegetables in this crusty new stuff Abbas seemed to think was *aish.* But Mona proceeded as daintily as she could.

Abbas watched with amusement until she finished. *"Kwayes. Kwayes awi. Kwayes awi-awi*—that was done very, very well. And now to bed." She took his hand trustingly as they walked down a corridor into a small room Abbas used for his occasional afternoon naps. Nights he spent in the lean-to in the garden. It would have been bad form for an unmarried manservant—even a *suffragi,* even the butler, the head servant, the majordomo—to sleep under the same roof as the virgin servant girls. "You can rest here."

Mona looked around the floor for the mat.

"No. Up here. On the bed."

She stared at the padded platform. It was covered with white sheets. It had a pillow. "But it's so high. What if I fall off?"

"Allah and the angels will watch over you. They sleep up in the air, too." He pulled down a sheet and tucked her inside. "Now you sleep. You've come a long way for such a little girl."

"Am I home now?"

He kissed her in reply and stood smiling over her until she fell asleep. Then he squared his shoulders and headed back to the kitchen to reckon with the mother.

"I tell you," Um Mona was saying to her cousins, "the sickness was everywhere. The malaria was the worst, especially for the children. But —*el-hamdulillah,* thanks be to God!—ours . . ." She looked up at Abbas, whose arms were folded in the pose of a listener.

"Go on," he said.

Um Mona avoided his eyes, and Khadiga and Fatima filled in the silence.

"My cousin."

"And mine."

"From Karnak."

"Our village."

"I know." Abbas was pleased, yet again, to be one step ahead of his staff. "Finish your work now, girls. I would like to speak to our visitor before she goes on her way." He waited while the maids scuttled off and Um Mona collected her wits. Finally he prompted her, "You are Mona's mother."

Um Mona nodded.

"It was a long journey for the child. A long way for a gossip with your cousins."

Nervously she noticed the ashy smudge of a *zabeeba* on his forehead. This Abbas must pray fervently for his prostrations to have left behind the bruise of piety. She hoped this Abbas wasn't a fanatic. She hoped he would let them stay.

"Why did you come?" Oblivious to her shadowed dark needy eyes, he stood as impassive as the grim stone statues of Karnak Temple.

She moistened her lips. "To work. To work here. I want to work for you. I'm a good worker. Strong. I can cook and clean. I'm very clean."

He looked skeptically at the dirty spots on her robe.

She followed his eyes and then stared at the polished floor.

He sized her up. Sturdy, accustomed to working hard, she had planted those large callused feet on the floor as though certain she would take root here. She had shown considerable spunk in coming all the way to Alexandria. But grit was not what Abbas looked for in a servant. More to the point was that she be honest, pliant, docile. Abbas was willing to forgive certain shortcomings in his slaphappy, absentminded Saidi staff. Every day he had to tell each of them exactly what to do, and every day each of them did most of what they did a little bit wrong. Sometimes an eggshell worked its way into an omelette. Sometimes a cockroach could be seen drunkenly dancing its way out of a rice barrel. As long as he was vigilant enough to catch such errors before they came to the attention of the al-Masris, Abbas was willing to mutter *"Malesh."* He prided himself on running not only a smooth household but a contented one. Weighing in on Um Mona's side was her kinship with Khadiga and Fatima. They were both good girls. Perhaps this one would slide easily into his family of servants. He would see what she had to say for herself. "But why have you come *here?* There is always work in the villages."

"The war. The war made it hard there."

"The war was here, too." He waited to hear if she would lie. He liked to catch Egyptians, especially Saidis, in their constant lies. Predictable behavior always pleased Abbas's orderly mind.

"My husband died in Kom Ombo. He was Nubian." She spoke the name of her husband's tribe with disdain, remembering too late that Abbas also was Nubian. She raised her eyes angrily to the heavens, as if Allah were to blame for suddenly allowing so grave an error to slip from her lips. She fell silent, determined not to mention Mona's illness. She did not want him to get the idea there was anything *dark*—anything so dark as a *curse*—connected with their trip north.

He dropped that particular line of questioning for the moment. "What can you do? You've worked before in a great house?"

"I can do whatever you want me to do."

Abbas raised his eyebrows. He hadn't expected her to be an experienced servant, but he *had* expected her to lie and say she was. Instead, she had neatly sidestepped his question. She was odd but intriguing. He would push her further. "I might need a woman to do some of the heavy work in the house. But the child. We don't need a child here. Perhaps, if you sent her back to the village . . . ?"

"No!"

"Why not?"

She either would have to leave or tell him the truth. "Mona was sick."

He nodded. Now they were getting somewhere.

She eitehr would have to leave or tell him the truth. "Mona was as she clenched and unclenched her fists. "Malaria. Then pneumonia. So many of the children are dying."

"So? What is that to me?"

She crept to her knees. *"La samaat. La samaat.* Please. Please." Except for her fists, she was the picture of humility. "Please sir. For my baby."

Abbas saw trouble in those fists and in this woman. But it was trouble he knew he could handle. He had decided to let them stay when he gave the child that meal on the good china. Once he had had a frail daughter like Mona far away in his old village almost at the Sudanese border. He had put Mona's mother through her paces because he firmly believed that people never respected anything that came too easily. He was still not ready to drop his show of reluctance. "Your child is not well. There are young children in this house. Children we must shelter. Protect. I don't want the al-Masris catching any of your Saidi diseases."

"No, sir." Her knuckles were white.

"And I don't want any trouble. The first whiff of sickness, the first problem, and back you go."

Understanding immediately that Allah had answered her prayers, Um Mona settled back on the stool and tried to bargain for more. "For my wages—"

He cut her off. "Room, board, and a pound and a half a month. You and Mona will share Khadiga and Fatima's room in the attic. Your job will be to scrub the floors. The child can help in the kitchen." When she tried to stammer her thanks, Abbas answered her in Kenuz to remind her that he had not overlooked that Nubian slur. "I do it for the child. I do it *only* for the child. She is beautiful. As beautiful as dawn on the Nile."

The autumn beach was deserted. The waves beat a dirty fringe of reeking seaweed on the sand. There was too much wind for the sailboats, but ghostly ships patrolled where the dark-gray sea met the light-gray sky. The official war was over, yet the British gunboats kept their sights trained on Egypt.

Mona danced into pools of water left by the retreating tide. Her mother paced morosely behind her, remembering that Abbas had promised to teach Mona to swim. Um Mona, who had herself always been too wary of the power of the river and the sea, would have liked to have been here for those lessons. Now, thanks to Abbas's curt dismissal, Mona would learn to swim without her mother here to worry and watch.

Um Mona huddled against the wind. Today she would return to the village of her youth and leave Mona alone in Alexandria. After six weeks working at the villa, Um Mona's first and last mistake had very nearly been a deadly one. It had begun in the scientific laboratory of that al-Masri doctor brother. How could Um Mona have known that there were cholera cultures in those test tubes she accidentally broke into shards? How could she have guessed that after she tracked those germs into the kitchen two of the al-Masris and one of the servants would fall so ill? Abbas had been merciful enough to tell her that if she wished, Mona could remain with him at the villa. For days Um Mona had tried to find work in another household, but finally last night she had sat defeated in that sad patch of dusty trees and brown grass which the al-Masris called their garden. Leave Mona? It would be like rooting out her own beating heart. She had tried to be logical, but weedy memories tangled her mind: herself, so desperate for a baby after those long years of barren marriage, making a midnight offering to an ancient fertility goddess and then submerging herself in a dark jade lake. Her own warm blood on her tongue as she insisted on biting off Mona's umbilical cord with her own sharp teeth, severing the skin and gristle that bound them as one. The *shaykha* cutting her baby's sex. Herself removing those ropes and promising Mona there would be no more pain with Ummie eternally by her side. Her own mother wrapped in the ultimate abandonment of cold shrouds when she herself was not much older than Mona was now.

Leave Mona? From the moment of her own mother's death, Um Mona had yearned only for the daughter who would more than replace her. She had thought they would never be separated. The birth pact gave a mother the right forever to be with her child, to watch her grow up and have her own babies, to laugh and grow old and finally die beside her. A woman's life, Um Mona believed, could hold no other—or greater—consolation. But still last night Um Mona had sat in the dying garden, for her mind had a thing or two to tell her heart. A good mother, the best mother, thought first of her child. Here in Alexandria were a soft climate, ample food, even a doctor living under the same roof. Here Mona might learn to read and write and maybe someday marry a fine city boy instead of a villager who worked the land and waited for the river to rise. And in Karnak? Was premature death all that waited for Mona in Karnak? One of Um Mona's earliest memories was her own mother crying over the shirt of one of her own dead babies. Was it better to have Mona die in her arms or live out of them? Um Mona had risen, shaken off her tears as a wet bird does the rain, and made the only choice a mother could make.

Mulling over that dreadful black night in that dreadful brown garden, Um Mona wasn't watching as her little girl edged into the water and was swept off her feet by a breaker. Mona screamed, and Um Mona ran to snatch her to safety before the child could be engulfed again. The wave had not been monstrous, the undertow had not been strong, but to Um Mona it seemed a bad omen.

"Ummie! Ummie!" Mona was choking on the water. "Hold me!"

"I'm here, *habibti*. I'm here." But knowing she would not be here tomorrow, Um Mona tenderly carried her daughter back onto the beach and her own wide lap.

"I was scared, Ummie."

Um Mona dried the child with her coarse black shawl. "It wasn't a big wave. Nothing is too big for my girl." Courage, she thought, was what Mona was going to need in the days ahead. "You must be brave, Mona. The sea didn't hurt you. You must not be afraid of the sea."

"I'm not!" Mona snuggled down into her mother. "I like the sea. It's better than the river. It moves."

"The Nile moves, too. Not so much as the sea. But you know, don't you, that the river goes into the sea?"

"It does?"

"Yes. Our Nile is spread out all inside the sea. The same water, the same *mayya* I used to carry in a jug on my head, is right here. That's why, in the village, we call the river the sea."

Mona shot out her tongue and licked the seawater off her lips. "But why is it so salty?"

Maybe, Um Mona thought, the salt comes from tears like the ones in my eyes. In the days, months, years ahead, Um Mona thought she might shed enough tears to flood another sea. But she merely told Mona that Allah, in His mysterious ways, seasoned this sea with salt. What mattered, she said, was that there was Nile in this sea.

Mona sighed with contentment. The sea was really the river? Her world seemed tight and secure.

It was time, Um Mona knew, to tell the child and make her understand. Later she would have to try to make herself understand. Um Mona wiped away her tears. "Do you like it here, Mona?"

"Oh, yes! There's Abbas and Khadiga and Fatima and everybody

41

else." Already Mona was the petted favorite of the kitchen. But then, afraid that Ummie would be jealous of her new friends, she threw her arms around her mother's neck and kissed her. "And there's *you!*"

Um Mona drew away from the embrace. "Do you like it better here than in the village?"

It was too abstract a question for a child who hadn't yet learned to compare. Mona searched her mother's eyes for clues on how she should answer. It could be that Ummie was about to scold her for liking her new friends more than she should. At last, unable to understand that look in those eyes, Mona said she thought she did like it better in Alexandria.

"Good." But Um Mona narrowed her eyes. Was Mona too light in her affections? For a moment she considered the danger in leaving her daughter among strangers. Could they steal Mona's allegiance? She would have to take that chance. "I have to go away."

"Away? Now where are we going?"

"I'll be living with my brother, Muhammad. In Karnak. The village where I was born."

"There?" Mona wrinkled her brow. "I've never been to Karnak."

"I go today."

"But what about Abbas and Khadiga and Fatima? Will they go, too?"

"No." There was a trace of jealousy in Um Mona's voice. "Your fine *new* friends are staying here. With you."

"Me?"

Um Mona nodded, unable for a moment to go on.

Mona stared at her mother. With a click of fear, she knew immediately and surely that Ummie was punishing her for being untrue. She had climbed up on Khadiga's lap. She had let Fatima braid her hair. She had even pretended sometimes that Abbas was her father. Mona had hoped her mother had not noticed these defections. But of course she had. Ummie knew everything. Ummie could even read her thoughts.

"I'm leaving you only for a while, *habibti*. Only for a while."

"No. I'll go, too. With you."

Um Mona shook her head. "I want to take you with me. Want to take you home more than anything in the world. But remember how sick you were in Kom Ombo? If you go back with me, you may get sick again."

"I won't." Tears streamed down Mona's cheeks. "I promise, Ummie. I'll be good. I won't get sick."

"Only Allah can decide that, Mona."

The little girl hardly listened to her mother's explanations about why Abbas was turning her out of the house and why Ummie thought it would kill her to be back in the village. All she knew was that she had no one to blame but herself. Ummie was leaving because she herself had not been good enough, faithful enough, lovable enough, to keep her here with her. Mona had failed the great love of her life.

"Don't cry, Mona." Her own jealousy now was forgotten as she tried to comfort her child. "I'll come back to see you every year, here in Alexandria." She hoped Abbas wouldn't deny her that.

"Every year? What's a year, Ummie?"

"Every time it gets hot, it's another year. When it's warm and sunny and the sea is calm, I'll come back to be with you."

It did not seem such a very long time to Mona. It had almost always been hot in Kom Ombo. She had never felt an autumn, a winter, a spring. "When it's hot?"

"Yes. Hotter than now." She thought of another possibility. "And we'll write letters."

"I can't write. And you can't either."

"No. But I'll tell the *shaykh* in Karnak what to write you. Someone here in the villa will read you my words and write back your answer." Um Mona forced a smile. "Maybe someday you'll even learn to read and write yourself. I would be *so* proud if you could do that."

Mona resolved to learn to read and write at once. If her mother was very proud, maybe she would want to show her off in Karnak.

"So I'm not really leaving you. My words will be here. I'll be here every year. And my heart, Mona—my heart will be here with you for always."

They smiled at each other through tear-filled eyes.

"I want you to be strong for me." Um Mona dropped her voice to a whisper. "Do you remember the day of your circumcision?"

The child nodded. She would never forget it.

"Remember how I told you to sit up straight and tall in front of those Nubians?"

The child sat more erect.

"Remember how I told you not to cry?"

The child stopped sniffling.

"I was so proud of you that day, *habibti*. So proud. You are Saidi, Mona. Remember that. You must be brave for me. Strong. As you are now!"

They slowly walked hand in hand back to the villa.

When the winter wind was stronger than the sun, Um Mona's first letter arrived at the Villa al-Masri. Mona had tried hard, in those weeks of separation, always to be the grateful guest. But she hadn't been able to hide the fact that she vomited every morning—sometimes in bed, sometimes at the breakfast table, sometimes while at work on her chores. The others, watching with concern, gave what comfort they could. Khadiga would kiss her and tell her how pretty she was. Abbas would buy her spun-sugar candy in the souk. Fatima would tell her fanciful stories when she tucked her into bed. But sometimes in the middle of the night, when Khadiga snored or Fatima turned over in her sleep, Mona would unconsciously try to nestle closer to her mother. Instead, groping the unyielding wall, Mona would wake to the realization that her mother was gone. She would lie dry-eyed, fingering her blue bead, until she heard the birds singing in the trees. To her, they sounded bereft.

Sensing some of this, Abbas saw urgency in the soiled brown envelope that the postman said was for Mona. Since neither he nor any of the other servants could read or write, he would have to ask an al-Masri to read it aloud. He ticked off the possibilities. There was Rafael al-Masri, the head of the family. But between his Cotton Exchange and his textile mills, the master was too preoccupied even for his own children. There was Madame Leah, Rafael's wife. But the mistress was more beautiful than kind, and besides, she couldn't even speak—much less read—Arabic. There were the five al-Masri children. But only the oldest boy could decipher Arabic, and Youssef would make a joke of reading the letter. That left only Rafael's younger brother. Of course, Dr. Baruch; it would have to be Baruch! Long ago Abbas and Baruch had been as close as brothers. Their friendship had since dissolved into the distance of master and servant, but still Abbas rather wistfully considered Baruch his favorite al-Masri.

That night, then, Abbas led Mona to the doctor's laboratory. Baruch was mumbling to himself and stroking his bushy black beard as he slumped over a table. When Baruch finally looked up, Abbas asked him to read a letter.

"From your wife and daughter?" Baruch peered nearsightedly at Abbas.

Patiently the *suffragi* reminded the doctor that both had died three years ago of typhoid.

Baruch blushed with embarrassment. Although not much over thirty, Baruch had already acquired the absentminded habits of a middle-aged man who was not much with people. The doctor had become a recluse after his own wife died, for Baruch was not a man to love— or lose love—lightly. Aside from his nieces, his nephews, and his patients, Baruch kept to himself.

"The letter," Abbas said, "is from our servant girl's mother."

"Of course." Baruch removed his eyeglasses. Without them, his long, ascetic, olive-skinned face looked too young and innocent to have sprouted a beard.

Abbas smiled to himself, recalling the family joke that Baruch's mother had once been far too friendly with an Arab peddler of nuts and dates. In a robe and turban, Baruch could easily pass for one of those scholarly young-old Arabs who debate the Koran at Cairo's al-Azhar.

44

Baruch rubbed his glasses almost clean on his shirt. When he put them back on the high bridge of his Jewish nose, he saw before him a timid child in a garishly colored dress. Her tight braids were neatly tied at the ends with yellow ribbons. He looked further at her extraordinarily soft eyes and dimples. He smiled and asked her name.

"Mona." She whispered the first word she had ever spoken to any of the al-Masris, then hid in the folds of Abbas's *gallabeiya*.

"I understand," Baruch said, "you've been getting some letters."

"Only one letter." Abbas didn't want the doctor to think this was going to be a regular imposition. The doctor had important work to do. Abbas had the impression that the doctor, here in this very laboratory, was about to find the cure for some dread disease.

"A letter from Ummie."

"Well." Baruch was shy except when he was discussing philosophy or diagnosing diseases. Sometimes he considered cracking an abstruse joke about the connection between life speculations and medical prescriptions. But he never had known anyone who would have smiled at such wit—if wit it was. "Well, well." Baruch was particularly shy with children. It was easier for him to make them well than to make them smile. To cover his confusion, he opened the letter and glanced at it. He gave the child a closer look. "Come here, Mona." He patted his countertop as if it were an examination table.

She took a few cautious steps toward him.

"No. Up here." He nodded at Abbas, and the *suffragi* lifted Mona up on the table.

Remembering Ummie's order to be brave, Mona swallowed hard.

Pretty child, Baruch thought. Looks to be about four years old. But too thin. So many of the Arab children were scrawny. And then too many of them grew up to be too fat. They lacked protein, for they counted themselves lucky to have meat once a month. They overloaded on sugar, for they put five heaping spoonfuls in every glass of tea. They compensated with starch, for they made do with meals of bread stuffed with potatoes and rice. "How old are you, Mona?"

"Six, sir. I'm almost six."

"She looks as if she doesn't eat enough. Why is that, Abbas? Surely there is enough food for her in our kitchen."

"She eats. She's gained four kilos since she came here."

"I was sick before."

Baruch's professional interest was piqued. "Sick?"

Abbas mentally thanked Allah for his unfailing memory. "Malaria. Then pneumonia. In the South. Last year."

Baruch nodded. Little, he knew, had been done to stem that malaria epidemic. It was always the same sad story. There had been neither enough quinine nor enough doctors, and forty thousand Egyptians had died. Little was ever done, in Baruch's estimation, to help the *fellahin*.

How any of them lived to be old was beyond him. Maybe, he thought, remembering the sight of seemingly ancient women nursing infants on the streets, they didn't live to be old after all. Maybe they just *looked* old.

Baruch sighed and reproached himself once again for wasting too much of his professional life on Alexandria's rich. He had become a doctor to help ease human suffering in one of the most disease-ridden places on earth. In Egypt lethal waves of malaria, typhoid, cholera, smallpox, and tuberculosis swept the masses. In Egypt eye diseases blinded tens of thousands each year. In Egypt not tens of thousands, not hundreds of thousands, but *millions* suffered toward slow and painful deaths from parasites carried by their river. In Egypt a child like this Mona had little chance of even living long enough to be blinded by the cataracts or sapped by the parasites. Yet instead of trying to alleviate this endless peasant need, Baruch catered to society women whose most serious malady was the onslaught of wrinkles. He tried to salve his conscience with three afternoons a week in his own free clinic. It was more than most of the other foreign doctors ever deigned to do. After all, Baruch regularly asked himself, how much could be expected from any one man? Baruch was quick to answer his own question. More: I must do more.

With an effort Baruch brought himself back to the matter at hand. This letter was, he thought, more the message of a lover than a mother. " 'Mona,' " he read, " 'Mona, *habibti,* my love.' "

Mona stared at the paper, imagining her mother speaking to her, her mother's arms around her, her mother's eyes upon her.

The doctor read the simple, emotional Arabic aloud in a low and steady voice. " 'I think of you at all times. In the morning when the sun comes up and I fill the water jugs. In the afternoons when I cook and sweep. In the evenings when I fill the jugs once more. I look at the river and think that the same water that passes by here will rush up to you. I wish that I were a drop of water so that I could be there, too. I want to touch your hair and kiss your eyes. Soon, if Allah wills it, I will. Be a strong Saidi for me. Do what Abbas says. Do not cry. I am with you in my heart.' "

The two blotchy lines at the end were the mother's attempt at a signature. The ink was smeared, perhaps by her tears, perhaps by the carelessness of the *shaykh* who had transcribed it.

Mona sniffled but did not cry. When Baruch handed her the letter, she tucked it inside her dress.

"And your answer? A letter like that certainly merits a prompt answer." Baruch was moved by the letter, but his European reserve did not allow him to intrude upon it. He knew that by now an Egyptian in his position would be wiping away his tears and clutching the little girl to his chest like a long-lost daughter. Sometimes Baruch wished he were an Egyptian so he could do things like that. Instead his voice was dry. "Now, Mona, you must write back to your mother." He took a blank sheet of paper. "So what do you want to tell her?"

"Ummie." Mona spoke very slowly. "I think it's getting hot here now and that you should come back. It's much hotter than when you left."

Baruch and Abbas exchanged glances. It was an unusually cold January.

"I am being good. I am sure, Ummie, that I won't get sick again now if you take me home with you. Everyone says I'm very strong now."

Baruch noticed once again the hollowed cheeks that made the child's eyes and dimples seem so prominent.

"Fatima tells me stories, but they aren't yours. I try to teach her our stories, but I forget them. Sometimes Khadiga kisses me and says I'm pretty. If I get prettier, can I come home? Abbas will teach me to swim soon. He says it's too cold now. But really, it's not. I think it's hot enough for you to come back." She paused. "Will I get letters from my Baba now, too? Can I send one to him in Paradise? Dr. Baruch will write one to him, too, I think."

The doctor's hand faltered.

"I will go tomorrow to the sea, maybe, and look for the water from Karnak. I think I will remember it." She nodded to Baruch. "That's all."

"You must sign it." He put the pen in her hand.

She squirted ink over the page. "Like this?"

"It will do."

Abbas stepped forward. "Thank you, Dr. Baruch. And now it's somebody's bedtime."

Baruch gave Abbas a look that the *suffragi* could not interpret. "I'll wait for you here, Abbas. Bring coffee later. And two cups. We must talk."

For the first time, as Mona thanked the doctor, she smiled shyly up at him.

"We will talk again, Mona, I'm sure, many times. Sleep well."

When Baruch was alone, he stared moodily down at his notebooks and his test tubes and his shiny steel instruments. He felt like tossing every bit of it into the garbage. His experiments were very likely of no importance. It was the same with his silly philosophical debates with himself on the purpose of life. All of it—his work, his thoughts—were no more than self-indulgence. While he was scratching his head, all around him people were living out their lives of heartbreak and misery.

Baruch straightened up and told himself sternly that he was once again getting too melodramatic. So a mother misses her child? So a daughter wants her mother? So why not take that at face value? Separations don't occur only in Egypt.

It was no use. He was, by now, too familiar with the hopelessness of Egypt's poor. All he had to do was spend a half hour in an Arab peasant's house, and down came this black despair. Baruch knew the real reason why he couldn't bring himself to do more for the Arabs. He felt too depressed—no, he felt almost paralyzed with despair—when he was around them. These people lived much as European serfs must have lived in the Middle—no, the *Dark*—Ages. They had no concept of sanitation or hygiene. If it weren't for Islam's admonishments that the faithful cleanse themselves—before prayer and eating, after sex and defecating—no one would ever wash at all. Even in Alexandria, this city that had been the pride of the ancient world, most of the hovels did not have running water, much less electricity. Holes in the ground served as toilets. Lice and fleas infested most of the date-palm sleeping mats. Baruch wished he were a tougher man. He wished he could throw himself wholeheartedly into serving the poor. Instead he fluttered impotently on the fringes, occasionally ministering from his safely elevated status as a healer. After an afternoon in his clinic's Arab quarter, Baruch wanted nothing more than to forget any of it existed. He would come home, throw himself down on a brocaded chaise, and put Mozart on the record player. But still he would be haunted by what he had left behind in the slums.

Baruch sighed. In an abstract way, he thought the squalor was emotionally harder on him than on the people who lived in it. It wasn't only that Western experience had taught him life did not have to be so arduous. It was also that his fine advanced education had failed to arm him with the spiritual comforts that made these peasant lives bearable. Most Arabs in their crumbling urban ghettos were more content than the rich Europeans in their French-facaded villas a few blocks away. Baruch despised clichés. He knew, too, that this last thought was not only a cliché but a cliché that the rich and the privileged had always used to justify their neglect of the poor and the oppressed. And yet there was a grain of truth in it. Islam gave the poorest of the Arabs an enviable measure of serenity. They trusted in their Allah not only as a child trusts in his parents but as a lover trusts in his beloved. As an outsider, Baruch had the worst of both worlds. He could see the filth in the Arab quarter, but he couldn't experience its joys. And so close brushes with Arab reality left him inconsolable.

Baruch reconsidered Mona's letter. He wished he had the mettle to take pleasure in the obvious devotion of that mother and this child. Instead, characteristically, he could think of nothing but how terrible it was to tear the two of them apart. He was hoping Abbas would be able to help him regain his equilibrium. If anyone could do that, it was Abbas.

Baruch nearly smiled to himself. Abbas had been his first—and, as it was turning out, probably his last—true Arab friend. Even as an adolescent, Baruch had been bored with the other Greek, Italian, British, and Jewish boys of his class. But Abbas had intrigued him. The dark-skinned Nubian boy had been Baruch's own age, and yet Abbas had embodied the mysteries of Egypt's seven thousand years. Abbas had dignity. Abbas had presence. Baruch had thought Abbas could help him unravel elusive Egyptian secrets. And so, when he went sailing eastward toward Abu Kir, Baruch would take Abbas along to serve him. They would tie up at one of the islands, and Baruch would share his picnic lunch as he plied Abbas with questions. What was it like back in Abbas's village? Were there crocodiles in the river? Dugout canoes? Did his mother wear a nose ring? Did his father have four wives? Abbas had laughed and set him straight: no crocodiles, no dugout canoes, an ankle bracelet but no nose ring, only one wife for his father. Once Baruch had asked why and how Muslims prayed. Allah, Abbas had answered, must be thanked for the richness of another day: for the light of each sunrise, for the heat of each noon, for the languor of each afternoon, for the peace of each sunset, for the stillness of each nightfall. Abbas had nearly upset the sailboat showing Baruch how to pray: always facing Mecca, beginning with arms out straight, then falling to the knees, finally prostrating in a salaam to God.

Often Abbas had harped on the theme of generosity. The most admired man in his village had been born rich but died poor because he gave away everything to those with greater needs. It wasn't enough, Abbas had explained, to be generous with what you did not want. Nor was it truly generous to give away only what you were sure you would, in one way or another, be returned. At its best, generosity was pure and unselfish and rooted in fairness and compassion. "It is," Abbas had said, "what makes us different from the animals." Abbas had spiced all his stories with jokes that Baruch at first had found silly. But Egyptian humor is the kind that improves with repetition. In time Baruch and Abbas would almost get drunk on the giddiness of those stories. "Baruch," Abbas would tell him, "Baruch, you laugh like an Egyptian. It is a great gift."

As Baruch sat waiting in his laboratory, he wondered when he had lost not only that good fellowship with Abbas but also that gift for laughter. Maybe some of it had gone away when he was alone in London studying medicine. It had been such a relief to come home and marry a Jewish dream named Daisy. It had been such a nightmare when she had died two years later. Since then grief had made Baruch forget he had ever known how to laugh. Baruch bit his lip. Daisy had been dead for eight years. Perhaps it was time to try to learn to laugh again.

Abbas brought in the tray with the tiny, silty cups of coffee sweet to the point of bitterness. Baruch gave him an encouraging smile. "I invite you to drink with me. It's been a long time, Abbas. A very long time."

Friendship so long neglected is not so easily repatched. Abbas had his pride. He served the doctor, but he did not touch his own cup as he related Mona's history. All things considered, Abbas concluded, it was best that Mona stay in the villa. Surely the doctor could see the child wasn't strong enough for *fellahin* life.

"Still, Abbas, that letter! It isn't right that girl has to feel so alone."

Abbas shrugged his shoulders. It was a gesture Baruch saw often in the Arab quarters, a gesture that managed to imply both sympathy and helplessness. "Life is difficult," Abbas said.

Baruch sighed on cue. He was doing his best to win Abbas over by respecting Arab conventions. A shrug, a word on life's hardness, a sigh: Egyptians appeared to draw comfort by eternally repeating that sequence. Baruch sighed a more sincere second sigh. "It makes my heart ache to look at her. There are so many like her. So many, Abbas. So many. I wish I could do something to make a difference for them all. I wish I could help. But what? What can we do?"

Abbas softened. He picked up his own cup, although he still would not drink from it. It seemed Baruch still had his tender heart. But there was only one possible answer to Baruch's old question. "Allah provides."

Baruch smiled at him. "Yes. You're quite right, Abbas. Allah does provide. After His Own fashion, in His Own inscrutable ways, Allah provides." But Baruch was considering some provisions of his own. Maybe, Baruch was thinking, maybe I could save this Mona. Maybe I could make a difference to this one fragile little Arab child. Maybe the most important thing I could do in my whole entire life is to focus all I have on saving this one child from her fate. Yet Baruch hesitated. He was too much the philosopher not to be aware that there were dangers in his plan. Who was he, after all, to play God? Who was he to assume that it was "saving" a fellow human being merely to provide proper food, clothing, health care, and education? And how could he be sure that, in the end, it was ethical to pluck this child, unasked, from her own culture into his? But, for once, Baruch decided he would act instead of just think about acting. By God, he was going to do it. He was going to make his stand, with this child, against all the dark forces in the world. And maybe, he thought, maybe what this is really all about is saving not only Mona but myself.

Baruch chose his next words with care. He knew how leery Muslims were of tampering with what they thought was Allah's will. "I think just this once, Abbas, that I will be Allah's helper. I can't help all those children. But I can, I think, do something good for one of them."

Patiently Baruch watched Abbas take an exploratory sip of his bittersweet coffee. He waited for Abbas to swallow it. And then Baruch put the proposition to him. They would make this little girl their model. They would give her love, learning, understanding. The two of them would give her the best that they had, the best goodwill that there was in an Arab and a Jew.

The two old friends grinned at each other. Baruch extended his hand with a flourish. Abbas smacked his own palm inside it, hard and solid, the traditional Arab sealing not only of a deal but of brotherhood. Baruch heard, then, what he had not heard for years. It was a somewhat worn laugh, a rough laugh, a laugh that was cracked at the edges. But Baruch could distinctly hear himself laughing once more like an Egyptian.

Mona sank up to her knees in the soft, sticky, pearly-gold mica sand of Agami Beach. Of all the many compensations of Alexandria—her talks with gentle Dr. Baruch, her prayer rug with its intricate weave of a Nile-like river, the blanket she had learned to roll in a ball and snuggle close to as if it were her mother—Agami stirred her the most. Never had she seen anything to match it. A strip of sandy mud along the river was the closest the village had come to a beach. The congested city seafronts, where peasant women kept on their long black robes even when beached like laughing whales in the fringe of the surf, weren't much better. Between the umbrellas, the tables, and the chairs, it had been difficult even to see the sand. Between the peddlers hawking everything from pistachio nuts to lice combs, it had been difficult even to hear the lap of the navy sea. But Agami Beach stretched in an infinite sandy cushion. Only an occasional white stucco chalet and a cluster of fig trees divided sand from sky. The turquoise water was here and there pickled lush brown by patches of seaweed. At the horizon all that separated the blues of the sea from the blues of the sky were misty, wraithlike silhouettes of great cargo ships. Today, however, a spring storm at sea made the water too rough for swimming. Watching the breakers roll in with a roar of churning water, Mona wondered if any of this azure sea had once flowed past her mother in Karnak. She didn't think so. This sea looked nothing like her Nile.

As Mona helped Abbas and Khadiga unwrap the foreign food for the al-Masri picnic, she was homesick for boiled *fool* broadbeans, spinach-like *mulukhiya* soup, and fried chickpea *taamiya* croquettes. Why didn't the al-Masris eat Egyptian food? Mona put aside her thoughts and carefully set out the sandwiches and cakes. Baruch had told her this outing was a test. If she did well today, she would be allowed to leave the kitchen and serve the al-Masris at their daily tea. Any minute now the women and children of the family were due at this secluded beach a slow hour's drive west of the city.

There was a flourish of shouts, and two good-looking big boys jumped out of the car and began clapping and laughing as they threw a ball around on the beach. A third boy—younger, not so handsome—tried to join in but instead consistently fumbled the ball.

Mona stared in fascination and then turned to her kind, plain cousin, who, it was rumored, was soon to be married to Abbas. "Khadiga? Who are those boys?"

"You don't know the al-Masris yet?" Khadiga looked up from the food baskets. "It's time you learned. The tall, fair-haired one is Youssef. The oldest boy. The dark one is his friend Hamid. Not family. But he's here enough that you'd think he was. The other one is Youssef's brother, Daoud."

When Daoud tripped on a rock and skidded to his rump, Hamid slapped his side in mocking laughter. Youssef appeared not to have noticed either the fall or the laugh. But as Hamid tossed the ball, Youssef stumbled in midstride and landed too gracefully on his rear. "You see that, Daoud? It's not our fault we fall. It's because the sand is so soft. Everyone falls on the sand." Daoud smiled in relief.

Mona smiled, too. "Khadiga! Youssef fell on purpose, I think, so his brother wouldn't feel clumsy."

Khadiga nodded. "That's our Youssef."

Mona shifted her attention to the knot of women and girls sitting not far away on the sand. A lady lay stretched on her stomach, a pile of cushions under her, a green-striped umbrella above her. Nearby a strapping woman with close-cropped hair sat on her rug with two little girls firmly in hand. "What about them? Who are they?"

"That's Madame al-Masri under the umbrella. She likes to keep her skin as white as yogurt."

Mona couldn't believe anyone so slim and beautiful was a mother. Her hair was as blond as an angel's, and her rhinestone sunglasses sparkled with gay glamour. Puffing elegantly on a cigarette in a gleaming black holder, she was wrapped from neck to ankle in a flowery robe that clung to the curves of her lithe body. This was a mother? She wasn't anything like Ummie. How could the al-Masri children ever climb up on this mother's lap? Ummie! Oh, if Ummie were only here today! Their letters weren't enough. But soon—it was hot enough today to sweat—Ummie would arrive for her visit.

Khadiga was still cataloguing al-Masris. "That bossy woman is the Swiss governess. Helga. The children hate her. And who wouldn't? But Madame says she keeps the children quieter than any of the other nannies ever could."

"And those little girls?" Mona missed her village playmates.

"Rachel and Lisabet." Khadiga peered at the girls. "They look so much alike that they could be twins. But Rachel's chubbier and older. Lisabet's your age."

Mona wished she could see what color their eyes were, how their hair curled, what they looked like when they laughed. But the girls were turned away from her to face a small boy frolicking with a puppy. "Who's the little boy?"

Khadiga laughed. "That, my dear, is Batata. They call him *Batata*—'Sweet Potato'—but his real name is Zvi. He's so cute. Always playing. Always laughing."

"And always falling." Mona watched him take another tumble and listened as his clear, high laugh rang out.

"He still doesn't walk very well. Doesn't talk much either. He's growing up nice and slow. But how that boy laughs! Allah keep him. Such a sweet potato."

"And the dog?" The round puppy had long, shiny, curly golden hair, a knob of a tail, and ears that flopped in front of its eyes. Mona would have liked to run over and romp with the two of them.

"What do I know of dogs?" Khadiga held up a fork. "One of these goes next to each plate. Spread them out so they look nice." By this time Abbas had the tea brewing on the kerosene stove, and Khadiga rang a brass bell to summon the children.

Youssef squinted in the sun at Mona. "I remember you," he said in Arabic.

She looked away, flattered but shy.

"Let's have a smile. Then I'll know it's you for certain."

She obliged. It was so easy to smile at Youssef.

"I knew it. You're the Saidi girl who was with that old woman. I thought I recognized you before in the villa." He nudged Hamid. "You remember. The one we threw the coin. So what's your name?"

"Mona."

"Stop distracting the servants." Helga spoke in rapid French, the first language of all Alexandrians of note. "And that's enough Arabic. No gutter talk at the table."

"How about on the blanket?" Stubbornly Youssef continued in Arabic. "Even you, Mademoiselle Helga, must admit this is not a table." Hamid and Daoud laughed.

"You heard me," Helga persisted in French. "I will not have you speaking that barbaric language during meals."

As the children devoured their lunch, Mona risked a peek at the little girls. Their gray eyes did not look her way. Their bushy dark-blond hair was trained in superior ringlets. But maybe they couldn't do everything she herself could do. When Abbas told her to bring wine over to where he was serving Madame, Mona balanced the bottle on her head just as her mother had taught her.

"Look at that." Youssef whistled in appreciation. "She doesn't spill a drop. Saidis all have such good balance."

"I bet you could do it." Hamid's grin was a dare.

The two boys seized the milk pitcher and minced away from the blanket in an exaggerated imitation of Mona. Everyone watched their clowning. No one noticed Batata and the puppy edging away from the blanket toward the water.

"Stop it! Youssef! Hamid! Come back here!" Helga ran after the boys when they continued to defy her. Meanwhile Batata splashed quietly in the shallows. When the puppy ran into the surf, Batata laughed and toddled after it.

Mona was on her way back to the others when, out of the corner of her eye, she saw a huge breaker roll over the boy and the dog. They were knocked under the water, another wave hit them, and then the undertow began pulling them away from the shore. Mona hit the water at a run. Wild high waves knocked her to her knees, but she knew no fear, since Ummie had told her not to be afraid of the sea. She caught the boy under his arms and pulled him to shore.

"Zibda!" The boy tried to crawl back into the water.

"*Zibda?*" It was the Arabic for "butter." "What do you mean, '*zibda?*'"

"My dog! Save Zibda!"

Forgetting that she still hadn't learned to swim, Mona went wading toward the flash of gold fur in the deeper water.

Batata, now in tears, screamed, "Zibda! Zibda! Zibda!"

Youssef and Hamid began running to answer the cries.

But Mona was floundering in the water. Repeatedly, as she made futile grabs for the dog, she was knocked off her feet. She tried to stand but instead her feet brushed stringy, spongy seaweed. She recoiled, screamed, took in a mouthful of water, and went under.

Youssef pulled her up by her braids. "Easy. Easy. Don't panic. You're safe." He dragged her, coughing, to shore.

"Zibda!" Batata pointed to where he had last seen his dog. When Hamid retrieved the cocker spaniel, Batata crept toward his pet. Zibda gave her tail a weak wag and nestled close to the boy. "Her!" Batata laughed and tugged at Mona's braids. "You saved me. And you tried to save Zibda, too! I like you!" Batata hugged her, Youssef pounded her on the back, and Mona hiccupped and tried to smile.

By now everyone but Madame was standing in a huddle over them. "*Pourquoi?*" Abbas, too excited to remember any more of his careful French, raised his voice in Arabic. "I'm asking you, Helga, *why* this happened. That boy is your charge."

Sulkily Helga looked over the al-Masris. "It's all Youssef's fault." Her harsh, halting Arabic became a whine. "I can't be everywhere at once. That Batata should be locked up in an asylum. All I did was turn my back on the little imbecile for one moment! And *why?* Because this one here was making a fool of himself with the milk jug. If Youssef weren't so spoiled, this wouldn't have happened."

Youssef took a menacing step toward the governess. "Don't say that about Batata! You take it back!"

54

Their shouts finally lured over Madame. She was annoyed not only at having to get sand stuck between her toes but also because her family was speaking incomprehensible Arabic. *"Qu'est-ce que c'est?"*

"Batata nearly drowned." Abbas's French returned of necessity. "Mona saved Batata. And then Youssef saved Mona."

"She tried to save Zibda, too," Batata added.

"Helga did nothing to help." Abbas glared at the governess.

"Vraiment?" Madame raised her perfectly plucked eyebrows.

"Not only that." Youssef wasn't going to let Helga get away with slandering his little brother. "Helga said Batata should be in an asylum. She called him an imbecile. We all heard her."

Madame sucked in her cheeks. She did not look pretty at that moment. "You will leave our house today, mademoiselle. *Comprenez?"*

"He is retarded." Helga went for the jugular. "You just won't admit it. Your little boy is an idiot."

"You can walk back to Alexandria. Your belongings will be out on the curb. *Bonjour,* mademoiselle." Madame was trembling when she looked down at Batata. He and the dog were sopping wet, and she was wearing a new mauve silk beach robe from Paris, but Madame swept the boy and dog up in her arms. She turned to make her way back to the car, but Youssef stopped her.

"What about Mona, Mama?"

"Who?"

"The little Saidi servant. The one who saved Batata's life. I don't think she could swim herself, yet she saved him."

Madame looked down at Mona. *"Merci."*

Batata and the dog slipped down on the sand, and the boy threw his arms around Mona. "I like her! Zibda does, too!" The dog barked and ran around Mona in circles.

"You children!" Madame rolled her eyes, but then blew them all a pretty kiss. "Just this once, the girl can ride back in our car instead of the servants' donkey cart." Madame put on her sunglasses, took Youssef's arm, and began picking her way off the beach.

In the back seat of the car, Batata insisted that Mona be next to him. As Zibda licked their faces dry of salt water, the two of them giggled and whispered secrets.

"And so," Abbas concluded as he served Baruch sherry in his study before dinner that evening. "Madame let Mona ride home with the al-Masris."

The doctor smiled as Abbas's tale came to an end. His Mona— Baruch thought of her as "his" now—had exceeded his expectations. His orders to feed Mona well, to clothe her warmly, to teach her how to pray, had been carried out according to the doctor's prescription. But when Baruch took it upon himself to show her how to use a fork and to curtsy instead of kissing an elder's hand, he had been surprised how much *fun* it was to watch the little girl laugh over these strange new ways of behaving. If Daisy had lived, if they could have had their own children . . . Baruch tucked away that regret. In the beginning he had thought of Mona as a worthy project. He had not guessed she would grow into a source of delight. Yet he knew he could not claim credit for what was the best of Mona. She had her mother, her Allah, and herself to thank for her courage and her character. It began to look as though Mona was well worth not only his past efforts but his future dreams. A new plan for Mona was already taking shape in Baruch's mind. Batata—poor, laughing little Batata—would be the catalyst. Baruch drained his glass and watched Abbas pour him another.

Baruch had noticed even when Batata was an infant that he did not respond to the world around him. As the child grew older, he had not been inclined to walk or talk but instead had clung to his family's eager arms. Then as now, Batata was everyone's favorite. Last summer a thorough physical examination had convinced Baruch the boy was retarded. After today's incident at Agami, it was time for Batata's parents to face reality. The boy was strong enough to hurt himself or others. Clearly, Batata needed special care. A governess who had to watch four other lively children was not enough, but a nurse who did nothing but fuss over him would be too much. Baruch's answer was to turn Mona into Batata's constant companion.

The doctor took a small sip of sherry and briefly considered whether Mona was becoming an obsession with him. It was true he longed for an excuse to teach her how to read and speak French and be as educated as a *lycée* graduate. Yes, he wanted all that—and more—for his Mona. But his neat, tender plan would help Batata as well. The difficulty would be getting Rafael and Leah to admit anything was wrong with their son. Idly Baruch sounded out Abbas. "Tell me, what do you think of Batata?"

Abbas smiled. The very mention of Batata always made them all smile. "Sweet, that one is. I love that boy. The way he laughs!"

"Wouldn't you say, though, that Batata is . . . a bit slow?"

"Perhaps it is the others who are too fast."

Baruch smiled. It was very Egyptian of Abbas to say that. "What I mean is . . . have you noticed anything *different* about Batata? He doesn't play as the others did at his age."

Long ago Abbas had decided about Batata. "The boy is special. A special child. Batata is one of heaven's favorites. The house is blessed by him."

"Blessed?"

Abbas patiently explained it to Baruch. "Most people—men, women, children—live out their lives as we do. A few are good. A few bad. Most in between, *nuss wi nuss*. Allah gave us our minds and our hearts.

And sometimes—and sometimes not—we use them well. But there are some who are so dear to Allah that He keeps their minds with Him in Paradise, so that all we see here on earth is what remains. A body without a full mind but with a pure heart. In the villages we call such blessed one saints. We revere them, we care for them, and we learn from them. In my village there was one such man. It was said he ate only straw and mud. He tore to shreds whatever clothes we gave him. He was a holy man, and we honored him as a saint when he died— too young—because Allah wanted him home. The women visit his tomb now to ask for special favors. Batata, too, is one of heaven's favorites. Praise Allah—*el-hamdulillah!*—for giving him to us."

Baruch lifted his glass in a toast to Abbas. He thought of the asylums he had visited in Europe and of the deep shame associated there with mental illness of any sort. *One of heaven's favorites.* The more Baruch learned of Egyptians, the more they moved him. Baruch knew Egyptians had many weaknesses. They often broke their word. They very nearly always chose the easy way out. They were inconsistent and easily corrupted and insincere. But at times like this, Baruch felt himself to be falling in love with this country and this people. "How right you are, Abbas. Our Batata is one of heaven's favorites."

Baruch girded himself with another sherry for the inevitable scene with Leah and Rafael. Leah, he knew, would cry and refuse to admit there was anything amiss with her son. Rafael would probably want to ship Batata off to an expensive Swiss sanitarium. But Baruch would do his best. Mona, by God, was going to be Batata's guardian angel.

On a sunny late-spring day Mona and Batata brought up the rear of a line of al-Masris bound for the zoo. In the lead, of course, were Youssef and his faithful Hamid. Daoud lagged a little behind them. The new governess, fat and placid Anne-Marie, held Rachel's and Lisabet's hands. Batata, pouting because he had had to leave his puppy behind, clutched the hem of Mona's starched navy and white uniform. Mona might be Batata's companion, but Leah had insisted on dressing her like a servant.

As the al-Masris wove their way along the zoo's teeming tar paths, Mona cast longing looks at the crowd. She knew she had more in common with the peasant women balancing baskets on their heads than she ever could with the Frenchified al-Masris. If it weren't for Batata, Mona would have long since begged Baruch and Abbas to allow her to return to the kitchen. She hadn't needed Baruch's telling her Batata was "one of heaven's favorites" to begin to love the boy. Often Mona would smooth back his thick mop of black hair just so she could look into his large brown eyes. Batata had quite the clearest and most trusting eyes she had ever seen. She was touched, too, by his vulnerability as he lurched about, never quite able to make his chubby arms and legs go exactly where he wanted them. Batata was her playmate and her friend and her joy.

On both sides of the pathway, men in pale *gallabeiyas* had stretched out blankets piled high with garishly enticing comic books and gaudy goldish necklaces and charms. There were straw hats with plumed feathers, balloons of red and orange, dolls dressed in pink spangles and fake fur. But most of all there was the food. Bite-sized bits of meat and cheese and pickles wrapped in bread that was flat or high, dark or light. Balls of sticky, spicy chickpeas fat-fried to a toasty brown. Ice cream in cups, cones, and perched at the ends of sticks. Round, delicately layered pastries encrusted with thick icing. Greasy little cakes plastered with cheese. Thin, dense fig bars dripping with nuts and honey. Candy, expensive pistachios, and cheap salted seeds and nuts. Berry drinks and fresh-squeezed juices of oranges, bananas, tamarind, and even an early stray mango. Tiny cups of sweet coffee. Tall glasses of sweeter tea. Bottles of cola and sugared lemonade. The al-Masris licked their lips but did not partake. Often their governesses had warned them such food was contaminated by the germs of the poor.

To stop Batata from whining that he was hungry, Youssef taught him a new word. The human sprawl all around them, he said, was called *baladi*. It meant more, he said, than its literal "sons of the good earth." *Baladi* meant city savvy that was streetwise and saucy. *Baladi* meant a mix of gaiety and cynicism, a gift for mimicry, an irresistible impulse to lampoon everyone and everything that smacked of authority. A *baladi* man considered himself better than any foreigner, for a *baladi* man thought his stock the oldest on earth. A *baladi* man knew he was better than a *fellahin* peasant farmer, for a *baladi* man was never dull-witted or easily gulled. *Baladi* was haggling with a fruitseller over a half piaster, then giving away ten times as much to a beggar. Being, at the same time, both sweet and tough, being able to swagger in rags, was what *baladi* was all about. *Baladi* didn't attempt to transcend misery. *Baladi* made a joke of it. Batata laughed happily at the women in *tobs*, the men in *gallabeiyas*, the children in striped pajamas. He bounced his belly to the quartertone beat of the wailing *mizmir* music. "I'm *baladi!*" he shouted.

Youssef always set a fast pace for his brothers and sisters, and it was beginning to be evident that he would lead the new governess around as well. Even Mona knew Youssef was the prince of the family. He looked like a fairy-tale prince, with that mane of tousled blond hair, those even features, and that lordly carriage. He acted like a prince, making his sisters blush with compliments, coaxing away Daoud's worries, keeping a close and loving watch on little Batata. Already Mona had spent many a meal covertly studying Youssef. He was always the last one to the table, and the children's forks would clink expectantly on china plates until Youssef would whip around the table and slide into his place with inevitable grace and assurance. For Youssef was a golden boy, one of the lucky ones born with good looks, money, and a nature so easygoing no one could hold any of it against him. Nothing—not even breakfast—ever seemed to start unless Youssef said it did.

What Youssef was saying now was that they would play a special game. In honor of Mona—he winked at her as he said it—they would converse only in Arabic. But since it was boring just to watch the animals in their cages—Mona already knew that Youssef had a great horror of being bored—they would while away the time deciding which animal each of them most resembled.

Youssef began the charade at the monkey house. He peered inside and, to Mona's amazement, seemed to recognize himself in a blond, gibbering monkey. But it *was* true that Youssef's mobile face was all laughing eyes and joking mouth. "How's this?" Youssef screwed up his face as a chimpanzee might. The children howled their appreciation. Youssef wouldn't stop scratching and gamboling until they bought a banana from the zookeeper and fed it to him.

Next came the seal pool. Youssef studied the sleek, slippery black beasts and then looked at Hamid. The other children—Mona included —immediately giggled. Sometimes, when Youssef wasn't looking, Hamid bullied the younger children. Mona had taken a particular dislike to him ever since the night he had put his hand on her knee under the dining table. She wondered why anyone like Youssef would pick anyone like Hamid for a friend. She had asked Khadiga this very question and had been told that Hamid came from one of the oldest and richest Egyptian landowning families. Hamid's father was not only a pasha but a pasha who shot ducks with the king. Madame al-Masri, Khadiga said, was mad for anything or anyone with a connection to Faruk, and so years ago she had encouraged Youssef to befriend Hamid. It was obvious to Mona that Hamid was shocked at Youssef's comparing him to a seal. It was equally obvious that Hamid was trying to decide whether a seal-like boy could still be considered debonair and dashing. But Youssef had christened himself a monkey, and so Hamid gamely tried to play the seal. "Ork?" Hamid flapped his hairy arms in front of him. "Ork, ork, ork!" Youssef gave the seals' keeper a speculative look but did not try to make Hamid eat a raw fish.

Then they moved on to the birds. They lingered in front of the glorious green-feathered parrots. They ambled past the serious pink flamingoes. In front of the gray, serene, dowdy turtledoves, Youssef pointed to Rachel and Lisabet. Obediently the girls dropped their heads and cooed. Mona smiled uncertainly. Her curiosity about the al-Masri girls was still unsatisfied. Although the pair kept aloof from her, Mona could not help studying their every gesture and examining their every frock. Already she had tried holding her teacup just as they did and shaking her hair with their same careless toss. Under her breath Mona made a little dovelike coo.

Youssef herded them to where the elephants stood by a fence shamelessly begging for food. One massive gray beast greedily scooped peanuts from the ground with a deep sucking noise. Of late the same sound had been heard at the al-Masri dining table, where one of their own company daily slurped her soup. Youssef bought a bag of peanuts and then threw one in Anne-Marie's direction. She caught it, ate it, and then ordered Youssef to give her the rest of the nuts.

Youssef noticed Daoud looking at the slinky striped tigers with something akin to envy. Already Mona had learned to feel sorry for Daoud. Awkward and skinny, he was always looking around to see if the others had noticed his continual mistakes. At the age of nine, Daoud already found life a struggle. He was nothing like a tiger—he was more like an ostrich—but Youssef granted Daoud his heart's desire. "I see a definite resemblance. No stripes, but the same walk. Yes, my brother is a tiger." Daoud paced with a sure, wicked step the rest of the day.

The children lined up at a mesh fence and held out crusts of bread for the shy, graceful gazelles. The creatures eyed the children with timid caution, but one of them finally crept up to look Mona full in the face. For a moment it was unclear whether Mona or the gazelle would be the first to turn and run. But then it bent to lick the crust gently from her before scooting away as fast as it could. Youssef laughed gently. "You, Mona, are our gazelle." She dropped her eyes and wished that she, too, could flee all that attention. But then she gave Youssef a grateful smile. The gazelles were the most beautiful animals in the zoo.

Although Batata was as helpful as he could be, Youssef couldn't decide which animal he most resembled. Batata eagerly roared like a lion, slithered like a snake, even lowered his head with the menace of a charging rhinoceros. At last Youssef hit on what would please Batata the most. "My brother Batata is a puppy." The boy barked agreement, went down on all fours, and did a creditable imitation of Zibda chasing her curly stub of a tail. All the children laughed.

It was when they finally headed for home that Mona's day was sealed in a glow. Youssef, for once leaving Hamid to fend for himself, hoisted Batata up on his shoulders. And to Mona's infinite delight, Youssef took her hand in his. All the way home Mona looked up adoringly at Youssef. This grand young al-Masri god—this aristocrat who had thrown her a coin, this hero who had saved her from the sea, this courtier who had told her she shared the beauty of a gazelle—had singled her out. With Youssef as her protector, she was no longer a stranger amid these glamorous al-Masris. Mona made a fervent wish and touched her blue bead for luck.

3 ~~~~~~

KARNAK, EGYPT / May 1947

From along the river road Mona thought she could detect smoke from the village fires rising to the predawn bronze sky. "Is it there, just there?" Mona tugged at Khadiga's and Abbas's hands. "Are we almost to Karnak?"

"Almost home!" Khadiga, long dismissed by her family as an unwanted spinster, was returning in triumph with her new husband by her side. She hummed a few *el-hamdulillahs* under her breath, thanking God once again for rescuing her from disgrace.

Cloaked in the soiled dignity of a starched white *gallabeiya*, Abbas silently swished through the dust. He would use part of this holiday to take Khadiga even farther south to visit his own Nubian village, but he was nervous about this extended visit to Karnak. He knew Khadiga's family, with their inbred Saidi hauteur, would not quite approve of his black skin. Abbas gave the mud hovels around him an unhappy glance. It was beyond him why the Saidis felt so superior. Any fool could see they lived in squalor. Abbas sighed. He would have preferred staying at the villa until the al-Masris returned from Europe in the fall. It was only to please Khadiga that he had agreed to this summer in the Said. Abbas gave his bride a shy smile. She asked for so little that he always found himself wanting to give her so much.

As the birds began to rustle awake in the sycamore trees, Mona began to dance in quick little steps. Every fiber of her body, every pore, every hair on Mona's head swelled with the joy of her homecoming. Coming home to Ummie! In the nearly two years she had been away, Mona had craved her mother in the mornings when she pasted a bright smile on her face, in the afternoons when she passed the time with whoever would love her, in the nights when she had tried to deceive herself that a wool blanket was flesh and blood. In her mind she had played and replayed what she knew would be the exact tints and textures of this morning: the lilac light of the rising sun, the homely assurance of dust and dirt between her toes, the misty kiss of the river breeze on her cheeks. Ummie had come to Alexandria only for one strained visit. Mona assured herself that everything that had gone awry then— Ummie's spats with Abbas and Baruch, Ummie's possessive commandeering of all her attention, Ummie's criticism of every slight change in her appearance and behavior—would not recur. This time they would be reunited for a season. This time they would slip back into their old heady oneness.

"Look over there!" Khadiga was already eagerly finding landmarks. "That's the date palm we used to climb to dive into the river. Even the girls did it!" A look from Abbas seemed to restrain her from trying it again. "And there!" She pointed to a dirt path trailing up toward the hills. "That's where my brother Magdi—Allah keep him!—used to go on his donkey for fertilizer. How I used to envy him. *He* climbed high in the mountains, while *I* had to make do with the river!"

As they all took in the Nile's dawn-purple sparkle, Mona broke away and ran down the bank. She dipped in her dusty toes and watched the river wash her clean. Mona laughed, bent, and cupped her hand in the river. She brought a mouthful of Nile to her lips and drank it down. A draft of the Nile, it was always said, guaranteed that the thirsty would always return to the river. She laughed again. "Abbas! Khadiga! I'm back!" Mona took a deep breath of the river air. Nothing human moved on the river. The dark slow Nile was all hers. Over it a hupi bird spread black wings. Across it green fields yawned and violet mountains pressed up to violet sky. Mona stretched out her hand toward a pure-white ibis in the shallows near her. But the bird was stalking a shimmer of light on the river's silken surface. With one quick dart of its graceful neck and one greedy gulp of its slender throat, the ibis ate a small silver fish. The bird fluttered its delicate white wings and flew off in the direction of the sun. Mona shivered as if from a sudden chill. What if Ummie was angry at her again? She was glad to return to her friends. She felt better when she took Abbas's hand in hers.

"Our beach!" Khadiga was pointing to a gentle jut of land that reached grittily into the river. "My mother, my sisters, my cousins would go there every morning to get water and wash clothes. There. Just there!" Mona began to drag her feet ever so slightly. That river-bank was so very like the spot where Um Hassan had thrown her circumcision blood.

But as they approached the village proper, the sun began to break free from the barren beige-on-beige hillocks to the east. The chunky flat-roofed houses and the dusty shadows of date palm were bathed in hazy light. Beautiful, Mona told herself. The village and the river are so beautiful. From the minaret of the mosque they could hear the *muezzin* begin his slow sleepy call to prayer. "*Allahu akbar,* God is most great!" All three stopped in their tracks, looked at one another, and then without saying a word knelt by the side of the road to perform the morning prayers. Mona felt the dust of her mother's village on her forehead. She wished those grains of dirt felt sacred and familiar, but instead the dust was just dust. She tried to fight off her feeling of foreboding when a pack of skinny dogs snarled a menacing welcome.

As they continued on their way, Mona was envious that Khadiga could read the news of her village very nearly in the tracery of dust on its walls. New drawings on the house of the *kuttab* teacher told her the old man had just been to Mecca. A new room precariously tacked to the house of one of her uncles assured her a cousin had taken a wife. Khadiga enthused that the storefronts in the souk were exactly as she had left them: the ramshackle cigarette kiosk just in front of the coffeehouse, the cloth store next to the grocer's next to the barber's. The domed mosque was on its corner, and the saint's tomb still slept by its side. "Home!" Khadiga said. "Karnak!"

Bound first for Um Mona and her brother, Muhammad, they turned down a narrow passage. It was very dirty, far dirtier than Mona remembered Kom Ombo. Donkey dung lay in piles. Dusty chickens clucked sleepily. Somewhere acrid garbage was burning. Khadiga pointed to a crooked little house leaning to the left behind a mudbrick wall. "There! That's it!" At the dead end of the lane, smoke from a cooking pot curled up from the house of Muhammad.

Self-consciously, Mona patted down her hair, smoothed out her dress, then broke into a run. "Ummie! Ummie! It's me! Ummie!" She burst through the unlocked door, and there was her mother and a fat man with a wooden leg. "Ummie!" She jumped into her mother's arms and let the tears flow. She clutched her with all the pent-up loneliness of those long months apart. She buried her head deep in her mother's chest to try to obliterate all that had happened since last they parted. Baruch, Batata, Youssef were not only—almost—forgotten but had never lived. All that mattered was that the two halves of the whole were one.

Um Mona was the first to pull away. She looked into Mona's eyes, sighed, and settled her daughter on her lap.

Kissing that beloved face, Mona concluded that Ummie had not changed one bit. She had the same tight lips, although just now they were soft and smiling. She had the same piercing eyes, although just now they were deep and dreamy. Mona put her head on her mother's breast in the gesture of a suckling infant. When she had longed most for her mother, it had been to be held just like this.

Um Mona was meanwhile scrutinizing her daughter as a Bedouin eyes a fine young camel in the market. Mona was cleaner and neater. Her skin was creamier. She had filled out all over. There was a new rosiness—almost a gaiety—about her child. Mona was not only different but better. In this robust little girl there were no signs of grief or sleepless nights or days of longing. Wondering how Mona could have bloomed so apart from her, Um Mona could not stop herself from pinching one of Mona's dimples very hard.

Mona recoiled and shot a quick, worried glance at her mother's eyes. Fierce. Ummie's eyes looked fierce. Mona shrank away. But then, when Ummie's eyes flashed with anger, Mona turned an about-face. She had not been away so long that she had forgotten either how to read her mother's eyes or how to try to appease them. "Ummie! I wanted to be with you, only with you, every minute!"

"Yes?" Only Um Mona's lips turned up in a smile.

Aware that something had gone very wrong, Mona desperately elaborated. "Oh, the al-Masris *try* . . ." In a flash of regret Mona was remembering how very hard they did try. Baruch would never have pinched her cheek. Youssef and Batata and Abbas and Khadiga would never have hurt her. Mona gulped and raced ahead. "I don't like their food. Or their clothes. I hate it there, Ummie! I hate it! All I want is to be with you!"

Um Mona looked deeply into Mona's eyes.

The girl tried to stifle guilty thoughts about how very, *very* nice her new friends were in Alexandria. But Mona trembled when her mother's lips pulled down into a thin frown and her mother's eyes lost their glow. Mona bowed her head. Ummie knew. Ummie knew how she loved it in Alexandria. But did Ummie know how she had missed her doting love? Mona took a deep breath, remembering what she had tried to forget about those other looks of Ummie's. Resigning herself, then, to the inevitable, Mona allowed her mother to draw her out. It wasn't long before her mother knew how she admired Baruch, how Abbas reminded her of her father, how reassuring she found Khadiga's arms. She prattled about Batata's sweetness and Youssef's jokes. With a sense of horror she heard herself boasting about learning to swim and trying to read Arabic. She even showed off her few words of French. But Mona couldn't seem to find the words to tell her mother how she had truly missed her, how she had lain awake listening to the sad birds, how she had looked at the sea and wished for the river. All she seemed to be able to say were the very things she knew her mother would hate to hear.

Um Mona stared down at the disappointment that was her daughter. She knew betrayal when she heard it. Mona's head had been turned by her fancy new friends. This child she had been willing to sacrifice anything for now thought she was better than her own mother. Um Mona's worst fear had come true. So! So she had not been able to win Mona's undivided devotion by the purest love mother ever felt for daughter? So she had endured these long months apart from her child, so she had suffered these fools in Karnak, so she had stifled her every maternal yearning? For what? For betrayal!

With hooded eyes Um Mona watched her daughter chatter on. Clearly it had been a mistake to allow her to fly so high and free. But, Um Mona decided, it was a mistake she could correct. Mona was here for at least the next three months—longer, if she wanted. She didn't ever have to send Mona back to Alexandria.

Um Mona clutched the child in her lap. She had almost forgotten how big and strong she herself was and how small and weak was this daughter. In Alexandria those al-Masris were teaching her French. In Karnak she would teach Mona other—harder—lessons she would never forget.

She would bring Mona down to the muddy brown earth of Karnak.

Patiently Um Mona bided her time. She brushed off Mona's anxious pleas to tell her what was wrong. She allowed Mona to spend hour after hour with Muhammad. She kept just a little bit aloof as she introduced Mona to her relatives in the village. But all the while Um Mona waited for her moment.

On the sixth day of her daughter's homecoming, Um Mona awoke to the certainty that today was the day to reclaim her. Already, in the early morning, she could feel the powdery sand beating against her face. The heavy air was dirty in her lungs. It was early May, and most of the fifty days of the dark spring *khamseen* season were past. But Um Mona was sure that this year's biggest *khamseen* sandstorm was on its way. Today infernal winds from the western desert would engulf the Nile Valley in stinging, golden sands. Today there would be neither relief, nor remedy, nor respite from that great hot wind. And today she would teach Mona there could be no escape from their dual destiny.

The storm began to build as the morning wore on. Muhammad had made for his landlord's fields to save what he could of the spring crops. When he did not return, Um Mona praised Allah. Her brother, who must have taken shelter near the fields, would not have the chance to interfere with her plan.

By noon the air was thick enough to see. It was so hot Um Mona wanted to shed her skin. Then the sultry winds began to blow. The fierce wind danced the sand and swept date-palm branches from roofs. Donkeys screamed in terror. In the uncertain shelter of their homes, men and women huddled under the stifling heat of blankets. At the height of the sandstorm Um Mona took her daughter by the hand and led her outside.

The sand cut Mona's eyes. The air glowed gold. She heard maddened dogs howling as if their hearts must break. She felt the sand inside her mouth, her nostrils, behind her eyeballs. She was gagging on the sand. "Ummie? Ummie!" Her mother's sharp pull on her arm was the only answer.

Step by step Um Mona staggered forward with her black robe and shawl covering even her face and eyes. By feel she crept forward to the souk and then, as if she were driven by a desperate desire for the coolness of water, she dragged Mona against the wind down to the river. At the Nile the wind knocked Um Mona off her feet. There was a strange smile on her hidden lips as she lurched back up, daring the storm to try to topple her again. She stood laughing with her arms outstretched in the wind, reveling both in the power of the storm and in her defiance of it.

Mona could not take her terrified eyes off her mother. Never had she seen Ummie like this. With that black robe whipping about her legs, Ummie looked like some wild spirit of the dead. She heard her

65

mother shouting at her. The river. Ummie was telling her to throw herself in the river. No, to *purify* herself in the river. Mona knew better than to argue. She eased down the bank and into the Nile. The river was so cool and black, so sane and serene, so safe from the wild hot desert winds. Around her everything—the sky, the ground, even the water—was gold. Everything was gold but her black-shrouded mother.

Um Mona pulled her from the Nile. Um Mona's black robes swirled around her as she moved along the walls from house to house. They cleared the souk, bypassed Muhammad's, and climbed the slight grade toward Karnak Temple. Why, Mona wondered, would they be going to one of the Old Places? Foreign tourists were the only ones who went beyond those looming stone walls. "There?" Mona tugged at her mother's arm. "We're not going *there?*" Her mother kept dragging her toward the temple. Mona looked up at the golden sky. Only a reddish smear hinted where the sun must be. "Allah!" Mona prayed silently under her breath. Scores of somber stone sphinxes crouched beside them. Then they were surrounded by a forest of pillars, each precarious enough to tumble down and crush them in this storm. "I'm afraid!" Mona was whining. "Please, Ummie! Let's go home!"

"But Mona, *habibti*. That's where I'm taking you." Ummie's high-pitched voice was eerie. "We're going *all* the way home, Mona." The storm seemed to howl its agreement.

Mona prayed harder under her breath. As they worked their way along a dirt path through a meadow, the wind made whips of the high grass lashing their bodies. Mona started to cry to herself as they crept against the wind. But even when they reached the cover of a large stone building, Um Mona wouldn't let them rest. She hissed that they were almost there, and pushed open a huge creaky door. They stumbled out of the wind into dark still coolness. They passed under many tall ornate stone doorways. Mona shrieked at the sight of a headless god sitting before her like an omen. Um Mona held her hand tighter and opened a final door into all but absolute darkness. "We're here!"

Mona was weak with fear, yet she thanked Allah she was out of the storm. Her mother was acting so strange today. It must be the *khamseen*. Sandstorms made everyone a little crazy. A full moon and a *khamseen* brought out the madness in everyone. That must be it. Mona shut her eyes in relief. When she opened them again, as her eyes became accustomed to the dark, she was not prepared for what was before her in this narrow enclosed well of a room. The chamber was so angled that the eye was drawn to its far end. Mona caught her breath. A hole somewhere in the roof sent a single shaft of golden light shining on a tall ferocious statue, a slim sleek statue of an erect gleaming black panther—or rather a lion—or maybe it was a woman. It was the black statue of a lady lion. Under the lion's head the statue's body was that of a young woman with small pointed breasts and lithe strong thighs. Mona shuddered. There was a supernatural and sinister sheen to the statue. There was an air of evil in this chamber.

"She is very old." Um Mona spoke as though the statue were a favorite cousin.

Mona looked up at her mother, silent as though in a trance. Mona's eyes were drawn back to the statue. She had no will for anything but staring at the statue. The statue was so slim, so straight, so grim. But beautiful. The statue was very beautiful. Her mouth was set in a grimace that held no mercy. Around her head was a black stone circlet. In her hand was a long shaft. Her left foot was slightly in front of her right, as if she were about to stride forward to subdue the world. Mona trembled. She was afraid of this statue. This lady lion was cold, dread, ravishingly cruel. She couldn't understand why her mother would bring her to such a place on such a day. But she couldn't tear her eyes away. "Ummie! Ummie! Let's go home!"

"We *are* home!" Um Mona's eyes were glittering.

As Mona stared at the statue, the light from above fired its eyes so that it seemed the blank black eyes of the goddess were lit from inside. "Who is she?" Mona whispered.

"I have heard she is Sekhmet. One of the old goddesses. I came to her as a last resort before you were conceived, Mona. It finally was Sekhmet who, with the help of Allah, made you. I've brought you back to her, Mona, so that you would know." Um Mona's voice was a low hiss. "So that you will never forget who you are. Where you came from. And *what* you are." Um Mona broke out in a loud keening scream.

Mona shrank back from her mother and the statue. She could hear the moaning of the wind. She could feel the gold dust of the desert itching next to her skin.

"You don't belong with those people in Alexandria. They can teach you French. They can show you how to write. But *this,* Mona, is what you are!"

"Allah!" Mona screamed for God's help.

Mona's mother was taking her by the hand and dragging her toward the statue. "Look at her, Mona. Take a good long look at her! Her eyes, Mona. Her eyes!"

Mona stared. And as she did, the light from the hole in the temple roof shone directly down into the statue's eyes. As the wind outside changed, the sand danced into the temple. It seemed, then, that the eyes of the goddess, too, were dancing. It seemed the goddess was alive! Mona shut her own eyes and almost swooned.

Um Mona very nearly smiled. With a curt nod toward the statue, Um Mona continued on with her business. She dragged Mona like a limp doll back the length of the temple, through the meadow and the forest of pillars, past the rows of sphinxes, outside the temple walls, through the village. Um Mona once again drew up on the bank of the Nile. "Wash yourself! Purify yourself in the river!"

Mona eagerly followed her mother's orders. But when she was submerged up to her chin in the river, she heard her mother's voice.

"Do you feel it, Mona?" She was still using that terrible eerie tone. "Do you feel your river coming to claim you?"

"What?" Mona couldn't make sense of what her mother was saying. "What?"

"Touch your blue bead, Mona! Touch your bead!"

Hastily Mona did as she was told.

"The curse, Mona. The curse. We have to combat the curse!"

"What? What curse?"

"You don't know, Mona? You don't know?"

Mona was sweating even in the river. "Know what, Ummie?" Her mother's black robe was swirling in the wind. All Mona could see was the black river, her mother's black robe, the gold-drenched air.

"Something evil happened on the day of your circumcision. When your sexblood was thrown in the river, someone defiled it. Someone cheated the river of its due. Do you remember that, Mona?"

Mona frowned. Of course she remembered.

"Cursed, Mona! You are cursed! From that day forward, by the river you were cursed! Your curse killed your father on the river, Mona! Your curse is strong enough to kill!"

"No!" Suddenly Mona felt the menace in every drop of water. Frantically she tried to scramble out of the river, but she slipped and felt the black waters closing over her. She splashed in panic and fought her way toward the muddy bank. She crawled to where her mother stood and grabbed for Ummie's legs. Sobbing and panting, she clung to her mother. "Save me! Ummie! Save me!"

Um Mona looked down at her daughter. It seemed that Mona was as frightened as it was possible to be. The *khamseen*, the black lioness statue, and the river's curse had woven their spell. Um Mona sat on the riverbank and took her daughter tenderly in her arms. "Don't cry, Mona. I'll save you, daughter. I'll keep away the curse, and the black goddess, and everything else that frightens you so much. Only *I* can save you, Mona! Only I!"

Mona looked up into her mother's eyes. She felt her mother lift her hand to touch the blue bead around her neck. Mona thanked Allah that she had her mother to save her from all the dread doings of the world.

There were four of them in the faded old cargo felucca drifting in midstream. Mona and her mother squatted together in the open belly. Muhammad leaned back with his hand on the rudder and the stump of his right thigh and wooden leg balanced on the side of the boat. Shinnying above them on the single mast, the boy Adil untied knots. The canvas flapped and unfurled. The lateen sail caught the wind.

Mona edged closer to her mother. That hot daze of two summer months had not blunted all her fear of the Nile. In those first few weeks after that *khamseen* terror, Mona had clung to her mother's skirts like a two-year-old toddler. When she had been awake, there was only her mother and the sun. When she had been asleep, there was only her mother, the sandstorm, the black goddess, and the river. The days and nights had been a fog of fear. But in time Um Mona had convinced her daughter that the blue bead—and her own presence—was enough to keep the worst of the Nile's curse at bay. By the end of June, Mona had been able to sit by the river without bursting into tears. By July she was coaxed into taking a journey by boat—at Abbas's expense—to visit his Nubian village. They had all sailed upriver, rested a week in the village, and now—since Abbas and Khadiga wanted to linger in his village—only the four of them were heading home in the sailboat.

The felucca was worn and rusty, its paint was peeling, and its fan-shaped sail was patched and patched again. But age didn't stop the low-riding boat from coming to life in the wind. Gracefully it rolled over slightly on its side. Mona made a grab for her mother's hand, but then touched her blue bead and laughed at her own timidity. They were on the river. Mona almost believed there was nothing to fear on the Nile.

It was nearly noon, and the orange sun beat down on the brown water. The river was swollen with its summer flood. High waters coursed the jutting banks. The river looked clearer, lighter, younger, almost Agami turquoise just *there,* where the sun hit it, a true blue just *here* when Mona leaned over the side and trailed her hand in the water. They glided near one shore, then the boat tilted and glided again to the other bank: back and forth in a slow repeated dissolve.

Mona reveled in how slowly everything moved when they were on the river. It was so snug to be in a world inhabited only by her mother, her uncle, and the boat boy, swimming in a world bounded only by the river and the shore and the sun. Mona stretched out on her back, blinked at the sun, and felt the fear bake out of her. She lolled on her stomach and, looking at the shore, surrendered herself entirely to the heart of Upper Egypt, to the African, Arabian Said swirling past them on the banks.

The sights changed little from second to minute to hour to day. Always it was predictably, peacefully the same. Forests of date palms were lush and stark against the golden sky. Stony rolling bluffs framed the palms. Primitive cavelike tombs, the legacy of a people so old that history had forgotten them, were cut into the rock. Banks were now sandy, now green, with terraced gardens side by side with dead reaches of dust. Women cloaked in long black robes clustered on the banks to wash clothes or fill jugs. From afar the long lines of shrouded women with burdens balanced on their heads looked like colonies of mute and muted insects. The fields ran sometimes smack to meet the water and at other spots stretched far back from the shore. There was a constant, deliberate, slow bustle in those green-brown fields, a stirring of men and of donkeys, of camels and of water buffalo. The shouts of the men mixed with the braying of the donkeys, the mooing of the buffalo, and the moans of the camels, blending into a bittersweet lament of back-breaking labor without a beginning or a middle or an end.

Separated for at least a few days from the real drudgery of that life on shore, those on the boat sighed at the dreamy beauty, the perfect symmetry, the splendid inevitability of those on the banks. There was serenity in ancient ways, comfort in the knowledge that none of it had ever changed and that none of it ever would.

To one of their company, however, it was no sweeter to watch this life than to live it. As they drifted north on the Nile, Um Mona refused to mellow. She would stare thoughtfully and nudge Muhammad when a village came into view. Behind those familiar flat-topped mud houses, some painted in pastel shades weathered to muddy beige and brown, some covered with date-palm branches, some open to the sun and stars, lived men and women who could be her brothers and sisters.

"There is a woman who cries because her husband is about to take a second wife," Um Mona said very sadly once.

"There is a man who cannot get enough water to his fields to feed his family," Muhammad answered.

"There is a girl who prepares herself for her wedding to a man she hardly knows."

"There is a boy bound for *kuttab* school, knowing he will never be able to remember the verses of the Koran."

"There are women chopping vegetables today as every other day."

"There are men digging into the earth, cursing it and loving it all the same."

"All this, Muhammad, is nothing."

"No, sister. It is everything."

In the idle hum of their voices, as the village slowly faded from sight, was the continuation of a debate that had begun when the two of them were only children. Mona looked from her mother to her uncle. This Muhammad was a man among men. She already knew that he had saved both her mother and her father. He had lost his leg—and four of Mona's kinsmen had lost their lives—defending her mother long ago against the shameful overtures of a former slave. Then many years later, when Muhammad was working the barges with her father, this uncle had extricated Baba from a steel fish trap and dragged him long miles to a doctor. When she had first met this uncle, she had been struck by his booming laugh, by his gentle manner, and—most of all—by how much he resembled her mother. They had the same mud-brown skin, the same broad face, the same high cheekbones. They had the same heavy hunched nose. They had the same double chins, jowly cheeks, grizzled black hair. They had the same thin lips, although Muhammad's were often splayed into a smile under his lean black mustache. But it was their eyes that set the pair apart. There was no rest in her mother's eyes, and there was no steel in Muhammad's. Her mother wasn't content with one single thing. Her uncle seemed content with everything. Mona leaned over and looked at her own reflection in the Nile. Was she more like her mother or her uncle?

Once Muhammad, inspired by a view of a serene stretch of fields with *fellahin* sleeping in the shade of nearby palm trees, told them a story he had first heard on the barges. A man from Cairo comes up to a *fellah* resting under a tree, contemplating both the river and his navel. "What are you doing?" the Cairene asks him. "Resting," the *fellah* replies. "But why," the city man asks, "aren't you working? The sun is up. You should be in the fields." The *fellah* yawns. "So? Why should I work?" The Cairene answers in a rush of words, "If you worked and worked and worked, instead of sitting here, then in time you could buy one *feddan*, one whole acre. And if you worked harder and harder, all day long and half the night, then soon you would have two *feddans*. And as the years went by, and you continued to work harder and harder, soon you would be a real landowner." "So what?" the *fellah* replies. "What would that get me?" The Cairene has an air of triumph when he answers, "Then you would be very rich and could rest." The *fellah* grins. "I'm resting now."

Um Mona did not even crack a smile. "Typical," was all she said. "That is *so* typical of Karnak."

Mona's eyes clouded with confusion. Which Said was true? Was this quiet backwater that Uncle Muhammad loved so much all gentleness and naps in the sun? Or was it as her mother said it was, as her mother had taken such pains to show her? Mona yawned. It was too hot for such thoughts. For now it was enough just to breathe in the Said and watch the flight of river birds.

Mona's favorites were the fine-boned white ibises of filigree wings and swirling airy flights. Once she thought she saw a glorious big fern-leafed tamarind tree covered with fair white flowers. But then there was a rustle and a flap, and the flowers flew up and made for the sun. Ibis birds filled the sky.

"Pretty," Muhammad said. "So pretty. Like women."

The hupis—those chattering, graying blackbirds marked with vivid scarlet and teal—careened overhead, then swooped at the river, clowning for the fish.

"Full of themselves," Um Mona said. "Like men."

71

Arrow-straight flocks of geese flew farther south in perfect formation.

"It must be a hard life for them, always moving, never at rest," Muhammad said.

"Maybe they're looking for something better," said Um Mona. "Maybe they find it."

Sometimes they saw fierce hawks and elegant eagles bent on errands more important than those of other birds. "They are the pashas of the sky," Muhammad said.

"And that one there," Mona asked, pointing to the one who flew the highest. "Is he the king?"

"Why not?" Muhammad said. "Why not?"

One afternoon Muhammad waved a fat finger at the river estates of a real king. Mona and her mother nearly tipped over the boat rushing for a glimpse of Faruk's flowers and hedges and trees. There were red blossoms as big as a donkey's head, bushes cut in the shape of great pyramids, tamer blooms of orange and white and purple and pink. King Faruk's gardens and fields stretched as far as they could see on both banks of the Nile.

"They say he comes sometimes in the winter," Um Mona told her daughter with reverence. "They say his train is all white, Mona, *white!*—and that it's so long you can't see where it starts and where it ends."

"They say," Muhammad added, "that he grows so fat that you cannot see where *he* begins and ends."

"You mock your betters," Um Mona said.

"I speak the truth." Patiently Muhammad tried to educate his sister. For sixty-five years the British had ruled Egypt as an overseer might boss slaves on a cotton plantation. And for sixty-five years hatred of the British had been the only political constant in Egypt. Egypt had never been a formal crown colony, had only briefly been a protectorate, but all the while had been economically dependent on London. Then, during the last world war, when Rommel's Panzers were almost to Alexandria, the desperate British had surrounded Faruk's Cairo palace and forced him to be their humiliated puppet. Muhammad spit in the Nile in the general direction of King Faruk's manicured gardens.

Mona watched the spittle float spiderlike on the crest of the water and then slowly—so very, very slowly that she forgot the reason for Muhammad's spitting in the river—dissolve and then disappear.

Everything was slow like that on the Nile. But nothing was as tantalizingly slow as the Nile's sunsets. Those special hours when the light turned sometimes silver, sometimes gold, were gloriously, glowingly, drawn out for hour upon hour. They watched it serenely, awash in the spectacle of every nuance of light as they glided soundlessly from bank to bank, at one with themselves, their land, and their river.

One night, eager to make up for time lost drifting without wind, they sailed long after nightfall. Mona was never to forget the blissful sweep of the water. Lulled by the gentle lapping, she slipped off to sleep and woke at dawn to find they had finally come to rest on a bed of tall reeds. But most nights, anchored at one of the sand islands dotting the midstream Nile, they lay on deck staring at the inky sky and counting the sprays of stars. As they watched, a shooting star almost always shook loose and streaked through the heavens, until the sky was black and their eyelids heavy and they slept.

On their last night, just a few miles from Karnak, Muhammad dug out his drum and Adil his lute. With the palm of his hand and with the tips of his fingers, Muhammad beat out an ages-old river rhythm on the taut donkey-skin drumhead. Adil answered him with the birdlike trill of the lute. Muhammad began to sing, and the crooning rise and fall of his Arabic chant was in perfect synchronization with the river, the shore, and the sky.

His music was answered by a faint echo carried by the wind from downriver.

"What's that?" Mona asked.

"Fishermen," Muhammad explained. "They're singing the song of the dancing fish." He smiled down at Mona. "Every night, as they wait on the river with their nets, they sing that song you hear right now. First high. Then low. Always sweet. They sing so well that the fish can't help dancing. They sing so well that the fish dance all the way into their nets."

"They do that?" Mona asked. "Dance into the nets?"

"They do," Muhammad answered. "They dance into the nets."

"It is a dance of death," Um Mona said.

"Both life and death," Muhammad countered. "Life for us. Death for the fish. But a happy death. They die dancing."

Mona fell asleep to the song of the dancing fish.

One hot afternoon toward the end of that summer, Mona sat watching her mother's stepmother, Zainab, grinding corn into meal. Over the months Mona had learned to like sitting beside this woman whose legs were made for dancing and whose tongue was made for gossip. It was so easy to be with Zainab, because Zainab always repeated herself.

"Yes, yes, yes." Sounding that one word as if it were a religious chant, Zainab nodded her still-pretty head to the beat of her words. As a girl Zainab might have been lush and lovely, but a loving trick of Allah's had transformed her into a real beauty in her middle years. Perhaps it was her good bones and her flashing eyes that made her face, always framed in black, so fine to look upon. But others who knew Zainab well might say that it was her heart that had performed this magic. Zainab was as soft as kitten's fur. "I tell you, Mona, it was a blessing on this village—it was Allah's gift to great Karnak—it was a *good thing*, Mona, when the old Omda finally breathed his last. Though it is always a sad thing—I cry, Mona, I always shed a tear—at the death of any man. I even cry sometimes—I weep, Mona, I have been known to weep—when I see so much as a dog lying dead in the street. Death!" Zainab dramatically flung her hand to her eyes, leaving a smudge of cornmeal or her lashes. "There is nothing so sad as death!"

Zainab made Mona want to laugh even at death. Perhaps that was why she felt so drawn to Zainab this summer. Mona had shied away from her stepuncle, Hussein, who was so rich from selling hashish. She had made very tentative friends with the mob of children who were her cousins. But she always liked to laugh with Zainab. On this particular day Mona sensed Zainab was working herself up to a story about Karnak's recently deceased headman. "The Omda? Did you know him, Grandmother? I bet you did. I bet you could tell me all about him!"

"Tch! Tch!" Zainab slowed her already slow grinding of the corn. She nudged the kernels between the two smooth rocks. As usual, she was putting most of her energy into her words. "Not me! Oh, not me, Mona! No, you'll have to find someone else to talk of the Omda! I would never, *never,* speak a word against the dead. Not me! Oh, not me!"

Mona settled back on her haunches. Zainab was obviously about to tell a story about the Omda.

"Ah, yes, Mona! Ah, yes! You won't hear a word about the Omda from me, not from me! *I* won't be the one to tell you about that terrible old man, that man who beat donkeys to death for eating his roses, that man who cheated poor farmers out of their patches of land! That one who fancied himself a pharaoh of old! No, I will not speak of that one. He was a murderer. No one else will say it. But I will. I wouldn't before—when he was alive. But now I will. He killed. The Omda was a killer."

Mona was disappointed. She had thought her stepgrandmother was about to tell her a funny story. Instead a frown etched creases in Zainab's forehead.

"My lips are sealed. I will say no more. Already I have said too much." Zainab made a few halfhearted swipes at her corn and then looked up at Mona. "You're like *her,* you know. She was beautiful like you. Kind. Though she used to laugh more than you do. They said she was the most beautiful woman in the village. I used to wish that I was like her. I married her Abdullah later, but I never could take her place." Zainab sighed. "It was terrible what they did to her."

"Who?"

Zainab went back to pounding her cornmeal. This time she pressed hard enough, angrily enough, to turn the corn to dust. "Pay no mind to me, Mona. I'm just an old woman who talks too much. That's all I am. Just a babbling old woman."

Mona wasn't going to let Zainab get way with telling her only half a story. She tried cunning where directness had failed. "I bet you were *more* beautiful than she. I don't even know what she looked like, but I'm sure you were prettier. No one could be more beautiful than *you,* Grandmother!"

Zainab's face lit up. "You flatter me, child. You flatter me!" Zainab *adored* flattery. But she thought it becoming to be modest. "No, no, no! I wasn't as pretty as your *real* grandmother. Not really! Though *you* may be someday, Mona. You have her eyes, her hair, her nature. You even have her name. I remember her when she was a little girl —when she was your age. If I didn't know better, sometimes I would think you *were* that other Mona! Allah help us! Allah keep you from her fate!"

Mona's hand crept up to touch the blue bead around her neck.

"So sad it was." Zainab was shaking her head, and there were tears in her eyes. "Not only to be murdered like that, but it was so senseless, Mona! It was so cruel! But the worst of it, Mona, the worst of it was how it changed your *own* mother!"

"Ummie?"

Zainab was no longer even pretending to grind corn. "She is what she is, as she is, because of what the Omda did. You know, Mona, you know what?"

Mona shook her head, bewildered.

"You know, Mona, I think the Omda as good as killed your mother when he killed your grandmother!" Zainab wiped her eyes and began to grind her corn very finely between her two rocks.

Mona let out a long breath. But although she sat in Zainab's house the rest of the afternoon, although she begged and pleaded and flattered and cajoled, Mona could entice her stepgrandmother to tell her no more.

The very next day, as Mona sat with Muhammad under the shade of a palm tree near the fields, she tried again. At first her uncle put her off. It had all happened so very long ago. Why call back ghosts? Muhammad finally relented only when Mona threatened to repeat what Zainab had said to her mother. He didn't want Um Mona starting another family feud with Zainab. It taxed all Muhammad's diplomacy to keep the peace between those two women.

Mona's grandmother had died, Muhammad said, when he was nine years old and Mona's mother only six. It had happened the same year that their baby brother had died in his sleep of a strange raging fever. It had happened when Karnak's Omda was a young impulsive man nervous that the recent peasant uprisings against the British would somehow shake his own reign. "I've thought about this for years, Mona. All my life I've tried to understand why my mother was killed. Maybe the Omda did it because he was afraid that if he let one *fellaha* break the rules, it would be the beginning of the end. Or maybe it was simpler than that. Maybe he just used brute force—yes, I think *fear* was the point—to keep us docile as donkeys."

Mona looked at her uncle doubtfully. She didn't want to hear about the historical roots of fear. She wanted to know how her grandmother had died.

She had been found, Muhammad said, with a knife in her chest floating in one of the jade-green irrigation canals one hot summer morning. No one had seen the murder, but everyone knew who had ordered it and why. The day before, Mona's grandmother had gone to the cigarette kiosk in the center of the village. She had purchased a packet of cigarettes and then lit one in plain view of all the men on the stoop outside the coffeehouse. That was the crime for which Mona's grandmother had died.

Mona couldn't believe it. She couldn't believe that would have happened in Karnak. She couldn't believe her grandmother had been murdered for smoking a cigarette.

Everything, Muhammad said, was different in the village then. Karnak wasn't so modern. It used to be, Muhammad said, as unthinkable for a woman to smoke in public as it would be for her to dance naked in the mosque during Friday prayers. Smoking was immoral. Only a very bad woman smoked. It was for being a bad woman that Mona's grandmother had been killed.

"But Zainab says that I am very like my grandmother." Mona touched her blue bead.

"Zainab has a loose tongue."

Mona swallowed hard. Uncle Muhammad had not denied that she was like her grandmother. Mona told herself she must not harp on that. "But *why* did my grandmother smoke if it wasn't allowed?"

"Ah. The eternal question. Rebellion. Why does a man—or a woman—finally rebel?"

"That's no answer."

"Perhaps she did it because she couldn't help it."

"I still don't understand."

"Nor do I."

Mona changed the subject. "And Ummie? What of her?"

Tears sprang to Muhammad's eyes. "Helwa. We used to all call your mother *Helwa*, 'the Sweet.' She was the sweetest, the gayest, the happiest little girl in the village. Can you imagine that? Mona, we both *love* your mother. But we both *know* your mother. Imagine, Mona, that everyone in the village once called your mother Helwa!"

Muhammad and Mona both sighed.

It was after the murder, Muhammad said, that Mona's mother changed. She grew very, very fat. She blamed all the other men, women, and children of Karnak for her mother's death. She thought they should have made the Omda pay for his crime. Muhammad sighed again. "As if they could take revenge on the Omda! It was Allah's will that my mother die that death. But your mother refused to accept Allah's will." Muhammad shook his head. "It was a tragedy. All of it—from beginning to end—was a terrible tragedy."

Mona mulled all this over that night as she sat by the river with her mother. She wished more than anything else in the world that she could comfort her. Poor Ummie, to have suffered like that! Mona could imagine how she herself might feel if someone as evil as that Omda had murdered her mother for something as silly as smoking a cigarette. *That* was the reason for the mysterious blackness of her mother's eyes. "Oh, Ummie!" Impulsively Mona threw her arms around her mother's neck. "You have me, Ummie! Always, you have me! And I'm like her! Zainab says I'm just like *her!*"

Um Mona gave her daughter a light hug. "Like Zainab? You're not a bit like Zainab. You—you, Mona, you're like—like a gazelle. But her—she's like a camel!" Um Mona laughed.

Mona looked at her mother very seriously. "No, Ummie. I didn't mean Zainab. I just mean . . . I mean, Ummie, I wanted to tell you that even though *your* mother died . . . like that . . . Ummie . . . you still have me. You'll always have me!"

Um Mona's eyes were very black and very wide. "What? What did you say?"

Mona stammered even more when she repeated what she now wished she had never said.

"So you know! You know!" Um Mona went as stiff as a corpse.

Mona tried again. "I'm sorry, Ummie. It must have been terrible."

Um Mona began to rock back and forth on her haunches. "Yes, oh, yes, it was terrible. I was there, Mona. I was there when they fished her out of that canal. My beautiful mother, Mona, was a swollen bloated corpse." With a sweep of her hand, Um Mona indicated her own obese body. "She was like *this,* Mona. Like I am now. Ugly! They killed my mother and made her ugly!" Um Mona stuffed one of her clenched hands into her mouth as if to choke off unspeakable words. But then she spoke once more. "It was *their* fault, Mona. Not one of them went to the Omda and said it was wrong! That's *why* he did it! He did it because he knew he could get away with it! They should have *tried!* And no one did, Mona. No one said a word. Not one word." Um Mona seized her daughter by the shoulders and shook her. "But you'll make it better, Mona! You'll be our escape. You're pretty, Mona. You can find a rich husband in Alexandria! Look for one, Mona. Find him, sink your teeth into him, and don't let go until you marry him. Do it for me, Mona! For me!" Um Mona began to cry in the small, steady shudders of a bereaved child.

Mona took her mother in her arms and nestled her large head on her small chest. She looked beyond her mother at the Nile. The sun was down. The river, the banks, the sky were a blackish gray. It was very quiet but for her mother's sobs. Mona wished she weren't such a little girl. Maybe if she were bigger, older, smarter, she could make her mother and herself feel better. But all Mona could think was that if both her arms were not around her mother, she would touch her blue bead.

Mona sighed so softly that she was sure her mother would not be able to hear her. It was late August. Abbas had said just the other day that they would be leaving soon for Alexandria. She would do as Ummie asked. She would hunt for a husband to save Ummie and herself. She hoped—she prayed to Allah with all her heart—that she would find one. Today, *now*, Karnak scared her. The river scared her. Her mother scared her. Yet she loved her mother, her river, her village —yes, even her village. They all touched her so much more deeply than anything that could possibly exist in Alexandria. She loved her Said, and yet she wanted to flee from it. Mona stroked her mother and dreamed of escape to Alexandria.

Looking out at the river—red and swollen at the height of the worst flood in years—Abbas was in a terrible temper. He should have prevailed on Khadiga to leave Karnak last month. But she had wanted to stay to celebrate the marriage of a cousin, and so they had been stranded when the river most unexpectedly began to rampage. The railroad tracks were under five feet of water. Karnak itself was a humpy island in the midst of a Nile as wide as a sea. Yet in less than two weeks the al-Masris were due back in Alexandria. Abbas had a villa to air out, dust off, spruce up. And here he was, marooned in Karnak. He had refused to be comforted by Khadiga's assurances that the river had crested, that maybe the Nile would start to recede next week, that the al-Masris would understand why they were late. He wasn't some shiftless servant who would use the excuse of a little bit of water to keep him from his work. He was a *suffragi*. He had been hired to make life run very smoothly at the Villa al-Masri. Madame and Monsieur would be furious if they returned to a dusty, stuffy house with nary a servant in sight. Abbas stood in the center of Karnak—the souk was now on the riverbank—and glared at the Nile. Clearly, they would have to take a boat on this inhospitable river.

So it was that only a day or two later Mona huddled on the steps of the mosque and pleaded with her mother to be allowed to stay in Karnak. She was sure that if she climbed into that rickety rowboat, she would meet her fated death on the river this very morning.

In the midst of the crowd of relatives, Um Mona laughed at Mona's fears. The boatman would avoid the swift currents by sticking close to the shore. With Allah's blessings, they would drift downstream to Qena in less than an hour. From there they would be able to hitch a ride north on a large motor-driven barge. "Don't be a baby, Mona. Get in the boat. Show some courage."

Mona's eyes filled with tears. Surely Ummie, of all people, must know that she had only very tattered shreds of courage. She looked out at the river. The Nile was the exact color of blood dried on white cotton. The Nile was wild and ugly and fearsome. A man, a woman, a child—especially a child—would court certain death on this river today. Her puny little blue bead couldn't possibly save her from something as powerful as this surly river.

Abbas crawled into the rowboat and helped Khadiga to his side. When Mona's turn came, she refused to budge. In the end Abbas had to carry her, sobbing, on board. She hid her head in Khadiga's lap when she felt the boat catch in the current.

But Mona had to look back at Ummie and Karnak. The village seemed a small island in a vast sea. And from her new vantage point, Karnak suddenly scared her more than the river. For as she waved, she saw her mother strike a new pose framed in the doorway of Karnak's whitewashed mosque. Um Mona stood straight and tall all in black, her left foot slightly ahead of her right, as though she were about to stride forward to subdue the world. Instantly Mona recognized the stance she had seen once in the *khamseen* and many times more in her nightmares. Her mother stood in the pose of the dread lion goddess of Karnak Temple. "Allah!" Mona prayed. *"Allah!"*

4 ~~~~~~

ALEXANDRIA, EGYPT / October 1947

Abbas tried to smile, not grin, at Baruch across the rickety tin-topped table in the coffeehouse. Abbas had heard before of foreigners so awash in Oriental mystique that they sank all the way into Egypt. Decked out in his brand-new striped *gallabeiya,* his hair wrapped in a tight white turban, looking more Arab than an Arab, Baruch appeared to be almost over his head in Egypt.

Baruch tried to cross his legs under the unfamiliar skirt of his robe as he examined the café. Sawdust and spit mixed happily on the floor, a ragged old man was reciting poetry in a corner, and on the benches at the rear the regulars were blissfully sucking on their water pipes. Egyptian. It was all so Egyptian. Once again Baruch congratulated himself for choosing to be Egyptian. As soon as he had returned from Europe, Baruch had formally changed his citizenship from Italian to Egyptian. Here and now, lounging in his robe, he knew that choice to be the right one. Let the rest of his family, like most of the one hundred fifty thousand Westerners living in Egypt, retain the legal status their ancestors brought with them. Let them enjoy the privileges of exemption from Egyptian taxes, from service in the Egyptian army, even—since foreigners were tried in special consular courts—from observing Egyptian laws. Baruch had heard his brother complain often enough that Egypt was going to the dogs because lately some of these special foreign privileges had begun to be eaten away. But, still, Baruch thought it unjust that to be a foreigner in Egypt was to be better than an Egyptian. Four generations of al-Masri had lived and died and become very rich in Egypt without ever judging themselves in any way accountable to this country. But never mind. Let the rest of his family be what they wanted to be. He himself, now, was by law what he felt himself to be—most of the time—in fact. To speed up his assimilation, he had engaged a tutor to teach him to read classical Arabic. He was boning up on pharaonic history. In time, by God, he might even make these fellows here in this café his friends.

But tonight he and Abbas were on a paternal mission. Last year Abbas had arranged the marriage of the café owner and Fatima, the former al-Masri maid. From time to time Abbas dropped in on Mahmoud to make the point that someone from Fatima's "family" was still looking out for her. Baruch offered Mahmoud a Soussa cigarette when he came to sit at their table, and they el-hamdulillahed at the news that Fatima was pregnant.

The smile vanished from Mahmoud's eyes as he indicated, with a nod of his head, that a man who had been bellowing nearby to a nest of his cronies seemed to be making for their own table. "Here comes trouble. He is, I think, Ikhwan el-Muslimin, a Muslim Brother."

Abbas shot a worried look at Baruch but then relaxed. Baruch did not look like a foreigner. This Ikhwan could not possibly be about to make trouble for Baruch. Abbas, like any moderate man of his time, was leery of the violent, self-righteous, ever-more-powerful Ikhwan. For years the Muslim Brothers had been painting anti-foreign slogans on the pavements of the public squares and haranguing crowds of passersby on the Corniche. Worse, far worse, two years ago the Muslim Brothers had assassinated one Western-leaning Egyptian prime minister and tried to murder his successor as well. Then, just last May, here in Alexandria, an Ikhwan bomb had killed several innocent foreigners when it exploded in the Metro cinema. Abbas thought the Muslim Brothers were an abomination.

The man stopped in front of their table. "You're Abbas."

"And you?" Abbas was as cold and formal as a *suffragi* can be. "Who are you?"

"A messenger." Ignoring both Baruch and Mahmoud, the man leered behind his bristly beard. "Merely a messenger. Not as exalted as that other Messenger, of course. Though my mission is similar, and my inspiration the same."

Abbas frowned. This man had the effrontery to compare his own coming to their table to the Prophet's bringing Allah's Word to the world.

"My own message, *Effendi Suffragi*, is that I suppose you'll be looking for a new job soon."

"I think not."

"I do. I really do, Abbas. Your 'family' will be leaving Egypt soon, *Effendi Suffragi*. Going to Palestine, no doubt."

Abbas sipped his coffee and ignored the insinuation.

The Muslim Brother leaned on the fragile table. "Oh, come on, now, *Suffragi*. Don't play dumb. Their name isn't really al-Masri. They're not really 'the Egyptians,' now, are they?"

Abbas stared back into the man's bloodshot eyes.

"They're Jews, Abbas. Jews. They don't belong here. And they won't be here much longer. Consider this a warning, *Suffragi*."

The café owner rose, apologized faintly, and led the Brother back to the other *Ikhwan*. It appeared that Mahmoud was appeasing them all with a free round of coffee.

Baruch sat staring into space. Why, he wondered again, had his great-grandfather bothered to change his surname from Morenu to al-Masri—"the Egyptian"? Few of the other foreigners had done so. Baruch supposed his great-grandfather had been afraid that someday, against all odds, Egypt's Muslims might turn against its Jews, just as Europe's Christians did so regularly. Baruch shook his head, then leaned back in his wooden chair. Jews had lived in Alexandria, mostly in peace and prosperity, for more than two thousand years. There was no reason, despite what had just happened, to think the situation was about to change. "You know as well as I do, Abbas, that Egypt's Muslims do not hate Jews." Baruch was embarrassed to say such an obvious truth out loud. *Of course* Egypt's Muslims did not hate Jews. This wasn't Nazi Germany.

Abbas nodded. Even when he was a boy, back in his Nubian village, he had been taught by his father that both Jews and Christians were People of the Book. Abraham was their common ancestor. Moses was a Prophet of the Muslims as well as the Jews. There were, of course, *differences*. Abbas would never have married a Jew. But neither would he have taken a Christian wife. To this very day, the distinction between Christian and Jew was not clearly drawn in Abbas's mind.

Baruch raised his cup and assured Abbas and himself that what had just happened was an incident aimed not at an Egyptian Jew like himself but at Zionists in Palestine. But he seemed to lose his taste for the Arab coffee as he remembered a few other incidents that everyone had been eager to dismiss as isolated. Two years ago in Cairo, fascist gangs had torched a synagogue, a Jewish hospital, a Jewish home for the aged, and a Jewish soup kitchen. Ten years ago bombs had been found outside Cairo synagogues. The police had defused the explosives, but on the fuses had been warnings that Egypt's Jews must not rally to Zionism. Too, there was the matter of that eccentric Egyptian pasha who had led an unsuccessful effort a decade ago to boycott all Jewish-made goods on the grounds that Jewish profits were inevitably siphoned to Zionist coffers in Palestine. Was all this cause for panic? Baruch thought not. "So one Muslim Brother gets carried away in a café? *Malesh*, it is of no importance."

Abbas forced a smile, pretended Baruch was right, and insisted on paying for the coffees as they made their way to the door. And yet, as Abbas caught the fanatic eyes of that Muslim Brother upon them, he was not altogether convinced.

Walking home in the season's first hesitant rain, Baruch considered what the hysterical Arab voices on the radio had to say about the escalating level of violence in Palestine. Clearly, all-out war there was being averted only by the presence of British troops. And, just as clearly, the British wouldn't referee it forever. Peering through the damp mist that hugged the sidewalks all around him, Baruch wondered just how vulnerable he and his might become here if one day Arab and Jew were to go to war. During the last world war Egypt had remained neutral for most of the hostilities. But the occupying British had seen to it that Italian residents were detained in desert concentration camps. Rafael had had to pay a wagonload of *baksheesh* to exempt the al-Masris from the roundup. Yet if worst came to worst now, during a Palestine war, Egypt's seventy-five thousand Jews—with their foreign or even "stateless" status, living in their enclaves in Cairo and Alexandria—could easily be herded into those desert camps for deportation. But was that really, Baruch asked himself, the worst that could happen? Dachau! Treblinka! Auschwitz! Buchenwald! Baruch's temples throbbed at the thought. He told himself, as they entered the front gate of the Villa al-Masri, that his imagination was running away with him. He had nothing in common with those sentimental, neurotic Jews who got so emotional over their lost land of Zion. It was absurd to imagine that the government and people of Egypt would ever equate an Alexandrian Jew like him with the Zionists of Palestine. The al-

Masris were hardly even Jews. The boys were circumcised at birth and had their *bar mitzvah* at adolescence. The girls were always married under a bridal canopy. The dead were inevitably buried in the Jewish cemetery. Aside from that, the al-Masris were precisely as Jewish as they were Italian—on paper but not at heart.

Baruch unwrapped his turban and handed it over to Abbas. As he mounted the staircase to his bedroom, he reflected on how his great-grandfather had come here from Milan in the 1860s. At that exact moment, to Ibrahim Morenu, Egypt must have been irresistible. With the American Civil War blockading rival crops, there had been a gold rush in Egyptian cotton. Too, the opening of the Suez Canal must have seemed such a great opportunity. And trade, tax, and legal agreements had promised to give all but the moon to any foreigner who would settle here.

Certainly, judging from the family's current worth in millions of pounds sterling, the move to Egypt had been a shrewd one. But had it been altogether wise? All his life, Baruch had lived on the margins. He was a nonobservant Jew in a land of Muslims. He had been Italian even though he had never spent more than an occasional holiday in that country. It was to end some of this ambivalence that he had taken out Egyptian citizenship. But, Baruch thought as he slipped out of his cotton *gallabeiya* and into an imported silk dressing gown, should anyone ask me, at this very moment, *what* or *who* I am, what would I answer? I am and I am not a Jew. I am and I am not an Egyptian. He wished he were as certain of his identity as, say, Mona must be.

Mona, on an evening a few weeks later, was being pressed into service for an al-Masri dinner party. It was highly irregular for her to help serve in the dining room, but Abbas's extra maid was ill. Tonight Mona would be two more hands at those crucial moments when it was necessary quickly to clear the table of one course and lay the china, silver, and crystal for the next.

As she puzzled over the difference between salad and dessert forks, Mona wondered why the al-Masris made everything so complicated. In Karnak everyone ate with his fingers. Karnak! Most of the time she missed it so. Ummie! She assured herself, as she always did, that she loved her mother more than she loved anything else in the world. Her mother, her village—they were her heart. Last summer, despite that *khamseen* madness, it had been such a relief to be with people who were exactly like herself instead of so different—as everyone, even the servants, were different in Alexandria. Mona could never be quite sure of anything here. Yet there was heaven in this villa. Screens on the windows kept out the flies. The beds were soft and without bugs. Meat was served every day. The bathrooms were white marble. There were no weird temples. It was all safe, so safe. Baruch would ask her sometimes to compare life in the villa with life in the village, and already she knew he was disappointed if she didn't answer in spiritual terms. Yet how could she explain her village to Baruch? How could he understand the whiteness of ibis, the gold of *khamseen*, the blackness of a goddess glowing in the dark? It was easier to talk to him of flies and *fool* beans. Mona smoothed down the lace-and-linen tablecloth. Surely, somewhere in the plenty of this Alexandria, there must be—if not answers—then at least the husband of Ummie's dreams.

In one of the upstairs bedrooms, Rafael and Leah al-Masri were sparring over the fact that tonight's gathering had a business motive. Next year Rafael would need more expansion money from the banks, and he was also planning to sell his cheap Egyptian-made cottons in the local department stores. Accordingly, he had invited Naim Benzion from the Egyptian National Bank and Joshua Nakattawi from the department-store chain of the same name. That they were both Jews was coincidental. That they might help his business was calculated. Of course there would be no business talk at the table tonight. But it couldn't hurt to have his guests, who did not have quite the cachet of the al-Masris, in his social debt.

As she slipped her rose *peau de soie* gown over her head, Leah was still grumbling. Both the businessmen's wives, she fussed, were disagreeable old cows with atrocious French accents. Moreover, Benzion had asked to bring along that son of his who had emigrated to Palestine. It was too bad, Leah fumed, that the notoriously ill-mannered Benzion boy had picked the night of her dinner party to make an appearance in Alexandria. She walked over and poured out a large measure of straight gin from the cut-crystal bottle she kept on her dressing table.

Sourly, standing in front of his mirror, Rafael watched the reflection of his wife drinking. Already Leah was into the gin. Tonight was sure to be one of those nights when she told all her guests the charming story of the time, so long ago, when she had once danced with King Faruk. Ah, well. The Benzions and the Nakattawis had never been here before, so perhaps they would be entertained with Leah's moonlight waltz with the king. Rafael cocked a weary eye at himself. He was tall and spare, and he kept his already gray hair barbered short and precisely in place. Rafael prided himself on his elegance. He would never be so indiscreet as to babble about his dreams and his disappointments to business acquaintances.

Leah was still nagging about tonight's party. To balance the table, since Baruch, too, would be with them, she had invited two of her Jewish women friends, who went by the most un-Jewish names of Lola and Blanchette. At least, Leah grumbled, *her* friends would be able to help keep the conversation civilized. Maybe Baruch would even take a fancy to one of them. Although, she added tartly, that was most doubtful. Baruch seemed to prefer the company of servants these days. She wouldn't even be surprised if Rafael's brother showed up dressed in one of those silly native robes.

Rafael was hardly listening to her. He was indulging himself in fantasies of cotton. Often he dreamed of cotton. Usually, however, he wasn't imagining when he would buy it and at what price he would sell it. Although no one else knew it and few else would have believed it, Rafael was in cotton for love as well as money. Rafael was a connoisseur of cotton. On his office desk he kept a blooming pod of cotton in a dainty crystal vase. He would never touch that pod of cotton when others were in the room. But often when he was alone, Rafael would first examine and then fondle the fluffy whiteness. He would admire how the light filtered through it and how it tickled when he rubbed it against his skin. When he watched Arab workers stomp cotton before it was baled, his soles would itch with the desire to join them up to their thighs in cotton. He bought cotton, sold cotton, ginned cotton, wove cotton. One of the disappointments of his life was that with all the difficulties put in the path of a foreign Jew trying to buy land, he had never grown his own fields of cotton. But although they might keep him from planting cotton, no one could stop him from dreaming of it. Often he dreamed he was floating free on a cloud of cotton. Wisely, Rafael kept all such fancies to himself this day and every day. It would never do, he thought as he restraightened his tie and headed downstairs, for others to know him for a man of passion.

A few minutes later Mona stood awaiting Abbas's orders in the doorway of the elegant main salon. The floors were covered with pink Persian carpets. The walls were papered in pale blue. When Mona touched one with her finger, she could feel the raised texture of satiny flowers and ribbons. The windows were draped in lace and damask. On the mantel of the large marble fireplace, next to the choicest of Monsieur's fragile porcelains, rested a solid-gold clock that chimed the quarter hours. Grouped about the room were couches and loveseats and chairs upholstered in silks and velvets. Mahogany tables had so many fresh flowers on them it seemed the drawing room was really a garden.

The doorbell rang ten minutes early, and the Benzion woman lumbered in wearing a shiny orange taffeta gown that bound her bulging midriff most unbecomingly. Kissing her in welcome, Madame al-Masri inclined her neck so that all would notice the curve of her own bosom and the slimness of her own waist.

As Khadiga poured the sherry, Leah was gushing in a pattering French that Mona was almost fluent enough to follow. "So glad you could come. Rafael and I have been too busy this season to see enough of our very dear friends."

Mona looked over at the Benzions, ranged on the sofa like those three bears in that story Batata liked so much. Papa Bear's bald head was shiny and pink as he grinned at Madame. Mama Bear was dowdy and garish as she peered nearsightedly toward Leah. And Baby Bear, their bushy-haired son, was looking more like the wolf who was about to devour Madame.

Leah prattled on. "We have been very naughty. But so much has been happening these days. Bridge. Canasta. The opera. The consular balls. I can hardly keep it all straight."

"I can't believe that." The Benzion man seemed to be trying to be gallant, as most men were around Leah al-Masri. Naim Benzion gestured at his son. "I was just telling Elijah here that nothing happens in Alexandria without Leah al-Masri at the center of it."

"You are too kind. Too kind."

Elijah was making an effort at being sociable. "Exactly what do you *do* here, Madame al-Masri?"

"Oh . . ." Leah made a pretty, airy gesture. "Everything. Just everything. With the war over, I've been too busy for words. Charity events for the orphans. Good works. That sort of thing."

"Fund raising?" Elijah's interest now was unfeigned.

"Oh, certainly. Certainly."

"My wife has a keener nose for money than a Greek." Rafael was laughing so hard he did not notice his wife's look of disdain.

Elijah leaned forward eagerly. "Then maybe you can help me. Fund raising. That's why I'm here. To get money for our people. In Palestine. For Zion."

Leah looked at him blankly.

"My son, here, is a bit of a firebrand." Benzion's tone was indulgent. "You know how it is to be young."

"*Mais oui!*" Leah hurried away from the topic of age. "Why, Youssef —our eldest son, we have three, you know—practically had to be dragged off to Europe with us last spring. Soccer. Cricket. Squash. Tennis. Rugger. Ah, *joie de vivre!*"

"I'm not talking about games, Madame." Doggedly, Elijah dug his heels into the carpet. "I'm talking about survival. About the survival of our people. Right now, this very day, in Palestine, our people are fighting for their lives."

"Yes, yes, very brave of them, I'm sure. Dashing. Very dashing."

Abbas was announcing the rest of the guests. Joshua and Sarah Nakattawi had arrived along with Lola and Blanchette. Baruch escorted them into the salon.

"Sarah!" Leah was cooing. "Sarah! It's been too long, *chérie!*" They kissed. Even Mona could see that this new woman's frock was too frilly for her years. Madame Leah's was, *au contraire,* everything it should have been. As were the dresses of Lola and Blanchette. Leah settled the Nakattawis on another sofa and stood for a moment next to Lola and Blanchette. The three attractive women made a charming tableau. Reluctantly, then, they took their seats, with the two young women perched on either side of Baruch.

They all sipped sherry, uncertain of what came next. Adept at filling silences, Leah took the initiative. She directed her comments, as always, to the men around her. "You're looking very well these days, Joshua. That shirt—French, isn't it?—suits you. Doesn't it, Lola?"

Lola made a suitable noise.

Joshua preened. "From my own shop. Silk. Easier to get these days with the war over. You have a sharp eye, Leah. French it indeed is."

"I knew it. I knew it." Leah clapped her hands girlishly. *"Très chic."* It was unclear whether she was complimenting herself or his shirt.

"No problem with the import taxes?" Rafael looked as if he hoped there had been. Even one sale of a single silk shirt meant less for Rafael's cottons.

"Not these days." Joshua smiled complacently. "I have, shall we say, friends at the Customs House."

"Corrupt!" Elijah put his glass down on the top of the marble coffee table so hard he nearly shattered the glass. "This entire country is corrupt. Now, in Palestine—"

"I've never been there myself." Rafael cut in before the young man could once again take over the conversation. "I've never wanted to go there, to tell you the truth. When I travel, I like Europe."

"Not so hot." Leah smiled sociably. "Such a nice change, Europe."

"And the shopping." Lola gave Joshua a bright look. "Begging your pardon, Monsieur Nakattawi, but it's so difficult to find anything *really* stylish here in Egypt."

"Perhaps you haven't visited Joshua's store recently." Leah tried to make her next statement sound sincere. "It is a little bit of the Rue St. Honoré!"

Abbas announced dinner.

Conversation was slower at the table. Even though Mona was in and out of the room, she could keep track of what was being said.

Over soup she heard Leah talking about a pasha in Cairo who had bought his twin sons a cheetah. Supposedly he was merely trying to keep up with a neighboring pasha who kept a declawed leopard on a leash in his garden. But the new owner had made a fatal mistake. He had forgotten to have the fierce cat declawed, and the cheetah ripped out the throat of one of the servants.

Abbas refilled their wineglasses.

Over grilled giant shrimps they talked of the latest scandal at the Greek consulate. A junior attaché had been caught in compromising circumstances with the wife of a Maltese barber, who had chased the Greek down the street with a razor. Lola herself had seen it.

All the women wagged their heads.

Over veal in champagne sauce they got down to serious gossip. The king's escapades—whether he had been seen in the company of this chic foreign woman or that much-married Egyptian matron of Turkish ancestry—were always the chatty centerpiece of every fashionable dinner party. But tonight's choicest morsel—Blanchette had it straight from her hairdresser, who also styled the locks of one of Faruk's second cousins—had less to do with sex than greed. The king, when visiting an elaborate Cairo villa, had hinted broadly to its owner that he wanted the house for himself. When his host did not respond, Faruk had pulled out a revolver and shot the crystal out of a chandelier. And the next day Faruk had confiscated the villa. From around the al-Masri table came a chorus of similar tales of the king. It was said Faruk stole snuffboxes, coffee cups, and *objets d'art* from the houses of his friends. Lola laughed and said their king was merely playful. Who could forget, she said, how he had poured icewater over the Swedish ambassador one night at a party and how he had cleverly had his car horn adjusted so that when he hit it it let out a screech like that of a dog being run over. Yes, Joshua said, that was Faruk. He repeated once more the old chestnut about Faruk's recurring nightmares of being chased by a lion. When one of his courtiers had told him he wouldn't get a good night's sleep until he shot a lion, Faruk had promptly gunned down two at the Cairo zoo. Inevitably, then, the dinner party chatter settled on Faruk's sexual adventures. It was said that he had women tucked all over Cairo in love nests to which only he had the key. Blanchette said that she had heard that every morning the king spread newspapers on his bed and watched as his pet rabbit mated on it. Because so many female bunnies were brought in to the male, the king had named the rabbit Faruk.

Leah put down her fork and said she refused to believe all this of "her Faruk." It wasn't so very many years ago, Leah said, that she herself had been the object of Faruk's attentions.

Mona watched the eyes of Rafael, Baruch, Lola, and Blanchette begin to glaze.

"I, you know, once danced with the king." The diamonds on Leah's fingers sparkled as she gracefully held her hand to her neck. "That was many years ago, of course. Before I married Rafael. Before dear Faruk got so . . . well, got so *fat*. He used to be a fine figure of a man, Faruk. It was at a hospital benefit. I was wearing white lace, and I had my hair down over my shoulders and a single red rose fastened at my waist. Faruk—I didn't know, then, it was His Majesty the King—sent one of his gentlemen over to ask me to dance. *'Mais oui!'* I said. *'Mais oui!'* I was led over to where he waited in white—I later was told it was the uniform of a royal admiral—and then he whirled me away.

They said we danced divinely together, Faruk and I. They said we made such a couple!"

Everyone smiled politely.

"But then my father hustled me away." Leah put down her fork and looked melancholy. "I never saw His Majesty again. My family made very sure there was never another *possibility* to see His Majesty. Even then, he had a reputation for being a rake!" Leah raised her glass and toasted herself. "But at least I know that once—once I danced with the king!" Out of the corner of her eye Leah saw Rafael subtly tap his wineglass. Hastily Leah set her own glass back on the table.

Mona noted that Madame looked far more subdued when Abbas and Khadiga were serving the salad. Without her gay initiative, the conversation sputtered, then settled on the latest duck hunt the Sporting Club had held on Lake Maryut. One of the visiting sportsmen from Cairo had bagged four hundred and thirty-six ducks in the space of only eighty minutes. It was a club record. No one at the table seemed to care about the shoot, the sportsmen, or the ducks.

It was over dessert, *crêpes Suzette,* that they ran out of small talk. Even Leah, who by now had a splitting headache, could not keep it going any longer. Standing beside the table with an extra tray of *crêpes,* Mona was able to hear what happened then from beginning to end.

Elijah apparently had been waiting for just this moment to plunge in. "I have just come back from Palestine. The situation there is desperate. Soon there will be war. We need money for arms. We are all Jews here tonight. We must work together."

The others looked at him as if he had broken wind.

Rafael threw the young man a patronizing glance. "I think, Elijah, that this is hardly the time or the place—"

"It is precisely the proper time and definitely the proper place." Elijah hurried on. "Don't you know what's been happening in the world, sir? The British are ready to pull out of Palestine. They've told the United Nations that they can't guarantee order there anymore. At this very minute, in New York, they're debating what to do with my country. Just yesterday, on the floor of the General Assembly, the Egyptian delegate said something I must repeat." He pulled a newspaper clipping from his pocket. " 'Arab governments will do all in their power to defend the Jewish citizens in their countries, but we all know that an excited crowd is sometimes stronger than the police. Unintentionally, you are about to spark an anti-Semitic fire in the Middle East which will be more difficult to extinguish than it was in Germany.' Gentlemen. Ladies. Now—whether you like it or not— Zionism is your struggle, too."

They all stared at him, surprised and embarrassed.

Leah finally found her voice. "I think that the gentlemen must be ready for their port and cigars. I think we can all, at least, agree on *that*. Ladies?" She swept out of the room toward the rear parlor, leading the rest of the women behind her.

Rafael nervously herded the men back into the drawing room. Abbas and Mona followed—he to keep their glasses full, she to keep their ashtrays empty.

As if there had been no interruption, Elijah began speaking once more. "I don't understand you all. You're Jews, all of you—"

"Every Jew is not a Zionist." Baruch spoke in the mild tone he used with his patients. "Some of us are not so political. So extremely political. Some of us don't see Nazis under every rock."

"Perhaps that's because you don't stop to turn over the rocks." Elijah's face was flushed. "They're there. Be sure of it. They're there. Why, six million of our brothers were killed. Six million! How can you not care?"

"I care about those six million. But that doesn't mean I care about Zionism." Baruch tried to keep his voice matter-of-fact.

"What Baruch is trying to say, son, is that none of us is without a heart."

Rafael thought it an appropriate time to plump for his bank loan by cozying up to the Benzions. "I don't mind saying that things are not all they could be for Jews here in Egypt. I am quite put out about that new Company Law that the Egyptians managed to pass last summer."

Joshua nodded in agreement. "Imagine the nerve. Seventy-five percent of my employees have to be Egyptian now. I had to fire some of my best people. Jews, most of them."

"Think of the problems it caused me." There was true emotion in Rafael's voice. "Forty percent of my board of directors has to be Egyptian now. It's a lot easier to find an honest, hardworking sales clerk than it is to find an executive of suitable caliber."

"It was the same at the bank." Benzion shook his head. "A lot of Jews had to go."

"And what did we have to replace them with?" Rafael spoke with rare passion. *"Egyptians!* All they do all day is drink tea and gossip. Lazy, every last one of them."

"Did you spend any time training them?" Baruch was beginning to let his anger show. "You can't expect people to be born knowing how to run a business."

"Some say Jews are." Elijah smiled smugly.

This boy's arrogance was getting on Baruch's nerves. "I wouldn't be too sure of that," he said.

"You would be if you lived in Israel." Elijah used the ancient name

Jews had begun to revive in Palestine. "What we have done in our country is beautiful. The most beautiful thing that has ever happened. We are making the desert bloom."

"My son here gets a little carried away sometimes."

"I can see that." Baruch did not even try to cover his irritation.

"What Jew can fail to be moved by Zionism? For two thousand, for almost two thousand years, we have been persecuted, have roamed the world dreaming of the sacred land which rightfully is ours. And now we're getting it. Taking back what we never should have left."

Baruch had had enough of this boy. "Stealing it, you mean. Stealing it from poor Arabs who have lived there for those same thousands of years. I don't call that glorious. I call that criminal."

Baruch and Elijah glared at each other.

Though Rafael, too, would have liked to turn that Benzion boy over his knee, he tried to smooth things over. He needed Benzion's signature on the bank loan. "I think all of us here can agree that there are some emotional and political reasons for the existence of Zionism."

"The Jewish Homeland!" Elijah's eyes shone.

Baruch snorted. "If all you cared about was a refuge, what you Zionists should have done was take the British up on their offer of land in the White Highlands of Kenya."

"Moses didn't lead our people to Kenya."

"No." Joshua Nakattawi was no lover of the British. "Leave it to the British to come up with Kenya—or Uganda, or whatever that plan was. They're the ones to blame for this mess. The British! That Balfour Declaration was what did it. Promising the Zionists a national home in Palestine!"

"November second, 1917." Elijah looked reverent. "A historic day."

"*That* was just a pretext for the British to take over all of Palestine after World War One." Baruch drained his port. "They didn't care about the Jews. They just wanted to grab Palestine from the Turks. So they could bleed it. As they've done here in Egypt."

"Really, Baruch." Rafael could never bear to hear a word spoken against his beloved British.

"I mean it." Baruch lit a cigar and signaled to Abbas for more port. "And once the British got Palestine, they did all they could to ruin it. First they told the Zionists they could settle there, and then they changed their minds. One day they'd encourage the Arabs, the next day the Jews. The British have made a mess of Palestine."

"I can agree with you there." Elijah lifted his glass and toasted Baruch. "For the past twenty-five years they've failed to protect our people. Those first kibbutzniks—our glorious pioneers—the British stood by and let them be slaughtered by Arab bandits. And then what about the way the British changed the immigration quotas just before World War Two? Just when the Nazis were starting to torture and gas our people, the British changed their minds and let only fifteen thousand Jews a year into Palestine. Do you know how many lives could have been saved if the British hadn't done that?"

"They were worried about their colonies in the Middle East." Joshua took pride in what he thought was his political sophistication. "They didn't want their Arabs joining up with the Germans. It was power politics, Elijah."

"It was unforgivable. The blood of six million Jews is on British hands, too."

"You go too far." Rafael was beginning to regret having arranged this get-together.

"No, not nearly far enough. Though we are beginning to deal with the British in our own way in Israel."

"Terrorism." Baruch all but spit out the word. "The Stern Gang. Irgun. I suppose you're proud of what they do, too."

Elijah quoted Lenin. "When you make an omelette, you have to break eggs."

"That's very tough." Baruch's eyes were hooded. "You are a very tough young man."

"I am a Jew." Elijah pulled another folded paper from inside his jacket.

"More quotes?" Baruch sounded sarcastic.

"No." Slowly, dramatically, Elijah opened a poster and held it up against his chest. It showed a bloody red dagger poised at the heart of a man in a turban and *gallabeiya*. "Do you know what this is?" Elijah did not wait for an answer. "The dagger is supposed to be Zionism. You're familiar with the robe, I'm sure. These posters are all over Egypt now. Anti-Semitism did not die with Hitler."

"I haven't seen one of them before." Rafael knew he sounded flustered.

"They don't have any in the Sporting Club." Elijah smiled grimly. "At least not yet."

"I can't believe Egyptians would produce anything like that." Joshua accepted more port from Abbas. "Egyptians just aren't like that."

"Who knows who's behind these posters?" Elijah leaned forward conspiratorially. "Some people even say the British are to blame. That they're funding efforts like these posters. That the British think if they can whip up the Egyptians against the Jews, the Egyptians will forget that it's the British who are sucking their blood."

"I object to your talking like this in my drawing room." Rafael had had more than enough. He stood up. "I think perhaps—"

"My son meant no offense. All the boy wants to do is raise some money for his friends in Palestine. He was going to ask you to contribute tonight."

"His begging is most aggressive." Baruch blew a smoke ring.

Rafael sank back in his chair.

"This is no time to stand on manners." Elijah ran his hands through his hair.

"The boy has a point." The poster had shaken Joshua. "You can count me in, Elijah. Come to the store tomorrow and we'll talk money."

"And you?" Benzion eyed his host.

Rafael knew his money was riding on his answer. But there were other banks. He could not truckle to this disagreeable young man. Bloodsucking British, indeed! "No. Not tonight. Not ever."

Elijah stood. "It's time to go, Father. I think we are not welcome here."

Both Benzion and Nakattawi rose.

As Mona hurried to help Abbas get the guests' coats, she saw Baruch and Rafael pour themselves a brandy. It was clear even to Mona that the dinner party had been a disaster.

Batata nudged Mona as they sat on the floor of the bedroom watching Youssef smear black shoe polish over his brown shoes. "Youssef! That's black!"

Daoud squinted at his big brother's shoes. "That's against the rules."

"I know." Youssef straightened up, smiled at his shoes, and then let them in on the joke. On this mid-May morning, Youssef was about to flaunt the dress regulations at very stuffy, very proper, oh-so-British Victoria College. Again Youssef smiled at his crudely camouflaged brown shoes. "What do you think, Daoud? Will they find me out?"

Daoud considered the odds. Youssef, who was the epitome of all a young British gentleman aspired to be, had most of his instructors wrapped around his little finger. He was a good sport, and he was good at sports. He was intelligent without being showy, and he was handsome without being pretty. Youssef was so many things Daoud wasn't. Along with most of the other boys at Victoria, Daoud would have given anything to be Youssef al-Masri for even a day. "You'll get away with it," he said.

"Batata?" Youssef grinned at the boy. "What's your verdict?"

Batata laughed his agreement with Daoud. As far as Batata was concerned, Youssef was smarter than any teacher in the world.

"Mona?" Youssef bowed to her.

She sighed up at him, so handsome in his uniform, so reckless in outwitting the authorities. If he were in her own shoes, Mona thought he might even try to outwit Ummie. Not, Mona, told herself hastily, that Youssef could win against Ummie. But it would be an exciting match. Mona smiled shyly at this bold, splendid boy.

As Youssef tucked his white shirt into his gray trousers, he caught her smile and returned it. Mona was a pretty little thing. In a few years she might be even beautiful. Youssef knotted his tie, winked at her, and laughed when she blushed. Already, at fourteen, Youssef was conscious of the uncanny effect he had begun to have on girls. Lately he had noticed the well-groomed misses from the British Girls College, the haughty mademoiselles from the Ecole Français, even the cat-eyed little *baladi bints* on the trolley all studying his face, then averting their eyes quickly before they thought he had seen them. Youssef knew that soon he would be the first of his friends to discover what was behind those long-lashed looks. Youssef prided himself on being first in his class. He had been the first to score a goal on the soccer field, the first to smoke cigarettes and hashish, the first to get drunk on whiskey, the first to shave. Soon he would be the first to take on the women of the world. Youssef slipped on his natty navy-blue blazer and smiled at his reflection. Very soon life was going to be even more wonderful than it already was.

Youssef was whistling when he met Hamid inside Victoria College's back gate. Hamid, too, was in on the prank. His part today was to slick down his hair with Vaseline, which also was against the rules at staid Victoria.

The two boys eyed each other critically. Youssef cuffed Hamid on the arm. Hamid smacked his palm on Youssef's. They were, as always, Arab brothers.

With careful nonchalance they sauntered under the arch of palm trees toward the gold-stoned halls of Victoria. Other boys waved or tried to join them for a pace or two. Youssef was the most popular boy in his class; Hamid, as Youssef's aide-de-camp, had nearly as much status. Popularity at swank Victoria was a dicey matter. It wasn't enough to be rich, well connected, or even royal. This very year the exiled, adolescent king of Bulgaria was a student at Victoria—as were the son of the former regent of Iraq, the heir to the throne of Albania, and the son of the sultan of Zanzibar. What Youssef al-Masri had that those princes lacked was not only innate glamour but the ability to radiate surplus glamour onto all those who ran with him. Others from Alexandria's glory set—the sons of pashas, bankers, landowners, and diplomats—were proud to count themselves friends of Youssef al-Masri. Surrounded by cronies, Youssef and Hamid strolled into English literature class.

An hour and a half later, having made it through Mr. Simpson's class undetected, the two of them were very nearly strutting down the hall. Hamid preened. "Rather good. I say, my friend, that we are rather good at being bad."

"I doubt Simp would notice if we came to class without our trousers." Youssef laughed. "But Barty's next. Old eagle-eyed Barton. We're home free if we can make it past him." Ian Barton, fresh from many years with the British army in Palestine, ran his history classes like boot camp.

As soon as they entered the room, the teacher glanced sharply down at the one's shoes, then up at the hair of the other. "Mr. el-Husseini. Come to the front of the classroom, Mr. el-Husseini."

"Sir?" Hamid smiled unctuously.

Barty took a white, well-pressed handkerchief from his pocket and handed it to Hamid. "Please wipe your hair."

"Sir?"

"The grease, Mr. el-Husseini. The grease that you seem to have plastered on that hair of yours. Remove it, please." The game was up, so Hamid glumly wiped off his hair. "That's better, Mr. el-Husseini. Now you may take that hair and that handkerchief to the office. There you will report your infraction. That will be all, Mr. el-Husseini."

Youssef had already slid into his seat. Barty looked him in the eye and then pointedly stared down at his shoes. Youssef gulped, steeled himself for his reprimand, and then wondered why none came.

He knew the answer a few minutes later when the senior prefect tapped on the door and exchanged a few words with the teacher, and then Barty turned to the class: "I have just been informed that classes will be suspended for the remainder of the day." The boys cheered, jumped up, and surged for the door. But Barty held up his hand. "Not so fast. Back in your seats. This is still, you will remember, a history class. I have not dismissed you." The boys reluctantly flung themselves back in their places. "The reason for your early dismissal is an event which I am sure will have great historical significance. And, for some of you, it may even have great *personal* significance." His eyes sought Youssef's. "Earlier today the British army pulled out of Palestine. No one can predict, of course, what will happen next. But I am informed that fierce fighting between the Arabs and the Jews has already begun." Barty ran a hand through his thinning hair. "It's war, boys, war. Another war." He looked at them for a moment, opened his mouth to continue, but then thought better of it. "Class dismissed." But as the other boys raced outside, Barty called Youssef back.

Now it comes, Youssef thought. Those shoes. Those stupid shoes. He decided to get it over with quickly. "I know, sir. I broke the rules. The wrong shoes. I'll report it immediately."

"That's not it. That doesn't matter. Not today. Didn't you hear me? About the war? The Palestine war?"

"Sir?"

"I am sorry for you, Youssef. This is going to be a bad time for you here."

Youssef still didn't get it. "Yes, sir. Of course, sir. Thank you, sir." He turned to leave.

But Barty was not finished. "This will be the last time I see you, Youssef. I'll be leaving Victoria. Leaving Egypt."

"I'm sorry to hear that, sir."

"I'm going to Palestine. To fight. I have family there. The only family I have, really. My wife's family. She was a Jew, Youssef. She's dead now, but she was a Jew. Like you, Youssef. A Jew."

Youssef blinked at his teacher, standing ramrod-straight before him. Barty clearly expected some sort of response. Youssef usually had the knack of saying exactly the right thing. More than anything he liked to say—do—the right thing. He liked to leave everyone laughing and happy. But now, embarrassed by Barty's intensity, Youssef drew a blank. Eager to get home, he gave his teacher a bright social smile. When he turned and left the room, he could feel Barty's disappointed eyes boring into his back.

"Did you hear?" A highly excited Daoud was waiting for Youssef at the trolley stop. "We're at war. Or almost. Against the Zionists in Palestine. We'll beat them. Everybody says so. Will Father be in the war, too?"

Youssef ruffled his brother's hair and steered him toward a waiting trolley. "Not unless they fight it with cotton."

In the Agami cottage where the al-Masri children had been packed off for safekeeping that summer, Youssef awoke very early one morning to find his youngest brother looking down at him. Batata was sitting on Youssef's bed. In his lap was Zibda, and there was a red ribbon around the dog's neck. Batata was smiling.

"Go away." Youssef shut his eyes again. "It's too early."

"But I have a surprise for you."

"I got it already. You woke me up." Grumpily Youssef pulled the sheet over his head, wishing it were as easy to hide from the fact that King Faruk had declared war on the Zionists the day after Israel came into being. Police nets had swept up suspected Zionists, Radio Cairo was threatening every day to drive the "Jewish bandits" into the sea, and there had been bloody anti-Jewish riots in Cairo. At first, since Youssef's father wouldn't let any of them go to school, Hamid had come to the Villa al-Masri every afternoon to keep Youssef abreast of Victoria's adventures. But after Hamid's older brother had volunteered for the army, the visits had become less frequent. Hamid had avoided his best friend's eyes and made lame excuses when Youssef invited him along for this Agami summer. Since then, Youssef had been moping and sulking. He would throw a ball to Daoud on the beach and watch, tight-lipped, as his brother fumbled it. Abruptly then, reminding himself that Hamid was never so clumsy, Youssef would tell Daoud to go play with the babies and stalk off by himself along the beach. There he would stare at the sea and try to puzzle it all out.

Just when his beard was starting to grow, just when everything was almost perfect, that stupid war had to begin. Youssef hated everything about the Palestine war. He hadn't liked it from that first curious look

Mr. Barton had thrown him in the classroom. Barty had seemed to expect something intense and soppy from him, something passionate and sentimental that Barty evidently assumed went along with being a Jew. Youssef despised this sudden focus on what it meant to be a Jew. He was Youssef al-Masri. He hadn't done anything wrong. And yet, reading the newspapers, eavesdropping on his father and uncle, it had dawned on Youssef that now it was suddenly wrong enough even to be a nonobservant Jew. For the first time, Youssef was being confronted by a wrong he couldn't right with a smile or a shrug. Sleep. Youssef wanted to go back to sleep and not wake up again until the war was all over.

Batata lifted the sheet, crawled under it, and whispered in Youssef's ear, "A present. I have a present for you."

"Hmmmmm?" Youssef yawned.

"A present."

Youssef turned to face his brother. War or no war, he resigned himself to humoring the boy. "All right, then. Let's have it."

"Zibda. That's what it is. Zibda."

"What?" Youssef was very nearly awake. "What about Zibda?"

"I'm giving her to you. You can be her boy. I want to give you my dog."

Youssef frowned. Batata had always been crazy about the dog. Youssef had a terrible thought. He knew his brother was retarded. Maybe Batata was getting worse. With all this trouble about the Jews and the war, he hadn't been paying much attention to Batata lately. Maybe his baby brother was slipping further away. Youssef chose his words carefully. "Are you mad at Zibda?"

"I could never be mad at Zibda."

The dog barked her agreement.

"So why do you want to give her to me?" Youssef looked into Batata's too-clear brown eyes as if for the first time. "I thought you loved Zibda very, very much."

"Of course I do. But I thought you needed her more. With Hamid gone, you're lonesome. You don't smile anymore. I don't like you to feel bad."

Youssef took a while to answer. He was relieved that his brother hadn't turned against the dog. Touched that the little boy offered Zibda to make up for Hamid. And shamed that he hadn't had his brother's heart. While he had been brooding on the beach, his mentally retarded little brother had been trying to devise a way to make him happy. Youssef made a snap decision. The hell with the war, the hysteria, the Cairo riots. He couldn't do anything to stop all that, but he *could* do something to keep those he loved from being touched by it all. If Batata was willing to give up his dog, Youssef would be at least as generous with himself. He looked at Batata gravely. "Oh, I don't know about that. You're right, Batata. I miss Hamid. I miss my friends. School, even. But I don't think Zibda is what I need."

"What then? Chocolates? I'll get Anne-Marie to buy chocolates."

"No. Not chocolates." Youssef leaned over and whispered in Batata's ear. "I need a best friend. Somebody to play with."

"Yes. I told you already. You can have Zibda."

"No." Youssef tickled Batata under the arms. "Zibda's too hairy. I choose you."

Batata squealed. "Me!"

"You." Youssef hugged his brother.

"Really?"

"Really."

"For all summer?"

"Longer. For always."

"Oh, boy!" Batata looked his adored big brother straight in the eye. "I won't be mad if Hamid's your best friend, too. When we go home."

Youssef tried to be as magnanimous. "And I promise not to be jealous of Zibda."

"Yes?"

"Yes." Youssef smacked his hand on Batata's open palm, brothers by choice as well as blood.

Late one afternoon Youssef, Mona, and Batata sat on the silver-gold sand playing their sunset game. Youssef had told them that the sun, as if it cannot bear to leave its favorite land, lingers in the Egyptian sky longer than anywhere else in the world. And then, Youssef always said, just when the sun is inches away from the horizon, it suddenly disappears, like a lover who cannot bear any more farewells and so runs off with the final word unspoken. But if they watched very, very closely, Youssef would always say, maybe one day—maybe today—the sun would not cheat them of its final rays. And so every day they stared, sunbound, but every day the sun always did its disappearing act just an instant before it should have sunk into the sea. It was the same today.

Mona missed the last melting away of the sun, for her eyes were fastened blissfully on Youssef. He had been so wonderful this summer. Youssef was always up just after dawn, walking down the beach, telling them all stories about the lands and the people on the other side of the sea. When breakfast was ready, Youssef would sit at the head of the table, making even Leah laugh at his jokes. Later Youssef would herd them all into the water, not letting them back on the sand until the salt felt crusted on their skins. With Youssef's great gift for making those around him feel special and privileged, gay and happy, he had made even Mona seem a princess. He had walked with her, talked with her, even wormed dark secrets out of her one day when the three of them went out on the sailboat. The craft had tilted far to the side in the gusty wind, and Youssef had teased Mona when he caught her stroking that blue bead she wore around her neck. As their boat cut through the waves, Mona had told him about the *khamseen*, the black statue, and the curse of the Nile. Youssef had laughed and said there was no such thing as an evil spell—unless Mona's bossy mother really was a witch. Mona and Batata had echoed Youssef's laughter. But when he ordered her to toss the blue bead into the sea, Mona had refused. Without Youssef always to protect her, ahead might be dark nights and even darker days when she might need her blue bead.

But that day in the sailboat, looking up at Youssef and laughing at Ummie's curse, Mona began to see Youssef as her savior. *Find him, sink your teeth into him, and don't let go until you marry him.* Why not Youssef? Why not? By night she began to dream of Youssef, and by day she began to hang on his every word. She would run to get Youssef a cold soda when she herself felt thirsty. She would laugh at his jokes a split second before the others found them funny. It was often just enough to watch how Youssef's legs moved when he ran, how his golden hair curled over his forehead, how his fingers stroked the sand as he lay in the sun. Mona kept secret the pictures of tall, fair-haired boys she scissored out of magazines. But she had begun to believe that Youssef returned her feelings one night when they all sat picnicking on the sand by the light of a full moon. As Youssef beat out a rhythm on the back of a saucepan, they all sang one of Um Kulthoum's songs of pain and lament and lost love, "*Habibti, habibti,* my love, my love." But suddenly Youssef made a speech. "Everybody! Look at the moon. Remember, always, no matter what happens, how it is tonight. How you can see nothing but black all but for the stars, the whitecaps, and the moonbeams. The moon looks almost shy. Soft, but giving all the light a man could ever need. *La lune, el amir,* the moon." Youssef had smiled at Mona, caught up in the web of his words. "The moon. So like our Mona. Our pretty little Moon-a." Mona had sighed to think that Youssef thought she was like the moon.

Batata was the only one who seemed to notice and approve her infatuation. And so now, playing their sunset game, Batata took a deep breath and uttered his heart's desire. "I want to be your little boy."

Youssef put his arm around his brother. "You already are. You're our little Batata. Everybody's. Mother's and Father's and Daoud's and Rachel's and Lisabet's and Mona's and everybody's."

"You don't understand. When I grow up, I want you to be my papa and Mona to be my mama. We'll all live together with Zibda and have lots of little babies and puppies."

Youssef laughed. "Well, Mona, what do you say? Is that what's going to happen when we grow up?"

Yes! Mona wanted to cry. Yes! That, too, was her own heart's desire.

But, too shy to speak those words, she searched the sky for the first glimpse of her moon. Youssef had said she was like the moon.

"You'll see." Batata spoke with great determination. "It will happen. And we'll all be together and live happily ever after."

Youssef smiled. There was a word, he knew, that every Egyptian said when anyone was so rash as to make predictions of the future. *Inshallah,* they all said—it will happen if God wills it. In that one word were equal measures of superstition and piety, for no one ever dared to tempt the fates. *"Inshallah,"* Youssef said.

Setting out briskly for work at six-thirty one sunny morning that August, Rafael al-Masri turned and then beamed back at his villa. More than two thousand years ago, when Alexandria had been the pride of the ancient world, a magnificent Gate of the Sun had sparkled on the site of his own home. From here, along what was now the Rue Fouad, the Canopic Way's white marble colonnades, temples, palaces, and tombs had stretched all the way to the Gate of the Moon, where the Minet el-Bassal cotton warehouses now stood. In Rafael's estimation, his Alexandria—where all roads led to cotton—had only improved over the millennia. He smiled at Youssef, who was trotting beside him like the most promising whelp of a litter. "Jolly good, this early start. We should be the first ones at the 'Change. Capital!" To Rafael, every day on the Cotton Exchange, with its aura of his wealth made and the wealth of others lost, was something to be savored. "The crop's in, and the buyers believe it's a small one. Prices have never been higher. The dollar shortage, don't you know?"

"Dollar shortage?" Glumly Youssef glanced down a side street toward the sea. Released only today from the strain of making a safe haven for the children at Agami, he longed to scout out his friends at Rushdi Beach. Instead his father was going to bore him again with cotton. As a small boy, Youssef had been entertained by these annual father-and-son pilgrimages to the Cotton Exchange. He had liked the shouting, the spitting, the fistfights that sometimes broke out between the buyers and the sellers. From his father's prime roost near the first-balcony railing, Youssef had taken in the circus. In the pit the Buddha-like ringmaster would tinkle a bell, the flunky on the ladder would adjust the price of cotton on a blackboard, and the businessmen would howl and gnash their teeth. But the thrill had palled for Youssef one hectic morning when he had witnessed what could happen on this Bourse. In his greed to sell, a Greek merchant had fallen over one of the ornamental railings on the fourth balcony, screeching all the way to the imitation-marble floor that he was willing to unload high-grade long fiber at rock-bottom prices. "Sell!" had been the Greek's last word on that, or any other, matter. Remembering that fatal day on the Cotton Exchange, Youssef dragged his feet alongside his father.

But halfway to their destination, Rafael stopped and peered behind the locked gates of the main synagogue on Nebi Daniel. Yes, the synagogue was still standing. In these uncertain times, he wouldn't have been surprised to see it in ruins. Egypt had gone mad at the outbreak of the Palestine war, and official Cairo was maddest of all at what it considered its Zionist fifth column. Two thousand suspected Zionists had been arrested and detained in the first days of the war. Then all Egyptian Jews, even those with foreign citizenship, had been blocked from leaving the country. It was then that Rafael had begun to worry about Cairo someday sequestering his villa, his bank account, his factories, his warehouses. Rafael had considered selling what he could and then funneling the proceeds to a secure account abroad. But he knew he would never get full value, since even the most discreet of transactions would still reek of panic selling. Weighing what he knew of Egypt and Egyptians, Rafael had decided to gamble and hold firm. There might be some unpleasantness during this war, but he was sure it all would evaporate with the signing of a peace treaty. Still, using Baruch's Egyptian citizenship as a shield, Rafael had taken the precaution of transferring his deeds and accounts to his brother's name. Rafael had congratulated himself on his foresight in late May, when the government began seizing the property of suspected Zionists. But then the police had begun rounding up even rich Jews who had never had anything to do with Zionism. When Rafael, too, was hauled in for questioning, he had emerged from two hours of interrogation with nothing worse than a queasy feeling in his stomach. Recalling last fall's dinner party, he had given sworn testimony against both Benzion and Nakattawi. Rafael had taken pills to quiet his stomach and had tried to assure himself that the worst that *could* happen *had* happened.

But then Egypt's suspicion of its Jews turned violent. In early June a month-long United Nations cease-fire had stunned an Egypt which had believed its own government's propaganda about glorious Arab victories. As if to make up at home for what had been stalemated on the Palestinian battlefields, explosions killed twenty in the poorest Jewish section of Cairo. Then, after the Palestinian fighting had resumed in early July, an Israeli aircraft—perhaps in retaliation for an Egyptian bombing raid on Tel Aviv—had dropped a load of explosives on one of Cairo's most densely populated slums. When hundreds died, the Cairo mobs had screamed for Jewish blood. Bombs had wrecked two Jewish-owned department stores, and for a week roving gangs of street toughs had roamed through Cairo searching for Jews but assaulting anyone who looked foreign. There had been reports of women raped on the streets, of rabbis murdered by a mob in a slaughterhouse, of men being dragged out of their cars and trampled to death.

American, British, French, Italian, and Greek diplomats had bitterly protested that at least two hundred had been killed by the mob. The Egyptian government, according to the rumor mill, had restored order only when Britain threatened to send over troops from its Suez Canal garrison. And still the outrages had continued. Only last week a policeman had come to the Villa al-Masri demanding a cash "dona-tion" of ten thousand Egyptian pounds for the war effort. Though they were sure that not one piaster of that money would ever make it to the "Palestine Fund," Rafael and Baruch had thought it prudent to contribute one thousand pounds. The betting at the Sporting Club was that the Egyptians had already been able to extort one hundred thou-sand pounds from the Cairene and Alexandrian Jewish communities.

With an effort Rafael steered Youssef away from the synagogue and turned his own mind back to cotton. "I've explained this to you before, Youssef. Since the war, there's been a worldwide shortage of American dollars. Egyptian cotton is a soft-currency article, and so demand for it has risen. The trick is to trade on that demand but hold back enough of the crop so the price won't break. Don't ever forget, son, that the larger the Egyptian cotton crop, the lower its price on the open market."

Youssef sighed softly under his breath. Cotton futures. Keeping down the size of the crop was his father's Eleventh Commandment. His own cotton future stretched ahead to infinity. Youssef hoped his brother Daoud would someday share his father's passion for cotton. Then maybe Daoud could inherit the business, and he himself would be free for another future.

The father and son crossed historic Muhammad Ali Square where, nearly seventy years ago, the mob had burned down the temples of foreign business, religion, and law. Those days of rage had provided the pretext for the enduring British Occupation. Youssef looked at the rebuilt facades of the Anglican Church where foreigners prayed, the Mixed Tribunals where foreigners were brought to trial, and the Bourse where foreigners bought and sold all Egypt on the Cotton Exchange and Stock Exchange. Pointing to an excited, chattering line of soldiers in front of the Bourse, Youssef asked his father what was wrong.

"Probably just protecting the mint." Rafael had been privately wor-ried over the past months that some Arab hothead would try to bomb the Cotton Exchange. After all, he reasoned, what better target was there than the Cotton Exchange? What else was more controlled by Jews and foreigners? What else, in the end, could ever be more impor-tant than the Cotton Exchange?

They breezed past the soldiers, strode by the entrance pillars, but then stopped and stared at the shut door. To it was nailed a garishly colored poster of a bloody dagger poised at the heart of a man in an Arab robe.

Rafael recognized the drawing Elijah Benzion had unfurled in his parlor nine months earlier. Some fool was making a very bad joke. Some madman had posted an inflammatory anti-Zionist poster on the very door to the inner sanctum. "Tear that disgusting cartoon down, Youssef. Tear it down."

"But what is it?" Youssef asked as he ripped away the poster. "What's it supposed to mean?"

"Hate, Youssef. The dagger stabbing the Arab is supposed to be Zionism. Now do you understand?"

Youssef bit his lip. Hastily, as the door to the Bourse swung in, he folded the poster so he could slip it into his pocket. A fat brown man in a white *gallabeiya* and a red fez loomed in the doorway, flanked by more soldiers with fixed bayonets.

"Abdel!" Rafael smiled at the doorman. The cotton brokers carelessly called all the doormen, the messengers, the bringers of coffee and tea Abdel, which in Arabic means "slave." Coupled as it usually was to another name—Abdel Muhammad piously meant "slave of Muhammad"—Abdel gave no offense. By itself Abdel was a slur. "Why are all these soldiers here, Abdel? Some sort of problem?"

The doorman folded his arms against his barrel chest. "No problem."

"Glad to hear it, Abdel."

"My name," the doorman said in halting English, "Wahib Ali el-Rahman. My name not Abdel. Rafael, now you call me right."

The sun glinted on the sharp points of the bayonets. "But of course!" Rafael let out a bleating laugh. "Ha-ha! Well, then, Wahib Allah . . . I mean Ali . . . el-Rashid . . . or whatever it is . . . *Sabah el-khair,* good day. My son and I will be on our way, now, as soon as you clear us a path so we can take our seats."

"Sorry. No seat today."

A soldier, noticing that the poster had vanished from the door, insolently eyed the al-Masris. *"Yahud?"* When Wahib Ali el-Rahman nodded, the soldier fastened another copy of the poster to the door.

"I think," Rafael continued huffily, "this had gone quite far enough. Either let me and my son pass, or fetch the secretary."

"Secretary sick today." The doorman grinned. "Secretary sick for many days. You want something, you tell me."

"I see." The secretary, Rafael knew, was a Jew. He glanced behind him. Bored soldiers had begun to drift over from their stations to see what was afoot. Remembering the recent Cairo bloodshed, Rafael looked anxiously at Youssef.

"Let's go home, Father. We have that appointment with the doctor. About Grandmother. We can't keep the doctor waiting."

Both of Youssef's grandmothers were dead. Youssef was trying to give him a graceful reason to back off. But, Rafael told himself, a man had to make a stand. He wasn't going to give in to a herd of Egyptians who couldn't even speak the King's English. He took one step forward. "I will pass."

The doorman held up one meaty hand. "No Jews. New law today from Cairo. No Jews on Cotton Exchange. Stock Exchange also. No Jews no more."

"That's preposterous." It was, Rafael decided, worse than preposterous. His people, his money, had *built* this Bourse. No one could deny it to him. He could compromise on almost anything, but never on the loss of the love of his life. Rafael took another step forward.

"I warn you, Rafael." The doorman shook his head. "You stop here."

"My name," Rafael said icily, "to you, *Abdel,* is Monsieur al-Masri. Now, run along, boys!" Imperiously he clapped his hands. "You—all of you—get to work!"

Goaded beyond control, the doorman swiftly pushed Rafael back so that he lost his balance and fell. Two soldiers pinned Youssef back out of the way. There was a blur of khaki as the soldiers closed in, kicking until Rafael was on all fours at the doorstep of the Bourse. Then the doorman, overtaken by that Egyptian sense of play which can turn cruel in the wink of an eye, whipped off his fez and placed it on Rafael's skull. There was laughter from the watching throng of soldiers. Warming to his task, the doorman called out for a basin and pitcher and then handed them to Rafael. "You, Jew. Wash my feet."

"No!" With a toss of Rafael's head, the red fez rolled to the ground and then tumbled down the front steps of the Bourse. Youssef shut his eyes as he heard his father grunt under the kicks of the soldiers. The doorman lifted his white robe to his knees and stuck one bare foot into the basin. "Wash feet, Jew."

"No!" Rafael's refusal was a howl.

There were more kicks, low moans from Rafael, and the soldiers with their bayonets moved closer to the prone man. "Father!" Youssef tried to break away from his catpors. At the sound of his son's cry, Rafael turned his head. Blood ran from one side of his mouth. His white shirt was ripped and dirty. His eyes sad and luminous and filled with tears, Rafael bowed his head. But when he lifted it again toward Youssef, his eyes were very bright. "We will always remember this, Youssef. We will be able to remember this, Youssef, because we will survive it. Go home, son. I don't want you to see this."

But Youssef stayed and watched as his father was made to wash the filthy feet of the doorman. Then another servant stepped to the front of the mob and demanded that his feet, too, be cleansed. But the officer in charge of the soldiers intervened, overturned the basin of water onto the marble steps, and made the servants cross the threshold of the

Bourse. Still, however, as Rafael scrambled to his feet, the servants mocked him with his own epithet, "Abdel!"

Grimly Youssef half-carried his father down the steps. But as Youssef was hailing a taxi, Rafael turned and raised his fist to the still-jeering servants and soldiers clustered around the front door of the Cotton Exchange. "Barbarians! Filthy Arabs! You'll be sorry! I'll make you sorry! Every one of you!" Quickly Youssef hustled his father into the cab.

Youssef lay in bed smoking a Soussa cigarette, waiting for Hamid to stumble into his room. It was nine o'clock on this cold February night, and Youssef had just awakened from his nap. Lately he and Hamid had felt the need for naps. They were up every morning at six-thirty so they could be at Victoria for their eight-o'clock classes. They weren't home again, except for lunch, until six in the evening. Usually they would skip dinner and sleep awhile, so they would be fresh for whatever came their way. As Youssef thought about what was coming their way this particular night, he blew perfect smoke rings into the air. Janetto Marsoni, one of the boys who formed part of their fast new set, had told him about the belly dancer his obliging father had hired for a "performance." His first woman! Correction, Youssef told himself, our first woman. His, Hamid's, and the other four boys who would be at Janetto's tonight. What would she look like? What would she feel like? How would he do? The others, he knew, would let him go first. He had to do it right. And he would, he knew he would. Despite all this year's evidence to the contrary, Youssef, at not yet the age of sixteen, still mostly believed that he could do everything right.

He stubbed out his cigarette. Where was Hamid? That one had the most amazing capacity for sleep. And, Youssef smiled to himself, Hamid no doubt would have a most amazing capacity for this other thing. Hamid. What would he have done without Hamid? They had been walking down a corridor together on Youssef's first day back at school, when that voice had rung out behind them: *Ya,* Hamid! What are you doing with the Jew?" Other voices had joined the chorus: "Do it, Hamid!" "Now, Hamid!" "Now!" Hamid had hesitated, looked Youssef in the eye, and then wheeled and spat at the sneering faces of the Arab boys behind them. There had been just enough time, before the free-for-all erupted in the hallway, for Hamid to smack his palm on Youssef's. Later, as the two of them had waited for their reprimand outside the headmaster's office, Youssef had rubbed his bruised cheek and asked Hamid why—"They always liked me!"—the Arabs had wanted Hamid to spit on him.

Hamid had insisted it wasn't just because Youssef was an enemy Jew. "You must know they've always been jealous of you, Youssef. Because of the way you look. The way you act. The way you *are*. It's not just your . . . your religion.''

But Youssef, remembering his father's humiliation on the steps of the Bourse, had known his world had turned sour only because he was a Jew. In the weeks that followed, Youssef noticed a change in some of his old Arab friends. A Palestinian he had befriended years ago would no longer speak to him. In physical training class a Syrian boy contemptuously chose him last for the soccer team. And always there were the whispers whenever he entered a room. When the other Arabs seemed to turn against Hamid, too, his friend had moved from the Victoria dormitories to a spare bedroom at the al-Masris'. Now Youssef and Hamid were always a pair.

Impatient for the night to commence, Youssef jumped out of bed. "*Ya,* Hamid! *Yalla, yalla,* let's go!" These days Youssef was often very loud. Ever since the armistice that had ended the Palestine war, there was a new coldness—almost a hardness—about Youssef. He had shown the Arabs. The Muslims didn't want him, so he had patched together a new crowd that was indisputably the hottest act Victoria had ever seen. "*Yalla,* Hamid!"

They took time out to loll on the balcony and smoke a little of their nightly hashish. Youssef, as always, prepared the cigarettes. He took a Soussa in his left hand, neatly sliced its paper open lengthwise with his thumbnail, and eased out some of the tobacco. He warmed the hard black nugget of hashish under a match and then swiftly flaked the now-gummy drug onto the guts of the cigarette. He mixed the hashish with the tobacco so the smoke would be even and full. He took a piece of *buffra* from Hamid's pack, licked the glue, and wound the rolling paper around what was left of the Soussa.

"Perfect." Hamid held the cigarette to his nose, sniffed it, and smiled. "Do some more for the party."

Lighting the reefers, waiting for the blurry sweetness to steal over him, Youssef looked out at his city. Early evening, when everyone was just rising, was the most pregnant time of the day. Trays were being readied with cold suppers and refreshing drinks. Diverting plans were being laid for the delicious night ahead. Youssef could hear the city stir, almost moan, under him from all sides. Like a woman, he told himself. I think, just like a woman.

At Janetto's, Youssef and Hamid threw a handful of hashish cigarettes down on the table next to the already opened bottle of Johnny Walker Red. Janetto signaled to the *suffragi,* who glided in with two more glasses and a bottle of mineral water. As Janetto mixed their drinks—whiskey, ice, a touch of water—Youssef looked around the room. The other four were already sitting on the red velvet couch and easy chairs, so Youssef settled on the floor and Hamid arranged himself cross-legged beside him. The others, watching Youssef and

Hamid assume the posture of Oriental potentates, wondered why they hadn't thought of sitting on the floor. Leave it to Youssef to do the right thing.

Janetto fumbled at the record player. To Janetto, Arab music was one long and grating catlike shriek. The belly dancer would expect Arab music, but Janetto couldn't find a suitable record. "Help him, Hamid," Youssef said. Hamid put the needle on a low throbbing instrumental. "The lights," Youssef said. "There's too much light." When he switched off the chandelier, at once Janetto saw the velvet-draped drawing room transformed, he thought, into the bordello of a man about town.

Youssef had already started the hashish around their circle when the knock came. The *suffragi* led the woman into the room. From head to toe, all but her face was muffled in a long black *milaya* wrapped like a sheet around her.

"Have you come to do the laundry or to dance?" The boys laughed nervously at Youssef's wit.

The woman smiled. She was missing one front tooth. She looked perhaps forty years old. "I . . . am Nervana!"

"Nirvana?" Youssef intentionally slightly changed the Turkish of her name. "Why do they call you that?"

"You will see. *Now* you will see." Already moving to the beat under the music, Nervana turned in a slow circle, unwrapping her *milaya* with one smooth and sweeping motion. For the rest of their lives, the boys in the room felt sure, they would remember Nervana's unrobing every time they saw even an old *baladi* woman discreetly covered up in her *milaya*. For under that drab black cloth, first they saw the skin of her plump brown shoulders and her soft smooth back. Then there was a flash of red, and they took in the low-cut scarf of the spangly material tightly molded to the curves of her breasts. Then came more skin, skin that bounced unbelievably, soft skin that jiggled before their eyes. The boys caught their breaths and waited for Nervana's final pivot. And there was the rest of her: a band of gold glittering low on her hips, a cascade of slit red skirt falling in a flirt to the floor, legs bare from thigh to foot. Janetto's father had known what he was doing when he hired Nervana. She was a boy's fantasy come true. All that flesh, that bare flesh.

"We see." Youssef grinned rakishly. "And Nirvana—not Nervana —you are."

While the other boys stared mesmerized at Nervana, Youssef lit another hashish cigarette. Hamid refilled their glasses, and the two of them whispered to each other.

"A bit fat." Youssef was more tentative than usual.

"Better for the dance. And what comes after. Watch that belly."

"But nice breasts."

Hamid smiled. "I saw a Bedouin dance once in the desert. Hers were bigger."

"Bigger than that?"

"Much."

"Did they shake like that?"

"More."

Nervana was just warming up. She danced around the room, her belly moving three times as fast as her feet, her hands waving dreamily, slowly, in front of her breasts, now leaning her body far to the left, now to the right. The boys caught a glimpse of something shiny under her skirt. Her panties were red satin.

"Oh." Janetto's eyes were glued to Nervana's thighs.

The music suddenly slowed to a low wail. The drumbeats, it seemed, were harder to hear than the thumping inside the chests of the boys.

Nervana's feet came to a dead stop. Only her belly moved, agonizingly slow, up and down.

Youssef smiled and leaped to his feet. He danced toward her, arms extended from his shoulders, his body aloof but interested.

Nervana grinned at him and waited for his advance.

He let his hips come close to her, then pulled them away. He had never performed this dance before, but he had watched it. His movements were sure and purposeful.

Nervana encouraged him with waves of her arms and grinds of her hips.

He danced a circle around her, sometimes almost close enough to graze her skin, sometimes almost painfully far away. At last, as he came to rest in front of her, only his hips moved to the music.

It was Nervana's turn. As the music grew faster, she heated with it. She danced in place—her hips, belly, breasts glistening with sweat. As the music reached a climax, her pelvis gyrated not quite—but almost —out of control.

Youssef casually pulled out a one-pound note and tucked it into the gold band around her hips, in the middle, just above where her legs met. He sat down to the congratulations of his friends.

The music began again. This time it was Hamid who got up and faced the dancer. She started shimmying. Only two parts of Hamid— his lips and his hips—responded. The corners of his mouth turned up in the merest suggestion of a leer. His hips, too, moved only slightly, subtly, so slowly that at first they seemed not to move at all. He used his hips to tease the groin of the belly dancer. She stopped smiling, and there was an intent look on her face. All eyes were on the magic inside Hamid's hips.

There was a new eroticism in the room. The boys were nearly panting. Youssef had danced well. Youssef had looked as graceful as a performer in a cabaret. But Hamid and Nervana gave off animal heat.

Hamid did not touch her, Hamid never moved a step closer to her, and Hamid did not even smile at her when he finished and sat down next to Youssef.

"You can take her first." Youssef, although he tried to pass off his offer as a courtesy, was anxious to save face. Hamid was clearly the natural leader tonight. Youssef was sure Hamid would show them all how to do it right.

Hamid did not have to be asked twice.

While the music ground on, Hamid once again approached the dancer. Again he held her with his eyes.

She reached around behind her and untied the scarf that served as her halter. Her breasts fell out. Their tips were big and brown.

Janetto laughed nervously.

Hamid did not look at the breasts. But when he pinched the tips with his fingers, the boys noticed that the nipples turned hard.

Nervana swayed, then reached down. She pulled her skirt and panties below her knees and then stepped out of them. She was as hairless between her legs as she was on her breasts. They could see her slit.

Hamid unbuckled his belt, unzipped his pants, and pushed the woman to the floor. She sprawled on top of her clothes.

Hamid kneeled, spread her legs, and pulled out his penis. He lunged forward on top of her. He fumbled between her legs for an instant, and then he got it inside.

"Ah." Nervana sounded relieved. "Ah."

"Ah." The boys echoed her sound.

Hamid moved his pelvis up and down, just as he had when he danced. He did not make a sound.

Nervana waved her legs in the air, then clamped them around Hamid's buttocks. "Higher. Put them higher. On your shoulders."

He pulled back a bit, grabbed her left leg, and put it on his right shoulder. Her right leg cracked and she moaned when he wedged it upon his left shoulder. They thrashed around, and then Hamid crawled off her. Carefully he tucked his penis back in his pants, zipped and buttoned up, and rose to his feet.

Gravely he walked over to Youssef, held out his hand, and the two of them smacked their palms together.

"Your turn."

Youssef got up and looked down at Nervana. Her eyes were closed and her legs still spread. He hoped he had an erection.

Youssef mimed Hamid perfectly. Kneeling, pulling it out, putting it in, hauling her legs up to his shoulders. He concentrated on the right movements, on doing the right thing, and at first he did not feel anything but the eyes of the other boys upon him. But then he felt suddenly different: hot, jerky, then wet and soft. He detached himself from the woman and nodded to Janetto.

The others silently took their turns, the music still whining, the hashish still lingering in a haze about them. None of the boys took off his clothes. None of them touched Nervana except to put it in and take it out.

Hamid watched them all and sipped his whiskey. When the last was through, he stood up again. He had heard, he said, that this other thing felt even better. He ordered Nervana to turn over.

Nervana sighed but did as she was told. She rolled over to lie with her belly and breasts against the rug. She had thought there would be none of this tonight. The man who had hired her had said these would be virgin boys. But this one didn't act like a virgin. She knew he was about to hurt her. She knew he would be too big for her.

Hamid kneeled down again, took it out, and put it between the cheeks of her buttocks. He pushed without effect for some time, but then he forced it in. Nervana screamed.

This time, as Hamid pumped, he began to make a sound, a low moan of a sound, a sound all of them had heard often, five times a day, every day, in the prayer calls from the peaks of the minarets. "A-l-l-a-h!" Hamid groaned once. He lay on top of her as if he were dead.

The other boys looked at one another. Were they supposed to do this, too?

Youssef stood up, already once again unzipping his pants.

Yes, they had to do it again.

None of them did it with Hamid's enthusiasm.

Afterward Nervana was bundled back into her *milaya,* and each of them handed her a one-pound note for *baksheesh,* her tips.

The boys were glad when she left. They were eager to talk all this over.

Janetto made sure they all had more whiskey. "Well." Janetto was intensely conscious of his role as host. "What did you think?"

No one said anything for a minute.

Hamid spoke first, stroking his chin. "I liked it. I liked it better even than hashish."

"Did you ever do it before?" Janetto leaned forward in his seat. "You *looked* as if you had done it before."

"Did you, Hamid?" It had seemed to Youssef, too, that Hamid had practiced.

"Not exactly." Hamid laughed. "Last summer, on the *izba,* a *fellah* showed me how to do it."

"And the girl?" Youssef wanted every detail. "Was she pretty? Prettier than this one?"

"A bit hairier." Hamid paused, then let them in on his secret. "She was a donkey. I did it to a donkey."

Janetto choked on his whiskey.

"An *animal?*" Youssef, too, looked about to choke. "You did *that* to an animal?"

"Women. Animals." Hamid shrugged. "It felt about the same."

Youssef's curiosity struggled with his sense of propriety. The stronger won. "What was it like?"

"We did it one night out in the fields. Ahmed said a lot of the boys do it. They don't stand a chance with the women in the village until they get married. So they get it where they can. The married ones use women. Some of the boys use each other. Or whatever else is there. Usually donkeys. Sometimes sheep. Or chickens."

"No!" Janetto was so flustered he knocked over his whiskey glass. "Chickens! That *can't* be true!"

"That's what Ahmed said. I was surprised, too. They're so little. And it would be hard to keep them still long enough. But Ahmed swore they did. The next time I go home, he said I could watch."

"I still don't believe they do it to chickens." Janetto was so rattled he didn't care if he *was* calling Hamid a liar.

"I don't mean to say they do it to chickens every day. And some of them just don't do it at all until they get married. But it happens. Believe me, it happens."

Youssef persisted with his original line of questioning. "So what did it feel like, Hamid? The donkey."

"Soft. Warm. A lot like Nervana. Only Nervana's skin was nicer. And she was softer inside. Wetter. Yes, I think it was better with Nervana."

Janetto breathed a sigh of relief. He was afraid that if Hamid had said it was better with a donkey, Youssef would have insisted they all try it.

Hamid was warming to his subject. "In the village last summer some of those old ones told me what to do. They were the ones who said it feels better to do it . . . the way I showed you the second time. They call that Greek style."

The boy sitting next to Janetto, a Greek by the name of Stefano, looked as if he didn't know whether he should be pleased or offended.

"And the way we did it the first time—you know, with her legs on our shoulders—they call that the Egyptian way. It's supposed to go in farther like that."

The boys all nodded as if they, too, had found that to be true.

Hamid turned to Youssef. "I forgot to try what else the men in the village told me. They said it's supposed to feel good for two men to do it to a woman at once. None of them had tried that themselves—not in *our* village—but I guess it would be all right with a belly dancer." He laughed. "*Anything's* allowed with a belly dancer."

"Two at once?"

"Yes. The one gets her in the front and the other in the back. They call it 'face-to-face.'"

Janetto felt sick. The look of interest on Youssef's face was unmistakable. He wished they all would go home. It was two o'clock in the morning. His parents would be back soon. He didn't think he could face his father tonight. His father would want all the details.

To Janetto's great relief, Youssef was standing up to go. It had been, they all assured each other, everything they had hoped it would be.

But on the way home, walking silently next to Hamid, Youssef felt sad. He had thought there would be lots of kissing. At the cinema there was lots of kissing. Youssef felt cheated at the way it had turned out. Was *this* all there was to it? Everything, he thought, everything was such a disappointment.

5 ~~~~~

KARNAK, EGYPT / July 1951

Mona was asleep, caught in the web of a disturbing dream that had begun to haunt her nearly every night since she had returned to the village. She tossed from side to side. Her eyelids twitched as her sleeping mind saw herself walking slowly down to the river, an earthenware jug poised on her head, her robe clinging to her breasts and buttocks as she swung to a slow sensuous music she alone could hear. There was no one else at the river. An early-morning mist rose from the water to cloak her in a cloudy spell. Mona set down the jug and then, with a dancer's fluid movement and a dancer's inborn grace, she threw off her clothes and slid into the river. The cool darkness carried her away, sweeping and swooning her under, until she could feel nothing but its silky cold caress. From nowhere then—unless it was from the depths of the Nile itself—would come a man, always a blond man, always a laughing man, to play with her and touch her, to trace the tips of her nipples with his smooth hands and lips, to make her smile and drift with the current. He would encircle her body with his arms and legs and she would relax into him in a long kiss until, urgently, he pulled her far under the water,—down, down, down—past breathing, past thinking, sinking deeper and deeper. But then just before the water filled her lungs, she would look up through the silty brownish water and see something floating on top. It looked like the body of a woman smothered in a heavy black robe. Mona, struggling toward that body, would try to thrash out of the arms of that laughing blond man. She had to see who or what it was on the crest of the Nile. Harder she would fight, frantic to reach that swollen dead or living body, kicking and punching, struggling, desperate. . . .

She woke up, gasping for breath and wet with sweat, tears, and her own femaleness. She always woke up at just this point. She never did discover who was floating on top of that water and whether it was living or dead. Why wouldn't Youssef let her find out? Mona began to cry quietly to herself until the dream faded. She did not know whether she wanted never to wake or never to sleep again, so disturbing was that dream.

She lay in the darkness and fought for control of herself. Ummie was fast asleep only a few feet away. Some of that dream was still with her. She could feel the freshness of the water and, as she deliberately touched the hard tips of her nipples, she felt a twinge deep inside her body.

She sighed and moved her hand away. Enough of that, she told herself sternly. She turned on her stomach and, pleased at the discomfort, pushed herself into the hard earth. She made herself think. Mona knew she was a bad girl to have such dreams. She had prayed to Allah to banish them. But hard though she prayed, the dreams still recurred. Ever since she had started to bleed each month, ever since she had come back to Karnak last spring, this dream had been with her. She wondered sometimes if it was her Nile curse tempting her to destruction. But then Mona shrugged off that thought. Youssef had told her years ago—it must be three whole years ago when they were all together at Agami—that there was no such thing as a curse from the river.

Youssef. It was Youssef who always beckoned to her, touched her, lured her in her dreams. She wished she had even a photograph of her Youssef. Except for the memory of his yellow hair and the sound of his laugh, it was only in her dream that she could conjure up Youssef.

Mona sighed again. Increasingly these days she had to make an effort to remember all that had been Alexandria. What was it about this village that seemed to blot out the possibility of any other life in any other place? She had been back in Karnak for only three months, and already her five years in Alexandria were faint.

Mona turned over on her back and looked up at the stars. There were so many glittering stars in the black sky over Karnak, so many more here than there had been in Alexandria. Mona wondered if she ever again would see the scant stars of Alexandria. The al-Masris had sent ten-year-old Batata away to a special sanitarium in Switzerland. Even Baruch had thought that with the government finally rescinding its travel restrictions against the Jews, it was time to have the specialists take a look at Batata. But just now must be, Mona thought wistfully, a fine time to be in Alexandria. The cabanas on Rushdi Beach would be packed. The king and the court would be larking about in limousines. Each night the sounds of music would drift all along the Corniche. Baruch had assured her that Batata would not be away for more than a year. In the meantime Mona was supposed to be once again getting in touch with her roots in the village. Mona had resented the entire idea. Did Baruch think she was a rose bush, that she could be so easily transplanted? Mona had been afraid to come home. She had feared that her mother would once again nearly scare her out of her wits.

Mona yawned. How could she have known that this time in Karnak boredom was to be a more insidious enemy than fear? Her life here had quickly settled into a mind-buzzing monotony. Each endless day was marked off only by the rise and fall of the sun, the five-times-daily prayer calls, and the slow rush of the river northward to the sea. These days and weeks and months by the Nile had been so very slow. It was as though, Mona thought, each minute itched under the skin, yet no one could even be bothered to scratch. For that, she thought, would make those itching minutes into a rash of hours, a disease of days. It was easier and better, she found, simply to tolerate those intolerable instants, those flushes of prickly desire, to feel their slow creep under the skin, and to do nothing. It could feel good, she now knew, to itch and not scratch, to feel the burning and let it go, to yearn into it and twist under it. After a while an itch either goes away or becomes part of what has to be, accepted and even welcomed without so much as an outward twitch.

Mona smiled up at the stars and stretched like a cat. She had discovered a voluptuousness, a hot and heady power, that comes with giving over the self to whatever has to happen. Her senses were glutted in Karnak. Promises of passion and hints of lust were everywhere. She saw it in those long languorous looks of the women, whose heavy-lidded almond eyes promised burning nights of slow ecstasy. She smelled it in that sharp scent of human and animal urine, in the heavy pungence of garlic and cumin and cardamom and coriander, in the sickly-sweet blooms of jasmine and bougainvillaea, in the fetid whiffs of rotten mangoes: all of it breathed in without discrimination. She felt it in the easy sweep of dust and dirt softly coating skin and soul, in the scorching caress of sun and heat that was all-embracing. She tasted it in the acrid dryness on the roof of her mouth, too parched to spit, too thirsty even to be slaked by the broad reaches of the river. She heard it in the low, sonorously sensual drone of the prayer calls, in the outraged laments of the donkeys and the camels, in the guttural grunts of the men, women, and animals rutting in the night toward relief if not release. It—all of it—drowned her senses, lulled them, overwhelmed them, until they were all that there was.

It was hard, then, to wake from the lassitude of those cloying minutes, hours, days, weeks, to shake them off as a dog shakes off river water, to blink hard and move about with purpose and resolution. It was hard, in fact, in this aimless daze, to move about at all. For although there was time—so much time, so terribly much time—Mona had little inclination to seize it. She had noticed early on, when she still had the energy for observation, that it was the same with everyone else. Men and women sat waiting and watching for hours on end, hardly moving, barely breathing, surely not thinking at all. The men would suck their endless cigarettes and drink their bottomless glasses of sweet tea. The women would chop their endless vegetables and suckle their insatiable babies. Slowly, always slowly, for why should they hurry when it was always the same? When one cigarette and one glass of tea were gone, there was only the next one. When one bulb of garlic was minced and one baby weaned, there was only one more potful and bellyful. Every so often, however, Mona would notice a man rising as does a sleep-walker and then making halting, spasmodic steps toward some fleeting goal. But then it was as if he would forget his mission and instead sigh and lie back in his coma, his wishful dreams no longer part of his waking life. Strangely, life here was both paralyzed and propelled by passion.

Mona felt her fingertips once again stroking the tips of her breasts. Angrily she forced her hand back off her body. That was the worst thing about this Karnak summer. Every damnable thing all around her led her to the brink of passion. Yet in her gut she knew there was mortal danger in the slightest surrender. When she woke up sometimes as she had this very night, her body damp with sweat, the heat moving through her, she wanted no more out of life than to moan and sigh until she could moan and sigh no more. She was nearly eleven—old enough for marriage. But with her mother's grandiose plans for her, there could be no quick and easy village wedding. And so, afraid of any other sort of passion, she would have to ignore the heat. Sometimes Mona envied the boys in the village. She heard the whispers about what young boys did in the shadows. She saw her male cousins wrestling on the riverbank with not quite the innocence of puppies. Once she had come upon two boys rubbing up against each other behind a sycamore tree. Mona knew the Koran condemned passion between two boys just as it did for un-married women. But in Karnak the sudden fancies of boys were winked at, whereas the slightest indiscretion of a girl was a matter of life and death.

Mona wiped the beads of perspiration off her forehead. It was so hot. It wasn't yet dawn, and yet it was so hot. All the Saidi summers were hot, of course, but this one seemed more ferocious than any of the others. Even when Mona arrived in April, it had been hard to move about in the afternoons. By now, in midsummer, life in the village had come to a virtual standstill during all the hours that the scorching sun was high in the sky. It was a numbing heat, so thick and heavy that it was hard to have two consecutive thoughts without forgetting the point of the first one. Men planted one row of seeds and then planted another row on top of the first, so muddled were they. Women forgot which babies were weaned and which were still on the tit, and listlessly suckled whichever child crawled to their breasts.

What made that heat seem even more killing was that this year the worst of it fell during Ramadan. Mona well knew that it was forbidden, by the direct command of Muhammad, who had been instructed by Allah Himself, for any good Muslim to break the fast between sunup and sundown. Keeping the fast meant not eating, drinking, smoking, not even swallowing spit. Until this year Mona had been too young to follow the Ramadan rigors. But this summer Mona's mother had decided that if her girl was old enough to menstruate, she was old enough to "keep Ramadan." Mona tried to console herself that she wasn't the only one finding Ramadan difficult. Ramadan was hard even when it fell in those chill, blustery weeks of December. But when it came in the summer it brought madness with it. For who could stand to be so parched, so weak and so parched, in such relentless heat? Maybe, Mona thought, it was the heat, the madness of the Ramadan heat, that was to blame. Maybe the heat caused that girl to act so crazy that those others had done what they had to do.

A shudder shook Mona's body. Khadra had been fifteen, Khadra had had flashing forget-me-not eyes, and Khadra had been overripe for marriage. For the past two seasons her father had been negotiating a large brideprice from a rich cloth merchant who was eager to take Khadra as his second wife. But Khadra, it seemed, had nursed another dream. Some of Khadra's womenfolk had warned her she was courting disaster when she was seen talking outside Karnak Temple and then walking by the river with Ibrahim, a handsome young carriage driver from a village on the far side of Luxor. Khadra had just laughed and said she was her father's favorite daughter. She was sure, she said, she would be able to convince her father to accept Ibrahim instead of the old cloth merchant.

Mona turned over on her stomach and hid her face in her hands. She would never forget that morning when her mother had dragged her down to the river to see Khadra's body. Khadra's father had slit her throat and, so that his daughter might serve as an example to the other girls of Karnak, he had thrown her body into a shallow pool of water along the bank of the Nile. Mona had tried to look away from the corpse, but her mother had made her examine it closely. There was a pink line on Khadra's neck, and already, since the heat of the night before, her body had begun to swell. But Khadra had seemed only asleep. Mona had not quite believed that Khadra's father could murder his favorite child. Yet later, outside the mosque, Mona saw Khadra's father wiping away his tears on the sleeve of his *gallabeiya*. It was said

116

that he wept not only for his daughter but because Ibrahim had escaped vengeance by fleeing north to Cairo. Very troubling to Mona was that no one, not even her gossipy stepgrandmother Zainab, could tell her just how far Khadra's indiscretions had gone. Had she kissed this Ibrahim? Had she let him touch her breasts? Had she let him lift her robe and touch her *there?* Zainab had lectured Mona for even daring to ask such questions. It must be, Mona finally concluded, that Khadra had been killed for the *suspicion* of doing something shameful with a man. Mona's mother had reinforced this harsh lesson every night thereafter when she would light a candle, watch until a moth flew into the flames, and make Mona chant the old chant: "Fire is better than shame." Since then Mona had been careful to keep her eyes to the ground and her mouth shut when any man other than her uncles came into view.

Mona shifted her position on the ground and wondered, fleetingly, if the woman floating on the river in her dream could be Khadra. Maybe she had had a premonition of Khadra's death months before it had happened. But no. The body floating on the water in her dream had to be either her mother, her grandmother, or herself. But why was Youssef always a part of this nightmare? Youssef had never even been to Karnak. Time and again Mona had postponed telling Ummie that she had found the bridegroom of their dreams. Youssef was far richer and grander than even Ummie expected. She would wait and surprise her mother when the match was settled. She wasn't ready to share her dreams of Youssef, even with Ummie.

Mona could hear the faint echo of the Ramadan drum a few lanes away. It must be almost dawn. The drummer was alerting the faithful to wake and fortify themselves with food and drink before the fast began at daybreak. Mona rubbed her eyes with her fingers and rolled over. She would have to wake her mother. Mona looked at the sleeping form so near her. This summer it had been hard to slip back into her old orbit around Ummie. After the tingle of those five free years in Alexandria, how could she again be Ummie's little girl? Baruch had tried so hard to teach her to speak up, to make her own decisions, to act instead of being acted upon. And so there had been a pushing and hauling between mother and daughter until Mona had finally given in. In her heart of hearts—Karnak, after all, still cut deeper than Alexandria—she liked it better Ummie's way. Yet no matter how docile Mona was, it was never enough to make Ummie into the kind of woman others would call Helwa. Just when Mona began to feel at one with her mother again, just when they would laugh over a small joke or she would see her mother's eyes light with pleasure, Ummie would say something to spoil it. It was as if Ummie couldn't bear to be happy.

Yet Mona sighed. This summer even her mother's scariest efforts had not worked their familiar black magic. True, she had once again been terrified when her mother had insisted on another visit to the black lioness of Karnak Temple. But this time they had gone at midnight by the light of a full moon to another lair of the black goddess outside the main temple walls. This time there had been many, many seated black statues ranged in a giant circle. This time Um Mona had whispered that these stone statues would spring to life and devour any man who walked the temple grounds after nightfall. But this time Mona had not been so afraid of the black statues as she had been of being bitten by a snake. She had heard that many, many poisonous snakes made their homes in the temples. It was supposed to be particularly dangerous to walk in the Old Places at night when the snakes hunted. Mona, as she prayed to Allah to keep away the serpents, had cringed at every uncertain step she had taken. But she had pretended to her mother that her lack of courage was that old baby terror. Anything to make Ummie happy.

Mona touched her blue bead for luck. Enough of such thoughts. If she did not wake her mother this instant, there would be no time to eat and drink before the fast began. Gently she shook her mother awake. It was time to begin another day, a day that no doubt would be exactly like the day that had gone before and the day that would come after. Mona stifled a yawn and wondered if she would ever see Alexandria again.

"Baruch!" Mona dropped the glass of tea, ran toward the tall lean man in their doorway, then stopped short of touching him. She would have loved to have thrown herself into Baruch's arms. But Baruch was a man, and Mona had learned well the lessons about what she could and could not do with men.

"Mona." Gravely Baruch extended his hand and saw Mona hesitate before she grazed it limply. When he had sent her south, his Mona had been a little girl. Now, ten months later, she was old enough to worry about the impropriety of touching her Uncle Baruch.

Um Mona escorted him to the guestroom's seat of honor, a noisily springed cushion that once had been the back seat of a taxi. As he waited for them to bring him the obligatory glass of sweet and tepid tea, Baruch allowed his eyes to roam the house where Mona lived. The walls were mudbrick, the floor was dirt, and only one window high in the wall let in a little light. Besides this dank room, it appeared there were two unroofed sleeping alcoves and another shed for the donkey. There was no sign of sink or toilet. The small primus stove where the women were stirring the tea was off in the courtyard. But, of all the amenities that were lacking, what seemed the worst to Baruch was the utter absence of decoration. The walls weren't even hung with a picture torn from a magazine. It was all so bleak and black and brown. No wonder, he thought, that poor Egyptians, like peasants everywhere, loved so to dress in glitter and spangles and the most garish of clashing oranges and purples and reds. He promised himself that never again would he look down his nose at the gaudy taste of the poor. What must it be like, Baruch wondered anew, for Mona to shuttle back and forth between this brown mud hut and a villa of velvet and lace?

He sat and drank tea with the mother and the daughter, repeating the Arab social formulas about health and happenings, thanking God for every fortune and misfortune which had been visited upon them. Finally Baruch settled down to the business at hand. Batata was due home soon, and so he had come to fetch Mona back to Alexandria. But from the sudden speculative look in Um Mona's eyes, Baruch knew she must be preparing to bargain. He hoped she would not be so crude as to attempt to *sell* him Mona. He had heard that sometimes happened in the villages.

But as Um Mona finally began to lay out her conditions, it appeared that she was concerned only with Mona's eventual marriage to a wealthy and pious man. A pretty girl like Mona, her mother said, should be able to have a man rich enough to own a barber shop or taxi. She wanted a son-in-law with the means to support not only Mona but herself, her brother Muhammad, and any future wife and children of Muhammad. If Baruch would promise that he and Abbas would find such a husband, Mona could return north with him. If not, she would keep Mona here and start hunting for a prosperous Karnak husband within the year. What was Baruch's answer?

Baruch lit a cigarette and reflected on this Egyptian mother's dream. Once an old *baladi* man had told him that all an Egyptian could dream of was meat for dinner. When Baruch had pressed him further, he had admitted that—oh, *yimkin,* perhaps—a man might also dream that the bus the next morning might not be too crowded. And what, Baruch had asked, about the dreams of a peasant farmer? "Meat," the old man had promptly answered. Then, after a moment's hesitation, he had thought of one more thing: "Good water to drink and enough water for the fields." Baruch had been unable to forget those Egyptian dreams. What must it be like to live a life where the most a man could dream of is meat for dinner, unpoisoned water, and enough room to stand up on a bus? At least Um Mona had the wit to dream a larger dream.

And so he smiled at Mona and her mother and, speaking for both himself and Abbas, agreed to find Mona a husband rich enough to bring her whole family north to Alexandria.

Then, just when the negotiations were almost concluded, Muhammad limped in from the fields. Afraid the bargaining would have to begin afresh, Baruch smiled uncertainly at this pleasant honest farmer who eked out a living as a sharecropper for one of the local landowners.

Yes, Muhammad was brushing off any suggestion that Mona's future be disposed of too hastily.

Baruch settled back on the taxi seat. Arabs being Arabs, Baruch knew it might now take days—even weeks—of indirect negotiations before he could leave with Mona.

And so, while Mona and her mother prepared them a feast of stuffed pigeons, the two men whiled away the hours pondering Muhammad's crops, Baruch's patients, and finally the changing political realities in Cairo. They were on their second *nargileh* of water-piped tobacco when Baruch finally admitted that it was the possibility of war that had sent him speeding down to the Said for Mona in this January of 1952. While Baruch listened to Muhammad's polite assurances that nothing so dire was probably in the winds, he tried to make himself believe that he and his had faced greater dangers when the Egyptian government had imposed so many restrictions against its Jews during the Palestine war. Baruch told himself the current problems might dissipate as easily as those others. Rafael was back on the Cotton Exchange. That "Abdel" who had made Rafael wash his feet had been fired. Concentration camps no longer bulged with suspected Zionists. Jews could once again come and go and work and play as they pleased.

Listening to Muhammad's tirade against not the Jews but the British, Baruch regretted once again that Egyptians were so obsessed by the British Occupation. Baruch knew that other colonial powers in other places were far more repressive. True, British economic dominance had turned Egypt into a giant cotton plantation to supply the Manchester textile mills. Baruch was even willing to admit that the British had never done enough to set up adequate health care and education here. And Baruch supposed there was intrinsic injustice to imperialism of any stripe. But the British, who kept only one military garrison at Suez, were hardly responsible for every evil in this country.

The two of them supped and sipped and smoked and discussed the crisis that had begun when Egypt had annulled its last treaty with Britain four months ago. Anti-British boycotts, strikes, and violence had spread through the country. Guerrilla bands largely composed of fanatic Muslim Brothers had begun clashing with British patrols. The British had retaliated by cordoning off the Canal Zone and inching their troops closer and closer to Cairo. Even here in Karnak, Muhammad said, men were ready to fight.

Yet that evening, riding the horse-drawn carriage for the two-mile trip back to the Winter Palace Hotel in Luxor, politics was the last thing on Baruch's mind. He would use the upcoming days of discreet squabbling over Mona to try to enjoy his first visit to the Said. He was thirty-six years old, he had lived in Egypt almost all of his life, and still Baruch had never before been south of Cairo. Tourists came to Luxor from all over the world to see the Valley of the Kings, Karnak Temple, and a bewildering array of other ancient monuments. Yet it was a rare Alexandrian who ever bothered to come here. And it's no wonder, Baruch thought, as he eyed the sooty lanes littered by orange peels and piles of rubble and rubbish. Luxor was as squalid, as bug-infested, as disease-ridden as any other Egyptian village Baruch had ever had the misfortune to behold. But the difference, Baruch thought, what made Luxor worth a sigh rather than a shrug, was that this was all that remained of once-great Thebes. Four thousand years ago this had been the grand and gold metropolis of the greatest of the pharaohs.

They were almost at Baruch's hotel on the bank of the Nile when the carriage driver turned and began hissing to him in English. "You want hashish, mister? A young boy? Or a woman, a big woman, ha-ha, big enough for you? Make good love." Although Baruch would have liked to slap the driver's sly face, he contented himself with invoking, in impatient and offended Arabic, the wrath of Allah on not only the driver but past and future generations of the driver's family. Baruch had heard much about the sapping heat of Luxor. He had known that it was hotter here than hell. But he hadn't heard that Luxor was over-ripe and very nearly rotten. He supposed that he shouldn't jump to conclusions. One venal carriage driver schooled to pander to the needs of soldiers on leave and tourists on holiday shouldn't prejudice him against a whole town. If there wasn't an eager market, the driver wouldn't be so bold as to try to ply him with sex and drugs. But then, as Baruch alighted from his carriage, as he had to shoo away a swarm of begging Arab children, as he had to endure a nasty fight over his fare with the carriage driver, Baruch felt a great weariness at the decay of Luxor.

It wasn't until a few hours later—after a bath, a light meal, and a gin and tonic—that Baruch's temper improved. Sitting with his feet up on the railing of his balcony, he wondered why he always felt such peace when he looked out over the Nile. Even when he merely sat alongside it at a café in Cairo, the river affected him like a drug. Here the Nile was narrower, cleaner, softer, and most certainly more beautiful. Docked just below him, gleaming white under the crescent moon, was a paddle steamer that shuttled tourists from Luxor to Aswan. Baruch could see couples dancing on the deck to the strains of "Stardust" drifting from a record player. Lights from the boat arced out on the river to illuminate groves of palm trees on the opposite bank. Near the steamship a neat row of humble feluccas bobbed in their berths. Colored lights were strung in the trees of one of those open-air cafeterias the Egyptians call casinos. From somewhere came the beat of a donkey-skin drum and the trill of a lute. Baruch threw on a *gallabeiya*, walked down to the water, and talked a boatman into taking him out in a felucca. The night wind caught the sail, and they slipped out on the black river. Spotlights picked out the gold pillars of Luxor Temple. Baruch lay back, lulled by the lap of the Nile under him. Suddenly, on an impulse he could not resist, Baruch slipped off his robe and dove in. He laughed and splashed like a young boy as he swam in circles around the boat, then floated on his back gazing up at the stars. Crazy. It was wonderfully yet maybe a little frighteningly crazy here. He wondered what the hell he was doing swimming in this polluted river at midnight. Had he lost his senses or found them? It was almost as though here in the river his conscious mind had drifted away, and his subconscious had risen to the surface. Was this what it was like here for Mona and the others? Did the constant sun burn away their consciousness? Baruch floated on the mesmerizing Nile. He had to admit the truth of at least one cliché about the Said. Nothing, they all said, was ever quite what it appeared to be in Upper Egypt.

The last thought, over Baruch's next week in Luxor, was to recur to him again and again. It seemed not only that was Mona happy and secure under her mother's wing but also that there was serenity in living by traditional values. But the converse, maddeningly enough, appeared to be just as true. He found himself constantly changing his mind about both the Arab present and the pharaonic past in Upper Egypt. Most days he found the stone obelisks and grim statuary of the ancient Egyptians too inhuman and humorless for his taste. But then, stumbling on a brilliantly colored wall painting in one of the tombs or catching the sun glinting on the face of a granite hawk god, he would be stunned by the grandeur of this oldest of all civilizations. He wondered why the villagers shunned the ancient sites. Was it simply that they found the old temples too pagan? Or were they embarrassed that their culture had fallen so far from its ancient glories? What, after all, could be said for a people who five thousand years ago had carved intricate gold-leaf drawings on solid walls of rock and who now made do with crude and unadorned walls of mud? Was it that, or was it that the Arabs resented rich tourists who saw so much to praise in a dead Egypt yet couldn't spare either smiles or thoughts for what breathed in Egypt now? Whatever it was, the villagers seemed indifferent to their own lost wonders.

But one day, when he and Mona were wandering through Karnak Temple, Baruch found more emotion than he bargained for. When they were in one of the side temples, Mona began to drag her feet and complain she was tired and wanted to go home. Nonetheless, determined to examine whatever the pharaohs had left, Baruch swung open a rusty door. While Mona clung to his hand and began to cry, Baruch looked in astonishment at the long dark chamber cunningly angled toward a chilling black statue that was both lion and woman. Baruch absentmindedly patted the sobbing Mona on her head while he riffled through his guidebook. Here she was. The black lioness Sekhmet was one of the most unpleasant of the Egyptian gods. The ancients had so feared her infamous wrath that they had placated her with annual festivals. She was the goddess of bloodlust and war and destruction— and of passion that has strayed to the dark side of love. But as Baruch moved forward for a closer look, Mona screamed and fled from the room.

It was only when he bought her a Pepsi and they sat by the stagnant green waters of the Sacred Lake that Mona finally told him her own Sekhmet story. Mona sobbed when she recalled how her mother had dragged her there at the height of the *khamseen*. Baruch held Mona in his arms and stroked her hair as she confided how she had been cursed at her circumcision. She told him how her grandmother had been killed for smoking a cigarette and how Khadra had been murdered for walking publicly with a man.

Enough, Baruch thought. Enough of all this brutal superstition, all this crippling fear. Enough. He marched Mona back home, listened to Muhammad's telling him to find Mona not only a rich but a virile husband—"She is Saidi," Muhammad said with a wink—and quickly agreed to what he had to so he could take Mona away with him. Yes, when Mona was sixteen, he would find her a proper husband. Yes, Um Mona and Muhammad and whoever else they wanted could come and live in Mona's married household. Yes, yes, yes. To himself Baruch made another promise. *Never again* would he allow his Mona to come back here.

That very evening he fetched Mona, and they set out together in the bluish-pink sunset light to walk the river road to the train station. Under the dusky shadows of sycamores, honky-tonk Luxor was at its peak. A howling mob jumped aboard the rusty hulk of the river ferry before it even touched shore. Women paced with baskets of food, cardboard cartons jammed with nuts and bolts, and brimming copper water tubs balanced on their heads. A carriage driver flicked his whip carelessly at his pair of prancing chestnut Arabians. Outside Luxor Temple peddlers tried to con tourists into buying fake mummy hands and feet. Nearby other peddlers hawked *fool* beans, salty white cheese, long-stemmed green onions, and loaves of flat beige bread. Motionless men with turbans wrapped like bandages around their heads sat as if they had been planted in the loose dust of the roadway.

An overburdened old blind donkey stumbled along ahead of Baruch and Mona. The donkey's backside was an open sore from the whippings of its sullen master, and the fresh fragrant clover was piled too heavily on the exhausted animal. The donkey balked, brayed, and shuddered to a halt. Its owner began striking it hard again and again, until the blood gushed.

Mona averted her eyes and touched her blue bead. She was so sick of omens and curses. Yet how could it be good luck that the way ahead was red with blood?

Savagely, relentlessly, the man lashed the donkey until the animal sank down into the dust. With one terrible last bray, the donkey died. Baruch took Mona's hand in his as the donkey's owner continued to beat the beast. But then the Arab shrugged and turned to the gathering crowd. There was a quick bargaining, an agreed price. Two men helped the owner load the carcass on the clover cart, and four others harnessed themselves in the donkey's place. All the way to the station Baruch and Mona trailed behind the cart piled high with the clover and the corpse.

Mona sat on the verandah of the luxurious Mena House Hotel sipping a lemonade and listening to Baruch expound on the wonders of the pyramids before them. On a whim during their train ride north, Baruch had decided they would break their journey for a few days in Cairo. He promised to show her not only the pyramids but some of the most famous and most beautiful mosques of the Islamic world. Maybe they would go to the opera; certainly they would visit the museum. Baruch was determined that from now on Mona would taste a sweeter life.

Mona stifled a yawn as Baruch embroidered on the magical pyramids. Baruch was in love with the pyramids. When he was just a boy he had climbed up inside their sloping passages to find nothing but a mysteriously empty coffin smelling not so mysteriously of urine. Since then he had watched, with great amusement, how the tourists gamely climbed inside seeking vanished wonders. It was the exterior of the great pyramids that still fascinated Baruch. It was strange, he told Mona, how their allure grew every time he saw them. They were such a big, straight, perfectly proportioned geometric progression. Once, when he was fourteen, he had gone riding out in the desert just after dawn one fresh spring morning. He had galloped across the sand and then suddenly there were the pyramids before him. A thick dawn mist had hugged their bases, so that all he could see were gold sand, white clouds, and their gray pointy peaks. They had looked as if they were packed in a world of dry ice. Another time he and his wife, Daisy, had decided on a moonlight winter visit to the pyramids. The moon had been full, the night had been freezing, and the peak of the middle pyramid—the one that still had its original smooth casings—had caught the light so that it looked as if the pyramid were covered in snow. Every time these beauties were the same, yet every time they were different.

Mona looked with disinterest at the gray points of the pyramids. Every time she went from villa to village to villa, she felt more disoriented. She had almost hoped that this time Ummie would keep her back in Karnak and find her a village husband. No one ever asked her what she wanted. Not that she would have been able to say. But right now, since she had been forced to take leave of her mother again, what she most wanted was immediately to settle back into Youssef's Alexandria. Yet she was so accustomed to doing whatever she was expected to do that she smiled and pretended to agree with Baruch about the pyramids. When he ordered her another lemonade, she drank it. She wasn't thirsty, but she drank it.

The next morning, instead of setting out early for the mosques and the museums of Cairo, Baruch overslept. When he finally woke and opened the newspapers, he began to regret his impulse to dally in Cairo. The Suez crisis had exploded. The day before a British commander had demanded that an Egyptian garrison surrender the town of Ismailia. When the Arabs refused, the British had opened fire and killed more than fifty Egyptians. Baruch sprang out of bed, packed their bags, and raced down to the lobby with Mona. But the concierge advised him that, on this twenty-sixth of January, it was best for foreigners to steer clear of the train station. Already there were wild rumors about what was happening on the other side of the Nile in downtown Cairo. Some said Egyptian soldiers had mutinied against a government which could allow the British to kill so many of their brothers. Others reported that the streets of Cairo were burning.

Baruch sat waiting out the crisis with Mona on the Mena House verandah. From time to time, hungry for news, he joined the worried knots of Europeans in the lobby. Before noon he heard that Cairo was being put to the torch by angry mobs who were throwing gasoline bombs at every symbol of foreign influence and power. The private clubs and the posh hotels, the coffeehouses and the cinemas, all were going up in flames. Finally Baruch heard that a mob was marching down the Pyramids Road and that already the nightclubs lining the boulevard had begun to burn. The hotel manager ran through the lobby, promising that the mob had been bribed to spare Mena House. But Baruch took Mona by one hand and their suitcases by the other and dashed out the front door. All along the horizon they could see smoke rising from Cairo. Men were running in all directions carrying valises, crates of goods, even a red plush sofa from the hotel lobby. They were throwing their treasures on donkey carts and lashing them atop camels.

"Taxi!" Baruch shouted. "Taxi!"

As if this were any quiet afternoon of any normal day, two black-and-white taxis were idling in the driveway. Baruch ran to the nearest, slid Mona and himself in the back seat, and threw their cases in the front. "Alexandria. Take us to Alexandria. The desert road."

The driver turned and smiled at Baruch. "Two hundred pounds. Pay now."

"Are you crazy? *Two* pounds. Not two hundred."

"Two hundred pounds." The man repeated the same sum, in the same tone, with the same smile.

"Get out." Baruch opened the door for Mona. "There's another cab right over there."

The driver's smile widened. "You prefer my cousin's taxi? Same price. Special price. For today only."

"Robber!" But then Baruch got control of himself. He wasn't bargaining for rugs at the bazaar. What he might be haggling for was his and Mona's life. He dug in his wallet. "One hundred and twenty Egyptian. It's all I have."

"Two hundred pounds."

"One hundred twenty and a gold watch."

The driver raised an eyebrow.

"One hundred twenty, a gold watch, and a ring." Baruch pulled off the jewelry, grabbed the banknotes, and held them out in his fist.

The driver smiled. "As you wish." He revved his engine and sped out the driveway toward Alexandria.

Mona and the al-Masri children were strung along the railing of the Corniche just above the point where the official yacht *Mahrousa* lay docked for its final royal mission. Beside them Leah al-Masri was casting languishing, long-lashed looks into the green eyes of the French diplomat Jacques Renard. But today Leah flirted without her usual *élan*. For on this hot July evening she had come, sentimentally dressed in a white lace gown with a red rose tucked at her waist, to bid adieu to the king she had once danced with in the moonlight. "Faruk," she sighed at Renard. "Oh, Faruk!"

Youssef edged closer to his mother and her latest lover in the hope that the diplomat was whispering state secrets in her ear. These last three days since the news of the *coup d'état* had flashed on the radio— "People of Egypt! The country has just passed through the most troubled period of its history, degraded by corruption and weakened by instability!"—there had been dancing in the streets, tanks in the squares of Cairo, and artillery surrounding the king's palaces in Alexandria. Cairo bulletins said a cadre of army colonels called the "Free Officers" had seized power and forced the king to accept a new prime minister. But although—*el-hamdulillah!*—there was the good news that only two soldiers had died in the coup, there was little hard information on what the revolution would mean.

In the five months since the mob had burned Cairo, the king had lost his grip on the country. Martial law had been imposed, guerrilla bands had been ordered to stop harassing the British, and transport and other services had been restored to the foreign troops. Three prime ministers had been appointed and dismissed, and king and army had been at loggerheads over who would lead the military. Faruk had been accused of collaborating on the sale of obsolete arms to his own army during the Palestine war, of subverting the constitution and selling every high office, even of burning down his capital city so he could ask for help from his British friends. Most of all, from Alexandria to Aswan, Faruk had been mocked as a dissolute playboy who was bringing Egypt to ruin. Ever since the coup there had been reports that the king—*à la Russe*—was about to be executed. But just hours ago a new rumor had swept the salons and slums of Alexandria. This morning Faruk had abdicated. Tonight he would be leaving Egypt on the royal yacht. Tomorrow he would begin a life of exile.

"There he is!" Renard pointed to a very fat, nearly bald man in an ornate white admiral's uniform coming down the steps of the Ras el-Tin Palace. "Faruk!" Behind him trailed Queen Narriman, carrying their infant son.

Leah turned pale. Behind those dark sunglasses she could hardly make out the features of her king. "Faruk? *Chéri?*"

"Two hundred and four!" Daoud announced. "He's taking two hundred and four boxes and suitcases. I counted them."

Renard watched the parade of Nubian porters carrying trunks, suitcases, and cardboard boxes. "They say that the colonels discovered Faruk was carting off half the gold from the Bank of Egypt. They say those whiskey boxes there are full of gold ingots. They say Faruk has been melting down gold statues and rings and pitchers in a special machine in the palace cellars. They say that some of the colonels wanted to threaten to bomb the royal yacht to get it back. But they decided to let him go and good riddance—that 'history would sentence Faruk to death.' And do you know what *I* say? I say it's a wonder Faruk didn't try to take the royal palm trees along with him!"

"Jacques!" Leah chucked him affectionately on the chin.

Youssef flinched as he watched his mother touch that man. Lately, as Youssef had been studying how his parents were with each other, he had noticed that she was never like that with his own father. How could his mother—his beautiful mother, his mother who always whispered in his ear that he and she were two of a kind—how could his mother carry on with this oily Frenchman? Why did she and his father fight so much? It seemed they didn't even like each other. Youssef wondered why they had ever married. Hamid said he thought Youssef's mother had wanted his father's money and that his father had wanted his mother's glamour. Still Youssef couldn't *understand*. That sort of marriage wasn't what he himself intended to have someday. He would marry for love or not at all. He shot his mother a look of reproach. "Mama! The king and queen. Look how he looks at her. How she looks at him."

But it was Mona who answered. "So romantic!"

Youssef smiled at Mona. At least *she* understood.

Renard whispered in Leah's ear. "They say that when the colonels broke into the king's private quarters at Kubbeh Palace, they found room after room of pornography. They say the soldiers have been using his sexual devices so much that they're already worn out. They say he kept a silver-handled whip in his dressing room—right next to an autographed photograph of Adolf Hitler."

"No!" Leah took a long look at the king who was rumored to have so many depraved royal prerogatives.

A cruiser in the bay began sounding a twenty-one-gun salute, and the sailors began to heave the mooring tackle.

"This is it!" Leah nearly swooned. "He's leaving us!"

But there was a stir in the crowd as an army jeep began to break through to the dock. Renard pointed to the squad in army khaki. "General Neguib. And three of the Free Officers."

"Monsieur Renard," Youssef asked, "are they going to stop the king? Is it true that Neguib will be king?"

"Never." Renard lowered his voice. "Neguib's a figurehead. The colonels are the power. We think a Saidi named Nasser is the real brains."

"A Saidi?" Mona looked at the diplomat in astonishment. "A Saidi deposed the king?"

"Our Mona's Saidi," Youssef explained.

"And a very pretty one," Renard replied.

Leah glared at Mona. "But this Nasser. Is he someone we have to worry about?"

"He is Saidi." Renard snapped his fingers. "A peasant." Leah and Renard laughed, and Mona blushed. "But I'll tell you what *is* causing some concern," Renard continued. "The colonels aren't going to stop with sending Faruk away. They say they're against colonialism and feudalism and imperialism. It's anybody's guess *what* they mean to do." Renard, as Faruk and Neguib paced the deck until they stood within earshot, leaned over the railing. "Quiet. I want to hear this."

Faruk was scanning what had been his subjects.

"Me! He's looking at me!" Leah waved to the king. "He remembers! He remembers!"

"Sh-h-h!" Renard put a restraining arm around her.

"Take care of the army," they heard Faruk say to the general.

"I wonder," Renard whispered. "Does he mean watch over, or watch out for, the colonels?"

"Faruk!" Leah blew her king a kiss and then threw the rose from her waist to the feet of the king. "Faruk!"

The deposed king, oblivious to the tribute of at least one loyal subject, took a last look at Egypt. "What you have done to me, general, I was getting ready to do to you." Faruk returned Neguib's salute, turned his heel on Leah's rose and his back on Egypt, and gazed out at the Mediterranean. The general and the colonels filed off, the sailors assumed their posts, and the white yacht that flew the star-and-crescent flag began to cut through the blue water.

"*Au revoir,* king!" Batata called out.

"Long live Egypt!" The crowd howled, and then, irrepressibly, couples began to dance along the Corniche. Daoud swung Lisabet on his arm, Rachel pirouetted with Batata, and Youssef spun Mona around in a spontaneous waltz.

"It's the end of an era," Renard said.

"The beginning of the end." Tears smudged Leah's mascara as she watched the yacht sail into the sunset.

Renard wiped away the tears. "Shall we dance?"

Leah gave a Gallic shrug, and Renard took her in his arms.

ALEXANDRIA, EGYPT / November 1954

Abbas carefully latched the front gate of the Villa al-Masri as he and Baruch left for their evening constitutional.

"I still don't agree," Baruch was saying. "Or perhaps it's just that I can't *understand* how you can *accept* that."

Abbas pulled his black wool *gallabeiya* tightly against him. It was a clear, crisp night. Too cold, Abbas thought, for a long walk. Abbas felt the freeze more than Baruch, for Abbas had spent his childhood in Nubia, where it was never cold, just sometimes less hot. But Abbas knew these walks were important to Baruch, and so Abbas resigned himself to a little discomfort. Once again Abbas explained his beliefs to Baruch. "Acceptance is easy. 'Acceptance,' after all, is the literal meaning of 'Islam.' To be a Muslim means simply to accept the will of Allah. Understanding is more difficult. Allah alone has that. For He has decided everything. We all merely do as He wills."

"But that's nonsense." Baruch was not so patient. "Each of us—you, me, Khadiga, everyone—has some choice about what we do. Like right now. We can walk through the center of town, along the Corniche, or back through one of the *baladi* quarters. It is our decision. Yours and mine."

"It is true that there are several routes open to us tonight. And we, of course, will walk along one of them. But who is to say how that has come to be? Or why?"

129

"*I* say. I—Baruch al-Masri—decide that we will walk along the Corniche. It is my own choice. There is no great Hand of Allah behind that."

"How can you be so sure? Perhaps there is a reason you cannot possibly comprehend for your desire to walk by the sea. Perhaps a beggar waits there for your *baksheesh*. Or a woman for your love."

"More likely a car to run me down. Some of these young fools are reckless."

"Possibly. Allah alone knows. May He protect us."

Baruch ignored the prayer. He and Abbas had had this particular discussion many times over, and still he could not resist it. "Don't you see where all this leads?" Baruch turned left, very decisively, toward the sea. "If it is as you say, as you persist in saying, then none of us bears any responsibility for what we do, how we live, whether we are good or bad. There is no reason for striving. There can be no expectations."

"Look around you." Abbas waved toward the streets beginning to fill with *baladi* men on the way to the coffeeshops, families en route to other families, hawkers wheedling their wares. "Each of these people has desires. For a good wife. Children. Bread. To be honorable. Generous. Pious. But none has the power to make any of these desires come to pass unless it is the will of Allah. It is true that we do not indulge in what you call 'expectations.' All they are is a fancy word for wishes. We would not be so presumptuous as to insist that our wishes always come to pass. We expect nothing. Only death. We know that we cannot control our own lives and cannot make our wishes come true. Is it not wiser to be as we are?"

Baruch made a face. "Easier, certainly. And serene. Definitely more serene. But not necessarily wiser. That fatalism is the greatest infection in Egypt and in every Islamic country. It holds you back. Why, no Muslim will even make an appointment to come and see me without qualifying with *inshallah*, 'if Allah wills it.' And half the time they do not, in fact, show up when they are supposed to."

"Then Allah did not will it."

Baruch would not smile back at Abbas. "And so they don't get to the doctor's. And so some of them die."

"Everyone dies."

"I am not disputing that. Only the waste. The terrible waste." Baruch shook his head. "And let me ask you something else. Isn't there danger in ascribing everything to your Allah's will? Doesn't it allow any man the possibility of violating every law of God and man, and then just shrugging and saying the result was fated? Think of the potential for evil!"

"Or for good. Aren't you forgetting that the Koran and the Traditions and Shariah law say very clearly how a good man should act? Yes, there is certainly the opportunity for men to do wrong. There is some choice and some responsibility. And in the end there is Paradise or the exclusion from it."

They were at the broad boulevard that runs along the scalloped shoreline. In silence they crossed the Corniche and leaned on the concrete wall separating city from sea. They looked out at the point in the harbor where once stood Pharos, the extravagant lighthouse that had been one of the seven wonders of the ancient world. Even now its feeble descendant was a beacon against the blank void of the darkness.

"Blind fate. The inscrutable will of Allah." Baruch shivered in the wind. "No. I won't believe that man is powerless, that each of us is caught up in forces beyond our control."

"No one is asking you to accept it." Abbas spoke very quietly. "You are not a Muslim. You're a Jew."

"Yes, yes." Baruch hurried on. "But do you know what *I* think, Abbas? I think that what is important in life is not the question of whether an individual should rebel against blind fate. What matters is *when* and *for what reason* each man finally does rebel. Ethics. Life comes down to the ethical basis for each man's rebellion."

Abbas smiled. "Or passion. What about passion?"

"Passion . . ." Baruch's voice trailed off. Passion had not filled a very large space in his life.

"Your problem, Baruch, is that you're trying to explain the inexplicable. These are spiritual questions. They will never be clear to you until you allow yourself simply to believe. Reason is not the answer. Belief is."

"And so we come again to that. Oh, Abbas, my mystical Oriental friend."

"Your Muslim friend."

"But my friend."

They smiled at each other and continued their promenade along the Corniche.

Baruch's love affair with all things Egyptian had progressed over the years from the nuances of classical Arabic to the masterpieces of Arabic literature. But every intellectual and emotional thread always led back to the skein of the Koran. Although he had thrilled to the Koran's lush imagery, still the essence of its poetry was a riddle. The more he understood, the more he did not understand. It always came down to what it had just come to with Abbas. Baruch had tried to study, to analyze, to dissect faith. But although it always eluded him, he refused to give up the pursuit. He spoke aloud. "It will make sense to me someday. I *will* understand. I will."

Abbas had the last word. *"Inshallah."*

They both laughed.

They were far from the center of town, walking eastward along the shore, when they paused to rest. Baruch leaned against the seawall. Passion. Abbas had mentioned passion. Not far from where they now stood, Baruch had lived with his bride fifteen years ago. It was just *there*, he thought as he looked at a row of villas, that we slept each night and rose each morning. To banish the pain of remembrance, he stared at the whitecaps cresting the black sea. It was just out *there,* in his creaking old sailboat, that Daisy had first said she loved him. Baruch told himself to stop it. Fifteen years was a long time. Long enough that a grown man should be able to walk down the street without wanting to cry. It was only when he was with his patients that Baruch felt like a grown man.

Resolutely he looked back at Alexandria's skyline. Think about this city and this country, he told himself. Concentrate on matters larger than your own personal tragedies. In the more than two years since Faruk had left the Alexandrian dock, the colonels had done their best to turn coup into revolution. The corrupt political parties along with the old titles of "pasha" and "bey" had all been abolished. Then the three-year interim military government had decreed it illegal for any man to own more than two hundred acres. But the land reform had not redistributed the wealth. The six percent of the old feudal aristocracy who had owned sixty-five percent of the land reinvested in city real estate and the suddenly booming construction industry. Worse, the glacial government bureaucracy was slow to parcel out land to the *fellahin.* But the colonels, now openly led by Gamal Abdel Nasser, had greater success persuading the British to abandon their toehold at Suez. After two years of hit-and-run guerrilla forays, the Egyptians finally forced the British to the bargaining table. Last month's treaty said the British would withdraw all eighty thousand of their troops from Suez by mid-1956. Seventy-five years of British Occupation was finally drawing to a close.

Hotheads in the Muslim Brotherhood, however, had not been appeased. Last week, here in Alexandria, a Brother had tried to assassinate Nasser. Immediately the government had countered with a massive crackdown. Six *Ikhwan* ringleaders were under sentence of death and five hundred were in prison. The bungled assassination attempt had also backfired on the figurehead of the revolution. Muhammad Neguib, accused of collaborating with the *Ikhwan,* was stripped of the presidency and placed under arrest. Nasser, already prime minister and chairman of the Republic of Egypt's Revolutionary Command Council, had assumed the duties of president. Yet still—Faruk or Neguib or Nasser—still there were this country's grinding poverty and ignorance and disease. Baruch sighed, and as he looked from the city to the sea and back to the shore again, he saw lights cutting the night. Idly he struck up a new conversation. "There must be a game tonight at Victoria. Youssef's probably there. Such a sporting boy, Youssef."

132

"Yes." Abbas's voice was chill.

"He'll be graduating soon. Then I suppose it will be off to university in Europe." Abbas didn't answer. "That boy was born with everything. Handsome. Good-natured. I always wanted a son like Youssef." And, Baruch finished for himself, I will never have one. But, preoccupied with the failures of his own past, Baruch did not notice the change in Abbas. A moment ago he had been Baruch's great friend. Now, standing at discreet attention, he was the servant out with the master. "Wouldn't you like a son like Youssef, Abbas?" There was no answer. "Abbas?" Baruch turned to look at him.

"Sir?"

"What's wrong?"

"Nothing, sir. Nothing at all."

"Yes there is. You have that *suffragi* look about you. Tell me what's wrong."

"It is none of my business, sir."

"That may be. But I'd like to hear it anyway. You and I talk about many things that are not strictly our business."

"This is different."

"So tell me."

"As you wish." Abbas paused. "It's Youssef. Your nephew."

"What's wrong with the boy? Is he ill?"

"Not in his body."

"What then?"

"In the coffeehouses they say he is wild. Whiskey. Hashish. Belly dancers."

"I'm surprised at you, Abbas. Paying attention to gossip. Youssef is a fine boy."

"He was. At one time he was. Now he and that Hamid are wasting themselves. They're headed for trouble. It's shameful. Shameful. And it isn't just hearsay. Some of it I've seen myself."

"Go on."

"I can smell the hashish in their rooms every night. And I know how much Youssef drinks, because I'm the one who serves him his whiskey, water, and ice. But his parties are the worst of it."

"Parties?"

"At the last one, there were nine boys and three dancers. Bringing prostitutes to his own parlor!"

"Maybe they weren't prostitutes. Maybe they were just dancers."

"The prostitutes were naked. One of them was older than you."

"You must have looked her over rather closely, Abbas."

"I had to dress her and carry her out to a taxi. She passed out."

"Oh. But Youssef is . . . sixteen?"

"He's at least twenty. An old twenty."

Baruch promised himself, before he and Abbas began their long trek home against the wind, that he would turn his attention to his favorite nephew.

Baruch and Mona were hesitating between this cake and that in the sumptuous display cases of Pastroudi's. Mahogany treasure chests trimmed with silver and lined with velvet made a jewel of each tiny cake. Baruch had almost settled on a white meringue with cherries when he caught sight of his lifelong favorites, the double chocolate marshmallow bars. Mona had her eye on the bite-size date cakes dripping with honey, but then she spied the heavy chunks of *vasbusa,* an even sweeter honey cake encrusted with nuts. The two of them exchanged worried looks of indecision, but then Baruch laughed. He ordered their hovering waiter to bring them a plate of all their favorites. So what if they already had ordered dishes of chocolate ice cream? So what if it was only a few hours before dinner? They were out together at Alexandria's most popular *salon de thé,* and Baruch was determined to make the most of the occasion.

He put a proprietary hand on Mona's shoulder and steered her from the cake gallery back toward the dark womblike snugness of the café itself. It was a late Saturday afternoon, and Pastroudi's was crowded with shoppers, browsers, chatters, and indolent passers of the time. Baruch stood in the doorway waving to acquaintances as he hesitantly scanned the crowd for an empty table. Finally he gave in and slipped the *maître d'* fifty piasters. Instantly a parade of waiters appeared carrying an additional table and two chairs above their heads. Baruch handed the headwaiter another fifty piasters and—magically—space was cleared for Mona and himself in front of the choicest ornate window overlooking the street.

As Baruch gallantly helped Mona off with her coat, he noticed with pleasure that she was wearing a new dress that he himself had chosen. On the shop hanger its white frills and touches of lace at collar and cuffs had looked so dainty, so sweet, so like Mona. But on her the dress was not quite right. It was too small, *there,* above the waist. With dismay Baruch noticed Mona had grown breasts. He adjusted his glasses and looked for reassurance that she still was his little girl. Her long black hair hung down her back in braids—no, in one braid. Why, he thought irritably, had she changed her hair? Two braids were more childlike. His eyes wandered the rest of her. Her legs were—*elhamdulillah!*—thickly encased in a schoolgirl's coarse black socks. And she was wearing flat pink shoes tied in front with a red ribbon. Baruch smiled with triumph as he handed their coats to a waiter. Her shoes were so ugly only a child would wear them.

They leaned back on their chairs and glanced around Pastroudi's. The soft Persian carpets, the dark wood paneling, and the hazy smoked-glass lighting transformed café into haven. Prosperous Muslim matrons, with their heavy black eye makeup and their stiff lacquered hair, sat plumply squeezed beside their spoiled children. Gray clouds of cigarette smoke hung in dark halos over the heads of frowning middle-aged Arab men leaning over splayed newspapers. Aging foreign women sat alone at tables for one, their raisin eyes searching the crowd for faces which would never again appear. Baruch called Mona's attention to one of the puzzles of fashionable Alexandria. Pastroudi's elegant floor-to-ceiling windows looked out at a parking lot for horse carriages. Mona laughed. When the windows were open in the summer, she reminded him, the stench from the parking lot was enough to poison the flavor of the sweetest cakes. For years she had associated the taste of chocolate with the smell of horse manure. Baruch noticed once again how Mona's whole face danced when she laughed. She was such a pretty girl. Such a very, very pretty girl.

With an effort Baruch tried to turn his attention to the reason for this *tête à tête*. Since that warning from Abbas, Baruch had been discreetly watching for signs of dissipation in Youssef. It had been easy to discover that Youssef and Hamid kept killing hours. Often they wouldn't roar home in Youssef's sleek new Jaguar Mark IV until three or four in the morning. After he put the liquor cabinet under surveillance, however, Baruch had concluded that the boys were abstemious compared to Leah and Rafael. Moreover, as Baruch continued to prowl around the villa, he had found disturbing evidence of the continuing deterioration of his brother's marriage. He couldn't help hearing Rafael and Leah's daily quarrels. Leah had always disliked the colonels who had forced her beloved Faruk off the throne. But when fourteen Egyptian Jews had been charged not long ago with spying for Israel, Leah had become convinced Nasser was a personal threat. Every day she nagged Rafael to sell everything and move the family to France. And every day Rafael called her a fool.

Baruch came out of his reverie as the waiter arrived with their ice cream and cakes. He smiled vaguely at Mona, unsure, now that he had her off to himself, how to sound her out about Youssef. Instead he asked her about her mother. Yes, Um Mona would be visiting once again this summer. Yes, Mona was still writing to her mother every week. Mona stuck the silver spoon into the silver dish and jabbed at the ice cream until it began to go soupy. She kept her eyes on the mess she was making as she continued to talk. "She says it's not long until I marry my rich man and she comes up here to live."

Baruch popped a white meringue in his mouth. He tried never to say a word to Mona against her mother. He thought he would let that beastly old woman's actions speak for themselves. He had hoped, when he rescued Mona from Karnak that last time, that the mother's hold on the girl would have been broken. But Um Mona seemed to be with her daughter even when she was far away. Baruch especially disliked the way Um Mona's yearly visits always made Mona so passive. If Mona had a fault, it was her inability ever to stand up to her mother. Thank God it wasn't a fault that would do too much damage. Baruch ate a double chocolate marshmallow bar. He supposed he expected too much from Mona. Every Arab child, boy and girl alike, was indoctrinated to obey every parental whim. And every Muslim girl was schooled forever to be docile. Part of Mona's charm was her shyness, her pliability, her eagerness never to offend. An Egyptian girl just couldn't be a bluestocking or some Joan of Arc rebel. He couldn't make Mona what she wasn't.

"Ummie says my husband will have servants." Dully Mona toyed with her spoon. She had begun to despair, over the past two years, that Youssef might ever want her. "And Ummie wants a red car."

"Is that what you want, too, Mona?"

"Ummie says it is the will of Allah."

There it is again, Baruch thought. He ate his ice cream so fast he got a sharp knifelike pain just over his eyes. But he held his tongue. He might question Abbas about Islam, but he had always taken care never to criticize Mona about her beliefs. It was important that she be a good Muslim. That she be good in every way. Abruptly he changed the subject. "What do you think of Youssef?"

She shot him a startled look. How, she thought, did Uncle Baruch know?

He wondered what that blush was all about. He rephrased his question. "Do you see Youssef much these days? You and Batata and Youssef used to be so close."

Mona looked relieved. "Sometimes we see him."

Baruch lit a cigarette. He disliked pumping Mona about his nephew. Yet he pressed on. "Youssef is an exceptional boy."

"Oh, yes." Mona stroked the ice cream with her spoon. "Batata loves him very much."

"How often do you see Youssef?"

"Youssef is very busy."

"Doing what?"

"Ask Hamid." There was a trace of bitterness in Mona's voice. She was jealous of Hamid. And once she had glimpsed Hamid doing something shameful with a naked old woman in the al-Masri parlor. She had not had the time, before she turned and fled down to the kitchen, to see for sure if Youssef and those other boys were egging Hamid on or trying to discourage him.

"I don't know Hamid very well. What's he like?"

"He smiles a lot." Mona tried to think of some other compliment she could pay Hamid. "He sits up straight at the table. Always."

"Does he?"

"Yes." Miserably Mona played with the spoon in her ice cream.

"But Youssef. You like Youssef, don't you, Mona?"

Mona smiled at her dish. "Youssef is wonderful. Maybe we'll all go to Agami again this summer, and maybe he'll play there with . . . with Batata."

"Instead of Hamid? Tell me, Mona, what do Youssef and Hamid do with their time?"

"Oh, they smoke a lot. And play music. Youssef likes to dance. He's a very good dancer. And they always go out at night."

"They stay out late."

"I suppose." Mona wished Baruch would stop this interrogation. She didn't even like to say Youssef's name out loud, except sometimes when she was sure she was alone. And then she would whisper it over and over again.

Baruch gave up. Mona didn't know any more than he did. Apparently she knew less. And she was acting strange. That conversation about her mother must have disturbed her. "It's too bad you didn't eat your ice cream. If you had finished it, I was going to buy you a present."

"Yes?" Mona raised a spoonful of liquid ice cream to her lips. "What kind of a present?"

"A new dress. A pretty one." And a dress, Baruch added to himself, that hides those breasts. He would buy Mona a *cute* dress.

Youssef opened his eyes and shut them immediately. The thick draperies were pulled tight to keep out hateful light, but still the bedroom dimness hurt his eyes. Youssef had a double hashish and whiskey headache. Why the hell was there so much noise coming from the street? With an effort he held up his left hand, willed his eyes open, and looked at his watch. Two o'clock. It must be two o'clock in the afternoon. He hadn't been in bed yet at two this morning, ha! He probably should get up. There was something he was doing today. What was it? Lunch. He and Hamid were going to lunch at Abu Kir to warm themselves up for that party tonight in Agami. A party at somebody's father's summerhouse. A party with no chaperons and many girls. Today promised to be worth the effort of opening his eyes.

He stumbled to the window, pulled back the curtains, endured the light. It was raining. A soft gray drizzle of a day. Good. He would have crawled back to bed if it had been unbearably sunny. He groped his way over to the mirror, afraid that what he would see there was a gray-haired, wrinkled old man with sick eyes. Any day now he feared that reflection would confront him. Yes, his eyes were streaked with veins of red. And there were two little horizontal lines in the middle of his forehead. He frowned at the lines, and immediately they deepened. *Malesh,* he told himself. Never mind. His was still the handsomest face in Alexandria. He was good for another day.

An hour later he and Hamid were drinking *café au lait* under the balcony awning listlessly ignoring the air, the view, the people bustling past them on the avenue below.

Hamid rubbed his eyes. "Abu Kir? Today?"

"Yes." Youssef yawned.

"But why? What's wrong with a little more sleep? It's raining. Why not stay in bed?"

"We have to make the most of our time." Youssef lit a cigarette and reflected to himself, gloomily, that there wasn't much time left for the two of them. These were their last possible months at Victoria College. Already they had conned the school and their parents into letting them stay at Victoria for two extra years. But soon Youssef would be packed off to university in London. He would hate to say farewell to what he was certain were the best years of his life, here with Hamid at Victoria.

Hamid, too, lit a cigarette. "I don't see why we can't make the most of our time in bed."

"You're lazy, Hamid."

The look on Hamid's face suggested what he did not have the energy to say, that Youssef was just as lazy as he was.

They smiled at each other and then smoked in silence, pleased that they shared the lack of any ambition other than staving off boredom. After a while—it could have been three minutes or three hours—Youssef yawned with finality, *"Yalla*—let's go." He stalked off the balcony, trailed by a still-protesting Hamid. They were almost to the stairs when Batata spotted them.

"Youssef!" When the tall strapping boy threw himself into his big brother's arms, the impact almost knocked Youssef over.

"Batata! What's the news?"

"It's my birthday. I'm twelve! Today!"

"Already? And what are you doing to celebrate?"

"Tonight's my party. A big one in the salon. Mummy and Daddy are coming. Mona told you last week."

"She did?" Youssef caught the frown on Hamid's face. "This is terrible. I can't come. Sorry, Batata."

The boy's face fell.

Youssef, remembering that only last week Uncle Baruch had reproached him for neglecting his family and his studies, tried to make amends. "I'll tell you what I'll do. I'll take you out to Abu Kir for lunch. Now. Just you and me and Hamid."

"And Mona. I want Mona."

Youssef nodded. "You get her and I'll ask Daoud." He found his brother, as usual, reading in his room. But Daoud shook his head and said he wasn't hungry. What he really wanted to say was that he hated to be around Hamid. He'd had enough of Arabs at school. Lately Daoud had become the butt of anti-Jewish pranks at Victoria. Sundays he simply couldn't deal with Arabs, even an Arab like Hamid who was very nearly family.

Youssef prodded his brother. "You should eat more, you know."

Daoud had been told all his life that he wouldn't be so bad-looking if he just put on some weight. But even when he ate so much sugary food that he almost made himself sick, even when he exercised with weights until his muscles ached, the only results were more pimples and a skinnier body. Daoud looked longingly back at his book.

"Come with us, Daoud. It'll be a change."

Owlishly Dauod stared up at Youssef. That incantation—it's a change, it's something new, it isn't so *boring*—did not work the same wonder on him. "Why don't you stay here? We can talk."

Youssef wavered. Uncle Baruch's criticism had hit the mark. He could skip the Agami party and go to Batata's. He could spend the afternoon cheering up this solemn brother. He never seemed to have time for Daoud anymore. "What's that you're reading?"

"It's about the Jewish pioneers." Daoud's eyes were eager. Often he thought how much he would like to share Herzl and Marx with Youssef. He would have liked to talk over Zionism and socialism with his adored big brother. "This one takes place on a kibbutz in Israel. You see—"

"Youssef!" Hamid cuffed him on the arm. "*Yalla,* Youssef!"

Youssef hesitated for an instant, then smiled winningly at Daoud. "Later. We'll talk about it all later." He whirled out the door with Hamid.

Batata was trooping down the stairs with Zibda by the leash. Mona was carrying Suker, Zibda's eight-week-old puppy, in her arms.

"Dogs, too?" Hamid despised dogs.

"Please?" Batata was pleading. "It's *my* birthday!"

Youssef ruffled his brother's hair. "If you two and the dogs sit in the back."

Even with the convertible's roof up, the rain dripped through the folds. As they swished toward the center of town, Batata kept up a steady chatter about his party, about Suker chewing Anne-Marie's false teeth, about the baby that Khadiga was expecting very soon. Mona silently studied the back of Youssef's perfectly formed head, while Hamid beat out a bored rhythm on the side of his car door. Peering out at the rain, Youssef allowed his thoughts to turn as gloomy as the weather. Soon, in England, every day would be as dark and cold as this one. To him, England was a bleak gray country of dour people who never, ever, would appreciate his own true worth. Two summers ago, when Youssef had last been in London, he had escorted a British girl to a Lebanese restaurant in Soho. When the music began, Youssef had jumped up on the stage and danced as he had learned to love to dance, moving his hips just so, using his arms to accent those wild hips.

The audience, mostly composed of tourists, had loved seeing a man dance like that. They had stuffed the front of his shirt with banknotes as he swayed near the tables, and he, Youssef al-Masri, had thrown the money to the band as if it were confetti in a parade. It had been a glorious moment. He had been shocked when he had returned to his table and found his girlfriend gone. Those British had no sense of fun.

Youssef cursed under his breath when they stalled in downtown traffic. He gave the black iron gates of the synagogue a dirty look. Just recently the anti-Jewish whisperings had started up again at Victoria. He supposed it was due to that sensational trial of that group of Jewish spies who had tried to bomb cinemas, a post office, and an American library in Cairo and here in Alexandria. But the attempted bombings had been duds. So why were the Egyptians so bloody paranoid? Youssef took a right turn on two wheels and picked up speed as he executed the twisting curves of the Corniche. They zoomed past the rosy walls of the former king's Montaza Palace and headed east on a dirt road. "Wait till you see this place, Batata. Abu Kir is beautiful. Rocks out in the water. Very good fish. And cats running around under the restaurant tables. Zibda and Suker will go crazy."

Batata laughed and patted the dogs. But then Youssef hit a hole in the rutted road at high speed, and Batata bumped his head hard on a roof strut. For at least four miles, there was no sound in the car except Batata's sobs.

Youssef, for lack of any other diversion, let his mind roam to the future. If a man worked at it, Youssef firmly believed, the present was almost always guaranteed to provide enough fun to keep the future at bay. But in England there would be no such guarantees. He would be starting all over, and he might never be able to work his way into his proper place. At Victoria College, he was the king. He was their Jewish king. He had shown all of them. Youssef had not forgotten that shame with his father at the Cotton Exchange—or even the smallest slight of the Arabs at school. But so it would seem that none of this was aimed at him and his, Youssef was always the first and the loudest to laugh it all off. He wished, however, as he pressed down harder on the gas pedal, that someday he could smash in the faces of a few particular Arabs. Passing the scrubby sandy farm-country fields, Youssef's eye was caught by a movement near the brackish scum of an irrigation ditch. "Hamid. There's two donkeys. Over there." Youssef pointed. "They're just like us, playing all day long. I would like to be a donkey." He took a pull on his cigarette. "An aristocratic donkey, of course. A beautiful one. One that doesn't work. One that plays all the time."

Hamid fell in with his mood. "I'd rather be a horse."

"No, not a horse." Youssef laughed without humor. "Horses think too much. Watch them. They're always thinking. I don't want to think. Not now. Not ever." He threw his cigarette out the window.

A voice piped up from the back. It was Mona trying to join the conversation. "I wouldn't like to be a donkey *or* a horse. But, especially, I wouldn't want to be a dog. One of those dogs that don't have a home and run around the streets. Abbas told me the police come around and shoot the dogs. Poor things!"

Youssef's lips narrowed into a thin line. Leave it to Mona. That one thought too bloody much. She was a real conversation-stopper. These days she was always making him squirm. The way she looked at him— what did she want? Mona needed to be loosened up. And—ha!—he and Hamid might be the boys to do it. They could take her with them to Agami tonight and show her what a good time was. Hamid had already called his attention to Mona's lovely breasts. And those whiskey-colored eyes! Youssef lit another cigarette and felt ashamed of himself. Mona was a sweet little girl. A good girl with amber—not whiskey— eyes. No, he thought to himself wistfully. Let Mona stay as she was. Everything, everyone, did not have to be gritty. There had to be something pure. She and little Batata were two of a kind.

It was the kid's birthday. He would make Batata happy. Youssef threw his brother a smile. "Did I ever tell, you, Batata, about the real story of Ali Baba and the forty thieves?"

"They all hid in a cave and somebody said funny words?"

" '*Fftaha ya semsem.* Open sesame!' But I don't think you know what it was that tipped Ali Baba off to those bad men in the cave. It was a little boy, a boy with black hair and brown eyes. And his dog, a gold one with long curly ears."

"Like Zibda?" Batata's eyes were shining.

Hamid gave Youssef an amused look.

"As a matter of fact, just like Zibda." Youssef shifted his gears with a flourish. "It was on the little boy's birthday, on a day just like this. . . ."

Youssef slammed a bureau drawer. Hamid padded back and forth on bare feet looking for socks that matched. They had returned to the Villa al-Masri long after sundown, and so they had skipped their usual naps and were rushing to get ready for the party. Grumbling, they drank their whiskey standing up and drew on their hashish cigarettes in fast little sucks. Hastily Hamid slicked down his hair and then swished up the ends in jellied curls. It would be at least a forty-five minute drive to Agami in this pouring rain. If Youssef and Hamid hadn't been sniffing so hotly on the scent of two young ladies, they might have decided instead to stay home for Batata's party. But tonight, they knew, was the time to close in for the kill.

Hamid carried the bottle of whiskey out the door in a paper sack. Youssef turned on the engine and swore when the windshield wipers barely moved. He shifted into high gear and sliced through slippery puddles. A heavy mist rose from the sea and snugged the roads. Youssef cursed again when he remembered that one of his headlights was burned out. He had meant to tell Abbas to replace it. Youssef signaled for the whiskey and took a long pull. Yes, that was better. He swung left where waves sprayed over the seawall of the Corniche. Between the smeared windshield and the deficient headlights, it was hard to see. Youssef switched on the radio. At least that worked.

Hamid passed him the hashish cigarette. "Tonight's the night!"

"Think you're ready?"

"You doubt me?" Hamid had on his wicked smile. "Dora is about to be one lucky Greek."

"As is the lovely Camilla."

"I'll drink to that."

They had been courting the two girls all month, for Youssef and Hamid were bored with belly dancers. You paid them, and they did it. Sometimes, especially for Hamid, they did it even without being paid. What Youssef and Hamid wanted now were persuadable girls from good families. Hamid had a secret yen for the rumored delights of Jewish girls, but Youssef was touchy about Jews. By default the field had been narrowed to Italians, Greeks, Armenians, and Maltese. After what had happened last year to Samuel Leon, they both knew better than even to dream of touching a Muslim girl. Hamid himself had heard Leon boasting at the Sporting Club of some late-night fun with a Bedouin girl. But the Arab father, after slitting the girl's throat, had gone to the police and accused Leon of rape. All the Leon money had not been enough to save Samuel from a vengeful knife thrust in his cell. Afterward Hamid had tried to convince Youssef that Samuel had died not because he was a Jew but because Bedouins were devils about their women. Hamid had repeatedly said that he didn't think Bedouins even knew the difference between Christians and Jews. But Hamid's explanations had fallen on deaf ears.

Hamid passed the bottle. "You know, Youssef, tonight I think—at long last—that we will finally make it."

"You think the girls are that easy?"

Hamid touched his crotch. "No, I think I'm just too hard!"

They both laughed. The plan was to offer the girls a ride home and then stop off at the cottage the al-Masris rented every summer. There, with the sound of the sea and the rain all around them, they were sure they would get what they wanted.

"Hell. I forgot the mineral water and the orange juice. The girls won't drink straight whiskey." Youssef steered a sharp bend with one hand on the wheel, his eyes searching for an open shop. Hamid had his head down to light another cigarette. Neither saw the black figure crossing the Corniche. But both felt the dull thump as the Jaguar hit and then ran over something that screamed just once. Youssef slammed on the brakes and gripped the steering wheel.

142

"It was nothing, Youssef. A dog. I'm sure it was a dog."

"Dogs don't scream."

"Then a cat." Hamid nodded as if he believed what he was saying. "Yes, it was a cat."

Youssef put his sweaty hand on the cold door handle.

"Don't get out, Youssef. *Yalla!* Come *on*. We're late. We don't have time to get out and look."

But Youssef was already out the door and walking slowly back on the Corniche. After a moment's hesitation, Hamid joined him. In the darkness lay a wet black form. Hamid nudged it with his foot, then kicked it until it rolled over. They stared into the wide-open eyes of a young *baladi* girl.

Youssef moaned. "No. Oh, no."

Hamid squatted to pick up a hand that sagged limp and lifeless. "Let's get out of here."

"We can't just leave her."

"You have a better idea? You want to get caught?"

Youssef had trouble focusing his eyes. He wished he hadn't drunk that whiskey and smoked that hashish. All he could think was that this couldn't be happening to Youssef al-Masri. He made Hamid help him drag the body off the road.

"There. Now let's go, Youssef. Now!"

Youssef leaned on the seawall and put his head in his hands. He pressed the tips of his fingers into his scalp. This was awful. He was sure they would get him. Someone must have seen. Someone always saw everything. He looked at the ramshackle tenements across the street. Even now someone must be running down and calling out to the others. Arabs would be pouring out on the road any minute. Even if he and Hamid ran to the car and screeched away, someone would re-member his car. There wasn't another like it in Alexandria. The police would come and get him. What had happened to Samuel Leon was going to happen to him. "It's no use, Hamid. They'll get me. And I'm a Jew. A *Jew,* Hamid. I don't stand a chance. A Jew killing an Arab girl. Oh, God!"

Hamid wet his lips with his tongue. He hadn't thought as far or as fast as Youssef. Until this moment he hadn't been very worried. Youssef wasn't the first boy he knew who had hit some poor soul in an unavoid-able mishap. All that ever happened was that the family had to be paid off to keep quiet. But Youssef's being a Jew *might* complicate matters. There were shouts from across the street as three men in *gallabeiyas* ran toward them. Hamid made a decision "Give me the keys. They'll go easier on me."

"I can't do that."

"We have no choice. No choice at all."

Youssef looked at him miserably.

Hamid held out his hand, and slowly Youssef extended his palm in almost the gesture of their old Arab handshake. But this time their flesh did not quite touch. The keys made a cold click as they fell from Youssef's hand to Hamid's.

Youssef moved his men on the backgammon board, then jumped up and readjusted the fan. "Bloody hot. It's so bloody hot. Bloody Egypt."

"I like the heat." Baruch took a sip of the tiny cup of Arab coffee. "Your move."

Youssef sighed and threw himself down in his chair. If he were in England now—as he was supposed to be—he wouldn't be sweating. But last February, after the Israelis had killed thirty-eight Egyptians in a lightning raid at Gaza, Nasser had canceled all exit visas for Jews. It was, Youssef thought, another stroke of this year's rotten luck. Once he would have done anything to avoid going to England. Now, after that mess over the *baladi* girl on the Corniche, staying in Egypt was a sentence. He no longer even had the consolation of Hamid. After the trial, after that new awkwardness rose between them, Hamid had been assigned by his new boss—Youssef's father—to spend the summer at the Delta textile mills.

Youssef sighed again at the backgammon board. Every night he sat in the parlor across from Baruch playing *mahoosa,* a meandering form of *tric-trac* in which it was crucial never to leave a man unguarded on a point. Every night Baruch would patiently explain the strategy of the game. And every night Youssef would nod and perversely pay him no mind. Youssef yawned and nudged one of his men so that two were left vulnerable. He had not slept well for months. He even hated to lie down on a couch and shut his eyes, for he dreaded the recurring nightmare of that black bundle of cloth with those sightless, staring dark eyes. No matter how much he drank, no matter how much hashish he smoked, those eyes were always waiting for him.

Across the board Baruch shrewdly assessed his nephew. He suspected that all summer long Youssef had been playing out a different game from backgammon. The farcical trial last winter had left its mark on the boy. Youssef had testified on Hamid's behalf. Hamid had cried on cue. The victim's family, dressed in new finery bought by Youssef's very thorough father, had even expressed sympathy for Hamid. There had been much talk of foul weather and no mention of drugs and drunkenness. The judge had ruled as he had been paid to rule, and Rafael had promptly paid the twenty-five pound fine. It was clear to Baruch that Youssef was still wallowing in guilt. Patiently, night after night, Baruch had been waiting for his nephew to unburden himself. "Are you sure you want to move that way? Take your time, Youssef. Think about it."

"I've thought. I think too much." Youssef gave his uncle a bitter look. "*This* is the way I want to move. It is the perfect move for Youssef al-Masri."

Silently Baruch froze two of his men atop Youssef's. "Sorry."

"Why be sorry? I deserve it." Youssef ignored his unguarded men and moved two more where Baruch could not fail to imprison them.

"Interesting move. An unusual strategy." Baruch trapped more of Youssef's men.

"Wait till you see *this*." Youssef guaranteed his loss of the game by leaving his corner diamond vulnerable. "And there is the finish. *Khelas*—it is over. I lose." Youssef experienced once again a small thrill that there was, at least, some justice in backgammon.

"You have, it appears, a real talent for defeat."

Youssef smiled. "So it seems. In many ways." He gave his uncle a stricken look. "I deserve it."

"Do you?" Baruch waited.

Youssef leaped up and poured himself a straight whiskey. He held the glass high in the air and drained it. His eyes were bright with tears as he sat down once more across the board from Baruch. "I can't stand it anymore."

"Then play a less reckless game, Youssef. Cover yourself. You know the rules. Play by them. There's no reason for you to lose."

"No?"

"No."

"But I killed her. I did. I did."

Baruch let him cry. He watched his nephew's face turn red and the tears course down his cheeks. He could have taken the boy in his arms and comforted him, but he didn't. Youssef, he thought, had had too much comfort over the years. He needed something else from his Uncle Baruch. Finally he handed him a handkerchief and set up the board for another game. He made the first move.

Youssef gulped. But he wiped away his tears, threw the dice, moved his men.

"Not that way. *Learn,* Youssef, from your past mistakes. This is a new game. Play it right this time."

Youssef looked at him in confusion. "But don't you know what I did? I killed the girl. Not Hamid. I was driving. I was drunk. And high on hashish. I did a terrible thing."

"Play."

This time Youssef left none of his men exposed.

"Good. Much better." Baruch took his turn.

Youssef threw the dice so hard that one bounced on the floor. "I don't do anything right. Nothing at all. I lied. I cheated. I even killed." But he moved his men cautiously on the board.

"You're just learning the game. And so you make mistakes. And so you lose. But there's no reason why you have to continue to lose." As if by accident Baruch left one of his men vulnerable.

"But you don't understand. I feel so damn guilty. What I did was *wrong.*" Youssef rolled double sixes, leapfrogged across the board, and trapped Baruch's men on dangerous points.

"Guilt? Did I hear you mention guilt? They say Jews have a patent on guilt." Baruch rolled the dice and after some thought moved his men. "You know, Youssef, sometimes I think that I've killed, too." He did not take his eyes off the board.

"You? I don't believe it." Youssef moved without thinking.

"Careless of you." Blandly Baruch imprisoned two of Youssef's men. "I don't believe you remember your Aunt Daisy. My wife. You were so young when she died. She died because of me, Youssef. If I hadn't insisted on treating the patients in the hospital cholera ward . . . I must have carried it home to her." Baruch did not roll the dice.

"But that's silly. You didn't do it deliberately. How could you have known?"

"In a way it was the same with you and that girl on the Corniche." Baruch lifted his eyes to Youssef's. "You didn't set out to kill her."

"But I was drunk. And I was driving too fast."

"Yes." Baruch snapped shut the backgammon board. "Shall we talk?"

Youssef nodded.

"If you were my son, we would have had this talk long ago. You have been, for some time, heading for a fall. You are—or have been—a superficial, self-indulgent child. You drink too much. Indulge in harmful drugs. Use women shamefully."

Youssef kept his mouth shut and listened.

"What makes your conduct even worse is that you were born with every advantage. I don't mean money. I mean a good mind. A fine body. And the opportunity to develop a sense of right and wrong. You were a lovely child, Youssef. A prince." When Youssef had the grace to hang his head, Baruch continued more gently. "I'd like to know what happened to change all that. What made you want to throw it all away?"

"You want to know? You really want to know?"

"If you want to tell me."

"It is because I am a Jew. They hate us here. All of us. And I hate *them* for it! Filthy Arabs!"

"Yes?"

"One of them made Father wash his feet at the Cotton Exchange. *My father!*"

"But was that because he's a Jew or because he insulted them? Think, Youssef. You were there. You saw it. Your father asked for it. He acted like some feudal lord."

146

Youssef lowered his eyes and chewed his lip. "But they laughed at me in school. They tried to get Hamid to spit at me. At *me!*"

"And did he?"

"No." Youssef rubbed his chin, remembering the bruises from the fistfight. "He spit at the Arabs."

"It would seem, Youssef, that all the Arabs haven't mistreated you. At least one 'filthy Arab' has stood by you. One has even perjured himself in court for you."

"Hamid is an exception."

"Listen to me." Baruch's tone was stern. "It is true, as you say, that bad things have happened to Jews here and elsewhere. The Nazis were a lot worse than the Arabs could ever imagine being."

"But it's *wrong!* It's *so wrong!*"

"Of course it's wrong. But what are you going to do about it? Cry and get drunk and feel sorry for yourself? Waste your life on trivial people? Hate yourself for being a Jew? Kill yourself as you did that girl?"

Youssef gave him a look of pure hate.

"Grow up, Youssef. It's your *life*. If you want to lose, as you've insisted on losing all summer here with me at the backgammon board, then that's your choice." He stood up and yawned. "I'll be here tomorrow if you want to play." He left Youssef sitting in front of the closed board.

Baruch had not misjudged his nephew.

They played again that next night and every night thereafter. As they marched their men around the board, they discussed the Palestine war and how it felt to be Jews in Egypt. They talked of friendship and loyalty and honor. They talked of women and love, of right and wrong, of guilt and forgiveness. Baruch was hard on Youssef. He neither exonerated him for his actions nor promised him a carefree future. Baruch told him, too, about his own conclusions about life. So few things are right and just, Baruch said, that it is absolutely essential that every man do his best to make his own controllable actions above reproach. Fury against every injustice is futile. What matters is picking the right time, the right issue, to stand up and be counted. And the road to ethical conduct, Baruch said, does not start with hashish and whiskey and belly-dancer orgies.

Youssef learned more that summer than how to win at backgammon. But Baruch wondered if his nephew had learned enough. He worried that Youssef's old escapades might cut deeper than one summer listening to an earnest, moralistic doctor. But at least, Baruch told himself, at least I tried. Baruch had always detested backgammon. It always gave him a headache. He had had one all summer long in the parlor.

7 〰〰

Youssef and Hamid were sitting, as they had on thousands of days and nights, on the al-Masri balcony at sundown. They were wearing their *gallabeiyas,* they were leaning back in their chairs, they had their feet propped up on the ironwork railing. On this balcony they had shared their first cigarettes, drunk their first whiskey, plotted the taking of their first woman. They had laughed themselves silly and shared their deepest dreams on this balcony. If something had changed between the two of them—if the fabric of their friendship had almost mysteriously frayed to a thread—neither was ready to admit it. For fifteen years they had been not only the best of friends but *best friends*. Each would have welcomed the opportunity to prove his loyalty to the other by a dramatic public act. But this sundown on the balcony, neither seemed able even to speak without weighing his words.

Hamid had just finished describing his summer—the big-breasted *fellaha* he had almost caught in the fields, the chic wife of the mill's French supervisor he did get between her own Porthault sheets—when Abbas carried out a brass tray of two glasses and a pitcher. The boys took exploratory sips of the golden nectar.

The applish taste of the tamarind juice made Hamid's lips pucker. He would have loved to spit it out. Even six months ago he would have done just that. But tonight on the balcony Hamid felt enough the guest that he could not reject his host's refreshments.

Youssef rolled the juice around his tongue. He, too, longed to be drinking whiskey instead of this swill that tasted like perfume. Youssef fought the impulse to dump the pitcher over the railing. From now on there would be no carousing until all hours, no drinking until his head hurt, no hashish smoking until the roof of his mouth felt like soiled cotton. After Uncle Baruch's principled coaching, Youssef was determined to be the man he was meant to be. Tonight he would try to inspire Hamid to join him in reform.

Youssef sighed when Hamid pulled a red cellophane wedge from his pocket. "None for me."

Hamid raised his eyebrows but then shrugged and rolled a hashish reefer. "You don't mind if I indulge?"

Youssef shook his head. For weeks he had been trying to phrase coaxing words to enlist Hamid, but now eloquence eluded him. "I did a lot of thinking over the summer. I guess it all started because of the . . . accident."

Hamid nodded with sincere concern. He was sincerely concerned that Youssef was about to rehash that unfortunate incident once again.

"Hamid! That girl's eyes haunted me all summer long. Do you remember how they looked?"

"In a way." Hamid could barely remember the accident, let alone the details of the peasant's features. Youssef was such a child sometimes. Most of the time Hamid forgot that Youssef was a *huwaga,* a foreigner. But at times like this, when Youssef went on with such naiveté, Hamid wondered what they had in common.

Youssef's nostrils flared at the tantalizing aroma of hashish. As he lit an unfiltered Soussa to busy his mouth and hands, Youssef began to spin out the story of how Baruch had persuaded him to change. He painted their former dissipation—their hashish, their whiskey, their women—as an adolescent stage which the two of them must leave behind as they became true men.

Hamid folded his arms tight against his barrel chest and willed the smirk off his face. Youssef's being self-righteous like this reminded him of the Muslims back in the village during the first few days of Ramadan. They all started off adhering to the rigid rules of the fast, not even swallowing the saliva in their mouths, and instead covering the ground with globs of pious spittle. Worse, they insisted on declaring to all who would listen—and even to those who would not—that it felt good to suffer so for their religion. But by the fourth week of the fast, many were sneaking cigarettes and tea, and none were talking about the pleasures of self-denial. Hamid seriously doubted if Youssef's reform would last even a Ramadan month. He knew that Youssef, like himself, was addicted to pleasure. But because Hamid had always loved Youssef like a brother, he decided to try to humor him.

"Certainly women and love are a necessary part of life." Youssef was speaking with great earnestness. "But from now on, I don't want to degrade either myself or them."

"Degrade?" Hamid could not keep from laughing.

"Yes, degrade." Youssef's lips were set in a prim line. "I want to treat women with respect. I want to be around women—ladies—whom I can admire. Women with good minds and pure hearts."

"And tits? What about women with good minds, pure hearts, and big tits?"

It was, Hamid thought, a very bad sign that Youssef did not see fit to laugh at his little joke. Youssef was parading his emotions as openly as a woman might. As Youssef began talking again about that accident on the Corniche, Hamid let his mind roam to his family: to his father, his grandfather, his three brothers. Never would he have heard such drivel from the lips of any of them. Many men of their station smoked hashish, drank whiskey, took their sport with belly dancers. As long as a man also gave alms to the poor, perhaps made the obligatory pilgrimage to Mecca, and in every other way showed the trappings of piety and generosity, few cared what he did in private. There was even, among some of the Turkish aristocracy like Hamid's family, a certain sensual pride in living above rules. Any worldly Egyptian who had the money and the opportunity might do the same. Sophisticated Muslims knew there was nothing sinful in a little pleasure

For a moment Hamid wondered if that was the difference between Youssef and himself. Youssef was a Jew. Maybe Jews put more stock in sin. Hamid narrowed his eyes at Youssef. This summer the newspapers had reported much about the Israelis' brazen forays on Egyptian posts along the border. Just this month the Israelis had attacked Gaza again and overrun the Egyptian outpost of El-Auja. Could it be that Youssef was beginning to identify with this Jewish business? Hamid rolled another reefer. No, Youssef couldn't have turned into a Jewish devil. His friend just felt guilty for running down that dratted girl.

Youssef was still hoping that his uncle's words, which had seemed so magical to him, would work the same on Hamid. But Hamid's thoughts were preoccupied with elaborate curses on the families of the upstart colonels who had deposed the king. If it weren't for them, Hamid wouldn't have to be sitting on this balcony, drinking boring juice, pretending interest in Youssef's sudden self-righteous yearnings to be good. Hamid should be looking forward to a life of ease and pleasure. By rights Hamid should one day be inheriting his share of his father's four thousand acres of prime Delta farmland. But that damned revolution had made it imperative for Hamid to dance attendance on Youssef. So far, by parceling out title to the choicest tracts to cousins and nephews and wives, Hamid's father had not lost much to land reform. But just in case Nasser someday went further, Hamid's father had told him to learn all he could about cotton from the al-Masris. Usually it was easy for Hamid to jolly Youssef along and draw out Rafael. But here and now Hamid had had enough of Youssef's new veneer of virtue.

At last, when Youssef ground to a halt, Hamid let the silence continue until Youssef could not help but inhale some of the hashish fumes lying over them in a blue cloud. Finally Hamid made his move. "Stephanos is having a party tonight."

"Tonight?"

"I hear everyone will be there." Hamid's voice was soft, persuasive. "You know, Youssef, I don't care so much about the taste of whiskey or the way the hashish feels in my blood or those belly dancers' thighs. It's the fellowship of old friends that I'd like to have tonight. I haven't seen most of the boys since we left Victoria." When Youssef admitted that he, too, missed their old friends, Hamid smiled. "I thought we'd leave around ten."

"I don't think I should go." Youssef nearly glared at Hamid. "I just told you I've finished with all that."

"With good reason. With very good reason." Hamid paused delicately. "I just don't think you have to turn on your friends just because you feel bad about that accident. Where's your loyalty? I thought you *liked* them."

"I didn't say I didn't like them."

"So we'll just go for a little while. We'll just talk to this one and that one. And then we'll come home and drink some more tamarind juice and get a good night's sleep." Hamid's heavy lids drooped so that Youssef could not see his eyes.

"Maybe." Youssef bit his lip and wished it were easier to be good.

Batata and the dogs raced in front of Mona and Youssef at the zoo. "Come on! The gazelles!"

Youssef was not quite in step with Mona as he slouched along with his hands in his pockets. Lately, as Hamid had continued to counter his talk of reform with delectable temptations, Youssef had made these outings with Batata and Mona almost a daily affair. Youssef always told himself he chose to spend time with Batata because it was a good work to try to make his mentally retarded brother happy. But he knew there was more to it than that. When he could cling to someone untainted, it was almost as if that dark night on the Corniche had never happened. When he was with Batata, Youssef didn't feel torn between his determination to be good and his inclination to be bad. He was out so much with Batata, Mona, and the dogs that dog hairs collected in fluffy golden balls on the back seat of his Jaguar.

While Batata and the dogs played fetch on the tar path, Mona stared off into space at the gazelle pen. What, Youssef wondered, could the girl be thinking about? He had noticed this fall a stillness, almost a waiting, about Mona. Although he had no idea what it was that Mona was waiting for, Youssef felt both tongue-tied and drawn to her. He stood near her and looked inside the pen where the graceful, delicate gazelles huddled aloof and tentative. "Do you remember when we saw them before?" Youssef sounded wistful. He had been so sure of himself then. Maybe those days had been the happiest of his life. Youssef felt a twinge of self-pity. It was tragic, he thought, for a young man of twenty-one to yearn for lost youth.

'I remember." Mona had not forgotten a single word that Youssef had ever said to her.

A memory came to him unbidden. "I called you a gazelle."

"I remember." As Mona turned and smiled at him, her eyes were gentler than the gazelles'.

Youssef looked deep into eyes that were amber, wide, wet, fringed in black. Eyes that we steady, achingly steady, as they looked back at him.

Eyes that were, above all, so innocent and pure that they carried with them the promise of bestowing both innocence and purity. Youssef blinked to break the spell, but then opened his eyes again, afraid she would be gone. How could he never have *seen* her before? Her skin, he noticed, was like honey—no, like custard and honey creamed together. The full mouth, the high cheekbones, the reddish-black hair were absolutely perfect. Mona, he thought fervently, was not merely pretty. Mona was beautiful. Mona was the most beautiful girl he had ever seen. He smiled a slightly inane smile and turned in confusion back to the gazelle pen. He said the first word that popped into his mind. "Scared."

"The gazelles?"

"Of course the gazelles." His voice was harsh from his trying to keep the sense of wonder out of it. Youssef told himself not to get carried away. He was Youssef al-Masri, a man of the world. This was merely little Mona, the nursemaid. "Look at them—huddled over there, as far away from us as they can get. They're beautiful, yes. But they have no courage."

Mona had waited for years for Youssef to look at her as he just had. She was not going to let him off so easily. "Perhaps they're not cowards. Perhaps they are right to be shy. Perhaps it's safer." She had revealed too much that was too tender about herself, and so she retreated. "The gazelles, I mean. People like us feed them too much. Make them sick. Tease them. Scare them with loud noises. I think it's right to fear something that can hurt you. Maybe they're wise."

As the two of them watched, a baby gazelle nuzzled its nose against its mother's neck while a male hovered protectively nearby.

It was all too cloying for Youssef. "Feed them, Mona." He bought bread and handed it to her. "They'll come to you. I know it."

"But they're happy as they are. Let's let them be."

"Then I'll do it." Youssef moved along the fence toward the animals and held out the bread as he shouted, "Here! Come here!"

When the gazelles cringed farther away, Mona crept close to Youssef and held out her hand. "That's not how to do it." She took some bread, tore it into small pieces, and threw it in the pen.

The gazelles looked at her and the bread. The male and the female did not move, but the baby gazelle tottered over and ate the bread where it lay on the ground. Mona tossed more closer to the fence. "Sh-h-h." She was afraid Youssef would frighten it off. They watched the gazelle edge closer and bend to scoop up the bread. Slowly, very slowly, Mona held a handful of bread through the mesh of the fence. After a moment of soft staring, the animal sidled closer, stopped and waited, then came so near they could see it trembling. Finally the gazelle lowered its head, nibbled the bread, and licked Mona's fingers. It turned then and scooted proudly back to its parents.

"See? You see, Youssef? The gazelle wasn't a coward. Only careful."

"But it knew there wasn't anything to fear from *you*. It wouldn't come to *me*."

"Was there anything to fear from you?" Mona smiled at Youssef again.

Baruch and Rafael were hunched forward on the edge of the sofa after dinner as they listened attentively to the shrill voice crackle in excited Arabic on the radio. President Nasser had just announced a massive eighty-million-dollar Soviet arms deal. It was, the announcer said, the beginning of the end of Western imperialist power over the Arabs. It was the beginning of the end of superior Israeli military firepower. President Nasser had shown the way. President Nasser had proved to all Arabs that their future lay with neither the West nor the East but as nonaligned nations that could benefit from all possible sources of aid. At this very moment, the announcer said, Arab brothers had taken to the streets in Damascus, Baghdad, and Beirut to shout their approval of Gamal Abdel Nasser.

Rafael leaned over and snapped off the radio. "That's enough. I won't sit here and listen to any more. I won't hear that madman praised in my drawing room. Nasser! To think the day would come when that bloody son of a postal clerk would do this!"

"Take it easy, Rafael." Baruch's voice had a professional concern. "Don't get so excited. You know your blood pressure. And the family history. Father might still be here if he had learned to take it easy. You know how Radio Cairo exaggerates. Maybe there's nothing to this at all."

"Not bloody likely." Rafael stalked to the liquor cabinet and poured himself another brandy. "Soviet arms for Egypt. A turn to the East. A slap in the faces of the British and the Americans. Another war in the making with Israel." Rafael swirled his brandy. "All the signs were there. I should have seen this coming." Over the past four years Britain and America had based their Mideast diplomacy on enlisting the Arabs in the Baghdad Pact's anti-Soviet military alliance. Iraq had joined. Jordan, Syria, and Lebanon were still being courted. But Nasser, still smarting from Egypt's long fight to eject the British from his country, had turned the West down flat. His punishment was that the British and the Americans refused to sell him enough arms to modernize his obsolete army. And as this troubled year had worn on, as Israel received Mystère bombers from France, as Egypt was humiliated three times over by devastating Israeli border raids, Nasser had unleashed his own guerrilla bands to harass the Israelis. Rafael paced the room. "And do you know the worst of it? Who do you think is going to pay for these arms? Me! Nasser has mortgaged *my* cotton crop for tanks to use against Jews! It's too much! Too bloody much!"

"Wait a minute, Rafael." Calmly Baruch reminded his brother that the cotton trade could benefit from the arms pact. Shortly after the revolution, Nasser had closed the Cotton Exchange because its wild speculations at the end of the Korean War cotton boom had been wrecking the Egyptian economy. Although Nasser had reopened the Exchange just this month under strict government controls, Rafael was still worried about the shrinking world markets. "At least now you'll be able to unload your cotton. What does it matter if it goes to Prague or Liverpool?"

"What does it matter? What does it matter!" Rafael struck his forehead with his fist. "The Russians are *Communists,* Baruch! The goddam bloody Communists will be taking over Egypt!"

"Perhaps you're jumping to conclusions. The Russians haven't landed in Alexandria yet."

"But they will. You mark my words, Baruch. Cairo will be Little Moscow. And it's all Nasser's doing." Rafael held up his snifter. "I drink to the demise of Gamal Abdel Nasser. May he die in pain!" Rafael drained his glass and then poised to throw it on the tiles of the fireplace. But he thought better of it. The snifter was very expensive Bohemian crystal.

As the brothers looked gloomily into their glasses, they heard footsteps on the staircase and barks in the hall. Youssef's voice rang out. "We're going for a walk."

Baruch frowned. "Youssef! I'd like a word with you, please."

Youssef was preceded by the dogs and trailed by Batata and Mona. Suker ran over and pawed Rafael's trousers. For some reason the puppy adored Rafael, but the feeling was not returned. "Get that animal away from me!" Rafael brushed off the dog hairs and held up his glass so it gleamed prettily in the light.

Youssef faced Baruch. "We're just out for a stroll."

"I don't think that's wise." Baruch pointed to the radio. "There's just been some bad news. The Soviets have agreed to sell Egypt millions in arms funneled through the Czechs."

"I think we'll be safe on the Corniche tonight, Uncle Baruch."

Baruch felt like a foolish old woman but persisted with his warning. "They're linking the arms sale with another Palestine war. The radio says there are pro-Nasser demonstrations all over the Mideast. Nasser is being hailed as a hero for taking a stand against the Israelis and the West. It might be better if you stayed in tonight."

Batata wailed. "But Youssef promised!" The dogs barked and chased their tails.

"We won't be long." Youssef gave Baruch his most winning smile. "When we come back, maybe we'll have a game of backgammon. I think tonight I may beat you. I feel lucky. Very lucky."

Baruch relented. Youssef was looking happier these days. Baruch was pleased, too, that his nephew was spending more time with Batata and less with Hamid. Baruch was sure Youssef's excesses could be traced to the influence of Hamid. "Rafael? If they avoid downtown? What do you think?"

"Make sure they take the dogs."

The hot late-September night was starry as they walked the long way down the length of the Rue Fouad to the sea. Batata chattered, the dogs sniffed every pungent gutter, and Mona and Youssef stole furtive glances at each other. The two of them had been shy in the week since their tryst at the gazelle pen. Youssef had thought of Mona often, usually when he was sitting by himself on the balcony or lying in his bed. But sometimes she would come to his mind when he was in the midst of a conversation, and a slight smile would play on his lips. All that week he had had to ask Hamid and his father to repeat much of what they said. Mona, too, had daydreamed away those seven days. She magnified the significance of Youssef's every word and basked in the memory of his every smile. That look, those smiles, were her morning tea and bread, her dinner meat and rice, her supper eggs and toast. All day she longed for night so she could go to bed and give herself over to dreams of Youssef. Her years of waiting, she hoped, she prayed—she *knew*, most fervently—were nearly at an end. Youssef, *inshallah*, was falling in love with her. Soon, *inshallah*, he would be admitting that he wanted to marry her. It wouldn't be long, *inshallah*, before Ummie and Uncle Muhammad came to live at the Villa al-Masri. She and Youssef would, *inshallah*, live happily ever after, as Mona long ago had prayed would be their destiny. Sometimes during that week Mona had taken the blue bead from around her neck and, as she tenderly kissed the talisman, had dreamed of the day—very soon—when she, *inshallah*, would be kissing her Youssef.

When at last they reached the Corniche, Youssef marshaled them across the busy street with an old man's caution. Life, with Mona just hand-holding distance from his side, was suddenly very precious.

On the far sea side of the sidewalk, where vendors were plying their wares, Youssef bought Batata fresh-roasted pistachio nuts. "Some say the best pistachios in the world come from Persia. But that's not true. The best pistachios are right here. The Greeks brought them. Better *pistash* here than in Athens."

"Athens." Mona let the word linger on her tongue. She wondered if sometime Youssef would take her to Athens. "Was it beautiful? I think Athens would be very beautiful."

"Not as beautiful as you."

Youssef and Mona smiled at each other. There was a curl of Mona's hair in her eyes. Youssef raised his hand to brush it away, but then stopped himself and instead reached his hand between their locked eyes, as if to catch and hold and treasure that look in the palm of his hand. They both sighed.

Youssef spied a jasmine seller holding up his necklaces of tiny blooms strung together with circlets of string. It was late in the year for jasmine. "The last flowers of summer. The last *ful* flowers." Youssef bought three necklaces of jasmine and held them out to Mona. "For you."

She smiled up at him from under lowered lashes and put the flowers around her neck.

In the moonlight all he could see were beige buds and amber eyes, all he could smell were sea salt and jasmine, all he could think about was touching her tenderly on her soft cheek.

"The beach, Batata." Youssef offered Mona his arm. "Shall we?"

Batata and the dogs bounded down the stairs and ahead on the sand.

Usually Youssef could think of innumerable sweet nothings to whisper to a young woman as they strolled together down a moonlit beach. Youssef was horrified, therefore, to hear the words that issued from his mouth. "That arms accord with Czechoslovakia is bloody bad luck."

Mona smiled up at him adoringly.

Encouraged, Youssef forged ahead. "What it means, of course, is that Egypt soon will be ready for another go against the Israelis. It means war, Mona."

"You won't have to fight, will you?" Mona looked worried.

Youssef put his arm around Mona as if to reassure her. With pleasure he noted that she did not draw away. "I have Italian citizenship."

"*El-hamdulillah!*"

"Would you care, Mona, if things were different? I mean, if I had to go to war?" Youssef stopped walking and faced her.

Her eyes, as she looked up at him, gave her answer.

Youssef bent slightly to lift a cluster of jasmine blossoms in his hand. He raised them and slowly, tentatively, but deliberately, he touched them to her lips. He rubbed the flowers gently over her mouth.

She breathed in the heavy scent, felt the soft petals against her lips and, closing her eyes, yearned toward the blooms. He bent closer and covered the jasmine with his lips, then found her own in a long scented kiss. When she finally made to draw away, he once more rubbed her lips with the flowers. Their kiss had been softer, sweeter, than jasmine in full bloom.

They looked at each other. She raised a hand and traced his lips with a finger, brushing away a jasmine petal that still lay there. He moved to hold her, but she turned and ran up the stairs, across the Corniche, and out of sight.

Youssef did not follow her. The kiss had been enough for tonight.

156

He felt at this instant that their kiss would be enough for his lifetime. Mona. He had kissed his Mona. His Mona.

As he ran far up the beach to join Batata and the dogs, never had the air, the breeze, the sand felt so glorious. Still running when he reached Batata, Youssef tried to swing his heavy brother up in the air. But Batata stumbled and they both fell, laughing, on the sand. Youssef kissed his brother. Youssef wanted to make Batata as happy as he himself was. He wanted to make everybody in the world as happy. "I bet you'd like an ice cream."

"Chocolate?"

"Anything you want."

But when they climbed the stairs to the seawalk, the vendors had vanished. If they were to go to Pastroudi's, it would mean ignoring Uncle Baruch's warnings by cutting through the center of town. *Malesh,* Youssef said to himself. On this night of nights, on the night he had kissed his Mona, they deserved to celebrate with Alexandria's best chocolate ice cream.

They ambled westward along the sea side of the Corniche. Across the street, cafés, restaurants, and cabarets were all bright lights and chatter. Pretending to listen to Batata laughing by his side, Youssef's thoughts were only of Mona's lips, Mona's eyes, Mona's hair. Tomorrow at breakfast they would look at each other in a secret new way. Perhaps some of the jasmine blooms would still be fresh, and she would wear them in her hair. She was so beautiful. And she loved him. He knew it. She had let him kiss her. She had kissed him back.

Crossing the Corniche, they joined sidewalks crowded with the usual flurry of men strolling for a free night's entertainment. Youssef admired the *élan* of *baladi* men in blue-striped *gallabeiyas* who, like *shaykhs* for the night, had wrapped soiled lengths of cotton rakishly around their heads. Youssef nodded at sleek Lebanese in tight white suits, bound for business even at this late hour. He tossed a ten-piaster coin to a legless beggar. Youssef's eyes came to rest on a gnarled, toothless old man who sat on the curb by his horse carriage. If Mona had still been by his side, Youssef thought, he would pile her into the calèche and show her Alexandria in style. They would look at the stars but neither touch nor kiss. They would thrill just to be together. Dreamily Youssef elbowed his way through the crowd, his arm linked in Batata's as the dogs slunk close by their feet. Youssef was too immersed in Mona's kiss to notice that tonight the sidewalk crowd was different from the usual polyglot. Apart from the industrious Lebanese, there were no foreigners on the sidewalk or in the cafés. No Greeks with black hair and carelessly stubbled chins, sipping coffee and argumentatively eyeing the crowd. No Italians strutting with their chests out, looking for loose and losable women. No Armenians, Maltese, Europeans. Only Egyptians, and poor ones at that.

There was another important difference that Youssef failed to notice. The crowd usually milled to and fro, around and back, in the streets as well as the walkways, aimlessly squandering time for the sheer joy of it. But tonight all the movement surged toward the square. Youssef, Batata, and the dogs were swept around the corner and into an impromptu rally in Midan Saad Zaghloul.

Brown work-worn faces were upturned toward a bearded man standing on a donkey cart and screaming in *baladi* Arabic. "They take the bread from our mouths! They grind us into the earth! Our earth, our land, our Egypt! And yet they steal the very dirt away from us!"

"*Aywah! Aywah!*" The crowd screamed not as one but in many hoarse voices. "Yes! Yes!"

"They live in their villas like pashas while we live like dogs! Like dogs!"

"*Aywah!*"

"And the Jews! *Yahud!*" The speaker spit. "They are the worst! While here in Alexandria they bleed us, while they drink our blood, their brothers have stolen Palestine from our brothers! The Jews want war with us! They attack us in Gaza, in El-Auja! War! We'll give them war!"

"*Aywah!*"

"It is as the Prophet said. Jews are unclean! They pollute us! We'll launch *el-Jihad,* holy war against the Jews! We'll wipe them out in Palestine! And we won't forget their spies here in Egypt!"

"A-l-l-a-h!"

"God is great and to Him praise!"

Youssef shifted on his feet and held Batata tighter. He had never before heard a Muslim claim that Muhammad had hated the Jews. Youssef offered an old man a cigarette and asked who the speaker was.

The old man smiled, lit both their cigarettes, and whispered, "I think he is a Brother."

"*Ikhwan?* The Muslim Brotherhood?" Youssef was alarmed to see the *Ikhwan* haranguing the crowd so openly. Last year Nasser had cracked down on the Brotherhood. He had imprisoned them, tortured them, even had six *Ikhwan* leaders executed. But in the excitement over Nasser's arms accord, in the spur-of-the-moment rallies and marches in the squares and boulevards of Alexandria, this Muslim Brother apparently had seized his chance to speak. Once again Youssef asked the old man if this speaker was *Ikhwan.*

"*Aywah. Aywah.*" Courteously the old man made room so Youssef and Batata could have a better view. The old man's voice tensed with excitement. "Listen to him. It is just as Nasser said today. We are Arabs! We are men! Now we'll get what we need to beat the Jews! Nasser outsmarted even the British! He spat in the face of the foreign devils! What a day! *El-hamdulillah,* what a day! Wait until I tell my wife. The chanting will start soon. And the music. It is like the Great Feast. There will be stories told about this day. Be sure of it. And I'm here! I'm seeing it! Me, Mustafa!" As if the words of the speaker were not so important as the spectacle, the old man did not seem to care that this blond young man in Western dress was obviously a foreigner.

Youssef looked up at the majestic gloom of the Koran chanter now standing in his long robes atop the donkey cart. Loudly, seductively, he droned the words of Allah as they had been revealed to the Prophet.

"Al-lah!" The crowd sighed and swayed to the music of the voice.

His fears allayed, Youssef lingered to listen. The sound of the Koran chanters always put Youssef nearly in a hashish trance. It was the same with the *muezzin* cries from the minarets. Youssef had grown up under the whine of Muslim prayer calls ticking off the stages of each day. To Youssef, Muslim chants were as beautiful and as stripped of religious meaning as the pealing of churchbells on a mossy English common. He never listened to the words being chanted, only the rhythm, the soothing rise and fall of the alliterated Arabic. Sometimes, standing outside the gay red-bunting funeral tents in the Arab quarters, watching the somber men in *gallabeiyas* and turbans and fezzes, Youssef would be strangely comforted by the rise and fall of a chanter's wavering deep voice. So now, too, Youssef drank in the sound of the singsong Arabic, reluctant to leave its sonorous embrace. This all, he thought, was the world of his Mona. Its sensuality was hers. Breathing deeply, he wanted to shut his eyes and be submerged in it and thus in her.

But the dogs were restless, and Batata tugged at Youssef's arm. "Ice cream."

"Not yet." Youssef wasn't ready to leave his dream world. But out of the corner of his eye he saw one of the *bowabs* from the Rue Fouad eyeing him speculatively.

The chanter stopped, bowed his head, and retired.

In his place sprang the bearded Muslim Brother. "You've heard the Sacred Words! We must purify ourselves! It is even as the Prophet said! No more foreigners! No more Christians! No more Jews!"

From nowhere a drumbeat began. Taking that rhythm as its own, the crowd began a one-word chant. "A-l-l-a-h!" They sighed like rapturous Sufi mystics being transported by glimpses of Paradise. "A-l-l-a-h!" They started it slow and steady but then picked up momentum from the energy and force of their own single voice. They began clapping as they screamed, in one voice, with one will. "Allah! Allah! Al-*lah!*"

As abruptly as it had begun, the chant stopped. In the stillness that followed, as the crowd panted like a pack of overheated dogs thirsting for water in the midday sun, as Zibda and Suker whined uneasily at Youssef's feet, the *bowab* from the Rue Fouad pointed an accusing finger at Youssef and Batata. *"Yahud!"* he screamed.

As hundreds of dark eyes turned on them, Youssef did not have the presence of mind to make a joke of the man's cry. Instead he hissed an urgent command to his brother. "Run, Batata, run!"

When the two of them darted out of the crowd behind the dogs, men tucked the hems of their *gallabeiyas* in their mouths and coursed after them. A few soon stopped to rewind their unraveling turbans. Others dropped out, panting, and tried to pelt the fleeing dogs with rocks. None hit their mark, and the Arabs laughed and lit cigarettes.

As Youssef ran, he prayed that Batata would not fall. The boy was laughing as he flew along, thrilled with this new game of Youssef's. They turned the corner and raced up the street. The dogs barked and ran in circles before them. There was only a small pack of Arabs still behind them. For in the square, *mizmir* music had begun, and most were more interested in it than running down a hot street in aimless pursuit of two lone Jews.

But, propelled by the memory of that brutality on the steps of the Cotton Exchange, Youssef urged Batata to keep running. He had to save his brother. He had to save little Batata. They zigzagged through the crowded streets. Youssef looked over his shoulder. Only four Arabs were behind them. But they couldn't stop just yet. Youssef led Batata down an alley. The boy tripped over loose garbage, and Youssef pulled him up by his arms. "Hurry, Batata. We must run like the wind!" They tore out of the alley behind the dogs and onto Nebi Daniel. The lights of the synagogue were before them, but the thick iron gate was locked. Down the street they ran toward the Ramleh trolley station. Youssef looked behind. No one was in pursuit. "Stop!" Youssef saw his brother slow to a walk. Youssef leaned against a wall and shut his eyes for an instant. "Mona, we're safe. We did it, Mona." He opened his eyes and turned to take Batata home. But his brother wasn't beside him.

The dogs, overheated by their high-speed run, had not stopped on the curb. Suker was already barking in triumph on the far sidewalk, but fat old Zibda had squatted in the network of trolley tracks. As a large puddle spread under her paws, a blue-and-white trolley was careening straight for her. Batata darted out to scoop his pet to safety.

"No, Batata, no! The trolley! No!"

In the next instant Youssef saw a number of discrete movements. He saw Batata reach Zibda. He saw his brother bend and grab the dog. He saw Zibda cringe close to Batata. He saw the leather soles of Batata's expensive custom-made shoes slip on the steel trolley tracks. He saw Batata's feet fly into the air as he lost his balance. He saw Zibda lick his brother's face as the two of them fell into a heap on the tracks. Youssef shut his eyes so he would see no more.

The metallic tinkle of the trolley bells rang on and on over the dying whimpers of the boy and the dog.

Youssef brought his brother home in a donkey cart. He walked behind it, holding Suker too tight in his arms. It cannot be, it cannot *be*, Youssef told himself over and over. Then he would look ahead at the bundle that was the body of his brother and over and over again, every step of the way home, he would curse the day that Youssef al-Masri had been born.

He could not allow himself to remember, then or later, how Batata's body had looked on the tracks. But he could reconstruct how the trolley had stopped. How the driver had sobbed and screamed and thrown himself on the body. How an old *baladi* woman had put her arm around Youssef and led him aside. How an old man had stripped to his diaperlike shorts so he could shroud Batata's sodden body in his shabby white *gallabeiya*. How others had hailed a donkey cart, pushed aside its load of clover, and tenderly loaded on the bodies of the boy and the dog. How many of them had turned away from whatever had brought them on the streets that night and instead trailed the creaking donkey cart to the Villa al-Masri in a grieving cortege of strangers. Nowhere in the world can there be, Youssef thought, a people who embrace death like the Egyptians. Nowhere are people so prepared, so unsurprised by death. It is as if mourning for one is mourning for all, as though the tears can flow so easily only because they are always waiting behind the blink of an eye.

At the gates of his house, Youssef dug in his pockets for *baksheesh*. A part of him could not believe that the crowd had gathered and followed him home for any other reason. He pressed money on the bent woman whose arm was still around him and on the old man who had wrapped Batata in his robe. The old woman frowned and turned away, fingering the amulet she wore around her neck to ward off the Evil Eye. "It would be bad luck to take money for the death of one so young." The old man was similarly offended. "I did not need the robe. It was meant for the boy."

Confused, distraught, yet touched in his misery, Youssef took refuge in his Arab manners. He draped his own linen jacket around the old man's shoulders. "This was meant for you." From his finger he drew a gold ring and forced it into the palm of the old woman. "For my brother. Please take it in memory of my brother." The money he had wanted to give as *baksheesh* he put in a pile on the back of the donkey cart. It might be that later they would give it to the poorest of the poor.

Youssef tried to lift his brother in his arms. But the clover-scented body was too heavy. To Youssef, forever after in his life, clover would smell like death.

Four Arabs picked up the corpse and followed Youssef to the door.

As he turned back to them, the light from inside illumined the scene. The four dark men, identically clad in long robes and turbans, holding the white bundle streaked with red stains. The worn wooden donkey cart surrounded by a huddle of hunched women in black. The heap of untouched metal coins gleaming in the moonlight. The gray donkey with the blistered backside standing so still and mute and unquestioning. The familiar towering villas giving the lie to the credibility of the rest.

His eyes swimming with tears, Youssef focused on the quartet of men before him. Their mahogany faces were so ridged at the cheekbones and foreheads that they seemed all bone and gristle. He looked at them more closely. It seemed suddenly to him that the four men had not eyes but tongues of fire where eyes should be. Youssef trembled, remembering from nowhere the tales he had heard of *afreets,* dark ghosts of the night come to wreak vengeance for deeds unpunished. He shuddered, then could not stop from looking once more at those eyes. This time he saw four identical pairs of dark staring eyes, the eyes of the *baladi* girl he had run down. Youssef screamed and covered his own eyes with his fists.

ALEXANDRIA, EGYPT / October 1955

Baruch leaned back in his chair, took another sip of sherry, and watched the rain pouring down outside the window of his study. It was early in the year for the chill winter downpours that made the warmth of the wine more welcome. In a moment he would ring for Abbas to light a fire. Baruch took off his glasses, rubbed his tired eyes, and allowed himself a sigh. Batata's death had hit his family hard. Maybe, Baruch thought, maybe Abbas had been right about Batata long ago. Maybe the boy had been one of heaven's favorites. Maybe the Villa al-Masri had been blessed by his presence. And maybe his death had taken away whatever grace had once dwelled within. Grace? Baruch stared glumly at his glass and decided he was giving his family too much credit. His brother, Rafael, had always been a snob who was gifted only at making money. His sister-in-law, Leah, was the decorative facade she had been born to be. And was he himself any better? So he tiptoed sometimes into the Arab slums to dispense a few pills and give a few injections? So he had meddled in Mona's upbringing and endured backgammon headaches with Youssef in the parlor? A fat lot of good any of it had done.

Baruch wished he could shake off this mood of despair. Once he had thought he could make better if not the whole world then at least the world of those he loved. But at moments like this, he doubted the wisdom of even trying to work his will on the tiny world of the al-Masris. If only he could believe that some action—any action—of his could make a difference! He supposed that nothing he had ever done —nothing anyone could ever do—much mattered. Vaguely he wondered what in the hell was happening to him. He used to be able to analyze a problem and then carry out a plan with every confidence of success. He suspected that his frightening new inertia was not due entirely to the creep of middle age. Somehow it was linked with his immersion in Egypt, in Islamic thought, in the hopelessness he felt to be all around—and finally even inside—himself.

Crudely put, it was Western, it was European, it was Enlightened, to believe that all things were possible for a man of goodwill. Putting it even more baldly, it was Eastern, it was Islamic, it was bitterly but deliciously mystical to heave a sigh and simply accept whatever calamities came. Baruch rubbed the tense muscles at the nape of his neck. He had not thought it would be so dangerous to dip into Islam. For in this matter, too, he was beginning not only to feel out of control but also even to wonder if it was desirable to *be* in control. He could not stop himself from sighing once more and shrugging his shoulders. Life, he mumbled to himself, was difficult. All his good intentions had come to nothing. Batata was dead. Youssef was back with Hamid and the belly dancers. Mona was preparing to return to that manipulative mother of hers.

Baruch poured himself another sherry and contemplated how pleasant it would be to get drunk this afternoon. Allah—or rather, *God* —only knew it would be easier to deal with Rafael and Leah at dinner tonight through the pleasant glow of three or four more drinks. On his lips, in his mouth, down his throat, the sherry was warm and sweet. Wouldn't Rafael be surprised if I came to the table roaring an Arab love song? Mona, Baruch thought giddily, was so very beautiful.

Baruch put down his glass and tidied up his thoughts. Rafael, who blamed all Egypt for Batata's death, would be outraged if he came to the table spouting Arabic. Alive, Batata had been an embarrassment to his father. Baruch remembered what Rafael had said the night he had told him Batata was retarded. "A drooling idiot locked up in *our* nursery?" But the boy's death had worked a transformation on him. The morning after the accident, Baruch had come upon his brother sitting on the staircase using his best imported tortoiseshell comb to groom the coat of Batata's cocker spaniel puppy. When Suker licked his cheeks and ears, Rafael had chuckled as if he himself were Batata.

Soon, even to the Cotton Exchange, Suker was trotting behind him on a polished Italian leather leash. Rising to even greater heights of devotion, Rafael had ordered all the snapshots of Batata enshrined in a gold-leaf book with the Hebrew letters *Zvi: Book of the Jewish Martyr* inscribed on its cover.

For Rafael had refused to listen to Youssef's stammering protests that only his negligence was responsible for Batata's death. To Rafael, it was an open-and-shut case of the Arab murder of his son the Jew. At first Rafael was content to pore over the scrapbook with Daoud. Later he was showing it to the new clusters of men who whispered of Zionism, Israel, the Promised Land in the al-Masri drawing room long after midnight. Rafael began frequenting the synagogue not only for Sabbath prayers but for daily benedictions. He insisted that the girls transfer from the godless Ecole Français to the Jewish School. He began wearing a *yarmulkeh* in the house and consulted earnestly with Abbas about dietary laws and the appointments of a kosher kitchen. It was only when he began preaching at Leah even in the bathroom that family affairs took a new turn. She called him a fool and a hypocrite. He called her a daughter of darkness. She moved into a separate bedroom. He was heard to mutter about the uncleanness of women. Leah's next act was to hire a good-looking live-in French tutor for Rachel and Lisabet. The dark-skinned young Moroccan Jew—God knows where he had picked up his impeccable Parisian accent—had muscles that rippled perceptibly under the tight-fitting French-cut silk shirts that Leah began buying for him. Baruch wondered idly whether he had more sympathy for Rafael or Leah—whether, in similar circumstances, he himself would turn to God or the flesh. He laughed out loud and without pleasure. Of course he would choose God. He had never had much of the other.

He drained the dregs of sherry in his glass. What was he going to do about Mona? He couldn't allow that perfect child to slip back into the sinkhole of Karnak. She was nearly fifteen, by village standards altogether ready for marriage. Her mother would auction her off to the highest bidder, and delicate little Mona would become the drudge of some illiterate lout. Baruch curled his lip at himself, disgusted at his distaste for the lives of peasants who were as human as he was. Usually he was great defender of the villagers. Usually he painted them in romantic hues the more vivid for his distance from the drab mud-brown villages themselves. But Mona, *his* Mona, lying under some farmer? Baruch, he said to himself, you are either supercilious or jealous. He poured himself another sherry and downed it like medicine. He tried to convince himself that Mona was like a daughter to him. When she had collapsed in his arms by the Sacred Lake of Karnak Temple, she had felt as crushable as a flower. He had been gentle with her then. He must be gentle with her now. She had been so needy. She needed him still. Instead of sitting here feeling sorry for himself, he should be formulating a plan to save her from what she would no doubt call her fate. It was damned annoying that Mona still seemed to confuse her mother's will with destiny.

Clearly, Mona was at a turning point. Long ago Baruch had decided —it was one of his favorite abstractions—that there are turning points, flashpoints, points of no return, in the life of every man and every woman. Everyone has good times and bad times, enough love and then a searing lack of it. He had observed that it was the tragedies, the disappointments, the unrelieved aches that make men and women mold themselves into what they finally become. Even in Egypt, Baruch thought, where the young grow old overnight, a boy can look at life with all the shimmering sparkle of shined-up silver. But since nothing irreparable has happened to him yet, no one can prophesy about the character of such a youth. Just so, an expectant, glowing girl longs for a husband and babies. But since she has not yet experienced the variegated heartbreaks that will surely come with them, it is impossible to predict whether her bloom will fade in months or years or never.

Sometimes, staring at the very young, Baruch wished there were some magic incantation with which he could prepare them for approaching doom. He was certain that every man and every woman sometime must face his and her own individual sets of shocks and outrages—few of them earned, none of them expected, but all of them as inevitable as night. What fascinated Baruch was how each man and woman chooses to respond: how they wither this one and break that one into jagged pieces, how they fire some in a crucible of hitherto-unsuspected strengths, how they allow a very few special ones to blossom into a richer and deeper sensibility. He thought that those last ones, those heroic ones, must know intuitively that they cannot control their catastrophes but that they do have some feeble and some not-so-feeble choices of how they themselves will respond. Baruch thought the secret of life, the key to contentment, lay in turning those random tragedies into personal triumphs.

Baruch looked over at the shelves where his collection of antique copper urns and plates and pitchers had taken on an iridescent luster in the fading light. If he were to pick up that worn old canister on the top shelf, if he were to rub it until a genie appeared and promised to grant him his dearest wish, it would be that he himself could be transformed into a spirit which could whisk through the world whispering wise words of consolation to every man and woman reeling from the first lick of life's capricious whip. He would tell them all that it wasn't their fault, that they had not been singled out for any special hurt, that they could be saved if they but had the wit to see their own suffering as a replica of the suffering of all. It had been that one clear and shining insight that had reconciled Baruch to the death of his wife so long ago.

Remembering the joys of Daisy, Baruch smiled to himself. He

supposed he *was* a little drunk. Perhaps, he thought, I should drink like this more often. Maybe what the world needs is not my sage advice but sufficient amounts of alcohol to anesthetize any pain. It had been from a hazy longing to heal the world's sufferings that Baruch had become a doctor. His thirst to heal, however, had not nearly been slaked with his eyedrops and his tongue depressors and his urgent requests to tell him where it hurt. He persisted in the belief that if he providentially happened to be present at the precise moment when a young man or woman faced that first stunning life crisis, if he could say the perfect words at the perfect moment, he might finally fulfill his vocation as a healer. He had hoped to do just that with Youssef when they had played their games of backgammon.

It hurt Baruch even to think of Youssef still in limbo. By the look of it, Youssef's adolescence was going to grind on and on. It was possible, in fact, that Youssef would never grow up. Baruch had made a hard decision not to take Youssef in hand again unless the boy either showed some signs of character or directly appealed to him for help. But he believed that Youssef's relapse was only temporary. There was gold in the boy somewhere. . . . But, now, Baruch was more preoccupied with Mona's own moment of truth. Obviously the girl blamed herself for Batata's death. Apparently she wasn't buying Youssef's excuse that he had sent her home that night because it was too late for a virtuous Arab girl to walk the streets. She knew as well as the rest of the al-Masris that she was supposed to be Batata's guardian angel. And yet she had been drinking tea in the kitchen when Batata's blood spilled on the trolley tracks. Was it preferable, Baruch wondered, to have too much or not enough conscience? He admired Mona all the more for not excusing herself too easily, yet he wished she weren't acting as if her scheduled return to the Said was a much-deserved penance.

It was nearly dark in his study, but Baruch put off summoning Abbas or even switching on a light. He had hoped that Mona would turn to him for advice. He had dreamed that she would look up at him with those wide amber eyes and ask him to set right her world. He had waited for one week, two weeks, three weeks after Batata's death, and still Mona had endured whatever she was enduring alone. Clearly, Baruch thought, clearly I'm going to have to take some action on my own. He drummed his fingers on the polished oak of his desk. He always told himself he hated to force his will on anyone. He was always criticizing the ingrained passivity of Muslim culture. He was less eager to admit that he himself hated to make hard and fast or even weak and slow decisions. He supposed that one of his own faults was that he spent too long trying to see every side of a problem.

But this time there seemed no other way around it. He would be damned if he let that girl go back to her mother's clutches. He would find Mona other work. He would train her as a nurse—as his nurse.

She could work with him in his office, maybe even help him with his evening experiments in his laboratory. He could enroll her in some classes at the hospital. She could still live in the villa. His brother and sister-in-law wouldn't care if half Mona's village lived in the attic, as long as Rafael had his religion and Leah her lover. He would help heal his Mona by steering her, too, into becoming a healer. To celebrate the pleasure—rare, these days—of deciding on a course of action that he felt was in his power to execute, Baruch poured himself another sherry. Under his breath he hummed a spirited little Arab ditty of love.

The two of them had their heads so close together over the laboratory table that Baruch felt Mona's hair curled against his cheek. "Sorry," he said in a fluster as he pulled away. "This doesn't seem to be working out the way I expected."

Mona stifled a yawn. It was ten o'clock, and still they were at it. Their work together began every morning in his downtown office and continued every afternoon in his *baladi* clinic. Sometimes she was at the hospital shadowing a nurse, and a few evenings a week they worked late like this. There seemed to be no end to what Dr. Baruch would teach Nurse Mona.

He had found her a dutiful pupil. She shepherded his patients to and fro in her starched white uniform. She found veins, gave injections, and seemed to try to memorize every word he said to his patients. But glancing down at her rough red hands which she seemed to enjoy drenching in harsh disinfectant, Baruch decided Mona was a little too obsessed with cleanliness. He had hoped that she would take more comfort in her work and in him. In vain he had waited for Mona to confide in him. If he wanted to give her the best that he had, he would have to take the initiative. "You know, Mona," he began as he shook together two vials, "your work with me has been excellent. You are by far the best nurse I've ever had." Mentally he asked his other nurses to forgive him. Mona did have a facility for helping others.

"Really?" She smiled shyly.

"Really." Baruch peered at the bottles in his hand. He hadn't been paying the slightest attention to what he was mixing. He hoped he didn't blow the two of them up before he finally made his speech. He motioned for Mona to hand him a test tube. "There are many different parts to doctoring. Techniques, theory, practical knowledge. All of it takes years to study and understand. But there's another side that can't be taught. Only felt. At the heart of it, a doctor is simply a healer. He—or *she*—gives hope to the sick because, I think, the healer has a certain sympathy for suffering. Usually that gift comes only to those who themselves have overcome suffering."

"Suffering?" She avoided Baruch's eyes. Nervously she touched the blue bead she still wore on a black ribbon around her neck. Thinking unhappy thoughts, she had lost track of Baruch's interminable experiment. She was grateful that the bustle of her new work usually left her little time to brood. If she allowed even part of her mind to wander from her work, all of it—dead Batata, grieving Youssef, grim Ummie, her own curse—claimed her. She would have little flashing whiffs from the past: the Agami sand kicking up under Youssef's heels, Ummie in the felucca under the stars, Batata tugging at her arm. Lost. All that goodness was lost. "Suffering," she repeated.

He poured the compound into the test tube and began mixing another. "You see, Mona, every one of us lives a life of pain. What distinguishes a good person from a bad one, a healer from a destroyer, is how we choose to channel that pain. We have very little to say about the dreadful things that happen to us. But sometimes, I think, we can use the pain rather than allowing it to use us."

She leaned forward as she strained to listen.

"What I'm trying to say, Mona, is that everyone suffers. Suffers terribly. Look around you at all the disappointed people. Everyone is disappointed. We are all alike. All, at one time or another, are in pain. If you can realize that, if you can accept deep inside you that it is pain that makes us all the same rather than something terrible that is visited so unfairly only on ourselves, then it may be possible to turn suffering into something else. Sympathy, Mona, sympathy. That's the key."

She tried to concentrate on Baruch, but instead she remembered jasmine petals and Youssef's lips. Batata was dead because she and Youssef had betrayed him. She had tucked those jasmine necklaces away in a drawer, where they had turned a brittle brown. If she were to tell Baruch why Batata was dead, would he still speak to her so kindly?

Baruch put down his bottles and test tubes. "You remember when you and . . . Batata . . . were studying science?"

She tried not to flinch at the memory of hot drowsy afternoons over their lessons in the old nursery.

"You remember about atoms and electrons and all that?"

She smiled. Batata had loved Baruch's science lectures. The boy had used clay balls and glass bottles and round hard cookies to reconstruct his uncle's theories. Once Baruch had hoped this interest in science might lead to other breakthroughs for Batata.

Sure he had her full attention now, Baruch sketched circles on a sheet of paper. "Think of all of us, every person in the world, as a little atom. And just as each atom has its nucleus with its own electrons revolving around it, so is each person born with the same drives whirling around his or her core. You could say that around the nucleus of each person revolve little electrons representing the desire to feel secure and to love and be loved." Around each circle he drew other, smaller balls. "But then life unfolds. And this little atom, compelled or maybe just responding to this irresistible electron and that insistent electron, wanting to be loved and secure, bangs into that atom over there. And then the second atom batters into a third. And that one into another. Maybe by accident, by chance, not by design at all. Do you follow me?"

She nodded. She never knew what to expect from Baruch. He fancied electrons were like being loved. She could almost feel Youssef's lips on hers. It was possible that there was electricity—so why not electrons?—in love.

"It's those collisions, Mona, that cause the trouble. Imagine, for a moment, that some atoms get hit harder than others and are so bent out of shape that it seems as if their electrons have gone wild. The atoms become distorted." He drew cancerous circles with bloated sides. "Some people are like that. They start off just wanting to feel love and security. But some terrible trauma happens to them. As a result, those two basic drives get twisted out of recognition."

She thought fleetingly of her mother, then frowned and willed that thought away. Her mother had nothing to do with what Baruch was saying.

"The point of all this, Mona," he continued as he put down his pen, "what connects suffering, sympathy, and all those frantic little atoms, is the understanding that all of us are the same. We all have the same simple needs, and yet not one of us ever gets entirely and exactly what we want. We are all brothers, suffering in our own lonely orbits. And those who suffer most are the twisted ones. Yet we must forgive ourselves—and others—for all those awful collisions we feel. If you can understand that, if you can allow yourself to experience your own suffering as the suffering of every one of us, if you can remember what it is to feel pain and see and feel it in others, then your own pain can become something fine."

"Sympathy?" Her eyes were alight.

"Exactly. Sympathy becomes compassion." Baruch smiled. "And that," he concluded, "is what leads to the next step. To be a healer."

"Oh." She reached over and folded up the paper on which he had scratched his thoughts. "Can I keep this?" She would wrap Youssef's jasmine petals in Baruch's sketch of pain. She paused. "Do you think you can teach me to be that? A healer?"

"I think," he said briskly, "that you can do that only for yourself. But I think it is possible, very possible, for you. Think about it, Mona. You can give yourself the gift of healing. If you want it."

In answer she threw her arms around Baruch and kissed him on both cheeks. Holding her crushed to him for a moment, Baruch had a feeling that she and he would one day harvest what had just been sown.

* * *

But those well-meaning words threw Mona into Youssef's arms instead. She mulled over what Baruch had said. Suffering. Sympathy. Healing. Batata's suffering was over through no willful malice of hers and Youssef's. Now it was Youssef who suffered and needed her sympathy. She had to help him forgive himself. She would heal him with her love.

She acted on her impulse shortly after dinner one night when she saw Youssef pull on a sweater and slouch out of the house. For some weeks Youssef had been going on solitary walks, always on the same route: down the Corniche to the deserted spot where he and Mona had kissed on the sand, then to the center of town and Saad Zaghloul Square, finally through the streets until he stopped at the intersection where his brother had died. Only when the night was old would Youssef roll some hashish, swill some whiskey, and lose himself in the cabarets.

No one had told Mona where Youssef walked these chill late-November nights. But she guessed that she would find him where she had lost him. She wrapped herself in a shawl and stole out of the house, and as she walked toward the sea she tried to quiet her fears. If she dared to help him, if she but took the risk, everything could be hers. From the sidewalk along the Corniche she saw his hunched thin figure silhouetted against the sea. Silently she joined him.

He neither acknowledged her presence nor moved away. He had not been alone with her since they had stood here together the night Batata died. Catching her staring at him sometimes over the dining table, he had resented her intrusions. Didn't she know that all they could be now were accomplices in his brother's death? He did not want any more reminders of his guilt. He had hoped this pretty little girl would go back where she came from—back to that dark village of hers —and leave him as he was.

She stood and waited for him to accept that she was there and was not leaving. She tucked her hands inside her shawl so that Youssef, when he finally looked at her, would not see that she was trembling. She felt a fine rain of sea salt on her skin.

They both looked out at the void of the sea. The sky was starless, and the new moon cast tentative light. A shivering wind churned the white waves smashing into the clammy sand.

Youssef bent to light a cigarette. Three times his matches sputtered. Mona stepped between Youssef and the sea wind and cupped her hands around his so that her fingers curled against his own. The match caught and held. He took a deep pull on the cigarette.

She remained where she was, although their hands no longer touched. She did not have to remind herself to be patient. Youssef was her destiny.

He still had not glanced at her. He knew what she looked like. Had he been an artist, he could unerringly have sketched the lilt in her eyes and the curve of her cheek. Just this month he had taken up with a dancer named Shu-Shu whose eyes were the cast of Mona's. A belly dancer suited him more than this little girl before him. Youssef wrinkled his nose. He could smell jasmine. Mona smelled of cheap cologne. It would, he thought, take more than five piasters of perfume to bring back that other night.

Finally she spoke, aiming directly at the heart of what had brought them together and also apart. "It was just here that you kissed me on the night Batata died."

Recoiling at the mention of that name, Youssef deliberately blew smoke in her face. Go away, Mona, he wanted to beg. Let it go. I don't want to destroy you, too. He had killed that girl on the Corniche. He had killed his brother. His eyes rested on the blue bead at her neck. He remembered her telling him once that she was cursed. Perhaps they were alike after all. He pictured Mona in a belly dancer's bra and skirt, then damned himself and her. Why wouldn't she leave him alone?

Mona ignored the smoke of his insult. She had a mission. She looked up at him, her eyes steadier and more confident than she felt. "Kiss me again, Youssef." She raised her arms and rested them lightly on his shoulders. "I'm here, Youssef. I'm here."

He looked down. Her face was pinched and somber, pleading and unpretty. She wasn't going away. She was standing so boldly near him. Not from desire so much as need, he could not stop himself from pulling her closer. For an instant he imagined that this night was that other night, that Batata and the dogs were just down the beach, that innocence was still theirs. He shut his eyes and saw his brother falling on the trolley tracks, heard the tinkle of that bell, smelled clover in the donkey cart. "Mona!" He spoke her name like death. His arms encircled her and still she was not near enough. He lifted her off the ground and into his arms. When he started to cry as he felt her cheek against his, he kissed her to stifle his sobs. Their second kiss tasted of salt.

At last he put her down. Their arms were still around each other. He let out a long sigh.

She wanted to say perfect words not only to solder him back together but also to graft him to her. But all she could do was will him to understand. With a fingertip she traced the path of his tears along his cheek. "I love you," she said.

"Let's walk," he answered.

They turned away from the wind. His arm was around her shoulders, her arm gripped his waist. She felt his fast stride sweeping her along the sand. He had not said he loved her. She turned her face to the sky. If she could see a single star, it would be an omen that all would be well. Allah, she prayed silently, give me a star. She tried to make herself believe that the sliver of the moon meant more than a star.

Shifting her closer to him, Youssef wondered where he was leading them both. What I should do, he thought, is give this girl a slap on the rump and send her away. Instead, reluctant to let her go, he plodded on. It could be as she said. It could be that she loved him. It could be that if she loved him, he might be better than he knew himself to be. But if that was true, if he was more good than bad, if there was any purity or decency left in him, he would send her away. She was a little peasant girl from the Said—without money, breeding, or much of a future. She was also a Muslim. He could never marry anyone like her, although no one would fault him much if he took what she was obviously so eager to give. Oh, God. He couldn't use her that way. "Go home, Mona." He said it under his breath and without conviction, and he did not lessen his grip on her.

Hearing only the fear in his voice, she kept pace with him. All Youssef needed was more time to realize that they belonged together.

Maybe he was wrong. Maybe the right thing to do was to let her love him. They could be a comfort to each other. Perhaps she really *did* love him. Perhaps she loved him so much that she would be able to save him, too. As long as he didn't dishonor her, as long as he left her intact, what harm, after all, could he do? He searched his soul. How did he feel about Mona? He remembered pulling her out of the sea at Agami, teasing her a thousand mornings in the nursery. For God's sake, she was like a sister to him. No, he didn't feel this way about Rachel and Lisabet. Mona was bound up in the yearning pity—was it pity?—he had felt for Batata. He wished she were still a little girl in braids and that he were still the unsullied prince of the family. He felt very, very tired. He guided Mona toward the cement stairs that led from the beach to the Corniche. He intended to walk her home and forget her.

Instead Mona settled herself on the second step and looked expectantly up at him.

He raised his eyebrows, shrugged his shoulders, and sat down beside her. Well, he had tried. Maybe he had only halfway tried to discourage this girl. But he had feelings, too. What he most of all wanted to feel right now was her breasts in his hands.

"I wanted to be with you, I wanted to hold you, the night Batata died," Mona said in a rush.

"Hold me now." He had his hands on her shoulders and was pulling her into his arms.

"We have to talk, Youssef." She averted her lips from his. "I think we should talk."

"Later." Eagerly he touched his lips to her smooth cheek, to the moist corner of her eye, along the translucent skin at her temple, down inside the scratchy wool of the shawl at her neck.

"Youssef?" Her voice was doubtful. She told herself not to panic. They had their whole lives to talk. They would always be together. They would marry and have children. The babies would all look like Youssef.

He turned her head and kissed her on the lips. Before his kisses had been as sweet as jasmine, as sad as tears, kisses like those she had sighed over at the cinema. But now Youssef's lips pressed hard into hers. She felt the ridges in his lips twist into hers. Under his sucking, grinding lips she tasted his hard teeth. "Mona," he groaned. "My Mona." When she tried to pull away, angrily he caught her closer to him. She opened her mouth to cry out to him to stop, but his tongue shot between her parted lips. He leaned the weight of his body over hers so the sharp edge of the stairs cracked into her back. She flinched closer to him, and he took that response as permission to run his hands down her spine. He grabbed handfuls of her buttocks and ground her up against his groin. She gasped, shut her eyes, and felt a hot rush as she twisted closer to him. She pushed her thighs into his, angled her breasts so their hard tips would brush his chest, closed her warm mouth around the lash of his tongue. He shuddered.

Flushed and dazed, they broke apart. She did not know whether to run or stay. Nor did he.

They avoided each other's eyes. When her breathing had slowed, she looked nervously over at Youssef. "It's getting late." When he didn't answer, she stood and smoothed down her dress. In a fit of modesty she pulled her shawl loosely around her so that Youssef, should he look up at her, would not be able to see what he had just touched. She looked down at the gold crown of his head. Tenderly she stroked his hair back into place. She did not want to leave with her mark on him.

"Tomorrow," he said firmly, still not looking at her. "Same time. Same place."

She hesitated, then nodded and fled up the stairs. She walked home alone and tried to forget the feel of his body.

Mona stood the next night before the mirror in her room, certain that signs of transfiguration must be reflected there. Since she had left Youssef on the beach, she had thought only of him. Surely he loved her. Surely he would be with her forever. She touched her lips where he had kissed her and traced the path of his lips from her lips to her eyes to her neck back to her mouth. She blushed when she caught herself sucking her finger as if it were Youssef's tongue. Almost slyly, she smiled at herself. Yes, her eyes were different. She fancied her eyes sparkled. So this was what it was to love. She was alone in her room, yet her dancing eyes swept through every corner to make sure she was not being watched. She stepped back from the mirror and looked at herself full-length. She turned sidewise and ran a lingering hand from her breasts to her waist to her hips. A little thrill ran through her body. Maybe she would let him touch her just a little. She caught a glimpse of herself preening and nearly burst into tears. Had she lost her mind? She could almost see before her the cruel pink slit from ear to ear on the neck of that girl fished out of the Nile back in Karnak. Had Khadra once felt like this? Mona peered anxiously into the mirror. Her mother's chant came back to her: "Fire is better than shame." She hung her head. She had played the slut with Youssef.

She prayed to Allah for forgiveness. In the back of her mind she heard again lines of Arabic poetry Baruch had once read her:

> It is as though every day my heart yearns more strongly
> for you
> And as soon as the wound is healed, a fresh scar is
> formed on my heart.

But the lover in the poem was meant to be God, not an infidel like Youssef. From the open window Mona heard the *muezzin* cry the faithful to prayer. She fell to her knees and felt the grain of the wood on her forehead. She banged her head on the floor as if with the desire to bruise herself. She was calm when she finally rose to her feet and began to dress for her assignation with Youssef. She could love Youssef, and Allah, and all that was good. Together they would bring forth the best in each other. Yet she could not stop herself from putting on her new pink dress that clung to her breasts, her waist, her hips. To show off her slender legs and ankles she wished she had silk stockings instead of her thick wool socks. She longed for high heels so that Youssef would not have to bend down so far to kiss her and so that she would have to cling to him for balance. She had a delicious fleeting image of herself shut away in Youssef's harem, waiting night and day for him to want her. She shook her head at herself. She touched her blue bead. She reminded herself she was a good girl. She turned out the light and went off to meet Youssef.

He waited impatiently for her on the sand. He, too, had been pre-occupied with thoughts of her: of her breasts, her lips, her tight thighs. She had come to him. She had begged him to kiss her. She had wanted him as he wanted her. He, too, had looked himself over in a mirror. He had coldly appraised his blond hair curled rakishly over his fore-head. He had caught the hard glint in his brown eyes. "You devil, Youssef," he had told himself. "You devil." He had tried to banish that thought, but it had persisted. He knew he had no business toying with Mona. Belly dancers were one thing, this sheltered Saidi another.

Several times that day he had decided to see her no more. And yet each time he had changed his mind. It could be, he thought excitedly if a bit dimly, that she could make him clean. And then he would remember the feel of her against him. Not for anything, not for any rules of God or man, could he keep away from their rendezvous. Whatever happened would happen, he had told himself, adding a one-word qualification that brought an ambiguous smile to his lips. *Inshallah.* It would all just have to be up to her Allah.

On the beach they ran to meet each other, but then, neither sure of what the other expected, they stopped just before they came together. Shyly, firm in her purpose to be chaste, she extended her hand. Swiftly he brought it to his lips and kissed the tips of each finger and then her palm. Her resolution not to kiss him receded just a little.

But he caught her mood and kept his distance. As artfully as a courtier, he held her hand as they walked along the beach. "I have thought of nothing but you," he said truly. Words he had heard on a Saturday afternoon at the cinema. "I could not sleep for thoughts of you. You are my life."

This was more like what she had imagined. She smiled to herself and let her hand relax in his.

"Tonight we will take a carriage ride," he said. "And we will talk. Would you like that, *habibti,* my love?"

She nodded, she hoped, very graciously. She was glad she had never ridden in one of those glamorous black calèches, so that her first time would be with Youssef. As they ascended the beach stairs, he tucked her arm inside his. They strolled up the Corniche, she thought, as a married couple might. Silently she thanked Baruch for freeing her from her servant's uniform and buying her this new dress that she thought made her look almost like a *huwaga,* a foreigner. Quickly Mona assured herself she didn't really want to be a foreigner. She had to admit, however, that she had frowned at her honey-colored skin today in front of the mirror and wished there were some cream or potion to bleach it just a shade lighter. She feared that eyebrows up and down the Corniche might be raised at the sight of a *huwaga* like Youssef with a Saidi like herself. She knew those gossipy *baladi* men on the street would assume she must be a prostitute.

She willed that thought away and, clinging more tightly to Youssef, stole a look up at him. He was so tall and strong and blond. He was the handsomest man she had ever seen. She shut her eyes and tried to freeze this moment in her mind and her heart. Remember the way the breeze tickles the hairs inside your nose. The way the pungent fish smell wafts from the restaurants across the street. The way the pavement feels beneath your feet, so rough and real. The way his arm fits snug in yours and guides your every step. She tripped over a loose stone and opened her eyes. But she had captured this moment for life.

Scooting across the Corniche, they laughed at the buses and the cars. Nothing, they knew, could hurt them tonight. They were still laughing as they climbed up the rickety metal steps of the calèche and settled down on the worn leather seats. The carriage was so imbued with the fragrance of years of assignations that the nightly-replenished smells of tobacco, sweat, and perfumes would never quite fade. Years from now, Mona thought, maybe Youssef and our sons and I will pile into this very carriage, and we'll catch a whiff of my—no, *our* —jasmine.

The carriage driver turned, leered, and began to chorus a hoarse love song. *"Habibi, habibi . . . !"* Youssef threw him a piaster and curtly told him to end his unwelcome serenade. The driver blew a lip-smacking kiss to Mona.

From the roof of the cab, curved to screen them discreetly from the street and the sky, dangled dirty gold fringe and little bells that jingled as the carriage lurched forward. Youssef grabbed the single worn blue bead, meant to ward off the Evil Eye, that bobbed amid the fringe. The carriage driver's coarseness had reminded Youssef that he was not the leading man in a movie but the would-be seducer of a girl he had always liked.

She put her hand over his. "Don't touch it. There is no evil here. Not with us. Not ever."

He released the bead but kept her hand in his. Her words ripped stitches from the seam of his pleasure. "Evil?" His tone was harsh. "What do you know of evil? A little girl like you."

He had put her back in her place. She felt like flouncing out of the carriage and letting him be as sullen as he seemed to want to be. But the braver part of Mona, the Mona who would be a healer, could not give up so easily. So she wasn't a fine lady. Youssef might not like it—or her, if she did this—but she would risk all and be firm with him. It might mean that he would not want her as his lover, but she would at least be his true friend. "I have known you, and loved you, for many years," she said softly. "And I think that you, too, know nothing of evil."

"You don't know me." Moodily he hit the Evil Eye bead until it danced. "You don't know me at all. No one does."

She turned her eyes resolutely out at the little of Alexandria the calèche cocoon allowed her to see. She studied withered palm trees flanked by leafless sycamores. At home in Karnak it was always summer, but here a gale wind blew. Inside the carriage, Youssef's cold hand over hers, she waited patiently for him to tell her more. On the city side of the Corniche she gazed at prudently shuttered cafés whose sidewalk seats were stacked elsewhere until spring. Outside Youssef's side of the carriage, Mona knew the sea would be black and cold and restless. She was beginning to examine the rows of villas on her side of the sea drive—the Greek pillars, the French facades, the Italian balconies—when Youssef finally broke the silence.

"I am nothing, nothing at all. *Mafeesh*—nothing. All I am is a shell. I smile and I laugh. I say what I'm supposed to say. But inside, *mafeesh*. I am like a wooden doll, painted on the outside but hollow inside. Or even one of those eggs that the Copts paint at Easter." He laughed, and his voice cracked. "You know what they do with those eggs? They suck out the insides! I am like that. Like that, Mona."

She was surer than ever that he needed her. "If all that is true, how is it that I love you?"

He gave the Evil Eye totem a savage punch. "You must be a fool. Or perhaps you don't love me at all. It's one or the other."

"Then I must be a fool, because I do love you." She disengaged her hand from his and took his head in both her hands. "Look at me, Youssef al-Masri."

Staring at her, he wished that he could steal for himself the gentleness that was in her eyes. That desire, too, filled him with despair. Seize it, steal it—is there no end to my destruction?

"You are not evil, Youssef. You are not empty. You are kind and good. I know that. *Batata* knew that. It is because of Batata, I think, that you feel this way, isn't it?"

His lower lip turned white as he bit it hard.

She decided to veer away from Batata for the moment. "I remember the first time you touched me. On the beach at Agami. When you saved me. Do you remember that, Youssef?"

He nodded dumbly.

"You were so kind to me. You are always kind." She stroked his cheek. "You always looked out for all of us. You made Daoud feel he wasn't clumsy. You made me feel that I was special. You told me I was like the moon. Like the moon, Youssef!"

He smiled at the memory of those golden days and nights at Agami.

She returned to what she sensed was the crux. "Batata loved you most of all. You made Batata happy. Someone who is empty inside cannot give so much to everyone else."

"Is that so? But Mona, I killed Batata! Me! It was my fault. All my fault."

"It was Allah's will, Youssef. The trolley killed Batata. Do you think that you are so important, so powerful, that everything happens because of you? You think both too much and yet far too little of your own worth."

"What?" There was the scent of absolution in her words, yet he could not quite breathe it in or believe it. "What did you say?"

She tried to keep her voice steady as she fought down the desire to cradle his head on her breasts. Had Ummie ever felt like this with her? She remembered her mother rocking her on the day of her circumcision. Yes, it had once been just so with her and her mother. Mona took a deep breath. "You're blind to the things that you do to make everyone happy. You refuse to take responsibility for your generosity and your goodness, as though none of that has anything to do with you. And yet you persist, at the same time, in having the nerve to think that you are responsible for everything bad that happens to any of us. As though Youssef al-Masri were Allah Himself! It was God's will that Batata die as he did. Not yours, Youssef. Even if you want to take on the burdens of Allah, it would not be possible. You are merely a man. The man that I love."

His face was somber. He could not quite believe what she said about God. But he could finally believe at least part of what she said. "You really do love me."

"Yes."

He lifted a handful of her heavy hair and tried to feel each strand. He wanted to know everything and to touch every part of this woman who had looked without disgust at what he had told her was inside him. He wanted to be just as she had insisted he was. He took her hand. If he spoke his wish out loud, it would make it so. "I love you. Truly I do. For now and for always." He put his arm around her and felt awed. She leaned her head on his shoulder and felt safe. They listened to hoofbeats on the cobblestones and breathed in the sharp clear air. It was from this moment in the calèche along the Corniche that they were to date their romance.

They sat with the motor running and the heater turned to high, looking out at the winter wasteland of Agami Beach. Above the horizon silver stars lit the dark sky.

"Tell me again, Mona." Youssef cupped her chin in his hand. "Tell me again about the stars you used to see in Karnak."

Always Youssef wanted to hear about her other life in the village. He was aghast that Mona's own grandmother had been murdered for buying a pack of cigarettes. He was spellbound over the bloodfeud that had cost Uncle Muhammad his leg. He loved to make her catalogue all the ways in which the Nile gave not only her whole village but her entire Said its life. And the stars. Always he asked her about the stars.

"The Karnak stars? They were like your eyes, Youssef."

He kissed her. *"Bi ainaya,"* he murmured. "You are my eyes."

She sighed. She had taught him that Arabic sweet nothing: *bi ainaya,* you are as dear to me as my eyes.

In the past two months they had been creeping off together whenever they could. At first their seclusion was the same as that of any new lovers, for their world was composed only of themselves and what they were beginning to build. Sharing it with outsiders might have degraded it. It was better to create their own universe of two. It was enough just to be together both in the flesh and also in the most hidden recesses of the mind and heart. They lived not only for their hours together but for their hours apart, turning over and over again what he had said and how she had smiled. Each word, each look, each kiss, was hugged to the heart until it took on a mythic glow. *This,* Youssef and Mona repeated over and over, is what life is all about. This is all that matters. This and nothing else.

But in time the world had intruded. Although they would still not admit it to each other, there was necessity as well as choice in their secrecy. If no one discovered their romance, then no one could cut it short. They also had to consider Mona's reputation. Who would ever believe that a rich playboy would court a poor nurse for any but one reason? Most nights, therefore, they made do with driving aimlessly and parking in Youssef's car. At first that winter, eager to know and tell all to this perfect other half, they talked more than they touched.

From Youssef poured first confessions, then confidences, finally dreams. He told her about his father's humiliation on the steps of the Cotton Exchange and how the boys at Victoria had hissed at him. He told her about the girl he had run down and how he had thrown away his hours on belly dancers and lost hashish nights. Listening with grave absolution, she would stroke his hair as if there were balm in her fingertips. In time he progressed to what, besides Mona, he wanted from life. He hated his father's business. Instead, he discovered even as he said the words, he wanted to use his life to right wrongs. He could be a lawyer. He could do his part to see that what had happened with that *baladi* girl's family in the courtroom would never happen again. They decided together that Youssef would brush up on his classical Arabic, enroll in the law academy, and in time become a respected Alexandrian attorney. Although Youssef went so far as to leaf through an advanced Arabic grammar every so often, he never forced himself to buckle down to serious study. He preferred to dream of marrying Mona and having many children. The first little boy they would call Batata.

Mona, too, tried to tell Youssef what she told herself was everything. She had surprised herself by crying over her father's death, for she had thought her father had not mattered much to her. More hesitantly she answered his questions about her mother. Vaguely Youssef remembered a fat old woman in black mopping his family's floors. He could not reconcile that image with the picture Mona painted of her mother. She would insist on telling him, over and over with great intensity, that she loved her mother very, very much. Youssef would try to lighten her mood by tickling her until she would vow that she loved him even more than she loved her mother. But sometimes, when he caught her stroking her blue bead, he would wonder. Sometimes he sensed that there were more mysteries to Mona.

But this night he was content to hold her in his arms until he was struck by an inspiration. "The Said! That's it! We'll go there for our honeymoon. We'll hire a felucca and sail from Luxor to Aswan! We'll be like Caesar and Cleopatra. After all, I'm Italian, like Caesar. And you're more beautiful than Cleopatra."

She drew a little apart. *"There?* You want to go to Karnak?"

"Of course I want to go to Karnak!"

She frowned. It wasn't only that Youssef wouldn't fit in the village. Ummie was in Karnak. Mona had begun to worry, as the first wondrous glow of her romance wore into a steady burnished gleam, about what her mother would finally say about Youssef. Ummie had instructed her to sink her teeth into a rich man, not to fall crazily in love with an infidel. Riches weren't the problem. Religion was. Now that she had Youssef, she wasn't certain what she was going to be able to do with him. Muslims and Jews didn't marry. "But Youssef. I thought you were going to show me the world when we get married. London. Paris. The pistachio nuts of Athens." She laughed.

He lit a cigarette. "I can't." In October and again in November the Israelis had successfully attacked outposts along the Egyptian border. In December, fifty-six Syrians had died when the Israelis retaliated for harassment of fishing boats on Lake Galilee. Arab *fedayeen* raids and anger against Israel were mounting. "Jews still can't leave."

There it was again. Yet from a mutual desire not to hurt the other, they never came closer than this to the chasm. Mona, with determined gaiety, told him her mother had always wanted to marry her off to a rich man so that the entire clan—"maybe even the chickens and the donkey"—could come to the city to live.

Youssef didn't answer. He assumed, of course, that Mona's mother would jump at the chance for their marriage. It was Youssef's conceit that only his own parents would object. Someday soon, Youssef reminded himself, he would have to face his father and mother and the truth.

"Ummie will be coming soon." Mona stared moodily into space. Waves of sickness had kept her mother away from Alexandria for two years, but still those letters had arrived every fortnight. "She says she can't wait until summer to see me."

Youssef stubbed out his cigarette. There was one sure way to short-circuit Mona's gloom. He put his arm around her. "I think we should call the second boy Baruch."

"And if it's a girl?"

"We could call her Ghazzela—Gazelle. After you."

They kissed until the windshield steamed out the night.

Um Mona's black eyes swept over her daughter after their first embrace in the kitchen. Something is different, Um Mona thought as she noted eyes that did not quite meet hers. Something has happened.

Mona, trying hard not to believe that Ummie could still read her thoughts, busied herself bringing her mother and uncle tea and cakes and settling them into the best chairs in the kitchen. As she worked around them, she chattered about her new studies with Dr. Baruch, the rainy weather, Uncle Muhammad's marriage, how terrible it was that Ummie had lost all her teeth after some epidemic or other had swept Karnak.

Um Mona watched her shrewdly. Mechanically she lifted cakes from her hand to her mouth, sucking the honeyed sweets until they could be swallowed as easily as mother's milk. When Mona had exhausted her news, Um Mona watched her daughter shift on the hard seat of her wooden stool. Finally she sent Muhammad away and allowed Mona to squirm awhile in the silence. At last Um Mona went fishing. "Is that all, *habibti?* Is that *all* that has happened?"

Mona gulped and looked her mother in the eye.

Um Mona pursed her lips. It was a boy. She knew it had to be a boy. And Mona did not want to tell her about it, so it was a boy she wouldn't approve. Probably some hot-eyed servant or a dashing *zabal,* one of those garbage collectors who rode in his donkey cart as if he were a desert prince. It was high time she arranged for Mona's marriage. Um Mona wished for a moment that she hadn't untied Mona's legs after her circumcision. Perhaps those Nubians knew what they were doing when they sewed up their daughters. She would have to make do with words instead of ropes. "You remember, *habibti,* when we used to play together in the village?" She smiled a gummy smile.

Mona made herself grin as if at a happy memory.

"I used to tell you stories. And you would laugh and laugh." Um Mona forced a laugh. "And then I would get a candle and we would light it and watch it burn. And so often the moths would come and circle the flame . . . closer, closer, until at last one of them couldn't resist, flew too close, and was burned to a crisp. Do you remember what we would say then, Mona?"

"Fire is better than shame," Mona chanted slowly, in the voice of a very little girl. "Fire is better than shame."

Um Mona nodded. "And do you remember what that meant?"

"It is better for a woman to die like that moth than to bring shame to her family." Mona spoke as if she was in a trance.

"Kwayes. Kwayes awi, Mona—very good."

Although Um Mona kept her sharp eye on Mona during the remainder of her visit, she could not discover which boy Mona fancied. Mona, even as she passed Youssef terse notes that they must be most careful while Ummie was in the villa, did not allow herself to consider the implications of her desire to keep Youssef under wraps. She told herself only that it was premature to share her secret with Ummie.

Meanwhile Um Mona tried to set the wheels of Mona's marriage in motion. Baruch and Abbas, as Mona's informal guardians, listened with anger and amusement while the peasant woman told them again what sort of son-in-law she expected. But for Mona's sake, Baruch and Abbas politely endured the old woman's demands. They both heaved sighs of relief when she finally returned for another year in the Said. In the summer, in the fall, they would begin to be matchmakers. Mona had just turned fifteen.

Mona and Youssef sat restless and tense, huddled miserably against their separate doors in the car. From where they were parked outside the cabaret they could hear tantalizing music and laughter. Their clandestine courtship was nearly a year old, and by now Youssef's convertible was an open-air prison.

All year they had done their best to keep their hands off each other. Trying to kiss with reverence, they assured each other that their aim was still an honorable life together. Youssef was clear, firm, and absolutely committed to the theory that he would never do anything to hurt his Mona. He had sampled sex with the belly dancers. What he wanted from Mona was more lasting. And yet he had made no move to publicize their engagement.

Waiting now wearily for Youssef to tell his parents, Mona lived and dreamed doubts. Just after her mother's visit, she had once again begun to be haunted by those old nightmares of floating in the Nile, of sinking in the embrace of a blond naked man, of glimpsing a bloated body on the crest of the river. Often when Youssef kissed her, she would push him away.

They debated whether they were lucky or not that things were as they were in Egypt that year. With all the momentous news on the minds of their elders, their romance had gone undetected. In January President Nasser had unveiled a new constitution that for the first time defined Egypt as an *Arab* nation committed to socialist reforms. Soviet arms were arriving in Alexandria and—after another deadly Israeli border raid—the Cairo newspapers began to chant that only an Eastern Bloc alliance could checkmate the Israelis. In February the World Bank had pledged to lend Egypt two hundred million dollars to construct a mammoth new High Dam at Aswan, and not long after Nasser was trying to use that offer to tease an even better one from the Russians. In May, to the growing annoyance of the Western powers, Nasser bestowed diplomatic recognition on Communist China. In June the last despised British troops honored their treaty and evacuated their Suez garrisons. But in July the Egyptian bubble burst. The West withdrew its promised aid for the High Dam, and the Russians admitted that they, too, had no immediate plans to finance it. What happened then on the twenty-sixth of July in Alexandria—in a speech Nasser delivered precisely four years, to the hour, that King Faruk had departed Egypt—galvanized the nation. Nasser nationalized the Suez Canal. Egypt would use its canal receipts to build its own High

Dam. That night Mona and Youssef braved the crowds and danced on the Corniche. But newspapers in London and Paris branded Nasser a "new Hitler" and an "insolent thief." Even Baruch began to be worried by a world that seemed to be lurching out of control.

Sitting in his car beside Mona, Youssef's mind was not on politics. Noble sentiments were in his heart and on his lips, but the summer heat had begun to creep under his skin. It would have been easier for him to stick to his resolves if his and Mona's world had been wider than the sultry front seat of his car. If only they could eat ice cream at Pastroudi's, hold hands at San Stefano's outdoor cinema, gad about to horseraces and parties! Instead, he would stare at her skirts tucked tight around the swell of her thighs. She would look everywhere but at the bulge in his trousers. Night after night they parked along the Corniche or out by the salt marshes, listening to the crickets and the buzz of the mosquitoes. With the heavy air weighing against them, they ran out of confidences. It was a season for touch and sensation, not for the quoting of tender little snatches of poetry. Often Youssef would snap at Mona and then cram his key in the ignition and roar her home. Sometimes she made excuses not to see him.

Youssef, squirming in his seat in the nightclub parking lot, finally couldn't stop himself from pulling Mona roughly against him and kissing her as he had once kissed her on the Corniche stairs.

She let him take her lips. But then when he moved his tongue inside her ear and then bit her hard on her neck, she felt dizzy. Fire is better than shame, she thought almost clearly. Fire is better than shame. She pushed him away. When he lunged for her again, she scrambled out of the car. "I'm a good girl." Fear made her haughty. "Do you think I'm one of your belly dancers?"

Stung, he leaped out of the car and strode past her toward the casino.

"Youssef? Youssef! Where are you going?"

"Inside. Where I belong. With Shu-Shu, belly dancer *extraordinaire*."

She waited for him in the car for an hour and a half before she finally walked home and cried herself to sleep.

Mona endured Youssef's ignoring her for two weeks before, in desperation, she turned to magic to get him back.

By then Youssef's love bite on her neck had faded so that she no longer had to hide it with scarves and high collars. She had been sorry to see Youssef's mark on her flesh disappear. Her days had been heavy and empty, and her nights had been long and lonely. Without Youssef she had been blank, inside and out. She had regretted ever coming to Alexandria. Pacing back and forth in her room, she had decided first to pack her bags and return to Karnak, then to stay and fight for Youssef. He had been taking his meals on a tray in his room to avoid her, but one day she had cornered him in the upstairs hallway. Although she had thrown herself in his arms and ground up against him like a belly dancer, he had pushed her away. This red-eyed stranger who reeked of hashish and whiskey hadn't even *looked* like her Youssef. Still she had not accepted that it was over. She had written him notes he never acknowledged. She had wished she could have cast off all she had learned in Alexandria and danced out her frenzy as she had sometimes seen the women of Karnak dance. She had wanted to tear at her hair and howl at the moon.

Instead, one steamy afternoon when everyone in the Villa al-Masri was fast asleep, she went out to buy a love charm. She wove through the alleys of a *baladi* quarter looking for the old *shaykha* who had been recommended by the hospital nurses. She found the *shaykha* squatting on her hanuches in a tattered robe on a tenement stoop. Mona wrinkled her nose and almost faltered and ran home. But then she reminded herself she had no real home. No one—certainly not Ummie, probably not even Baruch—would understand. She didn't need Baruch's sick little atoms and electrons. What she had to have was Youssef. No one ever had to know about this love charm.

When she blurted out what she wanted, the old hag laughed and pointed to Mona's breasts. "If *they* can't get you who you want, how can I? Can I make water flow from trees?"

Mona ignored the taunt and held out a one-pound note. The *shaykha* tucked the money inside her robe and ordered Mona to bring hairs from the head of the man she wanted.

The next afternoon, when Mona returned with some golden hairs collected from the front seat of Youssef's car, the *shaykha* looked at Mona with pity. "No. Go away. You don't want the love of a *huwaga*."

Mona gritted her teeth and handed over fifty piasters more.

Still the *shaykha* hesitated. "This charm will bind the two of you together for life. Take care. Once I weave it, it cannot ever be broken." When Mona impatiently pressed ten more piasters on her, the old woman shrugged. "So be it."

She led Mona inside to her lair. They sat cross-legged on the dirt floor of a cubbyhole under a flight of stairs. Mona could hear a baby wailing nearby and, from farther away, the sad beat of a drum. The *shaykha* squiggled ink inside twelve tiny boxes on a square of paper. With the flourish of a few more curlicues, she added the names of Leah al-Masri and Um Mona. There is, the *shaykha* explained, true magic flowing in the blood and the milk of mothers. No charm, she said, can ever be potent without the seal of mothers. For the miracle of birth, she added, carries the seeds of love and death. The old woman spit on the charm, stuck Youssef's hairs to it, muttered a few more mysterious words, and bade Mona hide the charm somewhere near where this blond *huwaga* slept. Mona kissed the *shaykha*'s hands, and running back to the villa, she told herself she had gone too far now for retreat.

But she nearly lost her nerve when she sneaked into Youssef's empty bedroom that night. What could have possessed her, she wondered, to believe that spittle and hairs and mothers' names could have anything to do with the fineness of herself and Youssef? It was only when the unmade bed reminded her Youssef was probably off with one of those lewd dancers that she stuffed the love charm inside his pillowcase. She dreamed that night that Leah al-Masri held her in her arms on the day of her circumcision, and that Youssef's mother laughed at her pleas to unbind her legs.

On his eighteenth day away from Mona—he knew he must have been keeping an unconscious count, for he did not have to consult a calendar to know how long it had been—Youssef awoke with a thudding hang-over. He lay in bed, sick at the thought of another false minute of a morning without Mona. He had frittered away the time apart in an unhappy blur. Nights he had spent in a hashish haze, drinking whiskey and weaving his way through that summer's crop of belly dancers. He had told himself this one had a smile like Mona's and that one could almost pass for her if he were dumb and deaf and blind. Days he had nursed his aching head and despised himself. Yet sometimes he had felt elated that he had broken away from the constraints of Mona's love. It had been so damn hard to be the man Mona thought him to be. It was so much easier just to let go and no longer try to be what he wasn't. Besides, in a way it was for Mona's own good that he had ended it. She deserved better than what he was. He had tried to forget that scene she had staged in the hallway. He had told himself she would get over him in time.

But, lying in bed on this eighteenth day apart, Youssef had to admit that hashish and whiskey and all those lies he had been telling himself had not altered the fact that he loved her. Remembering Baruch's words from that backgammon summer, Youssef decided that he *could* choose to be a man of action. It wouldn't be easy, but he would marry Mona. He knew there would be ugly scenes with his parents. He would do his best to win them over. And even if worst came to worst and they refused to give in, he would marry Mona anyway. He would live his life with Mona. And *that* would be *that*. His head cleared and he smiled. All of a sudden he was very hungry. He found Mona alone at the breakfast table.

Their reconciliation was silent and quick. He smiled at her from the doorway. She smiled back. They fell into each other's arms.

"Will you marry me?" he asked when they drew apart.

"Yes. Yes." She kissed his eyes, his nose, his chin. She must, she thought, never tell him about that love charm. She wished she could believe that Youssef had come to her on his own. She would just have to live with the knowledge that—Allah!—something dark had brought him back to her. "Yes."

"We'll have to ask—no, *tell*—my parents. And your mother, Mona."

She looked away, wishing there were some sort of potion she could slip her mother.

"Don't worry." He stroked back her hair from her forehead. "We're magic, Mona. Magic."

First they tried to enlist Baruch to their cause. They swept him off to lunch that very afternoon in the garden of the fashionable Beau Rivage hotel. While Youssef and Baruch chatted amiably about what Nasser's seizure of the Suez Canal might mean to Rafael's business, Mona looked from the goldfish swimming in the plaster pond to the chic men and women at the tables. This was her first time at the Beau Rivage. Except for the tall black Nubian waiters, she was the only Egyptian in sight. How scandalous, she thought, the people back in her village would find all these women mixing so brazenly with men. The sun glinted on gold jewelry and caught the shine of lipstick. These foreign women all looked so alike with their sleek hairdos, their pale dresses, their carelessly held cigarettes. Someday, Mona thought, I'll have to learn to look like them. Guiltily she remembered her trip to the *shaykha* for the love charm. Could that have led so easily to this?

Youssef leaned over and took her hand in his. "Uncle Baruch, I . . . we . . . have something to tell you."

Their grilled shrimps had arrived. *"Crevettes,"* Baruch said. "Nowhere in the world are there shrimps like this." Expertly he skinned one of its shell and took a bite.

"Uncle Baruch? Mona and I want to—are going to—get married."

Baruch bit a shrimp down to its tail. "Married? What did you say?"

"I said I want to marry Mona."

Baruch frowned.

"Mona and I are in love. We want to get married."

Mona smiled at Baruch. "We wanted to tell you first."

Baruch blushed and put down his knife and fork. Mona and Youssef? He looked from one to the other. It could not be. Mona wasn't old enough. Youssef wasn't good enough. He picked up his napkin to clean the spectacles with which he apparently had been unable to see what was in front of his nose. "How long has this been going on?" he finally asked.

"Since we were children," Youssef answered. The two of them laughed.

"So," Baruch said. "So." He looked at the two young people he loved best, holding hands in front of him with their faces hopeful and their eyes alight. He felt very foolish. He had thought, he had hoped . . . he was embarrassed at what he had thought and hoped. He tried to smile and hear them out as though he had no anxious emotional stake in this matter.

"Then you agree," Youssef pressed. "You agree?"

Baruch was solemn. "You're sure? You're absolutely sure?"

"I love Mona. I want her to be my wife. I want her to be the mother of my children. She will be my wife, my lover, my friend, my sister, my mother, my daughter. She will be—is—everything to me."

Baruch frowned at Youssef's pretty speech. "And you, Mona?

She was demure. She whispered to her plate of shrimps that she would always love Youssef.

"So it is like that." Baruch sighed. Once he and Daisy had spoken so to their parents. Oh, probably he had been more measured than Youssef. Daisy certainly had been more sure of herself than Mona. But still, it had been like this. Baruch blinked back tears and told himself it was better not to dwell on what he had lost. He tried to rid his mind of sentiment. Daisy and he had both been Jews. They had grown up attending the same schools, belonging to the same clubs, renting cabanas on the same beaches. "You know," he began, "that I want nothing but happiness for each of you."

Youssef kissed Mona on the cheek. "See! I told you Uncle Baruch would understand!"

It hurt Baruch to watch them together. Why in God's name had they made him their confidant? "I wish, Youssef, that it were that easy." He also wished that his errant nephew had left Mona alone. Mona was Baruch's own treasure. Why, of all the fair young girls in Alexandria, had Youssef stolen *her*? He couldn't imagine a more mismatched pair. He doubted if either of them was tough enough to withstand the forces that would be arrayed against them. They were both too sensitive and dreamy. But he supposed that was why he loved them both so much. Like it or not, it would now be his unpleasant task to try to bring them down to harsh reality. He chose his words with care. "The marriage you propose would not be easy. Marriage between a Jew and a Muslim is at best unusual. You must realize that neither your parents, Youssef, nor your mother, Mona, will be . . . overjoyed."

"I don't care." Youssef held Mona's hand more tightly. "That's *their* problem."

"Unfortunately," Baruch said, "I'm afraid it will be your problem, too. And there's something else. I hate to say this, Mona, but my brother and sister-in-law will object to your background. They would, in any case, probably balk at Youssef's wanting to marry any Egyptian, any Muslim, even a member of the former royal family. But Mona's a Saidi *fellaha*."

Mona flushed.

"She's the woman that I love. Nothing else matters. I *will* marry her."

Baruch sighed again. "I didn't say you can't. I just think you shouldn't delude yourselves. Think about how your parents are likely to react, Youssef. Are you willing to subject Mona to what they'll probably say? Are you willing to fight it out?"

Youssef shot back a challenge of his own. "Are you willing to help?"

Mona turned her eyes to Baruch. "Will you, Baba?"

She had never called him "father" before. He took a deep breath and gave in. Someone had to help these two innocents. "I will do what I can." They all smiled, and then Baruch picked up his knife and fork to attack the shrimps. "Eat." He swallowed his misgivings. "No sense in facing Abbas, Leah, and Rafael on an empty stomach."

The three of them went directly from the Beau Rivage to Abbas's kitchen. The *suffragi*'s first reaction was a quick shy smile for Mona. But then he turned his back and fumbled with the teapot on the stove. When he faced them again, he was impassive. "We will drink and talk." He was frank as he paced back and forth. Mona was a Muslim. Youssef was a Jew. A Muslim could not marry a Jew. That was *haram,* forbidden, absolutely forbidden. It was especially impossible for a Muslim girl to marry a man of another faith—Christian or Jew, it did not matter—because then, of course, the woman's religion would grow weaker as she fell under the sway of the man's persuasions. Abbas was courteous but most firm. Mona would never get his blessing.

Baruch asked if Abbas was speaking for Mona's mother.

"Of course. No Muslim would ever agree to such a marriage. It is against the words of Allah as revealed to the Prophet Muhammad in the holy Koran, as well as the Traditions and Shariah law. I'm sorry. Very sorry."

Baruch, Youssef, and Mona filed out of the kitchen. Baruch had hoped for more ambivalence from Abbas. Mona had prayed that Abbas would understand. Youssef couldn't get used to the idea of having to ask one of the servants for permission to take anything, let alone his heart's desire. They decided, however, that they would proceed that very night to sound out Leah and Rafael.

That afternoon was long and unlucky. Baruch was bitten on the leg by a poodle belonging to one of his rich patients. Mona broke a needle while she was giving an injection. Youssef signed the wrong requisition order and, to Rafael's fury, sent half a warehouseful of cotton to a dock where there was no ship. Even Abbas burned the roast.

But at last it was time for the family conference Baruch had called in the main salon. Rafael sat on the sofa with Suker in his lap. Leah drummed her long fingernails on the arm of her chair. Finally Baruch led Youssef and Mona into the room.

Leah looked up in surprise, wondering what Mona was doing in the drawing room. Then, by habit, Leah examined the skin under Mona's eyes. Lately, since those terrible blue circles had appeared under Leah's eyes, she had been unable to stop herself from looking for those same marks on every other female. Mona unfortunately had no dark circles. Leah frowned and then hastily composed her face so as not to make any more wrinkles. With envy the older woman noted the soft, uncracked dewiness of Mona's skin. My skin used to be like that, she thought. She stroked her cheek with a finger and felt dry and parched, inside and out.

Youssef came right to the point. "It is time that I marry." He smiled at Mona. "I am twenty-three."

"You *are?*" Rafael stopped petting the dog and told himself he should pay more attention to his family.

"Twenty-three is not so old." Nor, Leah told herself, was forty-six. Not if you took care of yourself.

Youssef plunged ahead. "I am here to ask your blessing. Mona and I want to get married soon. Very soon. We love each other."

"What?" Rafael stared at Youssef.

"I want to marry Mona."

"Is this a joke?" Leah asked acidly. "One of your stupid jokes, Baruch?"

"I'm afraid not, Leah."

Rafael was cold but courtly. Anger usually made him try to act as he thought an English gentleman would act. "It was *so* kind of you, Mona, to come here tonight. But now, if you will excuse us, I think we would like to talk to our son alone."

"Mona stays," Youssef said.

"She certainly does," Leah said. "That one just stays and stays. Even after her welcome has long ago been worn out. Even after Batata—"

Baruch cut her off. "I think, Youssef, that your father has a point. Do you want to subject Mona to any more of this?"

"I suppose not."

When Mona left the room with her head bowed, they all began shouting at once. "Quiet!" Baruch was louder than any of them. "Just for a moment, *please.*" He ignored their sullen looks. "Now. Let's try to talk about this rationally. Youssef wants to marry Mona. Mona wants to marry Youssef. They are in love. They know each other well—"

"Probably *very* well," Leah snorted.

Baruch warned Youssef with a wave of his hand not to talk back to his mother. "Youssef is acting honorably. Your son deserves a more civil reception from both of you."

Rafael nodded. "Very well, Baruch." He enunciated each of his words distinctly. "My eldest son will never marry a Muslim. Their children, as we all know, would not be Jews, for our religion begins in the womb of the mother. I would never permit such a match. Never. That is final and unequivocable. It is against God's law."

"The rabbi speaks." Even now, Leah could not resist jibing him.

Rafael's manners slipped. "Would you have our son marry a filthy

Arab?" A blue blood vessel at his temple was throbbing. "The scum who murdered our boy? Our little Zvi?"

"Of course not. The idea," Leah said, "is preposterous. Youssef married to a servant? Hardly."

"Quite. In this at least we agree." Rafael had regained his composure when he turned crisply back to Youssef. "Now look, son. You're young. A little wild. You are, after all, your mother's son. The girl, I admit, is a beauty. If you want her, take her. But let's not hear any more rot about marriage."

"I want to marry Mona. And I will. Whether you like it or not."

"That will be *all*, Youssef," Rafael said. "I forbid any further discussion of this matter. Now, would you be so kind as to leave your parents in peace for a moment? Go run off behind the back stairs with your pretty little tart. I think your mother and I want some words with my dear brother."

Youssef caught Baruch's pointed look. He slammed the door on his way out.

"I suppose, Baruch, that you've encouraged this?" Rafael looked at his brother with distaste. "One of your experiments in learning to love the Arabs, I presume?"

"I was as surprised as you are. But since you ask, I did give them my blessing. They're in love. Really in love. Don't the two of you remember what that felt like?"

Leah laughed bleakly. "Did we ever feel that, Monsieur al-Masri?"

Rafael looked suddenly older than his years. He ignored her question and instead reached for the dog.

"What do you expect these two young people to do?" Baruch persisted.

Rafael smiled thinly as he stroked the dog. "The same things all the rest of us do."

Leah got up and poured herself a drink.

ALEXANDRIA, EGYPT   /   October 1956

A few minutes' walk but a world away from the Villa al-Masri, Abbas threaded his way across the street from his home to the coffeehouse. At nine o'clock on this Thursday, the eve of the day of rest, the street swarmed with life. Young Arab men strolled arm in arm, a merchant in a striped robe lounged against a cigarette kiosk, other men filled every chair on the walkway outside the coffeehouse. Little boys played war games with sticks while a radio blared snatches of foot-tapping music. From a pushcart a peddler hawked the winter's first dates. A small boy hustled across the street holding aloft a tin tray packed tight with lukewarm glasses of tea. On the corner the smiling *cusharey* man ladled steaming gobs of rice and macaroni and hot pepper sauce onto flat stone plates. Most of the shops were still open, their bare electric bulbs casting pools of yellow light into the night. Old women were lined up at the government food shop, a widow haggled with the spiceman over the price of a handful of saffron, and in the shadows an ancient squatted with his lapful of tiny lemons for sale. The butcher had sold out his dripping hunks of meat well before noon, but the bloody sawdust outside his shop still drew packs of dogs. Bent over their ironing boards, the *muquaggis* spit mouthfuls of water onto faded blue and white and striped *gallabeiyas*. No women of childbearing age walked the streets, but on a flat rooftop clapping women squatted while a little girl practiced wiggling her belly. In Arab Iskandria, it was a night like every other night.

Abbas settled himself into his usual chair, called out to a waiter, and then looked up through a broken window to his flat. Yes, Mona was still there watching him. The morning after she and Youssef had declared their love, Abbas had packed her up and moved her from the Villa al-Masri to his own home. He had called Youssef a yellow-haired devil and given her the choice of either marrying a Muslim he selected or returning on the next train south to Karnak. Mona had finally chosen to stay. Days she worked under Baruch's close supervision, and nights she lit candles and wept and stood by the window watching Abbas interview her suitors.

For a moment Abbas stared back at Mona. She was as dear to him as a daughter. He would have acted precisely as he was acting for a child of his own flesh. For her he wanted a loving husband, bellyfuls of children, the security of a predictable life. But he couldn't help dropping his eyes and fiddling guiltily with his coffee. It was not so long ago that he had been young and had had his own dreams. Life, he sighed to himself, was difficult. To avoid Mona's stare, he looked up at the toothy picture of President Nasser tacked to a place of honor in a burst of patriotism following the nationalization of the Suez Canal. Abbas thought that Nasser, too, might represent a dream that would not quite come true. Since July, not only in Egypt but in Britain, France, and most of the diplomatic capitals of the world, the Canal takeover had become a crisis. From listening to Rafael rage that the West would never acquiesce to losing control of the Canal, Abbas had begun to worry about whether his countrymen had begun to celebrate their great victory over imperialism too soon. Opposite Nasser on another wall was a faded color portrait of the exiled King Faruk. As Abbas interviewed prospective husbands for hours at a time, his elbows resting wearily on the tin-topped table before him, he would look from this new image of the president to the old image of the king and wonder if Nasser's days of glory, too, were numbered.

Abbas brought himself back to the business at hand. Mona needed a husband to blot out that impossible Youssef. Abbas personally escorted her to and from Baruch's office each day, and Khadiga guarded her at night. But he couldn't keep Mona indefinitely under surveillance. Abbas had begun the husband-hunting within his own family. No brothers were currently single, and Abbas had politely demurred when one of them offered to divorce his wife as a special favor. His pious nephew Hesham was the first serious suitor. To save enough to buy his own taxi, Hesham held down jobs as both a hotel porter and a restaurant busboy. Ordinarily Abbas might have bethrothed Mona to him now and married her off as soon as Hesham saved up enough for his taxi and a suitable brideprice. But with that al-Masri devil lurking in the background, Abbas had turned down his nephew with regret.

To screen the neighborhood's marriageable men, Abbas had set up shop in this very coffeehouse that was owned by the husband of his old maid Fatima. Their marriage had turned out well, Abbas thought as he sipped his sweet black coffee and listened to the usual hubbub around him: the click of the wooden backgammon tokens, the rise and fall of the same old conversations about money and work, the singsong drone of an old man reciting verses of the Koran. Fatima had five girls and two boys. Abbas hoped he could do as well for Mona.

Abbas held high cards in this particular marriage suit. Mona was known to be very pretty and—*el-hamdulillah!*—was still thought to be virtuous. She could read and write, she could speak French, and the more enlightened men of this quarter did not hold her work as a nurse against her. Every man in the coffeehouse had at least a relative who had been interested in marrying Mona. Keeping in mind Um Mona's demand for a prosperous husband, Abbas had nevertheless turned down a prominent baker because he had never seen him praying at the mosque. He had rejected a wealthy hashish merchant out of hand. He had touched off a long, heated debate in the coffeehouse when he had refused to consider one of his fellow *suffragis* who already had two wives. Many of the men had divorced at least one wife, but few had more than one spouse at once. Still, most of them liked to gloat over the prospect that one day they might. Young and old had eagerly tossed contradictory Koran quotes like dice on the tables, debating the religious theory—although not their lustful interest—in this matter. But Abbas had not budged from his position. The Koran said a man could take as many as four wives only if he treated all his wives as perfect equals. That, Abbas had always insisted, was an impossibility.

At one point Abbas was so serious about a decent, balding barber that he had sent Khadiga to work talking to the man's neighbors about his habits and character. But the suit foundered when Baruch wouldn't agree to marry Mona to a man who couldn't read or write. It was only after Abbas threatened to send Mona back to Karnak that Baruch had promised to be more reasonable.

Abbas looked up as a plump middle-aged man in a police lieutenant's uniform came through the door. Hamuda el-Salem was a cousin of the grocer on the corner. He prayed often and publicly, he reportedly never touched a bribe, and he had recently been widowed. His age, his stability, and his public standing weighed in his favor. Mona needed a man strong enough to erase Youssef's memory. The responsibility of raising Hamuda's two children would be good for the girl. Abbas liked, too, Hamuda's gentle good humor and that paunch which bulged over his belt. Hamuda would love a good woman just as he so obviously loved good food. Surely Mona, too, in time could learn to love this man. Abbas rose gravely to his feet, smiled as wide as President Nasser, and saluted Hamuda el-Salem. The marriage might be arranged, *inshallah,* by the first of the year.

It was a week later, and explosions cut the night. A sound truck screeched in the street. But although the floor of the flat shuddered with the impact of the British bombing nearby at the harbor, Mona sat listlessly in Abbas's parlor. She hardly cared that three days ago Israel had invaded Sinai and that last night the British had destroyed the Egyptian air force on the ground. War or peace, invasion or independence, she pined only for Youssef.

In her hands were the matches and the half-gutted candle she was about to light, as she did every night, before she stretched out on the sofa. She looked around her bedroom, her harem, her prison. The undersized room, like every other prosperous *baladi* household, was cluttered by oversized furniture. There was barely enough room to walk between the sofa covered in cabbage-rose chintz and the six red velveteen gilt chairs and the square, oblong, and round wooden tables. Each table top was fussily draped with bits of lace and embroidery on which rested communities of gaudily painted figurines. There were donkeys, cats, and camels; fat little boys and round little girls; a sphinx and a pyramid; a bumblebee; stout women in long black robes; a man in a scarlet fez and white *gallabeiya* holding an umbrella.

From the walls, frozen in heavy gilt frames, stared part of the population of Karnak: faded black-and-white photographs of Khadiga's sisters and uncles and cousins as very young brides and far older grooms. Tucked into the corners of most frames were smaller, less faded pictures of brown-skinned daughters and sallow-skinned sons. In the largest photograph Abbas stood grim-faced with his hand sternly on the shoulder of a beaming Khadiga, while not far away their son Mahmoud grinned at the age of one month, six months, a year. Mona wished, for a moment, that her life had unfolded differently, that she could have been content to take her assigned place on this wall beside some bland young Muslim. She sighed. Hers was a different fate. She believed that to be true even though Abbas was doing all he could to make her join the gallery on the wall.

The explosions whipped the curtains at the open window near Khadiga's pride and joy, a massive china closet she and Abbas had purchased long ago with part of her brideprice. Seven feet tall and nearly as wide, it had lost its glass doors to the force of a stiff *khamseen* wind. On its shelves were blankets, books, and more bric-a-brac: unnaturally colored small glass birds, a candle stub stuck in a heavy black iron holder, misty pictures of rivers and mountains scissored out of magazines, and the unused silver soup spoons that had been a wedding present from the al-Masris. But what caught Mona's eye on the third shelf from the bottom was an orange-and-red plaster figure of a *fellaha*. A spring detached her midsection from the rest of her so that she eternally shimmied at the mere beginnings of a breeze. As the bombs dropped, the *fellaha* gyrated with the lewdness of a belly dancer. Mona stared at the crude figurine with distaste, as if it were one of Youssef's wild dancers. She had thought, so wrongly, that those women were her worst enemy.

She looked down at her candle and struck her match. She coaxed the flame from a blue dot to an orange blur. She held another lit match to the base of the candle until the wax was soft enough to stick onto a brass ashtray on the table before her. She studied the candle, wondering if tonight a moth would come to entertain her. Sometimes she told herself it was a good omen if a moth flirted with death. Other nights she was just as optimistic that her luck was turning for the better if the flame flickered and died without claiming a victim. Some nights she still believed that fire was better than shame. Still other nights she was just as sure that she had been playing with neither fire nor shame with Youssef. She had changed her mind so many times that she no longer knew exactly what she did think.

Tears were neither release nor comfort. The waiting was the worst of it. She had been waiting for a sign from Youssef for a month. They had not even been allowed to say goodbye. At first she had imagined a chance meeting on the Corniche. Or maybe he would fake an illness, and she would find him smiling up at her from a bed in one of the hospital wards. She had been so certain that Youssef would find a way to see her, that at the very least one day there would be a letter or a flower or a quick snatch of a meeting to give her hope. Once she had heard his raised voice arguing with Baruch in the waiting room. Several times she had glimpsed him standing across the street intently watching Abbas lead her home from work. Finally, three days ago, he had indirectly given her a sign that she hadn't expected.

Outside it was one long explosion. Like a sleepwalker Mona left the parlor, walked past the others cringing under the kitchen table, and climbed the ladder to the roof. The midnight sky flashed orange and blue and red. Silver planes dipped near the harbor, antiaircraft guns spat blue fire, and the thick smoky air stung her eyes. From the street a sound truck urged every able-bodied man to join and resist the expected French and British invasion. Every man, regardless of nationality, would be given arms to carry on the guerrilla fight with the imperialists in every back alley of Egypt. The French and the British might try to land at Port Said, but Egypt would never surrender. Already Radio Cairo had been bombed into silence, but the sound truck said that President Nasser was making the rounds of Cairo in an open car and that Nasser had stood in the pulpit of al-Azhar mosque and vowed that Egypt would fight on from village to village and house to house.

For three days hysterical rumors had been sweeping Alexandria. Some said the British were about to depose Nasser. There were fears that the military chiefs who had run Egypt for four years were about to take cyanide *en masse*. There were hopes that Arabs in Syria and Iraq and Saudi Arabia would destroy the oil fields and pipelines if France and England dared to land troops on Egyptian soil. There were even those who said the Soviets would drop atom bombs on London and Paris, if worst came to worst. Hordes of the panic-stricken had already fled inland from Alexandria. Shops were locked and shuttered for fear of looting. In the mass hysteria housewives were hoarding food and young men were rushing off to fight.

Dully Mona watched Alexandria burn. Youssef had been one of the first to volunteer. The day of the Israeli attack in Sinai, Youssef had left a note for his family that he had gone with Hamid to enlist in Cairo. The British bombers buzzed low to strafe the Egyptian artillery. Mona wished one of the bombers would sweep her own roof. Youssef would fight for Egypt, but Youssef hadn't fought for her. She stared at the fiery harbor and tried to make herself believe that Youssef had not been a lie.

Youssef stood inside the front door of a building across the street from Baruch's office, waiting to see if his ruse would work. He had paid a little *baladi* boy twenty-five piasters to lure Baruch out on a bogus medical mission. All he would need, he thought, was ten minutes with Mona. He would embrace her, tell her his plan, and by this time tomorrow the two of them would be halfway to Cairo. Ever since Abbas had slapped Mona under quarantine, Youssef had been laying his plans to elope.

So it would appear that he wasn't giving up too easily, he had pled his case again with his father and uncle. But after a heated argument in his office one day, even Baruch had finally told Youssef that he would not tread on either Rafael's or Abbas's religious convictions. The closest Youssef had been able to get to Mona was when she had passed by on a streetcorner. Youssef had decided to do nothing more to alarm his family or Abbas. He was coldly correct to his parents, sad but affectionate with Baruch, distant with Abbas. But bit by bit he had withdrawn money from his bank account until he had enough to last them for six months. How and where to marry Mona was the next problem. He had considered, but then rejected, taking her to their Agami cottage. The first place everyone would look for them was Agami. Reluctantly Youssef had taken Hamid into his confidence. If anyone could hatch a successfully devious plan, it was Hamid. Youssef had endured a few coarse cracks about hot-blooded Saidis and tried not to flinch when Hamid slapped him on the back and congratulated him on his conquest.

Hamid was less playful when he finally realized that Youssef wasn't simply amusing himself with Mona. Soberly he said Youssef would have a very devil of a time marrying an underage Muslim girl. Hamid doubted if any religious or state official in Alexandria would do it even if Youssef dangled thousand-pound bribes. Rafael al-Masri was too powerful and well known for anyone to marry Youssef without first checking with his father. Hamid was more optimistic, however, about Youssef's chances of finding some greedy official in Cairo to certify the marriage. It might take a few weeks—even a month or two —but in Cairo a bribe could buy anything. He advised Youssef to spirit Mona off to the capital, lie low until he could grease the right palms, and return home with a *fait accompli*.

Youssef imagined a month at the Mena House, sitting on the verandah facing the pyramids with an adoring Mona by his side. Crisply Hamid told him that was out of the question. Rafael would expect to find him at a luxury hotel. Youssef's only chance of success was to disappear into Cairo without a trace. Besides, even the shabbiest hotel in Cairo would chaperon Mona almost as carefully as Abbas. It was barbaric, but any hotelkeeper who didn't want to be arrested for running a brothel would insist that they stay not only in separate rooms but on separate floors. Hamid advised Youssef to rent a flat. Even that might be difficult, for no God-fearing Muslim would allow a foreigner to set himself up with a young Arab girl like Mona. Hamid had promised, however, to find them a Cairo hideaway as his wedding present.

Anxiously Youssef peered across the street. Where was that damned boy? He looked up as silver planes broke the horizon. The British were bombing night and day. He had heard they were even running air raids in Upper Egypt. Even so, Youssef was very nearly thankful for the Suez war because it would provide him with perfect cover for his plan. The day of the Israeli attack in Sinai, instead of rushing to

Cairo to enlist with Hamid, Youssef had booked a room in a seedy Alexandrian hotel. Tomorrow when Mona, too, disappeared, there was a chance that no one would guess they were together until it was too late.

Across the street Baruch darted out the door behind a boy in striped pajamas. Youssef waited until they turned the corner before he burst into the doctor's office.

Mona was sitting on a stool reading a magazine, and she did not look up when the door clicked shut. "The doctor is away," she said. "Come back tomorrow." She had lost weight. Her starched white nurse's uniform hung on her. He would fatten her up with grilled pigeons, with honeycakes, with bagfuls of those famous Groppi's chocolates. He would buy her new clothes. His love would put the color back in her cheeks. He would kiss away those circles under her eyes. He would pull that flowered scarf from her beautiful hair and comb it free with his hands. He cleared his throat and coughed. He wanted her to look up and see him standing there. He wanted to see her eyes catch fire at the very instant she knew he had come for her.

"I said to come back tomorrow. *Bokra.*" When there was no response but another cough, she looked up. "Allah!" Her hands flew to her headscarf. She bit her lips and, like a cornered animal, her eyes darted around the room. As the air-raid sirens began to sound, she stood uncertainly to face Youssef. After longing so to see him, all she could feel now was fear. The sirens drowned out her first words.

He had never expected this hesitancy. He had been sure she would throw her arms around him. He rushed to her, pulled her into his arms, and kissed her staring eyes shut. She was a dead weight against him. He tilted up her unresisting head and kissed her hard on her lips. He forced open her mouth, so that he felt that he was breathing life into her. She stirred, sighed, laid her head against his cheek, and began to cry.

"Easy. Easy." Impatiently he patted her head. "Baruch will be back any minute. We have to talk. Don't cry, Mona."

She sobbed harder. "Youssef. Youssef!"

"I'm here. I'm here. I've come for you, Mona."

"You waited so long, Youssef. I thought—" She looked up at him, and her eyes told him what she had thought.

"You love me, Mona?"

Numbly she nodded.

He kissed her lightly on the lips. "And I love you!"

She began to cry again.

"Will you marry me, Mona? Will you be my wife?"

"We can't! Abbas says we can't. You don't know, Youssef. You don't know! He's going to make me marry somebody else."

"Never!" The air-raid siren suddenly stopped, and Youssef's answer came as a shout. The alert had bought them a little more time. Still, Baruch could come storming back any minute. Youssef lowered his voice. "Tomorrow, Mona, you will pretend to be sick. Instead of coming here, you'll stay at Abbas's flat until they leave you there alone."

"They never leave me alone."

"I think, Mona, that tomorrow they might. I suppose you know they all think I've joined the army." He allowed himself a proud smile. "What you'll do is leave them a note that you're going back to the village. Then pack a small bag and make sure someone on the street sees you leaving with it."

"We're going to Karnak?" She half believed she would go to hell with Youssef if he booked her a ticket. But Karnak? She was sure now that Ummie was the very last person in the world who would be thrilled to see her with Youssef.

"We're going to Cairo!"

Her mouth fell open with surprise, and he could not resist kissing her again.

"We'll get married in Cairo. It's all arranged." He spoke with more confidence than he felt. But the key to the houseboat Hamid had rented was in his pocket. He had the names of some officials to see. It was true that at least *some* of it was arranged. "You'll go to the station and buy a ticket all the way through to Luxor, but then you'll get off at one of the first stops. At Damanhur. I'll be there waiting for you. We'll drive on to Cairo."

She stared up at him. "I don't know."

"You don't know *what?* You say you love me, that you want to marry me. Well, then, let's do it."

"We'll get married truly, Youssef?"

"Of course."

"You swear it, Youssef? You swear it?"

"I swear that I will marry you in Cairo." He pulled a ten-pound note out of his pocket and pressed it into her hand. "For your ticket."

The banknote was dirty and tattered and had been stuck together with cellophane tape. She looked from the bill to Youssef's face.

He cut off whatever she was about to say with a hurried kiss. "I have to go. I don't want Baruch to see me. Tomorrow, Mona. Damanhur!" He blew her another kiss and ran out the door.

The suitcase was heavy in her hand as she trudged toward the station. She stopped every few steps to resummon her courage as she passed the suitcase from one hand to another. She had repeatedly changed her mind about whether to join Youssef at Damanhur. She had been so sure, on those lonely nights by the glow of the candle in Abbas's parlor, that she would do anything to be reunited with him.

She had told herself she cared nothing for the old ways in the village. She had hated Abbas and resented Baruch. She had regarded every incinerated moth almost with envy. But now, when Youssef had acted as she had willed him to act, she was torn by doubts. It wasn't that she did not love Youssef—no, that had not changed. It was just that she couldn't forget that twice before—maybe three times before—he had left her: once when Batata died, again when he bolted into that cabaret, maybe the last time when he had seemed to accept Abbas's separation. Maybe he wouldn't even have come for her yesterday if it hadn't been for that love charm. Maybe the *shaykha* had been right. Maybe the love of a *huwaga* was a curse. Or maybe not.

Mona picked up her suitcase once again. She had dallied in Abbas's flat all morning long, still unsure whether she was running to Youssef or from him. She would buy her ticket to Luxor, and maybe it was to Luxor that she was bound. Youssef would be waiting in Damanhur, but maybe she would speed on south past him. She did not have to decide just yet. On the street before her Mona spotted a beggar woman and her four toddling children. Her impulse was to give the woman Youssef's ten-pound note and hurry on to her work with Baruch. She didn't have to flee either to Youssef or to Ummie. She could stay in Alexandria, she could marry the man of Abbas's choice, she could live the life of a respectable *baladi* matron. It didn't have to be a bad life. Probably just a dull one. She dug into her pocket and pulled out a bill. If it was the ten-pound note that had found its way into her hand, her decision would be made for her. She looked at a fifty-piaster bank-note, shrugged slightly, and handed it to the beggar. She heard the woman calling out Allah's blessing upon her as she crossed the street toward the train station. Nervously Mona shifted her suitcase from hand to hand. It would either be Youssef or Ummie, Damanhur or Luxor.

Alexandria station swarmed with soldiers awaiting shipment to Cairo and the Canal Zone. Mona kept her eyes modestly cast down and ignored the catcalls of the recruits. In peacetime they would never have bothered her, but the war had made them overbold. She joined a line of Egyptians buying tickets for the Said. Since the war had begun, most foreigners had been prudently staying off the streets. There were only a few furtive foreigners in the station, and even fewer women and children. Hers would be today's fifth train south. Poor Youssef would have been waiting for hours on the Damanhur platform. Four times he would have held his breath and watched for her to alight, and four times he would have been disappointed. By now maybe he would have given up. If she couldn't see him when she got there, it would be Allah's will that she end her days in Karnak. If she was lucky, back in the village Ummie would find her a husband who was as good-humored as Uncle Muhammad. She would take her place in a line of women carrying water jugs on their heads from the river to the village. She climbed on the train, took her numbered seat by the window, and settled down to wait. Damanhur was one hour south.

The train lurched forward, and Mona shut her eyes as she felt herself swept along the tracks. All her life she had been swept along: up to Alexandria, back to Karnak. With Ummie and without her. There had never been much choice. She wished there weren't a choice now. She was unaccustomed to choices. Ummie, Abbas, everyone Egyptian had always told her that everything was decided by Allah's will. That was what had been so heady about life in the Villa al-Masri. All the people there seemed to think they could have whatever they wanted. She, too, had almost been convinced that their lot was also her lot, that she, too, could have whatever she wanted—even Youssef. But the al-Masris were foreigners. Life worked differently for them. Mona's hand carressed her blue bead. The *shaykha*'s knife had cut deep on her circumcision morning. She squirmed in the train seat but could feel nothing, not even a twinge of pain, between her legs. How could she ever have considered running away with Youssef? She would never be anything but what she had been born to be: a Saidi. Youssef had promised to marry her in Cairo, but maybe Youssef was lying. Everyone lied. She looked out the window at the green fields, the brown palm trees, the sluggish brown-green irrigation canals. She could see women bent over planting cotton, men leading donkeys piled high with clover, children wading in a stagnant canal. She belonged among people like this: honest *fellahin*, men who salaamed to Allah and women who guarded their honor with fear and desperation. Youssef was asking her to go against all this. He asked too much. She would not get off the train in Damanhur.

Relieved that at last she had decided, she settled back in her seat. It had been so long since she and Ummie had been happy together. Ummie had not forgiven her for loving the easy life in Alexandria. But now it would be as it had once been in Kom Ombo. Maybe, in time, even Ummie's old wounds over her own lost mother would heal. To make Ummie happy! To make her rosy and smiling, to take her back to the days of her youth when the village had called her Helwa, the Sweet. Mona would never again see her beautiful dream of a city by the sea.

She would miss Baruch, Abbas, and Khadiga. And Youssef. She would have to live without Youssef. She heard once more in her heart his bitter words on their first calèche ride along the Corniche. He was more vulnerable than she was. She thought in the end he was more romantic. And so he would feel altogether betrayed by what she was about to do to him. It would be back to Hamid and the dancers and the drink. Youssef would be one of Alexandria's lost souls who haunted the cabarets and the hashish parlors, so jaded by the age of thirty that the Youssef she loved would be no more. She bowed her head and put her hands over her eyes. She could not save both Ummie and Youssef. She could not make both of them happy. It was one or the other.

But then she felt a surge of hope. Maybe all would go well in Cairo. Maybe, if she joined Youssef, they would be married in two or three days. Abbas, Rafael, Leah would have to accept their marriage. She could bring Ummie and Uncle Muhammad to live with them in a villa near the Corniche. Youssef could embrace Islam. She could have it all: Youssef, Ummie, Baruch, a leisured life in Alexandria. She could almost see herself and Ummie sitting in the shade of the Beau Rivage garden, sipping tea from china cups instead of glasses. Mona stared out the window. The train tracks ran parallel to a brackish irrigation canal where the Nile was dark and sullen. In a canal like this her grandmother's body had been found after she had violated the village laws. Mona tried to forget that deadly canal and remember instead the feel of Youssef's lips on hers. She must take this risk. She must be strong. She shuddered. She could do only so much. Love was strong, but fear was stronger. She would never forget Youssef. In all the long years ahead, she would remember that once she had loved truly, that once she had been truly loved.

The train slowed as it pulled into the cloud of dust and flies and sun-bleached buildings that was Damanhur. Men were grabbing suit-cases from the racks and thronging the aisles. Her eyes scanned the platform, and she saw Youssef running the length of the train, a ciga-rette stub dangling from his lips and desperation in his eyes. She huddled away from the window, but he saw her. He pressed his face against the dirty glass, but she shook her head and looked away. In a moment the train would leave Youssef behind. She started to cry.

But the train whistle did not sound. Instead she heard marching feet on the platform and looked out as a detachment of soldiers pushed Youssef aside. All around her in the compartment there was grum-bling as a steward cried out the news that the army had commandeered the train. Civilians would have to wait in Damanhur for the next train south. Weary men folded their newspapers and groped to their feet. *Malesh,* one traveler muttered to another as they gathered their bag-gage and poured out to the platform, resigned to yet another of life's daily annoyances. Mona sat rooted to her seat for one stunned moment, but then she rose, retrieved her suitcase, and walked with a heavy step out to Youssef's embrace on the platform. It seemed it was Allah's will that they be together.

The houseboat glowed gold before them in the curve of the silver Nile. Tender waves born by a passing rowboat lapped against the bank as if the river were the sea. In the sky the setting sun streaked clouds pink and purple, and there was a faint glitter of moonbeams and starshine. From far off a *muezzin* cry to prayer came as a sleepy yawn. Even the howl of nearby Kit Kat Square was as muted as the murmur of a million satisfied men turning over in their sleep.

Youssef put his hand on Mona's shoulder. It was the first time he had dared touch her since they had come together three days ago at Damanhur. The ride to Cairo should have taken three hours, but there had been military roadblocks, long waits for expensive stamps on their papers, suspicious soldiers who had demanded *baksheesh* not to arrest him as a spy. But the wait was worth it. He hadn't told her that their hideaway would be a houseboat, hadn't dared imagine that Hamid could have found them ready-made romance. He nodded toward the Nile, the sky, the silent riverbanks, as if he had conjured them up only for her pleasure. "You like it?"

"*Aywah!*" she breathed. "This can't be Cairo. This is a dream." Enduring the sweaty drives through the winding Delta farmlands, she had praised Allah for every moment's delay that kept Cairo at bay. She had watched the orange cloud of dust that hovered over the city move from the horizon and then closer and closer, until finally she had felt it in her lungs. Impacted in a Cairo traffic jam for much of the afternoon, she had morosely studied the teeming tenements, the seamy sprawl, the jittery clutch of Cairo. The last time she had driven through this city was with Baruch, when it was in flames on that Black Saturday in 1952. Then she had been glad to escape Cairo, and she stiffened her resolve to escape it again. In her pocket was her ticket to Luxor. She could catch a night train and be there by dawn.

But she lingered with Youssef on the crest of the bank. In the fading light she could see the dome and the minarets of Muhammad Ali's Citadel high above the stony beige cliffs of the Mukattam Hills. The Cairo skyline was a welter of shadowy spires. As she turned away from the river, she thought she could glimpse the gray triangle of a pyramid framed by the black squares of skyscrapers. Behind her were the slums of Imbaba, a *baladi* quarter like too many others. She looked back at her river. The houseboat Youssef said was theirs rode low on the water, tucked into its berth alongside a row of others painted in less regal whites and blues and grays. Theirs was a long gold-dappled bungalow with wide decks that lay like balconies over the Nile. The river here, north of the heart of the city, was cut tamely in half by the island of Zamalek, Cairo's preserve of the very rich. Royal palms lined the opposite bank where lived the old powerful ex-pashas and the newly powerful colonels, those born and those bred to arrogance and ease. At the tip of the island the grassy manicured knolls of the exclusive Gezira Sporting Club awaited pleasure. Flowery gardens swept lushly down to the shore, and here and there couples lazed over tea and pastries at the open-air casinos. She could almost hear their teasing laughter. Separating rich from poor, villa from tenement, was this slender streamlike branch of the Nile. The water looked to be as pure and clear as in the Said.

Mona gazed out at the river. She had not stood by her river for years, and its nearness calmed her like a drug. She took the measure of their houseboat. Surely there would be room inside for more than one bed. She was still skeptical of Youssef's promise to treat her as his sister until she was truly his wife. She had almost forgotten she had any tie other than fear to this tall blond stranger next to her. But as she watched her river, her innocent river, her inviting river, sweep past where they stood, it was the rest of the world that she could no longer quite remember. Who was she to question the will of Allah? She glanced back over her shoulder toward Imbaba, and unconsciously she stroked her blue bead. Was that what she wanted? Because she could not dare to take a risk, because she could not trust the one she loved most, would she take her place lower than the lowliest in a Cairo slum? She turned her back on Imbaba. Zamalek beckoned on the other side of the Nile.

From under lowered lashes she swept a sidelong smile up at Youssef. Uncertainly he smiled back at her, willing to follow her mood. She could feel Cairo dust coating her skin, and so to be free of it—to be free!—she ran down the broken stones of the bank to her river. By the time he caught up with her, she had kicked off her shoes and was wading in the Nile. He laughed and joined her in the sparkling crystal water. She splashed him as if they were children in Karnak, and then she danced and dove out of his reach, striking out on the river toward Zamalek. He caught up with her in the midstream current and they drifted together until their lips touched.

Her eyes flew open in horror. She had been right. This wasn't Cairo. But it wasn't a dream either. It was a nightmare, the familiar nightmare of her girlhood: the silvery river, the silhouetted palm trees, the wet tempting kiss of death. In a moment she would wake up back in her mother's house in Karnak or maybe on Abbas's sofa. She shut her eyes, surrendering to what had to be. She stopped treading water, and she let herself sink. Yes, this was the nightmare. She felt the water in her nose and mouth, Youssef's strong arms were around her. . . .

But he was pulling her not down but up. She looked wildly around for the corpse in the river. There was none. Mona blinked, coughed up water, and heard trilling *zaghareit* joy-cries shattering the silence: *"Ayyouy! Ayyouy! Ayouououya!"* No, this wasn't her nightmare. There had been no *zaghareit* in her nightmare. She and Youssef were swimming in the Nile outside their houseboat.

A pack of women were clustered at the railing of a nearby houseboat, trilling their tongues in *zaghareit,* shouting demands that he kiss her again. Their lips met, and they broke off only to laugh. Lazily they swam back to the shallows, where Mona bent and carried a handful of water to Youssef's lips. Later she would tell him why he had to drink, that everyone in the Said knew that the Nile was in your blood once you drank from it. He sniffed the water doubtfully but trusted her enough to drink. Solemnly he cupped his hands in the Nile and watched her drink without hesitation. Arm in arm they scrambled out of the water, up the bank, and down the gangplank. The women on the neighboring houseboat cheered as he carried her over the threshold.

Youssef burst through the door. "I did it!" He scooped Mona up in his arms, whirled her around, and kissed her, French-fashion, on both cheeks.

She caught her breath. She did not have to ask what he had done. Every morning of their four weeks on the houseboat, Youssef had been out trying to find someone who would marry them. First he had tried the rabbis, but every one of them refused him outright. President Nasser, outraged by the Israeli attack, had made it clear that as many of Egypt's Jews as possible should pack their bags and get out. The plight of a Jew loving a Muslim did not amuse the rabbis. Nor had his reception been any warmer when he had tried the *maazouns,* the Muslim officials responsible for certifying Islamic marriage contracts. Youssef had tried to pass himself off as a Muslim of Turkish descent, for some Circassians were as light and fair as he. But every *maazoun* had demanded proof of age, proof of nationality, proof of religion. Technically a girl coud marry whomever she wished, as long as she was sixteen years old. Mona wouldn't be sixteen until February. If Mona couldn't prove she was of age, the *maazouns* wanted the permission of her parents. Pressed by one *maazoun* at least to surrender proof of nationality, Youssef had reluctantly handed over his Italian passport. Although Youssef had insisted he was a Believer, the *maazoun* had been faithful to the letter of the law. As a foreigner, Youssef would have to secure a civil marriage certificate at a municipal office. The *maazouns* were specifically forbidden to marry foreigners and Egyptians.

It had taken Youssef more than a week to work his way through a web of Egyptian officialdom to the proper office. There he was told that no business at all could be transacted while Egypt was in a state of national emergency, with French and British troops occupying Port Said. Later, even weeks after the United Nations cease-fire, an undersecretary told Youssef that he must wait until the department chief came back from his wartime commission. The undersecretary always took care to settle Youssef in an upholstered chair, to see that he had fresh glasses of sweet tea, and to promise that his boss would surely return *"bokra, bad bokra,"* tomorrow or after tomorrow.

Mona shot only one question at Youssef. "When?"

"*Bokra!*" Youssef kissed her on the lips in triumph. "This time tomorrow, we'll be man and wife."

"Can that be possible?" She put her arms around Youssef's neck and looked deeply into his eyes. "This isn't a joke? You're sure, Youssef?"

"Positive." He thought she had never looked so beautiful. He had, at last, made her happy. He had, at last, done one right thing. "I talked to the secretary today. At eleven o'clock tomorrow, he'll marry us."

As he whirled her around and around, she almost forgot her tense weeks of waiting. She laughed out loud. She already had her wedding dress from one of the finest shops in Zamalek. Youssef had wanted her to wear white, as if they were marrying back in Alexandria. She had been drawn to gowns of red or orange, as if they were marrying down in Karnak. Her dress—her beautiful dress!—was a rose silk compromise with long sleeves and a flounced skirt. Every morning while Youssef went off to battle for their marriage certificate, she would unfold her wedding dress from its tissue paper, carefully ease it over her head, smooth it down over her body, and prance through the houseboat pretending she was truly a bride. There hadn't been much else for her to do on the houseboat, since Youssef had insisted on hiring an old man to clean their four rooms, shop for their groceries, and prepare their afternoon meal. Sometimes Mona wandered out on the deck in her bridal gown and drowsed and dreamed in the sun.

She would look down at the riverbank where the women from Imbaba squatted on their haunches, washing heads of lettuce and baskets of laundry in the Nile, gaily gossiping all the while. Often she would wish that she could share her secret with them, that they would toast her marriage by drinking together from the Nile. She learned, however, not to look too long at the *baladi* women, for then the boldest of them would beg her for *baksheesh*. At other times Mona had studied neighboring houseboats, hopeful she might find a woman friend there. But the other houseboats were strangely quiet in the early mornings, and it usually wasn't until after noon that she could see even servants stirring on the decks. She paid little attention to her neighbors after Youssef returned to their houseboat in the late afternoons, for then she had eyes for no one and nothing but him. He had been true to his word and had not tried to seduce her. They slept not only in separate beds but in separate rooms. They let themselves enjoy stolen kisses in the moonlight, but otherwise Youssef gallantly treated her as if she were Rachel or Lisabet.

He was cupping her chin in his hand and demanding she tell him her exact thoughts.

"That you treat me like your sister."

"Enjoy it. Tomorrow I won't."

"No?"

He pulled her closer and filled his hands with her heavy hair. "To-morrow!"

Her eyes teased him. "I can't imagine what you mean." She laughed as she kissed him, but then she broke away and shut the bedroom door firmly behind her. "Get dressed, Youssef. We're going out."

He rattled the locked door as if it were the bars in a cage. "No. To-night we stay in."

"Tonight we go out and celebrate."

"We can celebrate *here*, Mona."

"Oh, no. No we don't."

"You don't trust me."

"That's right."

He laughed and went off to bathe and change. Most nights they went out for a stroll and then a quiet dinner of kebabs and rice at one of the casinos lining the Nile. But Youssef decided this time they would stay out all night. They would not sleep again uutil they could sleep in each other's arms, tomorrow afternoon, after their marriage certificate was signed.

It was after dark before they were both ready for their night on the town. Mona was wearing one of the new dresses Youssef had insisted on buying her, amber taffeta to match her eyes, a bouffant skirt to bow to fashion, and a very high neckline secured by scores of small round but-tons to hide Mona's battered blue bead. They paid a half piaster apiece to cross their strip of the Nile in a rowboat, and then they walked hand in hand down Zamalek's quiet tree-lined streets past the foreign em-bassies and the palaces of the former pashas. Youssef was in an expan-sive mood, so he nodded to the doormen in their *gallabeiyas* sitting outside the blocks of luxury flats. He made Mona laugh when he pointed out a white marble palace where one of the richest landowners in the Delta lived. Youssef said the old pasha, whose greatest pleasure in life was the regularity of his bowels, was famous even in Alexandria because he kept a three-piece village band on his payroll—just so they could soothe him every morning by playing outside his bathroom door. Youssef said one of the pasha's sons had been in his class at Victoria, and that the boy swore he could tell by the crescendos of the flutes and the drums just how his father had fared every morning. Eventually Youssef steered Mona into a café, and they sipped cappuccino until it was past ten o'clock, a suitable hour for dinner.

They sat at one of the outside tables in the Casino des Hamam, down-river in Giza, just a few feet from the silent Nile, holding hands until the platters of pigeons finally arrived. Mona turned her nose up at the pigeons splayed open and charcoaled on a spit. At home in Karnak pigeons were always stuffed with rice and steamed to a tender crisp in charcoal ovens. Someday she would cook this great delicacy for Youssef, she promised, and then he would have to admit the superiority of

Saidi cuisine. They decided they would visit Karnak as man and wife in the spring. After Youssef was feasted and toasted by Mona's entire family, they would sail upriver by felucca to Kom Ombo so Mona could try to contact her father's family. She vaguely remembered her grandmother and three aunts and that old Shaykha Sameera.

After midnight they finally reached Auberge des Pyramids, the gaudiest nightclub in Cairo—and by the looks of the limousines and the taxis parked outside, the capital's most popular cabaret. Mona clung to Youssef's arm as they threaded their way through tightly packed tables in a hall as big as a soccer field. Everywhere on the walls and the dance floor were silver tinsel, pink and purple cutouts of cupids, and flashing neon. A forty-piece band was playing, it seemed, at least three different tunes, and at the same time a red-faced comedian was bawling bawdy jokes into a squealing microphone. Through the thick blue clouds of cigarette smoke Mona could make out mobs of young, middle-aged, and very old men, some in *gallabeiyas,* others in shiny Western suits, all of them shouting and laughing and slapping their sides.

Mona saw a woman in a low-cut red dress sitting on the lap of a man, smoking her cigarette not quite as carelessly as the ladies Mona had studied at the Beau Rivage. *Sharmoota,* Mona thought to herself—a prostitute. It was appropriate, she thought, that the word for prostitute was the same one that was used for the rags women used to clot up their menstrual blood. She was ashamed to be under the same roof as a woman like this. She held more tightly to Youssef's arm and kept her eyes on the sawdust packing the floor. Youssef ordered them a bottle of whiskey, ice, water, and more platefuls of food. It was, he whispered to her, obligatory to eat as well as watch. She used her fork to push the rice around her plate, daring only to shoot scared little glances at the parade of belly dancers who had replaced the comedian on the raised stage. She caught eyefuls of brown flesh, red skirts, bouncing breasts, hair hennaed to orange hanging down to thick waists. When the dancers worked themselves up to a climax, the band would begin to howl, and the men would scream "Umpah! Umpah! Umpah!" She heard plates being smashed to the floor, saw Youssef's eyes turn too bright as he gulped glass after glass of whiskey.

So this was what Youssef was like when he was his other self. She saw him seize two spoons and join with the band beating out the belly dancers' rhythm. She shrank farther into her seat when Youssef leaped to his feet and ground his hips in an obscene answer to the dancer. She started to cry very softly when he threw handfuls of banknotes at the wildest dancer of them all. She thought it must be nearly over at two o'clock, but they were still there when it was past four. Neither the band nor the dancers nor Youssef showed any signs of fatigue. Mona sipped her sixth glass of Pepsi and prayed with renewed fervor that no one from Karnak had seen her here.

But at last Youssef said they could go. He draped his arm drunkenly around her shoulders as they groped toward the door. From out of nowhere waiters, busboys, and sellers of cigarettes—even, it appeared, distant relatives of waiters, busboys, and sellers of cigarettes—hovered for *baksheesh*. Watching Youssef spray money in every direction, Mona felt sick to see her countrymen grovel. She was disgusted at Youssef's demeaning himself and them. No matter how much Youssef pleaded with her, she would never again accompany him to a place like this.

Over her protests Youssef directed the taxi to a riding stable out by the pyramids. She thought Youssef was too drunk even to sit—much less ride—a horse, but the predawn air seemed to clear his head. He routed the stableboys out of their sleeping stalls and demanded the two best purebred Arabian mounts. They would ride bareback out over the desert, Youssef said, and the pyramids would await them at dawn. She wanted to fall in with his mood of high romance, but she had to admit that she had never ridden anything but a donkey. *Malesh.* Youssef amended his order. They needed only one thoroughbred. She would ride pillion behind him. Mona remembered how sometimes at a Karnak wedding a bride would circle the village on a high-stepping horse borrowed from the Bedouins. This would be, in its way, almost the same. Youssef lifted her up behind him, she encircled his waist with her arms, and they were off galloping past a graveyard, through a pack of howling dogs, under the moon and the stars and the glimmers of the sun. The wind streamed through her hair as she held tight to Youssef. How could she ever have doubted him? As they pulled up on a dune overlooking the three perfect gray masses of the pyramids, the sun broke from the horizon in golden shards.

"Remember it, Mona. Our wedding day. Now it begins!" He slid off the horse, and as he lifted her down beside him, he kissed her tenderly.

She turned her lips away from the whiskey on his breath and looked anxiously up into his eyes. "You're sure there won't be any trouble? You're *sure* we'll be married today?"

"Of course." He kissed her again, less gently.

"I wished Batata could be here with us, Youssef. And Baruch."

"We'll get married again—in the synagogue—when we get back to Alexandria. Baruch can play your father."

She smiled. "And in Karnak can we get married again?"

"Whatever you want, Mona. Anything you want. I'll marry you in a temple, a mosque, a church. Everywhere, Mona. Anywhere."

He was once more the Youssef of her dreams. They sealed their pact with another long kiss.

They were both exhausted when, hours later, they finally staggered down the gangplank of their houseboat. After riding at the pyramids, Youssef had insisted on toasting the dawn of their wedding day with champagne and grilled shrimps at the cabaret atop the Semiramis Hotel. At a table by the windows overlooking the Nile, she had eaten *fool* beans and eggs while he worked his way through a dozen *crevettes* and a split of French champagne. There had been more belly dancers, another excessive band, more herds of obsequious servants. Youssef had offered any waiter in the nightclub a ten-pound tip to produce necklaces of jasmine for Mona. But the best they had been able to do was to give him the huge arrangement of roses that had graced the hotel's buffet table. Youssef, still unwilling to call it a night, had wanted to hire a calèche and ride with her through the streets of Cairo until it was the hour of their marriage. At six-thirty, when she had finally coaxed him home, they had both been surprised to hear music and laughter coming from the neighboring houseboats.

Youssef had insisted she make them coffee and that they sit and sip it together on the couch. He wanted them to talk, to touch, to talk and touch, until it was time to leave for the government office.

They settled back on the sofa. Youssef put his arm around her. Thinking they would drift asleep in each other's arms, she yawned and nestled close to him. Dimly she heard his voice and felt his lips brush her cheek. "Mona," he whispered. "My Mona. My wife. Today. Now. My wife." He held her tighter. She sighed and her eyes fluttered shut. But his body shifted, and then his hands were caressing her breasts. She moved slightly away. "No, Youssef. We can't." He kept his hands where they were and kissed her on the lips. She tried to pull back, but he wouldn't let her. "I want to touch you, to hold you," he murmured. "I've waited so long. And today we'll be married. At last. At last. Five hours, Mona. Five hours. Kiss me, Mona."

She was so tired. She hesitated. She didn't want to push him away once again. It could not hurt to let him touch her just a little. In a few hours, more than this would be allowed. She let her eyes close again, and sleepily she kissed him. His fingertips were tracing her nipples in wide, then narrow circles. Suddenly awake and alert, she wondered if this was supposed to feel good. All she could feel was fear in her stomach. She prayed she would not throw up the pigeons and rice and beans and Pepsis. Her right foot was so rigid it cramped. For a moment all she could think was how good it would feel to get up and walk slowly away from Youssef, down the gangplank and all the way home to Karnak.

He seemed not to notice how stiff she was in his arms. He was kissing her neck and lower down. He tried to work open her buttons with his lips, but then he swore and, with an impatient jerk of his hand, yanked open the bodice of her dress. She was too surprised at the rush of cold air on her skin, at finding herself so suddenly open and vulnerable, to do anything but gasp. "Your breasts, your breasts," he sighed, lifting her brassiere to behold brown nipples and dusky skin so soft, so light that he had to taste it, to kiss it, to suck it.

"No, Youssef, no," she pleaded. "Please don't do that. Youssef, please!"

He hardly heard her and did not stop. "Hold me, Mona, hold me," he murmured, lost in her breasts. She tried to slip away but could not move. He took her motion for passion and groaned. His body pressed down on hers, and his pelvis started to grind.

I have to stop him, Mona thought clearly. His body over hers was heavy and solid. Her body was so remote that she felt curiously untouched even as he probed it. Her cold, clicking mind was working as fast as his hot, urgent body. She loved him. She needed him. She had to keep him close to her, had to marry him. She could not anger him, could not risk a fight, not when she had to have him marry her this morning. Yet she couldn't allow him to touch her like this. This was all wrong. What she had to do was slip out of his arms and make him be content with his usual quota of kisses. She would talk him out of it.

She touched his hair with her fingertips. "Youssef," she crooned. "Youssef, I love you. Talk to me, Youssef. Tell me you love me." He seemed only to understand that she was pressing his head closer to her. "Youssef," she repeated, seizing his hair more firmly, prepared to pull it if necessary. "Youssef!"

In answer he raised his head from her breasts. His eyes were wild and unfamiliar. What was in his eyes scared but also thrilled her so that she could not have moved away if she had wanted to. She felt a sudden flash go through her. When he kissed her this time, both of their eyes wide open, she was as eager as he.

It was only when he drew away, fumbling with his trousers, that she got a grip on herself. "No, Youssef. No."

"Yes! Yes."

He threw himself back on her, his lips cutting off her words, his hands clutching at the hem of her dress. She tried to twist away from him, but he was too strong for her. "I love you, I love you," he repeated over and over. "You are my wife. Trust me. Trust me. I'll just put it in a little bit. Just a little bit."

She knew she would not get away. She could not get away. There was no hope. All she could do now was lie there. He was going to do it, her mind coldly told her, so she had better not make him angry. They would be married in a few hours. This was their wedding day. She could hold out no longer. Now she would need him more than ever. Now she had no hope except that he would do as he had promised.

She stopped struggling. As if she were watching Youssef from across the room, she saw him pull down the elastic at the top of her panties. They stuck between her tightly pressed thighs, and he had to lift her buttocks off the sofa and pry her legs apart to get them off. She lay there exposed for a second, absolutely still, and then he spread her legs wide. Something brushed against her pubic hair, and then there was a rubbing, a painful pressing, a final breaking. Very hard, very fast, he slid up and down inside her. Remotely she heard him pant and felt his sweat running down between her thighs. She waited for it to be over. He jerked, groaned, then let out a long sigh and was still. She felt something warm and sticky flow out of her onto the couch. She studied the uneven rows of timbers on the ceiling. None of this was how she had dreamed it would be.

She waited for him to say something to her, but all that came out of his mouth were little wheezes that must mean he was asleep. She twisted her legs slightly, and he slipped out of her. She had to get up. She had to clean herself—even though she thought she would never, ever, be entirely clean again. Slowly she slid herself out from underneath him, then covered him up with her dress. She could not bear to look at his pale body.

In the bathroom she washed off the blood and the sweat and the semen. She remembered that in the village, when a girl married, either the bridegroom or the midwife punctured the hymen with a finger so that her virgin blood would stain a white cloth. Everyone in Karnak would gather outside the wedding hut, waiting until the bridegroom emerged waving his bloody proof of his wife's virtue. Mona wrung out the rag she had used to clean herself and watched the pink water disappear down the chipped porcelain bowl to the sink drain.

She slipped a dress over her head and wandered out on the deck. The silver moon wavered near the gold sun, as if it were both night and day. Imbaba was waking. She could hear the donkey carts rumbling down the dirt alleyways. Already women were fetching water from the river. She watched them as they dipped their jugs into the Nile, heaved the jugs atop their heads, and moved off up the banks. Sharply she wished that she were one of these women. She heard a commotion on the next houseboat and looked over as two men and a woman waved drunken goodbyes. The woman, Mona saw, was wearing a black lace negligee. She felt hot tears on her cheeks. *Sharmoota.* The women on the other houseboats were prostitutes. All these houseboats must be brothels. Youssef had led her to a brothel of their own. Mona studied the woman in the black lace negligee: her hennaed hair, her scarlet lipstick, the cleft she could almost see between the curve of her breasts. She took a good look at what she hoped she had not just become.

Youssef smiled absently over at her as they sat facing each other on the two green leatherette chairs arranged at right angles to the secretary's massive, highly polished wooden desk. She fidgeted in her seat and wondered if she was still bleeding. It would be scandalous if she left a red stain on the secretary's chair.

The door opened—an hour and ten minutes late—and a swarm of male undersecretaries backed into the room, sheaves of papers in their fluttering hands, every one of them beseeching a word, a glance, a nod, from the chubby man who finally, with great weariness, followed in their wake.

Youssef sprang to his feet. *"Effendi!* Mr. Secretary! *Sabah el-khair."*

Mona stood silently and smiled wanly at the man who was to marry them. He was dressed in a worn green wool suit, and his crinkled hair had obviously been recently barbered in a scalped Western cut. But the secretary's mud-colored skin, his stocky build, his flat nose, his stubby hands told her that not so long ago—maybe only a generation ago—this man's roots had been in the land. He might be a government offi-cial, but he had the blood of a *fellah.* She wondered if he was Saidi or from the Delta.

Youssef and the secretary were shaking hands and smiling. The secre-tary was gloating over the great news with Youssef. Britain and France had finally bowed to international pressure and agreed to pull their troops out of the Canal Zone. Forgotten for the moment was the shame-ful fact that the Israelis, the French, and the British had needed only nine days of fighting to secure their hold on the Canal. Not to be men-tioned was that the Israelis had captured all Sinai, even the strategic Gulf of Aqaba stronghold of Sharm el-Sheikh. Neither Youssef nor the secretary mentioned that it was only combined American and Soviet pressure at the United Nations that had imposed the cease-fire and the tripartite agreement to quit the Canal. They both looked up at the portrait of President Nasser on the wall above the secretary's desk and praised Allah for giving Egypt its great leader. Finally the secretary or-dered them all glasses of tea. Mona sipped hers and remained silent. All she expected to do today was sign her name on the marriage contract. She thought that must be it over there, on top of the secretary's desk, not yet covered with stamps and seals. She itched to take it in her hands, to devour its every word, to kiss it with her lips. She reminded herself that the rings they had bought last week in the Street of Gold at Khan el-Khalili bazaar were in Youssef's pocket. Deferentially Youssef lit cigarettes for himself and the secretary, and the two of them chatted about the superior education that could be attained at Victoria College. When Youssef offered to help any sons of the secretary's gain entrance to Victoria, Mona wondered why the secretary's good-humored face was suddenly shadowed with grief.

But apparently it was time to get down to business. The secretary was waving his assistants out the door. An old man was removing their glasses encrusted with sugar and silty black tea leaves. Youssef flashed the secretary a private smile. Yesterday they had agreed on the price of the marriage the secretary was about to sanction. A marriage certificate cost sixty piasters, but Youssef discreetly arranged a stack of crumpled dirty banknotes on the secretary's desk. A certain amount of *baksheesh* had been necessary, the secretary had informed him, to overlook the matter of Mona's being underage. Youssef was surprised to see the secretary peel out the bills and count them openly on the top of his desk. The secretary, as if he were a *baladi* woman rejecting rotten tomatoes at a stall in a souk, refused to accept two ripped five-pound notes. Youssef produced two more crisp bills, and the secretary swept all of them —even the objectionable torn ones—swiftly into his pocket.

It was only when the secretary glanced through Youssef's passport that the look on his face changed from greed to alarm. "Italian? It says here you're Italian."

"A technicality." Hastily Youssef handed over ten more pounds to the secretary. "I was born in Alexandria. I'm as Egyptian as you are."

"I see." Absentmindedly the secretary pocketed the extra ten pounds. He lit another of Youssef's cigarettes and smiled sweetly. "You're Christian, no? The Church of Rome?"

"Yes," Youssef lied. "Yes, of course."

The secretary snapped shut the passport. "Then why does it say on your residency visa that you're a Jew?" The secretary was no longer smiling or listening to Youssef's quick denials. Holding the passport with the tips of two fingers as though it contained contagious germs, he tossed it back at Youssef with the ancient contempt of master to slave, of owner to dog. Mona was sure the secretary was Saidi. There was no greater Saidi insult than to throw something to another man like that.

"So?" Youssef finally said. "So what if I *am* a Jew?"

"Ah." The secretary smiled. "So the Jew does not choose to lie again." He stood up. "I cannot authorize this evil marriage. Nor, I can assure you, will any of my colleagues in the government. The girl is underage. I cannot break the law."

"But—" Youssef began.

The secretary paused at the door. His eyes were dark with bitterness. "My son died in the last war with the Jews. He was my *only* son."

It was when she had her back to Youssef in the houseboat kitchen that he saw the reddish-brown smear on her rose silk wedding dress. He came up behind her, touched the fabric, and saw that the stain was blood. "Mona? Mona, you're bleeding."

"*Malesh.* It's my monthly." She would not turn and look at him. She poured sugar into the pot and watched it brew with the tea leaves and the water.

"It was your monthly last week. You stayed in bed for three days last week, Mona. Why are you bleeding? Is it something I did to you? You know. *Last night?*"

She poured the tea into the glasses and handed him one. This was their first mention of what had happened last night on the sofa. She had awakened him just in time to leave for the government office, and on the way Youssef had avoided her eyes and chattered on about what he would say to the secretary. But now the subject of the secretary was an even greater taboo.

He looked at her intently and set both their glasses down on the kitchen table. He led her by the hand into the bathroom, where he drew warm water into the tub. He began to undress her as if she were his invalid daughter.

She let him take off her clothes. Why not? She had let him do more than that. She was utterly dependent on him now, even for her very life. Abbas, Uncle Muhammad, any Muslim who valued honor over shame, could kill her for what had happened to her last night. Yet in the harsh bright light of the bathroom she shrank away from Youssef, ashamed that he was about to look at her naked body. But he was ignoring her breasts and buttocks.

"Yes, you *are* bleeding. My God, Mona, you're almost hemorrhaging."

She pressed her thighs together to try to stop the trickle of blood that had begun the night before.

Tenderly Youssef lifted her in his arms and into the bathtub. The warm water was a caress. Mona sighed, lay back, and demurely folded her arms over her breasts. She felt Youssef stroke open her thighs. She heard Youssef gasp.

"Oh, my God!" He had never seen a woman who looked like *that* there. Parts that should have been there were missing. The skin that should have been reddish and slippery was white and puckered, drawn sloppily together, with red welts where once some sort of clumsy stitches might have been. The opening where he had taken her was still seeping blood. "My God! Who did this to you? My Mona. My poor Mona." He started to cry.

She reached up to touch his hair and try to comfort him. "It's nothing, Youssef. It probably won't bleed too much longer. Sometimes it happens like this. Once when a woman came to our clinic, Baruch said the wedding night reopened old wounds that never had healed properly. It's nothing, Youssef. It is like this with all the women. It is just my *tahara,* my purification. It's supposed to bleed like this for a while after a girl . . . marries."

He looked at her with disbelief. He had heard stories about female mutilations but had never believed them. Now he did. "How old were you when they did it?"

"Four."

"It hurt?" God, he thought, it must have hurt. It made *him* hurt just to look at it. He stifled his desire to touch his own penis and assure himself that he, at least, was still whole.

"It is the first thing I really remember in my life. A lot of people were there. The *shaykha* cut me. Yes, it hurt. Then they carried me down to the river, and the women had a big fight. Ummie tried to help me. I remember that. I remember." When she laughed, there was an edge of hysteria in her voice. "That's when I was cursed. That's when Ummie gave me my blue bead. Can you imagine, Youssef—*can you imagine!*—what my life might have been like if Ummie *hadn't* given me this blue bead to protect me?" She laughed again.

That bitter sound sent shivers down his spine. He ran his tongue around the outside of his lips. "When we . . . made love . . . the other night. Did it hurt?"

"Yes."

"I mean, did it feel good at all?"

"I was so frightened."

"My baby. My poor baby." He cursed himself. But how could he have known? How could he ever have imagined that Mona's body— maybe even Mona's mind—was so scarred? He resolved to be so gentle with her that he would never hurt her again. He stroked her breasts, her belly, and then brought his fingers down to where her legs met. "Open them, Mona," he whispered. He slid his fingers in her deep rut and tried not to cringe from the sight of what had been done to her. "Tell me how this feels," he said, in much the way Baruch would have instructed a patient. He touched her everywhere on the outside skin. "Does it hurt? How does it feel?"

"It burns a little near the . . . near *that*."

"But do you feel anything else?"

"No. Nothing at all."

He withdrew his hand and gently washed her body and patted her dry with a towel. His poor little mutilated Mona. He had thought her pleasure was just like his. He had thought it would be for her just like the belly dancers had always led him to believe it was for women. But then he had another thought. If in the village they had taken a knife to Mona when she was four years old and utterly innocent, what would they do to her now? He didn't have to ask. He had heard the grim stories of avenging brothers and fathers. Why the *hell* hadn't he waited until the damn marriage certificate was signed and sealed? It must have been the whiskey and the champagne. "Oh, Mona. I didn't know. I swear I didn't *know* what I was doing!"

She stared at the man she loved. No, he hadn't known. His world was so different. Wrapped in the towel, she swept back to her bedroom and swiftly dressed.

Youssef followed at her heels. "We'll get married. It's only three months until you're sixteen. When this war hysteria about the Jews dies down, it will be different. We can get married at the government office in Alexandria. Or we'll go away. We'll leave Egypt. I swear it, Mona. I swear."

She looked into his eyes. There was no turning back. Maybe she had never had much choice in this matter. Maybe Allah was not so compassionate as He was cruel. *"Inshallah,"* she said.

He tried to smile, and then he felt in his pocket for their gold wedding rings. Without speaking he led her out on the deck under the relentless afternoon sun. There on the houseboat, anchored on the green Nile between the tenements of Imbaba and the villas of Zamalek, he slipped a ring on her finger. "I, Youssef al-Masri, marry you, Mona Bint el-Hassan. I pledge before God that you are my true wife. Now and forever, so long as we live." He kissed her hands and gave her his ring.

Her eyes were swimming with tears as she slipped the ring on his finger. "I, Mona Bint el-Hassan, pledge before Allah that you are my true husband. Forever. For always. On earth and in Paradise."

10 ⌇⌇⌇⌇⌇⌇⌇⌇⌇

ALEXANDRIA, EGYPT / January 1957

Mona walked with a leaden step alone down the Rue Fouad toward the Villa al-Masri. The wind blushed her cheeks, and she shivered. Even after ten winters in Alexandria, the cold still gave her gooseflesh. Cairo had been balmier. They had delayed—and delayed again—their return to Alexandria. The last British and French troops had pulled out of the Suez Zone before the New Year. Soldiers were returning home from the front. The mails were creaking back into service. Even the telephones were working. They knew they had to go back home before Abbas, Baruch, and Rafael realized their ruse and came hunting for them. But still they had dallied in Cairo. Youssef had called their last fortnights there by an English word, "honeymoon," and he had always laughed when Mona mistakenly called them "honeyweeks." He had encouraged her halting efforts at English, for he said maybe they would go to London after they were married. But so far Youssef had found her anything but an apt pupil, at least in English. Mona remembered what else Youssef had been devoted to teaching her on the houseboat, and her memories flushed her cheeks redder than the wind had been able to do. Cold air swept up under her shirt. She was conscious of the flesh of her thighs rubbing together as she walked. He had kissed her just there this morning when they woke on their bed in the houseboat. Honeyweeks. Six honeyweeks together, almost as man and wife.

Mona smiled shyly to herself, and she glanced around her as if afraid a passerby could read her thoughts. Those *shebab*, those young Arab men lounging in a pack on the streetcorner, what if they knew? They

216

would spit at her, or maybe they would make a grab for her breasts, as she had seen boys like them do to foreign women along Kasr el-Aini in Cairo. Absently she wondered how those young men could be loitering on the Rue Fouad. The *baladi* quarters were on the other side of the city. The Rue Fouad was for the *huwagas* and those who served them. She kept her eyes demurely cast down until she passed by the young men. At least *she* belonged. At least *she* served. Mona walked a little faster to hasten her thoughts away from the precise nature of her service. The *pâtisserie* was just ahead. Maybe she would stop and buy Baruch something gooey and chocolate. He ate chocolate like a greedy little boy. He even licked his fingers of chocolate smears. But the *pâtisserie* was closed. Its windows were painted black, and there was a thick crust of dust on the padlock on the door. Of course, Mona thought. A *French* pastry shop wouldn't be open for business. Since the Suez invasion, it was a sin in Egypt to be French, British, or Jewish. Mona frowned, rested her suitcase on the pavement for a moment, and touched the blue bead. If Youssef were anything but a Jew, they would be truly married by now. Yet he wasn't even slightly religious, he never prayed, she had heard him mention God only when he slipped that ring on her finger. Surreptitiously she let her hand brush against the gold wedding ring lying between her breasts, under her dress on a thick gold chain. In three more weeks, when she was finally of age, she and Youssef would be able to get married. She would wear her ring proudly then. Youssef had promised her a fitting Karnak wedding present: gold bracelets, gold earrings, a charm with a quotation from the Koran that she could wear on her wedding chain. Only then would she do as he asked and throw her blue bead into the sea. No curse could strike at her when she was legally Madame al-Masri.

Mona wondered, as she continued on her way, if it really could be that simple. Could she shake her curse just by changing her name? In the foreign fashion, she had decided to take Youssef's name as hers. What did it matter that by giving up her father's name she would be defying yet another Egyptian tradition? She whispered the name that would be hers out loud: "Madame Mona al-Masri." The man passing by her in a *gallabeiya* and turban gave her a startled look. *"Pardon,"* Mona mumbled, and the man answered her in Arabic. She was conscious suddenly that all around her on the Rue Fouad, men were speaking not their usual argot of French, Italian, and Greek, but only Arabic. Some of the street signs, which always had been lettered in European script, had been freshly painted in swirls of Arabic. It was midday in the middle of the week, and there wasn't a foreigner in sight. It had been the same on the street where Baruch's office was located. The door had been boarded up. Mona shrugged slightly. She supposed the war must have hit harder here in Alexandria.

She could see the Villa al-Masri a block ahead of her on the corner, and she slowed her pace so she could put off having to lie for a little while longer. She hated the thought of lying, although Youssef always joked that everyone lied so much in Egypt that it was nearly as popular a national pastime as soccer. He called those little untruths that wives told husbands, that sons told fathers, that workers told bosses, "sweet lies," the slight accommodations of truth that sandpapered down life's small splinters, that maybe allowed people to hurt each other less. No, it wasn't that she shrank from sweet lies. She just wished she could be bold enough to tell Baruch no lies.

Especially, sharply, she wanted to tell him how she had stood on the bank of the Nile, how she had looked down at their houseboat, how she had *chosen* to be free. Only Baruch would understand—would maybe even share her joy—in the way she had rushed down the bank and thrown herself in the river. She would never have been able to do that without Baruch's years of gentle prodding. She was certain Baruch would sympathize. She could imagine Baruch's eyes filling with tears when she told him of their marriage vows on the deck of the houseboat. She could understand, now that she had been with Youssef, how lonely Baruch had always seemed. He, too, had once loved. But Baruch was different from herself and Youssef. Baruch had lost the one he loved. Youssef and she would not lose, not if they were discreet for just a few more weeks.

Mona was to return to the villa a week before Youssef. She was to take up her work in Baruch's office, pretend that she had been visiting all this while in Karnak, and treat Youssef—when he returned, supposedly from his guerrilla unit—as if he were no more than a flirtation from the past. It would not be so much a lie as acting out parts in a charade. They had convinced themselves, lying in each other's arms on the houseboat, that all would go well, that there was little danger of discovery, that they had been fools to think that Abbas could ever harm Mona. He might have acted like her father or brother when he hustled her off to his flat, but Abbas was Nubian, not Saidi. Abbas had left his old village behind decades and decades ago. Youssef maintained that Abbas wasn't any more in bondage to village taboos than Mona herself was.

Hastily Mona veered away from that thought, making a mental note never again to stroke her blue bead when she was worried. Instead she looked around her at the Rue Fouad. The usually bustling street was so quiet she could hear the wooden wheels of a donkey cart grating down the boulevard. Iron grills slashed shut shops. A police van was pulled up outside Solomon's, one of the city's fanciest shoe salons. Men in *gallabeiyas* scurried about, loading it with hundreds of boxes of Italian and French shoes. In the near-darkness of the shop Mona thought she could make out three policemen arguing with a merchant in a Western suit. She hurried past them, wondering what sort of business was being transacted. *Malesh*. It was none of her business. Mona waved to some of the *bowabs* stationed on their benches outside apartment houses on the Rue Fouad. At least that hadn't changed. By the looks of it, the *bowabs* hadn't budged for the entire two months that she and Youssef had been away. It would take more than a war to move the *bowabs*.

Mona hesitated in front of the Villa al-Masri. One soft spring over a decade ago she had first stood here on the pavement with Ummie. She had heard Ummie swear, and when she had looked up to catch Youssef's first smile, he had thrown her a gold coin. Waiting inside the villa that day, in the children's nursery, had been little Batata. Mona sighed under her breath. Batata had died more than a year ago. Today, in the weak winter sunlight, the balconies of the Villa al-Masri were shuttered. The draperies at every window were drawn. The wind scratched brittle brown leaves from a ficus tree along the front steps. Under her breath Mona prayed that Allah would forgive her for the lie she had to tell. Then she gathered her cloak closer to her body and slipped her key in the lock of the kitchen door.

Only Khadiga was there, stirring the contents of a skillet while she hummed a song Mona recognized from Karnak. Mona tried to remember the words. She listened for a moment, her eyes half closed, so that she could almost feel Karnak dust between her toes, Karnak heat on her skin. She willed away the past and set her face in smiles. "Khadiga! I'm back! I'm home!"

Khadiga wheeled in her direction, her cooking forgotten. The two women embraced: tears of welcome, happy kisses, ritual assurances that all was well, *el-hamdulillah!* Mona averted her face from Khadiga as she stammered out her story that she was just back from Karnak. Evasions, more smiles, a subtle turning of the focus from the village to the villa.

Khadiga's smile was fading. She was sighing. She had returned to the stove. "Sit down, Mona. Have some tea. You'll need it. I need it. All we do is drink tea now." Khadiga made an unhappy clicking sound with her tongue.

Mona settled on a kitchen chair while Khadiga, self-important with her gossip, poured out their tea from the simmering pot on the back of the stove. Khadiga brought out bread, cheese, hard-boiled eggs, pickled vegetables. Mona peeled an egg, popped it in her mouth, and chewed it slowly. She knew herself to be a poor liar. It might be easier to deceive Khadiga with her mouth full.

Khadiga handed her a glass of tea and sat down. "First of all, Youssef left. Joined the army or the guerrillas, we don't know. Monsieur al-Masri—Rafael, that is—at first was furious. Be he couldn't get any information from the war ministry. He couldn't even get through to Cairo on the telephone."

Good, Mona thought. So far so good. She slipped salty white cheese inside flat tan bread. But she decided she should show more surprise and concern. "He—Youssef—didn't get hurt, did he? In the fighting?"

"Only Allah knows, Mona. Allah keep that boy. He was always so much more trouble than the others. A good boy, maybe. A kind one, certainly. But trouble." Khadiga shook her head. "But that wasn't the worst of it. About a month later, the government came and took over Monsieur al-Masri's business. Just walked into his office near the Cotton Exchange, took his keys, and told him to get out."

"What?" Mona's eyes were wide.

"Yes. They told him it wasn't against him personally, of course. But with the war, with those British and those French and . . . those others . . . doing what they did, Nasser got mad." There was a small note of satisfaction in Khadiga's voice. "To get back at *them,* he took what was theirs—or rather, *ours.* Nasser says Egypt belongs to Egyptians. And, you know, Mona, I think Nasser was right. So at least for a while, while the war was on, he took some property of the French, the British, the whole lot. It wasn't just Jews. They just took the Jewish money first."

"But the *al-Masris?*" Mona shook her head. "I can't believe it."

Khadiga sighed. "But now I'm coming to the terrible part. Monsieur al-Masri had a stroke. That's what Dr. Baruch called it. A stroke. They had to carry him out of the Cotton Exchange on a stretcher."

"But he's all right? Youssef's father is all right?" Mona stared at the food on the table, hoping Khadiga hadn't noticed her slip. She must take care not to let everyone know she saw the whole world in relation to Youssef.

But Khadiga was intent on her story. "Depends on what you call 'all right.' He can't talk anymore. He has to write notes. And Baruch says it's hard to read them because his hand shakes so much."

Mona shook her head. "The poor man." She remembered Rafael al-Masri coldly ordering her out of the parlor. She took a sip of the very sweet tea.

"He still has to use a cane to get around. But—*el-hamdulillah!*—Dr. Baruch says there's a chance he might not need that for too long."

Mona sighed on cue. "Life is difficult."

Khadiga let out a long answering sigh. "And that's not all. You would think that would be enough, more than enough, to happen to any one family. . . ." Khadiga paused dramatically.

Mona munched her sandwich and prodded Khadiga to continue.

"Madame. Madame al-Masri. She left!"

"She's in Cairo?" Praise Allah that she and Youssef had for the most part stayed out of the luxury hotels.

"No. Not Cairo. She ran off." There was dire disapproval in the set of Khadiga's face and body. "The very day after the president went on the radio and told . . . the Jews . . . that he wouldn't stop any of them from leaving Egypt, she up and left. Took Anne-Marie and the girls—those sweet little girls of hers—and sailed off on one of those foreign ships. She left a note saying that she was going to Paris and wouldn't be back."

Mona could see Leah's face swimming before her in the parlor, Leah looking at her with contempt, Leah implying that she was responsible for Batata's death. Paris. The wicked woman was gone, maybe, surely, forever. Mona tried to be noble and feel regret. She reminded herself that after all, that woman had given life to Youssef. Maybe now it would be easier to be grateful to Madame al-Masri.

Khadiga wasn't finished. She leaned toward Mona conspiratorially. "We think—Abbas and I—that she took that fancy French teacher of hers with her. Because he's gone, too. Without a trace."

"No!" Mona rocked back in her chair.

"That's what we think." Khadiga's lip curled in scorn. "She's bad, that one. Leaving her sick husband and her children. And to think that I waited on her, hand and foot, for all those years. *Sharmoota.* That's all she was. *Sharmoota.*"

Mon swallowed hard. She picked up a pickled lemon and sucked it until her face puckered. Khadiga, if she knew the truth about her own two months away from Alexandria, might judge her just as she did Leah al-Masri.

Youssef raced down the pavement toward the sea. He was late. Mona had expected him at their bench along the Corniche twenty minutes ago. But he had had a very devil of a time getting out of his father's sickroom. Now they would be able to have only a minute or two together before Mona had to be back at the villa. Before he even crossed the Corniche he saw her sitting facing the sea with Suker lying abjectly at her feet. The poor dog never got a proper run anymore. Every afternoon Mona would walk the dog only from the villa to this bench. Ah, well. In a week Mona would be sixteen, and they would be married. Maybe in a few years, when all these Jewish war problems were over, they would buy a villa on the sea, and they could race down the beach with Batata's dog all day long. Youssef could almost feel the sand inside his shoes. Mona, he saw, was dressed like a twelve-year-old schoolgirl in knee socks, a dark sweater, a black skirt. She had a heavy black *baladi* shawl wrapped around her in some vague approximation of a disguise. But the sun caught the glint of his gold wedding chain outside her shawl. She was his, all right. He tapped her on the shoulder and tried to make his voice a low growl. "Could I see your papers, miss?"

She gasped and whirled around on the iron bench. Once again he thought that she was like a gazelle, so fragile, so easily frightened, yet sometimes she ate from his hand.

"Youssef! *El-hamdulillah!* I thought you were a soldier. I was just going to leave. It's late, Youssef."

"Father again. Sorry." He ran his hands through his hair and sat down beside her. They both looked out at the sea as they talked. They thought that anyone passing by would take them for strangers if they didn't look at each other. But the angles of their shoulders were inclined together. He had crossed his right leg over his left so that he almost encircled her. The small space between them on the bench narrowed with their every breath. Even from far away a half-blind beggar would know them for lovers.

"I'll have to go back in a minute, Youssef."

"I know."

They both looked out over the blue Mediterranean. It was one of those fair, crisp, sunny late-January days that made women like Youssef's mother fret about spring fashions. Behind them Alexandria glittered gold and rose and silver. A sailboat skimmed the waves not far from shore.

"You know what they used to call this, Mona?"

"Love. That's what they still call it."

He laughed. "No. I mean the bay. Long ago—two thousand years ago—when Alexandria was young, when the best of the Greeks and the Romans were at home here, they called this the Harbor of Happy Return."

Her dimples showed when she smiled. "The Harbor of Happy Return. It was and it is." They had slipped back into their old lives in Alexandria with surprising ease. Everyone was so preoccupied with Rafael's illness, Leah's disappearance, and the confiscation of the al-Masri business that no one had questioned them closely. Mona was living with Abbas and Khadiga and working for one of Baruch's old nurses at the hospital. Youssef was running his father's countless errands. While they bided their time, they felt secure enough to risk these daily meetings.

Youssef glanced over at Mona and lit a cigarette. "Hamid's back from the army."

"In one piece?" Mona's tone left no doubt that she hoped for some random wartime injury like the loss of all his arms and legs. She hadn't forgiven him for setting them up on the houseboat.

"Hale and hearty. Full of tales of glory."

"He was at Port Said?"

"No. At the clubs along the Pyramids Road. They gave him a fancy uniform and quartered him in Cairo. It sounded as if he was very ferocious with the belly dancers."

Mona snorted. "You told him about the prostitutes on the houseboat?"

"I did. He said it was the best he could do. He said he had had a lot of happy nights on those houseboats."

"A joke. Hamid thought it was a joke." Mona moved slightly away from Youssef. As often as she had explained precisely why she was angry with Hamid, Youssef had never seemed to understand. She rearranged the folds of her shawl as if she were a bird smoothing down her feathers. After a long moment, she gave in. *"Malesh.* It *was* a beautiful houseboat."

Youssef took a long, satisfied drag on his cigarette. "Any news, Mona?"

"I finally met him. Abbas brought my intended to the flat last night."

Youssef flicked off too much ash from his cigarette and had to relight it. He knew it was necessary to allow Abbas's marriage preparations to continue at the slowest of all possible paces, but still he was jealous. "And?"

"And nothing. We said about six words to each other. He gave me flowers. He stared at me a lot." Mona shrugged. "You know."

"No, I don't know. Did he kiss you?"

"Of course not. You know Abbas."

"I do indeed."

Mona laughed and continued to stare at the sea.

"So what did you think of him?"

"Who? Abbas?"

Youssef slapped her lightly on the soft honey skin of her hand. "Hamuda el-Salem. The man Abbas thinks you are about to marry. What was he like?"

Briefly she considered letting Youssef squirm awhile longer. She stole a look at him from under her lowered lashes, but he caught her and they both laughed. She took Youssef's hand in hers. "He's old. Fat. I think he must be as old as Abbas. Maybe forty-five or fifty. He wore his police uniform. He sweated a lot, even though it was cold in the kitchen. He hardly talked to me at all. He and Abbas had their heads together. Hamuda was telling him something about the al-Masris. He wants Baruch to come to his office today."

"What for?"

"I don't know. You know the police. Secrets. Intrigue. It makes them feel important. Hamuda's probably trying to get a reduction on the brideprice."

"So it's Hamuda now?"

"Yes."

"He gave you roses?"

"Just carnations."

He held tighter to her hand and was relieved. Mona liked roses. Thank God jasmine was out of season. The idea of that sweaty old man looking at Mona, imagining her in his bed! *Malesh.* Just a little while longer, and the charade would be over. Youssef had been busy with his own marriage preparations.

As if she could read his thoughts, Mona asked her usual question. "You went to the government office again?"

"I did, Mona."

"And?"

"The day after your birthday will also be your wedding day."

"Youssef!" She allowed herself one happy look at his face. Allah! He was handsome. When she was old and gray—when he was, too—she would still not tire of looking at him. "It's true?"

"It's true. I had to pay what was probably a record amount of *baksheesh,* but everything is in order. The trick was to find someone in the ministry who wasn't Muslim. I didn't want a repeat of that scene in Cairo. It took a while, but finally I found a greedy Copt. He says that as soon as you turn sixteen, he'll marry us."

"That's next week, Youssef."

"So soon?" Youssef's eyes were teasing. "You'll be sixteen so soon?"

She grinned up at him. "You won't get away this time, Youssef al-Masri. Next Tuesday you meet your doom."

"That's a promise?"

"It is."

"There's no way out of it?"

"There isn't."

"*El-hamdulillah!*"

They both laughed, and Youssef moved his other hand over hers. "I wish I could kiss you, Mona."

"Not here."

"I know. I haven't held you for two weeks! Can you imagine that? Fifteen days—fifteen nights!"

She glanced around the seawalk and could see no one approaching. She slid her hand up and down his thigh and then almost casually let her palm rest on his crotch.

"A tease. That's what you are."

"I just don't want you—any of you—to forget me."

"*Jamais.*" She thrilled him when she was bold. All those honeyweeks together on the houseboat, lolling on the bed. He had tried so to give her pleasure. She had succeeded so in pleasuring him. Slow love on the Nile in the afternoons, his hands in her hair, those full lips of hers moving down his chest. . . .

She broke into his reverie. "The rings, Youssef. I have to go soon. It's time for the rings."

He pretended to be tired of their game. "Again? We have to marry each other every single day, here on the Corniche?"

"Every day. I love marrying you."

He laughed and produced the ring. She slipped her own off the chain. They held each other's hands.

"I, Youssef al-Masri, marry you, Mona Bint el-Hassan. You are my wife now and forever."

"I, Mona Bint el-Hassan, pledge before Allah that you are my true husband. For always and forever."

They were quiet then, watching the tide go out.

"It will seem funny when we finally do it, won't it, Youssef? Sitting in some drab office, with some oily official counting his *baksheesh*. To have *that* count, and *this* not!"

"It doesn't matter. I'll marry you again every day of my life, if you'll have me."

"Just one legal time will be enough."

Youssef looked down at his watch and sighed. "You'd better go. It's late."

"You love me, Youssef?"

He looked at her gravely. "It seems so."

"Then say it."

"I love you, Mona." His eyes were steady, his lean face was earnest. A blond curl had fallen down almost in his eyes. She brushed it back. "And I love you, Youssef." Framed in *baladi* black, her eyes were dark shadows.

"Smile for me, Mona."

There were the dimples, the yearning amber eyes, the moist lips as she moved toward him in the sunlight. But before their lips could touch, she jumped up, blew him a kiss, and was running across the street with the dog.

"Tomorrow!" he called out after her. "Same time. Same place."

"I won't forget! *Jamais!*"

Youssef sat yawning on the chair he had pulled up beside his father's bed. On it Suker was snoring. Behind it Abbas was hovering. In the center of it Rafael was propped up on a mound of pillows, his silver writing tray perched on his lap. The tray held three small pads of ocher paper, a slender jewel-encrusted pen, and sheaves of loose paper covered in the spidery, child-size handwriting that was now so familiar to them all. Rafael picked up the pen, paused to admire its gleams of garnet, and began writing yet another message.

Ten to one, Youssef thought, it's another demand for the government to give him back his property. Rafael wrote to every possible ministry in Alexandria and Cairo, to the British consulate, to the Italian consulate, to his lifetime of business acquaintances at the Bank Misr. At first Youssef had followed his father's orders and delivered his messages, but now he merely pretended to knock on all those closed doors. Baruch had instructed him to humor his father but to stay out of the complicated family business. New, selectively enforced decrees from Cairo made it clear that Jews could no longer own their own businesses, could not practice law or medicine, could not engage in buying or selling, could not even touch their impounded bank accounts. As part of what Nasser called the "temporary wartime emergency," Jews were being treated as a Zionist fifth column inside Egypt. There were night raids and arrests of prominent Jewish businessmen and of Jews suspected of being secret or not-so-secret Zionists. There were rumors of new Jewish concentration camps in the Libyan desert and the Delta.

Baruch, since he had shut down his own clinic and office, made only occasional housecalls to his old patients. Most of his days and nights he spent racing around Alexandria trying to salvage what was left of his family from arrest and ruin. For although Rafael had signed his businesses and property over to Baruch years ago, he had often not informed his brother what he was doing in his name. Large sums were missing, and the police were demanding that Baruch account for them. Rafael's scribbled notes said the money had been dedicated to Zion. But since the police so far had been unable to prove that, they had made no move yet to confiscate the Villa al-Masri. The best Youssef could do for the family, Baruch said, was to keep his father from attracting any more government attention.

Youssef left his father's bedside and poured himself a glass of tea from the primus stove Abbas had set up on a table by the window. As he looked out at the street, he saw Mona crossing on her way to the hospital. She was still wearing that *baladi* shawl. Dressed in black from head to foot, she looked like a village woman. Youssef smiled to himself. Between her breasts she wore his wedding ring. He crossed back to the bed and idly picked up the scrapbook Rafael had dedicated to Batata. He leafed through the pages. Here was Batata holding a very tiny Zibda. Here were all his sisters and brothers—even that hideous governess Helga—on the beach at Abu Kir. And here was Mona sitting with Batata at their lessons in the nursery. There was even a leaf of dried clover from the cart that had brought Batata home. Suddenly depressed, Youssef thumped shut the scrapbook. It was an effort these days, with all the craziness around them, to hang on to the hope that very soon, when they were married, they would be able to recapture what had already been lost.

Youssef tried not to think very much about how these new Jewish decrees could hurt the two of them. Although he and Mona seldom talked of it, all around them was evidence that the world they had loved was crumbling. Every night as he and Baruch and Daoud sat around the dinner table, trying to ignore the fact that half the family was missing, Baruch would call the roll of more Jews who had fled. Nasser had told them they were all free to go, as long as they left their property and their money behind. Every Jew was allowed to take only a pitiful amount to start a new life. Each could carry out thirty Egyptian pounds in currency, which was hardly enough to keep a family of four solvent in Europe for even a week. Every Jew could take jewelry valued at one hundred and forty pounds, which, when pawned later, would fetch perhaps another few weeks of living expenses abroad. The only other legal items in the suitcases of the Jews were unlimited amounts of Egyptian-made clothing and shoes. So great was the panic, so fresh was the memory of what the Nazis had finally done to their Jews, that many of Alexandria's and Cairo's richest Jewish families were relieved to get out on Nasser's terms.

Families abandoned villas and estates, loaded their suitcases with shoddy Egyptian-made clothing into their chauffeured limousines, and fled the country of their birth. At the Alexandrian piers they were sub-jected to embarrassing searches. In their quest for secreted jewels, the Egyptians were even said to be ripping the seams from women's cloth-ing. Baruch had heard that one rich Jew caused a minor sensation when he snatched his wife's diamond watch from a customs inspector and ground it under his heel rather than allow it to be confiscated. Almost every day the ships left Alexandria with their cargoes of Jews. Most were bound for Marseilles. From there the most prudent of the Jews—those who had been gradually transferring their fortunes from Egypt to Europe ever since the first Palestine war—were heading for easy lives in Geneva, London, or Paris.

Stories were being whispered in the cafés that the French brothers at Alexandria's elite St. Mark's prep school had been carrying out brief-cases stashed with Jewish fortunes for years. Diplomatic pouches from the Belgian, Dutch, and Swedish embassies were still supposedly crammed with Jewish jewels. Baruch had even heard that in Cairo, one old Jewish millionaire roamed the quiet back lanes of Garden City, searching for an honest face in the crowd, for a likely Greek or Italian he could take a chance on trusting, for someone—anyone—who might carry out his jewels and cash and hand a percentage of it over to him later in Zurich. Jews like Rafael al-Masri, Jews who hadn't seen the writing on the wall quickly enough, faced a bleak future when they finally walked down the gangplank in Marseilles. There, instead of being aristocrats, they would be penniless refugees. It was said that France would let them stay for only a few weeks. It was rumored that neither France nor Britain nor any other country in Europe would give these Jews work or residency permits. A few with distant relatives abroad hoped they might be able to borrow a thousand or so pounds and emigrate to Brazil or the United States. Only the poorest Egyptian Jews—those who had lived side by side with *baladi* Arabs as their tailors and tinkers—even considered taking up the Jewish Agency's advertised offer of free passage to Israel. For although there were Zionists among

Egypt's Jewish upper crust, their Zionism was purely philanthropic. They had heard that if they went to Israel, they would have to live in tents or in the tin-topped shacks of refugee camps. In the salons of Alexandria's rich Jews, messieurs said to mesdames that they were not quite willing to offer their sons to Israel for cannon fodder. For Egypt's Jewish aristocrats, Israel was only a very desperate last resort.

Youssef rubbed the tense muscles at the back of his neck and thanked God that his father was too ill to be moved. So far his father's stroke had staved off any talk of their joining this enforced exodus from Egypt. As Youssef looked over at his father, one of those new waves of tenderness for the invalid washed over him. Always before his father had been so cold and remote. But now that his father was helpless, Youssef could allow himself to care for the old man. When Mona was his wife, together they would do all they could for his father. They would have to lead a quieter life, of course. There would be no more Sporting Club, no more cabarets, no more Agami summers. But they would make the best of it. In a little while he could get a decent job. Surely the hysteria would die down in a little while.

Quick steps sounded in the hall, and Baruch burst through the door. His hair was ruffled, his face was shiny with sweat, and he was breathing as heavily as if he had been running a marathon. He looked wildly from Rafael to Youssef to Abbas. "Daoud. Where's your brother, Youssef?"

"In school. At Victoria. He won't be home for another hour. You look terrible, Uncle Baruch. Sit down."

"I wish Daoud were here." Baruch threw himself down in Youssef's chair by the bed. By habit he picked up Rafael's palsied left hand, felt for his pulse, and checked his watch. Baruch looked grimly down at his brother. "How are you today, Rafael?"

Rafael wrote furiously. He held up a piece of paper. "The same," it read.

Abbas elaborated. "He ate both breakfast and lunch. I helped him to the bathroom. He still can't walk by himself."

"He's doing all right," Baruch snapped.

Rafael held up another paper. "I won't die. They can't kill this old Jew."

Baruch looked his brother over. Rafael's skin was colorless and damp. The stroke had left his face permanently twisted. Only Rafael's bright, restless eyes were unchanged. But there were traces of neither pity nor affection on Baruch's face as he sized up his brother. "Rafael, I have something important to discuss with you. You can understand me, can't you, Rafael?"

Rafael nodded vigorously.

"Youssef, you come here, too. Abbas, why don't you see if you can find me something to eat in the kitchen. And don't hurry back. We'll be having a family conference."

Abbas glided away on command.

Baruch waited until the door was shut. "I was at the police station today, Rafael. I was there—I thought on a social call—to talk with a lieutenant by the name of Hamuda el-Salem. Mona may marry him in the spring."

Rafael shrugged indifferently.

"Imagine my surprise, Rafael, when Hamuda el-Salem never mentioned Mona. Imagine my shock, Rafael, when he led me into an interrogation room, sat me down on a chair, and began asking me about you, Rafael. About *you.*"

Youssef sank down on the edge of his father's bed. He had never seen his uncle so angry. There were hard lines around Baruch's mouth.

"It seems the police think you're a Zionist, Rafael. Hamuda el-Salem thinks you've not only been siphoning our money to radical Zionist groups, but that a Zionist gang of which you are a member, Rafael, has been plotting to blow up bridges, government buildings, military installations."

"Father?" Youssef tried to laugh. But he was remembering his father's humiliation on the steps of the Cotton Exchange, his late-night meetings with those dark men in the drawing room, his sudden obsession with all things Jewish after Batata died, his heart failure at losing his seat on the Cotton Exchange.

Rafael produced a gobbling noise, the most that his vocal cords could manage.

"Easy, Rafael. Don't get excited. You don't want to have another stroke now, do you?"

Rafael's obedient stillness was sure testament to his determination to live.

"They say specifically, Rafael, that they have documents and witnesses to prove that you are planning to blow up the Cotton Exchange."

Rafael's features were a mask of sly cunning. But no answer.

"Rafael, this is serious. This was a warning today. Hamuda el-Salem was warning us, trying to help Mona's people. But you're—we're—all in danger now. You have to tell us. Trust us, Rafael."

Rafael gave them a calculating look, then bent and wrote on his pad.

" 'Fifteen Harat el-Pasha, Karmuz,' " Baruch read aloud. "What does it mean, Rafael?"

Rafael pointed his finger at Youssef and wrote another note. "Go there. Ask for a man they call Muhammad. Bring him here. Now."

The Alley of the Pashas—Harat el-Pasha—was in a quarter of the city that Youssef, like any sane *huwaga,* had never traveled on foot. But he knew about Karmuz. Everyone knew about Karmuz, mostly from jokes that would begin with a soldier and a *fellaha,* both of them innocently looking for a lost friend—the situation alone provoked laughter

—in Karmuz. It was a clamorous, congested rabbit warren that was home not only for destitute Arab families who had never had hope, but also for petty criminals, pimps, prostitutes, and sailors who had long ago abandoned ship. By night no one with even a spare half piaster to buy a glass of tea came to Karmuz. Neither taxis nor police patrols would enter this no-man's-land. Yet once Karmuz, the oldest quarter of Alexandria, had known glory. In the ashy dirt of Karmuz were the ruins of Greek pillars, Roman temples, Cleopatra's palace, and even subterranean early Christian catacombs with stone carvings of cobras and crosses. The conquering Arabs had built mosques in Karmuz, and finally—long centuries ago—Turkish pashas had walled away their women there. On the maps Karmuz lay in Alexandria's deep belly, inland from where the Ras el-Tin promontory juts out into the Mediterranean, far from the sea, closer to the salt swamps of Lake Maryut and the sludgy brown Nile branch known as the al-Mahmudiya Canal.

Youssef had been walking for hours before he was even in that part of Karmuz where the Alley of the Pashas was said to be. He had dressed in Abbas's oldest *gallabeiya*. Around his head he had wrapped one of the rags Khadiga used to mop the floors. Yet Youssef knew he couldn't pass for a native. He didn't have that stooped, shuffling walk. He didn't have that wily Karmuz knack of seeing and hearing everything but appearing to be deaf and dumb and blind. He knew little of suspicion, not nearly enough of fear. As Youssef had wandered from one bleak dusty street to another, his foreboding had grown. Back in the Villa al-Masri, he had bravely assured Baruch that he would return with this Muhammad before dusk. But now the sun had set, and as the darkness seemed to seep into the pores of Youssef's skin, he wished he had sent Abbas in his place. He stumbled along behind the boy who had, for a price, finally agreed to lead him to his destination. Youssef kept his eyes on where the boy's leathery bare feet slapped ahead in the dirt. Youssef tried to concentrate on sidestepping the stray bits of barbed wire and the wobbling pyramids of broken glass and garbage.

As if pretending to be invisible would make him so, he did not look up at those fierce men he sensed lurking in every doorway. He at first had tried to make himself believe that Karmuz wasn't so different from the *baladi* neighborhoods he and Mona had been so delighted to tramp on their adventurous last weeks in Cairo. Karmuz wasn't any dirtier. The peeling paint on the sagging buildings, the rusty metal shacks on the rooftops, the clotheslines of soiled laundry, weren't any more grim. *Baladi* Cairo, too, had smelled of urine and sheep dung and cooking oil fried too many times. The same reedy quartertone music howled from radios. Black-shrouded women, at his approach, pulled their coarse shawls around their brown faces with the same nervous gesture. Swarms of small boys, as always, begged for *baksheesh*.

But Youssef, in those *baladi* promenades with Mona by his side, had thought himself in love with the mysteries of all things Egyptian. He had seen beauty in squalor, hope in the ready *baladi* laughter, wisdom in the mumblings of old men outside the coffeehouses. Most of all he had thought he glimpsed something of Mona in every face in the crowd: Mona as a patient madonna when he saw a young woman pulling three children down the street, Mona as a tender guardian when he saw a child petting a sheep, Mona as the bravest of the brave when he saw a one-legged man in rags nobly setting out on an errand that was probably doomed. Loving Mona, he had loved not only what she had come from but what she had overcome. He had told himself that the life on a *baladi* street—its small hidden triumphs, its huge visible tragedies— was more real, more human, and maybe ultimately more merciful than what he himself had known in his golden frivolous life in Alexandria's villas and cabarets.

Karmuz exploded that myth. Those old women weren't carrying those jugs of water on their heads to be picturesque. There was no running water in the hovels of Karmuz. Those men salaaming on those reed mats weren't thanking their God for His rich bounty but pleading for the will to last another day. The blue bead on that baby there with the diseased eyes wasn't for decoration but to blunt the fear of death. Karmuz was as threatening and pathetic as thousands of broken lives could make it. Maybe, Youssef thought, maybe I'm seeing Egypt for the first time. And maybe I am seeing Mona, too.

The boy who was guiding him to Harat el-Pasha finally stopped and pointed to the left. At first Youssef could see no opening in what looked like a solid block of decayed buildings. But then he looked closer. An old man stood behind a wagon of rotting fish and screamed false claims at the top of his lungs: "*Samak!* Fish! Fresh fish! The pride of Alexandria!" Behind the peddler Youssef saw a large crack between two abandoned buildings.

"Harat el-Pasha," the boy said. "The Alley of the Pashas."

Youssef fished in his pocket for the twenty-five piasters he had agreed to pay the boy. Instead, in the darkness, he pulled out a one-pound note. The urchin grabbed it and darted off. Youssef let him go, relieved the boy had not abandoned him in some dark cul-de-sac where he might have been robbed, knifed, killed.

It was dark in the Alley of the Pashas, though Youssef noted with relief that the passageway widened once he had stepped away from the main street. But there was no light at all. Even the moonlight did not reach where he walked, for the buildings on either side were five stories tall and slanted outward, so that the alley was almost a tunnel. The vague outlines of what could only be ancient rotting wooden *mashrabiya* had been built precariously out from the walls and over the alley, blocking the sky's natural night light. He peered up, trying

231

to imagine what this must have been like four hundred years ago, when wives and concubines and eunuchs of some medieval pasha peeked down from behind the intricate carved wooden screens of the *mash-rabiyas*. Now no one, at least no one that Youssef could see, watched his halting progress down the alley as he looked for number fifteen.

But someone must have been watching, for suddenly Youssef heard an Arabic growl behind him. "What do you want here?"

Youssef froze in place. That sinister voice lay between him and the comparatively safe and bustling street. Youssef gulped. "Number fifteen. I'm looking for number fifteen, *Khamastasher Harat el-Pasha.*"

"Why?" The one word came at Youssef like a bullet.

"Muhammad. I have a message for a man . . . they call Muhammad."

"Who sent you?"

"My father. Rafael al-Masri."

"And you are . . . ?"

"Youssef al-Masri."

There was a silence, then a whispered conversation. Youssef began to tremble. There were at least two men behind him in the alley. Maybe there were more.

Each of his arms was roughly seized, and Youssef was propelled in silence down the black alley. They turned to the left, then to the right, where the passage was so narrow they had to walk in single file. Youssef heard a cat, or a baby, or something that was neither a cat nor a baby, scream. The men pushed Youssef through a door.

Youssef blinked in the sudden light. The tiny room, lit by a single kerosene lantern, moved with shadowy gray shapes. Gradually he could make out five men, plus the two who had brought him, surrounded by cartons stacked flush against the walls nearly to the ceiling. In one corner was a black box with knobs, buttons, and earphones. One man squatted at the shortwave. The others were grouped together around a man who was drinking white liquid from a glass and staring hard at . . . at me, Youssef realized.

"We found him in the alley," one of his captors was reporting. "He says he's Rafael al-Masri's son. Says he was sent here with a message for Muhammad."

The man who was most certainly their leader took a long pull on his milk. "And what was that message?" His Arabic was fluid and accentless.

"Are you Muhammad?"

No one answered.

Youssef hurried on. "My father wants you to come to his—our—house. There's a problem." When there was no response in the killing silence, Youssef rambled on. Anything to end that silence. "My Uncle Baruch was at the police station today. They told him my father was involved"—here Youssef let out a nervous giggle—"in a Zionist plot to . . . blow up buildings." He could not stop himself from staring at the cartons. Were they full of dynamite? "They said one of the buildings was the Cotton Exchange."

The leader stooped to put his glass of milk down on the floor. "What did your uncle tell the police?"

"Nothing. Nothing at all. He just came home and told me and my father. All my father did was tell me to come here."

The leader nodded and was silent.

His message delivered, Youssef appraised his questioner. On the street tall, blond Youssef would never have given this short, dark, shabby man a second glance. So what was it, Youssef asked himself, that made him feel such a callow youth next to this milk-drinking man who couldn't be far from his own age? It had to be, Youssef decided, something in his insolent, heavy-lidded eyes, something in the arrogance of the way this man held himself. Youssef had once known this same sureness in the halls of Victoria College. But this white man had the nerve to feel in control in the brown slums of Karmuz. Whoever he was, he intrigued Youssef. "Are you Muhammad?"

The leader did not answer but instead fired a barrage of questions at him.

"What is the name of your dog?"

Startled but eager to please, Youssef answered quickly, "Suker. We had another, but Zibda died."

"You had a governess—Swiss—when you were a child. What was her name?"

"Helga. Helga."

"And your history teacher at Victoria?"

"Mr. Barton."

The man seemed satisfied. "Sit down," he said, indicating the floor. He made a slight concession to graciousness. "Sorry about all those questions. But I had to be sure you were who you claimed to be. Before this, I had seen only your photographs." He paused but then went on before Youssef could ask what the hell he was talking about. "Youssef al-Masri, I now believe you are who you claim to be. My name is Moshe, not Muhammad. I can tell you all this because you are one of us now. Welcome, Youssef, to Little Israel."

It was after midnight when Youssef and the eight Israelis arrived at the back door of the Villa al-Masri. It had taken them nearly two hours to get here, for they had slipped through the back alleys in a roundabout way, intent on shaking anyone who had followed Youssef to the Alley of the Pashas. Along the way they had picked up another dark-haired man, presumably one of their comrades. Moving through the streets, Youssef kept telling himself that none of this could possibly be real. He would have a good laugh at this preposterous dream in the morning. Meanwhile, Youssef was uncertain of what precisely was happening, for the others were talking in low voices in a vaguely familiar language. He hadn't heard Hebrew since his *bar mitzvah*. The sad, grieving cadence of that ancient dead language he had muttered in the synagogue ripped off their tongues like machine-gun fire. He could understand only a word here and there.

"The servants?" One of the men addressed Youssef in Arabic as the squad looked around the kitchen. "Where are the servants?"

"Gone," Youssef said with satisfaction. "None of them sleep here anymore."

Moshe nodded. "Take us to Rafael."

Youssef led them upstairs to the door, but they barred him from entering.

"You, Chaim, go with Youssef," Moshe said. "Let him change into civilized clothes. Get the brother. And the other son. Then wait for us here. And *move!*"

Chaim watched Youssef pull on tan trousers, a clean shirt, a blue wool blazer. Youssef tucked his wallet inside his pocket and then—for luck—took his wedding ring as well. First they went to Baruch's room and stared down at the empty bed. No, Youssef thought. No! Baruch was the only one who could have straightened out Moshe. But Daoud was where he was supposed to be, sound asleep in bed. Youssef shook him awake. "Get up. Get dressed. Don't ask questions. But for God's sake, tell me what's happened to Uncle Baruch."

Daoud rubbed his eyes. "He was out helping some woman have her baby. What time is it, Youssef? And who's *that?*" He pointed to Chaim. When neither of them answered, Daoud dressed in silence. Chaim herded them back in the hallway just as the other Israelis emerged from Rafael's bedroom. One of them carried Rafael in his arms. Suker barked frantically at their heels. Rafael was smiling radiantly. In his arms he clutched Batata's scrapbook.

"Are you crazy?" Youssef was shouting. "Put my father down. He's sick. Can't you see he's a sick man?"

Moshe ignored Youssef. "Where's the other one? Rafael's brother?"

"Not here," Chaim said. "Out delivering a baby."

"We can't wait for him." Moshe's next orders were for Rafael. "Write your brother a note. Tell him where you and your sons are going. We'll leave the message on your bed." While Rafael scribbled, Moshe continued to think out loud. "There's no time to search the house for any stray papers. Not if we're to hit the tides right. Besides, they seem to know all about us already. Their intelligence network appears to be more efficient than their army." Moshe finally turned to Youssef. "We're leaving. All of us. Tonight."

"Leaving?" Youssef stammered.

"We go to Israel," Moshe said.

"Israel!" Youssef shook his head. "No. Not me."

"You don't have a choice," Moshe said. "We can't leave you here. Not now. Not with all you know."

"I won't tell," Youssef said. "I promise."

"You're stupider than I thought," Moshe snapped.

"But you don't understand. My girlfriend—no, my wife. I can't leave her."

Moshe paused. "Wife? What wife? Our intelligence said you weren't married."

"But I am. Mona. Mona is my wife."

Moshe cocked an eye at the man they had picked up en route to the al-Masris'. "Avi? Can you confirm that?"

"An Arab girl," Avi answered. "Used to be a servant here. Now is a nurse. The one he had on that houseboat in Cairo. But they're not married."

Youssef's mouth flew open in shock, and he looked quickly over at his father. Rafael was smiling smugly at him. His father must have known about him and Mona all this time. No wonder he hadn't questioned him about his supposed stint in the army. The Israelis had been spying on him.

"The girl, Avi," Moshe asked, "she is not a Jew?"

"No. She's an Arab, all right. Looks like one, talks like one, smells like one."

Youssef swung at the man who had profaned his Mona, but two of the Israelis pinned back his arms.

Moshe looked at him in disgust. "A fine Jew you are. I'd love to leave you here. You don't *deserve* Israel. But we—you—have no choice. Come *on*, lover boy." He turned and started running down the stairs.

"I won't go!" Youssef shouted.

"Gag him," Moshe called over his shoulder. "*Yalla*—let's go! The boat won't wait forever. And put that stupid dog back in the bedroom. We can't take a dog."

Marched between two burly Israelis, his mouth bound shut with a handkerchief, his eyes blurred with angry tears, Youssef staggered out the kitchen door. Two cars awaited them. They sped down the Corniche and out of the city on the road to Abu Kir. There they clambered aboard a motorboat and headed for the open sea. They were so far west that the lights of Alexandria were only a dim gold glow in the black night.

Baruch did not notice anything amiss in the villa when he arrived home just before dawn. He threw himself on his bed, depressed because the woman had died in childbirth. He slept fitfully.

Abbas and Khadiga arrived at the Villa al-Masri at six o'clock that morning. Khadiga made tea, and Abbas prepared Rafael's breakfast tray of eggs, cheese, and toast. He heard Suker barking behind the closed bedroom door when he was coming up the stairs. He threw open the door, and the dog began to howl. Abbas stared at the wild confusion of sheets and blankets and pillows on the empty bed. Mechanically Abbas put the tray down on a table, drew the curtains, and stared again at the bed. He saw Rafael's note, picked it up, and wished he knew how to read. He looked at the muddy footprints on the floor and hoped the police had not come in the night. Hamuda el-Salem had warned him that Monsieur was in trouble. Allah keep him, Abbas prayed. He looked down at the note again and debated whether he should collect Khadiga, head back to the flat for Mona and his son, and take all of them on the first train south to Karnak. No. He had served the al-Masris for more than forty years. He would not abandon them now. With the note still in his hand, Abbas checked the other rooms. Youssef's bed was still made. Daoud's had been slept in. Baruch was asleep.

Abbas looked down at his best friend. Without his glasses, Baruch looked like the child he had once sailed with out to the islands in the bay. Abbas sighed down at the last of the al-Masris, and then he tenderly shook Baruch awake. He told him Rafael, Youssef, and Daoud were gone. He thrust the note at Baruch and then remembered to hand him his glasses. Baruch started to read it out loud: " 'Gone to . . .' " But then Baruch darted a glance at Abbas and read the rest of it to himself: Gone to Israel with Y. and D. Police right. Take care.

The two men stared at each other. Baruch was the first to look away.

"The police?" Abbas asked.

"No. The enemy," Baruch answered. In a very quiet voice Baruch asked Abbas to wait for him down in the kitchen with Khadiga. He was determined not to implicate Abbas in what he knew he had to do.

When he was alone, Baruch threw cold water on his face, dressed, and read the note one more time. He had to believe the unbelievable. Hamuda el-Salem had been correct. Rafael—his foolish, bitter, sick older brother—had allowed himself to be drawn into some bizarre Zionist plot. Baruch shook his head. His blood relatives were all gone. Later he would have the time and the inclination to try to understand how this could have happened, how Rafael could have played a role in this hare-brained melodrama. But now Baruch knew he had to act. He lit a match to Rafael's note. He watched it curl in the flame and then turn to gray ash. Carefully Baruch searched the drawing room, his brother's study, and the bedrooms. He piled a stack of papers in the drawing-room fireplace and set them ablaze. When the police came—and Baruch was sure they would come very soon—there would be no incriminating evidence. Next Baruch rooted through drawers and cabinets, rejecting items of sentimental value but choosing those that could easily be converted to cash. He collected a pile of gold jewelry, silverware, and Rafael's immensely valuable porcelains. He carried it all to the kitchen and told Khadiga to pack it carefully in a reed laundry basket. After covering it on top with soiled towels, she was immediately to take it back to her flat for safekeeping.

It was time. There was, finally, only one thing that had to be done. Baruch knew he had to disassociate himself from his brother's politics, had to make it clear both to the authorities and to himself that he had no sympathy with Zionism. What he was about to do he had contemplated for many years, as he had delved deeper and deeper into the Arab mind, the Arab heart, the Arab soul. Now necessity forced his hand.

"Abbas. Go to the café. Bring back a man. A pious man. A Muslim. I need two witnesses."

Abbas silently swept out the door and returned only a few minutes later where Baruch waited in the parlor. With Abbas was an old Koran chanter who was much respected at the neighborhood mosque.

Baruch stood up, clenching his hands into tight fists. At last he spoke. "There is no God but Allah," he said slowly and very distinctly. "And Muhammad is His Prophet." There were tears on Baruch's cheeks. His family had made one choice, and he another. He was a Muslim.

11 〰〰

HAIFA BAY, ISRAELI WATERS / February 1957

Too tense for sleep, Youssef was pacing the deck just after dawn. For three days they had been at sea, bound for Haifa. First they had huddled on a Greek fishing boat. Then they had transferred to an even smaller and more rundown ship in a harbor at Cyprus. This creaky little craft with its gunmetal decks and cramped quarters flew the blue Star of David flag of Israel.

Youssef leaned on the rail and watched the heavy, wet fog hug the sea. As he remembered it—already Alexandria was taking on a mythic glow in his mind—at home the Mediterranean had always been calm and blue. Even the sea here was hostile and alien. Every unpleasant lurch of the boat took him farther from Mona and Egypt.

Again he reviewed the sorry facts. He had tried to explain, over and over again, to his father and to the Israelis, that he did not want to leave Egypt because he was pledged to marry the women he loved there. Neither his father nor the Israelis had been sympathetic. His father had scribbled him curt notes to stop whining and begin acting like a Jew. Moshe, even when Youssef had wrung his hands and said Mona could be killed if he didn't marry her, had shrugged and said more than that was at stake. He had tersely informed Youssef that he was no longer simply an Egyptian Jew—a member, Moshe stressed, of an increasingly despised minority—but an enemy of Egypt. Didn't Youssef understand that the Egyptian secret police, if they couldn't arrest Rafael, would make do with his son? The Egyptians would be able to find witnesses to testify that Youssef had visited their headquarters in the Alley of the Pashas. Prison and maybe even torture awaited Youssef in Egypt.

And even if Youssef didn't care about that consequence, Moshe did. Two years ago Israel had been internationally embarrassed by a sensational Cairo spy trial when Egyptian Jews had bungled a sabotage mission. Two were hanged, one committed suicide, and four others were still imprisoned. Moshe wasn't going to hand the Egyptians another propaganda tool named Youssef al-Masri. Moshe and his men had been sent to Egypt before the Suez war, when it was thought either that Nasser might be deposed by a popular uprising or that guerrilla fighting might be prolonged for many months. Moshe had aborted his mission, but he couldn't allow Youssef to turn it into a fiasco. Besides, Moshe had said, Youssef's Italian residency visa listed him as a Jew. Egypt was not allowing Jews back inside its borders. Youssef was in permanent exile.

Youssef stared through the thick swirls of fog. Moshe had to be wrong about Egypt. Moshe didn't know Egypt. It was true that the two wars with Israel had altered almost everything. But surely they had not twisted the character of an entire nation? The Egypt Youssef loved wouldn't unjustly persecute him. Egypt was neither violent nor hateful. The Egyptians—with their jokes and their sentimentality and their eagerness to settle for so little—were the most kind, the most generous, the easiest *malesh* of a people on earth. Yes, that was Egypt. But there were other Egypts: the Egypt of that "Abdel" on the steps of the Cotton Exchange, the Egypt of the Arabs who had ostracized him at Victoria, the Egypt of the mob who had screamed for blood the night Batata died, the Egypt of the bitter and greedy Cairo secretary who had denied their marriage certificate. Youssef remembered how these gentle sweet people could beat to death a balking animal. He remembered the fear that had shaken his bowels when he had walked the desperate lanes of Karmuz. Mona still carried a puckered scar between her legs as a souvenir of that other Egypt.

Maybe Moshe was at least a little right about Egypt. If only, Youssef thought, if only I could be sure. If only I knew the truth. If only I could be sure there *is* a truth. He longed to jump ship and swim back home to Mona, if by doing so everything could return to what it was meant to be. Instead Youssef gripped the rail and felt sick at his stomach. Had he done everything possible to protect Mona? Or had he simply allowed others to save his own skin? He remembered, from his medieval history class at Victoria, stories of monks who whipped themselves in their cells with little knotted pieces of leather. At the time he had thought that very strange.

Moshe had explained to him that of course no one would hold him in Israel again his will. He could go wherever he wanted, so long as it wasn't Egypt. The Jewish Agency could probably help him find his mother and sisters in Paris. But Youssef had not much liked Europe. Too, he had not forgiven his mother for the way she had treated Mona the night he had asked for his parents' blessing. No, he would not follow his runaway mother to France. Weighing in Israel's favor was his father's and brother's determination to settle there. Youssef didn't want to desert the two of them. Already he had done more than enough abandoning for a lifetime. At least Israel was in the Middle East. It couldn't be all that different from Egypt. It was close to home. When the political situation cooled down, maybe it would be easy to slip over the border. He would bide his time in Israel. But he would never give up Mona. Never.

Youssef clenched the railing as if, with the force of his hands, he could back the boat up and push it home to Alexandria. But the boat continued its steady vibrations toward Haifa. He heard a brisk hurried step behind him and turned as Moshe approached. Youssef straightened up and waited. Moshe made him nervous. He was always observing, judging, and finding everyone—particularly Youssef—not quite up to the mark. Youssef apparently had disgraced himself in Moshe's eyes by pining for an Arab girl instead of the Promised Land. Always Moshe treated Youssef with open contempt. Yet Youssef, in return, had been unable to stop himself from fawning on Moshe. He hated himself for it, but against all logic he wanted this overbearing young commando to like him, to respect him, to recognize—as everyone else always had—that Youssef al-Masri was superior in every way. And, too, for all Youssef knew, Israel might be full of Moshes. If he could learn to crack this one's stern facade, Youssef would have made a beginning. *"Sabah el-khair,"* Youssef called out in cheerful Arabic. He smiled too fully. "You slept well?"

Moshe grunted.

Even that guttural noise sounded foreign. Moshe, Youssef decided, must be grunting in Hebrew. As soon as they had left Egypt, the Israelis had refused to speak Arabic. Youssef tried a civil *bonjour,* remembering too late that Moshe also scorned French. "Sorry," he apologized in English.

Moshe consented to stand next to Youssef by the rail. He looked appraisingly out over the sea. "I wait to see the land," he said, in case Youssef was deluded enough to think he sought the pleasure of his company.

"Coffee?" Youssef asked, despising himself even as he spoke. "You want coffee? It should be ready by now."

"Milk."

Youssef went below to fetch two glasses of milk. He handed Moshe the fuller one. "We should be there any time now." Youssef tried to summon all his social graces. "Imagine. My first glimpse of Israel. I've been so many places. But never Israel." Moshe did not answer. "So tell me. What's Israel like?"

"Soon enough you will see."

"How does it compare with Europe? Is it as beautiful as France? Or Italy? It must be like Greece. Dry. Rocky. Barren."

"It is like nowhere else on earth."

Youssef persisted. "It must be like somewhere else. It's in the Middle East." He voiced his fondest hope. "It can't be all that different . . . say, even from Egypt."

"It is nothing like Egypt."

"How is it different?"

"How could it be the same?" Moshe sipped his milk and scanned the horizon for Israel.

As a sharp cold drizzle began to fall, Youssef turned the collar up on his blazer. Rain. We will arrive in the rain. It was, he thought, an appropriate beginning. "The sailors told me we're not far from shore. Maybe we could see it now if it weren't for the weather." There was no response from Moshe. Youssef stood in a silence he pretended was congenial. But he couldn't leave Moshe alone. "So what will Haifa look like? The sailors said it's built on a mountain. Mount Carmel."

Mosha's body tensed. "There it is. There!"

"Where?" Youssef looked into the gray oblivion.

"Ahead. To the right. Haifa."

The pelting rain had soaked through Youssef's wool jacket to the skin. He could just about make out a dark high mass through the fog. "Haifa?"

"Israel!" Moshe's voice was low, excited, throbbing. "Israel!" Moshe's face reflected the delight of a very young boy on his birthday and the anticipation of an ardent lover on his wedding night. "Israel!" When Moshe said it, it was a a caress.

"It's beautiful," Youssef said amicably.

"The most beautiful land in the world." Moshe was talking more to himself than to Youssef. "Our land. Our home. Our Israel. Every time I have to leave it, I ache. And every time I come back, I feel again what our people have always felt. Joy beyond all joy. Eretz Israel, the land of Israel!"

"Yes," Youssef said as he stared at Moshe in fascination. He had never seen such an overreaction to mere earth. "Yes."

Now Moshe was shouting. "Israel! Israel! At last!"

The others from his squad were crowding on deck and jabbering in Hebrew. Each face mirrored Moshe's. Some were crying without shame. Others were pounding their comrades on the back. One was praying.

Daoud came up from behind and put his hand on Youssef's shoulder. "Youssef! Israel! We're home!"

The two brothers looked out at the black coast through the silvery-gray slivers of rain.

"Do you feel it?" Daoud asked. "Do you?"

Youssef shook his head.

Daoud bit the smile off his face and patted his brother's shoulder. On the boat their roles had been reversed. It was Daoud who was the knowing one, Daoud who tried by example to show his brother how to be. "You will. You'll feel it. I know you will. Give it time."

"I wish I had your confidence."

"That's funny." Daoud smiled. "I always wished I had yours."

They were silent for a moment as they watched Mount Carmel fill the sky.

"Tell the truth, Daoud. Will you really be happy to get off here?"

"Does it matter?" Already Daoud had picked up the Israeli habit of answering a question with another question.

"I suppose not," Youssef answered.

Thoughtfully Daoud looked out at the land looming before them. "More than anything I know that I'm grateful to be coming here. Or maybe it's just that I'm relieved to be leaving *there*. But then, you left more . . . at home . . . than I did."

"Mona." Youssef hunched miserably down into his sodden jacket.

"I'm very sorry, Youssef."

"I know."

Daoud groped for words of comfort. "Mona was like my sister. It was easy to love her." He wanted to let Youssef know he would always stand beside him. "But you're not alone, Youssef. I'm here. Father's here. We're together."

"It's not right, Daoud." Youssef's voice broke. "It wasn't right to leave her."

Daoud sighed. "But Youssef, you didn't have a choice. So much of what seems to be happening all around us is not our choice. I used to think that when we grew up, we would be able to control our own lives. But now I wonder. Maybe none of us ever has control." He shrugged. "But definitely, now, everything is out of control."

"Yes." Youssef thought to himself that Daoud was beginning to talk like Uncle Baruch. His gentle, sad, reasoned voice even sounded like

Baruch's. He looked over at the one who had always been the lesser of the al-Masri brothers. Daoud's sandy hair still swept untidily down over the rim of his glasses, his nose was still too big and bony, he still looked as if he needed to be fattened up by a mother who cared. But something about Daoud had altered. Some of the old hesitancy—maybe even the air of the born victim—was gone. Maybe Daoud would have some answers. He asked Daoud what he would have liked to ask Baruch. "Was it all my fault?"

"It was none of our faults," Daoud answered, much as Baruch might have.

Youssef tossed his head toward the smudged coastline of Israel. "What I'd like to know, Daoud, is how the hell did we get here? And why? *Why?*"

"As I said, Youssef, it's all beyond our control. But at least we'll belong here. We're Jews. This is our country. Egypt never was. They didn't want us there. If we hadn't left, before long they would have thrown us out. You know how it was."

Youssef thought of Mona's arms around him as they rode through the desert at dawn toward the pyramids. "I know how it was. Egypt was Paradise."

"Youssef!" Daoud shook his head in exasperation. "You're not even trying."

Youssef, remembering that his brother had always been susceptible to Zionism, felt more alone than ever. He stiffened his neck and squared his shoulders. "Let's go get Father."

But as they turned to go below deck, Daoud held out his hand. "Youssef? I loved it, too."

Youssef smiled and smacked his palm, Arab-style, atop his brother's.

They found their father just inside the cabin door. Rafael had heard the commotion on deck and impatiently had dragged himself from his bunk. He was crawling toward the door as a three-legged spider might. His shirt had pulled loose of his pants, and the skinny, pale, freckled flesh of his back was showing. Youssef closed his eyes for a second at the sight of his father brought so low. But then Rafael lifted his head, and Youssef saw that his eyes were ashine with tears. Rafael's twisted face was glowing. His throat garbled a word that could have been "Israel." For the first time this morning, Youssef was moved. He had been embarrassed at Moshe's emotion and the weeping and praying of the others. But to see his once icy and self-contained father so transported eased a little of Youssef's own grief. It struck him that these men appeared to love this country as he loved his Mona. He would try to respect whatever it was about Israel that spawned such love.

The brothers carried the father on the deck and stood with their arms intertwined. The rain had slowed to a gentle spray. As their boat pulled into the crescent of Haifa harbor, the white sun broke through the charcoal sky. The silver sheen of raindrops seemed to add a luster of dew to the sparkling shore, and the gold rays of the sun refracted Haifa like a jewel. High, steep, verdant Mount Carmel was dotted with clusters of red-roofed, whitewashed villas and crowned at its center by a curious gold-domed temple. More houses were scattered low by the water, so that the mountain seemed a lush cushiony frame around the fragile shining city at its feet.

In its way, Youssef admitted to himself, Haifa was as lovely as Alexandria. He had not expected beauty in Israel.

The bald, busy bureaucrat shot a question at them first in Hebrew, then Yiddish, finally English.

"Youssef al-Masri."

"Daoud al-Masri."

The Jewish Agency official narrowed his eyes in a squint at Rafael's scrawled note. "*Vuss? Vuss?*" he muttered in Yiddish. "What? What?"

Youssef handed him their Italian passports, gave their religion as Jewish and their country of origin as Egypt. His father, he explained, was a stroke victim.

The official frowned. "English, Arabic, German, French, Bulgarian, Italian, Spanish. Isn't it enough? You can read this?" He thrust the note at Youssef.

" 'Rafael Ben-Yehuda,' " Youssef read.

"Another Ben-Yehuda." The immigration official inscribed the name.

"What's this?" Youssef faced his beaming father. "Ben-Yehuda?"

"Rafael, the son of a Jew," Daoud translated for Youssef. Daoud had conscientiously attended Hebrew class. He wouldn't have been able to buy a kilo of olives at the market, but he still had at least the basic vocabulary of prayer.

"I know." Youssef's tone was so sharp that the official's short temper appeared to be contagious. "But why, Father?"

Rafael wrote. " 'I will not be called al-Masri—the Egyptian—ever again,' " Youssef read aloud. " 'Proud to be a Jew.' "

"If you're finished with your family conference," the official was saying, "we can proceed. So you're all Jews, and you're all from Egypt."

"Alexandria," Youssef corrected him. He looked around the cavernous bustling warehouse at the pier with its long, gaudy queues of refugees from everywhere. He saw dark-eyed women in black robes and blond women in smart silk traveling suits. He saw men in tweed jackets and in tribal dress. He saw children who were barefoot and children who were wearing navy and white school uniforms. From the worried babble he could recognize French, Arabic, and German. Other shouts were incomprehensible. Some of the newcomers carried babies and boxes and baskets. Others, like the al-Masris, stood with very nearly empty arms.

"My father was in the Jewish underground," Daoud explained. "We would have been arrested if we had stayed. We had to leave everything."

"Yes," Youssef echoed. "Everything."

The Jewish Agency man yawned at the familiar lament. He himself had been lucky to get out of Austria before the war. Many he had known in his youth had not shared his good fortune. He had used up his meager reserves of sympathy, mostly in the middle of the night, brooding over all those who were no longer with him. To him, the plight of three Jews who had "lost everything" was unremarkable. They had no idea what it was to lose everything. "So. How much money did you bring?"

"Nothing," Youssef said. His eyes fell on the Batata memorial scrapbook in his father's arms. "We have almost nothing."

"The Egyptian government confiscated it all. We were lucky to escape with our lives." Daoud was apologetic about the melodrama of his words. He didn't know that in Israel, far more harrowing tales than theirs were run-of-the-mill.

"Any relatives?"

"None here," Youssef answered.

"So you'll be living on the state. At least, until you get jobs." The official looked appraisingly up at Youssef and Daoud. "Or until you go into the army." He checked off a few more boxes on the forms. "How's your Hebrew?"

"Minimal," Youssef admitted.

"Three penniless Egyptians with no Hebrew." The bureaucrat shook his head. "Jobs. What sort of jobs did you have?"

"My father," Daoud said, "was a broker on the Cotton Exchange. And an industrialist." Rafael stood a little straighter.

"But can he do anything now?"

"Now he's sick," Youssef said. "You can see that."

"And you two? What did you do"—the official absently paused as he looked over the forms—"in Egypt?"

"I worked for my father. Daoud was a student. We both went to Victoria College. In Alexandria."

As the clerk checked off more boxes, official Israel was classifying them as university graduates. "Ages?"

"I'm twenty-three. My brother is nineteen. Father is fifty-nine."

The official pounded their forms with a rubber stamp. "That does it. First the doctors will look you over. Wait outside for the medical bus. Then you'll be sent to a transit camp near Beersheva. You'll be able to use your Arabic on the rest of the North Africans. There aren't any pyramids, but there is more than enough sand. *Shalom.*" He waved them along.

But Rafael refused to budge. He scribbled a note. " 'We go to Jerusalem,' " Youssef read. "I was promised Jerusalem."

"You don't decide where you go. *I* decide where you go. We need settlers in the Negev Desert. Everyone wants Jerusalem. But you are going to the Negev. To Beersheva."

Rafael scratched another note. " 'Get Major Moshe,' " Youssef read. " 'The deal was Jerusalem.' "

The official's pink face was turning red. "You come here without a lira. Without Hebrew. Without job skills. Without family to help you. And you tell me where the state should send you? You have the *chutzpah* to bargain with me?"

"Be reasonable," Daoud said.

"Be smart," Youssef added. He wasn't going to be pushed around by a low-grade clerk. He folded his arms against his chest. "My father works for Israeli Intelligence."

"Mossad?" The official consulted his fingernails and then picked up the telephone. "Major Moshe *who?*"

"The one on our boat," Youssef said. "Just find him."

Muttering under his breath in a language the al-Masris did not know, the official made four phone calls, gave them a volley of dirty looks, and then settled down to wait. From a brown paper sack at the side of his desk he pulled a piece of apple strudel.

In time Moshe strode in. He squeezed Rafael on the shoulder, smiled at Daoud, and nodded at Youssef. The immigration official erupted in rapid-fire Hebrew. But Moshe, answering him in kind, seemed to be pulling rank. In less than a minute, Moshe was collecting their papers and offering Rafael his arm. "We're going to postpone your medical checkups. You have had, I think, enough of our bureaucracy for one day. To Jerusalem!" Moshe smiled as he whisked them out the door, down a corridor, and out into the sun. Youssef blinked. At least the sun here was as strong as in Egypt. Half-dragging their father between them, Youssef and Daoud rushed after Moshe toward a khaki-colored jeep. Moshe climbed in beside the driver, and the al-Masris crawled in the back. "Relax," Moshe said as they shot out of the parking lot. "Jerusalem is three hours away."

Youssef tried to think positive as he craned his neck out the open side of the jeep. They whizzed past familiar-looking dark and dumpy Arab storefronts near the port. Then they were in manicured neighborhoods of colorless and flat-topped cement houses. Fragile young trees straggled beside careful patches of flowers. It was very clean, Youssef had to admit. But it was also very raw. By the looks of it, this city had been erected overnight by a dull but efficient military contractor who was paid by the piece. The lively business district, thronged with scurrying, intent shoppers, could just as easily have been in Hamburg or Manchester or Prague. While the jeep idled at a traffic light, Youssef watched herds of stout European women in flowered housedresses and shapeless sweaters carrying bulging bags of groceries. Bold-looking, pretty, long-legged girls strode by with firm giant steps. Vaguely European middle-aged men shuffled in single file with news-papers tucked under their arms. At least on this street there were no beggars, no hawkers of lemons, no old women squatting on the pave-ment selling matches. Nor, at first, could Youssef spot a single Arab. But finally two tall, hawk-nosed, light-skinned men sauntered by in long belted beige robes partially covered by wool Western jackets. In-stead of turbans, they wore flowing white scarves held in place by woven black cords. Youssef chewed his lip. Bloody hell. This was a foreign country.

They sped south on the shore road toward Tel Aviv. Low golden dunes hugged a Mediterranean that was as blue and calm as in Alexan-dria. With longing Youssef sniffed the salt air of home. The rolling forested hills of the Carmel range were silhouetted against the yellow sky.

"Take a good look at those trees," Moshe said. "Except for here and the Galilee, we still don't have enough of them. It's going to take us a few more years to get this country back in shape."

"Back in shape?" Youssef repeated.

"As it was when we left it," Moshe said. "When it truly was the land of milk and honey. Before we were driven off and the Arabs ran it into the ground." Abruptly the terrain was flat. Orderly brown fields lay fallow for the winter. A few men worked on tractors while other labor gangs dug in the ground. "They're removing the rocks," Moshe explained. "Sometimes I think this country is one big rock. When I was on my kibbutz, the hardest work was the rock detail. Sometimes I thought I would break my back on those rocks. But we did it. We cleared those fields. And they will do the same here." They were pass-ing through farms of shiny-leafed, low-lying trees arranged in endless tight rows. "Orange groves," Moshe said. "And grapefruit. Farther south there will be bananas. We grow the best fruit in the world. Also the best vegetables."

"Wasn't this once swampland?" Daoud asked. "And didn't the first settlers—I mean the Jews who came here forty or fifty years ago—face epidemics of malaria and typhus?"

"It was bad here, but the real malarial marshes were near the Galilee. That's where my kibbutz is."

"Your kibbutz," Daoud asked, "is it religious or socialist?"

"How can a kibbutz not be socialist?" Moshe asked.

"How can anything with a conscience not be socialist?" Daoud retorted.

Moshe turned halfway around in his seat to grin at Daoud. With a twinge of envy, Youssef realized that Moshe had never smiled at him like that. Was this how his brother had felt, living in his own shadow in Alexandria?

Passing through the monotonous fruit forests, the afternoon sun lulled them into drowsy silence. Several times in the next few hours they were stopped by soldiers with machine guns. To Youssef these short, wiry, very young men seemed much like the commandos he had first encountered in the Alley of the Pashas. An entire country, Youssef thought sourly to himself, populated by socialist commandos. Youssef shut his eyes and tried to dream it all away.

When he awoke they were climbing twisted, boulder-strewn hills on a road that must once have been cut from sheer stone. "We're almost there," Daoud informed him. "Almost to Jerusalem." Youssef hadn't even known that Jerusalem was up in the mountains. "These are the Judean hills." Daoud sounded as if he had memorized a guidebook. "King David once walked here."

When they crested a final ridge, Moshe ordered the driver to pull over and park. Even as they helped Rafael out of the jeep, Moshe was pointing. "There! Over there you can see the Old City."

Rafael made a sound.

Daoud stared, then bowed his head.

Youssef squinted. Rooted in the stubble of a town perched on millions of stones he could glimpse tall turrets, graceful minarets, onion-shaped domes, spires topped by crosses. All of it was caught together in the bow of a high, winding wall that seemed to spring from the rocky innards of the heart of the earth. All the colors of the spectrum—the reds, blues, greens, yellows, black and white—had bled together, had died together, had been resurrected together, into the color of the walls of the Old City. They were rosy, umber, bronze, mossy, and violet. But most of all they were a tired yellow-gray, the most effortless color that there is: bleached and baked and stripped past all vitality. Yet there was a stirring patience to those exhausted, sallow rocks on those battered old walls that still, mysteriously, endured. Absurdly, Youssef felt like singing for the joy of those walls.

"We can't go inside the Old City." Moshe's eyes glittered with anger. "Since '48, Jerusalem has been a divided city. The Holy Places are in Jordanian territory. They won't even allow us to pray at the Western Wall, to visit our dead in our cemeteries, to maintain our old synagogues."

"But we can still see it," Daoud said. "Jerusalem." He quoted the Bible. " 'O Jerusalem, if I forget you let my eyes be blinded, let my right hand lose its cunning.' "

"You see that golden roof?" Moshe pointed toward the Old City. "The Dome of the Rock. The Arabs built it over the rock where Abraham was ready to sacrifice Isaac." The sun was shining full on the dome. "Jerusalem the Golden!"

"The sages believed that Jerusalem was the exact center of the universe," Daoud said.

"And they were right," Moshe said.

They all drank in the magic of Jerusalem for a moment longer.

"I'll have to take you to your camp now," Moshe said. "I hope you won't be too disappointed with your quarters. You—especially you, Rafael—might find it a little rough."

Rafael scribbled a note. " 'A bed of nails in Jerusalem is softer than a bed of feathers in Egypt,' " Daoud read aloud. " 'To be here is enough.' "

But before Youssef climbed back into the jeep, he lingered by himself at the edge of a cliff. As far as the eye could see, there were wild hills, barren gullies, dry wadis, and always those living-dead rocks. Youssef had never imagined barren stone could hold so much promise. Here and there were gnarled, windswept trees of olive staunchly growing from those rocks. If the rocks were inspiring, those stubborn gray and green and silver trees were a miracle. Youssef tried to take heart from those brave trees. If they could survive on these ferocious mountains, then maybe he, too, could take root in Israel.

Ma'abarot Asbestonin, their new home, was a squat shantytown thrown up on a dry gulch on the edge of Jerusalem, overlooking nothing but nothingness. To get there they had threaded their way southwest of the city proper, leaving the neat rows of three-story stone houses far behind, climbing up and around and finally down again a steep hill. At its very gut, when there was nowhere to look but up, the jeep jerked to a stop. The al-Masris looked out in silence at what awaited them. Row after row of sterile one-story wooden sheds with corrugated iron roofs marched deep into the gully below. The buildings, somewhere in size between military barracks and chicken coops, were identically colorless and unadorned. If the structures had been shaded by trees, humanized by the sights and sounds of even a few playing children, they would not have seemed so grim. But on this late afternoon there were no signs of life: only the silent huts, landscaped with mud from the morning's rain.

A smiling young woman with very red cheeks bustled up to them. "Shalom," she said, and then she and Moshe spoke in quick Hebrew. When the woman shook her head, Moshe pulled out a laminated white card and their immigration forms. Finally the woman nodded. "I'm Dafna," she said to the al-Masris in English. "Welcome to Israel. Welcome to Jerusalem. Welcome to Asbestonin."

Moshe indicated the mud and the huts with a sweep of his arm. "This is your ma'abarah—your transit camp. The Jewish Agency and the government run them for you newcomers. You'll stay here until you learn the language and are ready to go out on your own."

Clearly it was time to bid farewell to Moshe. All three of the al-Masris frowned. Moshe had known them at their villa in Egypt, when they still had been rich and proud and influential. In his custody on the boat, at the port, in his jeep, they had felt secure. But now they were reluctant to sever the slender cord connecting them to that other life.

Rafael, perhaps making the first move toward kissing Moshe Egyptian-fashion on both cheeks, took an uncertain step toward the major. But Moshe held him at arms' length in a half-embrace and then carefully, with the utmost respect, gave Rafael a smart military salute. When Moshe extended his hand to Daoud, Youssef noticed that, instead of the Arab handshake, Daoud pumped his hand firmly. "I hope we meet again," Moshe said. He nodded curtly to Youssef and jumped into his jeep without a backward glance.

The al-Masris turned and began plodding downhill through the mud after Dafna. The sun was fading, and a chill wind had begun to sweep down the mountain. Youssef wrapped his jacket around Rafael's thin shoulders. His father must be exhausted. They hadn't eaten since breakfast on the boat. As they slogged along, Youssef glanced inside windows. Motionless bodies lay on beds. Curiously quiet children played on floors. A woman stood over a table stirring the contents of a bowl. It was eerie to walk so far without hearing anything but their own feet.

"So what do you think?" Youssef whispered to his brother. Already they were in the habit of talking over their father's head. It was easy to forget that the old invalid on their arms had once wheeled and dealed in cotton, money, and power.

"It beats an Egyptian prison," Daoud said.

"But not by much." Youssef shook his head. "I just wish it didn't sound so dead. This is like walking through a cemetery."

Dafna ducked into one of the huts ahead, and they cocked their heads at the sound of raised voices in an Arabic dialect that wasn't Egyptian. A man shouted and a woman began a keening wail. Finally Dafna marched out toward them. "You'll be living here in this . . . flat . . . at least for a few days. Normally each family gets its own two rooms, but temporarily I'll have to put you in with some others." She smiled at the al-Masris. She had been educated at a British school in Jerusalem. After Hebrew, she was most comfortable with English. It unnerved her to speak Arabic, which she regarded as the language of the enemy. "You'll be sharing with Moroccans." She sounded apologetic. "They have been here for two years."

"You must be joking," Youssef said.

"It takes some longer than others to get what we call 'absorbed,'" Dafna said. "In this particular case we have a husband, wife, and six children who may never be properly absorbed."

"All in there?" Youssef thought the hut looked barely big enough for two people.

"They live in half of the building." Dafna nodded toward another

249

door. "Another family—more Moroccans, I think—lives in the other side."

Youssef's eyebrows shot up. He chose his words carefully. "Each of these buildings has two . . . flats?"

"Yes. For now, you'll be sharing half of one. That's what I was just telling them inside."

"Won't it be imposing?" Daoud asked.

"Here there is no such thing as an imposition." Dafna looked grim. "As I just reminded the others. But come. We'll go inside."

The small room was furnished with two cots, a small table, and two benches. On the table was a *menorah* without candles, a small three-legged primus stove, a few pots, and some jars and dishes. From nails pounded into the walls hung dresses, sweaters, a man's jacket and kaftan. Three open battered suitcases, piled high with more clothes, rested on the cement floor. Sitting in a row on the cots against the far wall were eight dark-skinned, unsmiling people. A man in a gray-striped kaftan glowered at them as he slowly and mechanically rubbed his beard with his hand. Next to him sat a fat woman in a long black robe and leggings with a black scarf pulled tight over her hair. In her lap lay a baby. Three other small children were squeezed next to her. Two older children sat huddled on the other bed.

"Shalom," Dafna said. When they didn't answer, she asked them in Arabic if they had made their choice. Still they were mute. "Very well," Dafna said briskly, in English, to the al-Masris. "I asked them to decide which of the rooms they would keep for themselves. Apparently it's this one. Follow me to your own quarters."

Through an open door was an identical room with one cot, a table, and more clothes strewn about. Dafna scooped the clothing up in her arms and deposited it in the other room. She returned quickly. "You look tired," she said to Rafael as she helped settle him on the cot. "Take a nap while I show your sons the camp and then get you some food." Rafael sighed and shut his eyes. "Well," Dafna said, looking around the bare room. "Tomorrow I'll see if I can get two or three more cots. One each for you fellows, another for the children next door. And you're entitled to a larger table and benches. I'll file a requisition to get you your own primus, but I'm afraid there will be a wait."

"A bathroom," Youssef said with the air of a first-class tourist trying to make do with a fourth-class hotel. "There *is* a bathroom?"

"Of course." Dafna led Youssef back past the silent Moroccans to a door at the far side of their room. The two brothers crowded in behind her. In a space the size of a closet were a flush toilet, a small sink, and a shower nozzle high on the wall.

"I think," Daoud said, "that compared to what some of the early settlers found here, it is luxury to have this bathroom."

Youssef, who assumed that Daoud was being sarcastic, ran the water in the hope that eventually it would have to turn hot.

250

But Dafna was turning a warm smile toward Daoud. "When my own parents came here from Poland, they lived in tents. No running water. No beds. And the mud. They still tell stories of the mud. You're lucky, you know. If you had come to Israel even five or six years ago, you might have had to live in a tent. There were so many new immigrants then that we had to build tent cities. These are palaces compared to what people had to live in then."

Youssef smiled uncertainly. In imitation of Daoud, he wracked his brain for a hardy and insincere sentiment. "A roof over our heads. Water to wash in. A dry place to sleep." Youssef remembered his father's homage to Jerusalem. "Just being here is enough."

"We try." Dafna beamed at the al-Masri brothers. Most of the new immigrants she processed were not so sympathetic. "It's hard, you know, to provide even this much. Since '48 we've had not thousands, not hundreds of thousands, but one million new citizens." Dafna loved facts, and now she spewed them out with enthusiasm. "We had six hundred thousand Jews here when the state was born. Eighteen months later we had three hundred and forty thousand more. By 1953 our population had doubled. And still there were more Jews who wanted to come home. I've heard the latest figures. Our Jewish population has *tripled* since '48. This has created enormous absorption problems. Helping a million Jews get on their feet, teaching them to speak a new language, finding them housing and jobs. It hasn't been easy."

Youssef wondered if anyone he had known in Alexandria had washed up here. "You've had other Egyptians?"

"Lately we've had a lot of everything," Dafna said. "Mostly North Africans. The Arabs have been expelling almost all their Jews. You hear so much about the Palestine Arabs in their refugee camps, but no one but us seems to care about the *Jews* who were forced out of their *Arab* homes. We take care of our Orientals. We've had hundreds of thousands of Moroccans. Many from Tunisia. A few from Algeria. More from Egypt and Libya. And that's not all. We're being flooded with Ashkenazim Jews from Hungary, Poland, Rumania. Even some from Russia. The Communists released communities of Eastern Bloc Jews after the Hungarian uprising last fall. Others they considered troublemakers were let out after Khrushchev denounced Stalin. We never know how many to expect, and from where. Our job is to take them all in so they can help build our country."

"Is this camp," Daoud asked, "just for Orientals?"

"Of course not. We're trying to *integrate,* you know. But don't worry. Everyone here isn't like your roommates. There are some you'll have more in common with."

"But we're Orientals," Daoud said. "We're from Egypt, remember?"

"You could pass for Ashkenazim," Dafna said. "No one would ever dream you were *Oriental.*"

"We don't want to pass for anything," Youssef said. He tried the water one more time. It was still icy cold. He turned off the tap with regret. "Being Egyptian is fine with us. In fact, I didn't want to come here."

"My brother," Daoud said, "was engaged to be married in Alexandria. He had to leave her behind."

Dafna's eyes clouded with concern. "But I'm sure she'll be leaving soon, too. The Jewish Agency will do all it can to get the two of you together. Tomorrow, if you like, I'll help you fill out the necessary forms."

"My fiancée is an Arab," Youssef said.

Dafna blinked at him, then dropped her eyes. But before she turned to lead the brothers back to their room, she gave Youssef's arm a sympathetic squeeze.

The Moroccan woman, as they were filing out of the bathroom, could contain herself no longer. She lunged toward them and held her baby up in her arms as she screeched. Youssef flinched. Dangling on a piece of string on the infant's forehead was a small blue bead. This despairing Jewish woman in Arab dress here in the Israeli transit camp could have been a *baladi* Egyptian. She could have been Mona's mother or sister or aunt. She could be Mona in twenty years. Youssef stared at the anguish in the woman's accusing eyes. A prickly sensation, almost like an itch, ran through his body. He felt in his pocket for the smooth, soothing contours of his wedding ring, and then he slipped it on his finger. He bowed his head and followed Daoud and Dafna into the back room.

12 ~~~~~~

ALEXANDRIA, EGYPT / April 1957

In the quiet darkness an hour before dawn, Mona stood facing Mecca on her prayer rug in Abbas's parlor. She had turned to Allah in formal prayers more often than was required in the three months since Youssef had abandoned her. With all devout Muslims she bent to the *muezzin* calls when the sun rose, when it was at its fullest, when it dimmed, when it set, and when the stars and the moon lit the sky. But she also prayed with the saintly in the dead of night and, as now, before the first light of every new day. She prayed for forgiveness, she prayed for guidance, she prayed for the strength to endure what it seemed Allah had ordained for her. The blue circles under eyes were testament that on this night as on many others, she had slept little. Around her eyesockets her skin was puffed with the residue of too many tears.

For the fifth time in this particular prayer sequence, she raised her open palms on either side of her face. "*Allahu akbar*—God is most great!" She folded her hands submissively on the new swell of her belly and recited the familiar opening chapter of the Koran, the verse that had been recited before her circumcision, the verse she once thought would bless her marriage contract with Youssef. "In the name of Allah, the Merciful and the Compassionate, praise be to God, the Lord of the Universe, the Merciful, the Compassionate, the Authority on Judgment Day. It is You Whom we worship and You Whom we ask for help. Show us the upright way, the way of those You have favored, not of those with whom You have been angry and those who have gone astray."

She hesitated and wet her lips with her tongue. At this point in her devotions she should add another verse of her choice from the Koran. Instead she pleaded to God as she knew later this day she would have to plead to her mother. "Allah forgive me! Allah help me! Allah, don't abandon me! *Allahu akbar!*"

So had she prayed when she had waited for Youssef on the Corniche on that last cold afternoon of January. The wind had lashed her as she waited on that iron bench for three hours, until finally she had stumbled back to the house of Abbas. She had watched with dull wonder as Khadiga unpacked that basket of al-Masri treasures. At first she could not believe that Youssef and his father and brother had vanished, that Baruch had become a Muslim, that the police were ransacking the Villa al-Masri for evidence against those who had already escaped. She had been sure Youssef was in hiding somewhere in Egypt. At the dawn of every new day she had listened to the birdsongs and had been certain that today Youssef must come for her. As each day slipped by she had polished her gold wedding ring on the loose black *baladi* robe she now wore over her European dresses. Each night before she tried to sleep she had brushed Suker's gold curls and cried as she remembered Youssef's head in her lap. Remembering how as a little girl she had vomited every morning after her mother left her in Alexandria, she had convinced herself that her morning nausea now was the same. Without Youssef she could not even eat. She had told herself it was only raw fear that had made her miss her monthlies. Without Youssef she could not even bleed.

She bowed her head and placed her open hands on her knees. "I extol the perfection of my Lord the Great; I extol the perfection of my Lord the Great; I extol the perfection of my Lord the Great. May God hear him who praiseth Him. Our Lord, praise be unto Thee."

She looked up toward the dark heavens, searching for the first rays of sunlight as she had searched for so long for signs of hope. For three weeks Baruch had been imprisoned in a Jewish detention center near

Abu Kir. Arresting an al-Masri had not only satisfied the secret police but given the government a pretext to confiscate the villa. After his release at the end of March, Baruch had begun sleeping on a bench in Abbas's kitchen while as a converted Muslim he petitioned to be allowed to resume the practice of medicine. It was to Baruch that she had finally poured out her story. He had examined her, then summoned Um Mona to Alexandria.

"Please, Allah, be with me today! *Allahu akbar!*" She leaned her hands before her for balance and abjectly brought first her nose, then her forehead to the rug. It had been easier to salaam when she was slim, before the contours of her body had rounded below her waist with Youssef's child.

"I extol the perfection of my Lord the Most High; I extol the perfection of my Lord the Most High; I extol the perfection of my Lord the Most High." She held her forehead to the nap of the rug an instant longer than was required, so Allah would be sure she was humbled to His will. If she was to die, she would die praising Allah. If she was to live, she would live praising Allah. She raised herself to a squat and sank backward on her heels with her hands on her thighs. *"Allahu akbar."* She bent her left foot under her and leaned back on it, taking comfort from the formulas of prayer. "Praises are to God, and prayers, and good works. Praise be on Thee, O Prophet, and the mercy of God, and His blessings. Peace be on us, and on all the righteous worshipers of God." She raised the first finger on her right hand. "I testify that there is no God but God, and I testify that Muhammad is His servant and apostle." She rose to her feet and repeated the opening chapter of the Koran, and then she waited once more for inspiration. She bowed her head, groping for hope that Allah, too, had not abandoned her. *"Allahu akbar."*

She held the palms of her hands before her like the pages of an open book. Now she should offer her petition to Allah. It was supposed to be couched in one of the verses from the Koran, but instead Mona spoke from her own heart. "Allah, send Youssef back to me. Allah forgive me. Allah help me, and the child I carry. Be with me today, please, Allah, when Baruch and I tell my mother. Allah keep her in her journey from Karnak. Allah lend her Your mercy, Your compassion, Your forgiveness. Be with me, Allah. Show me the way. Grant me the courage to submit to Your will. *Allahu akbar!*"

Um Mona swept into the small kitchen. At a glance her black eyes took in the wooden benches, the kerosene primus stove, the worn orange-patterned oilcloth on the tiny table. In the alcove behind the open curtain was a faucet of cold running water and a tin-lined toilet hole flanked by two raised porcelain platforms in the shape of shoe soles. "You *have* come down in the world," she said with satisfaction to Baruch.

The doctor, more gaunt and hollow-cheeked than ever, nodded. He took the first step toward winning the old woman to accepting him as Mona's future husband. "Allah provides. I have—*el-hamdulillah!*—embraced Islam."

Um Mona shrugged her shoulders. "Where is she?"

Baruch gestured toward the other room but did not invite her there. He intended to settle this with Um Mona alone. Already Mona had been through more than enough. For the past month the girl had been incapable of anything more than crying and praying. "I sent Abbas and Khadiga away. I thought . . ."

Um Mona lumbered into the parlor without waiting to hear what Baruch thought. Mona stood looking out the window with her back to them.

"Habibti!" As Mona turned slowly to confront her mother, Um Mona studied the pasty face, the slump of the shoulders, the redness around the downcast eyes. *"Habibti!"* Um Mona strode across the room and swept her daughter into her arms. Mona's sobs broke out as she clung to her mother. "Mona, Mona, Mona . . . I'm here, dear one. Ummie's here."

Baruch stood in the doorway, aware as he watched the two women plastered together that he had lost the first round. Um Mona was an illiterate peasant woman, but he must not make the mistake of under-estimating her.

"There, there . . ." As Mona sobbed in a high keening wail, Um Mona's hands came to rest on the new fatness at Mona's stomach. "Too much *tahina*, eh, my bride? You're getting more like me every day. My sweet, round little Saidi." Mona's head lolled on her mother's chest. Her shoulders shook, but she made no sound.

Baruch watched Um Mona lead her daughter over to the sofa. He told himself there was something he should be saying. But he was so at a loss that he left them alone while he fussed in the kitchen preparing their ritual tea. Over and over again in the past two weeks he had tried to rehearse the right words to salvage Mona's future. His plan was to marry Mona himself, but circumstances had forced him to send for the old woman. Although Mona was sixteen and he was both a Muslim and an Egyptian, everyone in Alexandria had heard of the police hunt for the missing al-Masris. Stubbornly, cautiously, the officials had insisted there would be no marriage without the consent of Mona's family.

Baruch poured the black tea into the thick, cracked glasses and measured out five spoonfuls of sugar into each of them in turn. To Allah, to Jehovah, to Jesus, even to the ancient pharaonic gods of Isis and Osiris, he prayed for the success of today's mission. He held himself personally responsible for what had happened to Mona and Youssef. He could still see the two of them holding hands at their table by the goldfish pond at the Beau Rivage. "Baba" she had called him that day. Had he tried hard enough to win over Abbas and Rafael? He thought not. He supposed that his own selfish jealousy, his desire somehow to keep Mona for himself, had played a part in thwarting their marriage. His heart had not been in helping them to get married. Then later, when he should have been suspicious about their joint absence from Alexandria, he had been too distracted by the fall of his own family's fortunes. He would try to make it all better today. He would marry Mona, and he would assure Um Mona that she and her brother's family could live with them forever in Alexandria. He gave the glasses a brisk swirl with a spoon and carried them into the parlor on a tray.

The mother and the daughter, still locked in a close embrace, did not seem to notice his return. He set down the tray, took a chair opposite them, and cleared his throat. "Um Mona, I am sorry if my telegram caused you any distress. But we have to talk today about something that is very important." His voice rang with the authority of a doctor informing a patient that the illness was terminal. "I thought it best for you to leave Muhammad at home this time so that just you and I can consider . . . what has to be done."

"It already is done. Mona and I are together." Um Mona smiled down at her daughter. She had not felt so tenderly toward Mona for many years. It was easier to love her when she was so needy.

"Yes." Baruch nodded his head. In a moment, he thought, he would have to try to regain the initiative. "Yes."

But Um Mona was a step ahead of him. "I suppose you called me here to settle the matter of Mona's marriage. She's finally sixteen. Her time has come. And by the way my daughter is carrying on, I suppose she doesn't want to marry the man of your choice. Am I right?"

"In a way," Baruch hedged.

"I may be nine hundred kilometers away from my girl, but I always —always—know what is happening with her. Don't I, Mona?"

Mona shuddered and buried her head in her mother's chest. She could hear her mother's heartbeat, but still, although she tried to blot out the voices above her, she could hear Baruch and Ummie.

Briskly Um Mona opened the negotiations. "So who is this man?" She narrowed her eyes at Baruch. This weak, bookish Jew would be no match for her. He would be easier to handle than that Abbas.

"There was one suitor. A police lieutenant named Hamuda el-Salem. A widower with young children."

"He makes how many pounds a month?"

"Twenty." Baruch paused. "But that suit came to nothing. I broke it off."

"A police lieutenant with twenty pounds a month?" Um Mona frowned, but then a great gummy smile spread over her wide face. "You found someone richer."

"You could say that." Baruch picked up his glass of tea and sipped it. "I will marry Mona."

Um Mona laughed. "You joke like an Egyptian."

"I am an Egyptian. And a Muslim."

"You are a *huwaga*. And a Jew. Mona is a Saidi. She can never marry you. Never." She stroked Mona's hair and brought her other hand around to make sure the girl was still wearing her blue bead. But she felt a second chain around Mona's neck, and before the girl could stop her, she pulled out Youssef's chain and wedding band. She looked at the shimmering gold. She picked it up in the palm of her hand and felt it not for its weight but its significance. "Whose?" Um Mona demanded of her daughter. "Who have you married? The policeman or this Jew?"

Mona averted her face. Youssef, she thought. Youssef! Why aren't you here with me now? Youssef.

Baruch fidgeted in his chair. He had warned Mona that at all costs they must not tell the old woman about Youssef and her pregnancy. He would dangle his riches before the old woman. "I'm a doctor. I make more—far more—than that policeman. I can offer not only you but Muhammad and his wife and children a home here in Alexandria. We'll have servants. And a car. We'll have everything you ever dreamed of. They've taken the villa, but in time I'll buy another one. A better one."

Um Mona was not listening to him. She seized her daughter by the hair and pulled back her head so that Mona could not avoid her eyes. She was sure the girl would never be able to lie to her. Um Mona's eyes burned into her daughter's. "Who?"

Mona could feel her mother's arms around her, her mother's eyes imprisoning her. She felt herself sinking back and shrinking, so that she was no longer the Mona who had loved Youssef on their houseboat but a very little girl in a world composed only of herself and Ummie. She could feel the familiar coarse cotton of her mother's black robe. She could see before her not only her mother's black eyes but also— Allah!—the dancing black eyes of the lion goddess Sekhmet. "He was rich, Ummie. You said . . . you said to get a rich one."

"Who!" Um Mona tightened her grip on her daughter.

"Mona!" Baruch was off his chair, reaching for Mona. If he could tear her away from her mother, he would have her forever. "Mona!" Baruch was shouting. "Remember what I've told you, what I've taught you! Mona! Tell her it's my ring, my chain, that we will marry. Say it, Mona! You can. You can!"

Mona could hear his small voice as a whisper from very far away. She looked up into Ummie's eyes, and as her mother rocked her, they were back together on the felucca, in the bosom of the Nile, with the starry black skies above them and the song of the dancing fish all around them. In the grip of a force stronger than any of Youssef's or Baruch's sweet words, she smiled up at her mother with infinite trust. "Youssef. We were to be married, Ummie. I was to be Madame al-Masri. We tried, Ummie. But no one would marry us. He left me with his ring and his chain and this." Mona patted her swollen belly.

In the terrible silence, Baruch froze. Later he was to reproach himself that if at this instant he had been able to pull Mona away from her mother, if he had been able to be a man of action rather than a man of words, he might have been able to make it appear to Mona that the will of her mother was not the same as the will of Allah. But Baruch froze.

Steadily, as Um Mona began to take deep breaths that turned into an angry animal panting, she stared at her daughter. Mona had betrayed her. Yes! Mona was a whore. Yes! Mona was unclean. Yes! Mona had to be punished.

Um Mona let the ring slip from her fingers and then slowly she swung back her arm and slapped Mona hard across her face with the broad flat of her hand. *"Sharmoota! Binti washka!* Prostitue! Dirty, low woman! *Sharmoota!"* Before Baruch could stop her, she rained blows on Mona's face and chest. Mona was enduring the beating without a whimper.

Baruch lunged to pull Mona away from her mother. But rage had swelled the old woman's strength, and she aimed a blow at Baruch that sent him sprawling against the tea table. She beat Mona until the girl slid to a heap on the floor. Um Mona tried to kick at the baby in her belly but instead caught her in the breasts. As the old woman rose to fling herself on Mona's body, Baruch grabbed her under the arms and threw her back on the sofa. But Um Mona rose, yanked off his glasses, and smashed them with her feet. "You!" she screamed. "It's your fault. You and that filthy Jew of yours who did this to my child. Where is he? Where's Youssef? I will kill him. Allah help me! First Mona, and then him! Allah guide my holy, avenging knife!" She made a step toward the kitchen to find a weapon to make good her threat.

But Baruch pinned her hands behind her and forced her back on the sofa. "Stop it. Listen to me!"

"Sharmoota! Binti washka!" Um Mona tried to spit on the prone form of her daughter. "I will kill you. Kill you, Mona!"

"I said to listen to me!" Baruch straddled the writhing old woman. "Your daughter is not a prostitute. She was an innocent. They tried to be honorable. They wanted to marry. But Abbas wouldn't let them. Youssef's family wouldn't let them. The *maazouns* and the government wouldn't let them. Youssef was forced to leave. He is far away. In another country. Mona is pregnant. She must have a husband. I'll marry her. I love her. No one has to know. We have to help your daughter."

"That one is no daughter of mine." Um Mona cursed the girl under her breath in a low, sibilant hiss. "I will have no whore for a daughter."

"Think, woman, think. She is the only child that you have now. Or ever will have. She is all you have. You love her. You know you love her."

Um Mona stopped struggling, hesitated, then looked up at Baruch. *She is all you have,* the Jew had said. Um Mona moaned. As life and strength ebbed from Um Mona's face, her eyes were transformed by pain so deep that Baruch looked away.

Um Mona began to cry. It was true. What the Jew had said was true. Mona was all she had. "My mother! And now her! Mona! Mona! I loved her!" The words seemed to be wrenched from Um Mona's gut. "And now this. And now this . . ."

Baruch felt almost sorrier for the mother than the daughter. He let go of the old woman. The worst was over. She would have to agree to his plan now. "There, there," he soothed the sobbing mother. "I will marry Mona. Here, today. I'm a Muslim. No one here has to know about Youssef. Isn't that true, Mona? Isn't that what we've agreed to do?"

Mona raised her head and looked from Baruch to her mother.

Um Mona sank back on the cushions of the couch. Her lip curled for a moment as she caught Mona's eyes with hers, but then Um Mona seemed to draw back into herself. She sank lower on the couch as her mind began to spin. It was possible, she thought, that all was not lost. It was possible, even, that much could be gained. Mona was a whore. Mona was unworthy of her love. But she could be paid back not by a quick twist of a knife but by a much slower, slyer blade. She, Um Mona, could turn this worst of defeats into a bitter but just victory. Um Mona slowly wiped the tears from her face, rearranged her robes, and sat upright on the sofa. When she looked back to Mona after a long moment, her face was composed and yet she pointed the hurt in her eyes like a weapon. She made her voice soft and wheedling. "You will not marry a Jew, Mona. Even a Jew who says today that he is no longer a Jew. No. You will come home to Karnak with me, Mona." Even as she spoke the words, Um Mona was shaping the years ahead.

The girl looked at her mother with astonishment.

"But they will kill her in the village." Baruch had not expected this quick recovery, this swift click of Um Mona's mind. He regretted ever sending for this wily old woman. He should have pawned every fragment of the al-Masri valuables and bought the cooperation of someone who could marry them. Or he should have left Egypt with Mona. He should have taken her to Israel and her Youssef. But now he pleaded desperately against the new terms Um Mona was making. "They would kill her in Karnak. You know that. You both know that."

"Mona, you know you deserve to die. Didn't we always say that fire was better than shame, Mona?" There was a hypnotic quality to Um Mona's voice. "But Mona, you know that if you do what I tell you from now on, Ummie won't let you die. You know that, Mona, don't you?"

"Don't listen to her, Mona. You don't belong in that village. You belong here in Alexandria with us, with Abbas and Khadiga and all the rest who love you. Your *work* is here. The . . . the *Corniche* is here. You can be free here, Mona. Free!"

Mona, still staring at her mother, did not seem to hear him.

"You were born in the village. When it is time, you will die in the village. It is your fate, Mona, to return to Karnak. It is the will of Allah, Mona, that you do as I say."

"Don't listen to her, Mona. Remember everything I've taught you, Mona. You have a free will. It is *not* inevitable that you do as she says. You can stand up to her. Now, today, Mona, *you* can decide. I'll help you, Mona. I'll never leave you, Mona. Be strong, Mona. Remember Youssef. Remember how you love him, how free you were with him, how you told me you felt when you stood on the shore by the houseboat and chose to run to the Nile and be free!"

At the mention of Youssef's name, Mona dully flicked her eyes over to Baruch. Once she had believed all the wondrous, tempting promises he and Youssef had made her. Once she had believed life could be different. Once, when she was braver and more full of hope, she had been able to defy all her mother had taught her. But now she touched the blue bead around her neck and bowed her head in resignation. She had squandered all her courage in loving Youssef.

"Get up!" Um Mona ordered. "Straighten your clothes, Mona. And stop sniveling. You heard me. Get up and sit here by me, Mona."

"No, Mona, no!"

Mona rose, shook out her robe, and sat down on the sofa next to her mother. On her face was a look of passive, peaceful surrender. She looked up into her mother's eyes and could do no more than sigh in relief.

Mona looked out the window of the train at the passing landscape. They—she, her mother, and Suker the dog—had left Cairo behind seven hours ago and now were in the dry, parched desert that skirted so perilously close to the gray, wide, serpentine Nile. She tried to swallow but could not. The air from the open windows was too full of dust. It choked her and made her cough. The dirt filled her lungs and brought tears to her eyes. Hastily she wiped away those tears before they could course down her cheeks. Ummie did not allow her to cry. Ah, she was safe this time. Ummie had not noticed.

Um Mona sat across from her daughter. She spied the tears, watched the girl brush them away, and—most important of all—saw Mona look over to see if she had been detected. Um Mona almost smiled. Good. Her daughter was too terrified to disregard her orders never to weep. Mona was learning.

Um Mona allowed herself the satisfaction of reviewing her last week's activities. All she had willed had come to pass. After that weak Jew of a doctor had tried to trick her into letting him have Mona, she had bullied Baruch into pawning some of the al-Masri silver so she would have the necessary hundred pounds for *baksheesh*. A few pounds here, a few pounds there, and she had discovered where to buy forged papers. For forty-five pounds she had obtained a document that made Mona the legal wife of one Muhammad Bahai el-Elemy, and another paper that proclaimed that same mythical Bahai to be a fisherman who had lately died at sea. After she had purchased their two second-class, one-way tickets to Luxor, she still had thirty-five pounds left.

She studied Mona's face. Despite all her recent sorrows, the girl was still a beauty. Um Mona thought it both perverse and unfair that one so bad could look so good, while she herself—an upright Muslim woman—was decidedly no beauty. There was no justice in the world.

But then Um Mona settled smugly back in her seat. It had not turned out so badly after all. Soon there would be the baby, the child of her child, to comfort her in the coming years. But what mattered more was that she had recaptured Mona, and that this time it was for good. Mona would live out her life as it was intended, next to her. Except now her own power was complete. Mona had no choice. All it would take would be a few whispered words about the truth of Mona's pregnancy, and the girl would die. Perhaps, Um Mona thought before she dropped off to sleep, perhaps there was a sort of justice in Allah's world after all.

Baruch sat with pen in hand looking at the blank sheet of paper. It was quiet in Abbas and Khadiga's kitchen. The others had long ago gone to bed. Baruch touched pen to paper. Ink, as he hesitated, ran in a rivulet and stained the crinkly airmail stationery. Baruch cursed, crumpled the paper into a ball, and readied a fresh sheet. He had to write to Youssef. He had a responsibility to tell the boy what had happened. By now Youssef must be half out of his mind with worry. Baruch raised his pen and then put it down again. How much should he tell Youssef? How much was it safe to say? How much was it right to say?

Baruch stared at the paper, then rose and fiddled with the primus stove as he made himself another glass of tea. It boiled and brewed too quickly. He ladled in sugar, stirred it, but could not bring himself to sit down again at the table and write the letter.

Instead he carried the tea into the parlor. He looked away from the sofa where Um Mona had won the day and the future. If only he had it to do over again! If only he had so much to do over!

He shook his head at himself and stood looking down at the street from the window. On the corner two young men stood laughing and smoking. In the coffeehouse a single yellow light bulb burned in the night. It was so quiet he could hear the surf breaking on the nearby beach. Mona, he thought, used to stand just here waiting for Youssef to rescue her. Here she waited, and here—finally—she could wait no more.

Baruch had failed to break through to Mona before her mother bundled her off to the Said. He had told her she didn't have to return to the village. He had told her he would somehow manage to marry her without her mother's permission or that he would go with her to Israel to rejoin Youssef. He had told her he knew she had it in her to defy her mother and live a better life. He had even slapped her face to try to bring her out of her trance. But looking into Mona's eyes, Baruch had known she couldn't even hear him. Baruch supposed that maybe he—and Youssef—had expected, always, too much from Mona. Both of them, underestimating the pull of her village, had judged her by the veneer they had together painted upon her. Her mother, knowing Mona better, had offered her the one thing Mona could not resist: inevitability, freedom from choice, blind obedience. Put to the test, Mona had chosen maybe what she had been born to choose. Like it or not, Baruch thought, Mona was lost not only to Youssef but to himself.

He could hear the whistle of a train coming into the station. Perhaps, Baruch thought, I'm being too pessimistic. The trains ran not only south but north. Mona's return to the Said was not necessarily permanent. He would try, with the weak but persistent power of his pen, to let her know that if she wished she could always change her mind. She could always make a home with him. Maybe, after the baby was born, after the reality of her decision sank in, she would find the strength to break away again. By God, even if Mona didn't like it, he would continue to dangle choice before her. He could not have misjudged her entirely. Somewhere in her was the young woman who had the strength to be more than she was born to be. Once she had been enough of a rebel to run away with Youssef. Maybe in time she could do it again. And maybe the next time she would run into his own open arms.

Baruch sighed under his breath. So tonight he had made one tiny, tentative, hopeful decision. He would keep the lines of communication open to Mona. He would always be here if she needed him.

Now he had to turn his attention to the other half of the separated lovers. What was he to do about Youssef? If he told him the truth, this already unhappy love affair could be elevated to tragedy. If he wrote that Mona was pregnant, Youssef would doubtless bull his way back to Egypt. He would be arrested at the airport or on the docks, he would be put on trial for espionage, and he would be sentenced either to hang or to live out the rest of his life in prison. The consequences of telling the truth would come too dear.

Or he could *not* tell Youssef that Mona was pregnant. He could lie. And then he would have to bear the responsibility for *that* set of consequences for the rest of his life. Baruch shook his head. Either way would have a moral wrongness to it.

Baruch shuffled back to the kitchen and riffled through his papers until he found the letter that had come from Israel via Paris. Desperation was in every line. Rafael was dead. His nephews were living a temporary life in a refugee camp. Youssef begged him to somehow, some way, get Mona out of Egypt. "Either she will come to me or I will come to her," the boy wrote. Yes. If Youssef knew, Youssef would come back.

Baruch drummed his fingers on the table. Since the Suez war, the Egyptian government—if not the people themselves—had hardened against its Jews. At the time of the first war with Israel in 1948, there had been mindless and random acts of violence against some Egyptian Jews. But this time official Egypt, instead of merely harassing its Jews, wanted them to go away and never come back. Nasser's secret police were mushrooming in importance. There was fear, now, in being a Jew in Egypt. Among the people Baruch encountered on the street every day, there was still no obvious hatred for Jews. Yet it would not be safe for Youssef to return. It wasn't even safe for Baruch to write more than this final letter to Youssef. The secret police had made it clear, when they had hand-delivered Youssef's letter to Baruch, that the continuation of such a subversive correspondence would put Baruch's new medical license in peril.

If he himself was afraid even to write to Youssef, how, in good conscience, could he write Youssef news that would inevitably put his nephew in worse jeopardy? Life had to be more important than love. Separated, Mona and Youssef would suffer. But at least they would both be alive. Baruch told himself he might as well face facts. The wounds between Arab and Jew in the Middle East were jagged with blood. Those wounds would not be healed for years and years, if ever. Youssef and Mona would be two of the living casualties. But already Mona was back in her village. In time she would reconstruct another life either there or with him in Alexandria. The best that could happen for Youssef was that he, too, give up hope of any reunion with her. By being cruel, Baruch in a way would be being kind. Youssef was young. Youssef would heal.

But still Baruch hesitated. Had he ever recovered from Daisy's death? Had he ever really healed? He admitted to himself that he never had and he never would. Yet he had gone on living, he had tried to make his contributions to the world in which he lived, he had even begun to love again. But his love for Mona—his unrequited love for Mona—was nothing like what he had felt for Daisy. A tear slipped down Baruch's cheek. Poor Youssef. Poor Mona. Poor me.

Reluctantly Baruch again touched pen to paper. He would do what he had to do. He would latch another lock on the door that had to be closed to Youssef. He would not give the boy a shred of hope. He would phrase what was happening to Mona in words that were vague yet unambiguous in their effect. He would imply that she was married. He would mention seeing the marriage contract. He would not exactly lie, and yet he would not tell the whole truth. Another tear ran down Baruch's cheek and made a blot on the letter. He balled up the paper, blew his nose, and began again.

13 〜〜〜

NEGEV DESERT, ISRAEL / July 1957

Even at night in the desert, Youssef was hot. Summer in an army desert bivouac. Of course it was hot. The days were a thirsty red blur. Nights in the pup tent weren't much better. The sun was down, but grains of roasted sand dug into his flesh. Youssef gave up trying to rub the small of his back free of sand. He rolled over, rooted in his pack, and stuck a bent cigarette in the corner of his mouth. He found matches inside his black soldier's beret. He wouldn't earn his fancy scarlet one for a long time, after his eight weeks of basic training, his year serving in the Nachal corps on a frontier kibbutz, and finally more advanced paratrooper training. Two and a half years in the Israeli army, learning to fight against the country he loved. And Israel? Could he ever learn to love to fight for Israel?

In his six months here, his feelings about this raw passionate land had fluctuated from dislike to indifference to a grudging respect. It had been easy enough to learn Hebrew. After all, he was accustomed to speaking more than one language, and Hebrew was almost as close to Arabic as French was to Italian. It had been more difficult to learn to feel at ease with the Israelis. How strange these people were: how abrupt, how graceless, how intense. They fought among themselves about everything from the choicest seats on a bus to whose turn it was to be waited on in a store. There didn't seem to be peace or contentment in any of them. When he had shared his misgivings with Daoud, Youssef had listened with great skepticism when his brother had repeated an old cliché. Native-born Israelis, Daoud had said, were called sabras because, like sabra cactus, they were tough and prickly on the outside but sweet and tender inside. Youssef had grunted that he didn't believe it. Daoud had continued to try to convince him. He had said it was Youssef's own fault that he hadn't made any friends. He had tried to coax Youssef into giving Israel time.

But Youssef had shrugged off Daoud's primer on learning to love the

Israelis. He would admit only to admiring their energy. They attacked work as if it were a well-loved sport. There was a sort of exhilaration about them. Youssef could not bring himself to confide in his brother that there was something else that he liked about Israel. He was still moved by the mystic clear air of Jerusalem, and he was still fascinated by the mysterious ardor these Jews so obviously felt for their country. Sometimes he would look around him at all the puny trees and rocky fields and wish that he, too, could romanticize them into milk and honey. At least then Israel would have been more bearable.

He shielded the match with his hands so that he wouldn't wake Daoud and the others. He turned over on his back and tried to relax as he drew the smoke deep into his lungs. Outside he heard a jackal howl in the desert. The beast sounded so forlorn. Once Youssef would have been able to empathize with that jackal. Now he merely wanted to kill it. What was one more death?

He had stood very close to death last month high on the Jerusalem cliff when they buried his father. He had to admit that the Israelis were very tough. They didn't bury their dead Jews in caskets. They simply wrapped them up in a piece of cloth and planted them in the ground, taking this idea of returning to the ancient Jewish soil to its most logical extreme. Looking down at the open grave, Youssef had pretended that it was he and not his father who was dead. The news that had come about the Egyptian government's seizing the Villa al-Masri had been too much for Rafael. Baruch had warned them before that a second stroke could be fatal, and Baruch had been right.

Youssef leaned over and picked up a handful of hot sand and watched it slip through his fingers as easily as time. The earth of his father's grave had been parched and rocky. He had imagined how it would feel packed around him entirely, pressing down on his flesh, its dry taste in his mouth. He still wondered why people shirked from talk of death and decomposition. It was a fact of life, you might say the last fact of life. Everyone was always telling him how he had to accept the way things were, that that was life. Youssef thought he would probably find it easier to accept death than life. He had stood with Daoud and Moshe in the new Jewish cemetery on Har Ha Minuhot, the Mountain of Rest, a windswept beige ridge overlooking all the other colorless Judean hills. In a way Rafael had all of Jerusalem at his feet. His father had yearned so for Jerusalem, and now what was left of him would lie on that hill forever. What had his father felt as he died? Did it hurt to die? Did everything all of a sudden just go black and stop? Or were there bright lights and rushes of good feeling? Youssef was almost certain what it must feel like. He thought he knew a thing or two about death, because it must feel as he had felt since he left Mona. He felt very blank. He felt not altogether here.

He had given his father's grave another longing look. The problem was that he wasn't quite *there,* either. He might feel as if he was at the bottom of a dark, deep pit, but every day he had to go through the motions of living. He was surprised sometimes when people spoke to him as though they thought he was still alive. He was even more surprised to hear himself mumbling responses. It was merciless how life kept going on and on all around him when he had already stopped inside.

Daoud had moved close by him when they began to throw the earth on top of his father. Daoud had wept, and Youssef had known it must be right to cry at your father's funeral. Since they had arrived in Israel, Daoud had seldom failed to do the right thing. But except for learning Hebrew, Youssef had made no effort to be more than a detached observer of Israeli life. He, a born aristocrat, had been almost amused to learn that the al-Masris did not rank naturally high in the Israeli pecking order. Those with the highest status in Israel were "Ashkenazim" Jews, Germans, Austrians, Hungarians, Poles, Rumanians, Yugoslavs, Russians—Jews who had survived the Holocaust, Jews who spoke Yiddish, fast-moving Jews with European ways and highly polished survival skills. At the bottom of the Israeli heap were "Oriental" Jews, Moroccans, Tunisians, Libyans, Egyptians, Iraqis, Yemenis—mostly poor and illiterate Jews who had been hounded from their homes after the birth of Israel, Jews who spoke Arabic, slow-moving Jews with Mideastern ways and not many skills that were marketable in Israel.

Daoud, even though he knew it would have been easy for the well-educated al-Masris to be accepted by the Ashkenazim, had taken on the cause of the Oriental underdogs. Daoud had tutored their transit-camp Moroccans in Hebrew, helped them fill out their complicated government forms, and tried in every way he could to rally them to demand their piece of the Israeli dream. For Daoud, from the first, had so loved Israel that he couldn't bear to see the new state on the fabled homeland be anything short of perfect.

But Youssef didn't care about the rift between Ashkenazi and Oriental. More disturbing to him was the poverty of his new life. Cold showers. Meals of tomatoes and olives and tough gray meat. A cot that wouldn't give. Rough clothes with loose seams. This was living? What had kept Youssef going these first months was the belief that Israel was nothing more than a temporary stopover on his way back to Egypt.

How many drab hours, how many hopeless days, how many frustrating weeks, had he sat in the Tel Aviv and Jerusalem ministry offices? *I want to go home,* Youssef had insisted again and again to the bureaucrats. He had learned to hate official Israel. The clerks were every bit as addicted to delays as the Egyptian bureaucrats had been. But the Israelis were also rude. There was no ritualistic drinking of tea, no sympathetic clucking of the tongues, no promises—even no hypocritical promises—that his problems would go away tomorrow or after tomorrow. Back at the transit camp it had been Dafna who had finally leveled with him. His circumstances were exactly as Moshe had warned him they would be. Egypt wasn't taking back its Jews. And even if by some miracle the Egyptians would let him return, the Israelis would do all in their considerable power to stop him. As Moshe had said, the Israelis weren't about to hand the Arabs a Jew with Youssef's history.

Dafna had found Leah al-Masri's address in Paris and advised him to send a letter through her to his uncle. Maybe, she said, Youssef's girlfriend could join him in Israel or Europe. While he waited for an answer from Baruch, Youssef laid few plans for a future in Israel. It was draining simply to endure the present and pine for the past. It had been Daoud's idea to bow to the inevitable and begin their army duty. Youssef supposed this was as good a place as any to wait for word from Egypt.

The jackal screamed once more. Youssef could probably bring the beast down with a single shot. Youssef was a good shot. He was, in fact, a good soldier. He liked the army's discipline, its rules, its demands. He liked the way they made him sweat and suffer. He liked how they had erased his identity and fashioned him into a machine that could kill. During a long hike across the desert, when he was at the outer limits of his endurance, when he was so thirsty he considered crying so he could lick his own salty tears, sometimes the familiar sadness would leave him. Physical pain washed away that other. It made him feel alive. It felt good to fight to be alive.

He had first felt that will to survive early in his basic training. The recruits had been running the obstacle course, crawling through fields of brambles on their bellies, scaling a high fence, dangling from a rope by their straining arms. At the end they had stood, perplexed, at the foot of a steep, sheer ridge they had been told they must scale. At that moment they had heard a rumble and looked over their shoulders as three tanks came at them. Soldiers shooting machine guns ran by the tanks. There was no time to pause and consider that the Israeli army wouldn't gun down its own recruits. Youssef had acted on pure instinct. "*Yalla!*" he had yelled in Arabic—"Let's go!" He had pushed and pulled Daoud and the others up the cliff. At the top he turned and flung himself behind rocks to take aim at the tanks and the soldiers below. For the first time since he had left Egypt, Youssef had felt right. Only Daoud and the others pinning back his arms had prevented him from shooting down at his officers.

Later his sergeant had taken Youssef aside to say he was officer material. Youssef had thought and fought on his feet. He had demonstrated both initiative and aggression. He was a leader. It was the first time in many months that Youssef had been assured that he was good at anything. When he thought about it, it was no particular surprise that he had a natural talent for war and destruction. Hadn't he shown that already in Egypt when he ran down that *baladi* girl, when he led Batata to his death, when he dishonored Mona? Sullenly he had answered the sergeant that he would never be an officer in the Israeli army. But he had kept his reasons and his gnawing doubts to himself. It was one thing to practice shooting at a turbaned cloth target, quite another matter to shoot with live ammunition at a soldier who might be Hamid el-Husseini. Maybe he could fight for Israel. But could he make war against Egypt? Youssef had told himself not to worry about that. Just last fall Israel and Egypt had been at war. It was unlikely there would be another one for many years, if ever. He could only worry about so much.

Youssef looked over at his brother. Daoud was sleeping on his side, his legs and his arms curled up so that he was a tightly defended ball. Daoud had little natural talent for soldiering. Youssef always stationed himself beside his brother, urging him onward when he seemed at the end of his strength, covering for Daoud as his brother had done for him in Israel in so many other ways. Still, Youssef wondered if in the end Daoud would turn into not only the better soldier but the better man. Daoud cared so much about so many right things. It was only when Youssef had been with Mona that he had known those certainties. Youssef sighed. He wished he could stop thinking and roll over and sleep like the dead. He stubbed out his cigarette in the sand. The Negev was one big ashtray, and he was one of the ashes.

Mona, he thought as he looked at the gold wedding ring on his finger. Mona, Mona, Mona. In English her name was a cry. A moan. In Arabic her name meant an impossible dream—that which all men yearn for and very few attain. Mona.

He wanted another cigarette, but the pack was empty. He lay back. Although he tried to sleep, his eyes kept opening. He turned his head and watched a bug creep very slowly over the sand. He raised his hand to kill it, but then he remembered that the ancient Egyptians had revered these scarabs as omens of good luck. He would let the beetle live. God knows he needed all the luck in the world. He used his hand to wipe away the tears that had been coursing down his cheeks.

When he came out of the supper tent the next evening, Youssef threw a minimal salute to the erect, gray-haired, vaguely familiar officer. Youssef had paid little attention to the rumor that top brass were in camp for a few days. If Ben Gurion himself had lined up next to him in the makeshift latrine, Youssef would merely have given the old boy a comparative once-over. But now, trying to place that face, Youssef stood stock-still. It was someone he had known a long time ago. Someone he wanted to remember from a happier time and a happier place. That familiar stiff-backed walk, that no-nonsense air. He was certain he knew that man. Youssef's mind turned crazily to shoe polish and hair jelly and Hamid. "Mr. Barton!" Youssef ran after the retreating figure. "Mr. Barton!"

When the officer stopped and turned, Youssef was certain he was looking at an older, bonier Mr. Barton. Or rather, Youssef noticed too late, Colonel Barton. "I'm sorry, sir. I forgot myself. But you see, I know you. Or rather, I knew you. Alexandria. Victoria College." Youssef was suddenly conscious of his unbuttoned shirt and his grease-soaked trousers. "Private Youssef al-Masri, sir. I was in your history class. At Victoria. You *were* at Victoria? You *are* Colonel Barton?"

There was a slight shifting of the deep lines around the colonel's mouth. Deliberately he looked down to Youssef's feet. "No shoe polish today, I see." A smile spread to his eyes. He held out his hand. "How are you, Youssef?"

"Mr. Barton! Oh, Mr. Barton! I mean, colonel!" He felt absurdly happy to see his old teacher. It was almost as if he were once again in history class at Victoria in the good old days, before the '48 war had begun the decay. "I can't believe it's really you." Youssef was holding onto the colonel's hand as if it were a lifeline. He tried to remember what Barty had said to him that day at Victoria when the Zionists had declared Israel a state. But he could recall only being very embarrassed. "Here. What are you doing here, sir?"

"My work. I suppose I could ask you the same question if the answer were not so obvious."

"Yes." Youssef grinned. "Yes, sir."

"Why don't we talk awhile, private." It was a command. The colonel began moving briskly toward the officers' tents. "It's not often that I have the chance to find out how one of my boys turned out. It's been ten years, Youssef. How *have* you turned out?"

Youssef blurted out the first thing that crossed his mind. "Bloody badly, sir." Aghast at the truth of his words, Youssef quickly elaborated on his family's flight from Egypt, his father's death, the loss of the al-Masri fortune.

The colonel led him into his tent, and Youssef sat at the edge of Barty's blanket. There wasn't even one grain of sand on that blanket. Leave it to Barty to make the sand behave in an orderly fashion.

"Your history, Youssef."

Evidently, Youssef thought, the colonel was not one for social amenities.

"You said that you have turned out 'bloody badly.' Explain, if you please."

Youssef looked the colonel in the eye. He could tell him to take his impertinent questions and interrogate some other poor recruit. Or— maybe?—he could tell him everything. Youssef had not trusted anyone but Daoud since he had arrived in Israel. He wasn't sure he wanted to trust Barty. But instead of bolting, he stared and waited.

Barty was the first to look away. He pulled out a canteen. "I think a little whiskey may be in order." He took a swig and offered it with a smile.

Youssef grinned and took a long pull. He hadn't been able to afford whiskey since Alexandria. Suddenly, with the sting of the alcohol on his tongue, he remembered those thousands of companionable nights sitting with Hamid on the balcony. A friend. How he needed a friend.

"You interest me, Youssef. You intrigued me even back at Victoria. I remember wondering whatever would happen to a young Jew like you. It couldn't have been easy, Youssef. I'd like to hear what it was like in Egypt these last years for a young Jew who seemed to have everything. Who turns up here in boot camp in the Negev, apparently much the worse for wear." Barty took another drink. "I'm an alcoholic," he said in a voice so low that Youssef wondered if he had heard him right. "Would you like to tell me how you came to be what *you* are, Youssef? Not as an order. As a request."

Youssef smiled at his old teacher. He wasn't Hamid. But by confiding that he had problems with drink, Barty had made a step toward friendship. Youssef would meet the colonel more than halfway. "It's a long story." Intentionally, Youssef left off the "sir." "I won't tell it unless you tell me yours, too."

"Agreed." Barty took another drink. "You go first."

Youssef leaned back on his arms and stretched out his legs. Those last long years at Victoria were worlds away from this Israeli army tent. The desert night felt suddenly too cold for confidences. But warmed by the whiskey and the unaccustomed glow of possible friendship, he allowed himself over the next hours to paint a picture of his fast company with Hamid, the girl he had killed, Batata's death, and the loving and leaving of Mona.

At the end Barty seemed to change the subject. "And what about your being a Jew?"

"It didn't matter, colonel. That really didn't matter. I *made* it not matter."

"Indeed. But it changed your status at school and with your friends. It lost you your fortune and the woman you loved. It made you abandon the life you had always known. It brought you here. And yet you say it hasn't mattered much."

"Look." Youssef was irritated. After listening to his life story, all Barty was interested in was his religion? "I'm not much of a Jew. I never have been. Even when I was a boy, I remember hearing my father make jokes about the religious Jews. How silly they were. Superstitious. Ignorant. It was only at the end, after Batata's death, that my father changed."

"Sometimes that happens. It must have been traumatic. Sometimes a shock like that makes a man question his values. Even change his values. How did your brother's death affect you?"

Youssef considered. "I fell in love with Mona."

"Yes. You chose to love not only an Arab but her country. Were you trying to be perverse, Youssef? Or pretending that the things you didn't like in Egypt had never happened?" The colonel ignored Youssef's glare. "And now you're in Israel. The *Jewish* homeland. What do you think of Israel, Youssef?"

Youssef shrugged and reached for the canteen. He drank deeply. "I suppose I just don't get it."

"What?"

"What they see in this place. On the boat, when the toughest commandos saw the coast of Haifa, some of them started to cry. Even my brother seems to be a little crazy about Israel. I just don't get it."

"Perhaps your problem is that you haven't thought enough about being a Jew. If you had, Youssef, perhaps seeing Israel might have meant something to you, too."

"I'm not a Zionist." Youssef felt like storming out of the tent. Instead, angry at Barty's inquisition, he repeated what he had heard Baruch say on many occasions. "The Jews had no business coming here. Taking the land from the Arabs."

"But you're here."

"Not by choice."

"Maybe you didn't arrive of your own volition. But they didn't abduct you into the army. What branch are you going to join?"

"Paratroopers." Youssef said it with pride.

"Is that so?"

"They're the best, colonel. I wanted to be with the best."

"Certainly the paratroopers are the elite. They're the ones we send out on our retaliatory raids over the Arab borders. Yet you seem to be nursing at least some loyalties to Egypt. I hope you'll forgive me, Youssef, for pointing out that there are some rather amazing contradictions in the way you have chosen to live your life. Does it feel as muddled as it sounds?"

"I'm a bloody mess."

The colonel paused and then spoke in a rush. "You had a great deal of potential, Youssef. You still do. That you have not lived up to it so far may be more a reflection of forces you cannot control than of those you can. It's true, nevertheless, that others have endured far more than you and yet have emerged less scathed. But those others don't interest me quite so much as you do. I suppose I think that you and I are alike."

Youssef drew in his breath. "Alike? How?"

"I'll let you work that out for yourself." Barty toasted both Youssef and himself with his canteen. "But I will say that you definitely have made some mistakes. Would you agree, Youssef, that you have a tendency to take the easy way out?"

"You sound like my uncle. My Uncle Baruch." Youssef smiled fondly. "He made me think about so many things. But in the end I suppose it didn't matter much."

"Perhaps you didn't think issues through to their obvious conclusion. Perhaps it is also a bit premature to give up on yourself. Your life is by no means over."

"Unfortunately." The familiar depression was back in Youssef's voice.

"I see self-pity is another of your weaknesses." The colonel took another drink. "That, too, can become a dangerous addiction. But my point is that much of what has happened to you, Youssef, occurred not because you're weak and unworthy but because you are a Jew. A Jew who happened to be in the wrong place at the wrong time—although there is some question in my mind whether any place but Israel has ever been the right place to be a Jew. But that's another subject for another time. What is important—very important, I think—is for you to see the connection between what has happened to you and what has happened to other Jews in your lifetime."

"I don't care if I'm a Jew or not."

"But others do. And I'm not so certain that you're being honest. I think you care a lot about being a Jew. It sounds to me as if you hate being a Jew."

"No! I am indifferent. That's all." As Youssef lit a cigarette, his hand was trembling.

"I seem to have hit a nerve, Youssef." Barty sighed. "You know, there are several ways to respond to the sufferings of being a Jew in our day and age. It can make you less a Jew or more of one." Barty unscrewed a second canteen of whiskey and took a thirsty pull on it. "I'm Christian myself, but I've spent many years in this land of the Jews. When it was Palestine. And now, since it's been Israel. I suppose you wonder how that all came to be."

"Yes!" Relieved to have his own tale-telling behind him, Youssef leaned forward in anticipation.

The colonel took a long drink of whiskey and used his hand to wipe away what remained on his lips. "I am Ian Duncan Barton, the third son of a coal miner and his Scottish wife. I was born in Wigan." He paused as if waiting for something. "That doesn't make you laugh? No? That proves you're not British. All the British laugh at the mere mention of Wigan. But it's not so funny to live there. It's dreary in Wigan, way up in the North, near Manchester. The sun seldom shines in Wigan."

Barty said he took a university degree in history. But when he couldn't land a proper job, he settled for the army. "In many ways my life didn't begin until I was shipped off to Haifa in '26. Palestine! I loved it so. . . ."

Youssef was rapt as Barty poured out his life and death story of the British Mandate. At first, like many of the working-class recruits, Barty was enthralled by the exotic Arabs. "We thought the Jews— those drab little socialists from the ghettos of Eastern Europe—didn't belong here. Palestine was a romantic, slow, sleepy little backwater. The Zionists were so jarring. Lord, how they worked! We couldn't believe it. They would work all day picking fruit or building roads or doing whatever menial work they could find. And then they would work all night long to build up their own settlements. I would think to myself, 'These people are mad. They can't work like this in the Middle East. No one can. They'll break. And soon.' I suppose, like a lot of people, I was looking forward to the day when they *would* break. When they would go back to wherever they came from and leave this country—and the rest of us—in peace."

Instead there was fighting. The 1929 Jerusalem riots between the Arabs and the Jews spread to Hebron, Haifa, Jaffa, even the farm communities. When it was over, two hundred people, almost as many Arabs as Jews, lay dead.

"I was sick of all of them by then," Barty said. "Both sides were impossible. The Jews didn't even act as if they could *see* the Arabs. And all the Arabs could see was more and more Jews. They were both so *damn* sure they were right. The problem was that both the Jews and the Arabs wanted, passionately, to throw out the British and establish their own state on the same soil. Palestine has always been blessed and cursed by too much passion. Although I think the curse has been the stronger."

In the early '30s Barty, who by then had become an officer, was transferred to another patrol unit south of Haifa. His job in Netanya was to halt illegal Zionist immigration along the Palestine coast. It was there that he met, married, and buried his wife.

"Hannah was the most tender woman who ever lived. She was very delicate. Slim. Ethereal. Some of the others used to joke that if a strong wind came along, it might blow Hannah away. They were so right. Perhaps they were seers. Jewish seers."

"She was a Jew?"

"I thought you knew that, Youssef. I remember telling you that in Alexandria. I don't speak of her often. I remember each occasion."

"So why do you keep telling *me* about her?"

"Who knows?" Barty took a drink. "Maybe because she was tall and blond and Jewish like you. She was born in Poland. Also, we never had any children. She died when she was pregnant. In 1939. During the Arab general strike."

"I was two years old then."

"I've thought of that." Tersely Barty continued his story. He had come across Hannah one morning in 1936 when he was on a solitary horseback patrol. "She was lying beside the trail with a badly broken leg. She was in great pain. She was crying." Barty lit a cigarette. "She was so beautiful even when she cried. Of course, I couldn't pass her by. It took hours to get a litter out to her in the wilderness. By the time I finally resumed my patrol, all that was left on a certain beach was an empty motorboat and many fresh tracks in the sand. I was furious. I was sure I had just missed a boatload of illegal Jews. I rode back to the post to confront the girl. She claimed she had broken her leg when she slipped and fell in the dune grass. But the doctor said that couldn't be. Her thigh was smashed as though she had been hit by a heavy object. I decided to keep her under arrest at the post until she told me the truth."

Barty smiled. "She was there for a month. She didn't tell me the whole story until I finally gave up and married her." Barty laughed, then grew somber. "As you may have gathered, the Jews were unloading a boatload of refugees just as I was riding up the coast. There were eighty-seven men, women, and children in that one motorboat. I don't know how they could have packed so many on it, but they did. Hannah was helping get them on shore when one of the Jews saw me coming. They had to do something to keep me away. It was Hannah who suggested that they break her leg and leave her on the trail. They used a sledge hammer."

"God!" Youssef said.

"Those were desperate times, and the Jews were a desperate people. Her leg never did set right. She walked with a limp after that." Barty paused. "That was what killed her. She couldn't move fast enough to save herself."

They were married with the blessing of her family, who, fortunately for Barty, were not religious Jews but radical political Zionists. They kept their marriage secret from Barty's superior officers, because they feared the army would have considered the match a breach of British neutrality. Barty visited her when he could at the Jewish settlement, and in time he was looking the other way when illegal boatloads of Jews washed ashore. "I don't think it's humanly possible, Youssef, to stay in Israel for long without choosing sides. There's right on both sides, you know. But it's the emotions that determine where each of us finally stands. That's why there have been so many wars. They have all been wars of passion." Barty lit a candle and watched it burn, in silence, for a few moments. "I loved her very much."

Hannah, he said finally in a flat voice, had been killed in the third year of the Arab general strike when transportation, food services, and —most of all—law and order were crippled. Hannah and two other women were trying to hitch a ride to visit Barty, who was on special duty in Haifa, when a carload of Arabs pulled over on the road. Because of her bad leg, Hannah couldn't run away fast enough. Her body was found the next day in a ditch.

Barty skimmed over the remainder of his story. In memory of Hannah he grew bolder helping the Jews. Eventually he even helped train the outlawed Jewish militia. It was then, too, that he began to take comfort from liquor. When World War Two broke out, Barty was kept in Haifa instead of being shipped to the front. After the war Barty's commanding officer suggested he resign. His drinking and his moonlighting for the Jews had not, after all, escaped official notice. It was then that Barty had taken the teaching post at Victoria. With the birth of the Israeli state in '48, he had returned to Haifa to be commissioned as a colonel in the Israeli army. "And that was that." Barty lifted the canteen and drained it. "Finished." He smiled. "I return to Haifa tomorrow."

Youssef tried to mask his disappointment. He had hoped tonight was the beginning of a comradeship. In his way, Barty was a little like Uncle Baruch.

"There's no reason why you can't come and visit me on your leaves." Barty pulled out a notepad and wrote down some numbers. "Call me when you get as far as Tel Aviv. I'll meet you at the Haifa bus station. Come anytime."

"I'd like that." Youssef stood unsteadily and pumped the colonel's hand. He hoped he wouldn't disgrace himself by acting as drunk as he felt. He was already out of the tent when he heard Barty call out to him.

It was three o'clock in the morning, and through the mist that hung over the desert, gray-haired Colonel Barton seemed more ghost than man. "You know what the point of all that was, don't you? I don't want you to allow your life to stop . . . the way mine did when I lost Hannah. Eighteen years, Youssef. I've been a dead man for eighteen years. Hannah. Mona. That's why you and I are alike, Youssef. Take a good look at me. And think it over."

The pale-blue airmail letter with French stamps was sitting in Youssef's letter box. He tore it open with trembling hands and sank down on the concrete floor next to the wooden nests of kibbutz mailboxes. He scanned the page of his mother's heavily underlined handwriting, then impatiently read the enclosed sheets from Uncle Baruch. He read Baruch's words again more slowly. He willed himself to concentrate not on what Baruch said about Mona but what his uncle said about himself. Uncle Baruch a Muslim? Uncle Baruch bowing and bobbing and sighing Al-*lah!* In a way it was not so hard to imagine. Harder to believe was that Baruch was living a *baladi* life with Abbas and Khadiga. Uncle Baruch living on the servants? No. That could not be.

For the third time Youssef read what else could not be. There were only a few sentences about Mona. Her mother had come and taken her back to Karnak. Baruch was certain her family would not harm her.

275

Baruch had seen Mona's marriage contract, and Baruch had to assume that by now in Karnak, Mona must be regarded as married. "Forget her," Baruch wrote. "What was the past was the past. *Khelas*—it is finished. What was between the two of you did not end well. But it has most certainly ended."

To distract himself, Youssef considered the carefully worded warnings in Baruch's letter. Under no circumstances, Uncle Baruch wrote not so enigmatically, should Yousef entertain any "village" travel notions. Baruch did not specifically say what conditions were like for Egypt's much-reduced Jewish community. In fact, the word "Jew" was never mentioned. But Baruch listed the Jewish families they had known who had packed their bags and left hurriedly in the night. Baruch repeated a phrase he heard much in the cafés, "Egypt was being rid of parasites." Baruch himself could testify to the dedication and attention to detail of the government's efficient secret police, for he had met them often after his family left for parts unknown. He had grown to know them even more intimately when he had served those three weeks in a desert detention center. Praise Allah, Baruch wrote, that the government had so graciously finally allowed him to resume the practice of medicine.

Baruch fleshed out his letter with chatty news that further drove home his message. Victoria College was being converted into a state school where students were taught in Arabic instead of English. The owners of Greek restaurants and Italian espresso bars were leaving in droves. He had run into Hamid on the Rue Fouad—it was renamed Sharia Hurraya, Freedom Street—and he could report that Hamid looked splendid in the uniform of a lieutenant in Nasser's army.

Yes, Baruch had concluded, it was a new world in Alexandria and Egypt. "Perhaps it is a mercy," Baruch wrote, "that one we knew well was spared it." Youssef thought Uncle Baruch must be alluding to his father's death. Yet he had not, apparently, thought it safe enough to mention Rafael by name.

With the compassionate help of Allah, Baruch concluded, President Nasser was beginning to right all that had been wrong in Egypt. But Baruch hoped Youssef would understand his position and not compromise him with any more correspondence. Youssef and the rest of his departed family would be always in his prayers. Allah's peace, Baruch concluded, be always with you. Youssef shook his head at the finality of Baruch's blessing.

Once again he read his mother's breathless greetings. How *nice* to hear from Youssef and Daoud! How *sad* about Rafael! She and Rachel and Lisabet were in *Paris!* So *many* of their old friends from the *Sporting Club* were here! Joshua Nakattawi—did Youssef remember *dear Joshua?*—was being *very dear!* She had been unable to resist reading Baruch's letter to Youssef before sending it along. Baruch was such a *character!* *Imagine* renaming the Rue Fouad! Poor Alexandria! Youssef and Daoud should *immediately* fly to Paris to join her and the girls! Leah did *so* miss her *little men!*

Youssef stuffed the letters into his trouser pocket and walked back to his barracks at the far end of the kibbutz. Last month, when he and Daoud had arrived at this frontier kibbutz near the Jordanian border for their year of army Nachal duty, flowers of yellow and blue and purple had carpeted the lawns. Now, at summer's end, the flowers were withered by too much sun, and patches of grass were burned brown. Already he could feel a shiver of autumn in the breeze that whipped his hair into his eyes.

He thanked God that the six bunks in his room were empty; for once on the kibbutz, he could have some privacy. Youssef threw himself down on his hard bed. He stared at the unpainted ceiling. What was he to make of Baruch's hints?

For so long he had lived only waiting for news of her. He had most feared that her family had killed her. But she was alive. She was only a few hundred miles away from him. When he drank his morning coffee, she was drinking her tea. When he was sweating through the afternoons, so was she. When at last he lay down to sleep, she, too, was closing her eyes. Youssef looked up at the sunshine streaming in his window. What was Mona doing at this precise instant? Was she down at the river, filling a water jug and carrying it home on her head? Perhaps she was preparing food. How did the *fellahin* cook? What did they eat? How did they live? Youssef didn't know. All he had was the most shadowy image of women in black moving silently among mud huts, maybe under tall date palms with the broad river flowing not far away. So that she could live on for him, he tried to embellish that picture with donkeys and camels and men in blue robes. But even as he concentrated, the image blurred and grew more dim.

Youssef covered his eyes with his hands and rocked silently on his bed. What was he to do? He had hoped that Baruch would write that Mona was living with him in Alexandria. He had dreamed it would be possible to get her out of Egypt. He would have joined her anywhere. If not in Israel, then in France, England, maybe even America or Brazil. Anywhere. He had suggested as much in his letter to Baruch. But Baruch had ignored that plea. Baruch had said most definitely that Mona had returned to Upper Egypt. Mona had been swallowed up in her Said. Just as he had left her, so had she left him. She was gone. She was as good as dead.

Baruch even thought she was married by now. While he had been pining for her in Israel, she had taken a husband who was more like herself. Oh, Mona! How could you do that? How could you forget? *"Jamais!"* she had called back to him at their last meeting on the Corniche. "Never!" He had thought she would never forget.

There might even be a child on the way. She could be carrying another man's baby. He remembered the look Mona used to get on her face when they talked of how beautiful their children would be. Now they would never be born.

Youssef pulled out the letter and read it once more. Baruch did not definitely say that Mona had married. Only that he had seen a sheet of paper and assumed she had. That was a strange way to put it. Maybe Baruch was wrong. Maybe she was still waiting for him to come for her. If he could get to Italy and wangle a new passport without Israeli stamps, he could fly to Egypt and find out for himself. But he didn't have enough money to get to Tel Aviv, let alone to Rome and then Cairo. Besides, he was in the army. He knew now what he hadn't realized when he had signed up. The Israelis would never let him out of the country while he was on active duty. But maybe, Youssef thought with growing excitement, he could borrow the money from Barty— even use the colonel's influence to get past the military police. He had visited Colonel Barton on three of his leaves, and there were signs Barty was beginning to regard him as a son.

But then Youssef forced himself to be realistic. Uncle Baruch had been most definite on one point. Egypt was the enemy camp. That was what he had been telling him with those chilling allusions to the secret police, detention centers, and the long arm of President Nasser. It must be bad if Uncle Baruch was afraid even to write to him. *Khelas,* Baruch had written. It is finished. Not only Mona but all that had been his in Alexandria was finished.

No, Youssef told himself. You cannot go to her. It simply is not possible to go to her. *Khelas.*

He heard the lunch bell in the dining hall. He would have to report for guard duty very soon. He would have to stand guard duty with his gun on the outer perimeter of the kibbutz, searching the scrub for enemy Arab infiltrators.

What was he do do about his mother's offer to come to Paris? It sounded as if Mama was having her usual gay time there. Apparently Joshua Nakattawi was paying her bills. Obviously his mother and the girls didn't need him. But did he need them? What sort of life would he have there, joining the *émigré* circuit of Sporting Club Jews? An empty life. A frivolous life. It was not what he wanted. At least here in this hardship life in Israel the people around him seemed to have a purpose. He lived on the fringes now, but it didn't always have to be that way.

He looked over at the table that the other North Africans in their barracks used to display their dearest possessions. Among them were framed photographs of dark-eyed girls who were the sweethearts of the men who slept in the crowded room. Youssef rose and pulled out the cardboard carton that held his father's Batata memorial scrapbook.

He flipped through the pages. Batata in his mother's arms. Batata with him and Hamid. Batata trying on Youssef's Victoria College blazer. Here she was. Batata and Mona, both still little children, holding hands on the beach. An older Mona walking behind Batata and Zibda. A snapshot, finally, taken just before his brother died, of Youssef and Mona and Batata and the dogs. Youssef stared at the photograph and then, as he pulled it from the album, a brittle brown leaf of clover fell to the floor. He stared at the clover that had once been on Batata's hearse, and then he pressed his lips to the image of Mona.

He asked himself a bitter question. What are you doing, Youssef? Kissing her goodbye? He looked down at the gold wedding ring on his finger. No, he would keep that on. He couldn't take it off. Not yet.

It was his first admission to himself that he might not be able to wait for her, without hope, forever.

14 〰️

KARNAK, EGYPT / *October 1957*

Mona yawned and stretched. The flies were awaking, and so was she. Although the *muezzin* call had not yet sounded, it must be nearly dawn. The heat of the day always began, contrarily, in the middle of the night, so that by now Mona's swollen belly and breasts were slippery with sweat. Still half asleep, she wondered about not only the exact temperature of today's hotness but also the precise date of this day. At the Villa al-Masri, where facts had seemed so ascertainable, a thermometer had been fastened to a wall fronting the garden. Even in the summer the mercury seldom rose above the hundred mark. This morning, without even a whisper of Alexandria's soft breezes, it felt like one hundred ten degrees. Alexandria. Baruch. Youssef. Mona tried to fall back asleep and dream of that lost time.

A flea bit her leg, and so Mona willed herself awake. Still thinking of Alexandria, she tried to puzzle out what month this must be. The Nile was in flood. The summer crops were ready for harvest. The midwife said the baby was due any day. She had last been with Youssef—ah, the houseboat!—in late January. Yes, this was late September or October. So hot. It was so hot. As Youssef would have said, it was "so bloody hot."

She brushed her sticky hair away from her damp face. If she rose now, she might be able to complete her first trip to the Nile before the call to prayer was sounded. Always she was the first to rise in her uncle's house. As part of her private penance for the wrongs she had committed —the houseboat, the houseboat!—she had taken extra duties upon herself. Even in her clumsy late pregnancy, she fetched not only water for their household but water to fill the public jugs scattered about the village to slake the thirst of passersby. The *zirs,* those six-gallon stone jugs that had always rested in front of the mosque, near the threshing floor, and by the lane that led to the fields, were symbols of her personal atonement. That it was difficult to keep them full to overflowing gave her satisfaction. She did not regret that she had sinned with Youssef. But as she had loved the seasons of their pleasure together, so, too, did she take pleasure from these seasons of her punishment. Allah and Ummie had shown her what she must do. She bowed to His will and fetched water and always—always!—she was careful to heed her mother's every command.

Despite the heat, despite the sweat, despite the fear, it was not a taxing life. In a way her return to the Said had been like falling asleep and never altogether waking. The dream had begun on the train south as she stared out the window at vistas that were unchanging for sixteen hours: brown earth, green fields, white birds. To the horizon it was flat but for the tall spindly palm trees with their tufts of tired green-brown leaves. Repeated brown villages of mudbrick, stacked against each other, blended so well into the landscape that Mona had to look hard to make sure they were really there. An occasional water buffalo, donkey, man, woman. Canals. The sky. Always the river. From her seat on the train she had been mesmerized by the monotony. She had drunk it in when half asleep, and still she had seen it sketched in a sort of dream.

Life in Karnak had been the same. After the tense excitements of Alexandria—after Youssef!—there was even a comfort in the sameness and the slowness of every inevitable night and day. Each shuffled past, much like the one before. Units of time, so clear and measurable in Alexandria, now stretched out into a Karnak infinite. Lateness was calculated not in minutes or hours but in days. A man was to come to see Muhammad on Thursday morning, but when he arrived the next Monday night, no sincere apologies were offered or expected. *Malesh.* Thursday or Monday, it was all the same. All that was required was breathing out and breathing in, until a man or a woman breathed no more. The *muezzin* woke them up each morning, and they ate because their bellies were empty. The men went to the fields. The women went to the river. The men sowed and reaped. The women cleaned, cooked, and bore babies. When a new problem arose—when there was a dispute over land or water, a shortage of tea or sugar, a brideprice that proved difficult to collect—they waited for the problem to disappear. If it persisted, voices grew loud, threats were made, and gradually, in time, the sharp contours of the conflict dissolved, then drifted into the past. The men sat with the men. The women sat with the women. They talked and drank tea, only half listening to what came from the mouths of their friends, sure that they had heard it all before and would hear it all again. There were long, comforting silences in the middle of their conversations, and no one rushed to fill them with empty words. Sometimes as Mona sat and drank and sighed, hours passed and she thought of absolutely nothing. Only the rise and fall of her chest assured her she was still alive.

In the vocabulary of not only Karnak but every other village in Egypt, there was even a word for this comfortable trance. *Kaif*, it was called, when a man or a woman, worn down by the impossibility of relief from every vexing problem, succeeded in entirely turning off the mind. A *fellah* in the fields, a *fellaha* by the river, could sit for hours without movement or action or thought, drowsy in the dry white heat under the cobalt sky. The very air of Karnak was druglike and dopey and dizzying. The heat fed the draining dullness that in its turn spawned *kaif*.

At first, too, she had been so afraid of everything. In every chance glance of a villager she had feared that her secret must—now—be discovered. Every gleam of a blade chopping vegetables, a sickle cropping wheat, had made her stare and wait for the blow that would be her own. But she had been afraid, too, of everyday life. Every bug that bit her body might have been a malarial mosquito. She had hesitated to drink the Nile water that for a certainty carried bilharzia and might have even contained the bacilli of cholera or typhus. She had been afraid to eat food that she knew could be contaminated. She had avoided drinking the unpasteurized buffalo milk that could have brought tuberculosis. These fears, she had known, were reasonably grounded in the most basic hygiene principles she had learned from Baruch. But to live she had to eat and drink, and so she had swallowed her fears. Less logical, deeper dreads had also gripped her. She had been so afraid of scorpions that every night she had shaken out her woven date-palm mat before she lay down to wait uneasily for a poisoned sting. Snakes, too, had been part of her litany of fear. Always, imagining a serpent in every rustle, she had watched the rushes at the edge of the river. She was cautioned always to tread with a heavy step to the river. She was warned to steer clear of the pharaonic temple nearby, especially at night when it was rife with creatures that slithered and scuttled. So far, despite or because of her vigilance, she had spied not a single snake or scorpion. But she was beginning to learn that the heat could be as deadly as any viper. The heat sapped her vitality. No matter how many hours she slept, she was still tired when she awakened.

At this very moment she was very tired. She heard a stirring around her on the dirt floor. Without looking, with her eyes resolutely shut, she thought that Ummie must be waking. Ummie must have at least one eye open to watch her. Ummie kept a constant watch over her. She had the feeling sometimes even when she was off by herself in the fields or at the river that Ummie was stalking her behind a palm tree. But so far Ummie had kept her part of the bargain. She had not breathed a word of Mona's shame even to Uncle Muhammad, much less to his wife, Bahia, or his two small boys. The villagers had accepted her tale of a dead husband without suspicion. Um Mona had documents which the Karnak *shaykh* had read and pronounced genuine. Mona wore Youssef's gold wedding band and his gold necklace. Um Mona flashed the wad of banknotes she claimed was what remained of the brideprice. In a way Ummie was once again her protector. Sometimes, falling back on instinct or perhaps just habit never quite forgotten, Mona even felt thankful for her mother's constant vigilance. For if there was terror in her mother's eyes, there was also safety.

She had first felt this confusing mix of fear and security when Ummie had beaten her in Abbas's flat. In her desperation, she had clung to her mother as the only certainty in life. Youssef was gone, but Ummie was still here. So long ago, that day of the *khamseen* and the trip to Sekhmet's temple, Ummie had said that she and only she could save Mona from sure destruction. It was hard for Mona to remember sometimes that all Ummie was promising to save her from was Ummie's own dark side. It was all so bewildering. Ummie loved her and Ummie hated her. Ummie protected her yet Ummie never let her forget she had the power to destroy her. Mona sighed under her breath and wondered what she herself felt for her mother. There had been a time, during those heady years in Alexandria, when she supposed she had felt sorry for her mother. Imagine feeling pity for Ummie! More often than she remembered those years of estrangement from her mother, Mona thought of the years when she had accepted Ummie as the love of her life. It was odd how when she had been in Karnak, the world had revolved only around Ummie. Yet when she had been in Alexandria, her world had been an orbit of Youssef. Ummie and Youssef, Youssef and Ummie. What would have happened, she wondered, if, that day in Damanhur, the train had not been commandeered for the troops of the Sinai war? It had been her intention that day not to choose Youssef but to come back to Ummie. Well, here she was after all.

Mona could hear a body turning over in the next room. Muhammad's family, too, must be waking. So far Mona had been tentative in her friendships with Bahia and her children. She had tried, too, to shy away from her stepgrandmother, Zainab, and she always cast down her eyes when her stepuncle, Hussein, came to call on Muhammad. Partially she kept to herself because she knew Ummie would not tolerate emotional defections. But maybe more of it had to do with Mona's trying to hang on to the hope that her life in Karnak was only temporary. If she did not allow herself to take root here, she could still believe in a future with Youssef. Yet it was hard to live in such isolation. If it weren't for Batata's cocker spaniel, Mona would have felt entirely alone. Suker's fine, glossy coat was the same color as Youssef's curly blond hair. Having the dog with her was having some of Alexandria as well.

Of course, it had been difficult to keep the only pet in the village. Karnak's dogs were scrawny, half-wild beasts who lived in the lanes hoping for occasional scraps of meat. By day they slinked in the shadows, fawning on any human who came their way. By night they ran in packs, growling from dusk to dawn, turning the village lanes into a no-man's-land. When Mona took Suker out for a walk, the other dogs would try to attack him. Mona had begun carrying a heavy stick to protect the little animal. She had been worried that some night Suker might get out of the house. She had made even Bahia and the children promise never to leave open the front gate. Poor Aunt Bahia, that kind of woman who seldom raised her voice except in prayer, moaned in fear every time she saw the golden dog. "An angel will never come inside a house where a dog lives," Bahia had said many times. The Prophet, Bahia would whisper, called dogs unclean. But even though Muhammad's wife would mutter little prayers under her breath to counteract the evil presence of the dog, she endured the animal. Bahia watched how Mona held Suker, how she petted it, and even, when she thought she was unobserved, how she kissed it on its hot black nose.

Mona smiled to herself. When her baby was born, when she was ready to put her sketchy escape plan into action, she would take Suker with her. When, in these months of lassitude in Karnak, had she awoken to the possibility—no, the necessity—of escape? Had it been when she finally realized that nothing she could ever say or do would recapture that old closeness with Ummie? No, it must have been when she first felt the baby kicking. Until then she had been able to deny her own yearnings for Youssef. After all, he had left her. In the trance of Karnak, it had been almost hard to believe that Youssef had been more than a dream. But that was part of *Youssef* kicking inside her. She reproached herself now that she had not been able to stand up to her mother in Alexandria. She should have known enough to stop Baruch from even sending for her mother. She should have known she wouldn't be capable of confronting her mother.

Mona stroked her belly and wondered if she would ever have the courage to defy her mother. Even now, as she plotted how and when she would get away, she planned to do it like a sneak. Not for anything would she pit herself directly against Ummie. She would wait until she recovered her strength after the baby was born, and then she would creep away in the night to wherever Youssef waited. If he couldn't come to her, she would run to him. Sometimes Muhammad would return from the souk with coffee or spices wrapped in a funnel formed from the page of an old Cairo newspaper. Mona would smooth out *al-Ahram* or *al-Akbar* and eagerly read for a scrap of news that would mean peace between Youssef's new land and hers. From what Baruch had said, she knew Youssef couldn't come for her until there was peace. But never had she found even a shred of evidence that day was nearing. The columns in the newspapers had bristled with threats against the Zionist dogs.

She would just have to make her way to Baruch in Alexandria, throw herself on his mercy, and hope that somehow he would help reunite her with Youssef. Baruch's letters seemed to promise that he would help her in any way she wished.

Mona reached blindly to pet the dog, who always slept curled up in an uneasy gold ball near her. First she would walk Suker, and then she would fetch the water. Today would be like every other day. But her hand came back empty. Mona opened her eyes and scanned the dirt floor. Then she sat up and examined the small room where she and Ummie slept in opposite corners. Maybe Suker was asleep on that heap of reeds Ummie was preparing to weave into baskets. Awkward in her ninth month, Mona rolled over on all fours, eased to her knees, then crawled to her feet. The dog wasn't bedded down in the reeds. She hoped he had not gone next door to Bahia. Muhammad's wife would be terrified if she found Suker near her. Mona waddled into the other room. The two large bundles of cloth were Muhammad and Bahia, the smaller mounds the boys. Suker wasn't here.

Mona told herself there was no need for alarm. Seeking coolness, the dog must have wandered outside in the night. He would be waiting for her, his tail wagging, in the courtyard where they cooked their food and entertained their visitors. She stood in the doorway. The dog was not in the courtyard. Worse, the front gate was ajar. She closed her eyes. It could not be. Everyone knew the door had to be firmly latched each night. She always checked it herself. Last night when the others had finally fallen asleep, she had gone to the door and it had been latched.

She rushed out into the crooked lane and looked to the left and the right. She whistled as Youssef had taught her, but the dog did not come running. She walked toward the center of town between the high mud walls of her neighbors. "Suker!" she called softly. "Suker!" In the twilight of the rising sun there was no sign of the animal. She turned and retraced her steps, following the curving lane as it led toward the river. Streaks of dawn-white flashed the dark sky beside the still-bright moon and stars. Ahead were two circling black buzzards. Lower and lower they flew, and finally they landed beyond the next twist of the lane. She prayed to Allah that they and she were not seeking the same lost dog.

She found the birds of death feeding on the remains of Suker. She looked down at his guts and gore. Some animal, maybe a pack of animals, had cornered him during the night. The flies, too, had been at work. Gold fur lay in congealed blood.

Slowly Mona walked back to their house. She found the small hand hoe that Muhammad used in the fields, and with it she buried Suker in the soft mud near the river. She sank down under a palm tree and looked out at the gray Nile. The sun was breaking over the purple mountains, and the sky was shot with violet sparks. The river was melting to liquid silver. The birds from their nests in the sycamore trees were singing to the sun. Nothing moved on the serene river, and Mona drank in its stillness. Always when she had remembered the village, she had yearned to sit like this, alone with her Nile. But the river didn't have to live in Karnak. Its swift current passed by the village's life-and-death struggles as it coursed north toward Alexandria and the sea. Lucky Nile. The river, she thought, was so much luckier than she.

Had the front door blown open by accident? There had been no wind in last night's heavy heat. Who could have tempted her dog to that sorry death? Bahia, even though she feared the dog, could never be so mean. Muhammad and the boys had always liked to play with the dog. None of *them* would ever have hurt Suker. But there was one in their household who was capable of enticing the dog to destruction—one who would be eager to drive home the lesson that freedom and death went hand in hand. Could Ummie have unlatched the door? Could Ummie have suspected that Mona still dreamed of freedom and Youssef and that other life? In the heat Mona shivered with fear.

But then, as she began to weep, a sharp pain cut through her lower body. Mona cried out. She, who had assisted Baruch at so many birthings, knew this must be her first contraction. She was beginning her labor. In hours or days she would no longer be alone. Suker was gone, but in his place would be a human reminder of Youssef and Alexandria. She stroked the blue bead around her neck and gazed at the Nile as the *muezzin* call sounded—*"Allahu akbar,* God is most great!"

Um Mona stood over her straining daughter. She had been in labor for only seven hours, and already the midwife was acting as if the birth was imminent. Um Mona shook her head at another of life's injustices. Mona's hips were so narrow she had been sure Allah meant to punish her with days of hard labor. When she had given birth to Mona, she had suffered three days of agony. Remembering that pain, Um Mona glared at her daughter. Mona hadn't been worth a second, much less a lifetime, of pain.

"It's coming! The baby's coming!" Zainab screamed loud enough for heaven to hear her. Characteristically, Zainab yelled the news again. "I can see the baby coming! The baby is about to be born!"

In the small dark room where the mother and daughter always

slept, Mona was panting through the cotton rag Um Mona had stuffed in her mouth. She had been afraid the girl would cry out Youssef's name. Mona was gagging on the cloth. Um Mona watched her with satisfaction. But then Mona's wild terrified eyes met hers. Mona was shrieking. Um Mona heard her muffled cry, "Ummie!" Um Mona's expression softened, and tenderly she wiped the sweat from Mona's face. For a moment she was sorry it—all of it—had to be this way.

Um Mona shifted from her daughter's head to a position near the base of her squatting body. Mona's legs were wedged apart by a giant circular sieve held perpendicular to the ground. Bahia and a cousin crouched behind Mona. As they supported her back with the weight of their bodies, the women leaned down to help Mona push out the baby.

"Ummie!" Through the gag they all could hear Mona's cry. "Ummie!"

Um Mona stood beside Zainab and watched as the midwife pulled the baby from Mona's body. She heaved a silent sigh of relief. Its skin was dark—almost as dark as Um Mona's husband's skin had been. Um Mona had been afraid the child would be fair like that accursed Youssef. She had had nightmares of yellow hair which even she would never have been able to explain.

"A boy!" Zainab was squealing in triumph. *"El-hamdulillah!* A boy!" She and Bahia and the cousins and the midwife let loose with *zaghareit* shrieks of joy.

Mona opened her eyes, seeking her son but seeing only her mother. "Ummie!" She held out her hands, and Um Mona filled them with her own. "Ummie!"

For a second, staring down at her daughter, Um Mona forgot all about the newly birthed infant. "Mona . . . ?" Um Mona leaned closer and tentatively stroked back the hair from her daughter's wet face. "My Mona."

"A boy!" Zainab was holding the baby up to the light as she shrieked. "A boy! Mona has a boy!"

Um Mona swiveled her head away from her daughter. For a moment she had forgotten. For a moment, as Mona, at the peak of her pain, had called out her own name, she had forgotten the girl's shame. She dropped Mona's hands and stared at the newborn bastard in Zainab's arms.

"A name!" Zainab struck the baby on his rump until he howled. "What will be the name of this new son of Karnak? Mona, what will you call your little boy?"

Um Mona feared the girl would want to call him Youssef. "Ali," she said quickly. "His name is Ali."

"Sabah el-khair, Ali," Zainab cooed down at the dark-brown flesh

in her arms. "Look at him! He's laughing!" She smiled over at Um Mona. "Is he like his father? His poor dead father?"

"I hope not." The words had slipped out before Um Mona could stop herself.

"Why do you say that?" Zainab was not paying much attention to Um Mona as she whispered "Allah!" in each of his ears.

"Only that his father died so young." Um Mona smiled down at her grandson. "Ali will be different. Allah will bless him with a long life. Here at my side. Forever."

Zainab looked up, fearful the Evil Eye would strike down the baby for his grandmother's tempting of the fates. "Inshallah," Zainab amended as the midwife severed the cord with a knife.

Um Mona seized the infant. In her arms the flesh of her flesh began to cry. She held him tighter, and Ali again began to howl.

"My son!" Mona held out her arms for Youssef's baby. If she could just touch her son, if she could hold his flesh in her arms, the past would be the future.

Um Mona stood above her daughter. By all that was holy, by all that was right, by all that was just, this little son of the infidel Jew should never have been born. Yet as she stared into the small brown face, she couldn't help smiling. Whatever shame had given life to him, she had a grandson. He would love her as Mona never had. He would be her own. Her own Ali.

But Zainab was snatching the baby away. Zainab was handing him to his whore of a mother.

Um Mona stood looking down at the mother and son. Mona was nuzzling the small head, kissing the tiny fingers. Um Mona bent lower. "Ali, Ali . . . ," Mona was whispering. "Our Ali, Youssef. Ours." Um Mona stared at her daughter so hard that she was sure Mona would have to look up at her.

But for once Mona did not obey the force of her mother's eyes. She continued to caress her baby. There was infinite comfort in the realization that if she had the son, in a way she had the father as well.

Mona sat with her baby in her lap in the house of her stepuncle, Hussein. All of them—Um Mona, Muhammad and Bahia and the children, Zainab and the sisters and the cousins—always assembled for every Thursday-night radio concert delivered by Um Kulthoum, Egypt's most beloved singer. Her songs were heart-wrenching, tearful wails that reverberated with the sadness and suffering of lives gone awry. That Um Kulthoum was Saidi—that she had been born in the poverty of a village much like Karnak—endeared her all the more to the sisters and cousins and aunts and nephews in Hussein's front room.

On this particular night, to the heartbeat rhythm of a drum, Um

Kulthoum was introducing a throaty new song. *"Ansek, ya salem, da el mish mumkin abadan,"* it was called—"How can I ever forget you?" The gutty violin strings of the *kamenga* wailed with heartsick longing. "I will never forget you," Um Kulthoum moaned. "It is impossible. Never! It is impossible! It's impossible! Can my heart move and love another you? Never! Never." Mona nodded. Um Kulthoum knew. It was just so with herself and Youssef. "No night and day have I tasted sleeping. No night and day have I tasted sleep. Where is your heart?" The music wailed. "Where is your pity? Where is your heart?"

Mona drew her shawl around her face to hide her tears. Um Kulthoum would never forget, and neither would she. "Why? Why? Why?" sobbed Um Kulthoum. "Why would I love again? It's impossible to love again. Never. Never."

Mona began to sway to the music. Around her grown men, who seemed such unlikely vessels of grand passions, were openly weeping. "Memories! Memories! Of my love and yours! I can't forget it. I can't speak of it. But my days are all dreams, all dreams of you. And all that I live for is you."

Mona felt her mother's eyes boring into her, but tonight Mona would not allow her mother to steal even this vicarious solace. Instead, cradling Youssef's son in her arms, she abandoned herself to Um Kulthoum's song. "We had the most beautiful story," Um Kulthoum cried, "in all the ages. Many years have passed. And still the beauty is the same. I will love you. All things are beautiful between us. It remains the same, though I be far from you, and you be far from me. *Ansek?* Forget *you?* Never! *Ansek!"*

Mona crooned *"Ansek!"* to her son. This song, she knew, was meant especially for her. *"Ansek! Ansek!* Forget you? No!" It was so sad, but it was so beautiful. It had been exactly so with herself and Youssef. They had had—they still had—a great love. Through no fault of their own, fate had separated them. There was some comfort in having had a secret love, a lost love, a love that was doomed. There was—there could be—even a perfection in a love that was so tragic that Um Kulthoum sang of it. *"Ansek!"*

As the song ended, a sad but contented smile was on Mona's lips.

But then her mother leaned over to whisper in her ear. *"Ansek?* I, too, Mona, will never forget."

The smile died on Mona's lips.

Mona sat under a palm tree nursing her baby and drowsily watching the river drift by her. It was winter, a time to eat raw onions and salt fish to ward off colds that were strong enough to kill. It was winter, and the blue current of the river seemed to mock her as it raced freely north toward Alexandria.

From time to time Bahia, who sat next to Mona watching her own two boys, would repeat gossip that had been stale a season ago. Ali gurgled, and Mona put him against her shoulder to burp him. She hummed a bar of a song—"*Ansek!*"—under her breath, covered her breast, and settled the baby on her lap for a nap. Soon—in a few minutes, maybe in an hour, certainly by the time the sun crossed to the other side of the river—she would return to the house of Muhammad to help prepare their supper. She yawned. There was no hurry. There was no hurry about anything. Once, before Suker died and Ali was born, she had thought it was only a matter of time until either Youssef came to her or she went to Youssef. The problem was that she had lost any grip she had ever had on time. *Inshallah,* there would come a time when again they were together. Maybe tomorrow or after tomorrow, she would go to Youssef or Youssef would come to her. But for now, the winter sunlight was making her too drowsy to think of all that.

"Mona! Mona! Are you there, Mona?" The urgent voice of Zainab drifted on the wind. "Where are you? Mona!"

Lazily Mona listened and waited for Zainab to find her.

"Mona!" Zainab threw herself down beside them on the riverbank. "Mona! You have to come to my house. Now, Mona! A surprise! There's a surprise for you at my house!"

For a moment Mona could hear her heart hammering in her chest. Youssef had finally come. Youssef had come for her and was hiding in Zainab's house. But then she told herself not to get her hopes up again. He had been gone a year. If he returned—her faith had ebbed enough so now she had to think "if"—he would go to Baruch, and Baruch would send for her. Youssef didn't even know Zainab. How could he possibly have searched out Zainab in Karnak? No, it wasn't Youssef. Zainab was just trying to trick her again into taking care of some sick soul. Mona regretted ever telling Zainab about her medical training in Alexandria. Since that single confidence, Zainab had unceasingly nagged her to cure every ill in the village. No matter how often Mona told her stepgrandmother that she had not completed her training as a nurse, no matter how much she pleaded simply to be left alone with her infant son, Zainab would not leave her in peace. That's all she wanted, to be left sitting by the river dreaming of her past with Youssef and her future with Ali. "Your surprise is just that somebody's sick again. Isn't that so, Grandmother?"

"A surprise has to be a surprise," Zainab said gaily. "How can it be a surprise if I tell you what it is? If I tell you what it is, how can it be a surprise? What do you think I am, Mona, a fool?"

Mona smiled fondly at her stepgrandmother. If Zainab was a fool, then the world was unwise in wanting to be anything else.

"Get up, Mona! Come on, Mona! *Yalla!*"

To humor her stepgrandmother, Mona allowed herself to be pulled to her feet. Bahia and her two small boys trailed behind them on the path back to the village.

"Chocolates!" Hassan was saying.

"Pepsi!" Fathi was saying.

"It has to be chocolates or Pepsi!" The boys tugged on Mona's robe. "You'll give us some. You will, won't you?"

Zainab's courtyard was a knot of worried relatives. Mona recognized three of Zainab's sisters, four cousins, a niece, somebody's stepchildren. No, Youssef wouldn't be hiding in the midst of these talkative strangers.

"So I was right," she muttered to Zainab after she had properly greeted every one of the adults. "Somebody's sick again. What is it this time? A mangled leg, influenza, a sore back? If your surprise is what I think it is, then *I* have a surprise for *you,* Grandmother. I'm not a doctor. I'm not a nurse. I'm just Mona."

"Sh-h-h." Zainab held a finger to her lips. "Quiet!" She led Mona through the guestroom into her own sleeping room. There, lying on a mat, was a tiny bundle of rags that was making a raggedy little noise.

"I thought so," Mona said.

"Surprise!" Zainab grinned in triumph.

Mona averted her eyes from the infant on the floor. "Take the child to the health center."

"The family is afraid of the doctor. No one goes to him. Besides," Zainab said, "the clinic is closed. You know it's almost always closed."

"Then the midwife. Fetch the midwife."

"The midwife said she could do nothing."

"How can it hurt, Mona?" Bahia was pleading. "How can it hurt to take a look at the child?"

"Touch him," Zainab said. "Pick him up." She nudged Bahia. "I bet all she has to do is touch him. I know that. I know all she has to do is touch him. Her hands. Just one touch of her hands."

Mona looked down at her hands. In Alexandria she had almost believed Baruch when he told her she had it in her to be a healer. But she had had a purity about her then. Now . . . now she didn't even have the strength to heal herself.

"If it were Ali there," Bahia said, "you'd help him."

Mona held her son tighter. Yes, if Ali lay dying, she would move heaven and earth to save him. She took one step closer to the bundle on the floor.

"Do it Mona! Do it!"

For the first time Mona took a good look at the baby crying on the floor. He was so tightly wrapped in dirty rags it was a wonder he could breathe at all. The least she could do was take off those clothes, wash him, and try to see what was wrong. Absently she handed Ali to Bahia and knelt down beside the sick baby. Carefully she peeled off the rags.

A bulb of garlic, an onion, and four blue beads fell to the ground. Poor little thing. No wonder he was crying. She called for hot water, soap, clean layers of cloth. She washed the scrawny body. The baby was all bones. "Does anybody *feed* him? Get me the mother."

Zainab returned in a moment with a frightened young woman of twelve or thirteen.

Unconsciously, as Mona pointed to the girl's breasts, her voice took on the ring of Baruch addressing a patient. "Have you milk?"

The terrified girl whispered to Zainab.

"She says it dried up. She says the Evil Eye was on the child. She says her husband says it's her fault. Her husband says if his son dies, he'll divorce her."

"And no one else could feed him? No sisters, cousins, aunts out in the courtyard?"

"They say the baby is cursed. They're afraid to touch it."

"So!" Mona's eyes softened as she stared at the young mother. Fear. She knew what fear felt like. Curses. She knew about the whispered power of curses. She sighed under her breath, remembering Baruch's words years ago in the al-Masri laboratory. He had said sympathy was the key. If you can feel it, he had said, if you can allow yourself to feel the sufferings of others as your own remembered pain—if you can feel compassion—then you can do it, Mona. He had said she could be a healer. He had said she had the power to make herself a healer. But did she want to be a healer? No. All she wanted was to be left alone with the flickers of her dreams.

The baby, liberated from its rags, was crying hard enough that he woke her own son.

She could turn away from this hungry baby. No one would blame her if she, too, denied him what he needed. But that look on that young mother's face! Slowly Mona drew open her bodice. She bent, lifted the boy to her breast, then signaled to Bahia to put Ali at the other one. As she felt the tugs on her nipples, she held the babies tight to her breasts. She raised her eyes to Zainab. *"Ayyouy! Ayyouy! Ayouououya!"* Zainab let loose with *zaghareit* shrieks. Bahia joined in, then the starving baby's mother took it up, and finally there was an echo from out in the courtyard.

"Didn't I tell you?" Zainab crowed. "Didn't I *say* she was a born *shaykha?* A born *shaykha*, by Allah! I always said, I always knew, even when Mona was a little girl, that she was touched by Allah. She'll bring that little boy back to life! She'll save him. She'll save him with her own magic. *El-hamdulillah! El-hamdulillah!* That Allah has sent us our own Shaykha Mona!"

Mona looked down at the two greedy mouths feeding at her breasts. *Shaykha*. If Zainab had her way—and Zainab was so hard to resist she could probably convince the villagers that a camel was a goat—then soon all the rest of the women would be calling her *shaykha*. If only they all knew, if only they knew of what she had done with Youssef, some of them might even take up rocks and stone her. She had to be the most unworthy woman in Karnak. But she nestled the two babies closer to her. A healer. Could there be redemption in being a healer? Sympathy, compassion, healing. She nursed the two babies and her thoughts.

15 ~~~~~~

TEL AVIV, ISRAEL / April 1958

Youssef stood in Tel Aviv's central bus station at the peak of its holiday howl. He had just said goodbye to Daoud, who was bound for Jerusalem to keep Passover with Moshe. In a half hour Barty would be picking Youssef up outside the bus station and driving them down to a Seder at his in-laws' kibbutz near the Gaza border. Youssef balanced his rucksack on his shoulder, leaned against the gritty wall, and fought off bewilderment at the very nearly hysterical confusion swirling around him. One by one, two by two, rank by rank, Israelis swarmed past with their suitcases, duffel bags, and bunches of vegetables, fruits, and flowers. From open mouths came the gabble of Hebrew, Yiddish, English, Arabic, and Polish. Tanned, tired, but bright-eyed olive-drab soldiers flooded the hallway. A homing pigeon of a private flew past, obviously on his way to visit his mother or his sweetheart. Youssef felt a stab of envy. None of the buses could take him to the woman he loved.

Youssef watched another soldier stride by with an unlit cigarette dangling from the side of his mouth and a laughing girl soldier clinging to his arm. It was easy to imagine what they would be doing this weekend. Sex, Youssef thought, *love*. What good was it anyway? It probably wouldn't work out for this couple either. Youssef saw the eyes of other soldiers linger to admire a ripe pair of breasts or an especially enticing set of buttocks. Men, Youssef thought, were fools. Stupid, randy fools. He himself had given all that up. If he couldn't have Mona—and, increasingly, he had to admit that seemed to be the case— he would have no other. In the winter he had taken off his wedding ring because he was sick of having to explain it to curious acquaintances. He slipped his hand in his pocket and fingered the ring as if it were worry beads.

A baby-faced airman hurried by carrying his black Uzi submachine gun tucked under the same arm as a bouquet of fresh flowers. The gun bumped into the backside of a plump Ashkenazi housewife. The woman turned, shoved the Uzi away, and uttered a few pointed words in Yiddish before bustling onward. The soldier looked first confused, them embarrassed, and finally folded the gun and the flowers tight to his chest as if they were his beloved children. Youssef's bitterness melted into the old, sad, familiar grief.

He lit a cigarette and looked around for Arabs. Sometimes, when he was especially homesick for Egypt, he would try to conjure it up in the faces of passing Arabs. If there were any passing Arabs. Often he would wonder where the hell the Arabs were in Israel. The Arabs as good as lived on reservations. In Israel, distinctly, there were Jewish cities and settlements and Arab villages and quarters. The sectors were divided by a mutual desire not to mix. Between the two uneasy communities any contact except some necessary buying and selling was rare. Even in public places like this bus station, the Jews and the Arabs remained aloof.

He spotted a thin, sullen old Arab peddling cigarettes and chewing gum from a spread blanket. By the look on his face, the old man would rather have been selling his Israeli customers primed grenades. As Youssef watched, a policeman ordered the Arab out of the corridor because he was blocking public access. The Arab sucked out his lips as if he were about to spit. But then he blinked and very slowly swallowed hard, as if what was in his mouth were bile.

Youssef went back to observing the restless, rushing Israelis. Many were managing not only to hare through the pack but to wolf down their lunches at the same time. A frizzle-haired girl with an armful of books crammed nuts in her mouth as she shot past on her trajectory. A kibbutznik—he must be a kibbutznik with those ill-fitting, carefully ironed blue denims of his—munched a felafel sandwich and dripped gooey *tahina* sauce on the floor as he raced on his way. A little girl, wide-eyed and fearful, chewed nervously on a fat cookie as her mother dragged her by the hand. That was it; that was Israel. Everyone was so nervous. Youssef stamped out his cigarette.

At last he spotted two genuine Arabs. Even if they had not been wearing robes and *kefiya* headdresses, he could have identified them by their pace alone. They sauntered by as if watches and timetables had no place in their world. They moved in Arab slow motion while the others blurred past at Jewish double time. Early on in Israel, Youssef had learned it was futile to try to talk to Arabs on the street. Many, sizing him up only as one of the conquering soldiers, pretended not to understand his heavy Egyptian accent. Some would stare through him unseeingly. A few would sidle up too close, willing to sell him whatever they thought he wanted. The Palestinians were as much a mystery to Youssef now as they had been the day he arrived. All he knew was that compared to Egyptians, Palestinians were tall, lean, and light of skin. And sullen. They looked so brooding and sullen. He felt another homesick pang for his jolly fat Egyptians.

He lit another cigarette. It served little purpose to lean against the wall and catalogue the many ways in which he was unlike all who crossed his path. Israelis, Arabs—it was beyond him. He was having enough trouble finding his *own* place in his adopted country. He was beginning to think it might be on a kibbutz. It had been Daoud's idea for the two of them to serve this optional one-year stretch at their partially army-staffed kibbutz. But it was not Daoud but Youssef who had found he liked running with the kibbutz pack. He enjoyed the pickup games of basketball, the casual banter in the dining hall, the rambling late-night coffees in the rooms of the members. Most of all he liked the constant, inevitable company. On the kibbutz he was rarely alone with his thoughts.

Youssef was troubled, however, that Daoud didn't feel the same way. Daoud had nursed such high hopes that the kibbutz would be a socialist utopian dream come true. Instead, Daoud had become increasingly obsessed with the plight of the Oriental immigrants. On the kibbutz the few Moroccans were assigned the worst work details. The native-born sabra girls refused to keep company with the Tunisians. Most of the Orientals were housed together in the most dilapidated dormitory. Daoud spent his free hours in meetings and protests and political discussions, trying to change all that. Wearily—perhaps a bit guiltily— Youssef tried to catch his brother's political fever. But even though the kibbutz *did* discriminate against Orientals, Youssef would be sorry to leave it next summer when he and Daoud moved on to their specialized paratrooper training.

Youssef watched a soldier strut past in the coveted paratrooper's scarlet beret. He would have to ask Barty today for details of the training. Over the months he had drawn closer to the colonel. He had even confided to Barty his doubts about ever actually taking up arms against Egyptians. Barty had clapped his arm around Youssef's shoulders and advised him not to torment himself about a war that might not come. Youssef should learn to shoot straight and let the generals worry about where the guns were aimed. Instead of wasting valuable energy brooding about Egypt, Youssef should be counting his lucky stars that he was in Israel.

Youssef sighed under his breath. If he wasn't quite ready to call it a lucky star that had led him to Israel, at least he could say that the land was beginning to seem less alien. Besides the easy comradeship on the kibbutz, Youssef had taken a shine to Barty's in-laws during his frequent visits to the colonel's house in Haifa. Hannah's cousins Sasha and Hagar were the salt of the earth. Their sons were good company. He was more ambivalent about Hagar's daughter, Rivka. Like so many Israeli woman, Rivka was too bold for Youssef's taste. She was tall, skinny, and sharp-tongued. If it weren't that he was forever finished with women, he might have responded to her blatant flirting just long enough to teach her some manners. It was indecent that she always wore such short shorts to show off those long, lithe legs.

Youssef consulted his watch and hurried down the dark tunnel that connected the station to the street. Lurking in the shadows was a fat Moroccan beggar woman. She held a baby in her arms, and two more wailing children clung to her long black robe. The scene was so reminiscent of home that, automatically responding as if he were on the Corniche, Youssef dug in his pocket for *baksheesh*. But behind him someone impatiently cursed in Hebrew that he was blocking the way. Youssef fumed to himself that the Israelis were always in too much of a rush for the small gestures that gave life grace. But then he shrugged, hastily flipped the beggar woman his coins, and hurried on his way.

As he stood in the shade of a crabapple tree, Youssef looked down at his reflection in the sun-dappled surface of the fish pond. The tall blond soldier was framed in roses, heather, morning glories, and daisies. Behind him were palm trees, maples, and pines. There was even a strangely twisted small tree that looked vaguely Japanese. The shouts of children drifted over on the wind. An old woman sat knitting on a bench. Despite the peeling paint on the dairy barns and the jerry-built buildings, Kibbutz *Chozrim*, Kibbutz Homecoming, had such an air of comfort about it that Youssef would have liked to settle down under a tree and drowse away the day.

Youssef gave the pastoral scene a last look of longing. He wasn't supposed to be daydreaming on the kibbutz green. At Hagar's insistence, he was supposed to be finding Rivka at the dining hall so she could show him around the settlement.

He could hear Rivka even before he crossed the kitchen threshold. "Not that way! That is definitely *not* the way to prepare matzoh-ball soup."

"How would you know?" Youssef could hear another woman's angry retort. "You keep telling us you're the best tractor driver on the kibbutz—*not* the best cook. So while you're assigned to my kitchen, you do as I say. You wash the dishes. *I* make the soup."

Youssef could see at least eight women stirring, cooking, and cleaning in the stainless-steel kitchen which, according to the large brass plaque on the wall, was a gift of Myron and Sophie Greenblatt of Shaker Heights, Ohio. "Rivka! I'd know that temper anywhere."

She looked up. Her face was flushed from the steam of the sink. She had pinned her black hair behind her ears, but some of the strands had escaped to dangle in strings around her face. She was wearing a dirty pair of shorts and a blouse that was wet enough to cling to the outlines of her brassiere. "Oh, *no*. You're early."

"Who's this?" A woman from the far end of the kitchen sized up Youssef. "One of your many boyfriends, Rivka?"

"A fine young man." The old woman who was the evident boss of the kitchen peered at Youssef as she stirred a huge metal soup caldron. "You could do worse, you know, Rivka?"

"Don't mind them." Rivka wiped her hands on her shorts. "They don't know what they're talking about."

"You laugh." The woman stirring the soup pot seemed oblivious to the fact that Rivka most definitely had not laughed. "But you're not getting any younger, you know, Rivka? I had three sons when I was your age. If I were you, I'd be grateful for this soldier. You lost out with that volunteer from South America and that boy from the Galilee. This one's a little skinny, but what can you do? It's not like you're a prize yourself."

Youssef wasn't surprised they all knew Rivka was in search of a suitor. But the poor girl looked mortified. He walked over to the soup pot. "Smells good." His smile to Rivka implied that they were the only two in the kitchen. "Your mother thought you might be able to show me around the kibbutz."

"I have work to do."

"Work? What work do you ever do?" The soup woman poured Youssef a bowl and handed him a spoon. "Eat. You need it. And Rivka. As soon as this soldier finishes his soup, you show him what we've built here. And take those pins out of your hair. You'd have such nice hair, Rivka, if you'd wash it once in a while. And don't forget to show him the swimming pool. My son Yaakov proposed to his wife up there, you know? It's a very romantic spot. Better than the cemetery."

Youssef laughed, finished his soup, and complimented its outspoken cook. He caught up with Rivka outside, where she was already setting a brisk pace with her flashing tan legs. He tried to put her at ease by making light of the scene in the kitchen. "That's the first time anyone has called me skinny. But she was right about your hair. How often *do* you wash it?"

"Often enough." She pointed to the left. "The children's houses are over there. The laundry and the library are on the other side of the trees. First we'll go to Monument Hill for the view." She sprinted ahead of him up a tree-lined path.

When he drew abreast of her, he noticed that she had tucked her shirt into her shorts and taken the pins from her hair. He smiled to himself.

"Do you have a girlfriend, Youssef?"

296

His smile froze. He thought Barty's in-laws knew all about his past. The colonel believed in getting everything out in the open. "I think so," was all he was able to mumble.

"The cemetery is on that nubby hill over there." She kept walking. "Now I remember. An Arab girl. In Egypt. What *was* her name?"

"Mona," Youssef said unhappily. "Her name was . . . *is* Mona."

"Pretty name. I suppose she's pretty, too."

"Beautiful. Mona is beautiful."

"The green down there is where we hold our weddings. My mother planted most of the flowers herself."

"Must keep her busy."

"It does." Rivka was once again walking a few paces ahead of him. "You used to wear a wedding ring, but you don't now. Does that mean you haven't heard from her lately?"

"I haven't heard from her at all." He couldn't take his eyes off Rivka's thighs. They were as tough and muscled and obvious as her line of questioning. He wondered if the skin would be soft to the touch. "You know my situation."

"I just thought you might have heard something by now. You've been away for—what—more than a year? For all you know, she might be married. You know how those Arabs are. Marry young. Breed like bunnies. She's how old now?"

It was an effort to be polite to this girl. But he was, after all, the Passover guest of her family. "Mona is seventeen."

"Almost an old maid."

Youssef could no longer control his anger. He didn't want to talk to anyone—he especially did not want to talk to Rivka—about Mona. "Like you?"

She seemed to shudder, but then she stopped and turned. Her brown eyes were bright. "You're so right, Youssef. An old maid is precisely what I am. Only I suppose there's not much hope for an old maid who looks like me."

Youssef was filled with remorse. He hadn't meant to hurt her. Israelis, especially Israelis who lived on a kibbutz, married young. It could not be pleasant to have your fellow kibbutzniks needling you about your single state. He would be decent and explain that he was committed to Mona for life. "My uncle wrote to say he thinks she married someone else." Youssef paused. He had not intended to tell her the truth. "I thought she was waiting for me."

Rivka looked cheered. "So it's over."

Youssef began walking again. He wished he had not encouraged this girl. "Mona is my wife."

Rivka scrambled behind him. "Wait a minute. You just said you thought she married someone else."

"Legally we're not married. But we exchanged private vows." He pulled the wedding ring from his pocket and held it up to the light. "She is my wife."

"How very romantic. I wouldn't have thought you were such a romantic."

He was irritated again. "How would you know, Rivka? How would you know anything at all about what I am?"

Youssef breathed in the salt air at the top of Monument Hill. Beyond the white dunes the sun was sinking into the gray Mediterranean. Below them the kibbutz spread in clusters of neat green fields, beige flat-topped housing units, efficient work and play centers. To the south he could see the gray shadows of the Gaza Strip's teeming refugee camps and barbed-wire borders. Egypt was less than three miles away.

Rivka walked over to the tall bronze statue of three brawny men and one hefty woman. "The defenders of Kibbutz Chozrim. In the '48 war our one hundred and forty-four kibbutzniks held out against two thousand Egyptian soldiers for six days." Her voice was tight and dry. "Because of Chozrim's valor, the main force of the Egyptian army was not able to approach Tel Aviv until our army was ready for them. Twenty-six men and women—including my father—died in that battle. Chozrim fought against impossible odds. We were desperate. We were stubborn. We still are." She strode over and stood directly in front of Youssef. "As that bitch said back in the kitchen, I'm no prize. I'm not pretty enough for you, Youssef, am I?"

Her face was almost level with his. He didn't know how to answer. But as he groped for kind words, she shut her eyes and leaned closer to him with her lips parted. Pity moved him to kiss her very softly. He could feel her fingers in his hair. From not far away he heard the kibbutz dining-hall bell sound. She angled her slim body into his. Just as he forgot all about pity and would have pressed her closer to him, Rivka turned and ran. "Save me a seat at the Seder," she called back to him as she disappeared down the leafy path.

He had feared Rivka would make wistful eyes at him all during the Seder, but instead she was a boisterous comrade. If it weren't that she arrived with freshly washed hair and wearing—wonder of wonders—a skirt, he would have thought that he had imagined their kiss and their words on Monument Hill.

The Seder lasted far into the night. Aside from the generous amounts and traditional types of Passover food, the fete had little in common with any Youssef had attended in Alexandria or Jerusalem. Passover at Kibbutz Chozrim started off with all rising to sing the "Internationale." Then the kibbutz secretary delivered a stirring speech honoring those who had died for freedom not only on their own kibbutz battlefield but also on the Sinai and Golan fronts. The choir sang modern songs in Hebrew. Sasha's wife read a poem she had written for the occasion. There were many mentions of Zion but none of God. Groups of children performed Hebrew folk dances under the admiring eyes of their families. At last came the Haggadah service commemorating the exodus of the Israelis from their ancient bondage in Egypt. Sasha narrated, and when he posed the most famous of the ritual questions— "Why is this night different from all other nights?"—Rivka winked at Youssef. Others in the dining hall were making merry as well. Barty was already into the sweet dark wine. Hagar was nibbling on the matzoh before she should be. The folding chairs seemed to rattle with laughter. Youssef found himself smiling at strangers as if he had known them all his life.

At last, as they feasted on the chicken and drained their glasses, Rivka made clear what had been implicit. Chozrim was not a religious kibbutz. The founding members were political radicals from their Polish youth in Hashomer Hatzair. Their progressive kibbutz federation had excised some of the religious sentiments of the Haggadah and substituted words that celebrated the freedom and founding of the Jewish State. Pious Jews in their long frock coats, Rivka said, could make what they wanted of Passover. They could go on and on about the dreaded pharaoh who had made slaves of the children of Israel. They could smear symbolic blood on their doors. For all she cared, they could even try to reenact the parting of the Dead Sea. But to the people of Chozrim, Passover was a time to break unleavened bread with their family of friends and to rejoice in the freedom they had carved out for themselves in the modern land of their ancestors.

Youssef, as he allowed himself to flirt just a little with the boyish woman at his side, considered the irony that he, Youssef "the Egyptian," felt so at home at this Israeli feast to celebrate the leaving of Egypt. He slipped his hand in his pocket to assure himself Mona's ring was still there. He asked himself if by kissing Rivka, if by liking her kibbutz, he was betraying Mona and Egypt. He considered the alternative. Could he go on forever living a temporary life in Israel? He was so tired of being a stranger in a strange land. It was possible, of course, that he could live out the rest of his life in Israel as bitterly as he had begun it in that transit camp. Would Mona want that? Did he? He could not help laughing at Sasha's broad jokes, clapping wildly along with everyone else at the children's songs and dances, and exchanging irreverent comments behind his hand with Rivka. She wasn't a beauty. Whatever he might be able to have with her would be nothing like what he had shared with Mona. Yet Baruch said Mona had married. . . . A woman like this Rivka could never quite match Mona, and so in a way he would still be being loyal to his love. But would that be fair to Rivka? Wouldn't she want more of him? Youssef swirled the wine in his glass, then shrugged and toasted Rivka with it. What, after all, was the harm in this? He liked Kibbutz Chozrim, he liked Sasha and Hagar, and—yes—he was beginning to like Rivka. He bit into a matzoh and winked back at her.

Youssef was smoking and staring at the ceiling of the paratroopers' barracks as he tried to talk to his brother. Daoud was sitting on the floor fiddling with the radio dial. "I just don't know what to do about her," Youssef repeated.

"Do?" Daoud said absently. "Why do anything?"

"You don't know Rivka. She's like a bloody octopus."

"You and your women!" Daoud grinned at his brother. "Still the same old Youssef."

"No. It's not the same. If you mean my old belly dancers, it's not the same at all." Moodily Youssef blew smoke rings. "Last spring, Daoud, I didn't even like her. Then I felt sorry for her. And now . . . now I don't know. Everyone—Barty, her family, her entire kibbutz—considers us practically engaged." Youssef glared at the ceiling. "Goddam bloody aggressive Israeli women."

Daoud didn't answer. He was bent over the radio listening to static.

"Daoud? Daoud! You're not listening."

"Maybe it's because I've heard it all before. At least with the radio I can turn the dial and hear something new." Daoud's laugh took the edge off his words.

Youssef forced a smile. He tried so hard to make Daoud understand. But his Orientals were all his brother had time for these days. "You don't think I should worry about Rivka?"

"I think you'd be better off if you spent less of your life mooning over women and more time worrying about things that matter."

"Politics. You know I don't care about politics. What good has politics ever done either one of us? If it weren't for fanatic politicians, we'd still be at home in Alexandria."

Daoud looked up from his radio. "You still miss it—and *her*—don't you?"

"Always."

Daoud began pacing the room. "You know, Youssef, I miss it, too. I miss crazy things. The sound of the prayer calls when I'm half asleep in the morning. *Tahina*." Daoud smacked his lips. "They don't make *tahina* here as they did back in Egypt. I guess they don't use enough garlic. And I miss those silly jokes the Egyptians used to crack just when they had me so infuriated I was ready to scream. I'd end up laughing even if I didn't want to."

"You? You feel like that?"

"I. I feel like that."

"I never would have guessed it."

"Why? Because I love Israel, too? There are other ways to mourn, Youssef, that are just as full of grief as crying yourself to sleep."

"I haven't done that for months. For weeks, anyway." Youssef rolled over on his side so he could look his brother in the eye. "Just what, exactly, are you trying to tell me?"

"My Orientals. They're my Egypt here. Why do you think I can't leave them alone? I'm closer to home when I'm around them. It's a way, maybe, of keeping a foot in both camps."

"I thought you just couldn't resist the oppressed."

Daoud laughed. "There's that, too." He sat down on the edge of Youssef's bunk. "You know, I've been thinking that when we get out of the army, we might work together in Jerusalem. With the Moroccans. We could be together, Youssef." Daoud blushed. "We could do something *fine*. We could live with the Orientals—it would be almost like living in Egypt—and yet by helping them we'd also be doing something—I guess this sounds crazy to you—we'd be doing something to make not only ourselves but Israel better as well."

Before Youssef could answer, there was a crackle on the radio. Daoud sprang to his feet and bent to listen intently to the announcer. In Haifa's Moroccan slum of Wadi Salib, a drunken brawl in a café the night before had exploded into a full-scale riot. One Moroccan had been shot resisting arrest. Enraged Orientals were encircling the police station screaming for not only revenge but justice. Wadi Salib was in flames.

Daoud looked up from the radio. "This is *it*. Now it will change. Now the government won't be able to ignore the Orientals any longer. Are you with me, Youssef? Are you?"

Youssef looked away from his brother and the radio. "But I'm still not sure what to do about Mona and Rivka. If only I could be sure Mona was really married. If only I could go back and see her and talk it all over with her, then maybe I'd know what to do about Rivka. Maybe you and I could try to slip over the border—make a lightning paratrooper raid of our own, a little personal reconnaissance. I mean, I like Rivka. She's good company. But I don't love her. Not as I love Mona. What do you think, Daoud? Daoud! You're not listening. You never listen to me."

Daoud threw Youssef one brief, dismissive glance of disappointment. Then Daoud twiddled with the dial of the radio until the announcer's voice was loud and clear enough to drown his brother out.

Youssef and Rivka were stretched out in the warm autumn sun on the opposite ends of a blanket on the kibbutz beach. Youssef munched the last of the cookies and lit a cigarette. His eyes were half closed. Very soon, soothed by the gentle lap of the surf, he would nod asleep.

Rivka had other ideas. "We should talk, Youssef."

"Hmmmm," Youssef mumbled. He did not move a muscle, but inside he went rigid as he primed himself for the assault he knew was coming. In the year and a half he had been keeping company with Rivka, he had learned to know her moods. That tone in her voice meant trouble.

"You get out of the army in two more months," she said.

"You know what they always say: 'You're never out of the army. Civilians are just soldiers on eleven months' leave.'" Youssef's mind wandered back to his and Daoud's first parachute jump. Twelve hundred feet above the ground, they had exchanged terror-stricken looks in the belly of the army Dakota. The green light had snapped on, and the al-Masris had edged closer to the open door. When his turn had come, Youssef had silently cursed the army for insisting that they had to leave the plane head first. It was horrifying to have to let go, to whoosh out there into nothingness, to free-fall for three seconds until the chute finally opened. He had wet his pants. He was almost as nervous at this very instant, because he was sure Rivka was intent on snaring him into a commitment. "Did I ever tell you about my first parachute jump?" He flashed her a winning smile.

"Many times." She tried another tack. "Is Daoud still talking about going into social work? Barty says he's trying to find him a job."

"You know Daoud and his Orientals."

"He'll probably have to work in one of the cities."

"That's where the Oriental slums are. I think he wants Jerusalem."

"He's the only family you have here. Does that mean you'll be going with him?"

Youssef sat up. "Be direct, Rivka. Out with it."

"Will you marry me?"

He blinked. He had expected some intermediary questions. He would try to remember never again to ask an Israeli to be frank. "I don't know." He lay down once again and covered his face with his arm.

Rivka waited. Youssef had developed the bewildering habit of prefacing explanations of what he knew by first claiming that he didn't know. But this time he did not elaborate. "I wish I'd thought to bring some coffee," she finally said. "I could use some coffee."

He didn't answer. He had been dreading this confrontation for months. Rivka was more buddy than sweetheart. He knew she would have been willing to sleep with him long ago, but he had kept their intimacy to a minimum. He wanted, so badly, to act honorably. He did not want to betray the woman he loved or mislead a woman he liked.

After a while she doggedly continued. "I mean, you like the kibbutz. And everyone likes you. You fit in. You could have a good life here. That counts for something, doesn't it, Youssef?"

He liked her less when she was pathetic. He sat down and faced her again. "You didn't ask me to marry the kibbutz. You asked me to marry you."

"I thought I would have a better chance if I came with the kibbutz."

He smiled. She always made him smile. That was one reason he liked her. But she knew very well that he could join Chozrim on his own. What held him back was that he knew she would never leave him alone if he did. He tested her resolve. "Do you really want to marry me, Rivka?"

She nodded.

"Why?"

"Why? *Why!* Why do you think?"

He wished he hadn't asked. She was tracing a pattern in the sand with her finger. He followed it with his eyes. She was forming the Hebrew letters of his name. "I don't think I'll ever get married," Youssef said gently.

"You're still in love with Mona."

"Yes."

"I didn't ask you to love me." In the sand she was spelling out the final characters of "al-Masri." "I just asked you to marry me."

"I think the two should go together."

"What should happen doesn't always happen."

"No," Youssef agreed. His tone was final.

She finished with his name, then savagely blotted it out with her fist. She looked at him. "All my dreams are always destroyed. All of them gone like that. Youssef, you have destroyed all my dreams."

He bit his lip hard. The last thing he had wanted was to hurt Rivka. He had never made promises to her that he couldn't keep. Nevertheless, here they were. Once again he was guilty. For God's sake, he didn't want to destroy her dreams. He knew how that felt. Maybe, he thought, maybe I just haven't tried hard enough with Rivka. Maybe I haven't tried hard enough with anything. Why—why!—had she accused him of destroying her dreams? His life was a litter of broken dreams. He lay down with his back to her and started to cry.

"What's wrong, Youssef?"

As he cried, he wished he had never met Rivka. He should never have thought it could be good with anyone but Mona. All he had done was inflict his misery on someone else. He had drifted into an empty relationship with her just as he had drifted into the army and would doubtless drift into a kibbutz.

Rivka was stroking his hair. "I'm sorry, Youssef. Really. I'm sorry. I shouldn't have said anything. I don't want to put you through all this."

It was easier to deal with a badgering Rivka than a noble one. But at least he was able to stop crying. When he looked up at her, she smiled at him and brushed the sand off his face.

"You look like a pretty poor excuse for a paratrooper."

"Cigarette. Give me a cigarette." She lit him one, and he took an exploratory puff. "I don't know." She waited. "I want to tell you the truth," he continued. "But I don't want to hurt you."

"You were the one who was crying."

He knew he had lost considerable strategic ground. He rubbed his eyes with his fingers and then looked back at her. She was still there waiting. "You know I love Mona. That I wanted to marry her."

"You've told me. I know she is your . . . first choice."

"I haven't seen her for so long." To himself he added that it was exactly two years and seven months.

"I want to marry you. I love you."

"I know. I know that." He hesitated. "Would you still be willing to marry me? Knowing how things are?"

"Yes!"

"And what if there's peace, and I could go back to Egypt?"

"You know Jewish law. A man can divorce his wife just about anytime he wants."

God, he thought. How desperate she is for me. How could she settle for this? How could she be so eager to settle for this? "Let's go over this again. You want to marry me. Knowing that I want to marry someone else. Even realizing there might be a divorce later."

"Nothing is ever certain in life. Divorce is always possible."

"But how many of your dreams would I destroy then?"

"I'll take my chances. Maybe you won't leave me."

"I don't know."

"Children. We could have children. You'd like that. I know you would. You'd be a wonderful father."

Youssef wished she hadn't said that. He had always wanted a son.

She was watching him closely. "Then it's settled. I was born on the kibbutz, so we'll be in line for a decent room. And we'll have to decide what sort of work you can do. I thought that if you don't like working in the fields, you could teach in the high school. English and Arabic. I already talked to the chairman of the education committee. He was very enthusiastic."

Youssef stared at her. Surely there should be more to it than this. It seemed less that they had just agreed to get married and more that he had just been recruited. But he let her talk. At least Rivka could have her dreams.

16 ———～～～～

KARNAK, EGYPT   /   January 1962

Shaykha Mona stood looking at the sharpened knife as the girl and Bahia and Zainab and Um Mona stood in a circle in the back room. No, Mona thought, I can't go through with it. No matter what my family wants, no matter what the village custom says the girl needs, I can't cut the clitoris of Muhammad's daughter.

Out of the corner of her eye she saw Ali creep through the door and hold Soad's hand as all the women recited the opening chapter of the Koran.

"No boys!" Zainab slapped Ali on his rump. "Out! Wait outside! You can't stay, Ali. No boys allowed."

"But I want to watch. I'm not just a boy. I want to be a doctor. Can't I stay, Mother? Let me stay. I want to learn to be just like you."

"Boys don't do *tahara."* Soad, usually so adoring of her cousin Ali, now was scornful. "Even boy doctors don't do it. Only *shaykhas.* You're not a *shaykha."*

"Can't I stay, Mother?"

Mona shook her head.

"But you can walk beside me in my procession," Soad said with the graciousness of a princess dispensing a very great favor. "You and my mother and Shaykha Mona can be right up front."

"I can?"

Mona nodded, and Ali ran out to boast to his friends about the parade.

Mona watched her relatives undress the child. Soad was nearly four. Muhammad's daughter was not yet four years old. Mona herself had delivered the girl. Every day she had watched Soad playing with her own Ali. Now she was supposed to mutilate little Soad?

Zainab was fanning the incense. Mona caught her mother's eyes on her. Yes, Ummie was remembering the day back in Kom Ombo when that Shaykha Sameera had dug out Mona's flesh with another knife. There were tears in Ummie's eyes. Mona looked back to the knife. Ummie had sharpened it herself this morning. It was very sharp. Mona had plunged it into a flame to sterilize it. It was very clean.

Mona moistened her lips. Four years ago, when she had put that starving baby to her breast as Zainab had known she would, her career as a Karnak healer had begun. Now she was both an occasional nurse at the government's health center and one of the village *dayas,* a midwife who not only birthed babies but ministered to the real and imagined ills of Karnak's women and children. Mona had always contended there was no mysterious miracle in the survival of that infant she had fed. But the baby's mother and father, his uncles and aunts, his grandparents and cousins, had all been determined to believe otherwise. Mona, the beautiful young widow with an infant of her own, had saved that child from the certain death of a terrible curse. It hadn't taken long for others to hear embroidered versions of the miraculous cure, for there were few secrets in the village. The more Mona said she had no special healing gifts from Allah, the more the others praised her for her humility. No one had forgotten—no one ever forgets anything in Karnak—that it was always Mona who took it upon herself to fill the village's public water jugs. It was even recalled, in whisperings that could easily have been traced back to Zainab, that on the day of Mona's Nubian circumcision she had entered into a mystical communion with the Nile itself. Confidence had quickly grown in this sad, quiet one that all were soon addressing as Shaykha Mona.

"Shaykha Mona!" An old woman's querulous voice called out from the courtyard. "Shaykha Mona!"

Mona still cringed when anyone called her by the respectful title of *shaykha*. She knew she often was held up to the young girls of Karnak as an example of how a modest, unassuming, selfless young woman should behave. Only Mona and her mother knew better. Her mother never let her forget the dishonor she had brought down on her family by running away with Youssef. "*Sharmoota!*" her mother would sometimes hiss when they were alone. But the insults were unnecessary. If Mona singlehandedly cured every soul in Karnak of whatever ailed them, her past would still be the same. She could never regret her love for Youssef, but public honors in the village only increased her sense of guilt. Sometimes when she sat by the river on a lazy afternoon, she would look at her reflection in the Nile. She would study the grave, unsmiling young woman of twenty-one and wonder why she was still cursed with good looks. Her life in the village would have been easier if she had been so plain that no man could ever want her for his own. Instead she had had to fend off a series of marriage proposals. One of the waiters from the Luxor Hotel had wanted her. A night watchman from Karnak Temple and the spiceman's son had proposed. Even the old *kuttab* teacher had approached Uncle Muhammad. Steadfastly Mona had refused them all. Marriage would be an admission that Youssef was never coming back. As long as she masqueraded as a widow, she could still hope for a reunion. And there was something else as well. Suppose, Mona sometimes thought, I married a village man and gave him a son or two. Reading the Cairo newspapers from year to year did not allay her fears that someday there might be another war with the Jews. Ali could someday face his father in battle. But only sons of widowed mothers were exempt from the army. If she did not marry, if she did not give birth to another son, the worst could never happen. And so she had refused all her suitors.

"Shaykha Mona! It's me! Um Mustafa! I need you! My eyes! My eyes hurt!"

Zainab clucked her tongue in impatience, but when Um Mustafa appeared in the doorway it was too late to turn her away.

Glad for the delay, Shaykha Mona held Um Mustafa's face up to the light. Yes, her eyes were getting worse. By the looks of it, this one wasn't using her medicine. Um Mustafa said the health center had run out of eye ointment again. It was expected to arrive, *inshallah*, tomorrow or after tomorrow, which Mona knew could translate into next week or next month or next year. In the meantime the clerk had given Um Mustafa tablets which she had been diligently grinding into powder and rubbing into her eyes. Examining the pills, Mona was not surprised they were aspirin. The only items the village pharmacy was ever sure to be stocked with were aspirin and cough syrup. Carefully Mona explained to Um Mustafa it would be better to wash her eyes out three or four times a day with boiled water. Um Mustafa nodded but joked that maybe, after all, her eyes had seen enough in her forty-eight years. As long as she could make her way to the river—and she was sure she could do that even if she was blind—she would praise Allah for His mercy. All the women sighed in unison. Um Mustafa lifted her water jug back to her head. Mona watched her continue on her slow and steady inevitable path to the Nile.

"Now," Zainab said, "the circumcision!"

Mona stared at the knife. Was this knife, this act, as inevitable as everything else in Karnak? Was it an inevitable consequence of allowing herself to become a *shaykha?* Until now, because Mona refused to perform circumcisions, the *tahara* ritual had fallen to an old midwife whose eyes were very nearly blinded by cataracts. Two months ago a little girl had hemorrhaged so heavily after her circumcision that she had had to be hospitalized in Luxor. Last month another little girl had died. Mona heaved a profound sigh. If she didn't circumcise Soad, that old butcher woman would take a knife to her small cousin. But if Mona performed the gentlest of circumcisions, she could make sure Soad hardly bled. Yet she cringed at the thought of presiding at the ritual. That day—that sweltering, excruciating day by the Nile in Kom Ombo—had scarred her for life. How, now, remembering all that, could she turn from victim to victimizer? And yet how could she not? The circumcision would be performed with or without her help. It would be better for Soad if she was the one to do it. Wasn't Soad's life more precious, Mona asked herself, than her own sense of right and wrong?

Mona wished there had been time to write Baruch and ask what she should do. Often Mona wrote Baruch for advice. To her complaints that she didn't know enough about medicine to practice it, he replied crisply that already she knew more than most of the other healers in Karnak. Of course she couldn't function as a doctor. But she could deliver babies, clean wounds, give injections. Maybe even more important, Baruch always wrote, was that by practicing *compassion,* she would be giving a great gift not only to others but to herself. And so with Baruch pushing and prodding her, with Zainab and her kinswomen bringing her patients, Mona had done her best. As the years passed, it seemed Baruch had been right. She did have a certain gift for soothing the sick. Kind words and aspirin couldn't stop cancer or cholera. But basic hygiene, common-sense nursing, and a sympathetic listening to litanies of aches and pains sometimes could work wonders.

Still undecided about cutting her cousin, Mona sank down on the floor next to Soad. She looked around the room at the rapt faces of her family. The typical Karnak way of resolving a dilemma like hers would be somehow to trick the others into believing Soad was circumcised or to foist the responsibility for the ritual onto someone else. But Mona decided against the easy way out. She would, for once, make her own free choice.

Mona stroked the little girl's hand. *El-hamdulillah,* she thought, that in Karnak circumcisions were not as colorfully gruesome as they had been in the Nubian village of her childhood. In Karnak they didn't paint girls with henna or bind them with ropes. In Karnak they didn't throw the remains of a girl's sex in a bloody offering to the Nile. In Karnak they didn't chant about bridegrooms and penises and shame. In Karnak all that was required was that the tip of the clitoris be excised. Then they would form a procession and dance Soad down to the Nile. Finally there would be a dainty feast of tea and cakes. Mona wished she could believe that, like so much of what happened in her village, there was no lasting harm in the matter-of-fact circumcisions of Karnak.

Sometime over the years Mona had made her peace with the village. At first all she had been able to see was the bleakness of the mud huts and the blank despair of the poor souls fated to live there. When she was alone in those first years, she had found herself saying over and over again, even out loud, that she wanted to go home. That she *was* home—that she had been born to live and die in Karnak—was a feeling that had crept over her gradually with the years. Sometimes she was even able to take comfort from the idea that everything that happened to her—Youssef's love, Baruch's imparted wisdom, her own loneliness—was part of a pattern whose design was becoming apparent only here and now in Karnak. Perhaps it was her destiny only to be the mother of Ali and one of Karnak's healers.

Mona made herself smile into Soad's trusting eyes. Remembering the helpless dread she had felt when her aunts had pinned her down at her own circumcision, Mona spoke gently to Soad. "I want you to spread your legs, *habibti.*" Mona showed the knife to Soad. "Then I want you to hold very still." Mona spread her own fingers on her black robe and deliberately—swiftly—she sliced through the tip of her own little finger.

Soad watched her cousin's blood stain the black robe. "Does it hurt?"

"A little," Mona admitted. "It will hurt you, too, just a little. But if you're still and I'm quick, it won't be too bad for a brave girl like you."

Soad looked up at her mother. Bahia blew her a kiss.

"You understand?" Mona asked.

Soad pulled her legs wide.

Mona stared at the cleft. She had done all she could to minimize the risk of infection. She had tried to reassure Soad by taking a knife to herself and telling her what to expect. Now she had to do it. As she delicately felt for where the clitoris must be, she remembered Youssef examining her in the bathtub of their Cairo houseboat. How appalled he had been. What would Youssef think of her now, poised with a knife in her hand? How could she ever make him understand? Still, against all hope, she waited for him. Always, still, when she walked through Karnak's bustling souk, her eyes darted from robe to turban to face. She had learned to live with the grief of not having Youssef, but still she nursed the belief that someday he would come for her. From time to time she would think she spotted a disguised Youssef in the back lanes of Karnak. Any tall stranger in a *gallabeiya* and turban might be Youssef. But then one stranger might smile, and she would see his yellowed teeth. Or another might walk out in the sunlight, and she would see his pockmarked face. She would sigh then that once again her eyes had been playing tricks on her.

Looking down at Soad, Mona remembered her own wantonness with Youssef. What shame could have been hers if she hadn't been circumcised? Everyone said *tahara* was for a girl's own good. Maybe everyone was right?

Mona shook her head. She would not lie to herself. Female mutilations were *wrong*. Her honeyweeks with Youssef had been *right*. For a moment, remembering the joys of the houseboat, courage came back to Mona. Someday, she told herself, she would have to be brave enough to stand up for what she knew was right. Today could be that day. She opened her mouth to tell them she would never, ever, be a party to a circumcision. But she reconsidered. Soad might have to pay with her life. Were her own scruples worth that much?

As she wavered, Mona felt mother's eyes on hers. There was triumph in Ummie's eyes. Suddenly Mona saw it all. If she did this, if she bowed to village superstition or custom or whatever *tahara* mostly was, Ummie and the ways of the village would have won. She would be theirs. Mona fingered the hilt of the knife with resignation. What choice, really, did she have? What she had to do now was the price for being one of them. Mona dropped her eyes from her mother's.

"Hold still, now, Soad, and it won't hurt so much." Mona lifted the knife. Neatly she cut the tiniest possible sliver of her cousin's clitoris.

"Ow! That hurts!"

Quickly Mona applied the antiseptic. The small cut was barely bleeding. She applied a gauze bandage, slipped Soad's pantaloons back on her, and kissed her cousin.

"That's all?" Soad asked.

Bahia, Zainab, and Um Mona parted their lips, fluttered their tongues against the roofs of their mouth, and trilled their joy cries—"*Ayyouy! Ayyouy! Ayouououououya!*"

Mona buried her head in her hands.

Mona latched Muhammad's door behind her and called out to Soad, who was playing by herself in the courtyard. "Ali? Where's Ali?" She was exhausted from helping a woman through fourteen hours of labor. "I told him to come back here and not to leave the yard."

"He went away with Um Mona."

"With my mother?" Mona sat down beside Soad. Always she tried to keep her mother and her son as far apart as possible. When she was away from home she worried about what her mother might do or—especially—*say* to Ali. That her mother was devoted to the boy did not lessen Mona's fears. By now Mona was too well aware of the dark side of her mother's love. Already she had caught her mother telling him grisly stories about their enemies the Jews. How could Ummie be so deliberately cruel? She knew that someday Mona would have to tell Ali the truth about his father. Allah only knew what Ummie was saying to Ali at this moment. "Are they out shopping at the souk?"

"No. Not the souk."

"Are they down by the river?"

"No. Not the river."

"Well, where are they?"

"It's a secret." Soad avoided Mona's eyes. "Um Mona said an evil spirit would come and get me if I told you where they went."

"Is that so?"

Soad dropped her voice to a confidential whisper. Since her circumcision a year ago, she had grown even closer to her cousin the *shaykha*. She wanted to tell Mona her secret, but she was afraid. "She wouldn't let me go with her. She said only Ali could go with her today."

At once Mona jumped to a conclusion. Then she told herself she was being foolish. Her mother wouldn't dare! But just to be sure, she made her next question a statement. "She took him to Karnak Temple."

Soad's mouth dropped open. "How did *you* know?"

Mona sprang to her feet. As she slipped out the door, she broke into a run and looked up at the sky. At least today there was no

khamseen to help her mother. Today the grayish winter sun was encased in smoky clouds. It was one of those rare blustery afternoons
when cold desert winds caused palm trees to shiver and moan on high.
Behind the brown mud village walls women, sitting on their haunches
sipping tepid tea, burrowed in the warmth of their heavy black flannel
robes and shawls. Along the winding lanes old men, bundled in robes
and turbans and rags that served as scarves, rubbed their hands together over small steaming dung fires.

Mona suppressed a shudder as she passed through the temple entrance. How afraid she had been that day when her mother dragged
her here in the sandstorm. She ran faster. By Allah, her mother wasn't
going to terrorize her son, too!

She was lost for a moment in a forest of tall pillars, but then she
spotted the path that led through the meadow toward the Temple of
Sekhmet. She passed tourists snapping their cameras, guides recalling
the past in foreign tongues, watchmen sleeping in the dust. How long
had her mother had with Ali?

She caught her breath as she approached the courtyard that led to
Sekhmet's temple. She would steal up quietly and stand in the doorway so she could hear whatever her mother was saying. Maybe she
was wrong about her mother's intentions in bringing Ali here today.

The door to Sekhmet's temple was ajar. As she crept closer, she could
hear her mother break out into an eerie howl. Gooseflesh rose on
Mona's neck. Soundlessly she stepped inside.

"See her! Fear her! Sekhmet!" Um Mona howled again.

Mona's eyes followed her mother's pointing finger. Despite herself,
she broke out into a sweat.

"I see her," Ali said. "I've seen enough of her. Let's go look at the
pharaohs. They're so big. I like them better."

"Sekhmet!" Um Mona howled again. "You belong to her! Sekhmet!
I belong to her! Sekhmet! Your mother belongs to her!"

But Ali was looking at not the statue but the ceiling. "There's light
up there. It shines on her eyes." There was pride in Ali's voice. "Imagine building this room so the sun would shine in her eyes! Those
pharaohs!"

"That's not the sun in her eyes, Ali. That's life in her eyes." Um
Mona grabbed Ali's hand and pulled him toward the black statue.
"Come meet Sekhmet. Come meet the one you owe so much."

"As you wish," Ali said, obviously bored.

The grandmother and the boy walked to the foot of the statue.

"See her and fear! Sekhmet!"

Ali reached out a curious hand and felt the thigh of the statue.

Mona caught her breath. She herself had never had the courage to
touch the dread statue.

Ali was yawning. "I saw her. I touched her. *Now* can we go home?

Or the lake. Let's go over to the Sacred Lake. Some of the boys in the village say they saw fish in the lake. But I don't think they're telling the truth."

"No! Here we started and here we remain! Sekhmet!"

As Mona watched her mother desperately pluck at Ali's robe, she saw white foam at the edges of her mouth. How, Mona thought, could I ever have so feared this room and my mother? She looked at her young son. Not yet seven, and Ali was already too old for the childish fears that Mona herself still sometimes felt in the night. Was Ali braver and finer than she had ever been? How could he stand in this ghastly chamber and not be awed into fear? Still, now, even though she could see this temple and her mother as the sham of power that they were, Mona could not quite bring herself to look the black lioness in the eye. She braced herself to rush into the room and snatch her son to safety.

But Ali was reaching for his grandmother's hand. "Are you sick? You look sick. Poor Grandmother."

Um Mona looked at Ali in bewilderment, sank down on her haunches, and began to cry. Ali stroked her hair and crooned to her under his breath.

Mona hesitated in the doorway. Her mother had tried her damnedest and failed to intimidate her son. By rights, Mona thought, I should storm inside this room and tell her in no uncertain terms to leave Ali alone. But she asked herself if that was necessary. Ali was doing well enough without her. And her mother would never forgive her for witnessing Ali's defiance of the power of Sekhmet. She would spare her that humiliation. She would allow her mother at least the illusion of her old power.

Mona looked around the darkened chamber. Part of her, maybe a dark part of her that she would have liked to disown, did not quite want to believe there was no ultimate power residing here. Once there had been a sort of delight in the terror of this room and the ferocity of her mother's love. It linked her and Ummie still. If she admitted that spell was broken, if she proved to her mother that it was finally ended, what would the two of them have left? She had been forced to break with Youssef. But nothing was forcing her to break with Ummie. Mona still shrank from the ultimate confrontation. Still she wanted that tie intact. She told herself she felt sorry for Ummie. She told herself it was pity that kept her rooted to her position in the doorway. She told herself that, just as Ali had said, his grandmother was a sick woman. Yet more than anything, Mona wished it were she and not her son who was stroking her mother's matted hair. She would have liked to stroke it with the tenderest of touches.

Before Ali could coax his grandmother home to Muhammad's, Mona turned and retraced her steps through the temple grounds. She assured herself that she had nothing to fear, now, from her mother.

The bursting, heavy scarlet blossoms of the flame trees drooped velvet-soft almost in the river. Ali and the other children, boisterous with spring high spirits, climbed palm trees on the far shore to dive like hupi birds into the wide green Nile. Mona sat only half listening as Muhammad talked of the crops and the price of wheat and whether the new government cooperative would tell him this year to plant cane or wheat. Ali, at eight years old, was already taller than all of his friends. He would be tall and slim, like his father. She watched him dare the other boys to climb as high as he on the palm tree. He was a natural leader, like his father. In her mind she composed another of her imaginary letters to Youssef: "From far away, when I see our son walking toward me, it's as if I see you striding up to me on the Corniche. He laughs like you. And brave! Our son is very brave. You would be so proud, Youssef, if only . . ." She was in the midst of a reverie about how one day, when Ali was a famous doctor, Youssef would run into him by chance on a boulevard in Paris, when something Muhammad was saying caught her attention. Painkillers. He was asking for pills for the pain. She narrowed her eyes. "This pain, Uncle. When do you get it?"

"When does the sun shine and the moon glow?" Muhammad laughed. But, nervously, he made as if to stroke his mustache.

Mona frowned as she noticed, for the first time, the bare skin on his upper lip. All the men in the village grew mustaches as badges of their virility.

Muhammad looked sheepish. "I'm like a young boy, eh? It fell out. So did the hair on my chest. Bahia tells me I'm not the man I once was. But she's not complaining. I keep her happy."

As he patted her hand, Mona noted that his fingernails were flatter and wider than was normal. Her brisk tone was nurse to patient. "Have you been tired lately, Uncle?"

"Who isn't tired?"

"After you eat, what then?"

Muhammad made a burping sound. When she didn't laugh, he touched his side above his belly. "Here it hurts. But that's good, isn't it? My heart is *here*. I have a good heart."

Muhammad, Mona thought, had always had a good heart. She looked back at the river. How was it that so many of the important events of her life took place by the Nile? She watched the water drift by. So much changed—Batata died, Youssef left, Ali was born—and yet the river hardly changed a ripple. It wasn't decent that the river always was the same. She picked up a rock and threw it as far as she could out into the Nile. There was a small splash, a few waves, and then it was as though the rock had never been.

For a long time she had been worried about the endless hours her uncle spent in the fields. How elated Muhammad had been when the government allotted him two *feddans* of land to work as his own! A Cairo official had announced that plots of land confiscated from the rich were finally being parceled out, for purchase over forty years at very low interest rates, to the poorest *fellahin* in the villages. All his life Muhammad had dreamed of a patch of land for his own. As far back as she could remember, he had scrimped and saved so he could someday buy land. She remembered how he would dig up his pitiful sack of coins from his hiding place under his sleeping mat. "You see this?" he would say as he let the coins dribble through his fingers. "*This* is the land!" But he had never had enough money to buy land. And then, wonder of wonders, President Nasser had made it possible for him to have two inexpensive acres for his own. Since then, day and night, Muhammad had worked up to his knees in the stagnant water of the fields. Mona had cautioned him over and over again to be wary of that treacherous Nile water. Parasitic worms lived on snails that thrived in still waters. The worms entered the body through the skin and settled in the bloodstream. The disease called bilharzia was the result. There were injections to cure bilharzia in the early stages. But when the *fellahin* inevitably returned to their work in the fields, they were infected again. The same river water that was their life was their death. Years later, sometimes five or ten or twenty or thirty years later, the farmers died of a host of bladder, kidney, and liver diseases linked to bilharzia.

From the familiar symptoms—the hair loss, the spreading fingernails, the fatigue, the pain over the liver—it sounded as if Muhammad might have cirrhosis. If what she feared was true, if Muhammad persisted in spurning her injections and continuing to work in the polluted waters, he would face a lingering death after some other infection struck his weakened body. She glared at the river. "You'll be fine, Uncle, if you just stop working the fields."

"I have two sons, a daughter, a wife, a niece, and a grandnephew who all have to eat. And you ask me to stop working in the fields? What happens if I don't do as you say?" Muhammad caught her chin in his hand so he could read what was in her eyes. "Allah!" He let go as if her judgment had burned him. As bad as that?"

She let her silence tell him the worst. She kept to herself the knowledge that, in cases like his, there were complex and expensive operations that could be performed in London and Paris but not in Karnak or Cairo. All she could do was help delay the end by giving him glucose injections to bolster his liver. If he did not give up working the land, Muhammad would surely die.

They were both silent.

"They say," Muhammad finally said, "that when the High Dam is completed, all our troubles will be over."

"Think, Uncle. What will happen when the dam is raised? There will be more water, so you'll be able to flood your fields all year round. More bilharzia and sickness—*that's* what the High Dam will mean."

"So, then, how long do you think I have?"

"I'm not Allah," she snapped. She was angry at Muhammad, at the fields, at the river. "You have time," she finally said more gently. "I'm not certain. But I think there's . . . some time."

Muhammad brightened. "So maybe I'll live so see my grandchildren." He spoke first of his oldest son, who already worked beside him in the fields. "Hassan's only twelve. But I've talked to Zainab already about one of her nieces. Saheer. She's always laughing. She's so like Zainab."

"Another Zainab? *El-hamdulillah!*"

Muhammad laughed. But then he frowned as he considered the future of his younger son. "There's not enough land for Fathi, too. Hussein wants to put him to work for him in the hashish fields. But already Fathi is saying he wants to go to Saudia to work. I don't know about that. To work like a slave for the Bedouins? We always thought they were like the animals. No civilization! No history! But a little bit of oil and—pffft!—they think they're kings. Yet I suppose Fathi has to do what he has to do. It's better than Hussein's hashish fields."

"Death is better than the hashish fields." Mona could have bitten her tongue. Usually she was so eloquent when talking of death to her patients. But with Muhammad, with this fine old man who had always deserved so much more than he had ever received, she seemed to have lost all her tact.

Muhammad, however, had not flinched. "I suppose what's most important is to find a husband for Soad. She's only seven. But it's never too early to worry about marrying off a daughter." He paused significantly. Long ago he and Bahia had agreed. Cousin marrying cousin was the most suitable of all matches. "Ali has been like a son to me."

She shot him a sharp look. Surely Muhammad wasn't being manipulative. He had endured his illness for years. Had he brought it up now just to maneuver her into a marriage contract for Ali? But when she saw the tears in Muhammad's eyes, she was ashamed. He was only trying to take care of Soad, just as she was only trying to forge the best possible future for Ali. "My son," she said, "is only a boy. It's too early to talk of marriage."

"Later might be too late for me. You know?"

Mona kised Muhammad on both cheeks. It was only decent that she let the old man have some solitude. Of course he would need some time alone to try to reconcile himself to his illness. "Tomorrow we'll have the doctors take a look at you. Maybe I'm wrong. Maybe all you need is a rest. Meanwhile . . . meanwhile we'll think all this over."

Back in the room at Muhammad's which she used now as a makeshift clinic, Mona busied herself arranging every bottle of pills, every needle, every steel implement. She soaked everything in disinfectant, scrubbed them all hard, and then rearranged them again. When there was nothing else to do, she sank down on the date-palm mat and thought.

Ali married to Soad. It would be very neat. There would be no dangers. Already they were like brother and sister. Pear-shaped Soad, who was as dear to Mona as a daughter, was sweet and uncomplicated. She was gentle. She was kind. There would be no anguish for Ali with Soad. The family would most certainly welcome the inevitability of the match. It was strange, Mona thought, that I never considered this possibility myself.

The men and women of Karnak would think her mad if she spoke her mind about what she thought was the most necessary component of any marriage. Love matches occurred sometimes by chance in the village, but no one would openly reject a possible marriage because a couple wasn't sentimentally attached. Yet someday, when Ali was ready for marriage, Mona wanted it to be for love. She wanted her and Youssef's son to have it all. How, by pledging him at this early age to eventual marriage to Soad, could she cheat Ali of the chance for real love? Could she just pair him up with his cousin as Muhammad mated two buffaloes who walked forever in circles around the water wheels?

Loving Youssef, she thought, was the brightest act of life. Oh, it was wrong. Or, at least, it was not altogether right. I've spent years atoning for it. But at the hour of my death, it will be Youssef's name—not my mother's, not my own son's, not even Allah's—that I cry out. It always was, always will be, only Youssef. Next to him—and our son—nothing else matters. I lost him. I don't have him—and *it*—anymore. But once I did. He was—no, *is*—the music of my life.

She looked around the room at the tools of her trade, at the everyday clutter that helped her fill the hours. She couldn't care so much about her patients, she couldn't touch them as gently as she did—maybe she couldn't even help heal them at all—if she hadn't had those months and years with and then without Youssef. How could you love many people, love everyone or anyone, if you had not truly loved and been loved in return? How could she deny her own son, the son who was a living reminder of Youssef, the chance for a great love?

And yet she wasn't sure. It was true she wanted all that for Ali. She would have liked to give it to him wrapped up in bright papers and ribbons, as they used to decorate Batata's birthday presents in Alexandria. But she knew only Ali could fall in love. And what if someday he fancied a girl who didn't love him? Or what if some bossy mother set her daughter out to get him with sly smiles and wiggling hips? Already she and Ali had made a pact that, when the time was right, they would send him to Cairo to study to be a doctor. Someday Ali would be a young man of great prospects. Maybe after a year or two in Cairo, he would come home with a distressingly starry-eyed tale of misplaced emotion. As if it were yesterday she remembered—with a click of sudden understanding—the shock and distaste on the faces of Youssef's parents in the al-Masri parlor.

Soad's weakest suit was also her strongest. There would be no risks in making Soad his wife. If at first there was no great passion, at least there were no seeds of tragedy. Just as there was wisdom in so many of Karnak's ways, perhaps there was prudence in this traditional method of marriage. She wanted not suffering but peace of mind and heart for Ali. She had to admit, too, that she had her own selfish reasons for maybe agreeing to the marriage. If someday Ali did go to study in Cairo, having Soad here as his wife would be another assurance that in the end Ali would come home and live out his life near her.

And there was something else to be considered as well. She and her mother and Ali had lived under Muhammad's roof for years. They owed this dying uncle more than they could ever repay.

How was she to weight all this? What values could she assign to love and peace and tradition and loneliness?

She supposed there would be no harm in an informal agreement with Muhammad that someday Ali and Soad would most likely marry. Who knows? Maybe, *inshallah*, Ali *would* develop a passionate attachment to Soad. Maybe Ali would be luckier in love than his mother and his father had been allowed to be.

"Shaykha Mona! Shaykha Mona!" A woman's voice called out from the courtyard. "Are you there? Shaykha Mona, I've come for a love charm."

Mona smiled wryly to herself. She could always try writing a love charm for Ali and Soad.

17

KIBBUTZ CHOZRIM, ISRAEL / November 1966

Where the hell *are* they, Rivka fumed to herself as she buzzed around the room like a wet wasp, making it even more ready than it already was for Yossi's arrival with the children. It was four thirty-five and Yossi was, as usual, late. She could hear the excited cries of the other neighboring children already at their parents' rooms. Hers were always the last to arrive when it was Yossi's turn to fetch them. She smoothed down the blue-and-white spreads on the beds and pulled back the matching curtains to let in the remaining daylight. As she fluffed the pillows once again, she frowned at their fraying seams. She stalked to the closet and clucked her tongue at the disarray. Yossi never cleaned up after himself. She guessed that even though Yossi didn't complain to her about how it felt to have had much money and now none, he must miss having servants. But then, Yossi didn't talk to her very much about what he felt.

She flicked her wrist and consulted her watch. Four-forty. It was not hard to deduce where he was and what he was doing. He was gossiping somewhere between the Infants' House, the Tots' House, and their room. Yossi was incapable of passing anyone without turning a casual *shalom* into a long-winded chat. But you would think, Rivka told herself, that he could have made a special effort to be on time today.

It was their seventh wedding anniversary. The honey-currant cake— Yossi's favorite—was waiting in the cupboard beside the bottle of wine. Mother had allowed her to pick a bouquet of flowers from one of the less prominent beds. Rivka eyed the blossoms critically, swore, and could not stop herself from arranging them once more. The vase was on the cluttered table Yossi used as a desk. Chozrim's leaders were fervent socialists, and so—of course!—Yossi had embraced their political ideals with the zeal of a convert. Rivka stared at his books and pamphlets as if they were the enemy. *They* were what kept him from her. Or, at least, they were one of the many things that kept him from her. She sighed, sank down on the bed, and picked at her fingernails.

They had been married for seven years: not a lifetime, but long enough. Rivka supposed those years had been successful ones, at least for her country and her kibbutz. Food shortages and rationing were mostly past history. Dead Sea mineral deposits were now being mined, an oil pipeline ran from Eilat to Haifa, and the new Jordan Valley waterworks would soon be pumping life to the parched Negev. Most of the money to pay for all this came from Jewish communities abroad, German reparations, and American aid. But since it cost so much to keep the army ahead of the Arabs, inflation was a new fact of life. Too, there was the troublesome question of immigration. The deluge of Jewish immigrants had slowed to a trickle, and last year more Jews had left Israel than had arrived. Israelis joked that someone should put a sign up at the airport, "Will the last one to leave please turn out the lights?" Yet even though the refugee camps no longer overflowed with disoriented Jews, the Orientals were still a nagging problem. Orientals struggled with high unemployment, suffered the worst from inflation, and were outraged because newly arrived Russian immigrants easily outranked them in jobs and social acceptance.

Rivka yawned. Because of Daoud and that earnest Moroccan he had married, she heard more than she ever wanted to hear about the

Orientals. He and Simha worked together in the Oriental neighborhoods of Jerusalem. Rivka supposed they talked politics even in bed. Maybe that's why they had been married for four years and still were childless. Rivka had to admire the couple's dedication, but she had little sympathy for their obsession. Aside from Yossi, there were few Orientals at Chozrim.

Their kibbutz had boomed in these last years. The new canning factory was such a success there was talk of opening a second. No one debated anymore if assembly lines compromised agrarian kibbutz ideals. Factories made money, and Chozrim needed capital for new housing units that would boast fully equipped kitchens in each member's room. As a child Rivka had witnessed emotional debates over whether it was corrupting to the collective spirit to allow hotplates in the bedrooms. Now they were to have refrigerators, sinks, everything but air conditioning.

Yet despite prosperity, Chozrim—and Israel—still had to live under constant Arab threats. A grim-faced Yossi often translated venomous Radio Cairo for his comrades. Palestinian terrorists launched frequent raids from Jordan and Lebanon and occasional ones from the Egyptian-occupied Gaza Strip just south of Chozrim. Last summer a tractor driver had been killed while plowing a field on their own kibbutz. And then lately, after Egypt and Syria announced a mutual-defense treaty, some Israelis had begun to panic. But Rivka liked to think there was no cause for alarm. As a lesson to the Arabs, three days ago Israeli tanks and armored cars had laid waste to a Jordanian village. Every once in a while, Rivka thought, it was necessary to remind the Arabs not to trifle with Israel.

She sighed. None of this bothered her as much as what happened each day and each night in her own little world.

That world, she thought, was bounded by the four constricting walls of this very room. Seven years. They had been married for seven years. All of their married life spent in this little room. And most of it spent waiting. Waiting for Yossi to come and waiting for Yossi to be ready to go. Waiting for something unnamed and yet necessary, for something that had never happened.

On interminably hot afternoons and on damp days when the chill cut all the way through, she had sat in this room, waiting. Her pregnacies, one after another, had been impatient waits for the son who would change everything. But instead she had given him only three daughters. She looked down, noticed she had picked apart another fingernail, and sat on her hands to keep herself from doing any more damage.

She had to admit that Yossi doted on their daughters. He had named each of them himself. The first he had mysteriously given the uncommon name Ayala, "the Gazelle." Yossi had been even more evasive than usual when she had asked him why. The second he had called Talli, "Morning Dew." It was a kibbutz fad to name children after nature, and Yossi was always quick to follow every fashion. The youngest girl was Naim, "the Nice One." It was a boy's name yet Yossi had insisted on it. He said it was because everyone on the kibbutz, in the interest of true equality of the sexes, was beginning to call the girls by boys' names and vice versa. But Rivka was not deceived. She knew her old enemy desperation when she saw it. He had wanted a boy and was pretending he had one. Yossi was like that. If he couldn't get what he wanted, he pretended he had.

It was the same with their marriage.

No one on the kibbutz would ever have believed that there was anything wrong. Toward her in public Yossi was always, in exactly the proper degrees, attentive, good-natured, and teasing. He never so much as looked at another woman, although God knows enough of the women looked at him. She had been more than right that day on the beach when she asked him to marry her. Yossi had become one of the kibbutz stars. He was seldom in their room except to read and to sleep. His students in the secondary school were always running after him. He coached the boys in basketball and spent frequent evenings talking with them in their rooms about God only knew what. Yossi was never at a loss either for words or for an audience. Most evenings were crammed with kibbutz activities. He gave popular adult lessons in colloquial Arabic, and he never missed a gathering of the Marxist study group. This year, since he was also chairman of the work committee, he was on call every afternoon and evening to iron out the usual problems of keeping four hundred people productively resigned to their work. Yes, everyone liked Yossi.

She knew that none of them liked her quite as much. There were eyebrows raised in the dining hall when she could not stop herself from arguing with him over minor matters. She was hypersensitive. Her feud with Ayala's nurse in the Tots' House had grown serious enough to require the attention of the entire kibbutz at a Saturday-night meeting. Then there had been the ongoing squabbles over her work assignment. Since she was a child she had wanted to drive a tractor. She had achieved that high-status job only briefly after her marriage. But then her pregnancies had driven her from the fields. Presently she was on temporary assignment in the laundry. Her own husband was chairman of the work committee, yet she had drawn one of the least desirable job rotations. Not that that was surprising. Yossi denied her in other ways as well.

Still, it grated. This was *her* kibbutz. She had been born on it. Her father had died defending it. And yet, compared to Yossi, she was the outsider. There is nothing, she thought, as miserable as not fitting in on your own kibbutz. Four hundred pairs of eyes judging your every mood. All those people knowing you so well, and not much liking what you had no chance to hide. She thought she knew what the others thought about her. To them she was that bitch married to wonderful Yossi Goshen. It was so unfair. He owed her everything—even his name. Before their marriage she had tried to bully him into Hebraicizing it. Egyptians had killed her father, and to assume a name that meant "the Egyptian" in *Arabic* was too much to ask. At first Youssef had balked, but as usual she had worn him down. Yossi was a Hebrew form of Youssef; Goshen was the Biblical name for part of Egypt at the time of Moses. The entry on the kibbutz marriage rolls was under the name of Goshen, although legally Yossi still refused to make the change. Rivka suspected there was more to this than stubborn sentiment. In some fundamental way Yossi was still "the Egyptian." He still believed their enemy was his ally. Yet the kibbutz members couldn't see through him. It isn't fair, she seethed. It is all so terribly unfair.

The others didn't know what Yossi was like. Under that charm, under that gleaming surface of his, was a cold man. It had taken Rivka most of their marriage to admit to the unpleasant fact that they were never easy with each other. Oh, maybe at first, when she could still make him laugh, there had been hope. But somewhere along the line, as she brooded over their every unsatisfactory encounter, she had lost her sense of humor. She had thought it would be enough simply to marry him. But she had been wrong. The most she could say was that their bodies fit together very well. It was strange, she thought, that they reached their peaks of passion when they were angry with each other. But even that was never enough. What she wanted, after his physical need was slaked, was for Yossi to put his arms around her and confide all his thoughts and feelings and hurts. Instead, even after seven years, he still eluded her. The reason for his distance was no great mystery. Mona. At the thought of that woman, Rivka felt the familiar twitch under her right eye. She had named that unruly nerve Mona. Rivka hated every thought of Mona. She had been surprised Yossi hadn't wanted to name one of their own daughters Mona, so that he could hold a Mona in his arms every day. To test him, Rivka had allowed him to choose their names. But here, too, Yossi had evaded her trap. He had never suggested the name Mona, although Rivka suspected a Mona connection in calling their oldest girl "the Gazelle." Ayala was Yossi's favorite.

Hoping to subdue that ugly twitch, Rivka closed her eyes. Often she would ask Yossi if he loved her. He would always smile, ruffle her hair as if she were some fawning dog, and vow that he did. But he never volunteered it. Over the years Rivka had developed the dangerous habit of asking him if he loved her at just the precise moment when she knew she had especially irritated him. One of these days—would she like it or not?—she would catch him in the truth.

Rivka opened her eyes. The twitch was still out of control. She blinked hard, but Mona did not go away. Why, she asked herself, why do I love him? Why in the world do I love him? I don't think I even like him, yet I love him so much. I was so desperate to get him. I wanted him from that first day I saw him—so handsome yet so lost and disconnected—coming up the path to Colonel Barton's. I thought I could connect him. I thought he could be so wonderful if he were connected. And I thought I could do it.

She stroked the skin under her eye. Sometimes she would draw the curtains, tie a scarf around her right eye, and wait in darkness for the twitching to stop. She could sit like that for hours, and still that little blue, eyelash-thin Mona would remain untamed. But today she didn't want Yossi and the girls to find her sitting blindfolded in the dark. Instead, she forced herself for once to be honest. Certainly she had wanted to help Yossi. But also she had simply wanted him. Wanted to walk down the kibbutz paths with him so tall and good-looking by her side. Wanted to show all those others that she could get not only a man but a man among men. Well, Rivka thought, I did it. I got what I wanted. Everyone else thinks my man is splendid. But still they don't like me much. And neither does Yossi. He married me because he felt sorry for me. Oh, God. Why does it have to be like this? How could it have turned out like this?

Rivka looked down at her watch. Five minutes of five. She heaved to her feet and over to the door. As she opened it, she saw them coming. Yossi! Her despair fled. Yossi! So straight and so golden. Yossi! Naim was swaddled in his arms. Talli and Ayala—carrying a bouquet of yellow and purple flowers—were by his side. Mine, Rivka thought: all mine. All of them. They are mine. Rivka crouched and held out her arms for Ayala and Talli.

"We were picking you flowers, Mummy."

"We picked them ourselves."

"I picked the most."

"No! Me! I picked the prettiest!"

Rivka smiled. So that was it. Here I was, half out of my mind, and they were picking flowers for me.

"Happy anniversary." Youssef kissed his wife. "And don't tell your mother we raided the beds on Monument Hill."

To her she gathered the bouquet and the baby. Yossi must never know how I feel when he is apart from me, she thought. He must never know. He wouldn't like me at all if he knew. She laid the baby on the bed and set the kettle on the hotplate. In a moment she would bring out the cake, and they would toast their marriage with a glass of wine. Maybe, she thought, maybe this year will be better.

"Colonel?" Although Youssef had one of Barty's gin and tonics in his hand, he sat at the very edge of the armchair with military formality.

He knew his mission today was far from social. He braced himself. "Colonel Barton, is there going to be a war?"

"On a beautiful April day like this," Barty said, "you come all the way to Haifa to ask me that? I'd rather talk about your girls. How many teeth has Naim cut? And Ayala? Is she still saying she wants to be a soldier when she grows up?"

"I'd rather talk about whether *I* want to be a soldier when *I* grow up."

"Yossi!" Barty poured himself another whiskey and smiled genially. "Don't tell me you're still worried about *that*. I thought we cleared all *that* up years ago. You've been in the paratrooper reserves for—what?— seven years? I've talked to your officers about you. You're not only a soldier. You're a *born* soldier."

"Colonel Barton, *is* there going to be war with Egypt?"

Barty began picking nonexistent lint from his trousers. "I believe you know the meaning of 'security,' Yossi. Surely you don't expect me to gossip about classified matters."

"So you're talking about war."

"Read any newspaper. It's the Arabs who are screaming for war."

"So you think it will be war against Egypt?"

"Ice. We need more ice. Excuse me, Yossi, while I get us more ice."

Youssef watched the colonel's stiff retreating back and wished with all his heart that there was no need for this interview. But over the past months Youssef had grown certain another war was brewing. Arab terrorist raids had increased to two or three each week. Russian arms were pouring into Syria and Egypt. Worse, Israeli warplanes had just downed six MiG fighters in retaliation for the shelling of Jewish settlements near the Syrian border. After the dogfight, the Jewish pilots had circled Damascus in a cheeky warning that the next time they could attack the Syrian capital city itself.

Youssef looked out the window at the sea. It had been while he was sitting alone on Chozrim's Monument Hill, looking out at this same sea, that he had come to his decision. If there was a war with Egypt, he would not fight in it.

Youssef gnawed his lip, uncertain, now that he was about to tell Barty of his decision, that it was the right one. How, he asked himself one more time, could he *not* fight? In the ten years of his exile, Israel had been kind to him. Rivka might not be a perfect wife, but she was his wife. The girls—his girls—were his treasure. He was a model kibbutznik and paratrooper. On the outside there was nothing to indicate that Youssef al-Masri, better known these days as Yossi Goshen, was anything but a fervent citizen of the Jewish State.

Youssef felt in his pocket for Mona's ring. How *could* he fight? How —despite wife, children, army, kibbutz—could he take up arms against the land and people of his birth? How could he war against Mona?

He stood and paced the colonel's parlor as he had paced atop Monument Hill. How, he asked himself, could he still be so confused about all this after so many years? For a long while, now, he had kept his doubts to himself. But still they had eaten away at him.

Youssef sighed. Once again he tried to sort out what his conflicting loyalties would and would not allow him to do. If Israel were to go to war against only Syria or Jordan or any other state except Egypt, of course he would fight. But he could not fight against Egypt. He had learned to live away from Egypt. He had even accepted that he might never see it—or *her*—again. But he could not take up arms against it. Always, even when as a raw recruit he had excelled on the firing range and in the field, he had dreaded that it might come to this. Was it more moral—did it require more courage—to fight or to refuse to fight?

Youssef threw himself back down on his chair and buried his head in his hands. All he knew was that he could not, would not, take aim and fire against Egyptians. He supposed the Israelis would court-martial him and put him in Ramla Prison. His only hope was that, against all logic, Barty would say that Egypt would not be the enemy in the approaching war.

The colonel set down the icetray, shot a worried look at Youssef sitting in such an obvious posture of despair, and made them fresh drinks. "Now suppose you tell me what this is all about."

Youssef straightened up and repeated his question. "If there's a war, do you think we'll fight it against Egypt?"

"Use your head, Yossi." The colonel's tone was kind, but there was finality in his words. "Egypt is the only Arab country that counts. If there's a war, of course it will be against Egypt."

Youssef went ashen, then stood as if to say goodbye. He had thought he would confide in Barty today, but now his nerve failed him.

"Not so fast, Yossi. Sit down. Tell me what's wrong."

Youssef hesitated, then sat. "You won't like it."

"Indeed?" The colonel waited.

"Well, then." Youssef took a deep breath. "If we go to war against Egypt, I won't fight."

Colonel Barton blinked.

Youssef moistened his dry lips.

"Did I hear you right?" There was a flush on the colonel's cheeks. "You won't fight?"

"Not against Egypt. No, colonel. I won't fight."

Barty slammed his drink down on the table. "That's treason, Yossi. You're an Israeli citizen. You've lived here most of your adult life. You're a trained soldier. You have a wife and children. And you say you won't fight to defend them?"

"I'd fight if it were just the Syrians. If a terrorist broke into the Tots' House on my kibbutz, I'd shoot to kill. But not in a war with Egypt."

"What the hell do you think this is, Yossi, some silly study group on your kibbutz? In a war, private, you don't draw the lines about who you will and will not fight. You're a soldier. It's your duty to fight *wherever* and *whomever* you are commanded to fight. Who the hell do you think you are?"

Stubbornly Youssef shook his head. "Go to war against Egypt?" There was a tremor in his voice. "A war against my own country? No."

"Your own country!" Barty shouted. *"Israel* is your own country!"

Youssef dropped his eyes, and his words were almost inaudible. "They'll put me in prison, won't they?"

"That's what we generally do with traitors," Barty snapped. "I suppose that girl in Egypt is behind all this?"

"Partially. But it's more than her. My uncle. Hamid. It would be wrong—for me—to fight against them."

"And what about your family and friends here?"

"It's time I do what I believe to be right."

"Is that so!" The colonel downed the remains of his drink. "I suppose you've considered how hard this will be on your family. Rivka. The girls. Daoud. Your fellows and *my* family on the kibbutz. You would put them through all this because of some sentimental *claptrap!"*

"Call it whatever you want, colonel." Youssef's voice, now, was steady. "But I won't fight."

Barty poured himself another drink. "The army will crucify you if you tell them what you've told me. You'll be destroying everything you've built here. You know that, don't you?"

"I told you, colonel. I can't fight. It's . . . call it a matter of conscience."

"I call it a matter of *cowardice."* Barty downed his whiskey. "If I had known, Yossi, that it would come to this, I would *never* have let you become part of Hannah's family. *My* family!" There was contempt in every line of the colonel's face. "What is it, really? Are you afraid you'll ruin your handsome face in a war?"

Youssef colored. "I see, now, that I shouldn't have told you. I just thought you might . . . I remembered, colonel, how you told me you were loyal to your Hannah. You went against the orders of your officers and helped the Jews during the Mandate."

"That wasn't the same. That was honorable." But some of the anger drained out of Barty's face as he sat thoughtfully sipping his whiskey. He looked at Youssef as if measuring his resolve, then he sighed. "Tell me, Yossi," he finally said, "would your . . . delicate sensibilities . . . be offended if you went through the war—if there is a war—as a non-combatant?"

Youssef frowned. "I don't understand."

"You speak and read Arabic."

Youssef nodded.

"It's possible," the colonel said to himself. He narrowed his eyes at Youssef. "There's a way out. It would kill Rivka and damn near ruin the lives of your girls if you went to prison over this. For *them*—not for *you*, you understand—I might be able to get you transferred. A friend of mine runs an Intelligence unit that translates nonclassified Arab broadcasts and newspapers. But first you'd have to promise me— if your word means anything—that you'll never do anything to betray Israel."

"Of course I wouldn't betray Israel. I don't want to betray anyone or anything. That's what this is all about."

"Is it?" He stared at Youssef as if he were a stranger. "Go back to Chozrim. Tell no one. I'll do what I can. But Yossi . . ."

"Yes, colonel?"

"You are dead to me, Yossi. Dead. You understand that?"

"Yes, colonel."

"You are a traitor, a coward, and a disgrace to your country. A disgrace to Israel, Yossi. *To your country.*" The colonel's voice broke. "And to me." He pointed to the door.

Youssef met his brother's worried eyes in the hush that followed the news bulletin that had crackled over the radio. It had just been announced, on this nineteenth of May, that United Nations forces—at the request of the Egyptian government—were withdrawing from the buffer zones between Israel and Egypt. Already the armies of Israel, Egypt, and Jordan were on alert. Now, with war almost a certainty, Youssef was very nearly disappointed that Barty had managed to transfer him to Intelligence. In the past days, he had heard the Arab threats on the radio. The head of a Palestinian terrorist group had boasted that there would be "practically no Jewish survivors." The most popular song on Syrian broadcasts had as its grisly refrain: "Massacre them, bring back their severed heads!" In this atmosphere of hate and fear, Youssef had begun to feel that his decision not to fight might have been wrong. But he couldn't manage *another* military transfer. For him, there would be neither the purity of battle nor the justice of a court-martial. For him, this was going to be a war of regrets and guilt.

Wooden chairs scraped on concrete as the members and visiting relatives of Kibbutz Chozrim began dispersing in twos and threes to brood over the coming war. Youssef took another look at the men and women of his extended family. Under the threat of war, they had grown more tender with one another. Lately, each night in the Tots' House, there had been more fathers than mothers tucking the children in. One man even insisted on sleeping on the floor next to his son. Usually undemonstrative couples held hands in public. In the kibbutz shop the first wartime shortage was film, as family after family clicked snapshots that soon might become emblems of the last days before grief.

Youssef and Daoud walked into the starry, fragrant summer night. The heavy scent of honeysuckle, the sharp tang of mint, the cloying perfume of roses almost took the edge off the news of armies and war. But from the fields Youssef caught the scent of clover, and he remembered the night Batata had died. He put his arm protectively around Daoud and was glad, as he led him back to his room, that their wives were off with his children. It was so long since his last good talk with Daoud. And you never knew—*you never knew*—Youssef thought as he poured them double shots of whiskey, when and if they would be together like this again.

"Simha and I will be going back to Jerusalem tomorrow. Our battalion—I mean my battalion—will call me up there."

Youssef nodded and then cleared his throat. "I think, Daoud, that maybe tonight I should tell you something."

"All over the country tonight, every man and every woman is confessing and promising everything imaginable. Why should we be any different? Go ahead. I'm listening."

Youssef took a swallow of whiskey. "It's about my transfer. Barty arranged it after I told him I couldn't fight against Egypt." When Daoud's head jerked up in surprise, Youssef held up his hand to keep him from interrupting. "Hear me out. I've been a long time coming to this. It's not what it might sound like. I'm not a coward."

"You're my brother. You don't have to tell me that."

But there was not only disappointment but anger in Daoud's eyes. Youssef began pacing the room. "I thought—hoped—that maybe you would understand. I've always admired the way you stand up for what you believe in. Now it's my turn. Your fight is the Orientals. Mine is even more unpopular. I just can't fight against the Egyptians. It's not in me."

Daoud poured them each another drink. "Not fight to defend your home? You've heard the Arab threats on the radio. They want to exterminate us."

"What they threaten to do and what they'll be able to do are not the same. The Arabs lost the last two wars. They'll lose this one. Israel can win without me."

"You sound more confident than our generals. Call me a pessimist, but I happen to think this will be a war of survival. And you won't fight?"

"This isn't a whim. I've been thinking this over for years. I told Barty that I was ready to face a court-martial and prison. It was his idea to have me transferred. To spare the family."

"Facing Rivka would have been worse than a firing squad. She would have thought it was the ghost of Mona at work again."

"And you? What about you?"

"Frankly, if anyone but you were telling me this, I'd be throwing a punch by now. But you're my brother. I suppose you have to do what you think is right. I don't agree with you. I don't like it. But I should have seen this coming. You and I have never seen Israel and Egypt the same way. But I thought you'd turned around over the past few years."

"I tried. God, how I tried."

Daoud looked at him for a moment. "So you've made two decisions. The first was not to fight. The second was to allow Barty to fix it so you wouldn't pay the consequences."

"As you said, as Barty said, it would be too hard on Rivka and the girls."

"True." Daoud frowned. "But just a few minutes ago you said you liked the way I stand up for what I believe in. And that you wanted to do the same. But if what you're trying to do is get some self-respect—"

"That's cruel, Daoud."

"Maybe." Daoud's eyes flicked on Youssef for an instant. "I could be even more cruel. But let me finish. Morality goes by strict rules. There are few easy compromises, if what you're really concerned about is doing the right thing."

"You think I should go to prison?"

"I think you should do what your conscience dictates. If your objection to fighting in the war were on political grounds—if, for instance, you thought Israel had no right to exist—then, yes, you should either leave the country or stand up for your convictions in some other way. That's not the case, is it?" When Youssef shook his head, Daoud smiled in relief. "So, then, your feelings for Egypt are more tied up with Mona and the Corniche and Agami summers. Should you go to prison because you long for a time when you were happy?" Daoud threw his hands up in the air. "I can't say. But whatever you do—or don't do—you know I'll always stand beside you." Daoud poured them more whiskey. "But I have to say that I'm going to miss *you* standing beside *me*. Literally. You know you're a better soldier than I'll ever be. I always thought I'd be safe with you next to me."

"Me? The original bad-luck boy?" Youssef tried to laugh.

Daoud stared off into space. "I wonder where I'll fight. Sinai, probably."

"I hope it's not in the Golan. Those Syrians are supposed to be devils."

"Even so, I'd rather go against the Syrians." Daoud made an admission. "I'd just as soon not fight against the Egyptians either." He ran his fingers through his hair. "Yes, I suppose I can understand how you feel." But then he reached inside his shirt pocket and extracted three envelopes. "Just in case . . . I wrote these this morning. One is for Simha. One for Mother. And one for you. If something happens, will you see that the others get them?"

"Nothing will happen." Youssef slammed his glass down on the table. "Nothing will go wrong."

"Humor me."

Youssef looked at the letter addressed to him. For many years he had thought Daoud knew secrets that had always eluded him. Just in case Daoud had finally written them down, Youssef would have liked to rip open his letter here and now. Instead he tucked the letters in the flap of a book, then looked over at his brother. What of his loyalty to Daoud? Maybe his little brother *would* be safer if he fought by his side. But, no. It was too late to change his mind. Daoud would have to go this one alone. Youssef poured them more drinks. "Do you ever think of Egypt, Daoud?"

"Of course I do. Sphinx, pyramids, dirt, flies." But there were tears in Daoud's eyes.

"Batata. I'd give anything if he were here with us tonight."

"Yes. Sometimes all that seems so long ago and far away. And then it seems as if it all happened the day before yesterday."

"Victoria College."

"Your belly dancers."

"Mona." Youssef's voice was a whisper.

"If you don't mind my asking, do you still feel . . . I mean, Youssef, is your not fighting in the war some sort of declaration of love for Mona?"

Youssef toasted his brother with his glass. "Sometimes I can't remember what she looks like. And then I see a woman on the street who is a little like her, and I suddenly remember everything. I haven't forgotten her. But she's not so much the woman I love as the one I lost. I think I would have been happy with her all my life, Daoud. Yes, this one is for her."

Daoud made another confession. "I was a little in love with Mona myself, you know."

"No!"

"Not that I stood a chance. But she was so beautiful. Inside and out. And the way she used to look at you with those eyes of hers!"

The brothers sighed.

With a faraway look in his own eyes, Youssef poured them more whiskey and settled back on the bed. When Rivka and Simha came looking for them some time later, the brothers were back on memory lane, drunkenly singing sentimental children's songs in Arabic.

Daoud crouched low. He signaled to his partner to stay where he was. He jumped into the corridor of the Arab house to face a savage soldier whose gun was aimed at his own chest. Daoud gasped. The soldier's uniform was splattered blood-red and eaten away by scorches of sulfur. But it was the look in those eyes that made Daoud press his finger to shoot to kill. It would be a mercy forever to shut the animal eyes of that soldier. As Daoud was emptying his machine gun, he saw the enemy doing the same. Daoud braced himself for death, but instead all he felt was pinpricks on his arms and legs. He looked down in surprise at the shards stuck in his uniform. A mirror. He had been shooting at a mirror.

Daoud called to his partner to advance to the next room, and then he leaned against the wall. Eight hours of combat in the Battle of Jerusalem, and he had been reduced to shooting at what he had become. But at least he was alive. At least he was fighting against not Egyptians but Jordanians. And at least he was battling not for the meaningless sands of Sinai but for his home, for Jerusalem! How he and his comrades had cheered in the orange groves of Givat Brenner when they were told they were to have the glory of liberating Jerusalem. With the Egyptian air force already destroyed on the ground by a preemptive air strike, Daoud and his comrades were about to be the vanguard of a stunning Jewish victory.

Daoud looked around the small stone house in East Jerusalem. Arabs had lived here. He studied the prayer rugs, the cooking pots, the picture of Mecca on the wall. What glory was there in fighting for this? In the first long hours of gruesome fighting for the Police School and Ammunition Hill, forty of the five hundred men of his battalion— along with more than a hundred Arab Legionnaires—had died. The Jewish paratroopers had been trained as nightfighters in open territory, but their task had been urban guerrilla fighting in a heavily defended, densely populated sector of the ancient city. For the past nineteen years the Jordanians had dug into their positions with bunkers, trenches, and barbed-wire obstacles. Snipers lurked at open windows. Even women and children could be throwing grenades. Every inch of Arab territory had to be taken by house-to-house fighting. In those first hours of war, all Daoud knew was where he put his own two feet, what he had to do in the next three seconds, how far he was at every instant from the next Jordanian machine-gun nest. A comrade fell headless. The guts of another poured into a street. Once he shot an Arab Legionnaire at point-blank range, and the bullets had made meat of the Arab's belly.

After those hours of gore, Daoud had thought himself inured to horror. He had fought, killed, triumphed. The paratroopers had taken their first objective. Then, after the fighting spread through the Arab-held American Colony, Daoud's orders were to mop up house-to-house on streets already secured by advance shock troops. But this mission held new personal terrors. He would scream a warning in Arabic, then he and his partner would enter each house shooting. While one stood with his back to the wall just outside the door, the other would kick it open and fire into the room. They never knew which room might hold a nest of Arab snipers and which might be sheltering terrified children. Each time they succeeded in clearing another house, Daoud closed his eyes and thanked God. He couldn't have endured it if, by mistake, he gunned down some little Arab girl. And now to have come face to face with himself and to have pulled the trigger! If Youssef were here beside him, Daoud would have put his head on his brother's shoulder and wept the tears of the damned. But at a cry from his partner, Daoud readied his machine gun and sprang back into action. Later, every day of his life, he would have to live with himself. But now his duty was to shoot to kill.

Two days later Daoud sat motionless in the courtyard of the Rockefeller Museum. A few Arab artillery shells burst not far away, but Daoud was too exhausted to take cover. He and what was left of his squad had been waiting and grousing and grumbling for the signal finally to take the Old City. Every few hours an officer circulated in the courtyard to tell them that even though they had it surrounded, international politics were delaying them from the prize. The Israeli high command, fearful of world reaction to their takeover of the Holy City, still hesitated to give the order for the final advance. Daoud listened to the bitter complaints of his comrades. So many had already fallen. For them—not only for this week's casualties but for *all* the centuries of Jewish dead—the paratroopers wanted to storm the Old City walls. Should the United Nations step in and impose a cease-fire —as it had in each of the two previous wars—Jerusalem must be theirs.

Daoud looked over at the exhibition rooms where some soldiers wandered as though they had nothing on their minds but fragments of three-thousand-year-old pottery. What sort of army was this, anyway? What soldiers other than these Israelis could fight so savagely, then turn around and trip through a museum like the gentlest of scholars? As he lit a cigarette, Daoud could not help but feel a flash of pride that he was one of these soldiers. But then he coughed as the rawness of the nicotine burned his lungs. Yesterday, after they had finished that painful house-to-house fighting, Daoud had started smoking. He ground out his cigarette. He wondered whether it—all of it—would be worth it when he and the others were finally at the other side of the ancient walls. He wished Youssef were here. They could talk. There had to be something they could say to each other to make all this better. There had to be *something* they could have said. Despite Daoud's pride in what he and his comrades had accomplished so far in this war, he had begun to wonder if maybe Youssef's answer to this war *had* been the right one. Three wars in nineteen years. Three terrible wars of Jew and Arab. Daoud wished he could believe this war was the last. But he had heard the sounds of Arab bloodlust. He had listened to the battle cries torn from his own throat and from his comrades who in normal times were farmers and teachers and bus drivers. Whoever won, whoever lost, the battles would not be over when this next cease-fire was finally proclaimed. Maybe there would always be another shot that had to be fired.

But then there were cheers in the courtyard. Daoud grabbed his

Uzi and moved out with his fellows for the final assault. He stood with his squad and watched, breathless, while Jewish guns raked the Muslim Quarter of the Old City. Somewhere in there, to the left of where the artillery was aiming, was the sole remaining Western Wall of Solomon's Temple. Two thousand years ago, when the Romans had destroyed all but that one Temple Wall, the worldwide scattering and humiliation of the Jews had begun. To take it back, to regain the Wailing Wall, might in part restore millennia of lost Jewish pride, hope, dignity. The Wall could help make whole not only Jerusalem, not only Israel, but maybe in a small way every Jew in the world. Maybe, Daoud thought, even one glimpse of the Wall would redeem these last days of killing. Running toward the walls of the Old City, Daoud felt his battle despair fall away. Jerusalem! They were about to conquer the heart of Jerusalem!

Ahead there was only scattered resistance as Jews were bursting through St. Stephen's Gate. Daoud joined the rush of scrambling paratroopers. They were the first inside the walls of the Old City! They would be the first Jews in nineteen years to stand before the ancient Western Wall!

By the time Daoud got through the gate, paratroopers were pounding each other on the back in triumph. The news spread from man to man. Jewish soldiers were at the Western Wall. Their brigade commander had already roared over to the Temple Mount in his jeep. A delegation of Arab leaders had pledged that the Old City would not resist. New orders were shouted out. There was to be no shooting. The Old City was Jewish territory. The paratroopers were to fan out and make sure each serpentine street and each stony tunnel was not sheltering a sniper. The peace of the city would be preserved now and forever and ever.

Daoud leaned against the hoary stone wall. It was over. Thank God it was over. He had survived, and the city was theirs.

Soon he would follow the order to police the streets. But first he had another, higher order. Eager for a glimpse of the Wall, he joined a pack of soldiers running through the maze of twisting streets. When the war was over, when the cease-fire reigned, he would come here with Youssef and Simha. He would write down his prayer on a slip of paper and wedge it into the Wall. He already knew what he would write on his paper. Peace. Now, always, he would pray for peace. And he knew he would not be alone. In the years ahead the Wailing Wall would be a litter of thousands of Jewish prayers for peace.

Listening to the rat-tat steps of rushing soldiers ahead and behind him, Daoud sprinted toward what must be the Wall. Then, from the top of a long flight of stairs, he could see it. The Wall. It had to be the Wall, for in front of it were banks of Jewish soldiers. Weeping, praying, bloodstained soldiers. A legion of battle-weary soldiers with prayers on their lips.

Daoud sighed and was putting his right foot on the step when the single shot rang out. He clutched his chest and looked up in surprise at the face of the Arab in the window. He cried out, and his body tumbled forward. He hit the worn stone steps, he stared sightlessly at the Wailing Wall, and then he died.

18 ~~~~~

ALEXANDRIA, EGYPT / July 1967

Baruch checked and rechecked the kidney dialysis machine. Already he had analyzed the donor blood to make sure it was not only the right type but also free from microbes that could kill. He fussed for a few minutes over the machine, then smiled down with false cheerfulness at Abbas in the hospital bed. "I'm almost ready. You, my friend, are about to be a new man."

Abbas yawned and settled back in the bed. This was his seventh blood transfer, and Abbas was bored with the procedure.

But when the nurse shuffled into the room, Baruch frowned at the interruption. What now? The day was already going wrong. A pack of the world's lustiest cats screeching outside their kitchen window had kept him awake until dawn. At breakfast, because of the continuing food shortages, there had been neither tea nor bread nor eggs. His careful plans had gone awry at work, too. The competent nurse he had lined up last week had not reported for work. Instead he had drawn a slow-moving, dim-witted young woman whom he would not have trusted to bandage a finger. He growled at her to go away.

But behind the nurse was a messenger from the superintendent's office. The son of a Cairo colonel had gashed his leg during a soccer match on Victoria's playing fields. Dr. Baruch was ordered to stop whatever he was doing and attend to the boy in the emergency room.

Politely but firmly Baruch demurred. "Today is my day off. I'm not even supposed to be here." He had come to the hospital only to oversee, personally, this one special blood transfer. "Tell the superintendent to get someone else."

Baruch turned back to his work. He tinkered a bit more with the dialysis machine. He checked the tubes in Abbas's arms, took his blood pressure, tested even the electric current. The first indication of Abbas's illness had been extreme fatigue, then back pain. Tests had shown evidence of advanced uremia, probably a result of the bilharzia he must have contracted swimming in the Nile in his youth. Abbas was a very sick man, but he could live for many years as long as he was regularly hooked up to the dialysis machine.

Just as Baruch had Abbas plugged in, just as his bad blood was flowing out and the fresh blood was flowing back into his veins, three more men crowded into the little room.

"Dr. Baruch al-Masri, you are ordered to report to the emergency room immediately."

"I'm busy," Baruch said. He was used to the hospital's bureaucratic overkill. It didn't surprise him three men had been sent to deliver the nagging order. But he spoke with finality. "You can see I'm busy."

The second messenger smiled unctuously. "You are indeed very busy for such a very junior member of the staff. For such a *replaceable* junior member of the staff. The superintendent orders you to report to the emergency room. At once."

Baruch waved a dismissive hand. "Tell the superintendent that I will come as soon as I can. I will be where he wants me to be within an hour." But there was a new crease of worry in the lines around Baruch's eyes. He did not have to be reminded how tenuous his appointment was.

The third messenger walked to Baruch's side and hissed in his ear, "The superintendent wishes to remind you in your file it is noted that once you were a Jew suspected of Israeli espionage. Come to the emergency room now, and there will be no trouble."

Baruch did not have to be told that if the hospital supervisor said the word to the secret police, his case could be reopened. Since last month's disastrous war with Israel, it had become more precarious than ever to have Jewish connections. After Egypt's terrible defeat on virtually every battlefield—after the Arabs lost the Sinai, the West Bank, Gaza, the Golan Heights, and *especially* symbolic Jerusalem—Egypt had once again begun to treat its Jews as a potential fifth column. Four hundred of those five thousand Jews who had stubbornly stayed in Egypt had disappeared from their homes and jobs at night. It was said that one hundred and fifty who held foreign passports were deported after a few weeks. It was thought it would be years before the other Jews were released. Baruch had no illusions. The same thing could happen to him if the hospital supervisor turned him in. Baruch would not even have been surprised if at least one of the messengers standing in this room was a police informer. As he knew, as everyone knew, the government's spies were everywhere. Of all President's Nasser's policies—his hit-or-miss pan-Arab statecraft, his laudable land-reform and social-welfare policies, his thrilling construction of the

Aswan Dam and takeover of the Suez Canal, his blanket nationalizations of industry and commerce, his seizure of the wealth of the foreigners and the native-born—it was only his drive to transform Egypt into a police state that was frighteningly efficient. No one ever made the mistake of underestimating the secret police. The prisons were crammed with Communists, Muslim Brothers, former aristocrats, and fools who had made the mistake of complaining too loudly in public.

Abbas put his hand on Baruch's arm. "Go. Don't worry about me." He smiled at the nurse. "I'm not so old and sick that I won't welcome some time alone with you."

All Baruch's instincts told him he shouldn't leave Abbas alone with this sorry excuse for a nurse, but he knew he had to comply. He calculated he should be back from the emergency room in, at most, a half hour. He took the additional precaution of slipping the nurse a one-pound note to be sure she would not leave Abbas's side. Long ago Baruch had been forced to accept the prevailing hospital ethic of *baksheesh*. He even accepted bribes himself, for patients were convinced that without it doctors would allow them to die. Besides, Baruch needed the money. Abbas was too ill to work. Khadiga's job as a servant brought in only five pounds a month. Baruch earned twenty pounds, and their rent took most of that. He had to be grateful for whatever *baksheesh* he was offered.

Still, Baruch hesitated by Abbas's bed. If he had learned one thing for certain at this hospital, it was that anything that *could* go wrong *did* go wrong.

"*Yalla!*" the messengers chorused.

"Go," Abbas urged him. "Go, my friend."

Baruch muttered to himself when he skidded and almost fell rushing down the corridor. Herds of bent old men made periodic attempts to wash the floors, but all they did was slosh water around until quitting time. Men lay on damp blankets along swampy hallways, ignored by nurses who sat laughing together as if deaf to their moaning patients. El-Muasa, Alexandria's largest state hospital, was as teeming as a *baladi* slum.

A cluster of shrieking, black-shrouded women were coming toward him leading what appeared to be a newly widowed crone. Baruch had seen far too much of such mourning since last month's war. That war —that terrible June war—as he thought of it he cursed it again. It was a calamity that thousands of young soldiers had died in the war. But it was a tragedy that the defeat had cost Egypt her greatest resource, the easy good nature and trust-in-God hopefulness of her own people. Baruch wondered how history would finally judge Nasser. He had tried—yes, he had truly tried—to improve the lives of the poor. But Baruch thought Nasser had gambled—and lost—too much trying to be a messianic leader. Idolized after the Suez war for his defiance of the West, Nasser had been distracted from domestic problems by fantasies of uniting all the Arabs. But, instead, Nasser had squabbled bitterly with Iraq, wasted years on an unsuccessful union with Syria, and bogged down his army in a civil war in Yemen. Of all these foreign misadventures, however, the worst was last month's war with Israel. How, Baruch wondered, could Nasser have waged a war Egypt was neither prepared for nor could win? Now the entire country was in mourning—just like those *baladi* women shrieking down the corridor —for that June disaster.

As Baruch took a shortcut through a ward, once again he decided that these gloomy caverns of the sick looked like leftovers from another century. There weren't enough beds or medicines or equipment. Doctors fawned on patients who were rich or influential, but poor souls viewed coming to the hospital as a death sentence. Most, rightly, preferred a more dignified death at home.

On nights when Baruch couldn't sleep, he wondered how all of it could have come to this. He had thought, on the day he stood in the parlor of the Villa al-Masri and bowed his head in submission to Allah, that he was choosing a life of noble simplicity. He had been ashamed that an accident of birth had made him an aristocrat in a nation of peasants. He had romantically longed to be poor. But the worst surprise of poverty was its grinding dullness. There was only his draining work at the hospital, his desperate companionship with Abbas and Khadiga, their monotonous meals of rice and beans. Sometimes, when he woke up in the morning almost paralyzed with dread, he would remember how he used to admire Egyptians for their celebrated patience. Now, unhappily, he realized they were only resigned. And he knew that was the difference between him and them. He had accepted Islam, but he still could not accept the terrible injustice of these lives. For a long time now he had known himself to be living on the outer edge of his emotional strength. He remembered how when he had first come to live with Abbas he had been excited at the thought of finally, absolutely, testing himself. Arrogantly, he now knew, he had been certain that hardship would force him into being a finer man. Instead he had discovered he was more frail than he had suspected.

Lately he had found himself being afraid of what would happen if he pushed himself so far that he broke. It was possible that already he was beginning to collapse inside. He could not accept the knowledge that he was powerless to alleviate the suffering around and inside him. Twice in the last month when he was in the middle of a crowd crossing busy Hurraya Street at the height of the howling commercial rush hour, he had been unable to stop himself from opening his mouth and screaming. He had screamed from one curb to the other. What scared him was that no one heard his cry over the honking of the buses and the cars. Worse, no one thought it extraordinary that a grown man was coming toward them on a busy street almost totally out of control. Yes, he knew he was at a danger point. He could not comprehend how Egyptians survived lifetimes of this. Maybe long ago all of them had been broken. Maybe all they had left was their stubbornly silly humor. He shuddered now when he heard them say *malesh*. People had to care about something, didn't they? A whole nation could not just give up?

He sped into the emergency room. The hospital supervisor was hovering beside a young woman in a smart white linen suit. Gold glittered at her ears and neck and wrists. Her hair was lacquered into an extreme bouffant. Her lips were ruby-red, and her eyelashes were coated with heavy black mascara. Baruch stared. He had almost forgotten that women like her existed.

The supervisor seized Baruch by the hands and informed him this very sophisticated Cairo lady—her father used to be a pasha!—had demanded a civilized doctor who could speak French. The woman's Egyptian husband was, the supervisor whispered, a man of influence. During the union with Syria he had reorganized much of the Damascus civil service. During last month's war, he had been cited for bravery under fire. Her husband was one of the few military leaders who had not been tarnished by the terrible defeat.

The supervisor waved his hand toward a child lying on a cot surrounded by five nurses. That boy, he said, must be treated with the utmost care. Baruch moved impatiently toward the cot, but instead the supervisor guided him to the mother. An aide served them all tea as the woman reviewed Baruch's credentials. When she heard he had trained in London, she nodded her approval. Harrods, she said, had the best woolens in the world.

At last Baruch was permitted to examine the boy. The chubby little fellow was dressed in the same Victoria College soccer uniform Youssef had once worn. He had a deep knee-to-ankle gash in his leg. Baruch would clean and stitch it, then he could be on his way back to Abbas. He called for antiseptic solution, and eight nurses looked at him in surprise. Antiseptic, he repeated. White uniforms fled in all directions.

Baruch looked down at his watch. He had been away for forty minutes. The blood transfer must be complete by now. Still the nurses did not return. Baruch shifted from foot to foot. He heard the mother promise to take her son to Pastroudi's.

The supervisor bustled over. There would be a slight delay while they searched the wards for antiseptic. *Malesh*, it would take only a few minutes. He clapped his hands and ordered a Pepsi for the boy. Another round of tea arrived as well. The supervisor, the mother, and Baruch lit cigarettes.

Ten minutes later a nurse finally, triumphantly, handed Baruch a bottle filled with yellow liquid. A glance told him it was liniment. Again he sent the nurse away for the antiseptic.

Baruch told himself not to worry. He had checked everything before he left Abbas. He had bribed the nurse to stay with him. Nothing would go wrong.

Finally the antiseptic arrived, Baruch poured it over the wound, stitched and bandaged the cut, and pronounced the boy good as new. He turned to shake the mother's hand and be gone, but instead he heard her complaining about eye disease in Egypt. Could the doctor please check her son's eyes? Baruch's boss nodded and smiled and gushed that Dr. Baruch would be honored. Baruch did as he was told. He worked quickly, but the examination took ten minutes more.

Outside the emergency-room door, Baruch broke into a run. He prayed nothing had gone wrong with Abbas. He raced up two flights of stairs, through a ward, and down the corridor toward the dialysis room. Just before he rounded the corner, he glanced inside a small waiting room where many of the nurses liked to sit and chat. Abbas's nurse was listening to a blaring transistor radio. As she nodded her head in time to the music, she played with a pair of those cheap plastic toys that were sold by sidewalk vendors for five piasters. In her left hand was a crude little doll in a black dress. In her right was a doll in a red *gallabeiya*. There must have been magnets in the heads of both dolls. For when the nurse held the dolls inches apart, the two were drawn together in a metallic kiss. Every time the dolls clicked together, the nurse giggled. Baruch smiled too. His fears had been groundless. The blood transfer must have been completed just as he had ordered.

But as he turned the final corner, he heard the purring of the dialysis machine. Why would the machine still be on? He stood in the doorway. The only light was shed by a bare electric bulb dangling from the ceiling. It revealed a small room bathed in the blood of Abbas.

Oh, my God. My God. There was blood everywhere. All over Abbas, the sheets, the walls, the floor. The blood was purple on the walls, brown on the sheets, black on Abbas's very still, dark skin.

Still the dialysis machine hummed. Baruch walked toward it. He knew it was too late, but he switched off the machine. With part of his mind he reconstructed what must have happened. The tube that led to Abbas's left arm, the tube that pumped in the strong new donor blood, was still held in place by the adhesive tape. But the tube on Abbas's right arm that pumped out Abbas's polluted blood had slipped free of the machine. Even now the blood was squirting up in an arc. Baruch forced himself to look at his friend. What was more horrible even than the blood everywhere, what was more ghastly even than the fact that Abbas was surely dead, was that Abbas's eyes were wide open. He had watched himself bleed to death.

Baruch stood over his friend. Though he knew it was hopeless, automatically he felt for Abbas's pulse. Abbas was dead. Baruch's own hands were covered with the blood of his best friend. But no, no, no! No man could die like this. No man could watch himself bleed to death while his nurse played with a child's toy not twenty-five feet away. Tenderly he closed the lids of Abbas's eyes.

Baruch sank to the floor and buried his face in his hands. From his throat came a high, piercing howl. This was too much! His fault. It was his own fault. He should have stayed by Abbas even if the head of the secret police lay dying in the emergency room. No! Too much! It was too much. Baruch looked down at his own hands, wet with Abbas's blood. Inside him he felt a great dizziness. He could almost not hear his own voice screaming. Mad, he told himself. This time you are going mad. If you don't stop yourself, Baruch, they will throw you into one of the hospital mental wards. Baruch thought he heard himself laughing. Why not! Why not be crazy! Why the hell not!

After a while Baruch could feel arms dragging him to his feet, could hear voices murmuring soft words of consolation. It is the will of Allah, someone was saying. *El-hamdulillah,* another was intoning. Such a good Muslim, Baruch thought almost clearly. Thanking God even for this, even for this. Great sobs tore through Baruch as he looked at his dead friend. *El-hamdulillah?* Thanks be to Allah? How could anyone praise God for this? How? How? I can't do it! I won't think that! That's wrong! No! But then, somewhere deep within, Baruch felt something black and batlike move. It coursed upward through his body. It was in his lungs, and he breathed it out. He opened his eyes and thought he saw something dark float to the ceiling, then pass out of sight.

He sank down in a chair. He felt lighter and younger and somehow free—yes, free! Surely the others were right. He could see it now, yes. Of course they praised God for ending the suffering of Abbas. What else could you do? What else? How naive he had been. He had thought that when you had too much, you broke. But what happened was that you bent instead. Of course it didn't make any sense that this had happened. But maybe it wasn't supposed to make sense. Allah must, however, know why. Surely Allah must know. Yes.

Baruch sighed and shrugged his shoulders. Abbas looked so peaceful and content. Baruch wiped away his tears and then stroked Abbas's cheek. His friend had not died in vain. Baruch had lost Abbas but had found Allah. God would help him endure even this.

19 〰〰〰

JERUSALEM, ISRAEL / August 1967

The scorching summer sun beat down on Youssef as he walked the byways of Musrara trying to find Simha's flat. Always before Daoud had led the way. Now he would have to find it on his own. With Daoud gone, with Barty turned against him, with Rivka more and more alienated, Youssef was trying to become accustomed to being alone.

Daoud's last letter to him had made him mourn his brother all the more. When he had finally been released from his active army service, Youssef had opened Daoud's letter on Chozrim's Monument Hill. He knew it by heart now: "You have had so many losses already that I grieve to be yet another one for you. Sometimes I think that of the two of us, your lot has been by far the harder. It was easier for me to leave Egypt and make myself at home here. Everything is easier for those of us who get what we want. I am sorry that I won't be able to be with you in these next months, because I hope—and I *believe*—that sometime soon there will be a peace of your own making for you. I know you well enough to realize that you are looking for magic answers from me here now, as you always did when you talked to Uncle Baruch and Barty and the others. Maybe the best thing I can tell you is that there aren't any. None of us knows any more than you do. I don't ask you to look after Simha, for she's stronger than either of us could ever hope to be. Just take care of yourself, big brother, as I always knew you could."

Youssef wandered lost through Musrara, thinking of his lost little brother. Daoud stumbling on the beach at Agami, trying and failing to intercept the ball. Daoud standing before the tiger cage at the Alexandria zoo, believing his big brother when he told him he paced like a tiger. Daoud at the rail of the boat in Haifa Bay, crying out, "We're home!" Daoud huddling with his Orientals, fighting for the weak and the despised. Daoud drunk on his bed at Chozrim, singing in Arabic. Daoud had always tried *so hard*. And in the end Daoud had been one of only six soldiers killed by snipers after the Old City fell. "I always feel safer when you're beside me," Daoud had said. Once again, Youssef thought, I've failed. He wondered if it was supposed to be a consolation when people said that the good died young.

Uncertainly he searched for his brother's house so he could deliver Daoud's last letter to Simha. Musrara, which since ancient times had lain in the shadow of the walls of the Old City, had been a no-man's-land for the last nineteen years, wedged between the commercial bustle

340

of West Jerusalem and the walled-off Arab quarters of East Jerusalem. The Old City walls had become a menace, for Musrara had been in rifle range of Arab Legionnaires who sometimes sniped at stray Jews shuffling through the border streets. The June Israeli victory had transformed Musrara. The Jews had quickly pulled down the make-shift brick-and-barbed-wire Jordanian wall. Now the glorious gray-gold walls of the Old City drew the eye up from Musrara's streets. Houses which Jews had entered for nineteen years only from their rickety back stoops looked out in surprise at the New Gate to the Old City's Christian Quarter.

But, to Youssef's way of thinking, Musrara had not changed enough. It was still terribly overcrowded. The poorest class of Moroccans had moved in here as squatters after the War of Independence. Yet there were signs that once Musrara, when it had been a prosperous Christian Arab enclave, had been a bastion of the middle class. Youssef could pick out an intricate bit of iron grillwork on a balcony, a long stair-case that swept majestically up from the street, an arabesque arch over a rounded window that once could have been fitted with stained glass. These touches of grace made Musara seem all the more des-perate. Unsure of his bearings, Youssef remembered his last afternoon in Alexandria when he had gingerly picked his way through Karmuz seeking a man called Muhammad in the Alley of the Pashas. In Mus-rara, too, women in long black robes avoided his eyes. Men lounged idly, insolently, on streetcorners. The whine of North African music came from broken windows. The music had almost, but not quite, the aural assault of Egyptian quartertone *baladi* rhythms. But the same longing, the same beseeching hope, was in every beat. Youssef wondered anew how much of Daoud's devotion to the Orientals was pining for the Egypt he had left behind. It was a way of neither rejecting Israel nor spurning Egypt, of living only at those weary Israeli points at which Arab and Jew intersected. Once Daoud had said as much to him. Once Daoud had suggested they be partners in Musrara. Youssef couldn't even remember why he had said no.

Finally Youssef moved down some alleys, up a back staircase, and along a crowded corridor. He knocked on a vaguely remembered door and braced himself to comfort a grief-stricken widow.

Simha was sitting with an old woman at a table over by the window. His brother's wife—she of the dark eyes, dark hair, dark skin, and (Youssef had always thought) dark ideas—was all laughing animation, speaking fast in a patois of French and Arabic. She waved Youssef over to a couch.

As he waited for her to finish her business, he looked around for clues to what he had never understood about his brother. The room was crowded with heavy, overstuffed chairs and hulking chests that looked even more out of scale next to dainty spindle-legged tables cluttered with bits of glass and lace. On the walls were wedding portraits of Simha's family: squat, dark-skinned men and fat, sweet-faced women. From the kitchen came the smell of bubbling oil and simmering spices. The room was an echo not of their old villa on the Rue Fouad but of the parlors of scholarship Arabs they had known at Victoria College. Yes, Youssef thought, Daoud, too, missed our Egypt. He sought it out and lived in its resurrection here.

Simha ushered her visitor to the door, fetched Youssef a glass of too-sweet, too-dark tea, and settled down with her husband's last letter. She read it slowly, then she smiled and tucked it into the front of her dress next to her heart.

"What did he say?" Youssef still hoped that Daoud had left those he loved some of his answers.

"He said what I already knew." Simha smiled again. "That he loved me. That we were happy. That he knows I'll carry on the work he couldn't finish."

"That's all?"

"What else was there to say?"

Youssef shifted on the sofa. "And what will you do now? I mean, is there anything I can do?"

"*You?*" There was a hint on Simha's face that she thought there had never been anything that Youssef could do. But then she seemed to soften. "No. I have my work. What was *our* work." She paused. "Daoud wrote about you, too. He asked me to help you. Do you know what he had in mind? Is there something *I* can do to help *you?* Daoud worried about you. Often we talked of you."

Youssef's mouth was dry. He took a sugary sip of the lukewarm tea. "What did Daoud say when you talked?"

"He said he had always failed you. That he had never had enough left over for you. He used to hope that you would come here and live with us."

"He never told me that. At least, he didn't mention it . . . recently."

"He thought he was just being selfish. He said you were probably happier at Chozrim." Simha leaned back in her chair. "Are you?"

"I don't know."

Simha was not practiced in the art of drawing out Youssef, and so she did not wait for him to continue. She looked at her watch and jumped up. "I'm due—I'm *overdue*—on a call to one of my favorite families. Make yourself at home. We can talk later if you like. If you want to stay over, you can sleep on the couch. Otherwise . . ."

"I was just going." Youssef stood, took a last look around the room, and followed his sister-in-law out the door. They parted with the traditional Arab farewell of near strangers: two dry kisses on each other's dry cheeks.

Youssef, as he walked slowly the long length of Jaffa Road toward the central bus station, mulled everything over. It seemed to him that he had made his usual muddle of things in Israel. At first, yearning only for Mona and his old days and nights in Alexandria, he had despised everything Israeli. But he hadn't been able to endure feeling like that forever. And so he had turned an about-face and thrown himself into the best of the Zionist dream on a kibbutz, and a good kibbutz at that. Still, however, a part of him—the very innermost part of him—had not quite joined in. And so eventually he had tried to make a stand—any stand. He had tried to be true to himself by refusing to fight in the war. But in that, too, he had gone only halfway. He had leaped at Barty's solution to serve in the war but not fight in it. And then during that war, when he had been awash in those hideous Arab threats to exterminate Israel, he had wished he were fighting on the Jewish front lines. Israel wasn't his true home. But this country had most assuredly taken him in and given him a life. In return he had given very little back to his wife, to his children, to the people of his kibbutz, to Israel itself.

Walking through Jerusalem on this sweaty summer day, Youssef admitted he was still an outsider. He looked at long-legged women in blue denim shorts and dreamed of short women in long black robes. He had thought, from time to time, that maybe he would be happier living among Israel's Arabs. But he had seldom been able to strike up a conversation—let alone a friendship—with the few Arabs who had crossed his path. To them, he was the enemy, the usurper, the feared and hated conqueror.

For years on the kibbutz he had not only studied but lived the best of Zionism. When he was immersed in the most stirring books of Zionist thought, he was proud to be an Israeli. But it had always bothered him that the Zionist dream was at the expense of another whole people. The early Zionists had written of Palestine as if no one were living there when the Jews had decided to come back. "A land without a people for a people without a land"—that was the old Zionist slogan. It was wrong that Jews had been persecuted wherever they had landed in the world. But it was wrong, too, that the Palestinian Arabs had been made to leave. He remembered, on the night of his reunion with Barty at that desert boot camp, what the colonel had said about Israel. Not only that there was right on both sides but that no one could remain in Israel for long without passionately, emotionally, taking sides. Youssef reflected that, as a Jew, the choice of which side he had to take had been made for him. Still, he couldn't forget that so many Arabs had been forced out and that they had not been allowed to return. He knew how it felt to be a refugee barred from home. Whether militant Israelis were willing to admit it or not, the founding of the Jewish state was based on a terrible injustice.

But, on the other hand . . .

Why, dammit, when he turned all this over and over in his mind, was there always an "on the other hand"? There couldn't be so much ambiguity. There *had* to be clearcut right and wrong.

But there wasn't.

On the other hand, Jews had to live somewhere. He himself had been chased from Egypt, just as other Jews who had survived Hitler's extermination camps had been hounded from Europe. Without Israel, what would have happened to him and to all the other Jews he now lived beside? It was true, too, that during this last war, when he had had to translate the venom that came from Cairo, his loyalties to Egypt had been strained very nearly to the breaking point. Maybe, Youssef thought, I'm no swaggering, oh-so-sure Israeli. But neither, I think, could I be part of this new Egypt of Nasser's. More and more, instead of seeing Jewish and Arab rights, Youssef was stunned by their individual wrongs. Each side had made so many tragic mistakes.

He reached the bus station, fought his way to the front of the ticket line, and then sat down on a bench to await the bus home to his kibbutz. He watched the crowd surge around him. It seemed to him that all the things he found the hardest to accept about the Jews in Israel —their arrogance, their brashness, even their smug self-righteousness— had doubled since the Six Day War. The Israelis were such poor winners. They had been much more lovable before this war, when their raw bravery had been tempered with tenderness. But it was true that Jews had thousands of years of experience at being victims and only nineteen years as struggling victors. Maybe, in time, Israelis could learn to be more graceful winners. Maybe that's what he should concern himself with in Israel.

In the aftermath of the great victory of the Six Day War, Israel could not only make peace from strength but finally address the moral problem of a generation of dispossessed Arabs. Youssef shook his head at himself. Greater thinkers than he had not been able to solve these problems. He was a good basketball player, a decent teacher of Arabic and English, a loving father. He wasn't a diplomat or a politician. But what was it that Daoud had written him? Youssef took his brother's letter out of his pocket and read it once again. "None of us knows any more than you do." Youssef raised his eyebrows. The world was in worse shape than he had thought if what Daoud said was true.

He settled into a seat by the bus window. He could not, he knew, go on forever as he had been for the past ten years. Neither hating Israel nor loving it without reservation had worked. He looked out the window as the bus passed near Har Ha Minuot, where his father by now must be part of the Jerusalem dust. What I'll try, Youssef promised himself, is to be honest. I don't like what Egypt has become. And I don't think I like everything that Israel is becoming, either. Maybe no one at all will like me for it. But from now on, I'll say what I think.

He lit a cigarette as the bus began its long descent from the heights of Jerusalem.

Youssef stood at dusk on the kibbutz green trying to screw up his courage. In a little while he had to enter the dining hall for what promised to be a meeting he would never forget. He picked up a pebble, threw it in the fish pond, and watched ripples spread. He supposed, like anyone trying for the first time to be angry or loving or strong, or anything else that doesn't come naturally, that he had been clumsy in his first attempts at honesty. Looking back at the chain of events leading to tonight's meeting, he realized he might have charted a more delicate course. But it was too late to undo what had been done.

Rivka had been the first victim of his new candor. Only a few hours after Youssef arrived back at the kibbutz, she had hung on his shoulder and asked him once again if he loved her.

He had looked her in the eye. "Sometimes I do. And sometimes I don't."

Her mouth had dropped open. Characteristically emphasizing the negative, she had whispered another question. "When *don't* you love me?"

"When you ask me. You ask me too much. Too often."

"Really? Really!" Rivka's voice had risen. "Mona. It's because of *Mona*, isn't it? *Isn't it?*"

"No. It's because of you."

And that had been that. At the time Rivka was crying too hard to say any more. She fought Youssef off when he tried to put his arms around her. Later she froze him out with silence. They became roommates who shared the custody of the children.

It had taken a while for anyone else on the kibbutz to notice the change in the Goshens. It wasn't extraordinary for a married couple to sit at different tables—even at different seatings—in the dining hall. Maybe Rivka was touchier than usual. But Youssef—gregarious, busy, likable Yossi—had seemed his old self.

Youssef sank down on a bench and looked up at the sky. Tonight there would be no moon. It would be such a dark night. He sighed.

The first public clue he was changing came in his Tuesday-night Marxist study group. For years he had been sitting down with five or six others to split hairs over the classics of communist thought. Long ago Youssef had learned the catechism, but usually he deferred his hesitant opinions to the more strident views of his comrades. On this particular night, however, Youssef broke new, and apparently heretical, ground. It all began when they were idly discussing the aftermath of the war. Youssef suggested that with so many more Arabs now under Israeli control in the West Bank and Gaza, Israel had become a colonial—maybe even an *imperialist*—power. Angrily his comrades had shouted him down. One word had led to another. Before Rivka's cousin Sasha could soothe ruffled tempers, Youssef had been called a "bloody Egyptian," and worse.

After that Youssef had been ostracized by the study-group members. One averted his eyes when he passed him on the paths. Another stared through him in the dining hall. A third, who used to walk back with him every night from the Tots' House, found a variety of excuses to avoid him. In a way Youssef regretted having spoken his mind. But he had asked himself what truth there was on his kibbutz if there wasn't room for dissent.

And so this other matter had arisen. Listening one day to his secondary-school students butcher Arabic in class, Youssef decided they obviously needed more conversational practice. To help them, he devised a plan that might even in a very modest way bridge the gap between Jews and Arabs. The Gaza refugee camps, under Israeli control since the Six Day War, were only a few miles away from his kibbutz. Why not, Youssef thought, bring young Arabs over to Chozrim for a visit? In the morning his students could practice their Arabic with them in class. In the afternoons the students could show the Arabs around the kibbutz. In the process the Jews might learn the Arabs were not all bloodthirsty killers and barbarians. The Arabs might learn a similar lesson.

But he had run into resistance when he presented his idea to the education committee. The chairman protested it wouldn't be *safe*. A middle-aged soldier, who had just fought in Gaza, said the Arabs lived there like rats. He reminded Youssef that most of the Arab terrorists had been recruited from Gaza. He said he doubted the Israeli military would even *allow* Youssef's kind of fraternization. When the committe unanimously voted down his proposal, Youssef stubbornly insisted on bringing it before the general membership of the kibbutz.

Youssef consulted his watch. It was almost time for the meeting. He knew what he was in for. The education committee and most of the Marxist study group were saying Yossi Goshen had lost his senses.

Youssef shook his head. He had wanted only to begin to play his part to make his kibbutz and his country better. But he knew how kibbutz disagreements could mushroom into ugly rifts. Here at Chozrim he had watched more than one fervent member leave over issues like why women rarely worked in the fields or whether the kibbutz was becoming too materialistic. He didn't want that to happen to him. At least he didn't *think* he wanted that to happen to him. He supposed that in the aftermath of a war in which eight of Chozrim's young men had died or been maimed, this wasn't the most diplomatic or strategic time to urge them to entertain Arabs. Those on the kibbutz who weren't mourning the dead were swept up in the near delirium of national pride that they had, once and for all, beaten back the enemy. But when *would* be the right time to urge reconciliation

with the Arabs? Long ago, in that Alexandrian summer of backgammon and regrets, Uncle Baruch had told him each man must
choose with care the ethical issues on which he makes a stand. Although
day trips for young Arabs were not a matter of life and death, it seemed
to Youssef that it *was* a beginning.

Youssef squared his shoulders and made for the dining hall.

More than the usual number of members had already assembled.
He noticed Rivka sitting with his former comrades from the study
group. He saw them bend their heads and whisper and point as he
took a seat between Hagar and Sasha. Throughout the meeting the
two of them neither verbally condemned nor supported him. But
sometimes Hagar would take his hand and pat it, and Sasha would
give him small smiles of encouragement.

Youssef fidgeted nervously as the kibbutzniks talked of who was
entitled to long vacations this year, when the rosebushes would be
sprayed with bugkiller, and what the deadlines were for nominating
candidates for the standing committees.

Finally the education chairman gave his report. "Yossi Goshen
made a proposal in our committee last week. Most of you probably
know all about it already—intra-kibbutz *communications* being what
they are." He paused for the titters that all references to gossip always
triggered. "The education committee did not agree with Yossi's proposal. To help the children in his classes use their Arabic, he suggested
we bus in some Arabs from Gaza for the day. But maybe I'm not the
best man to tell you about it. Yossi?"

Youssef rose. His face was composed, but when he opened his mouth
to speak, his first words came out in a high-pitched squeal. "Sorry. I
guess I'm a little nervous."

"Don't worry, Yossi!" someone called out from the front row. "You
may not be much of a speaker, but you're still the best basketball
player on the kibbutz!"

Although the comment was meant to put him at ease, Youssef
flushed with anger. This was no time for jokes. By God, he would
make them take him seriously for once! "I'm not here to talk games,"
he began stiffly. He had intended to stick to a watered-down explana-
tion of his Gaza plan. But instead out came something else. "What
I want to talk about is where we are and where we're going as a
country and a people. It seems to me that's what we should be doing
now. While we still can." He paused. There was absolute silence in
the hall. There was nothing on earth that thrilled the members like
the blood sport of a political fight. "Last June we won the war—"

"Did we *ever!*" someone yelled.

"—but I think that now it's time to talk about winning the peace."
Youssef's voice was steady. "Specifically, just what are we at Chozrim
going to do about all those Arabs—maybe more than *one million*

Arabs—who are now under our control? What is this going to do to our country? Are we going to be colonialists? Will we grow fat and smug? As most of you know, I wasn't born in Israel. I came here only ten years ago. And so maybe I don't have the same knowledge of this country as those of you who were born here or came here before I was ever born. But it seems to me that sooner or later our country—*Eretz Israel*, the land of Israel—is going to have to deal with the Arabs—"

"*They're* the ones who deny *our* right to exist!" someone shouted. There were angry, agreeing murmurs.

"That's not what I mean," Youssef said. He looked around at the men and women who had been his brothers and sisters for nearly a decade. He didn't want to offend them. Why was he standing up here making himself a target for their abuse? He tried to be conciliatory. "Maybe most of the fault is theirs—"

"All! It's *all* their fault!" came a voice from the left.

"Hear me out," Youssef said. Desperately he tried to win them back to his side. "All I'm saying is that there are two cultures in the Israel that I know. There are the Jews. And there are the Arabs. And now there are even more Arabs than ever in the . . . occupied territories."

"You mean within *our* borders," a shrill female voice interrupted. "Our *new* borders."

"Our *defensible* borders," another voice said.

"Call it what you will," Youssef continued. He longed to plead with them all to understand. How could he let them know he hadn't *meant* to offend? He groped for the safety of a middle ground. "The reason I brought all this up in the education committee is that I think it's important that we here on the kibbutz do what we can to bring those two cultures together. How many of you have Arab friends?"

"How many Arabs are *your* special friends?" someone shouted back.

Youssef reddened but continued on. "Maybe my plan to bring in Arabs from Gaza is a little unrealistic—"

"Crazy, you mean!" a woman cried. Youssef looked over and saw that it was Rivka. "You're crazy, Yossi!"

Youssef remained only barely in control of himself. "I was just about to say that I admit there are security reasons for not bringing in boys from Gaza." He was speaking rapidly and loudly to drown out the catcalls. "But not every Arab within the State of Israel is an armed thug. I certainly, at least, don't believe that's the case. If there are those of you here who *do* believe that, I guess I have nothing at all more to say."

"Then sit down!" someone yelled.

"Or go back!" Rivka screamed. "Go back where you came from!"

Youssef opened his mouth, but no words came out. He sat down. A few voices were raised to defend him. Someone said something about how they all had to guard against arrogance. Someone else said it was about time they talked less about security and more about liberty and justice: for the conquered Arabs, for the Orientals, for the larger group outside kibbutz boundaries. But they were in the minority. Most of the men and women Youssef had considered his comrades thought Yossi Goshen was a traitor. He had, it seemed, gone too far.

It was later that night, when he was bedded down on the floor of Sasha's room because he didn't want to be near Rivka, that Youssef decided he hadn't gone far enough.

He couldn't remain at Chozrim. Not after what had happened to-night. Like it or not, it seemed that forces beyond his control were making him homeless again. It wouldn't be so hard to leave Rivka. He knew they had long ago reached the point of no return. But his three little girls? He would try his best, somehow, to take them with him.

He did not have to ponder long where he would go. He supposed, lying here on Sasha's blanket, that he had really made up his mind on his walk up Jaffa Road after visiting Simha. He would go to Jerusalem and begin where Daoud had ended.

He lay sleepless all through the night as he tried to come to terms with it all. The irony did not escape him. He had made his last stand on the kibbutz he loved, defending Arabs he didn't even know. *Malesh,* he comforted himself. Never mind. Maybe how this had come about was not as important as the result. It was past time to leave the kibbutz and finally go it alone. There was not only fear and trembling but a little exultation in that thought. Uncle Baruch—if he knew, if they could write, if that border weren't so irrevocably closed—might even be proud of him. And Mona? He liked to think she would be proud as well. At the age of thirty, he was finally beginning to act like a man.

20 ~~~~~~

KARNAK, EGYPT / October 1970

Mona paced inside the front room trying to marshal her courage for the showdown with her mother. The room was gloomily draped in mourning for the recent death of President Nasser. Muhammad had squandered two pounds, thirty piasters for the black cloth that hung on the walls. To it he had affixed his collection of portraits of Gamal Abdel Nasser at the Aswan Dam, Gamal Abdel Nasser reviewing a military parade in Cairo, Gamal Abdel Nasser grinning on the Corniche in Alexandria. Mona looked the dead president in the eye. She would rather face the ghost of Nasser himself than her mother. She went to the wall, pulled back some of the black cloth, and peered out from a crack at where Um Mona sat in the courtyard weaving her Nubian baskets. Day and night for nearly thirty years, as others in Karnak threw together their slapdash containers, Um Mona had stubbornly woven her tight, sturdy, undervalued date-palm baskets.

Mona thought it was probably unjust that her mother's baskets were not appreciated in the village. The difficulty, Mona knew, came from the color of the dyes Um Mona always used to decorate her baskets. The other villagers used oranges and purples, bright blues and greens. Um Mona never compromised on her preference for browns and blacks. Mona felt a thrill of fear run down her spine. If her mother wouldn't give in on the color of her baskets, how likely was it she would change her mind and agree to keep Ali in school? Yet that was exactly what Mona had to accomplish today. Ali was thirteen and ready for secondary school. Um Mona had made it clear she wanted him to quit this education nonsense and work for Hussein as a runner to the Qena hashish fields. Mona, however, had another plan for her and Youssef's son. Baruch had moved to Cairo after Abbas's grisly death. Tomorrow she would take Ali to Baruch and ask his help when Ali was ready to attend the university. She had made up her mind to follow this course with or without her mother's permission. Mona gritted her teeth, marched out, and escorted the old woman down to the riverbank so she could say what had to be said in private.

The sunset's rose and gold and silver were reflected in the sparkling calm of the river. Eager to postpone the confrontation, Mona chattered nervously. "The Nile didn't used to be like this. Before the High Dam it was different. Wilder. Freer. Richer. Ten, fifteen years ago, you never knew what to expect from the river. If it weren't for the new dam, we wouldn't be able to sit here like this now."

"Karnak would be an island," Um Mona said with satisfaction. She, too, had preferred the fickle power of the old Nile.

"I suppose," Mona continued, "that it's better for farming with the dam holding back the river, letting it loose when we need it. And I suppose it's good that we have electricity now, even though we can't afford anything to plug into the sockets. But I loved the old river more. It left the land so rich after the floods. You could pick up a handful of the mud in the fields and feel the life in it. The soil was redder. Now it's so black, and it needs so much fertilizer."

Um Mona shrugged. She knew Mona hadn't brought her here to talk about the river. She was ready. Ali would do what she told him to do.

"But I suppose," Mona continued, "everything has to change." She could not help fingering her blue bead for luck. "Ali—for instance—is almost a man. He's even trying to grow a mustache."

Um Mona shot her daughter a bitter look. In the past few years she herself had sprouted a coarse coat of hair on her upper lip. Children in the village taunted her about it. She steered the conversation away from the growing of mustaches. "Hussein says he'll give Ali ten pounds a month."

"He'd make more than that as a doctor."

"But Ali won't be a doctor."

"He will if Allah wills it."

The lines were drawn. Mona moistened her lips with a discreet flick of her tongue. In her mind she replayed all the arguments for keeping Ali in school. The family was better off since Muhammad had his two *feddans*. Mona earned more every year with her nursing. Ali contributed a little from his afternoon work on one of Hussein's tourist feluccas in Luxor. Even Um Mona brought in a few piasters from her unpopular baskets. There was enough now to buy meat twice a month, a water buffalo to help in the fields, even the expensive commercial fertilizers from the government farm cooperative. They could get by without Ali's working full-time. If Ali eventually could stay with Baruch in Cairo, there was no reason why the boy couldn't remain in school. Already Muhammad had suggested this course of action to Um Mona, and already Um Mona had vetoed it. But Mona couldn't allow Youssef's son to spend his days at a hashish merchant. She was willing to endure her mother's bullying of herself. But Ali . . . Ali! Ali must have more. She tried reason on her mother. "He wants to be a doctor. His teachers think someday he might be able to pass the university examinations. It would be a great honor not only to the family but to the whole village."

"How strange that the word 'honor' comes so easily to your lips." Um Mona continued on more kindly when she noticed Mona's flush. "Give it up, daughter. Keep him here. You don't know what will happen if you let him go. Surely you remember what happened the last time a member of this family left the village."

"*That* had nothing to do with *this*," Mona said faintly.

The thought of what had happened in Alexandria caused Um Mona to bow her head, rub her fingers over her eyes, and rock on her haunches.

Mona touched her mother's shoulder. "I'm sorry, Ummie."

Um Mona lifted her head. Her voice was tender. "Ali is a good boy, don't you think? He's not bad looking. He works hard. He does well at school. He's very pious. Ali reminds me, in fact, of another child I once knew. Do you know who I'm thinking of, Mona?"

"Don't do this to both of us, Ummie."

"Tell me, Mona, tell me who once was like this!"

"I suppose you mean me." Mona wondered if her mother remembered it right. Was she ever so good and strong and pure? But at least she understood now why Ummie didn't want Ali to go to university in Cairo. Across the river she watched a line of women dipping their jugs in the water. It didn't tax her imagination to consider what her own life would have been if she had never known the al-Masris and Alexandria. She would have been like every other woman in Karnak. By now she would have been married for twenty years and the mother of six or eight or twelve children. But she couldn't allow herself to believe it would have been better that way. She couldn't make Youssef a regret. No. Ali, too, must have his chance in a world wider than Karnak. Surely, she thought, Ali will be wiser.

"Of course," a more composed but angrier Um Mona was continuing, "your son is not without his faults. But I suppose he can't help it, considering his parents. That business with the depraved English infidel didn't surprise me one bit."

Mona blushed. Ali wasn't the only boat boy who had succumbed to the temptation of money and homosexual sex with the tourists. The problem was that Ali had been caught in the act. But at least Ali had been acting the part of a man when his Uncle Hussein came upon them in the belly of the boat. Mona told herself it could have been worse. There would have been far more shame if he had been playing the woman with the infidel. She primly tucked her robe around her feet. "All that is over and done with. It hasn't happened again."

"Ali couldn't be trusted any more than *you* could." Um Mona narrowed her eyes and spoke her next words in a hiss. "You went away as perfect a child as there ever was. And you came back with a Jewish bastard!"

Mona shrank away from her mother. Seldom had Ummie been so brutal. "Ali will not fail . . . like that."

"How do you know?" Um Mona was warming to her attack. "How can you be so sure? The boy has bad blood."

Was there, Mona thought wearily, to be no end to this? Maybe it would be better to tell everyone the truth. Maybe that's what I should do tonight, starting with Ali. So they would have to kill me. Would that hurt any more than this? But no. I have to think of Ali.

"You listen to me." Um Mona punched the air with her finger for emphasis. "Your son stays in Karnak. He will work for Hussein running hashish. He was born here. And he will die here. There will be no fine life for him, strutting around in Cairo, puffing himself up like his father's family."

So there was more to this than fear of what might befall Ali in Cairo. Ummie intended to punish Ali, too. That was too much. In a very thin voice Mona defied her mother. "Tomorrow morning I'm taking Ali to Cairo to see Baruch. He is—as you and I know—Ali's great-uncle, as close to him by blood as Muhammad is. I think Baruch will let Ali live with him while he's at university."

"You think so?" Um Mona hesitated, locked her jaw in determination, then played her trump card. "*I* don't think so. For if you do, Mona, I swear by the Beard of the Prophet that I will be forced to tell them the truth. I will tell Muhammad and Hussein that their saintly niece lay with a Jew and give birth to a bastard." Um Mona folded her hands in her lap.

The two women stared at each other. Mona was the first to blink and look away from the black eyes that could still terrify her. Always she had dreaded it would come to this. In a way it would be a relief to have all these years of shame and fear finally at an end. But then Ali would be left alone. And what would be worse even than her own death would be Ali's shame in discovering that his father was a Jew. Ali wasn't the only boy in the village to play at war games against the Jews, but often he was foremost in the pack. She had made occasional feeble efforts to tell Ali how kind the Jewish al-Masris had been to her. But she knew that had not been enough to counteract Karnak's mounting anti-Zionist sentiment. In the classroom where Ali sat every day, there was a map of Israel outlined in black tacked to the wall. "Remember Palestine" was inked below it. After the everlasting shame of the crushing '67 war, it seemed everyone in Karnak truly hated the Jews. Ali was too young to be able to handle the knowledge that Youssef al-Masri was his father. Earnestly Mona appealed to her mother. "No. No. You couldn't—wouldn't—do that."

As she uttered those words, Mona saw a flicker of some half-screened emotion on her mother's face. Could it be? With sudden certainty, Mona knew what she should always have known. Her mother, too, had much to lose by revealing their secret. Why, after all, had Ummie concocted that fake marriage story? Why had she brought her back to the village? Of course! Ummie didn't want to be alone. She wanted, Mona thought, to have me forever. Mona wrinkled her forehead and studied her mother's face. In some dim, twisted way, Ummie did it all because she loves me. Would she be able, now, to try to have me killed? Putting the worst possible construction on it—even if by now she more hates than loves me—would she give up her power over me? Would she let all the village know that her only child was a fallen woman? Of course not. *Of course not.* Mona let out a deep sigh of liberation. In a firm voice, she risked everything on that one telltale shadow that had crossed her mother's face. "Tell them if you must. But tomorrow Ali and I will be on the train to Cairo."

Um Mona caught her breath. To hide her confusion, she made herself laugh. "You'd like that, wouldn't you? You'd like to die!" She stared at the river. The sky had turned gray, and there were only a few slivers of rose above the mountains to the far side of the river. The Nile was black. It seemed to rush past faster at night. It was a much colder, less human force when the sun was down. Um Mona turned her situation over in her mind. She had never thought Mona would call her bluff. Should she tell? That had never been her intention. But, by Allah, now she knew that someday she would. Someday she would repay the girl for this defiance. One day before she herself died—*just* before she died—she would tell everyone the secret. But she hated to think of it coming out now. She couldn't bear to think of Muhammad killing Mona. She wouldn't do it while Muhammad was alive. She would wait. She wasn't ready to give Mona up just yet. Tonight—now! —she would make her way to Sekhmet's Temple and think all this over. She wouldn't let Mona know she had won this round. She would let Mona worry. Let her go to Cairo tomorrow not knowing whether she faced death upon her return. Let her suffer. Let her lose sleep. Without another word Um Mona swept past her daughter and away from the Nile.

Mona sat on the riverbank. How, she asked herself, could she have been so stupid all these years? Of course Ummie wouldn't tell anyone. As the fear that she had felt for her mother all her life began to lessen its grip, Mona felt free enough to begin to be bathed in love and pity for her mother. Poor Ummie. Poor, desperate, twisted Ummie. She remembered Baruch, back in his Alexandria laboratory, telling her that she should feel compassion for those who had been broken by life. Tears sprang to Mona's eyes, and she felt a great welling tenderness for her mother. In a way, after all her own troubles, she could understand why Ummie was as she was. Maybe one reason she herself had been able to endure all she had had to was that she was her mother's daughter. Clearly, surely, she had inherited her own spirit and passion and will from her mother. But she had been luckier than her mother, for she had had Baruch to help her from closing up and turning love into hate. Maybe now she could play the same role with Ummie as Baruch had played with her. Maybe in time, with love and with patience, she would be able to help patch her mother back together. Remembering how, when Ummie had been a little girl, she had been called Helwa, "the Sweet one," Mona smiled to herself. Maybe if she herself could finally be the daughter Allah had meant for her to be, someday Ummie would be called that again.

At dawn the next morning the old familiar fear was in Mona again as she stood with Ali at the Luxor train station. Remembering how it had felt to be held too tightly by her own mother, always she had tried to curb her desire to protect him too much. She had been determined Youssef's son would grow up to be brave and free, and so she had tried to school herself from the beginning to let him go someday. But still she was afraid for him. He was so young. Today the child in him had insisted on dressing in his best blue-striped *gallabeiya* even though its freshness would be spoiled on the long dirty train ride. He had swaddled his head in a long white cotton turban that emphasized his high cheekbones and the flash of his white teeth against his dark-brown skin. She studied her son's face. He had flatter and coarser features than Youssef had had. But maybe that was all for the good. She didn't think anymore that the best things in life came with beauty. Mothers in the village, fearful always of the Evil Eye, worried the most for their handsome children. Mona fingered her blue bead and took comfort that at least Ali had character.

Aside from that one lapse with the British tourist, Ali had never disappointed her. He was bright, good-hearted, and—most unusual and noteworthy of all—he had always scorned the easy lie. Even as a little boy, when Ali had not been afraid of Sekhmet's statue, her son had been so brave. There was so much *life* in him. She fretted, however, that maybe he was too eager, that maybe it would be too easy for him to be led astray. He didn't have any idea of Cairo's temptations. Moved by the urge to help and to warn him, she considered telling Ali —here and now—the truth of his real father and herself. Instead, on impulse, she quickly untied the string that held her blue bead at her neck. "Ali. Ali, I want you to wear this."

"Oh, Mother!" Ali rolled his eyes. "Don't be silly. Those are for women and little children. I'm almost a man."

"Do it for luck." Firmly she tied the talisman around his neck. "Promise me you'll wear it. That you'll never take it off. My mother gave it to me, and so now I give it to you. Think of me when you touch it, Ali."

He looked around to make sure no one had noticed. He tucked the blue bead inside his *gallabeiya* so no one would think him a baby. Then he laughed and leaned down to kiss his mother on both cheeks. He would do anything for his mother.

In the yellowish early-morning light the people on the platform seethed with nervous excitement. In Luxor, in Karnak, in every village up and down the Nile, only the trains kept to a schedule. The panic of being left behind infected the pushing and hauling men, the scrambling and shrieking women. Like Ali, most of the men wore the long blue or striped *gallabeiyas* of the Said and had wrapped checkered or solid gray lengths of cotton rakishly around their heads. But here and there minced Arabs in fastidious Western dress. Young men in tight black trousers and brightly patterned polyester shirts lit foreign cigarettes with torchlike butane lighters. Older, plumper men in dark suits stood off a bit by themselves, self-consciously angling in the light so no one could miss the flashes of gold at their necks and fingers. But most of those waiting for the train were *fellahin,* sprawling and squatting on the cement floor with their parcels and baskets and cardboard boxes spread out in circles around them. Here a youngish woman nursed a baby, there an older one kept a sharp eye on her cages of chickens.

Mona steered Ali down the platform where the crush of people and luggage and animals was not so great. When the train pulled in, everyone would race for the same first few crowded compartments. Long ago her mother had taught her always to make for the cars in the rear. How had Ummie felt so many years ago, that first time when they had stood on this very platform to go north to Alexandria? Had Ummie's emotions been so mixed? If she had been able to see into the future, would she still have made the trip? Apprehensively Mona took Ali's arm. "Stand a little closer to me, son."

They heard the whistle, then felt the rush of hot air as the long gray train pulled into the station. The mob howled, and men tried to force their way into the doors and windows before the train had even ground to a halt. Mona allowed herself to be carried along behind her son. He waved their purple cardboard tickets and leaped up the steps and into the third-class compartment. "Come on! Cairo!" He pulled her up behind him. They squirmed inside a car already nearly full of passengers from Aswan, Kom Imbo, Edfu, and Esna, perching on the hard wooden seats and spilling over onto the floor. Ali strode to the back of the car and triumphantly found space on a seat near the window. With a lurch the train moved north. "Cairo!" Ali's eyes were shining. "We're going to Cairo!"

He spat on his hand and smeared the spittle onto the window to better their view. A top layer of dirt came off on his palm, but the glass remained dark and murky. By the looks of it, no one had cleaned the exterior of the windows for many seasons. Their view of the Nile and Egypt would be framed in a filthy gray grime.

But Ali was fascinated. He pressed his nose to the window, trying to catch sight of his uncle and cousins working in the fields. To be on the train to Cairo, to be looking out at the fields instead of up at the speeding train! From his vantage point the Nile looked smaller, more silvery, slithering like a serpent along the lush farmland of the Said. His river, his Nile! Always he had felt himself pulled northward with the rush of the river. He would have liked to have floated like a great brown fish all the way to Cairo on the current of the Nile. He grinned at his own foolish fancy. Yet he thought that the green river—fringed by the high arch of the sycamores, with the lacy leaves of the tamarind trees trailing in the water—was as happy as he was this morning. He nearly jigged in his seat. Cairo! He was going to Cairo!

For as long as he could remember, his mother had talked to him of a world wider than Karnak. He had heard so much of the Corniche in Alexandria, of tea parlors and taxis, of streets made not of dust and mud but of stone and cement. Now he would see it all for himself. He was going to the undisputed capital of the Arab world, to the city that had lived for more than a thousand years, to the citadel that had been Saladin's and Muhammad Ali's and even great Nasser's. He would walk through the bazaars, pray inside the famous mosques, maybe even would find a home away from home among the religious scholars of al-Azhar. Cairo! The greatest city in the world would someday be his. Ali hugged himself in wonder at it all. He wasn't only going to Cairo. He was going to Cairo—by Allah!—to see about being a doctor. He was going to learn to be just like his mother. No, he corrected himself, allowing just this once a bit of preening. Maybe he would be even slightly better than his mother. For she, after all, was a woman, and he was a man. She was a midwife, but he would be a doctor. But then he smiled to himself at the incongruity of ever being better than his mother. He would settle for being just as good as she was—as gentle and as wise. He would be his mother's son in every way.

Ali turned his attention to his fellow travelers in their compartment. The *fellah* men, hunched on the floor, smoking their cigarettes, staring into space, were nothing new. Nor were the black-swathed *fellaha* women, already munching their lunches, their babies and children spread noisily around them. But facing them a few seats away were two women who looked like the spun-sugar dolls sold on the eve of the Prophet's Birthday. They were wrapped in gauzy rainbow-colored hues of lavender, rose, azure, and peach. In their ears and through their noses were old-fashioned chunks of flashing silver. When they caught him staring, they giggled with their hands held over their mouths. "What *are* they?" Ali nudged his mother and whispered.

"Sudanese," she guessed. "They must have taken the boat to Aswan."

"The Sudan! Someday I'll go there, too."

They ate the sandwiches Mona had packed and bought glasses of dark, sweet tea from an old man in a dirty white jacket.

Ali went back to looking out the window at the river, the irrigation canals, the fields, the tall date palms. They were two hours north of Luxor. "It looks the same as in Karnak."

"It looks the same all the way to Cairo." Already the monotony of the thirteen-hour ride was under her skin. Irritably she surveyed the compartment, imagining that all her fellow travelers were her patients. Many of them, sitting in a stupor, looked sick enough. A doctor sent south by the Ministry of Health had told her that nine out of ten of the *fellahin* were dying slowly of bilharzia. Infections of the eye were the next most common ailments. She counted cataracts on the eyes of the old and watched the young rubbing their lids as if they had the perpetual itch of trachoma. Others who coughed and wheezed were no doubt victims of the respiratory diseases brought on by the dust. Depressed, she let her own eyes droop as Ali began a conversation with a man sitting near them. How Ali loved to talk. Youssef had been like that, too. He had said so much to her, and so little of it in the end had come true. She drifted off to sleep, lulled by the rock and clacking of the train, made drowsy by the heat. The wails of the babies, the rise and fall of the guttural voices around her, were familiar and soothing. She dreamed in uneasy snatches of other journeys and other sounds of wheels. She was in the train with her mother, going first north and then south. She was in the car with Youssef, careening down to Cairo and their fate on the houseboat.

When she awoke hours later, it was very hot and Ali was still excitedly talking. Mona smiled sleepily at her son. She herself had never been quite as agog with the wonders of the train. If he was already so dazzled, what would he think of Cairo? She yawned. It was noon, and every hair on her head was soaked with sweat. Her bones rattled against the hard seat. The compartment was gray-white with smoke. Better to shut her eyes again and try to sleep. She only half awakened when they lurched into each station: Assuit, Manfolut, Mallawi, Minya. She dreamed of men in gray robes with turbans wrapped over their faces, of women in black who opened their mouths yet couldn't seem to utter a sound. Mona pulled herself up from her dozing hunch and looked at the men in gray and women in black ranged round her. She resolved not to fall back to sleep again.

Ali was deep in conversation with his neighbors. The man opposite him, an old soldier in a fancy military uniform, was confiding a dream he had had just a month before the last terrible war with Israel. "I was walking up a hill, up a high, rocky hill in the mountains. I think it must have been in Jerusalem. And all of a sudden I saw a beautiful young girl in a robe as blue as the sky. She told me she was the Virgin Mary."

"No!" Ali said.

"Yes," said the soldier. "She told me there would be another war, and she promised me that this time we would win. 'But first,' she said, 'you must take Jesus Christ as your Lord.' "

"But you couldn't do *that!*" Ali said. "Allah!"

The old soldier nodded. "You're right. I looked at that woman, and I said, just as loud and as clear as I could, 'There is no God but Allah, and Muhammad is His Prophet!' And she disappeared in a flash of fire."

Ali shuddered. "So then what happened?"

"I woke up," the soldier said. "And it was then that I knew that we could not win the war, not with the Christians—the Americans and the British and the French—backing the Jews. That woman in my dream was a devil sent to tempt me." He leaned forward and whispered. "If I hadn't been so strong, if I hadn't been true to Allah, who knows what might have happened? Maybe I would have lost my soul, but we would have won the war!"

Mona rooted in her basket for what was left of their food. She was sick and tired of all these preposterous excuses for the Arabs' loss of the '67 war. Dreams indeed. Ali had appeared to believe every word of the soldier's story. She wished he weren't so gullible. It wasn't only in the Said that everyone and everything was not what it appeared to be. She handed Ali an egg, some bread, a lump of cheese. She thought again of important words that she had long left unsaid to her son. Soon they would be in Cairo, and he would take his first steps away from her. But it still wasn't the right time to tell him about his father. Ali was too young. He would always, she feared, be too young. He had spilled tea on the front of his *gallabeiya,* and there was a crumb of bread on his cheek. She reached up and brushed it away with a finger. Was wiping his face all she could do for him?

"Giza!" Ali cried. "The sign says this is Giza." He craned in the dark for the pyramids. He could see only railroad cars, a few dusty roads, and men moving slowly past in *gallabeiyas* and turbans. Surely these men must be different from the *fellahin* of the Said. But they walked the same, they spit on the street the same, they talked with their hands the same. He consoled himself that they were not quite to Cairo yet.

Mona began to worry about getting to Baruch's. Cairo for her had centered on the railway station and Youssef's houseboat on the Nile. What she remembered most about Cairo was its vastness, its chaos. She rummaged in her basket for the letter from Baruch. If he couldn't meet her at the station, she was to take a taxi to his flat in Sayeda Zainab. Allah only knew where that was. Absently Mona wondered if Baruch would find her very much the worse for wear. She glanced down at her wrinkled black robe and rearranged the black shawl that hid both her hair and her forehead.

As the train stopped, men and women were screaming and cursing and laughing in a rush for the platform. Mona was pushed this way and that, and she fought her rising panic when she lost sight of Ali. But then she was being squeezed out the door, and she felt her son's arms around her as she landed on the platform. "Welcome to Cairo!" he said.

The platform was awash in a mob headed in one direction. Ali's head swiveled from left to right. On the cement floor sat a woman in black, a baby at her breast, two other toddlers by her side selling matches. A one-legged boy in green-striped pajamas peddled newspapers. A porter, wheezing like the donkey he resembled, pulled behind him a cart unsteadily stacked with an entire carload of luggage. Men put the hems of their *gallabeiyas* in their teeth so they wouldn't trip and be crushed in the stampede. Slim soldiers in khaki green and taller ones in black and scarlet swaggered on their way. Stout women in black dresses, black hose, and black shoes stepped smartly as if they were alone in their villa gardens. *Baladi* mothers clutched small children by the hand, and vendors darted in the thick of the crowd hawking candy and cigarettes, cola and biscuits, key rings and flashlight batteries.

"Cairo!" Ali shouted over to her as they rushed along. "*El-*

hamdulillah!" They followed the crowd down one flight of stairs and up another, emerging in a cavernous gray hall where moonlight streaked moodily down through broken panes of the high glass ceiling arching overhead. Uncertainly Mona looked around her. This central station hall had changed with the years. That huge mosaic mural of a smugly smiling Nasser still dominated one wall, but now it faced a poster of Sadat decked out in military whites and medals. From one end of the hall to the other, tattered banners of black and purple mourned Nasser. There was a new sadness, an almost palpable air of decay in the station. Cairo before had been gay, wild, full of irrepressible life. Now it seemed tawdry. She stood there a minute to get her bearings and watched a bent old man sweeping away litter. Carefully he brushed it into a pile. As he turned and picked up a dustbin, the handle of his broom scattered the garbage back over the floor. There were soldiers and police everywhere, and some of them had huge, snarling dogs barely restrained at the end of their leashes. She clung to Ali's arm and steered him to a far door.

The mother and son paused on the threshold of Cairo. A mammoth granite statue of an ancient pharaoh rose smack in the middle of the square before them, staring as if in perpetual disdain at what swirled at his feet. Cars, taxis, trucks, donkey carts, camels, horse carriages, and bicycles careened in every direction, even high in the air on swaying concrete-and-steel overpasses. Old men, young men, women, and children moved with dogged determination on the streets, over the fences, alongside the cars. Garishly painted kiosks and food carts fought for position along the street under the angry red and orange and green gashes of neon signs. Over it all was the constant hellish howl of horns: tooting, beeping, crying, wailing, nearly talking in their own hooting jargon that is Cairo. Smoke from hundreds of cars, thousands of cigarettes, enveloped everything and everyone in a haze made yellow by the flickering electric lights.

Mona caught her breath and searched in terror for a taxi. When she felt a hand on her arm, she steeled herself for another level of assault. Instead she looked up into the warm brown eyes of Baruch.

"Mona!" He folded her into his arms.

She was saved. "You're here!" He was grinning down at her, as reassuring and solid in his dark cotton suit as he had always been. He looks the same, Mona thought. More gray, but the same. And not so old. I used to think he was so old. She remembered her manners. "Ali, I want you to meet Baruch al-Masri."

The man and the boy studied each other, then gravely shook hands.

"How did you know?" Mona asked. "How did you know we'd be here today? We didn't even know for sure ourselves until yesterday."

"I've been meeting every train from the Said all week. I couldn't

360

do any less, now, could I?" Baruch shooed them toward a waiting taxi. "Let's get out of this madhouse."

He settled Mona in the back seat beside him and positioned Ali in front so he wouldn't miss any of the sights. As they crawled down Ramses Street, Ali and the driver kept up a constant patter over the clackety drone of Oriental music coming from the taxi's cassette player. Ali grinned at the nearly naked pink plastic doll of a foreign woman that bobbed above the dashboard. He reached out to touch the orange sequins the driver had lovingly pasted on the steering wheel. And he whirled in his seat and gaped out the windows at Cairo. Never before had he seen even a traffic light, let alone Cairo with every shop open and every light ablaze. The buses were huge red-and-cream monsters, so overflowing with passengers that boys and men hung onto their steps and tried to wiggle inside by the windows. "Look at them!" Ali cried.

"Twenty-seven people were killed on this street last week alone," Baruch whispered to Mona. "They drive their buses like tanks. If Nasser had made these bus drivers his tank corps, the Israelis wouldn't have had a chance."

Stalled in the traffic, their taxi was besieged by beggars seeking alms and by peddlers selling boxes of tissues and brightly painted plastic dolls. Throngs of people threaded their way fearlessly through the banks of stalled cars. Ali ogled men in Western suits and in Arab robes, modest women with their hair covered discreetly in lacy wimples and shawls, a brazen woman in an orange wig and tottering silver high heels.

"As soon as you can get out of this mess, take the Corniche," Baruch told the driver. "We can't let Ali get his first impression of Cairo only from Ramses Street." They inched up one ramp, sped down another, and the Nile was finally before them. "Stop the car," Baruch ordered. "Everybody out. I want you to see this."

Ali stood between his mother and Baruch and looked down at the Nile. It was the same river he had watched every day of his life in Karnak, but this Nile took his breath away. The reflection of gold, red, but mostly green fairy lights winked and shimmered over the surface, so that the river seemed on fire. "Ah," Ali sighed. "Ah." Across the river a tall golden lotus-like tower, glittering higher than the highest palm tree, pointed to the orange halfmoon in a sky mottled with navy-blue clouds. From gaily lighted casinos sprawled along the banks drifted the sounds of Arab love songs. Fleets of tiny rowboats floated in the center of the river packed with families enjoying a hot night out. Never had Ali seen the Nile more full of inviting, unbreakable promises. Leaning on the railing, the breeze rippling through his hair, Ali caught the scent of jasmine and roses. *Muezzins* atop a thousand minarets began their call to evening prayers. *"Allahu akbar! Allahu akbar!* God is most great!" Ali, Mona, and Baruch bowed their heads and murmured the familiar words. When they opened their eyes, the river awaited them in all its glory. "I'll never forget it," Ali said. "I'll never forget how this looks and feels!" He threw himself into his mother's arms, and she looked over his head at Baruch. Take care of him, her eyes pleaded. Take care of my son.

Mona and Baruch sat on rough gray stones at the base of the Great Pyramid. It was late afternoon and a hot wind was blowing in from the desert. Not far away were the camels and their drivers, the donkeys and their carts, the straggling herds of tourists who littered the Plain of the Pyramids. Somewhere above them Ali and a Bedouin guide were climbing to the peak of Cheops.

Alone with Baruch, Mona longed to ask him not only what he thought of Ali but also what he had heard from Youssef. But she was shy about how to begin. Before Baruch had been not only a generation above her but also the one who smoothed out her problems and knew all the answers. But in the past week of their visit, with Ali between them, she and Baruch had been on a more equal footing. Demurely, timidly, she tucked her robe around her legs. Then she waited for him to tell how it was to be between them.

Baruch, too, waited. He had waited for her for years. He was willing to wait a little longer. Surely under that deathlike black robe was the core of the girl he had once known so well. But Mona was a full-grown woman. With him she would have to act like one. He would find out in his own good time not only how deeply the Said had claimed her but how she had finally reconciled her two lives. She had once walked a tightrope between her mother's Karnak and the al-Masris' Alexandria. Finally, when she had lost her balance, she had fallen back to the village. In her dress and behavior there were no clues that once she had dared to run off with her Jewish lover to a houseboat on the Nile. Obviously, over the years she had channeled her passion into Youssef's son. As the three of them had visited the Cairo mosques and browsed in the bazaars, Mona had seldom taken her eyes off Ali. Her attention had wandered from him only when she had sensed she was in the presence of someone or something that was suffering. It seemed to Baruch that Mona had a sixth sense for suffering. Walking through the crowded streets, he had seen her straining toward every scab and whimper along the way, as if she wanted nothing more than to stop and nurse Cairo's battalions of the walking wounded.

She must have endured these years by learning not only how she could suffer but how she could heal. I, Baruch thought, never taught her that. It was true that the great mass of Egyptians had an almost limitless capacity for suffering. Perhaps she had been born to it, as some are born with an innate ability to dance or sing. But what set Mona apart was that she appeared to know not only how to suffer but how to transcend suffering. There was a new nobility about the Mona sitting beside him. Baruch lit a cigarette and smoked in silence. Noble Mona might be. But she was still too passive for her own good. She was waiting, he knew, for him to take the initiative. Of course he had already agreed that Ali could live with him when he was ready for the university. He would use his slight influence to help Ali gain admission to medical school. He would sell the remaining family porcelains to buy books and Western clothes for this last of the al-Masris. He would also probably have to give up his two-room flat and take a small room to share with Ali. Otherwise, on his pittance from the hospital, how could he feed the boy? All this Baruch would do willingly. But he would not assume the full responsibility for whatever relationship he was to have with Mona. He would not speak first. He was not finished with trying to teach Mona how she could be.

"Well," Mona said finally. "What do you think?"

He blew smoke rings. "About what?"

"Everything."

"I think I told you long ago what I think about most things. But perhaps you've forgotten."

"I remember all of it. I wish sometimes I could forget how to remember." When he didn't answer, she went on hesitantly. "Ali's a good boy, don't you think?"

"In what ways?"

"You've seen him this week. He's so excited. I've never seen him so excited. I felt old watching him. I can't believe I ever felt the way he looks."

"You were different, Mona. Much less sure of yourself. I always wanted to take you by the hand and lead you every step of the way."

"And now that I'm old and gray?"

He looked at the premature silver in her dark hair. She wasn't even thirty. He wanted to kiss every gray hair. "You're even more beautiful than you were as a girl."

She smiled to herself. There it is again, she thought, that preoccupation of others with the way she looked.

"That's it exactly," Baruch said. "That look on your face right now. *That's* what makes you look so beautiful." He pointed to the valley before them where the Sphinx had lain waiting forever. "That secretive, suffering smile. As if you understand all the mysteries in the world and find them, at the same time, both sad and a little funny. That's what is different about you now."

They exchanged shy smiles.

"You've changed, too, Baruch." She laughed. "I don't remember your being so courtly."

Courtly? *She knew.* Baruch was befuddled. He tried to put himself on a more even keel. "Cairo. How does Cairo seem to you now?"

Mona gazed toward the smoky huddle of minarets and skyscrapers along the horizon. She fancied she could hear those infernal horns even out here. "As if it all fell apart years ago, and no one cares."

"It was the wars that did it." His voice was tense with emotion that had less to do with Cairo and more with having Mona so near him. "All the lost wars with Israel! All the money went for tanks and troops and bullets. And all for nothing. The worst was the last war. To lose what we did in '67! You've put your finger on it. Since the war this whole city—maybe this whole country—has been suffering from mass depression. You take the sense of honor away from millions of Arabs, you replace it with shame at losing so much to the Jews, and you get what we have here."

"But Nasser tried. Surely you agree that Nasser tried."

"I liked Nasser. Even though he hounded my family and all the foreigners until they left, he did try to make things better. But almost everything he did backfired. He cut rents in half, and so landlords neglected their buildings so badly that many of them collapsed into the streets. He promised government jobs to anyone with a university degree, then he made the universities free. Now it seems that half of Cairo is on the government payroll. Tens of thousands of overeducated, underemployed bureaucrats sit in their offices, drink tea, and act as if it's their job to paralyze the government. Whatever anyone tries to do, it creates a bigger catastrophe. After the last war Nasser kept shelling the Israelis across the Suez Canal. All that happened when the Jews fired back was that Cairo had to absorb a million refugees from our bombed-out Canal cities. There was nowhere for them to live, no work for them to do." Baruch shook his head. "Even the rich complain that the telephones don't work, that it takes half the day just to drive across town in all the traffic. Wherever you look, whatever you try to do, it all seems so hopeless."

"And you?" Mona asked. "What about you? Have you given up hope, too?"

"I used to look around and see only the smiling faces. But the deeper you go, the more you tap into the despair. I suppose it's better to laugh than to weep. But Allah!" It was a plea. "I'm just hanging on."

She was afraid. Baruch was supposed to be the strong one. "What happened? What's happened to you?"

"Abbas. I wrote you about Abbas. *That's* what happened."

Mona took his hand. "I loved him, too."

He cleared his throat, but he could not keep the pain from his voice. "Do you know what the rich say about life before the revolution? They say it was Paradise."

Mona looked out over the pyramids plains, remembering a dawn ride behind Youssef on a galloping Arabian stallion. They had thought they were to be married that day. Instead . . .

"So what do *you* think, Mona? Did we lose Paradise?"

She flinched and let go of his hand. "I think of all of . . . that . . . as a dream. Karnak is my real life." She eased away from freshly reopened wounds.

Baruch shrugged his shoulders and sighed. "My niece Lisabet married someone with a most un-Jewish-sounding name, so it's safe to correspond with her in Switzerland. Her letters are full of dinner parties and holidays at the seashore and private schools for her children. Sometimes I can hardly believe I ever lived in a world like hers."

Mona tensed. "What else does she write?"

"Maybe you wondered why I never told you about any of them. With things as they are, I didn't want to implicate you if there was any trouble. Sometimes they still open my mail."

"I thought as much. But tell me now."

"Rafael died long ago, and Leah remarried. She and Rachel and her husband still live in Paris."

"And the others?"

Baruch could not help looking around nervously to make sure no one could overhear. Nasser was dead, but his secret police lived on. "Daoud died in the '67 war," he whispered. "In the Battle of Jerusalem."

"Allah keep him!" Mona bit her lip. "And?" she prompted, afraid that he was leading up to news of another dead al-Masri.

"I don't know much about Youssef. We haven't corresponded for many years. The last I heard, maybe ten years ago, he was going into the Israeli army."

"How was he then?"

"All right. I asked him not to write again. It was too dangerous."

"You know nothing else about him?" Mona persisted.

There was no point, he reminded himself, in making Mona suffer more. Just as he had never informed Youssef about Ali, he had already decided not to tell Mona what he knew about Youssef's marriage, children, and divorce. "All I can say is he must be alive. The only news I get about my family is the dates that they die."

"Yes. I would have known, I think, if he had died."

"You've not heard from him then?"

"No." Mona shut her lips firmly, as if Youssef's silence were a pact.

Baruch's curiosity overcame his compassion. "How do you feel about all that now?"

"I have Ali. He is like his father, isn't he?"

"From far away, in a dim light, I could swear he was Youssef. The way he moves. The way he laughs. The way he is around people. But, you know, there's a lot of you in him, too. I don't think Youssef ever really saw the beggars, the cripples, the lost ones. Ali, I think, is more sensitive than his father."

"Youssef was sensitive."

"Perhaps." Baruch paused. "You haven't told Ali anything about *that?*"

"Not yet. Mother threatened to tell everyone. I've always been so afraid of that. But all of a sudden I realized that even she could never go so far."

"Don't be too sure." Baruch had not forgotten the confrontation in Abbas's parlor the day he had lost Mona. "Don't underestimate your mother."

"I think I know her better than you do." There was a smugness in Mona's voice. "I told her to tell them."

"And she didn't? Mona! If you had been able to stand up to your mother back in Alexandria, everything would have been different. It still can. It's not too late. Don't go back to Karnak. Stay with me. We'll send Ali to secondary school here."

"Here? Oh, it's too late for that. Too late for me. I've had my good years. No. I belong in Karnak now."

"You're still young." Baruch plunged ahead. "I asked you to marry me once before. Will you marry me now, Mona?"

"Baruch!" Mona blushed. "I will never marry. Not unless . . ."

Baruch fumbled as he lit another cigarette. "You're still waiting for him."

"Yes." Mona smiled again to herself.

Baruch hid his sigh by inhaling deeply on his cigarette. He hadn't expected to ask her to marry him. Perhaps, he thought, I've been imagining all along that Ali is *my* son, not Youssef's. Enough. I'll have to be satisfied being Uncle Baruch. He smoked his cigarette down to the filter. When he spoke again, it was briskly. "I wanted to ask you something else. About Ali. Don't you think you should tell him about Youssef?"

"Sometimes I think he must know."

"What kind of answer is that?"

"He's too young. He's only thirteen."

"You're not still afraid, after all these years, that they'd kill you in the village?"

"For a Saidi, it's never too late for vengeance. But that's not the only reason I haven't told him. I just think it's better if Ali doesn't know his father is a Jew."

"Ali hates the Jews that much?"

"He's an Arab. All his life he's heard how the Jews took away Palestine from his brothers. That we have to win it back. I can't tell him yet. But I will. Someday I will." Her voice softened. "You know, Baruch, I don't think it's over yet. It's unfinished between Youssef and me."

"Then finish it, Mona. Tell Ali. Tell him today."

"Not yet." She shook her head. "Not quite yet. But when he's here with you in Cairo, maybe you can talk to him about the Jews. He knows you used to be a Jew, but I think he admires you. Maybe you can help prepare him."

"So someday you *will* tell him?"

"I must." But her voice lacked conviction.

"Any more instructions for me? Besides teaching this young Arab to love the Jews?"

Mona smiled. It seemed she and Baruch were to be friends. "I think sometimes about Youssef and Hamid in Alexandria. I worry about Ali's choosing his own friends. He's too trusting."

"As you were?"

"Maybe." For a moment Mona seemed to grieve. "If you could look out for the likes of Hamid, I'd rest a little easier. And girls. Make sure he doesn't get into any trouble with girls."

As Baruch pledged his word, he looked at Mona thoughtfully. He wondered how much of the father she did see in the son.

21

JERUSALEM, ISRAEL / October 1973

Youssef padded quickly around his room as he dressed with unusual care at five-thirty on this Sabbath morning. He ran a comb through his slightly thinning hair and tucked the sheets around the frame of his single bed. But as he tiptoed into the hallway, he could hear sounds coming from the kitchen.

Ayala—blessed, thoughtful Ayala—was standing over the stove cooking breakfast.

She whistled as she looked her father over. *"You're* all dressed up today."

"And *you're* up very early. You didn't have to do this."

"I wanted to. Someone had to take care of you." She poured him a cup of coffee. "Besides, I had to be up early anyway for my nature walk. Today we're going to the Dead Sea."

"You won't change your mind and come with me?"

"I'll meet her tomorrow."

Youssef sipped his coffee. "You're going hiking with Reuven?"

"With him and thirty others." But Ayala was blushing.

As he ate his eggs, Youssef reflected that his little girl was growing up. "You're seeing quite a lot of him."

"Can I help it? He follows me everywhere." Ayala laughed, but then she became serious. "You like him, don't you?"

"Reuven?" Youssef lit a cigarette. Yes, he did like that good-natured, open-hearted young man who already seemed to be courting his daughter. "I just think you're a little young for this."

"I'm thirteen. Not so young. And Reuven's eighteen."

"How long has this been going on?"

"Since we were children."

Youssef poured another cup of coffee and remembered when he had said just that about Mona to Baruch in the garden of the Beau Rivage Hotel in Alexandria. So it was like *that* with his daughter and this young man. "Tell me more about this. You met him at Chozrim?"

"Years ago, at a kibbutz federation meeting. You know how it goes. Marrying someone from your own kibbutz would be like incest. So the kibbutz elders—matchmakers one and all—have all these *very* political get-togethers so girl can meet boy. It worked for us."

Marriage. She and this young man were evidently talking of marriage. "And what does your mother think of this?"

"You know Mother!" Ayala rolled her eyes. "Do you know what she said about him after they first met? She said he was nice, but his arms were too hairy. She's never satisfied."

"Remember, that's your mother you're talking about."

"How could I forget?" Ayala stirred some coffee into her milk. "But what do *you* think of him?"

"I think you're too young to be serious about anyone."

"Anyone but you, you mean?"

"Something like that."

They both laughed.

"Don't worry, Father. I'll be around here for a long while. We want to wait until I'm nineteen or twenty. When we're both out of the army and Reuven has his degree. Maybe if we settle up on his kibbutz in the Galilee, you could join it, too."

So, Youssef thought, his little girl had the future all planned. This new generation was so sure of itself. But maybe the young were always like that. He, too, had once laid his elaborate plans. Now he lived from day to day.

Remembering with a start that today was not just like every other day, Youssef gulped down the rest of his coffee, kissed his daughter goodbye, and turned up the collar on his jacket as he stepped out into the semidarkness of tree-lined Borochov Street. It was colder than he had thought, and he faced a long walk. If this had been any morning but Saturday, he could have caught the Number 18 bus on the corner. But this was Shabbat. The powerful religious factions made sure that buses never ran on the Sabbath. From here in the southwestern hills of Kiryat Hayovel, it would take well over an hour to walk to the center of Jerusalem. He consoled himself that he needed the exercise. He was thirty-eight years old. Keeping in shape was one of his small, nagging daily worries.

As he concentrated on maintaining a brisk pace, he reflected that it did him good to walk all the way into town. It reminded him of his roots. He looked down the gully toward the transit camp where he had first stayed with his father and brother. What had happened to the immigrants who had been his neighbors there sixteen years ago? The East Europeans were probably officeworkers and teachers and stalwarts on the *moshav* collective farms. Some of the Orientals must be laborers in the Galilee and Negev border towns. Others would have settled in the slums near Tel Aviv's factories. Many, as he knew all too well, were still on the dole. Since he had left his kibbutz, Youssef had been a caseworker in Jerusalem's welfare department.

There wasn't a car or truck or bicycle on the main road that twirled down the rock-strewn mountain. It was damp, but not as damp as it would be in a few months. Jerusalem winters were always a shivering shock. Six of them he had endured, and still they always caught him by surprise. They were not only very cold but wet. As if to remind him that winter was not far away, a fine, clammy drizzle began to fall. Youssef hunched his shoulders and burrowed into his collar. It was lighter out now. He could see spread before him the clean, tall mercantile towers of Jewish West Jerusalem. Over there, hacked into and perched atop the mountains, were low-slung monuments and museums and other architectural gems. Tucked into the hills were the well-groomed suburbs of the academic and governmental elite. Much of it was so new the trees around the houses were saplings. Construction on this side of Jerusalem had boomed since the last war.

He wended his way down Mount Herzl past the military cemetery where Daoud was buried. Even with so many graves, the cemetery was still not full. Another war, Youssef could not help thinking, should do it. He looked not far away, at the crest of a hill, where another cemetery was home to another al-Masri. Youssef mumbled a prayer under his breath for his brother and father.

In the outskirts of middle-class Jerusalem, on the quiet streets of yellow-gray, single-family stone houses, Youssef consulted his watch. There was time for a detour. He pulled a *yarmulkeh* out of his pocket and set it on the back of his head. He made for where the bus carried him every day, to Mea She'arim, the colorful Orthodox bastion of Jews who still lived almost as if they were in a nineteenth-century East European *shtetl*.

Today, as every day, he wandered under arcades of fragile balconies slung along the narrow, winding streets. Men hurried past him in fur hats and homburgs, in long frock coats and black stockings, in elaborate gray and white prayer shawls. Even after the two years that Youssef had been working in Mea She'arim, he was still intrigued by the people he tried to serve there. They asked little of him except his help in avoiding every hint of government interference. He visited them in their *yeshiva* schools, their ritual baths, their synagogues.

At one time, during those lonely years before Ayala had come to live with him, he had even flirted with their religious ecstasies. When dancing with the Hassids had not moved him, on impulse he had joined the Christian processions on Fridays for Stations of the Cross in the Old City. Then, for good measure, he had even taken off his shoes and knelt in motionless meditation in the mosques. But instead of being enlightened by all these forays into faith, he had been disturbed by the aura of musty, primitive mysteries in those synagogues and chapels and mosques. The Christians called this the Holy Land, but their gloomy shrines sent shivers down Youssef's spine. He watched Jews and Christians and Muslims come close to worshiping the mammoth rock where Abraham was supposed to have been willing to sacrifice Isaac. Although in a way Youssef envied the certainties of the faithful, he had come to realize that religion was not his personal salvation.

Then, in his search for answers that could comfort, he had turned to art. He had attended the symphony, wandered the museums, bought tickets to the ballet. Yet being a spectator to culture had touched him only a little. For a while he had tried going to foreign films every week at the Semadar Cinema in the German Colony. But he would always feel like crying at that moment—that terrible moment—when the lights came on and he was face to face again with his own life.

In desperation, finally, he had tried nature. He had walked the Jerusalem hills, on mountain trails near the Dead Sea, through the deserts of the northern Negev, in the flowery pastures of the Galilee. As the months passed, as the beauty of his adopted country washed over him, he had wondered how it could have taken him so long to *see* Israel. Politicians and philosophers and demagogues could argue forever over who had the better claim to this land, but there was no question in Youssef's mind now about its worth. More than religion, more than art, he had found comfort in the beauty of this land. If he had it to do all over again—if he could at least relive his years in Israel—he thought he might have been more content simply to try to make plants and flowers grow in this rocky, stubborn soil. But he supposed it was too late to try to make another start.

Coming toward him down the street were two little Orthodox boys who were, like all the children of this quarter, solemn beyond their years. He had a sudden impulse to stop and tell these boys jokes, to buy them ice cream, to do whatever was necessary to coax them from their premature anxiety. The purity and hopefulness of his children —his three girls—had been his chief comfort. Without them he might not have been able to endure. At first he had been able to be with them only in the summers. But then, when Ayala was old enough for secondary school, even Rivka had agreed she could get a better education in Jerusalem. Talli and Naim would come to live with him, too, in a few years. But they wouldn't be staying with him forever. Already precocious Ayala had her young man picked out. He would have the girls for a few more good years, and then once again he would be alone.

Removing his *yarmulkeh,* Youssef walked down two streets and across another until he was back in his old neighborhood of Musrara. He had hoped, in his first months here as a social worker, that he would find he had the makings of a saint. He had imagined that he would be so hardworking and patient the poor would flock to him. Instead, there had been years of gritty plodding work.

Youssef lit a cigarette and looked moodily over Musrara. In these streets, these alleys, these cul-de-sacs, he still saw another missed chance for peace in the Middle East. When he had first arrived here, fresh from the ideological ferment of the kibbutz, he had been struck by the superficial resemblance of Musrara to the *baladi* quarters of old Alexandria and the Palestinian Arab villages and towns. The Oriental Jews were enough like the local Arabs to pass for their distant cousins. Both groups spoke Arabic. They ate the same kinds of foods. They were at the bottom of the economic and social scale. They were religious and fatalistic. They were superstitious and family-bound. He had thought his life's work would be to fashion an obvious alliance between the Orientals and the local Arabs.

If only he could have helped to make that happen, so much could have been different in Israel. The Oriental Jews were already a majority in the country. If they had made common cause with the Palestinian Arabs, the East European Jews could have been forced to give up their militant control of the country. In time, then, Israel could have become again what it had been: a Levantine country populated by Jews, Arabs, and Christians. There could have been peace. But the Orientals had made short work of his grand scheme. Back in their old homes in Muslim North Africa, the Orientals had spent generations trying to convince their colonial French masters that they were not only different but a cut above the Arabs. In Israel, as if they were afraid the Ashkenazi would lump them together with the Arabs, the Orientals scorned any contact with them. At election time the Orientals voted mostly for the worst of the right-wing politicians. There seemed no possibility now of any alliance between the Oriental Jews and the Palestinian Arabs.

Youssef crushed the cigarette butt with his heel and continued his stroll. Although he had failed to bring Arab and Jew together here, he still regarded his Musrara years as happy ones. For he had had one shining success in Musrara. He and others like him had helped to galvanize Moroccan street gangs into a protest movement that had touched the conscience of the country. Borrowing a name from the Americans, Musrara's Black Panthers had dramatized the plight of Israel's Orientals better than decades of painstaking social work by men like Daoud. Laws had been passed to help Orientals stay in school and succeed in the army. Plans had been drafted for new types of housing. Youth detention centers had been overhauled. When Youssef was in one of his optimistic moods, he told himself that Israel was at last beginning to grapple with the first of its two great problems. In time, it seemed, Oriental Jews were going to be more than second-class citizens.

He stood looking out over where the Arabs lived in East Jerusalem. If only now, he thought, Israel could bring itself to address its second, and even greater, problem. Someday, somehow, there had to be justice for the Palestinians. Often Youssef wished he weren't so emotionally drained. There was so much that could be done—there were whole lifetimes of work to be done—about Israel and the Arabs. Feeling as he did, he thought he probably should join one of the leftist groups who were trying to talk sense about the Palestinians. But he knew he was just too tired for another cause—especially for what was probably another *lost* cause. There had been a time, after the Six Day War, when political compromises with the Arabs might have been possible. But now, after all those airplane hijackings, after the massacres at Lod Airport and the Munich Olympics, Youssef was afraid that Israel was swinging to the right.

It was a pity, but Jew and Arab seemed further apart than ever. Youssef sighed under his breath. Despite his concerns about human rights for the Arabs, what he wanted more than anything now was simply a normal life for himself and his children. He wanted some peace. He wanted to be able to get on a bus without worrying if a bomb was planted on it. He wanted to be able to turn on the radio without his heart beating a little faster for fear of another terrorist attack or even another war. Life in Israel was one long nerve-shattering siege. Yet Youssef could at least take comfort from one thing. Whether he was optimistic or pessimistic about the future, whether he was anxious or disappointed about the present, whether he was sad or guilt-ridden about the past, he no longer doubted where he belonged. Imperfect Israel was finally home.

He consulted his watch again. If he didn't hurry, he would be late. As he skirted the walls of the Old City, he felt a rush of love for Jerusalem. He wished he had the leisure to double back through the early-morning shuttered lanes of the Old City. He would have liked to wander through the Muslim Quarter before the hawkers were shrilly awake, then saunter over to the Western Wall to watch the Orthodox sway in prayerful adoration. He never tired of wondering about the thousands of hopes and fears on those slips of paper they wedged between the stones of the Western Wall. The Old City now, forever, was the innards of Jerusalem. He stopped, turned around, and gazed at the walls. They had inspired him the day he had arrived in Israel, and for him, even now, they were still magic.

On sweet spring dawns he climbed the Mount of Olives to watch the sun turn the city's millions of rocks to gold. On noisy summer nights, with floodlights on King David's Tower, the air was heavy with spices and ripe blossoms and deeds that called out to be done. But now, as he lingered on a steep cobblestone hill, he decided quintessential Jerusalem came on still, silent Shabbat mornings like this one. There were too many distractions when the streets were thronged with hurrying Jews, soft-stepping Arabs, and awed tourists pouring over their eternal maps. Only on a morning like this, with the rain falling and the mist curling on the hoary walls, did it seem to him that the very heart of Jerusalem lay open. For the two thousand years of their exile, Jews had longed to die in Jerusalem. At times like this Youssef understood why.

There was no more time to hang around and gape at the walls. He was late, and the one he was to see would not take kindly to delays. She was not at all Levantine. She assumed things would proceed on time and as planned. In the seventeen years of their separation, his mother's expectations had not changed.

He had been surprised at the cable heralding her arrival. Until then there had been no hint that his mother had any desire to see her sole surviving son, much less that most Jewish of countries where he had made his life. Last night he had met her at the airport and sat beside her in the limousine to the King David Hotel. There had been time only to register that the cold, lovely statue that had been his mother was now an old woman. Her beauty must have fled long ago, but that coldness had remained. Yet she still had presence. The cane she leaned on was a graceful walking stick of ivory and gold filigree. Her frock—his mother had never worn dresses, only frocks and gowns —was *très chic*. Her silvery-blond hair was regal. Even now, heads turned to wonder who she was. She still never passed a mirror without swiveling for reassurance of perfection. Perhaps, Youssef thought, today I'll finally be able to see beyond my mother's facade.

The King David waited in its cold and marbled rosy hilltop splendor. Once this hotel had been a symbol of imperial British arrogance. Once the British Mandate's headquarters had been centered here. And once, before the first war in '48, Jewish terrorists had bombed this hotel. But that old colonial aura of power and privilege still endured. Instead of visiting British dignitaries, however, the King David now catered to rich foreign Jews who came here as philanthropists and patrons. On floors polished to a slippery shine, under glittering cut-glass chandeliers, well-bred guests glided with assurance. Outside the hotel the liveried doorman looked Youssef over with a barely disguised sneer. Once, back in Alexandria, no lackey would have failed to fawn on the young scion of the al-Masris. But Youssef was long out of practice at appearing to know and have it all. In a gilded lobby mirror he peered at his reflection. His well-pressed khaki trousers were a bit short. His heavy cotton shirt was shabby. His jacket was out of style and wet from the rain. His clothes were adequate for his station as a social worker but clearly not good enough for the King David. Surely they—and he—were not going to be good enough for his mother.

He called up to the suite of Madame Leah Nakattawi. She was breakfasting in her room. Youssef should join her there. He took advantage of the opportunity for exercise and ran up the four flights of stairs. He was a little out of breath when he knocked on his mother's door.

"Entrez!" Leah, as always, still clung to her French. Last night at the airport she had already informed him that his accent had become *très déclassé.* In between gasping at how afraid she had been of being hijacked or gunned down while waiting for her luggage, she had chided him that he really should work on his French accent.

She was seated at a table in the center of the room. It was seven o'clock in the morning, yet his mother was turned out with as much care as if it were opening night at the Opéra. Her makeup was flawless, her lavender silk dressing gown cascaded to the floor, and every hair on her head was precisely where she wished it to be. "Mama!" When he bent to kiss her on both cheeks, her skin felt as papery as a corpse.

With disgust she appraised his clothes and complained first of the coffee, then of the croissants. Youssef agreed that the Nescafé was third-rate. He proposed they order Arab coffee.

She frowned. *"Jamais!* Nothing that reminds me of *there.* My husband used to drink it. Joshua was always going on and on about Egypt."

For a moment, assuming that she was making some reference to his own father, Youssef was confused. But she was remembering the man who had made her wife and widow a second time. Three years after Rafael's death, she had married the man who had been considered good enough to invite to dinner at the Villa al-Masri only once. But even before the first Palestine war, Joshua Nakattawi had been prudent enough to begin transferring profits from his Alexandria department store to a Swiss bank account. When he first fled Egypt, he had invested his savings in the Dutch diamond-cutting business. By the time he ran into Leah in a Parisian *émigré* salon, he had more than doubled his money. First as an act of charity, later as an act of love, he had begun to support Leah and the girls. He made the liaison official when his long-suffering wife Sarah finally died. Youssef supposed there were greater betrayals than his mother's. She had abandoned Alexandria—and all of *them*—when that life went sour. But at least she had taken care of the girls. "How are my sisters? Last night you spoke only of their marriages and their children. How *are* Rachel and Lisabet?"

"Oh," Leah said airly, "they're fine. Just fine. I told you that Lisabet lives in Geneva, *n'est-ce pas?* Taxes. The Swiss are so much better than the French about money." A shadow crossed her face. "Less anti-Semitic, too. The boys are in school there. The lake is as lovely as ever."

"But what is Lisabet *like?*"

"Pretty. Very pretty. She has my looks."

Youssef smiled indulgently. He had forgotten how breathlessly pretty his mother had been. Once—yes, once—he had admired her so.

"Rachel, I think, must take after your father's side of the family. She's turned to fat. Tch!"

"I've gained a little weight myself." Afraid of his mother's censure, he sipped his coffee without his customary sugar. "You see her often?"

"Every day. Her children are fat, too. She has a fabulous cook. What she should do is fire that man. Or give him to me. But she won't listen. She just keeps filling her face. She's so greedy. She reminds me of your father."

"Father was thin."

"But greedy in other ways." There was a silence. "He's buried here," Leah said.

"Yes."

"On the Mount of Olives? I hear that's *the* place."

Leave it to his mother to know the best of everything, even the best place to molder to dust. "Father died when the Mount of Olives—and all of what we call the Holy Places—was under Jordanian control. He was buried on another hill. At state expense."

She raised her eyebrows. "I should not have thought that Rafael would end like that."

"Uncle Baruch," Youssef said, delicately changing the subject to the relative he still missed the most. "Have you heard from him?"

She gave a Gallic shrug. "Not for years. He let me know in no uncertain terms that he would not write to me again."

"The same with me. I suppose we can't blame him. It can't be easy there. But at least he had the courage to stay."

"He always was a fool. Now he's a *Muslim* fool. If he had to convert, why couldn't he have become a Christian?" Leah's voice was wistful. "He writes to Lisabet. Her husband's a Gentile."

"So what's the news from Egypt?"

"Baruch's in Cairo. When Abbas died—"

"When? And how? Old Abbas!"

"I can't be expected to remember something as trivial as *that.*" Leah carefully dabbed at her lips with a linen napkin.

So Abbas was dead. He, too, had opposed the marriage to Mona. If it hadn't been for the three of them—his dead father and Abbas along with his mother here—he and Mona would have been man and wife.

Leah seemed to read his mind. "What about, *chéri,* that little Arab girl of yours?" She rolled her eyes. "Your first *mésalliance?*"

Youssef gripped the bone-china handle of his coffee cup. He still felt a twinge when he thought of her. Sometimes, when the loneliness got the better of him, he would take out their old wedding ring and sigh over what was lost. But he did not allow himself to do that very often. Again, now, he changed the subject. "I suppose you'd like to visit Father's grave."

"No." Leah shuddered. "I detest cemeteries."

"Daoud's grave isn't far from Father's."

"Poor little Daoud. To die so young. And for nothing. He was always nothing."

"Daoud," Youssef said stiffly, "was *something*. I think that I would die a happy man if I had a son like Daoud."

"Death. All this talk of death." Leah forced a bright smile. "I didn't come here for that."

"Perhaps I could help more," Youssef said diplomatically, "if I knew just why you *have* come."

"Why," Leah said gaily, "to see *you!* And, of course, for the sights. I've been all over the world, and never to Jerusalem. People are always surprised when I tell them I've never been here. I suppose they think that every Jew belongs here."

Youssef smiled. "Maybe they're right."

"Oh, God, Youssef, not *you,* too! I could see Rafael and Daoud swallowing all that Zionism. But you? No. You're too much like me. You always were." She chucked him under the chin with her long fingernails. "You still are!"

He touched his chin to see if she had drawn blood. Was she the source of what he had tried to shake for so many years? Did the emptiness that still haunted him sometimes come from the genes of this silly painted old woman? Maybe once they *had* been alike. But maybe all the sadness he had endured was worth it, if in the process he had become different from her. If it had been possible for him to live life as his mother had, maybe he would have ended up just as she was now.

But all Youssef's years of manners—so carefully learned, so deeply ingrained—came to his rescue. She was here for only a few days. She was his mother. He might never see her again. "You flatter me, Mama."

She laughed, pleased at what she took for a compliment. "You're a terrible correspondent, Youssef. So few letters over so many years. Aside from that unfortunate marriage of yours, I know so little about your life. I was so relieved at your divorce. A little Polish Communist for *my* daughter-in-law?"

"Socialist, Mama. And three little Polish—no, Israeli—socialist granddaughters."

"Your girls. Are they pretty?"

Youssef nodded.

"How pretty?"

She would not rest until she could compare herself with them. "See for yourself." He opened his wallet and handed her his photographs. "Ayala is the oldest. She lives with me here in the city."

Leah smiled at the image of the sweet-faced blonde. "That one is like *us,* Youssef."

"Naim's almost nine, but she's still our baby. A little butterball. She reminds me of Batata."

"*Oui.*" Leah sighed.

"That one's Talli. She's bold, like her mother. But, thank God, she's easier to get along with."

Leah studied the slim, tanned, sloe-eyed girl. "She looks foreign." Leah put down the pictures. "While we're on the subject of the women in my son's lives . . . tell me about Daoud's wife. I can never remember her name."

He slapped the snapshots back in his wallet. "Simha. You know that, Mama. You remember her name very well."

"Some things I suppose one *wants* to forget. I *do* remember that she was Moroccan. Was she *noir?*"

"She was—no, *is*—just about as dark-skinned as my sisters' old French tutor. Surely you remember him. He was the one you left us for when you went running off to Paris."

"You're not as charming as you once were, Youssef. You seem to have picked up some bad habits in this country."

Restlessly he walked to the door leading to the balcony. "I've seen the walls of the Old City from just about every possible angle. But never before from here. I think that maybe this is the best view of all." His lips turned up in an almost smile. "But then, that's what I always say. I suppose I just like to look at the Old City. Come here, Mama. You don't want to miss this." He tried not to notice how hard it seemed for her to stand up and hobble to the window. She had moved with more grace last night. Had that been—or was *this*—an act?

The morning light shimmered on the gold and silver domes. Minarets and cupolas and spires reached into the gray sky. But it was the thousands of prickly television antennas that caught Leah's eye. "They should do something about those aerials. They're so ugly. And it's all so *dirty!*"

Youssef's patience was nearing an end. If his mother cared so little about her family, if she refused to be moved by what lay before her very eyes, he couldn't imagine why she had come here.

She saw the look on his face. "Once on the Riviera, Youssef, I saw King Faruk. He was so fat that his toadies almost had to carry him around on a litter. And he had been so *magnifique* when he was young. When I was young, too. When I danced in the moonlight with the king. He's dead now. Faruk is dead." She swayed and caught at Youssef's shoulder. "Everything has been such a disappointment. Don't you be, too." Her shell seemed to crack with her voice. "I'm dying. Cancer.

It's in my bones. I came here to see you before I died. I'm so afraid, Youssef. I don't want to die!"

He put his arms around his mother and tried to feel as much sympathy for her as he would for one of the frightened old Moroccan grandmothers of Musrara. He would do his best to comfort his mother. It was probably never easy to die. It must be especially hard for his mother. Remembering how it had felt to be hollow, he held her with a delicate tenderness that could not crush. She would be with him for two weeks, until the Yom Kippur holidays were over. He could manage to be a good son for that long.

On Yom Kippur, Leah, Youssef, and Ayala walked through the Jewish cemetery on the Mountain of Rest. The three generations—one old and blond and faltering, one middle-aged and blond and uncertain, one young and blond and vibrant—stood over the grave of Rafael Ben-Yehuda.

"What was my grandfather like?" Ayala asked.

"Rafael?" Leah tried to laugh. "Don't ask me. I was only his wife."

"In Egypt he was very rich. In Israel he was very poor." Youssef thought for a moment. "I suppose he would have liked to be remembered as an ardent Zionist. Once he was brave enough, or foolish enough, to plot to blow up half of Alexandria. But when I think of him, it's as a very important man in Egypt. A cotton king."

"Is that how you remember him?" Leah shook her head. "Not me. He didn't have it in him to be a king of anything." Behind her heavy makeup, her eyes were bitter. But then she turned to Ayala with some of her old sparkle. "There are things you don't know about your old grandmother. When I was your age—no, just a little older—once a *real* king romanced me. King Faruk. Once . . ." She stopped her reminiscence when she saw Ayala shrug her shoulders.

"What do I care about kings? But at school we're studying how the Arabs expelled all the Jews after the War of Independence. What about that? My father never talks to me about Egypt. Maybe you'll tell me, Grandmother. What was it like?"

"Once it was heaven. Your own father, Ayala, always used to have two or three belly dancers in his sports car. Now, *he* was a little prince! Alexandria!" Leah sighed as she stared down at where Rafael lay. "Then it all fell apart. Do you remember, Youssef, how your father called me a 'daughter of darkness' after Batata died?"

"I remember," Youssef said. "I remember everything."

"And that awful day on the Cotton Exchange!"

"What's that?" Ayala asked.

"Ancient history," Youssef said.

"*My* history," Ayala retorted. "Tell me. I want to know."

Reluctantly Youssef told her. "After the '48 war, feelings were running high against the Jews. On the day the government banned Jews from the Cotton Exchange, your grandfather and I tried to go in. There was . . . an incident. Your grandfather insulted the Arabs at the door, and one thing led to another. They made him wash the doorkeeper's feet."

"No wonder you left Egypt!" Ayala's eyes flashed. "So it was just as they tell us in school. Even then, the Arabs hated us."

"No," Youssef said. "It wasn't like that. It was a lot more complicated than that."

"Certainly the Arabs hated us, Youssef." Leah dug her cane into the crust of Jerusalem soil. "You just could never see it. That Mona had you bewitched. What was it you used to call her? 'Your little gazelle'— that was it."

"What?" Ayala took her father's arm. "Gazelle. That's what you named me. Who was Mona?"

"A girl I used to know."

"A pretty little Arab," Leah said. "He was crazy about her. If your grandfather and I hadn't stepped in, I actually think he would have married her."

Ayala stared in fascination at her father. She had never thought of him being young or in love or coupled with anyone other than her mother. She opened her mouth to start grilling her father about Mona, but then she heard a shout from not far away.

"War!" A man was waving a transistor radio. "War! The Arabs have crossed the Canal!"

Youssef and Ayala looked at one another in alarm.

"I can't believe it, I can't believe it," the man with the radio was mumbling over and over as he walked toward them in a daze. Ayala snatched the radio and turned up the volume. Egyptian troops had just burst through the supposedly impregnable Israeli defenses on the east bank of the Suez.

Youssef broke into a run.

"Youssef?" Leah, who had not understood a word of the news in Hebrew, querulously called out to her son. "Where are you going? Youssef!"

Ayala took her grandmother's arm and turned to lead her out of the cemetery. "I think he's going to war."

"You'll be seeing the kibbutz at its best," Youssef said as he swung his mother's rented car up the road to Chozrim. In the seven years since he had left the kibbutz, Youssef had not been back even to pick up the children. He had missed the kibbutz so much that he hadn't trusted himself to revisit it. It was only because it was one of his mother's dying wishes—Leah had a never-ending list of dying wishes—that he had agreed to bring her here today.

"All the flowers will be in bloom," Ayala said. "My grandmother—my other grandmother—plants most of them. She even planted some of these trees along the road."

"Another industrious Israeli," Leah said with distaste. She had intended visiting Israel for only a fortnight but had stayed five months. At first she had been stranded when the October War had suspended commercial air traffic. Later, as her cancer had worsened, she had lingered for months at the Hadassah Medical Center.

Youssef looked anxiously over at his mother. He had been so afraid she would die while he was on active duty during the war. But then, those terrible weeks of war had been fraught with more cataclysmic fears. More than once, especially at first when the Arabs had been winning, he had wished he were fighting on the front lines instead of translating Arabic broadcasts. This war was so different from the last. This was a war that Israel had very nearly lost. Even though at the end the Israelis had turned the tide and had been in a position even to conquer Cairo, what mattered more was that Israel had been proved vulnerable. Maybe peace now seemed more elusive than ever, but at the same time it had become more imperative. Youssef looked out at Chozrim, where seven years ago he had been shouted down at a meeting for suggesting the time was ripe for reconciliation with the Arabs. He wondered if the members would act the same way now. But then, weary of such speculations, Youssef smiled over at his mother. She had lost thirty-five pounds in the last few months. The doctors said her current remission wouldn't last. "How do you feel?"

Leah pulled a mirror out of her handbag and patted her hair back in place. "A better question," she said tartly, "is how do I look?"

"Beautiful, of course." Ayala squeezed her grandmother's arm. In her months of nursing her grandmother, Ayala had concluded that flattery worked better on her than chemotherapy.

"I look like an old woman. A dying old woman. What will your sisters think, seeing me like this for the first time? I shouldn't have come."

Ayala ignored the old woman's fretfulness and continued to point out the kibbutz landmarks. Youssef noted with astonishment the many changes in Chozrim. There were new housing clusters, a second factory, and a museum to commemorate the battle here during the '48 war. The laundry looked large enough to accommodate the dirty wash of Tel Aviv. Even the dairy barns had a fresh coat of paint.

"Shabby," Leah said. "Is every kibbutz this shabby?"

Youssef tried to see Chozrim through his mother's eyes. There had been *déjà vu* in squiring her around Israel these last few weeks. She had complained of the spartan ugliness of the cities, the rudeness of the people, even the parched rockiness of most of the scenery. Youssef remembered well when he, too, had carped just so about Israel. But instead of agreeing with his mother, he heard himself frequently leaping to his country's defense. He looked again out the window at Chozrim. Maybe the kibbutz did look too utilitarian. Certainly it was no match for Paris. But there was pride in every blade of grass. "We like it," Youssef said.

Ayala looked hopefully over at her father. She and her sisters had always dreamed that someday their father would come back here again to live. But they had been told about the bad feelings that had surrounded his departure. A man or a woman who had left a kibbutz under a cloud hardly ever came back. Besides, she doubted if even an enlarged Chozrim was big enough to contain both her mother and her father.

Talli and Naim were upon them before they even parked the car.

"So big!" Leah peered out at her granddaughters. "My God, Youssef, your children are giants." She reached out the window and touched Naim's black hair. "You're so like your Uncle Batata. My youngest son."

Talli nudged Naim. "You know. The martyr. The one in the scrapbook from Egypt."

Youssef helped Leah from the car, and she gripped Talli's chin. She studied the angles of her face. "It looks as if the gypsies left you."

Talli broke into what she thought was a brilliant improvisation of a gypsy dance.

Leah laughed. "Yes. I can see that we *are* related. Back in Alexandria . . ." Suddenly Leah leaned her head on Youssef's shoulder and began to cry. "They're so young! So young!"

Youssef told the girls to go and make them tea while he showed their grandmother around the kibbutz. He picked Leah up in his arms.

At the crest of Monument Hill, Youssef and his mother sank down on a bench.

Youssef looked around, awash in memories. He used to like to come up here and think. He used to look south to the Egyptian border and Gaza. He used to look west at the Mediterranean and take comfort that Alexandria was a boatride away. It was here that he had decided not to fight in the '67 war. It was here that he had first kissed Rivka. "Rivka . . ." He didn't realize that he had said her name out loud.

Leah pulled out her compact and powdered away the remains of the tears. But she had heard what her son had said. "You're so secretive, Youssef. That Rivka. Tell me. Was it a very bad marriage?"

He shrugged his eyebrows. "She gave me the girls."

"I was married twice. Neither one was any great success. Maybe you and I don't have much wedded bliss in us." She smiled almost coquettishly. "I was always much better at love affairs. You were, too."

"Maybe." Youssef looked out again at the Mediterranean. Once he had sat here and dreamed of sailing home to Mona and Egypt.

"You never got over that first one, that Mona, did you?"

His eyes clouded. "No."

"I suppose you think I failed you that day when you told us you wanted to marry her." Leah took her son's hand. "I was never much good to you, was I, Youssef?"

"I was never much good to myself."

"But maybe I can make up for that now." Leah cleared her throat. "I've decided to leave you my money. Rachel and Lisabet don't need it. You'll get about three million francs. You'll be a rich man, Youssef. My little prince will be able to live like a king again."

"Leave your money to me?" Youssef took his mother's wasted face between the palms of his hands and looked into her cold eyes. All that money hadn't redeemed her life. What use could it be to him? Money couldn't buy back his youth. Even three million francs couldn't carry him back over the closed border to Mona and Baruch. It couldn't bring back Daoud or even let him live contented and without doubts. Yet he supposed that much money could change his life in some ways. The irony was that he wasn't sure he wanted or could endure much more change. He had tried so hard to carve his life into what Daoud had once called "a peace of his own making." Yet he still hadn't altogether succeeded. He stared into his mother's eyes. She, too, had found life such a disappointment.

"Rich, Youssef! I'll make you rich!"

Youssef kissed his mother on both cheeks. The old woman had so little time left. He would do his best to pretend to her that her final legacy was enough to make up for all those other things he had inherited from his mother.

Ayala and Reuven were in the lead, Talli was close behind, and then came Naim. Youssef played his flashlight on the trail that seemed to curl up and away to infinity. He gasped to catch his breath as he called out to Sasha, "We're almost there. Almost to the top. If Moses could do it, so can we."

They had crawled out of their sleeping bags at two o'clock in the morning and set out on the well-worn path to the summit of Mount Moses in the heart of the Sinai. Leah had died in late spring, and Youssef was using some of his inheritance to treat his family and friends to a holiday through some of the most awesome terrain in the world. Once the children of Israel, after their escape from Egypt, had wandered the Sinai for forty years before finally being shown the Promised Land. Youssef and his companions were making do with a week careening around the occupied Egyptian territory that hardy Israelis had turned into a wilderness playground. There were bus tours of the Sinai, organized hikes through the Sinai, even camel treks through the high plateaus of the Sinai. But Youssef and his family had hired a retired army jeep and a retired army scout to show them the glories of this desert wasteland that had been a battleground for four Mideast wars. Yet it was not the wars of the Sinai but the peace—the utter spiritual peace of this virtually untouched virgin land—that had moved them. They had swum over coral reefs in the Bay of Sharks, camped out under the moonless velvet skies, and stood wonderstruck in cathedrals and canyons of stone. Now they were about to have what everyone said was the most gloriously mystical experience in the world: sunrise at the top of the very mountain where Moses had seen the burning bush and been given the Ten Commandments.

But the climb was not easy. Youssef squinted down the trail for Sasha. The old man needed time to catch up. "Rest!" Youssef shouted. "I have to take a rest."

He sank down on a rock and watched as the three girls and Reuven danced down to him in flushed excitement. Talli aimed the fancy new camera he had bought her. Naim pulled chocolate bars from her pocket. Ayala unscrewed the canteen and passed it around. At last a puffing Sasha stumbled into sight and threw himself down beside Youssef. "I was meditating," Sasha explained.

"Sure you were." Youssef grinned at Sasha. He had not forgotten Sasha's loyalty in those dark days when he had decided to leave the kibbutz. Even after the divorce from Rivka, Sasha had remained a faithful friend. Back at Kibbutz Chozrim, Sasha had taken it upon himself to watch over Youssef's daughters.

Talli insisted they group together for a family portrait. But just before she snapped the photograph, Naim ducked out of range. "No. No pictures. Not without Mother. It's not right without Mother here."

"Naim!" Ayala scolded her little sister and put a reassuring arm around her father's shoulder. She still wasn't sure how he felt about their mother's recent—and most surprising—marriage to Colonel Barton. There was, she knew, some ancient grudge between her father and the colonel. "You know she couldn't come. You know she's on her honeymoon."

Youssef tried to soothe his youngest daughter. "I feel the same way you do, Naim. I invited them. But the colonel decided against it."

"Him!" Talli snorted. She still couldn't believe her mother could marry anyone as old and stern as Colonel Barton. Everyone on the kibbutz had been shocked. No one had known the two of them were even courting.

"He took our mother away." Naim began to sniffle. "It's not the same on the kibbutz without Mother."

"I'll say it's not the same!" Talli whooped with joy.

Ayala patted Naim's hand. "You want Mother to be happy, don't you? Remember how her face looked the day she got married."

"I've never seen her smile like that!" Talli giggled. "*My* mother a *bride!* I just hope Colonel Barton knows what he's getting into."

"But she's gone!" A tear slipped down Naim's cheek. "Now it's like we're orphans. Daddy doesn't live with us. And neither does she! We're all alone."

Ayala, Reuven, and Sasha exchanged glances. When Reuven nodded as if to encourage her to go on, Ayala bent her head close to Youssef's. "Father? We've been thinking . . . all of us . . . Reuven, too . . . that maybe now that Mother's living in Haifa, you might come back to the kibbutz."

"Chozrim?" Youssef rubbed his chin with his hand. "Come back? To the kibbutz?" He shook his head more in surprise than refusal.

"We could all be together," Naim said.

"The way it used to be," Talli added.

"I miss the kibbutz." Ayala was holding her young man's hand. "And Reuven could come and live there, too."

"We'd like to have you, Yossi," Sasha said. "We've talked about it at a Saturday-night meeting. Most of the members—not all of them, mind you, but *most*—think now that it was a mistake to let you leave as you did."

Youssef was silent as he remembered the trauma of his last Saturday-night meeting at the kibbutz. Could Chozrim have changed so much?

"We've done some soul-searching since the last war," Sasha continued. "I like to think we've all grown up a little. I know it wouldn't be easy to come back. But we need you. And I like to think that maybe you need us."

"The sun!" Reuven saved Youssef from having to answer too quickly by pointing to the sky. "The sun's almost up. Come on! We have to get to the top for the sunrise."

Talli and Naim scrambled up the path. Ayala put her arm around Sasha for the last leg of the difficult climb. Reuven linked his arm in Youssef's. "Father? Can I call you Father? Will you let me help you, Father?"

Youssef ducked his head so Reuven would not see how moved he was. In the thin clear air near the crest of the mountain he was almost dizzy with emotion. His children, Sasha, his old brothers and sisters on the kibbutz wanted him to come home? He didn't need time to think it over. He would do as they asked; he would do as he wanted; he would return to the kibbutz he had never ceased to love. And Reuven had called him Father! Youssef allowed the young man to guide him along the trail. It wasn't only his daughter who was in good hands with this Reuven. It was good to lean on this strong young man. How he had always longed for a son!

They all stood in a huddled knot on the windswept mountain and watched in a hush as shards of light broke over the green and brown and now golden nests of misty mountains to the east. As they held their breaths, the sun rose.

"Let there be light," Reuven said.

384

Ayala kissed him on the lips, then rested her head dreamily on his shoulder.

"Look at it!" Talli pirouetted and held out her hands as if to embrace the sun, the air, the mountains. "Sinai! Our Sinai! Ours!"

"Egypt's," Youssef said in a whisper. "Not ours. Egypt's."

"If there's ever to be peace," Sasha said, "someday we'll have to give it back."

"Give this back?" Talli shouted. "Never! Never again!"

Youssef shivered to hear his own daughter utter the war cry that Isareli soldiers had made their own. Some army units, before they took their oath of allegiance, ran up the mountain at Masada where once Jews had committed mass suicide rather than surrender. "Never again!" the soldiers all shouted at the crest of Masada.

Youssef looked around the barren mountaintop. It was here or on a mountaintop near here that the moral commandments that were to provide an ethical guide for much of the world had first been written on stone. Thou shalt not kill, steal, commit adultery, bear false witness against God or man. Youssef regretted that there had not been a few more commandments to come from this mountaintop. Thou shalt not wage war. Thou shalt not covet thy neighbor's land. Thus shalt forgive thy enemies and thy friends. Youssef looked north toward Israel and west toward Egypt. There were tears in his eyes as he wondered if the history of the world would have been different if Moses—or God—had so commanded his people.

22

CAIRO, EGYPT / October 1975

Baruch riffled through the pages of *al-Ahram,* trying to deduce the real news behind the government propaganda. He was as adept at this word game as any full-blooded Egyptian. Baruch bypassed the political "news." First things first. He glanced at the headlines trumpeting no food shortages, then looked at the breakfast table before him. There were no eggs and sugar, although today at least there was tea. If he bothered to go to the window, he knew he would be able to see the mob of black-robed *baladi* women at the doors of the *gamiya.* They would be praying today they would be able to use their ration cards at the government store for scarce sugar, eggs, flour, butter, and tomato paste. He read further in the article. Yes, here it was: the telling contradiction. The Minister of Supply—the man Baruch always thought should be called the Minister of Shortages—said that soon the egg distribution system would be fully operative, that they expected enough meat for next month's Great Feast, that there would be more flour maybe to-morrow. Baruch tucked briny white cheese in the cavity of his flat brownish bread. It would be some time before he—and everyone else—could have a better breakfast.

He skimmed the international news, if news it was. The Israelis were shelling southern Lebanon. The PLO disowned a failed attempt to hijack a plane. One headline said there were two hundred casualties in the continuing fighting in Beirut. On the same page another story claimed the Lebanese cease-fire was holding.

Baruch eyed the photographs heralding the second anniversary of the October War. That "great Arab victory" Egyptians celebrated with such rejoicing was not altogether true, either. When the Americans and the Soviets had forced the cease-fire, the Israelis had been nearly to Cairo and could have taken Damascus as well. Yet this last war *had* restored a measure of Arab pride and dignity. Egyptians had crossed the Canal. Syrians had surged to the Golan. This time an Arab war could boast Arab heroes. Baruch stared at today's pictures of the most celebrated of those heroes.

The president was watching the biggest military parade in Egyptian history. Flanked by Vice-President Mubarak and War Minister el-Gamassay, Sadat beamed at surface-to-air missiles, midget submarines, and Mirage F-1 fighters. He smiled beatifically at paratroopers passing on the double, token armored units, and heavy artillery mounted on splendid tracked vehicles. It was just last January that crowds of workers and students, tired of inflation and food shortages, had rioted on the streets of Cairo. "Hero of the Crossing," they had screamed, "where is our breakfast?" Any half-wit who walked the streets knew Sadat was tolerated only as the architect of the October War. Sadat spawned affection only in those few who had benefited so much from the thriving black market, the tourist industry, and the construction of luxury housing. Maybe Sadat was too busy making international head-lines to take a hard look at his country's grinding poverty, its disease, its underemployment, its exploding population. But then Baruch gave Sadat the benefit of the doubt. Perhaps there was method to the seem-ing madness of his government's policies. Or perhaps there was nothing more that he—or anyone else—could do for Egypt.

Baruch looked around the new room he shared with Ali. There were two narrow cots, a table and chairs, and a metal cupboard running the length of the room. Ali at the moment was down the hall in the bath-room they shared with six other families. The communal kitchen was a few doors away. It was a far cry not only from the Villa al-Masri but even from Baruch's old two-room Cairo flat. From his thirty pounds a month salary, he used to spend twelve pounds on rent, nine pounds on cigarettes, and a meager thirty piasters a day for food. Ali's arrival had brought economies. Rent on this new room was only three pounds a month. To cut down on cigarettes he bought them singly instead of by the pack. Still, he had less than eighty piasters a day to feed himself and Ali. Even with government food subsidies, that wasn't enough for an eighteen-year-old's ferocious appetite. Baruch was reserving the last of the al-Masri porcelains for the textbooks Ali would need over the next six years and the boy's occasional trips back to Karnak.

Clearly, he had to get more money from somewhere. He didn't have the twenty-five thousand pounds it would take to set up a lucrative office-dispensary. But he supposed, like many of the other doctors at the hospital, he could moonlight. One doctor he knew even specialized in restoring hymens. For twenty pounds he would help a young woman hoodwink her husband on their wedding night. The procedure was simple and safe enough. The weding date would be set for just after the beginning of a girl's menstrual period. The doctor would sew her up while the blood flow was strong. With luck, if the girl kept her legs tightly together for a day or so, she would be able to stain the requisite bit of white cotton when the crucial moment came. For fifty pounds the physician would do a neater job of suturing a bit of sheepskin to her opening. Hastily Baruch decided he would leave that specialty to the others. He himself would merely treat common colds and fevers and aching backs from the bedroom he and Ali shared. With luck, he could earn enough to make ends meet.

Baruch rustled the newspaper pages. Each day the drumroll was sounded of projects too good to be true. Finally he found a cornucopia of domestic tidbits buried at the bottom of a page—five million pounds for low-interest reconstruction loans, four hundred thousand pounds for Alexandria's water pipes, a quarter of a million to pave roads, fifty thousand to clean Cairo's streets, two and a half million to bring water to villages still lacking it. Baruch wondered why the government bothered to write such fiction. No one believed it.

Ali entered, toweling dry his face. He munched bread and cheese and pointed to *al-Ahram.* "What's the news?"

"*Mafesh.*" Baruch wrapped their lunches of bread and cheese in the newspaper. "Nothing. Nothing is new."

Ali could hardly breathe in the smoky, sweaty air of the bus. He was wedged in between two men and one doughy woman. The rough edge of the woman's basket was digging into his arm. "*Malesh,*" the woman predictably shouted at him. She pulled a live, squawking hen out of her basket by its feet, and a wing flapped against Ali's cheek. Around them everyone laughed, so Ali obligingly forced a smile. He wondered if he was losing his sense of humor. A vaguely familiar young man with fair skin and extraordinary wet brown eyes nudged him. "Twelve thousand Cairo buses for eight million people," the boy said, smiling just enough to show his even white teeth. "Sadat!" The fellow made as if to spit. Ali, remembering that he had seen this boy in his neighborhood and on campus, almost smiled back. But then he recalled promising his mother he wouldn't dabble in politics. Dutifully Ali turned his back on the boy.

The bus lurched along the rutted road. Ali, angling for a little more space with these strangers pressed against his skin, admitted to himself his earlier enthusiasm for this city had waned. Cairo had robbed him of confidence in his own glorious destiny. Except for Baruch, he hadn't been able to make friends in his three months here. He was barely keeping up with his studies. In the spring, before he could be admitted to the medical school at Kasr el-Aini Hospital, he had to pass examinations in nine subjects, from chemistry and physics to Islamic Civilization and English. Then it would be at least six more years before he could return to Karnak as a certified doctor. Should that day ever come, he planned never again to leave the village. As Ali, son of Mona, nephew of Muhammad and Hussein, his position there had been as fixed as any star in the sky. Here he was just another dark-skinned, bewildered boy from the backwaters of Upper Egypt.

Ali sneaked a look at the handsome boy in the bus. If only he had a friend! Baruch was both more and less than a friend. His mother had said that Baruch had once been like a father to her. Was this what it was like having a father? Baruch was the only one he could talk to about everything that confused him. Baruch tutored him in his studies, counseled him with his problems, and spent his days off showing him Cairo. They made a weekly ritual of visiting different mosques for Friday prayers. Once Baruch had guided him through a forest of al-Azhar's slender columns to a knot of bearded scholars sitting in a circle of rush mats, debating how man could have free will if Allah had predetermined all that was to be. If only there could have been more moments like that in Cairo!

But Baruch had once advised him not to worry so much about being unhappy. What's important, Baruch had said, is becoming a doctor. So it hurts a little en route? So what? Only a fool thinks life should be one big happy afternoon in the sun. Ali had grumbled to himself that there were undoubtedly some rewards to being a fool.

Baruch was kind. But Baruch was sad, just as his mother had always been, too much of the time. Ali missed his mother, he missed the rest of his family, and he missed his friends. Letters weren't enough. More than anything he wanted to hear his mother's voice and walk with her along the river. As he thought of his mother, Ali longed to finger her blue bead that he still wore around his neck. But there was no way he could extricate his hand from the tangle of arms and bellies binding him. As the bus neared the Giza campus, Ali pushed his way in terror to the door. He hated jumping off the bus as it moved. He had seen boys tumble off balance onto the pavement, their arms or legs in that odd angle that portended broken bones. Once he had witnessed a truck driving over a boy as he lay groaning in the street. It was hard not to think of sudden death in Cairo.

When he hit the ground intact, Ali breathed a sigh of relief, then braced himself for the next ordeals. First chemistry, then math, history, physics, and finally English. The straight slashes of the trees in front of the university buildings were a reminder of how little greenery there was in Cairo. He thought of the long, lush lines of the sycamores along the river road to Luxor, of the soothing softness of the Nile, of the wide quilted fields of clover and cane baking in the sun. January in Cairo was so cold. It had never been cold in Karnak. For warmth he drew his chilled hands up into the sleeves of his sweater as he hurried off to class. A thousand seats in the auditorium, and still some had to sit on the floor.

In the classroom, as in the rest of Cairo, there were hints of past splendor. A worn mosaic tracery was on the floor, and the slightly cracked ceiling arch was a handsome sweep of arabesque. Carefully he chose his seat close enough to hear the professor in case the microphones weren't working again.

He hoped he wasn't the object of the giggling he could hear from the *baladi* boys behind him. He had tried so hard with those fast-talking, saucy young men who always moved in laughing herds. But all they did was mock him for his dark skin and his drawling Saidi accent. He had avoided them ever since he overheard them calling him el-Bowab, after those black Nubian and brown Saidi doorkeepers who sat on benches outside the houses of the rich. He might be a peasant from the country, but he had his pride.

He looked up as a trio of rich boys swaggered into the classroom. Once again he wondered how much they had paid for the thick gold chains they wore around their necks, for those flashy red and purple sweaters, for their tight imported blue jeans, for the transistor radios they carried in lieu of books. A whole family back in Karnak could live almost forever on what those clothes alone must have cost. Once again he doubted if what he had been told about the revolution was true. Nasser supposedly took the money and the land away from the rich, so that now all Egyptians were absolutely equal. No one seemed to have told the rich boys the news. They had never favored Ali with even a look.

He heard a droning flutter at the door, signaling the arrival of a contingent of Muslim Brothers, the *Ikhwan*. First came the men in their long white robes, their tight white turbans, their bristling black beards. Just behind them were the women in floor-length, rainbow-colored robes and white wimples. Today one woman had even her face covered in sky blue. Over the twin eye slits were perched an absurd pair of pearly glasses. Some said the Saudis paid the *Ikhwan* forty pounds a month to dress up like this. He watched the Brothers take the choice seats in the front row. They dominated the classrooms and interrupted any professor who dared utter a syllable they thought contrary to the words or spirit of the Koran. At first Ali had been not only fascinated by the Brothers but also flattered by the attention they lavished on him. He had prayed alongside them and even had visited some of them in their homes.

But even though Ali admired their piety, he had shied way from any deeper involvement with the Brothers. He didn't like their fanatic eyes and the way they hissed in low voices about the conspiracies of the godless corrupting Allah's holy laws. He liked them even less when Baruch warned him the government kept a sharp eye on the *Ikhwan*. It was as dangerous to be a Muslim Brother as it was to be a Communist. Ali didn't want to spend his life rotting in a concentration camp, or a detention center, or whatever you called those prisons in the Western Desert. He opened his notebook and slid farther down in his seat, hoping class would begin before one of the Brothers began haranguing him.

It was when he was crossing the mall on his way to his last class that he felt the tap on his shoulder and whirled around to behold the boy from the bus. "I'm Karim." He fell into step beside Ali. "We seem to be headed the same way."

"Ali." He smiled uncertainly as he tried to keep pace with Karim. He took in the thick black hair, the hawk nose, the flick of dark eyes appraising the oncoming students as if for a quick sale. Like the rich boys, Karim was wearing tight foreign blue jeans that cost seventeen pounds even in the duty-free shops at Port Said. But instead of a woolly sweater, Karim had on a navy T-shirt and an olive-drab jacket with "U.S. Army" stenciled on the flap of a pocket. "You're not American?"

Karim laughed. Again that flash of well-scrubbed teeth and this time, as well, a hint of red tongue. "Not me." There was a swagger to Karim's walk. "I'm Palestinian."

There were said to be thousands of Palestinians on the Giza campus, but this was the first who had talked to Ali. "Palestinian!" He dogged Karim's heels. This handsome boy—the handsomest boy Ali had ever seen—reeked of cologne and glamour.

"I've seen you in the neighborhood." Karim lowered his voice. "And on the bus." Again he puckered his full lips as if to spit.

Ali wanted this boy to like him. "Sadat." He, too, dared to whisper.

Karim seemed pleased. "I wasn't sure about you. You never know." He waved to some boys on the path. "There's a meeting today. If you're interested."

"Meeting?" Ali squinted at Karim.

"Just a few of the boys. Nothing official. I'm going there now." Karim stopped, offered him a Marlboro, and fired their cigarettes with the whoosh of a butane lighter. "We don't ask just anyone. I probably shouldn't have mentioned it."

Ali hesitated and drew on his cigarette. "I have English class."

"We speak Arabic." Karim smiled again, and Ali, looking helplessly into the other's eyes, allowed himself to be led toward the university gate.

Not far off campus, eight young men were sitting with glasses of tea on the floor of a small smoky room. Ali squatted beside Karim and watched and listened and hoped he wouldn't do anything wrong. He noticed that the others—dusky boys who spoke with the nasal twangs of the Persian Gulf, fat ones in gray robes who did not speak, olive-skinned fellows who needed a shave—seemed to defer to Karim. No one acknowledged Ali's presence. Through a babble of voices Karim was saying something about eighty pounds a month and Iraq and honor. Someone muttered that the Syrians were paying a hundred pounds. Karim spit on the floor, and there was laughter as Ali was handed a joint of hashish for his own. He puffed and felt the dreamy slowness steal over him. "By living you learn to die," Karim was saying. "And by dying you learn to live." The light filtering in from the window had lessened, and Karim's face was in shadows. Such eyes he had. Such fierce and tender eyes. The tea was sticky on Ali's furry tongue. He sighed when Karim stood up to leave.

The horns, the traffic, the rush of hurrying people were not enough to break the spell. "You had the sense not to say anything," Karim was saying as he hailed a taxi. "We need men who are discreet."

"For *what*, exactly?" Ali asked. But he knew.

Karim was haggling with a driver. He waved Ali into the back seat and put up a finger. "Later."

It was the second taxi ride of Ali's life. Karim gave the driver a cigarette, and the music on the radio drowned out any possibility of talk. The driver ran red lights, laughing. Karim leaned back in the seat and smiled with his lips at Ali. In the traffic jam of Tahrir Bridge, Ali looked out the window at the gray sparkle of the river. The hashish made a time warp of the hour. He wished he could smoke more in the taxi. Looking up at a crowded bus, he wished this luxurious ride would never end. They crawled past the machine-gun-guarded British and American embassies, down Sharia Maglis el-Omma, and alighted on a Sayeda Zainab corner by a herd of scavenging goats. Carelessly Karim peeled a one-pound note from a wad of bills tucked into the front of his jeans. "Now," Karim was saying, "for some bread and salt."

Ali was dazed with happiness. Bread and salt. Sharing bread and salt, by Egyptian custom, sealed a friendship forever.

Karim strode past Baruch's building and turned down a dark and narrow unpaved alley. Ragged little boys threw a ball back and forth. Foot-tapping *baladi* music drifted down from an open window. Damp laundry flapped over their heads. Sly dogs slunk close to the walls.

"You've read Gorky?" Karim asked after a while.

"No." Ali had never even heard of Gorky.

"I'll lend some to you. You should read Gorky. It's like this. Even in Russia, maybe especially in Russia, it was like this."

Karim turned right again through an ash-colored hole in the wall. They stepped over three motionless women sitting in the dust. "My aunts," Karim explained with a wave of his hand. They walked single-file along a passage that snaked as far ahead as Ali could see, with doors and ladders and huddles of women indicating the residence of a great number of families. Karim stopped at a door and pounded. There was a shuffle, and the door was opened by a fat woman. "My mother."

Ali tried to hide his surprise as he mumbled her the ritual greetings. He thought Karim would have sprung from someone more grand. In the room, too, he had expected something better. The mudbrick walls had been carelessly half-plastered, then painted in spots with a color that might once have been pink. A long wooden table covered with pots and jugs and old newspapers sat squarely in the center of the room. Against the walls were benches topped with straw mats. On them slept boys much younger than Karim. "My brothers." He shouted to his mother to prepare tea and food, whispering to Ali as they filed into the back room that the old woman was nearly deaf. There was a double bed, two padded chairs, and hundreds of books lying in heaps on the floor. Ali glanced down at the titles. Some were in Arabic, others in English, French, and a language he had seen before only on cardboard cartons. He picked up one of them. "What's this?"

"Russian."

"You know Russian?"

"No," Karim admitted. "And I can't read much French or English either. I just like books."

The walls were studded with photographs, some framed, some merely nailed to the cracked plaster. Ali guessed they were all of Karim. A bald baby Karim. A little boy Karim. A Karim as he was now, shot from every conceivable angle. Ali didn't even have a single snapshot of himself. But he couldn't blame Karim for having so many. If he looked like Karim, he, too, might arrange a gallery of his own photographs.

"My room," Karim said, lighting stubs of candles. "Do you like it?"

"Very nice. But the rest of the family all sleep in the other room? And you have this one all to yourself?"

"I'm the man of the family. I get the bed."

That explained it. "Your father is dead?" Karim nodded and Ali smiled. "Mine, too. He died before I was born. What about yours?"

Karim was yelling to his mother for the tea. She silently shuffled in with the two glasses, then left them alone again. Karim was launching into a stream of complaints about the university. The classes were too crowded. The teachers were reactionary. It was impossible to get anything he needed from the library. "Every day I go there and I think to myself that this is the greatest university in the Arab world. And yet look at it! It's a disgrace."

Ali didn't have to answer, for Karim was on his feet again, pulling a cassette recorder out from under his bed. "You like Bob Dylan?"

"I don't know. I like Egyptian music."

"You'll like Bob Dylan, too," Karim promised. He rummaged through a basketful of cassettes and fitted one in the machine. Intense, whiny, off-key music filled the air. "Passion. Need. Hear that passion!" Karim pounded his fingers on his thigh in time to Bob Dylan.

Ali was more fascinated by Karim than by this strange music. He was trying to find the right words to comment on Bob Dylan when Karim was on his feet again, pacing back and forth.

"This music makes me crazy. Do you hear it? Do you feel it? Ah!" Suddenly he wheeled on Ali. "Well, you've had enough time to think it over. Are you with us?"

"I guess I'm not used to how it sounds."

Karim scowled. "Not the music. Us. The Palestinians. The meeting."

Ali took a gulp of his tea. "I'm not sure what it's all about."

Karim threw himself down on the chair next to Ali. "Freedom, that's what it's all about. Honor. Justice. *Vengeance.*" He repeated what he had said at the meeting. "By living you learn to die. And by dying you learn to live."

"You're *fedayeen?*"

Karim threw him a superior smile. "They'll make posters with my picture, Ali." Karim glanced at the walls. "Better pictures than these. In color. I look good in uniform. They'll put my poster up on the walls, in the streets of Beirut, Amman, Damascus, Baghdad. Everywhere my people are. At least that's *something.* Who knows? Maybe you'll even see some here in Cairo. You'll be walking down the street, and you'll look up, and there I'll be. And maybe you'll feel sad when you remember how we sat here today."

Ali bit his lip. Karim must mean those "martyr" wall posters he had seen of Palestinian commandos killed in action.

Karim pulled a carton out from under his bed. "Here's one of me training in the Lebanon." He threw Ali a black-and-white shot of a younger Karim with a rifle slung on his shoulder. "And this one is in Algeria last summer. I think it's the best. It's in color." This time Karim was posed aiming a submachine gun at the camera.

"Fatah," Ali said, looking at the camouflage green-and-brown trousers in the photograph. "This is Fatah's uniform?"

Karim snorted. "You think I'm in Fatah?"

"You tell me."

"I can see you need some educating." He turned away from his photographs with some reluctance and sat down again next to Ali. "Fatah—Arafat's group—is the biggest and, I think, used to be the best. They were the first to start the raids on a large scale. But then Arafat started playing politics more than fighting the Zionists. Fatah got cozy—too cozy—first with the Syrians and later with Nasser. Then Arafat took over the PLO, and although Arafat is a great leader, our best leader, *a great man,* he doesn't order enough raids now. He keeps his boys on a tight leash. We think he'll jump at the first chance to negotiate with the Zionists."

"We?" Ali prompted.

"I'm ALF—Arab Liberation Front. *We* don't make compromises. *We're* in it to the end. Wars of national liberation, Ali. All over the Middle East. Arab brotherhood, Ali. None of Arafat's mincing around about a negotiated settlement for *us.* In Baghdad—"

"So you're aligned with the Iraqis?"

"Iraqi brothers give us money, arms, everything. The Baath Party has been a big help, especially since they started getting all that aid from the Russians. It used to be that Fatah, with their filthy Saudi riyals, were the only ones who could afford the best weapons and uniforms. But now someday we'll be on top."

"So that was an ALF meeting today?"

"We're recruiting. Usually I don't invite anyone I'm not sure of. But with you, Ali, I was . . . very sure, right away." Karim's lips turned up in a smile. "I get one hundred and twenty pounds a month. But we'll pay you eighty—now, while you're still in school. Later—when you're on active duty—you'll get even more."

"Aren't you afraid the secret police will arrest you?"

In the shadows Karim's brown eyes had changed green like a cat's. He whispered, "I'll tell you a secret. Sadat's in on it, too. Half our salaries come from Iraq, the rest from the Egyptian government. You see, the ALF is the rival of el-Saiqa, the Syrian Baath Party *fedayeen.* Cairo doesn't want to see the Syrians get any more powerful than they already are. The Egyptians can't support us openly—you know how crazy Sadat is for dollars—but he helps us on the sly. It's safe, Ali. As safe as working in a government office."

Ali felt dizzy. Fatah, ALF, PLO, el-Saiqa, Sadat? He shook his head. "Politics. They're not for me. I just want to be a doctor and go back to my village."

"A doctor?" Karim brightened. "We need doctors."

"So does my village." He hesitated. "It's not that I don't sympathize." He looked over at the photographs. His grandmother, his uncles, all the villagers would be proud. But would his mother? He touched her blue bead and shook his head again, this time more firmly. "No, Karim. Sorry. It's not for me. All I want is in my village."

Karim's mother waddled in with a round tin tray cluttered with dishes of meat, rice, macaroni, and salads. They washed their hands, ate in silence, and lit a pair of Karim's Marlboros. Regretfully Ali told himself it was time to leave.

But Karim was not through with him. He ordered more tea from his mother and peppered Ali with questions about his village. What was it like at dawn on the river? On market days? What did the old men talk about? How was it in the fields? What were the jokes? And why, *why* was he so eager to return to it? Ali relaxed and talked of Karnak. As he wound up a story of swimming in the Nile on a glorious, starlit Ramadan night, Karim smiled. "I like you, Ali. And do you know why?"

Ali leaned forward in his seat, eager that Karim was going to tell him something splendid he had never realized about himself.

"Because you're normal," Karim said.

"Normal?" Ali was deeply disappointed.

"Yes. Normal. You're lucky. Very lucky. When you pray every day, make sure you thank Allah for that. You don't know what a gift that is." Karim's eyes were pools of darkness. "I and all my people lost our past when we lost our country. Maybe if you tell me how it is in your village, I can know how it was in mine."

Karim looked so sad that Ali wanted to stroke his hair and smooth out the lines in his forehead. Their eyes met, and they both smiled.

"Bread and salt?" Karim offered Ali his hand.

Ali slapped his on top of Karim's. It was a pact. They would not be comrades in arms but nonetheless they would be friends.

Mona and Ali sat becalmed in the belly of the felucca drifting in midstream. On this, Ali's fourth day home, they were off on a sail south to lush Banana Island. Uncle Hussein, who never let the villagers use his tourist feluccas for their private pleasure, had insisted that the doctor-in-training be his guest. Ali was now a great man in the village.

Mona leaned back against the wooden hull, rapt at every word that issued from her son's mouth. He had finally succeeded in growing a mustache. He was enough taller that his *gallabeiya* showed his ankle bones. He had passed his first-year examinations and was bursting with tales of adventure and triumph. In his eagerness to tell her everything, he skipped from story to story like *fool* beans hopping in hot fat. He mimicked the Muslim Brothers—dire, pious, bristling with indignation—entering a classroom. The boat rocked as he showed her how the Sufis danced the night of the Prophet's Birthday. He snapped his fingers and laughed and told jokes about his bumpkin behavior in those first months away from her. He was as Youssef had once been —so *sure*, so eager, so deft. Tears stung her eyes.

He was touched, thinking that she cried because he loved being away from her. In his absence Karnak had grown smaller but his mother had grown dearer. Unlike the others—the women who were babbling the old clichés about marriage and babies, the men who were repeating the old complaints about money and crops—his mother *understood*. She, too, had lived apart from the Said. While she was eager for the most minute details of his life in Cairo, the eyes of the others glazed over just as he was beginning to tell them what it was like away from the village. He trusted her enough to tell her what he didn't like about Cairo: the bus accidents and the cats screaming at night, the *baladi* boys who mocked him, and the terrifying babble of lectures delivered in English. He described the rich boys at the university and how wrong it was that some lived like pashas in Garden City while others made do in hovels in Sayeda Zainab. "Was Alexandria like that, Mother?"

She trailed her hand in the water. Baruch had once asked her if Alexandria had been Paradise. She must not think of that. "I was living with the rich myself, in a villa as grand as a palace. But I remember when I was just a little girl and my mother left me there. I vomited every day for three months."

"Allah!" He had never thought of his mother being a lost little girl. She looked so sad, remembering. He shouldn't have reminded her of another life in another place. He changed the subject. "You know, sometimes I pretend that Baruch is really my father."

She seemed to grow sadder still. That day, years ago, when she had sat beside Baruch at the pyramids, she had refused his marriage proposal. But often she had caught herself wondering what it would be like to marry Baruch. For nineteen years she had waited for a word from Youssef. Was it right to wait forever? She sounded out her son. "There was a chance, once, that Baruch could have been your stepfather. He offered to marry me when his family left and he became a Believer."

"And you didn't do it!" There was regret in his voice.

Mona retreated in loyalty to Youssef. "Your real father had just . . . gone. I couldn't marry someone else. When you've had what I had with your father, you can't forget it." She moistened her lips. Should she tell him now? The impulse faded. "Besides, by then I just wanted to come home."

"I know. Everyone, everything, is here."

She smiled at her son. "I wanted you to have what I missed when I was very young. The peace of the village. Its certainties."

He reached over and squeezed her hand. "But to come back here after living in a palace!"

"I had you. My mother. The family. And later, I had my work. I belong here. I never altogether belonged in Alexandria." And with Youssef? She asked herself if she had ever altogether belonged with Youssef.

But Ali was voicing a fear that sometimes held him. "Didn't you wish sometimes that you hadn't come home? That maybe you didn't want the village anymore?"

She had been waiting for this and had her answer ready. "Hardest of all was living in both worlds. As you are now. But I know the Said. And I know the city. I think you'll choose the Said."

"Choose? *Choose?*" He hadn't dared to think of his return to Karnak as less than an inevitability. He stood up and pretended to search for a breeze that would send them on their way. He looked out at the palm trees, the mud huts, a line of women filling their water jugs. Give this up forever? "I'll be back. Don't worry. I'll be back. I promise you I'll be back." But he was looking north, where the river rushed to Cairo.

She searched his face and was afraid. "I'm sure it's very lonely for you in Cairo."

"At first." He squinted at the sun. "But there's Baruch. And Karim."

She tucked her robe tighter around her legs. "Tell me about your friend."

"You'd like him, Mother. He's very handsome. He studies history at the university."

"Yes?" she prompted. So far Ali had told her little of what she wanted to know about his new life in Cairo. Baruch, her trusted ally, was not a threat. She feared only cat-eyed *baladi* girls who might be scheming for her son, and boys who might be carbon copies of Hamid el-Husseini.

"Did I tell you he's very handsome?" Ali smiled to himself. "He lives near Baruch. We go to the cinema to see American Westerns." Ali pretended to pull a gun from the pocket of his *gallabeiya* and shoot at Nile fish. "He takes me out to eat kebabs. Cairo is beautiful at night, when you can't see the dirt." Ali tried to think what his mother would like to hear. "And we pray together."

"He's not a Muslim Brother?"

"Oh, no." He had heard the disapproval in her voice. "Not Karim. He's *fedayeen.*"

She tried to hide her alarm but could not. "I've told you, Ali, that the one thing I will not allow is for you to be involved in politics. I suppose this Karim tried to recruit you?"

"At first he did." Ali touched his blue bead as if it were a pledge. "Now we don't talk about that at all." It was a small lie. Sometimes Karim couldn't help talking about the training camps in Lebanon, his childhood in Gaza, his father and brother who had died for the cause. "Mostly he likes to hear about Karnak. He tells me I'm lucky *I* still have *my* village." Ali groped for a neutral fact to disarm his mother. "He likes Bob Dylan. You know Dylan?"

She would not be sidetracked. "Does Baruch know Karim's one of the *fedayeen?* And have you told Karim that Baruch was once a Jew and has family in Israel?"

"Palestine. We don't call it Israel, Mother. We call it Palestine."

She shivered in the heat. This Karim was getting to her son. "I asked you a question, Ali."

"*I* haven't told him. I have just this *one* friend. And this *one* guardian." He thanked Allah when a slight breeze began to riffle the sail. He busied himself angling it in the wind and then took hold of the rudder. "Life is difficult enough."

She sighed. She had seen a new stubbornness in his eyes. Youssef, too, had been willful. She looked away from him as the felucca skimmed over the water. It was the first time she had ever heard him say life was difficult. Boys didn't say that, but men did. She would write Baruch and ask him to try to break up this friendship. Maybe Ali would listen to Baruch. Obviously Ali thought he was too old to have to pay heed to his mother. They sat at opposite ends of the boat and did not talk.

Later, even after they had docked at the island and picked the season's first mangoes from the shiny-leafed trees, there was still an uneasiness between them. Mona made tea on the primus stove Hussein had so thoughtfully provided with his boat. It was time, she decided, to bring up the other matter. In a calm, even a distant, voice, she told Ali that Muhammad would probably die soon and that it was his wish that Ali and Soad marry before long. For a while they talked of what could and could not be done for Muhammad.

Finally Ali shook his head. "Uncle Muhammad dying! And Soad finally for my wife!" It seemed to Ali that he had been betrothed to Soad all his life.

"You like her?" Mona almost hoped he would say that he had always detested his cousin.

"How could anyone *not* like Soad? It's just that I have so long still to go in school and no money for the brideprice."

"Muhammad says your prospects are enough for him."

"Little Soad." Ali reflected that it would be a marriage like all the others in the village. Soad would not ask much of him. "What do you think, Mother?"

"Ah! You still value at least some of my opinions." But then she softened. "Do you love her, Ali?"

He smiled fondly. "She's like my sister."

"I mean, do you love her like a wife? Love, Ali. True love. There's nothing like it."

He flashed her a superior smile. "You're very sentimental."

Mona flinched. Sentimental? Was that what she was? Perhaps, she thought, perhaps I'm wrong in wanting him to wait for a great love. Maybe he doesn't want it. Maybe he's different from me. She was disappointed. She had thought he was the same.

As he drank his tea, Ali considered that his mother seemed to be saying he didn't *have* to marry Soad. Thus far he had spent little time thinking of girls. What was the use, when he couldn't touch any of them except for the one he finally married? But he had always known he would marry Soad. He remembered, however, that he was an educated man with advanced ideas. "Don't you think, Mother, that I should ask Soad first?"

He found her singing softly to herself as she stirred *fool* beans in a pot in the courtyard. Um Mona sat close by weaving her inevitable baskets. Yes, he could ask her now in the presence of a chaperon. How strange it was to have to worry about village conventions before talking to this cousin who had always been his playmate and confidante. He wished for a moment he could tweak her braids and tease her into laughter. They could climb a tree, swim the river, steal oranges in the souk. Instead, he cleared his throat uncertainly. "Soad?"

She looked up, blushed, and dropped her spoon.

Gravely he handed it back to her. "Soad."

She blushed again. "Ali."

She looked pretty with her honey-colored skin so rosy. He had never thought of her as pretty before. He studied her delicate childlike features and those new rounded breasts and thighs. He noticed she was batting her eyelashes at the pot of *fool* beans. Could Soad be flirting? When he stammered that he wanted to talk to her, she took the beans off the fire.

He sat down gingerly beside her. "Hot today."

"Yes."

"Probably hot tomorrow."

"Yes."

Shyly she was avoiding his eyes. Ali realized she was nervous, too. She must know what he was about to say. "I'll be going back to Cairo soon."

She nodded.

"I wish you could come with me."

Her eyes were dancing as she laughed up at him. Modestly she covered her mouth with her hand, but she could not hide the eagerness in her eyes.

Ali felt braver. "I want to marry you, Soad."

She sighed a deep sigh of joy but did not dare to look at him.

"Your father approves. I thought we could sign the first contract before I go back. We could be married in a year or two." He waited for her answer.

She was smiling to herself as she stared at the ground.

"Soad? Will you?"

Her smile broadened. It seemed she thought her answer too obvious for words.

Yet Ali had to hear it. He had to have her free consent. "Will you marry me?"

Her brown adoring eyes finally met his. "Oh, yes! Yes, Ali, yes! *Of course* I'll marry you!"

But as the young couple bent their heads together to laugh and dream, there was one in the courtyard who watched and listened and did not smile.

In the past few years Um Mona had lost so much of her fire that she seemed more ash than ember. Once or twice the night watchman at Karnak Temple had escorted the old woman home in the dead of night, for Um Mona haunted Sekhmet's chamber whether the moon waxed or waned. Fearful of the snakes and scorpions which were said to lurk there, Mona chided her mother as Um Mona once had scolded her. Increasingly all of them—Mona, Muhammad, Bahia, Ali—more pitied than feared the old woman.

But as she sat over her Nubian baskets, Um Mona weaved a pattern of their insults. Ali had the cheek to ask Soad to marry him, but none of them had thought to ask her permission for the match. She knew her grip over Mona—over everything—had been steadily slipping ever since her daughter had dared her to tell the others about Youssef. Ali —that haughy Jewish bastard—ignored his grandmother completely. Even Muhammad, who once had consulted her about everything, seemed to be going over to the other side. Um Mona decided they would all pay for this someday. On a day, at a time, of her own choosing, they would pay. They could make their plans. And so could she.

That summer she began to paint her baskets not brown or black but red.

23 ~~~~~~~

CAIRO, EGYPT / November 1976

A fly flitting on his face disturbed Ali's dream of his mother and the river and Karnak. His eyelids fluttered, and for a moment he wasn't sure where he was. The fly was far smaller than those in the village. But it was a persistent, maybe even a sophisticated fly. When he brushed it off his lips, it danced on his nose. It was acting like a *baladi* fly. When he flicked at it with his hand, it landed on his eyes. It was on his lips again when he heard the first wails of the dawn prayer calls that, thanks to the loudspeakers, seemed to be coming from only a few feet away. He groaned and shut his eyes. He was in Cairo. In his dream his mother, her eyes swelled by fear, had been about to tell him a secret. He tried to will himself back into the night web. "Prayer is better than sleep!" As the *muezzin* chanted, the dream receded. Damn the *muezzin!* At once Ali called back his curse. All praises to the holy message of the *muezzin!* He rubbed his eyes, saw that Baruch was still asleep, and stumbled over to the window.

In the tenuous pearly light, the fairy-tale minaret of Sayeda Zainab was ethereal. Beyond it more than ten hundred minarets rippled like whitecaps all the way to the horizon. Some gleamed like silver or burned like copper. Others pierced the ghostly sky like the needle-sharp obelisks of Karnak Temple. "I extol the perfection of Allah!" In the call of the *muezzin,* too, there was a sonorous perfection. One Ramadan nightfall he and Karim had climbed the worn, twisting staircase of Bab Zuwaila's minaret. At its crown, in the mauve-and-purple light of sunset, they had caught their breath in awe at Cairo spread before them: at the glittering serpent that was the river, at the proud gray distant peaks of the pyramids, at the city waking from its daytime fast to pray and to eat and to live. In a symphonic swell, the almost synchronization of a thousand prayer calls had echoed all around them. They had laughed out loud with joy at witnessing the essence of Cairo together. Karim. Today he had to talk to Karim. He had promised Baruch that tonight he would talk to Karim. And after he said what he had to say, he would no doubt lose that one who was closer than a brother.

The morning seemed less bright. Soon he would have to dress and set out for another confusing blur of a day at medical school. This year all the classes were taught in English. Why couldn't they train them to be Arab doctors curing Arab diseases in Arabic? The lectures were packed with the sons of colonels and government ministers and rich import-export brokers. Ali was even more out of place this year than last. In medical school what mattered was not *what* but *who* you knew. There were stories of highborn but fumbling students who managed to place in the top ten of every class because their fathers paid *baksheesh* to the professors. Some students never even came to class because they had already purchased transcripts of the lectures to memorize in the privacy of their Zamalek or Maadi or Garden City villas. The classrooms were so overcrowded that the best seats were sold to the highest bidder. Ali spent long hours in the library, for he couldn't afford to buy some of the more expensive textbooks. Praise Allah that Baruch tutored him for free. His classmates had to pay as much as a thousand pounds a year for private lessons to make up for the deficiencies of the professors' lectures. Medicine was a rich man's profession. Never was this more apparent than in the mobbed dissection labs, for he had to stand too far away to see the operations. The rich boys bargained with the professors and—thirty pounds for a human arm or leg, eighty for a skull—they took home part of a corpse to examine at their leisure. There were endless corruptions to becoming a doctor. His classmates were contemptuous of the government demand that they work for a year in a village clinic. Most planned to buy their appointments elsewhere or, at the very least, to be assigned near Cairo so that they could get by visiting a village clinic only a few hours a week. Ali tried to shrug off all the things he could neither understand nor accept.

Below on Sharia Maglis el-Omma, a man trundled a wheelbarrow laden with clover and fruit. The wide and dusty boulevard, half paved with cobblestones and bisected with gleaming steel trolley tracks, ran through this ancient *baladi* bastion of honest and thieving peddlers, smug and lazy government clerks, generous and conniving small shopkeepers. Sayeda Zainab was not far from the most sacred mosques, the legendary medieval city gates, the fabled bazaars and spice markets of Khan el-Khalili and the Muski. The Nile lay somewhere beyond the gray-brown streets and maze of rooftops. How many people lived and died in Cairo? Some said seven million. Others insisted it was more like twelve. In the netherworld of this urban sprawl, it was easy for millions to wander lost and uncounted.

He had to get a grip on himself. It wouldn't do to start off a day so pessimistically. He tried to focus on the other side of Cairo: on its laughter and its music and its sense of life lived past the hilt. Cairo was denser than ten thousand villages. The flat mudbrick skyline of this metropolis—with laundry waving in the mist, with rubble lying in ash-colored heaps, with date-palm shacks stacked crazily in the air— was Karnak multiplied to infinity. Already the animals were awake. He could see goats, pigeons, sheep, and—of course—cats. Cairo was a paradise of cats. They were everywhere, creeping in the shadows, mating in the sun. The only thing more emblematic of Cairo than the cats was the carcasses of animals that dangled on metal hooks outside the meatsellers' doorways. Across the street the butcher was already setting up shop, for this was Thursday, the one day of the week meat was for sale. Souk el-Etnein, the Monday Market, was beginning to buzz. Ali looked down at the black huddle of huts and tents, at the wooden and stone walls and counters. On the burlap sacks, on date-palm mats, on tiny carpets, Allah was salaamed. While old men hunched near open fires drinking tea, their sons were unloading the carts. Ali could almost taste the sweet guts of oranges, the tart chalkiness of white cheese, the bitter crunch of lemons. That cart must be full of prickly pears, this one of aubergines, that one of dates. He smiled, his hunger overriding his gloom. He could hardly wait to take a bite of Cairo. But first he must fetch water so that they could wash and then wake Baruch so they could pray. He would need all of Allah's blessings and the earth's bounty on this night of nights, when he told Karim they could be friends no longer.

That night, one of the last sultry nights of summer, Ali and Karim walked the streets of Sayeda Zainab arm in arm. Every other man and boy in Cairo capable of making it to the streets was out along with them. On sidewalks outside the coffeehouses, men sat on wooden chairs sipping their *masboot* and smoking their *nargilehs*. Young men stood together laughing and talking and puffing on their Cleopatra and Nefertiti cigarettes. Little boys kicked soccer balls back and forth in the center of streets that would always be too narrow for cars. Irrepressibly gay *baladi* music rolled out from open windows and distant balconies. Vendors hawked bolts of cotton, coat hangers, and plastic sandals. Karim stopped to bargain for dates from a pushcart and fed Ali one from his own hand. The sweetness stuck to the roof of Ali's mouth.

They sauntered toward Khan el-Khalili and their favorite café. In a city of infinite dirt and seediness, in a city that nonetheless was sometimes as satisfying to a man as mudpies are to a child, the café of Fishawi was mecca to artists and students and believers in causes. It was an ancient coffeehouse, and it looked it. Conquering Turks had swaggered here under the gilded mirrors that now were a cracked and dull smoke-gray. Nubian slaves had attended their masters on silken divans that now were tufted by straw and covered in hairy blankets. Plots against caliphs and sultans had once been hatched under the intricate shade of those now rotted wooden *mashrabeiya* screens. Now Muslim Brothers, Communists, boys who would be men, and tourists mad for local color flocked to this dim café set in the heart of the bustling bazaar.

Ali and Karim sought out their usual table in a back room where the filthy, tarnished, ornate brass chandeliers cast a murky light. Ali leaned back on a musty wooden panel painted with a picture of a cherry tree whose blooms were more like petunias. A little boy in blue-striped pajamas delivered their coffee.

Ali sighed. He had to do it now. He prayed for tact. "You know, Karim, that I couldn't continue my studies without Baruch."

"Allah keep him!" Karim lit a Marlboro for himself and another for Ali. He listened closely to the tremor in Ali's voice.

"He helps me with money and he helps me with my studies."

"A good man. A generous man."

"Yes. He treats me as a father would. And so I owe him the respect of a father." Ali coughed and cleared his throat. "I haven't told you everything about Baruch. About his past. He used to be a Jew. He only became a Believer when the rest of his family left Egypt after the Suez war."

"So?" Karim blew smoke rings. He was willing to be magnanimous to all those Ali loved. He had no quarrel with Baruch or with converted Jews who lived in peace in Cairo.

"You don't understand. His brother and his two nephews went to Is—to Palestine. One nephew still lives there."

"A Zionist!" Karim bared his perfect teeth. "The son of his brother is a Zionist!"

"That's not all. I told my mother you're *fedayeen,* and she told Baruch. They're afraid I'll join you, and so Baruch forbids me to be your friend."

Karim raised his eyebrows. "Your mother would not be honored to have you fight with us?"

"I've told you before. She hates politics. All politics."

"Your mother is only a woman." Karim shrugged. "All mothers worry. But all men fight."

"Baruch says he'll have to send me back to Karnak unless I stay away from you."

Karim laughed. "An idle threat, Ali. He won't send you home."

Ali shook his head. "I promised to do as he asked."

"That old man means more to you, Ali, than I do?" Karim looked hurt. "Ali, Ali. I thought you were my friend."

"I am! Forever, I am."

"But you give me up so easily."

"I've been arguing with Baruch since I went home to my village."

"Yes. Since you agreed to marry your cousin." There was, as always when he referred to Soad, a note of bitterness in Karim's voice.

"I did that for my Uncle Muhammad."

"And yourself, Ali? Do you ever do anything for yourself?"

"I owe them all my life."

"So." Karim calculated for a moment. "So. So this is to be our last night, Ali!" He sighed. "Life is difficult." But then he smiled sadly. "We will have to make a celebration of our parting, eh, Ali?"

Ali had expected recriminations. "Celebrate?" It was his turn to feel slighted. He had thought Karim would fight to keep his company.

"But we must put a good face on it, yes?"

"I suppose."

"A celebration, Ali. What shall we do?" Karim snapped his fingers. "I know. The *hammam*. We'll go to the baths."

Ali hesitated. He had never been able to afford the sybaritic delights of the baths. But it was late. What he should do was go home and study his chemistry. He had thought Karim would stalk off in anger as soon as he told him.

"Our last night, Ali! You must be my guest. I claim that right."

Put like that, it would be an insult to deny Karim a second time. Ali nodded and followed his friend down the length of the bazaar, past Sudanese boys still hawking crocodile skins, past old men hunched over *tric-trac* backgammon boards outside shops of polished brass, past little boys hurrying with trays of coffee and tea, past stray tourists trying to learn to haggle over silver and alabaster and gold. Their last night. This was the their last night together. Ali tried to catch Karim's holiday mood but instead was resentful and very sad. Clearly, Baruch was wrong about Karim. His friend, gliding ahead of him in the narrow aisle of the souk, was so great in spirit that he met the end of their friendship with yet more generosity. He would never get used to Cairo without Karim.

At the elaborate dirty red tile entrance to the *hammam,* Karim dropped his voice to a whisper. "You know what they say." Karim rolled his eyes as though all superstition were a joke. "Evil *jinn* live inside here in the water. We must pray as we walk over the threshold. And make sure you step inside with your left foot." Ali forced a matching laugh. But both boys prayed as they entered with their left feet forward.

They were in a grand, gaudy chamber domed like a mosque. Ali craned his neck at archways gilded in ancient red Arabic script, at glazed skylights glowing with the moon, at the cracked white marble fountain spouting icy water. Exhausted, fat old men and wriggling, very young boys reclined on worn black marble benches. From one end of the lounge to the other, hung even in the outer recesses of the dome, was a tangle of damp towels and sheets. The air was moist and cloying and as familiar as the inside of a mother's lost womb. Beardless, lithe boys who smelled of hashish called Karim by name. They joked and patted his backside as they whisked off their clothes.

"Sometimes I come here at night, after I leave you." Karim laughed. "A man must take his pleasures where he can." Ali touched the blue bead he had refused to surrender to the bath boys. He shrank away from a glimpse of Karim's rippling, smooth, glamorously shaved body. He breathed a sigh of relief when the boys tucked almost dry sheets around their waists. As they made their way down a dim corridor, the wooden *hammam* clogs slapped on the wet stones. They passed sour-smelling latrines and closet-sized chambers whose doors were not shut tightly enough to screen the low moans issuing from inside. Ali clutched his sheet closer to his body. It would be better not to tell Baruch that he had been here. There were dirty stories about what happened in some of the *hammams* late at night. Thank God he was here with a man he trusted as much as Karim.

The steam room was vast and misty and crowded with an excess of prone naked flesh. Swimming before Ali's eyes were another domed ceiling and archways, a steam geyser from a white marble fountain, and olive, brown, and pink skin reclining on black marble benches. The walls dripped with moisture and sweat. The plaster on the ceiling was cracked from a thousand years of wet heat. In the vapor, shrouded figures—rubbing, coaxing, fondling—bent over still bodies. Ali's sheet itched like a blanket. The thick air made his breath come in shallow animal pants. In slow-motion, dreamlike gestures, Karim waved away a swarm of attendants who had appeared from the fog to minister to them. "You will let me serve you tonight, Ali? Of course." Karim's voice sounded hollow in the wet chamber. "Of course you will. You are my guest." Karis drew off his sheet, signaled for Ali to do the same, and then made him lie face down on a hot marble bench. "Relax, Ali, relax. You'll like this. I'll make you feel so good, Ali. So good."

Karim straddled the small of Ali's back. When he leaned forward to rub Ali's neck, their slippery flesh slid and stuck together. "Relax, Ali, relax." Karim's practiced hands kneaded Ali's body until his joints cracked.

"Ahh!" Ali groaned. It was very hot. Perspiration oiled their bodies. As Karim worked his neck, his arms, his thighs, he could feel the tension and suspicion oozing from his pores. He stopped thinking and went limp. Karim was rubbing the soles of his feet with something very hard and prickly. Darts of exquisite pain shot up Ali's legs and, with snaking hips, he groped for more. Again Karim was kneading his body with his bare hands, but this time his touch was so gentle Ali sighed with his eyes shut.

The only sound was hissing steam and muffled moans echoing off the moist walls. Karim's fingers trailed up his arms, down his back, and then, feather-soft, at the very tip of his thighs. Ali shuddered and rolled over on command. Teasing now, very sure of himself, Karim stroked him everywhere but the taut skin between his thighs and his belly. Ali tensed, aching for the forbidden touch. But Karim laughed softly, slapped the very tip of his penis as if by accident, then retreated to a bench only inches away. Ali turned over again, ashamed both of his erection and that Karim had ignored it. A pained Ali and a smug Karim lay quietly for a very long time. Ali flexed his fingers. Just when it seemed it must be his turn to rub Karim, his friend led him by the hand into the bathing room. He clapped his hands, and one of the boys fetched a copper bowl full of steaming-hot sweet water. Karim soaped and rinsed Ali, this time touching every part of him with fingers as impersonal as a mother's.

Ali stood docile and trembling. He would have traded his heart, his soul, all of his ambition either to control his embarrassing erection or to have Karim touch it. Instead Karim handed Ali the copper bowl and the soap. Ali worked up a lather on Karim's slick and gleaming honey-light skin. With every stroke Ali's confidence grew. Karim was hard now, too. They held their arms and thighs and bellies against each other and joked in tight, strained voices first at how fair Karim was and then at how much bigger Ali was. Karim reached for him, but Karim's timing was off. It was Ali's turn to tease, to retreat, to watch with smug power. Ali plunged into the hot tub, under a steaming waterfall that cascaded into the tank from the vaulted ceiling. They lay apart there in lazy dizzy languor. Ali praised Allah when he finally went limp. He would make himself forget what had almost happened. He would blame what had almost happened on the heat and the emotion of parting from a true friend.

At last, very slowly, nearly drunk with heat, they retraced their steps the length of the *hammam*. An attendant handed them crisp fresh sheets, and they wandered into a salon full of gossipy regulars sipping coffee and smoking. "Tch!" Imperiously Karim demanded a private room for their private rest. He whispered other requests to the attendants. Smirking boys led them through a passageway, then disappeared. Karim pushed open a door onto a fragrant white marble room large enough for only one long, narrow red marble bench. "After you, Ali." Before he could protest, a procession of boys arrived. One carried two Pepsis on a tin tray. A second held a water pipe. A third had a live-coal brazier, tongs, and a cube of hashish. A fourth waved a wand of incense and a candle. A fifth had a small brass table. In front of the bath boys, who were arranging their offerings in the cubicle, Ali was ashamed to turn down Karim's hospitality. He settled down beside Karim on the bench. He refused the hashish, he took a sip of the warm syrupy cola, and he lay back and breathed in the sweet fumes of the incense and the drug. He shut his eyes. In the heavy, woozy air, it would be so easy to drift asleep.

"Light," Karim said. "There's too much light." He kicked shut the door and lit the candle.

Ali couldn't help watching the candlelight play on Karim's high cheekbones, his glittering eyes, his mouth that was almost smiling.

"Our last night, Ali. Can you believe it? Our last night!"

"A perfect night."

"It doesn't have to be the end." Karim's voice was pitched very low. He brought his hand up to his chin and very slowly ran the tip of a finger along his lips. "It could be the beginning."

As if in a trance, Ali followed the progress of that finger with his eyes. Karim was sucking his own finger. He was drawing the finger in and out of his mouth.

"No, Karim." The hoarseness of his own voice surprised Ali.

Karim leaned over and took his wet finger from his mouth and very gently touched the blue bead around Ali's neck. "For luck. I touch it —and you—for luck." He stroked the skin around the amulet that was supposed to ward off the Evil Eye. "All that brown skin. That luscious brown skin."

Ali wanted to say something, but he was locked onto Karim's large, wet, hooded eyes. He was conscious of his every breath, of the heat in the room, the darkness, the heaviness of the air.

Karim moved his fingers up to Ali's mouth and touched his lips as he had his own, the tip of his finger tracing slowly, very slowly, along first the bottom, then the top. Ali's lips were so full that this took him a very long time.

Never before had each ridge of Ali's lips felt so warm and tingly and alive. As Karim let his fingers trail down Ali's chest, his belly, to his erection, Ali shut his eyes. As he sighed, his lips parted. He felt Karim's lips on his own. He felt Karim's lips moving hotly against his. Karim's burning lips edged down to where his hand slithered. . . .

"No! Allah!" Ali broke away, stood, and looked wildly down where Karim smiled at him with those magic lips.

"Didn't you *know*, Ali? I always knew." Karim laughed. "If you're a good man, Ali, you'll leave me tonight. But if you're a bad man, you'll stay." Karim's laugh was as silky as his caress had been. "But remember, Ali. Even if you leave me tonight, remember that I'll be here waiting for you. Tonight. And tomorrow. And after tomorrow. And you'll come back, Ali. You'll come back."

That laugh followed Ali as he bolted out the door, down the corridors, and dressed on the run. He tore out of the *hammam* and raced down the dark alleys toward home. He threw himself down on his safe, narrow, chaste bed in Baruch's room. He would never, he promised himself, never, *ever*, see Karim again. Karim wanted him to do dirty things. Allah! Once he had done that with an English infidel, once he had been shamed almost beyond redemption, but never again would he do it. It was wrong for men to kiss each other as Karim had kissed him. The Koran condemned it. It was unnatural. It was against the laws of God and man. It was *haram*, forbidden. That so many still did it didn't make it any less wrong. How could he have almost let that happen? Ali tossed on his bed. Oh, Karim. He would miss him. He would miss his company. He would miss that feeling that Karim was his perfect match. "Don't you *know*, Ali? I always knew." No. That couldn't be. He would make other friends. He would work harder at his studies. He would spend more time with Baruch. Ali looked over at the sleeping man. Thank God Baruch didn't know. Or did he? Had Baruch guessed about Karim? Was that why he had forbidden their friendship? Ali blushed in his bed. He could never tell anyone about tonight. He was forever done with Karim.

Yet in the next months, as Ali walked to Kasr el-Aini beside Baruch, as he shuffled home alone at night, as he ambled through the souk buying bread and fruits and vegetables, Ali seemed to see nothing but *shebab,* young men walking arm in arm. Some strutted with their arms intertwined at the waists. Others whispered softly in each other's ears. When he passed a knot of young men smoking on a corner, he doubted the innocence of their pouting lips. Everywhere he looked he saw lips, eyes, broad shoulders, and—especially—round buttocks. It was strange how covered up the women were and how open to the senses were the men, particularly the swaggering, hot-eyed *shebab* in their tight trousers. At night, except for an occasional old woman, there were only men on the streets. He wished his mother lived with them in Cairo. He even wished his grandmother were here. Anything to fight off this feeling that he lived, worked, breathed in a world only of men. A world of men who were almost but not quite like Karim. No one looked exactly like Karim. No one was as straight and tall, as fair and handsome, as tense and charged, as Karim.

He tried to immerse himself in his studies. He talked to Baruch about his work as a doctor. But no matter how hard he tried, still he found his fingers straying to the blue bead around his neck. Then Ali would remember his steamy night with Karim, and his mind would trail away from his studies.

In the dim winter afternoon, from outside on the street Ali and Baruch could hear the rumble of tanks, the static whirl of a bullhorn, the crack of shots. Ali lunged for the open window, but Baruch tackled him to the floor. "Down! Get down, Ali! That's gunfire!" There were screams, more shots, the retreating sound of tank treads gnashing against cobblestones. A sharp, burning cloud of yellow tear gas seeped in from the street. A donkey brayed, and then the silence was broken only by low moans.

Ali and Baruch stared at each other with wide eyes. The rioting had spread even to their street. Yesterday President Sadat had bowed to international pressure to stabilize the economy by ending the billion-dollar government subsidies of vital goods. Today bread rose from one to two piasters a loaf. The price of a canister of butagas, the necessary heat and cooking fuel, increased by fifty percent. Tea, rice, and sugar almost doubled in price. It was the beginning, the president had vowed on the radio, of a new era of "struggle, resolution and sacrifice." Instead, what had begun on this eighteenth of January was bloody spontaneous rioting from one end of Egypt to the other. In Alexandria sailors sacked the beach house of Vice-President Mubarak. In Aswan a mob destroyed a triumphant arch that was to welcome Sadat and Yugoslavia's Tito. In Cairo, Muslim Brothers stormed the nightclubs along the Pyramids Road. From atop eight-story downtown buildings boys and old women hurled bricks at the police below in the streets. Quickly forming gangs forced buses to stop, smashed the windows, and set the hulls ablaze. In Tahrir Square a mob armed with bricks and clubs battled police in armored command cars. A ten-foot poster of Sadat was ripped to pieces and burned by howling rioters. "Down with Sadat! Nasser! Nasser! Nasser!" In the stalled traffic on Tahrir Bridge boys kicked in the windshields of fancy German and American cars.

Smoke bombs, tear gas, and fierce small fires hung over the city. "With blood and our lives," chanted a mob in Opera Square, "we will bring the prices down!" In Dokki police used machine guns to clear nests of rooftop snipers. Streets were cordoned off so Helwan steelworkers couldn't storm government buildings. Roadblocks were not in place quickly enough to stop Sadat's political party headquarters from being put to the torch. Everywhere shop windows were broken, police stations were attacked, streetlights were smashed. At four o'clock on this wild Tuesday, Sadat ordered army units back from the Sinai border with Israel, to enforce a curfew against Egypt's civilian population.

It was just after four o'clock now. Coughing, his eyes running with the effects of the gas even with a rag protecting his face, Baruch crawled along the floor, reached up, and switched on the radio. "Stay inside!" a voice was shrieking. "Curfew! Stay inside! Everyone on the streets will be shot on sight! Remain inside! Be calm!" But even in the background of the radio broadcast, there was the sharp rat-tat of machine-gun fire. "The television center!" Ali clutched Baruch's arm. "They must be trying to take the television center! It's a revolution!"

"A revolution?" On the day of the Free Officers' 1952 *coup d'état,* there had been almost no shots fired. The only civil disturbance that even approached today's anarchy was Black Saturday, when he and Mona had had to flee for their lives from Mena House. "No, Ali. This isn't a revolution. Here revolutions are quiet. This is a riot—a bread riot." Baruch's voice was bitter. "They're fighting—finally—only so they can eat." Baruch listened intently to the noises from the street, then stood and began packing a bag of medical supplies. He seemed to shrug off years as he shrugged on his coat, so that it was a very young and shining-eyed Baruch who turned to Ali. "Come on. You want to be a doctor, Ali? You can start right now."

"But the curfew!" From not far away enough, he could hear gunfire.

"Ali! Men and women are dying out there!" When Ali still hesitated, Baruch threw his coat at him from the peg on the wall. "Use your head, Ali. The wounded are on the streets. They can't go to the hospitals because they'll be arrested for rioting if they're caught there. *Yalla*—let's go!"

Sharia Maglis el-Omma was dark and quiet. The Souk el-Etnein was as black and unmoving as death. Night was falling, but the streetlights had been broken or shot. Metal gates stretched tight over every shop. A wrecked *cusharey* cart lay on its side, slimy macaroni and beans vomited onto the steel trolley tracks. From open windows drifted the whine of frenzied radio bulletins. The air was foul with gas and smoke. At first it seemed that nothing moved on the street, but then they could make out dark forms wavering over prone bodies. When Baruch approached one such huddle, there was a flap of black cloth like the rising of flies from a dead animal carcass. "Mercy! Mercy!" Two old women shrank into the gutter. As he reassured them that he was a doctor, Baruch bent over the wounded old man who lay mutely with his eyes wide open, too afraid to groan. Baruch turned the man over and shined a torch on his back, which had been superficially grazed with what looked like buckshot. "Running," the old man whimpered. "I was running from the tanks."

Baruch sighed with relief that the government—at least here—hadn't used full-caliber bullets to scatter the crowds. Later he would dig out the pellets, but for now he told the women to carry their brother upstairs to his room.

Slowly Baruch and Ali moved from body to body. Most had fallen from buckshot sprays in the back. But a little boy's crushed leg bore the mark of a tank tread. A young woman's face had been shredded by flying glass. Three men had been brutally clubbed about the head and chest. Many screamed that they had been blinded by the gas. It wasn't until they were blocks away, near the district police station, that they came upon the dead bodies. Women, their terrified grief more terrible for its utter silence, tore their hair and clothes over lost husbands, fathers, sons. Baruch ordered Ali to keep collecting the neighborhood wounded while he himself began to work back in their room.

Keeping close to the buildings, his ears cocked for a return of the tanks, Ali swept through first the streets, then the warrens of the alleys. Some of the wounded could walk. Others had to be dragged by their women back to Baruch's. Everywhere there were groans and curses and cries of "Long live Egypt!" He hid once when a military patrol raced toward Garden City in a jeep, and later he watched a swarm of boys loot a store of televisions, radios, and space heaters. His eyes tearing from the gas, his body blackened by smoke, Ali had worked his way back to Maglis el-Omma when he saw a familiar figure staggering not in the shadows but down the center of the street. "Karim!" The Palestinian had a blood-soaked rag tied around the crown of his head. His shirt, his jeans, his jacket were wet with blood. "Karim!" Ali caught him in his arms.

"CIA!" Karim waved an empty tear-gas canister stamped "U.S.A." "American gas. They're using American gas." Karim stared at Ali as if he were a stranger. "Al-Azhar. Machine guns. The army fired into the crowd by the mosque. Holy men. Children. They gunned down little children. Boys and girls. Dead."

Ali drew Karim into the doorway of a shop, tore the shirt from his chest, and struck a match. Karim had been strafed by buckshot. But unlike most of the others, none of Karim's wounds were on his back. Karim—so brave!—a guerrilla even on the streets of Cairo!—had not run from the soldiers. Ali counted ten, twenty, more than twenty, bleeding black pits in Karim's muscled skin. He bent over Karim, kissing every wound, wishing he could suck out the lead like snake venom.

Karim seemed finally to know him by the feel of his lips on his skin. "Ali?" Karim sighed. "I knew you loved me, Ali. That you'd be on the streets with me tonight." Ali kissed him on the lips and the eyes and held him close. The sky burned red. He could hear gunfire and the sickening crunch of tanks coming closer. He clutched at Karim as if he were the only sanity in this world. Then, tenderly but quickly, Ali dragged Karim across the street, up the stairs, and into Baruch's makeshift hospital.

For hours, all the night long, Ali worked by Baruch's side in their bedroom, in the long corridors, in the kitchen and sleeping rooms of their neighbors. They worked by the light of lanterns and flashlights, for Baruch had cautiously blacked out the windows so they wouldn't be raided by an inquisitive army patrol. Baruch was tireless. He cracked jokes as he dug out buckshot, prayed to Allah as he twisted tourniquets, soothed hysteria as he washed out eyes. Ali fumbled alongside him with unpracticed hands. But always Ali's eyes went back to Karim. For him, there was only one patient that mattered in this room.

It was nearly dawn when Ali finished tending Karim himself. The wounds had looked worse than they were. Some of the thirty-seven pellets had barely pierced the skin on Karim's face, chest, arms, and legs. One—*el-hamdulillah!*—had missed his testicles by a centimeter. Finally Baruch checked Karim's wounds and slapped Ali on the back. He suggested that Ali go get a few hours' sleep at Karim's. Ali would be needed back here before long, when the next batch of wounded straggled in.

Karim had recovered enough to walk on his own strength. But the two young men had their arms around each other as they weaved down the stairs, along the alleyways, and inside the room where Karim's mother and brothers lay sleeping. They stood on the threshold of Karim's bedroom. Ali knew there would be no turning back once they crossed to the other side.

They lurched in. Karim bolted the door. When he turned, Ali put his arms around him. Karim's kiss was hard and tense and violent and sweaty. Ali licked the caked blood on Karim's ear. "Ali." There was anger in Karim's voice. "Ali, Ali, Ali." They fell down on the bed and pressed hard against each other. Their shirts were unbuttoned, their

412

trousers were off, they were next to each other's bare skin. They writhed together, and then Karim was kissing Ali's belly, and lower. Karim went to roll him over, but instead it was Ali who twisted and pushed into Karim. Afterwards Karim held him in his arms as Ali wept.

"I love you, Ali," Karim crooned. "Don't cry, Ali. Don't cry. Just love me."

Ali tried to smile as he watched Muhammad initial the marriage contract in his daughter's name. Ali's hand shook as he bent to sign the document. He hoped it wasn't a bad omen when the ink splashed in blots. It was thought the most contented marriages began on the eve of the holiest day of the week, and so Ali and Soad were being wed on this Thursday night in late spring. But the mood in the marriage broker's office was bittersweet. Ali had been summoned home for this hastily arranged ceremony when Muhammad took a turn for the worse. Before he died, Muhammad wanted to see his daughter not only safely married but, *inshallah,* pregnant as well.

Ali hoped, as he promised aloud to take Soad forever under his protection, that this, too, was not a lie. These last months since the bread riots had been so full of deceit. Ali had learned to lie to Baruch about where he spent his evenings. He had learned to lie to his mother in letters that never mentioned Karim. He had learned to lie to himself in the guilt of sleepless nights. Now was he going to learn to lie to Karim about Soad?

The men filed back to the waiting women in the courtyard. Soad's skin glowed with the gleams of henna, her vivid orange dress ruffled to the floor, and her face was bright with triumph. *"Ayouya! Ayouya! Ayouououououya!"* Zaghareit joy-cries swelled from the throats of Mona, Bahia, Um Mona, Zainab, and the cousins. Ali and Soad were man and wife.

Woodenly Ali endured the feast and the dancing. But finally he and Soad *and* Bahia *and* Mona retired to a back room for the ritual deflowering. Why, he wondered, did his mother have to be the *daya* who watched? The room was so crowded. Was Karim hovering in the shadows as well? Ali managed an erection only by remembering Karim lying on the red marble bench in the *hammam.* But Soad wasn't Karim. She felt drier and tighter. She screamed once when he pushed inside her. He would have to do this to her forever! Karim. Ali wiped the blood off his penis, and his mother and aunt left the room brandishing the stained cotton, proof of Soad's virtue.

He lay down beside his cousin. When he put his arm around Soad, she hid her head against his chest. She was so cold and trembling and afraid. In a little while, when the heat of his body maybe stilled her shivering, he would inch over his hand to stroke her breasts as gently as was possible. How could skin be as soft as Soad's? She was so shy and

413

yet so yielding. How vulnerable this woman was. Were all women like this? Awash in tenderness, he held her closer. Of course it wouldn't, couldn't, be the way it was with Karim. She was too fragile for the caresses he lavished on Karim. The pleasures of a woman were so different from the pleasures of a man.

She risked an anxious smile up at him. "I pleased you?"

He covered her lips with his own. He wanted suddenly to protect her from every pain and doubt and risk that might ever come her way. She was his wife. If Karim . . . *once* Karim . . . left his life, Ali had a glimmering he might even be content with this woman.

Tentatively he touched her breasts. This time, when he grew hard, he wasn't thinking of Karim.

Arm in arm, languid in the summer heat, Ali and Karim walked across a bridge that spanned the Nile. But when a nymph of a boy winked suggestively at them, Karim flushed and gripped Ali so hard he almost cried out.

Ali thanked God that hadn't been a girl flirting. These days Karim's jealousy of women was even violent. He had badgered Ali for every detail, not only of the wedding but of his most intimate dealings with his wife. "Did she do this to you?" he would ask in bed. "And this? And this? And *this?* Tell me, Ali. Tell me!"

Resolutely Ali had refused to talk about the two weeks he had shared with Soad. It was enough, he thought, that he had betrayed each of them already by being faithful to neither. When he was with Soad, he had thought he would end it with Karim. Instead they had grown closer. The emotional pitch of their loving had intensified. They had fought and wrestled naked and lain wet in their own mingled sweat. As they sat moodily sipping expensive Pepsis at "their" table in a river-bank casino, as they listened to Bob Dylan in bed, as Karim caressed him even in public, a heady new torment had soldered them together. Ali had tried—and failed—to convince Karim his marriage was for the best. Before the wedding, when Karim had been trying to soothe Ali's conscience, he had said women were for marriage, for having babies, for cooking and for cleaning and for all the other domestic trivia of life. But only men could share reason, honor, and souls and bodies of a kind. Karim had once said they would love while they could. Then they would go their separate ways after they were both married to the women their families thought best.

Karim, however, no longer saw it that way. He accused Ali of be-traying him. He demanded daily proofs of Ali's love. He teased him with tales of his own past couplings—an Egyptian officer in the Gaza camp who had seduced him with promises of eggs and meat, a German who had lured him to his room at the Hilton, taxi drivers and *hammam* attendants and boat boys on the river. Fiercely, now, each no longer quite sure of the other, they loved with jealousy and possession and the urgent deadline of borrowed time.

As they crossed the sidewalk toward the entrance to the casino, Karim looked over a cluster of pushcarts and then stopped dead. "Ali! Prickly pears! They're selling prickly pears!"

Ali shrugged. "I'm not hungry."

"No, no, you don't understand." Karim was ashen. "It's summer, Ali. They aren't selling dates anymore. *I have seen my last harvest of dates!* The last, Ali. The very last."

Ali held Karim more tenderly. He knew that behind his lover's volatile moods was a growing fear of death. Once, twice, three or four times, Karim had received orders to be ready to leave for active duty in the Lebanon. But after the Israeli elections brought Begin to power, a new set of orders had come for Karim. He was to stay in Cairo until the fall, when the *fedayeen* answered the expected Israeli hard line with a coordinated wave of raids inside Palestine. Frequently these days Karim hadn't been able to help saying farewell to every evidence of life: his last Ramadan, his last *khamseen,* and now his last harvest of dates.

"So," Karim said as they settled at their Nile casino table, "so I am to die not in the summer but the autumn. I always thought it would be summer."

Ali drummed his fingers on the table. The river was flush with so many rowboats that sometimes they banged into one another, and waves of laughter rippled from shore to shore. Plaintive Arab love songs drifted over the water. It was morbid to talk of death on a night like this. If this was going to be one of Karim's self-pitying jags, Ali thought, he would go home and study his pathology textbook. He reminded himself that Soad was not so complicated. If only he and Baruch had more space in their bedroom, Ali might have sent for his wife. Sometimes he thought he would have liked to while away the summer with sweet Soad.

But then Ali took Karim's hand in his. He loved Karim not despite but *because of* his complications. How could those innocent nights with Soad ever match the intensity of hot afternoons with Karim? Soad had been soft and vulnerable. But Karim was as hard and needy as life itself.

Ali tried to reason away Karim's despair. "Why are you so sure you'll die? So you go on a raid. You blow up a bridge or a road. If all goes well, you can get back over the border. I've never understood why you always say you'll die on your raid."

"Many comrades fall," Karim said darkly. "But they'll never take me prisoner. I'll die where I long to live. In Palestine. My stolen home. By living you learn to die, and by dying you learn to live."

Under his breath Ali sighed with impatience. Yes, this was going to be one of those nights. He could understand Karim's wanting to fight to regain his homeland. If rich foreigners came in and drove *his* family from Karnak, it would only be honorable that he dedicate his own life to recovering what had been lost. What Ali couldn't comprehend was why Karim was dedicating his *death* to it.

But Karim was smiling as he looked out at the river. "They say it's beautiful . . . Palestine. Old men in the camps used to tell us about it." Karim's voice was as tender as love can be. "Orange groves and olive trees. Goat herds covering the hillsides. So many *muezzin* cries over the walls of Jerusalem that you can hear them all the way to Bethlehem. Soon I'll see it for myself, Ali. Soon I'll be going all the way home!"

Thinking not of Palestine but of Karnak, Ali gazed at the Nile and was swept up in Karim's wave of longing.

"Maybe I'm wrong, Ali. Maybe I won't die on my raid. Maybe my raid will be the one that does it. Maybe the Israelis will finally wake up and realize it's time to stop all this killing. Maybe we'll *all* be able to go home. Wouldn't that be *something*, Ali! Wouldn't that be something!"

"Yes." At this instant Karim looked even younger and more innocent than Soad. To string this moment out—to stave off for as long as possible Karim's inevitabe return to the realities of raids and refugees—Ali asked him what kind of life he wanted in a Palestine at peace.

"You'll laugh."

"No. I promise you, Karim. I won't laugh."

"Well then." Their Pepsis had arrived, and Karim took a sip of the sweet cola. "I want to be a poet," he whispered. "I want to write the most beautiful poems that were ever written. I'll write of our country— its beauty, its peace, the glories of its nights and days. I'll write of our suffering when we lost it and our triumph when we won it back. How the struggle has changed us, *how it's made us fine!* I have it in me, Ali, to write all that. I know it."

His warrior love a poet? Yes, Ali thought, *yes!* His poems would have his fire. "Can you show me some of your poems now, Karim?"

"Poetry? Now?" Karim frowned. "Everything I write now is . . . You wouldn't want to see it, Ali. Even *I* think they're too depressing. Now's the time to wage war, not write poems."

Ali sighed. Karim was back to the old refrain.

But not quite. Karim leaned forward. "Come with me, Ali. *Be my comrade!*"

Ali shook his head at the familiar entreaty. He was training to be a doctor, not some wild-eyed romantic who might kill women and children in the name of slogans that sounded more just than they were.

"I'm not asking you to fight, Ali. I know how you feel about that. But you could be one of our doctors. Maybe they'll bring me back, bloody, on a stretcher. And just as on the night of the bread riots, you'll be the one who nurses me back to life."

Gently Ali shook his head again. But as he watched the light die in Karim's eyes, he wished it were possible he could someday heal his lover not of battle wounds but of all the wounds he seemed to carry inside.

24 ~~~~~~

KARNAK, EGYPT / November 1977

Um Mona sat watching her brother die. It was sometime before dawn. Bahia and the others were asleep. They had taken turns sitting with Muhammad so that he would never, as long as he lived, be alone. If there were any changes in his condition, if it appeared that his time had finally come, whoever was with him was to call the others. Mona, seeing the end nearing, had sent for Ali two days ago. They expected him on one of today's trains.

Muhammad opened his eyes. "Helwa." That barely audible voice was all he had left. "Oh, Helwa, you're here."

She held both his hands in hers.

"It will be soon, Helwa, soon. I feel it. Soon."

"I'm here, brother."

"Many people are here. I can't see them. Not yet. But I feel them. Mother. Father. Your husband." He smiled. "They're all together."

Um Mona shuddered. She had had little use for her husband or father when they were living. She liked being near them even less in death. But she leaned forward. "Our mother. Tell me. Can you see her? How is she? Ask her, Muhammad. Tell me!"

Muhammad shook his head slightly. "I can't see any of them. But they're here. They've come so I won't be alone when I die. When I'm no longer with you and the others, I'll be with them." He seemed to remember something. "Bahia. Soad. My sons. It's time, Helwa. Call them."

"Fathi's in Saudia. The rest are asleep. We don't have to call them yet." She had shared her brother with all these interlopers for too long. She would keep Muhammad to herself for a little while.

"Bahia! My wife!" He made a feeble try at raising his voice. "Bahia . . ."

"We're together now as we were when we were children." Um Mona looked down at her brother tenderly. "Do you remember, Muhammad?

When Mother died, and you held me, and we cried. When we sat by the river and wondered what our lives would be like. When you took me down the Nile in the felucca from Kom Ombo. The birds, Muhammad. Do you remember those birds?"

"Get my wife. And my children. I must say goodbye. Bring them now."

"There were ibises. And hupis. And eagles. There was a whole treeful of birds. We thought they were flowers, and then they all flew away."

"Helwa. Please." His voice was getting weaker. "I want my family."

She stared down at her brother, and her eyes were no longer tender. *"I'm* your family."

"I want them. Bahia. My children. Helwa, help me. Please."

It was just as she had thought. Muhammad had turned against her. He didn't care about her. He cared more about that hag Bahia and his miserable, mediocre children. Those children he married off without even so much as asking her if she thought it for the best. "I've loved you, Muhammad, all our lives. I thought you would never turn against me. That's cruel, Muhammad. Very cruel."

He was looking up at her with pleading eyes. He tried to speak, but no sound came out. His lips formed his wife's name.

So, Um Mona thought. So it's Bahia you want at the end. Well, my brother, you won't have her. As she looked smugly down at Muhammad, a new thought came to her. She had only been waiting for Muhammad to die before she finally put in motion her plans for Ali and Mona. She had decided to spare her brother the knowledge of Mona's whoring. She had wanted him to die in peace. And what did she get for all that consideration? At the hour of his death, Muhammad turned against her. It would serve him right to tell *him*, too, about Mona. She folded her hands in her lap. He deserved it. In the end, he was as faithless as all the others. "Muhammad. Muhammad, there's something you don't know about Mona. She didn't marry a fisherman. She—" But Muhammad did not seem to be listening. "Muhammad?" There was no movement in his bed. "Muhammad!" She shook him hard. "Muhammad! I'm talking to you! Listen to me, Muhammad! I'm not done. Muhammad! Muhammad!"

Her brother was dead. She shut his eyes and lips and carefully arranged his body. In a moment she would let loose a mourning shriek to wake the others. She would tell them he died in his sleep, that he never woke up, that he slipped away before she could call them all to his deathbed.

But first she would sit awhile with her brother. She crooned to him in the low, musical voice of her girlhood. "I always loved you the most, Muhammad. You and Mona and Mother. You were the only ones. We had such good times, Muhammad. You remember them. The

418

best of all, I think, was when we sat in the felucca looking at all the birds as we floated along. We sailed all night one night, and in the morning we had come to rest on a bed of reeds. It felt so soft. Do you remember that, Muhammad? Don't answer. You don't have to. I know. I know."

Ali walked toward Karnak tired and alone. Baruch was on special duty this week and so had been unable to come and do what he could. Besides, Baruch had said, there wasn't much he could or probably should do for Muhammad. It would be a mercy if the secondary fever finished off Muhammad's wasted body before he had to suffer more.

Resting by the river, Ali looked out at the calm sweep of the Nile. He supposed Baruch was right about Muhammad. Why prolong his inevitable death? This fall, since Ali had secured special permission to join the hospital rounds with the more advanced students, his knowledge of pain had become more intimate. He himself would prefer a quick death to what they had to endure.

Ali watched the swift current of the river and remembered his first day on the wards, as he hovered on the edge of the herd of sixty gossiping and joking students. Already he knew that the students complained they seldom had a chance to examine living patients, that some of the greedier sick men even extorted three pounds from the student doctors before they would recite their medical histories. The supervising doctor had paused beside a few patients only long enough to order them—"What? You're still here?"—to go home so their beds could be used by the gravely ill. In vain had an old man whined that he had no home in Cairo, that he needed outpatient care, that his village was far away. The doctor had spent more time shaking his head over a man whose mangled legs, like so many others in this ward, were the result of a bus accident. "It's in the hands of Allah," was all he had said before he turned away. Ali could remember that morning exactly, for it was on that morning he had begun to wonder if he really wanted to be a doctor.

He leaned over on the riverbank, collected a handful of stones, and began skipping them on the surface of the Nile. When he had shared his misgivings with Baruch, he had expected him to condemn the uncaring doctor. Instead Baruch had been philosophical. That doctor, Baruch had said, was as much a victim as the patients. That doctor made thirty or forty pounds a month. He was a poor man whether he was a good doctor or a bad one, whether he helped twenty patients or passed by two hundred and twenty. Kasr el-Aini was a free state hospital that lacked the funds for proper food and medicine and any but the most primitive equipment. How could the system not brutalize the doctors as well as the patients? There were so many sick and so few resources, Baruch had said, that a doctor had to pick and choose those who might survive. Although many doctors saved the rich and the influential, Baruch concentrated on those who would cause the most hardship if they died: men with seven or eight children or three wives or who worked as engineers or teachers or doctors. Playing God, Baruch had said, was the most terrible price of being a physician.

At the time, embarrassed by Baruch's sudden tears, Ali had lowered his eyes and let the matter drop. But as the days passed, his despair had mounted with his experience. He saw men lying in their own blood on the emergency-room floor while their doctor went off to pray. He saw too much. As the weight of it beat him down, his doubts about being part of this for life multiplied. Between the hospital miseries and Karim's elaborate preparations for death, it was a relief to be once more back in Karnak. Maybe he should stay in the village. Maybe it would make more sense simply to remain here forever and till the fields with an honest, blunt steel hoe. Ali let out a long Egyptian sigh.

But as the wind shifted, he could hear the faint sounds of shrieking. He gathered his belongings and broke into a run. When he was close enough to pinpoint the source of the mourning wails, he knew he had come too late.

Their courtyard was packed with weeping, screaming, dancing women in black. Linked in a sorority of death, they tore their robes and shuffled back and forth. One figure surely must be Ali's mother, another his wife, but he couldn't pick them out. It was his grand-mother, in the shredded outer robes of chief mourner, who caught his eye. She whirled like a dervish and howled like a dog. Shrieking as if she had lost all reason, her features masked by dye and mud, she looked the very spirit of death. As Ali searched the press of women for his mother and his wife, his attention was always drawn back to his grand-mother. Her wild eyes were so bright that Ali wished he had thought to bring sedatives. Just as he was vowing to himself to be especially kind to his grandmother, Um Mona ran screaming to encircle him.

"Dead!" She began pulling Ali toward the house to view the corpse. "Dead!"

Mona, her face contorted almost beyond recognition by the blue dye and black mud, materialized at Ali's side. She kissed him and mumbled the details of Muhammad's passing as they staggered into the house with Um Mona. The old woman broke away from them when she caught sight of the white-shrouded body capped by the empty red fez. "Birds!" she shrieked. "Eagles! Hupis! Ibises! Do you see them, Muhammad? Do you hear them? Birds!" Her eyes rolled out of focus as she gyrated in front of the corpse. "Brother! Come back! Come back to your Helwa!" Muhammad's stepbrothers and nephews and friends muttered "Allah!" under their breaths as they tried vainly to subdue her.

Mona reappeared and waved a plate of cakes very nearly under her mother's nose. "Eat. Eat, Ummie. It's time to eat." Um Mona stopped in midstride. Saliva dribbled down her chins as she sniffed the cakes. "We'll go sit down in the other room," Mona said as she steered her mother toward the back of the house. "You and I and Ali will have tea and cakes."

"Ali?" Um Mona looked around the circle of faces for her grandson. "Ali's here? Ali? Come to Grandmother, Ali. Come. Sit and talk, Ali. I must talk to Ali."

His *gallabeiya* stuck to his body as Ali crept through the close, heavy air down to the river. It was after ten o'clock and no one else stirred under the pale full moon. The other men from Karnak and the neighboring villages were still in the hot front room listening to the blind Koran chanter mourn Muhammad with the Sacred Words. For four hours his voice had droned on and on, first soft as a sigh, then as sharp as a shriek. Exhausted from sitting up on the train all the night before, Ali had repeatedly flirted with sleep. But he knew that soon, when the death rites ended, he would have to be gracious to all the guests. A quick swim in the Nile might refresh him. Ali slipped off his undershorts, waded in the shallows, and then threw his *gallabeiya* off his body and onto the bank.

The cold black river washed away not only his sweat but the tears he had shed for Uncle Muhammad. He churned through the water with the pent-up energy of a long night and day's strained nerves. Then he floated on his back along with the current, looking up at the star-scattered sky. If he shut his eyes and just went with the river, eventually it would carry him all the way back to Cairo and Karim. Was that what he wanted? He fought the current and treaded water in place. Between Um Mona and the funeral, he had had little time to digest the news that Soad was pregnant. In the late winter he would be a father, for little Soad had managed to conceive on their wedding bed. Ali smiled at the moon, thinking of that belly already swelled by his son or daughter. He might love a man, but there could be no doubts now about his virility. He was delighted with Soad. After the funeral he had fixed a plate of food for his wife and fed it to her with his own hands. He had settled her onto their mat and sat stroking her hair until she slept. Soad, about to be a mother, had become—like him—a half orphan. He would have to be father as well as husband and cousin to his Soad. It was like a poem. Allah had his will and life had its rhythms; an old man dies and a baby is born. Of course they would have to name their son Muhammad.

"*Ay-iee! Ay-iee!*" A woman's death howl shattered his reverie. By the light of the moon he could see a figure in black on the bank near where he had shed his clothes. "*Ay-iee! Ayiee!*" He tried to ignore her. He was naked. He could not go ashore until whoever it was went away. "*Ayiee!* Ali! Ali! Come! We must talk!"

Afraid some fresh calamity had occurred in the village, he paddled closer to the shore. He crouched modestly in the shallows and peered at Um Mona. "What's happened? My mother? Soad? Bahia?"

"*Ay-iee! Ay-iee!*"

He would have to get out of the water and calm her down. "My *gallabeiya!*" As she bent to throw it to him, Ali saw something shiny flash in her hand. Carefully he eased his robe over his body as he climbed up the bank. She looked so pitiful with her robe still in tatters and her face still caked with dye and mud. "Now tell me what's wrong. Sit down here beside me and we'll talk."

She sidled closer and sat warily, poised like a wild animal either for attack or escape. "*Ay-iee!*" When Ali tried to put his arm around her, she edged farther away. "Don't touch me," she hissed. "Not tonight. Not ever. Not until you're clean. Not until you've wiped this family clean of its shame. For now I'll tell you, Ali. Now I'll tell you everything."

She was still talking as if she were possessed, though she sounded less demented than when she had danced around Muhammad's corpse. "It's late, Grandmother. You're tired. We can talk tomorrow."

"Now! Fire is better than shame! *Ay-iee!*"

Ali looked back toward the village, hoping to catch sight of a brawny man to help him coax his grandmother back to the house. But they were alone. He supposed he would have to humor her for a while. "So tell me, Grandmother. But do it quickly. The Koran chanting will be over soon."

"Ha! So you want to know, eh? Well, my boy, I've waited more than twenty years for my vengeance. You must kill her. Tonight, Ali, tonight! You must kill your mother tonight!"

He ignored the prickle of gooseflesh that was spreading from his back along his arms. Clearly Muhammad's death had unhinged her. In his opinion Um Mona had never been altogether sane. He would talk to her as if he were a doctor on the psychiatric wards. "Muhammad was a good man. We all loved him. We will miss him. But it was nobody's fault—certainly not my mother's nursing—that he died. It was his time. He's in Paradise."

"Muhammad?" She sounded almost lucid. "I'm not talking about Muhammad. I'm talking about you. And that whore, your mother."

"Yes, yes." Ali was used to her name-calling. He tried to pat her hand, but she shrank from him. "Come now. We'll go home." He tried to stand.

She pulled him back on the ground. "You'll sit here and listen to me. It's time you knew who and what you are. Who your real father was. What your mother did!"

He still wasn't really hearing. "There are cakes back at the house. And meat. We'll go back and eat and drink. You must be hungry, Grandmother. Come. I know I'm thirsty."

"Blood! Blood!" She pulled a knife from the folds of her robe.

Ali decided she was hysterical enough to do anything. "I'm listening," he said very carefully.

She laughed. "Oh, you'll listen." She bent her head toward him. "Your father wasn't a fisherman. That was a lie. There never *was* any marriage. You're a bastard, Ali. And your mother is a whore! *Ay-yeeeee!*"

She was talking like a lunatic again. He would have to gain her trust so he could get that knife away from her. "So who," he asked, as if he cared, "*was* my father? If he wasn't that fisherman?"

"You can't guess?" She laughed again. "Think, Ali, think. You're so smart. You're at the university. You're going to be a *doctor.*"

"Tell me, Grandmother. Tell me."

"A Jew, Ali. A Jew. Your father was one of *them.* Youssef al-Masri. That blond devil Youssef al-Masri! She lay with him like an animal, Ali. Like an animal! And then when he left her, when he went to Palestine with all the rest of those swine, she had a bellyful of Jew. That was you, Ali. You!"

He was paying very close attention to her now. What she was saying was of course just a delusion. He wondered if she had dreamed all this up today, or if she had nursed this sick fantasy for years.

"Mona came back here with me. I lied for her. I bought those fake marriage and death certificates for her. I did it, Ali. Me! Because I didn't want to see my little girl die." Um Mona started to cry. "She was such a good little girl. My sweet little Mona! I loved her, Ali! I loved her. I didn't want to see her die."

"Of course you didn't, Grandmother. Of course you love her."

Um Mona suddenly stopped weeping and spit out a bitter stream of invective. "I love her no more. I was wrong, Ali. I was wrong to save her. Sekhmet says so. Allah has cursed our family because of her shame. Muhammad died because he did not know enough to avenge her filthy act. We're all doomed, Ali—doomed!—unless you do it. Unless you kill her. Kill her as she should have been killed before you were born." She waved the knife in the air. "Plunge it in her heart. Plunge it into her whorish heart. It's not right, Ali. It's not right. Everyone thinks she's such a saint. *Shaykha!* They call her *shaykha!* It makes me sick when they call her *shaykha!* But no more. No more! You take this knife, Ali. It's sharp. I made it sharp. You kill her. And then you throw her body in the river, where she belongs. What's left of her will swell up and rot, as my mother did in the canal. She won't be so pretty then." Um Mona laughed and laughed.

Ali sucked in his breath and tried to remain calm. He would reason with her about the Saidi code of vengeance, as if she were sane. "But I'm not her father or her brother. Even if all you say is true, it is none of my affair."

Um Mona narrowed her eyes. "You're of age. You're her closest male relative. The family's honor is in your hands. You have to do it." She lowered her voice. "That is, you'll do it if you're really both an Arab and a man."

Ali was aghast. He had heard it said, once, that something like this had happened in Qena long ago. A son had killed his mother—and then himself—when his mother was accused of having betrayed his dead father. But then Ali caught himself. This was only his sick grandmother's rantings. None of it was true. It *couldn't* be true.

She read the doubt on his face. "You don't believe me, eh? You don't think that precious mother of yours would have done that. But she's always been a sentimental fool, Ali. She still dreams of that Youssef. I see her mooning around, singing *'Ansek!'* That's why she wouldn't marry anyone else. All this time she's been waiting for him to come back. Didn't you think it was strange that she didn't have a wedding picture of your so-called father? That she never told you much about him? That she never took you to visit any of his family? It's true, Ali. It's true. Baruch knows. He offered to marry her to cover her shame. He's your great-uncle, Ali. Just like Muhammad." She started to cry again at the thought of her dead brother.

Ali stared at his grandmother in bewilderment. It couldn't be true. She must be crazy. His mother couldn't have given herself to a man like that. A *Jew*. She couldn't have lied to him always, about everything. Yet his mother *was* sentimental. She never had said much to him about his father. She always did go on so about the Jews. And she had admitted that Baruch had offered once to marry her. Suddenly he felt so dizzy he held his head in his hands.

"Ask her yourself, Ali. I don't think she'll lie. She'll tell you."

Ali looked into his grandmother's burning eyes and was afraid.

"I see that maybe now you believe me." She took the knife and put it in Ali's hand, closing his fingers, one by one, around the handle. "You must do what you must do." On her face and in her voice sorrow had replaced rage. "There is no other way. You're an Arab, Ali. You must be strong."

Ali looked at her for another long moment and then stood, the knife almost forgotten in his hand, before he turned to go and hunt for his mother and the truth.

The guests had already drifted away from the quiet house as Ali moved silently through the courtyard and the guestroom. Men who had come from far away for the funeral were stretched out on the floor already snoring. He crept up the stairs and past the room where he could hear Bahia softly sobbing.

His mother was sitting on her pallet, watching a single candle burn in a saucer. He stood in the doorway, his fist wrapped around the knife, until she looked up.

She saw her son, his white *gallabeiya* streaked with mud, framed in the moonlight. His face was a mask of horror. He had the knife in his hand. She did not have to be told what had happened. He knew. Her mother had finally done it. Ali had come for her.

"Sit down." She was surprised that her own voice sounded so calm. Had she been waiting for Ali? Had she been waiting for this moment all his life? "We'll talk, Ali. I see that we . . . finally . . . will talk."

He acted as if he had not heard her. He continued to stare, with dilated pupils, at the place where she sat.

"Son. Please sit down. We can't talk with you in the doorway. We'll wake the others. Sit down, Ali." She patted a place beside her.

He looked wildly around the familiar room, at the window, the date-palm mat, the robes hanging from the nails in the wall. His eyes focused on his mother. She was still wearing her tattered black robe and had not yet washed the blue dye and mud from her face. She didn't look like his mother. He stumbled toward her and sat down on the dirt floor, so that the candle was between them. He cradled the knife in his lap.

"So it has finally come to this." Her voice was a whisper.

"Come to what?" Ali was hoarse with dread. It couldn't be true. In a moment she would tell him his grandmother was mad. They would have to take care of her night and day. A woman as crazy as his grand-mother could do something violent.

"My mother has talked to you?" Mona wanted to be absolutely sure. Perhaps she was wrong. Please, Allah!—she still didn't have to tell him. "She sent you here," Mona said, pointing to the knife, "with *that?*"

Ali nodded, not trusting himself to speak.

Mona stared at the candle. "I didn't want it to be like this. I wanted to tell you myself, someday when you were perhaps old enough to understand. When you'd lived more. When maybe you could for-give."

"Forgive *what?*" He had to hear it from her own lips. Apparently at least part of what his grandmother had said was true. But she must have distorted it. Which part of what she had said was the lie? Was it worse that his father was a Jew or that he had not married his mother? Allah! It could not be as Grandmother had said.

She sat silent, wondering how to explain. How could she make him understand how it had been—was—with Youssef? Young, golden, laughing Youssef. It was not so very long ago that they had stood on the deck of the houseboat and he had vowed so much. Remembering, her courage came back to her. Youssef! "We were in love, Ali." Under the mud and the dye Mona's eyes were luminous. "Truly in love. We loved for many years. Since we were children. It was a great love. A true love." She tried to smile at her son. "You have not yet, I think, felt such love in your life. I hope someday you will. And that maybe then you'll be able to understand."

Ali shut his eyes and wished for the blessing of eternal deafness.

"We wanted to get married. Youssef . . ." She hesitated when her son shuddered at his father's name. "Youssef promised to marry me." She looked at her finger. "He gave me this ring. Baruch was the only one who approved. Youssef's parents didn't want a poor Muslim girl for their rich . . . Jewish son. Abbas, the *suffragi* who was my joint guardian with Baruch, alo forbade the marriage. He wouldn't let me marry a Jew."

As the truth began to sink in, Ali opened his eyes and stared at his mother.

She was intent on making him understand, as if a recitation of the circumstances, the details, the reasons, would matter in the end. The words tumbled out as if she had rehearsed and refined them into a pattern of sense. "I wasn't quite sixteen when the war broke out. The '56 war. They wouldn't let us see each other. Abbas was trying to arrange another marriage for me. We *had* to do it, Ali. We *had* to be together." She hardly heard Ali moaning. "We ran away to Cairo and tried to get married. We went to the *shaykhs*, the rabbis, the *maazouns*. No one would marry a Muslim and a Jew. Especially not then, just after the war, with the Israelis attacking the Canal, with Nasser screaming about the foreign devils. But we found one clerk who said he would. The night before we were to marry—" Her voice broke, she stopped, she continued again. "*It* happened. We didn't mean it to, Ali. It just happened. We were alone on that houseboat for weeks. And we loved each other, Ali. We truly loved."

"No, no, no," Ali moaned. "It can't be true. It can't."

"When we went back to get married, the clerk discovered that Youssef was a Jew. He refused us. There was nothing for us to do but go back to Alexandria and wait the few months until I was of age and could marry without anyone's permission. But . . . but . . . Youssef's father was a Zionist. There was some plot. The Israelis came and took Youssef and his father and brother away in the night. I'm sure he didn't *want* to go, Ali. I'm sure he really *meant* to stay and marry me."

"My father?" Ali was still struggling to comprehend the only facts that mattered. "Youssef al-Masri is my *father*? A *Jew*? You weren't married to my *father*?"

She seemed not to have heard him. There was more she had to tell him. If she found the perfect words, he would understand. She reasoned with Ali as she had reasoned with herself for twenty years. "He didn't know I was pregnant. He still doesn't know that you even exist. But I'm sure he'd love you, Ali. And he'll come back one day. One day when there's peace. The only reason he hasn't written to me, the only reason he hasn't come back for us, is all these wars."

His eyes drilled into her. The mother he had always adored could never have done what this woman said she had done.

She tried to hold on to the comfort of Youssef. A moment ago she had felt so close to him that it had been almost like having him here in this room with their son. But Youssef was gone. All he had left her was Ali. Too late she began to fear that now she must lose her son as well. She wished she hadn't admitted everything to him. If she had lied, it would have been her word against her mother's. She kissed the hem of Ali's *gallabeiya*. "It was wrong, son. I know it was wrong. Every day since then, since I came back here with my mother, I've tried to atone for it. Forgive me, Ali. Please!"

He flicked his robe away from her. The rage of a man, an Arab, a son of the Said, was welling up from his chest to his head. "Allah! The shame! The shame!"

She looked at the candle sputtering between them, and once again she was remembering another time. "When I was a little girl, Ummie would sit me down before a candle like this one. We would watch the moths circling it, and then one of them would fly into the flame. 'Fire is better than shame,' my mother would have me say. 'Fire is better than shame.'" She looked over at her son with compassion. "Ummie wants you to kill me."

Ali was breathing heavily. As he looked down at the knife in his hand, the blade seemed to glow red. He touched it to see if it was hot enough to burn, not cut, through flesh. Shame! The worst shame of all! He brought his eyes up to that other face flickering in the candlelight. "Woman, do you deny that you deserve to die?"

"That it must come to this." Mona sighed almost to herself. She could no more stop what was about to happen than she could stop the sun from rising or the Nile from running. There was peace in that thought. "So this is how it must end. You know, I didn't think it was all over. But I never thought, never dreamed . . ." She nodded. "Yes."

Ali stared at the candle until he felt its flame must blind him. He held the knife up in his hands. As if from a great distance, he could almost see the blade glinting toward the one who had shamed them all.

"So you'll do it, Ali? You'll kill me?"

Ali grunted and inched on all fours closer to her.

"If this is Allah's will," Mona said as she closed her eyes, "then so be it." Her lips moved as she prayed. When she opened her eyes again, Ali was so close to her that she could see the perspiration rolling like tears down his cheeks. Her son . . . their son. "Oh, Ali! For you to have to kill me! To have to kill the one who gave you life!" She shook her head and reached for the knife just as he was drawing it back so he could stab her with all his strength. "No, that is too cruel. Too much. Give me the knife, Ali. I'll do it. I'll kill myself. I can't let you do it. You're my son."

He froze and began to tremble just before the knife could touch her. "You'd kill yourself to spare *me?*" The waves of redness began to recede from before his eyes. This was his mother! What was he doing with this knife and his mother? Allah! His mother! Through his tears he saw his mother's eyes, nose, hair. She took him in her arms and cradled his head on her breast. "Don't cry, Ali. It's all right. I'm not afraid to die. I deserve to die. You're right. I've always known it. It is my fate. My curse." She loosened the knife from his grip and held it in her hand. It had a keen edge. Her mother must have sharpened it. She stared at the blade. It had passed from her mother to her son, and now she drew it almost lovingly to her chest.

Ali snapped out of his trance, grabbed the knife, and threw it away. He was shouting. "No! I can't let you do it! No! You're my mother! Allah help me! Allah forgive me! But I can't kill you! And I won't watch you die!"

There were sounds of running feet. Others had heard them and were coming. A groan escaped Mona's lips. "I'm sorry," he thought he heard her say. As the candle sputtered and died, his mother's face grayed in the moonlit shadows. Ali turned and ran blindly from the room. Karim. He needed Karim.

He ran down the Cairo platform, darting in and out of the crowd, almost tripping over a shouting newsboy, racing toward Karim. A soldier, suspicious of anyone in such a hurry on this very special day, demanded his identity papers, and Ali had to pay him twenty-five piasters *baksheesh* before the soldier would let him go. What he wanted, all he wanted, was to tell Karim and then to forget. To feel Karim's arms around him, to have Karim hold him!

Ali stood outside the teeming station and sized up his route to Sayeda Zainab. It would take too long on the footbridge and along the sidewalks. He plunged into the stream of Ramses traffic, weaving in and out between cars, trucks, donkey carts, motorbikes. He scaled the seven-foot iron fence dividing the road and jumped down on the other side through another lane of traffic. He tore down the streets next to the banks of parked cars. All night long, hiding in the belly of the felucca, staring at the Nile, he had endured only by thinking of Karim. When he saw the glow of lanterns, when he heard his mother and Soad calling his name, his desperate thoughts had turned only on Karim. If he had talked to his mother again, he would have had—impossibly—either to kill her or to forgive her.

As he ran past a bus, the boys hanging on its sides dared him to race it to the corner. But Ali had no time for games. He was as single-minded racing down the streets as he had been hiding behind that pillar at Luxor station, his heart beating faster every time he saw a figure in black draw near. He had allowed himself to think no further and no deeper than escaping from this nightmare to Karim. He had smoked, one after another, three packs of cigarettes during the interminable train ride. They had made his throat hurt, and he had puffed harder so he would have to think of that pain. But, unbidden, his mother's face would flash before him: his mother gray and weeping, his mother singing *"Ansek!"*—his mother forever so sad and alone.

His lungs choked as he kept up his pace through the howl of the news criers of Opera Square and then along the deserted sidewalks in front of the king's old palace. He could hear not only his feet thudding on the pavement but his heart hammering in his chest. All day long as he squatted among the cigarette butts and candy wrappers and cast-off newspapers on the train floor, he had stared at the cages of frantic chickens beating against their date-palm bars. He had thought about the sharp blade that would soon cut off their heads and had shuddered at the thought of a knife and of blood. Almost he had killed her. Allah! He had told himself, over and over, that he would not break, would not cry; he would go to Karim and Karim would make him better. When the train had broken down north of Minya, the passengers had speculated that there must be a split in the tracks or that a wheel or axle must have shattered. One more fanciful man had suspected Israeli sabotage. Ali had flexed his fingers and wanted to take that man's skinny neck and wring it between his bare hands as he would a chicken's. Instead he had wrung his own weak—Jewish?—hands as he fought back the tears of shame.

He veered into the maze of Sayeda Zainab's alleys. Right here, then left, then right, right, and left. "Karim!" he shouted at the dilipidated wall of his lover's house. He sidled through the hole in the wall and pounded on the door. "Karim! Karim? It's me!" When there was no answer, Ali pushed open the door and walked through the empty front room into Karim's bedroom. Something hard and cold was pushed into the small of his back, but then Karim laughed and embraced him.

"It's you! Really you! Ali! *El-hamdulillah!* I thought it was the police!" Carelessly Karim threw his pistol onto the bed next to his open suitcase. "Thank God you got here in time."

"In time?" Ali pulled away from Karim. "What's wrong? What's happened?"

"Surely you've heard. Even in that village of yours, you must have heard."

"Heard what? Why are you packing?"

"Your filthy traitor of a president says he'll go to Jerusalem to make peace with the Zionists. Sadat! I spit on Sadat! It happened today. It's in all the papers."

"What?" Ali had paid no attention to the screams of the newsboys in Cairo station and on the streets.

Karim sank down on the bed. "None of us could believe it. The Americans must have bribed him with millions of dollars. I hope he chokes on them. Crawling like a dog to Jerusalem—*our* Jerusalem!"

It was almost enough to make Ali forget his own shame. Desperately he tried to think. He pointed to the gun and the suitcase. "And this?"

"I'm leaving, Ali. There's no telling what the secret police will do. They know who I am—hell, they've been paying me for years—so I'm flying to Damascus tonight before they can arrest me. Then I go to Beirut."

"Oh, no, Karim!" His last hope was leaving him. "Not now. You can't leave me now."

For the first time Karim took in Ali's stained *gallabeiya*, his dirty face streaked by tears and sweat, his bloodshot eyes. "What's happened? Your uncle died? I'm so sorry, Ali. He was a good man. Like a father to you." The tears welled in Ali's eyes. Karim pushed aside the gun and the suitcase and pulled Ali down on the bed next to him. He took his lover in his arms as a mother would a child. "My poor Ali. You look as if you haven't slept for days." Karim stroked his hair. "That's it, you can cry, Ali. You're with me now. Your uncle is in Paradise. It's all over." Ali sighed and nestled closer. Karim kissed his hair, his cheeks, and then slid down so he could kiss his lips.

But Ali pulled away when he felt Karim's mouth on his. First he had to tell him all of it, and then he could lie in Karim's arms before— Allah!—they too had to say goodbye. Ali took his last crumpled pack of cigarettes from his pocket, lit one slowly, and then drew on it. It was going to be harder to tell Karim than he had thought. He would have to repeat all that had happened. He would have to say the very things he hadn't allowed himself to think. He shut his eyes.

"Ali? Ali, what's wrong?"

Ali's eyes shot open. "Everything." If Karim judged him innocent, the blame would be gone from him forever. "My uncle was dead when I got there. My grandmother came and gave me a knife. She said I had to use it to kill my mother!"

"You always said she was a little crazy. My poor Ali. Did you have to put your grandmother in a hospital?"

Ali stared at him. "She wasn't really crazy. That's not it." He stubbed out his cigarette on the floor and took a deep breath. His voice was flat and dead. "She told me the truth. What she's known all these years. My mother was never married. My father wasn't a fisherman in Alexandria. I'm a bastard. Grandmother told me I had to kill my mother myself to avenge the shame."

Karim pursed his lips. "Barbarous. That's barbarous. Allah! How *could* she tell you that? How?" He caught his breath. "You didn't do it, Ali? You didn't kill your mother?"

"I went to her. I didn't think it could be true. But she admitted it."

"You killed her!" Karim was horrified. "Oh, Ali!"

Ali looked at his hands. "When I had the knife right to her chest, she said she would kill herself. That she didn't want me to have to do it." Ali buried his head in his hands and began to cry again.

Karim recoiled. "So she's dead."

Ali raised his head and shook it.

"No? She's not dead?" Karim sighed in relief. He took a handkerchief from his pocket, wiped the tears off Ali's face, and made him blow his nose like a child. "Barbarous peasants," he muttered, so low that Ali couldn't hear.

"I threw the knife away," Ali finally whispered. He blew his nose again. "I couldn't do it. And I couldn't let her do it. She's my mother."

"Of course you couldn't kill your mother, Ali. No man could."

In relief at Karim's approval, Ali began to talk compulsively. "The train broke down on the way back up here. A man said that maybe the Jews blew up the tracks. I wanted to kill him with my bare hands. But then I looked down at them. At my hands. Jewish, Karim. Jewish!"

"You're upset, Ali. You're confused. You're getting Sadat mixed up with this business with your mother."

"Jew." Ali was still examining his hands. "He was a Jew. My father was a Jew."

"What? Ali, *what* did you say?"

"The man my mother did that with." Ali looked at Karim in bewilderment. "I told you. I'm sure I told you. He was a Jew."

"A Jew!" Karim spit out the words. "What Jew? Where?"

"Baruch's nephew. My mother worked for them. She said they tried to get married."

"Where?" Karim leaped to his feet. "Where is this Jew who took one of our women? I'll kill him. I'll kill him tonight."

"He's in Palestine."

"Allah!" Karim cast his eyes to the ceiling. "Your father was a Zionist! He dishonored your mother, then went over to the enemy!" Karim paced from one end of the room to the other. "Oh, my God, my God! Allah, Allah, Allah! It's monstrous! Your mother lay with a Zionist! With the enemy, Ali. The murderers of our people. Of *my* people!" Karim glowered down at Ali.

"But she's my mother," Ali said softly. "You just said—I heard you —that no man could kill his own mother."

Karim drew his arm back and slashed Ali across the face, as a man will do to his much-despised wife.

Ali cringed and touched his stinging cheek.

"Get out of here!" Karim's voice was full of hate. "You're no Arab. You're no man. For all I know, you're a Zionist spy. How I could have loved you, I do not know. You're a Jew, too, Ali. A sneaking, lying Zionist. Your father's son. A Zionist and a coward. Get out of my sight before I lose my temper and kill you myself."

Ali rose to his feet. All the emotion of the past days centered on anger at Karim. "That's despicable. Low and despicable. For *you* to say that to *me!* You will beg my pardon."

"I will beat you senseless. Jew! Zionist!" As he taunted Ali, he tried to punch him.

They circled each other in the small room, then Ali kicked away the table between them. "All I wanted was to be with you, Karim. I needed you. I thought you loved me. But you don't. You never did. All you care about is your stupid war games against the Zionists. That's probably a lie, too. You probably sell copper pots in Beirut!" He punched Karim on his perfectly formed jaw.

Karim reeled and swung at Ali. "Jew! Jew!" The blow fell harmlessly on Ali's arm.

"That's the best you can do?" Ali hit Karim twice more in the face. *"That's* how you learned to fight? A lot of good you'll be on that glorious raid you're always talking about! You can't even hit me! And I'm only *half* a Jew!" He punched Karim in the chest, and Karim crumpled to the floor, the wind knocked out of him. Ali stood there looking down at him until his own breathing slowed. Still, when Karim didn't move, Ali's rage began to ebb. He had hoped Karim would rescue him from the trap and the tangle of his own emotions. He supposed he had expected too much. Now it was over with Karim, too. But how he had loved him! He couldn't leave him here like this for the police. He picked Karim up in his arms, laid him tenderly on the bed, and felt for his pulse.

Karim's eyes fluttered open, and he groaned. "You can fight, Ali. I didn't know you could fight."

"You know it now." There was the ghost of a smile on Ali's lips.

"You fight like an Arab, Ali."

"I am an Arab. And Karim, if you're trying to apologize, you'll have to do better than that."

Karim cursed. His eyes were hard with speculation. "You're stubborn."

"I'm an Arab. And a man."

"Prove it, Ali."

"I just did."

"Really prove it, Ali. Come with me. Join us. I'll get you the right papers. We can leave tonight. We'll be together."

Ali chewed his lip. There would be a perverse perfection in that end.

Karim began to coax. "It's the only way. Erase the shame. Do it, Ali. Do it. Come with me. Show me you're no Zionist. That you're an Arab. A man. Choose your side. Don't stay here and die of shame. Live, Ali. Live and be proud."

"No. No." But Ali waited for more persuasion.

"What do you have to lose, Ali? You can't go back to your village.

If you do, you'll have to kill her. You know that, Ali. What else can you do? Walk out that door and go sit by the side of that Jewish doctor, in that pit of a hospital you say you hate? Is that what you want? To join your Jewish uncle?"

Ali stared in fascination at Karim, waiting to hear more. He could not do it just to be sprung from his trap. If he did it, it would have to be for only one reason.

"I love you, Ali." Karim reached up and touched the blue bead around Ali's neck. "You're like my brother and my father and my son and my husband and my wife. Come with me, Ali. We'll be everything to each other. Everything!" When Ali shuddered, Karim smiled. "I take back what I said before. I was wrong. You're not a coward. Not a Jew. You're an Arab. The man I love."

Karim's lips were red and glistening. It seemed to Ali that it was his fate to bend down and kiss Karim.

It was less than an hour later when Ali left Karim on the corner and stole up the staircase to Baruch's room. It wouldn't take him long to get some fresh clothes, his favorite pictures—of Karim, of Soad, his photograph of the whole family at his wedding. Although he thought Baruch would still be at the hospital, Ali slipped his key silently into the lock.

Baruch was sitting at the table. "I've been waiting for you, Ali. Sit down."

Ali ignored him and threw his shirts, trousers, and underwear down on the bed. He rooted in a box and found the two photographs he wanted. He picked up a piece of newspaper and began wrapping his belongings.

"So you're running away, Ali? You're going to turn and run?"

Ali pretended Baruch wasn't there and quickly stripped off his stained *gallabeiya*. He shrugged on a shirt and pulled on trousers.

"Your mother telephoned me, Ali. She got through at the hospital this morning. She's frantic, Ali. She thought you might have killed yourself. They've looked all over Karnak and Luxor for you. In the irrigation canals. Along the river."

Ali tried to walk past Baruch, but the doctor held him back. "Don't touch me, Baruch. I'm warning you. Let me go!"

"Go where, Ali? Where are you going?"

"Let me pass. It is no business of yours."

"No? No? I think it is. You're *my* flesh and blood, Ali. My brother's grandson. And you're going to listen to me." Baruch shoved him back on the bed. "Listen to me, Ali. You owe me that."

"I owe you nothing." But Ali, remembering Baruch's past kindnesses, sat and listened.

"Your mother should have told you years ago. Or maybe I should have done it for her. So many shoulds! Allah! To find out as you did!" Baruch stopped and sighed, aware he was fighting for Ali's life here and now just as he had once fought for Mona's in Alexandria. He had lost that other round to Um Mona. He could not fail again. He sat down next to Ali and spoke very gently. "It wasn't the way you think. I was there. In Alexandria. Youssef—"

Ali spat in the general direction of Baruch. But then, embarrassed at his rudeness, he flushed and looked his great-uncle in the face. Was there a family resemblance? How many days and nights had he wished that this wise man was his father? Allah! It was too much.

"Hear me out, Ali. Your mother, your father, you . . . I've loved you all as if you were my own children. Good people, decent people, to be caught up in this! Youssef wasn't much older than you are now. Mona was younger than Soad. That's no excuse for what happened. But they would have been married if it weren't for his being a Jew—"

Ali's sympathy snapped at the reminder. "Whore. She's a whore. My mother is a lying traitor of a whore."

"I don't think you really believe that. Ali, I've never seen two people more in love. Your father didn't want to leave. He loved Egypt. His letters . . . I wish it had been safe to save his letters. He was forced to leave. He might have been killed, Ali, if he had stayed. It was nobody's fault. Not yours. Not your mother's. Not your father's. There's been enough tragedy in this family already. You can end it, Ali. Don't make it worse, I beg of you. End it, Ali. End it now."

"That's exactly what I intend to do, *Uncle* Baruch."

"I'll telegram—no, try to *call*—your mother. She'll come here. We'll explain it. You'll understand. I'll marry her. I've always wanted to. We can all live in Cairo. No one has to know. Soad's baby is due soon. Think of her, Ali. What about your wife?"

There was a sadness in Ali's eyes, but he shrugged.

"You've got to try to understand, Ali. Your mother and your father have suffered more over this already than you can imagine. Think of what it must have been like for your mother, living with this all these years. Having Um Mona hold it over her head. The humiliation, Ali, the fear! Think of it. To endure it all, and then to have that woman put a knife in your hands."

Ali looked down at those hands. "I couldn't do it. Tear her flesh? Make her bleed?" He shook his head slowly back and forth. "She said she would kill herself before she let me do it. Can you imagine that, Baruch? Can you imagine?"

"Yes. Mona would do that."

"If only she hadn't lied so much. Everything she ever told me was a lie. She's a dirty woman." Ali could feel the anger once more surging through his veins. "My mother is a dirty woman."

"Ali, forget what you've been told about Arab vengeance and honor.

Listen to your heart. And your head. You're an educated man, not a Saidi peasant. Decide for yourself. Forgive her, Ali. You can. You have a mind. A soul. Free will. Use it. Make that choice."

"Everything will be as it has to be," Ali said with finality. "As Allah wills it."

"No, Ali! You decide. You act. Forgive her, Ali. Do what you know to be right."

"Inshallah." He stood and tucked his package under his arm. "I'll write to you, Baruch."

"From where? Where are you going?"

"Where I have to go."

Baruch had watched him pack Karim's picture. "You're going off with that boy. You're going to Palestine, aren't you, Ali?"

"I am going to meet my fate."

"Are you trying to kill yourself or your father?"

Ali half smiled and took a step toward the door.

"Just tell me one thing, Ali. One more thing. Why Karim? Why did you go to Karim? I was here. I was waiting for you. Why Karim?"

"You don't know?" Ali laughed. "He's my lover. I had to go to my lover. After all, I'm my mother's and my father's son. A child of passion. It was my fate."

He ran down the stairs to where Karim waited. As they ran, Ali could hear Baruch calling out as he chased after them. They lost him in the confusion of Liberation Square.

25

THE LEBANESE COAST / *March 1978*

Ali sat—pen, paper, a photograph, and envelope in hand—on the outer fringes of the men around the campfire. In a little while, after the midnight briefing, he and Karim and the eleven others in their squad would make for the boats to carry out their objective. In his four months at the rival training camps, Ali had practiced with his Kalashnikov rifle on the range, he had learned to throw grenades, he had drilled to run and to shoot and to win under fire. Before the split came and they left the Arab Liberation Front, he had yawned through interminable lectures on Arab socialism, guerrilla warfare, the inevitability of the historical process. He had wondered if Mao and Che and Ho Chi Minh, too, once felt this frightened yet exhilarated, this trembling but uncertain. He had also wondered if those revolutionary giants ever had been as sick as he was of the endless wrangles over tactics, theory, and policy.

In Cairo he had paid little attention to Karim's elaborate dissections of Palestinian politics, but here he had been thrust into the thick of it. In the first shock of Sadat's pilgrimmage to Jerusaem—they said he had actually kissed Golda Meir at the airport!—he and the other ALF commandos had waited for the signal from above to sweep into Palestine and liberate every square inch of Arab soil. Instead, the weeks dragged into months. Begin conferred in Ismailia; Arabs leaders met in this capital or that to disagree on what must be done; Israel brazenly kept opening new settlements on the West Bank. But in the guerrilla camps the only fighting was with fists, among the *fedayeen* themselves. The ALF, supposedly hewing to the Iraqi party line, formed an alliance with one guerrilla group on Monday and broke it on Wednesday. Yassir Arafat, biding his time in the slender hope that Sadat's gesture might force Israel into recognizing the rights of Palestinians, kept a lid on his men for three months.

In February the ALF lost patience and sent two of its men to Cyprus to assassinate the editor of Cairo's *al-Ahram*. Karim, furious that he and Ali had been passed over for this plum of a mission, publicly denounced the ALF. Ali hadn't much cared when he and Karim then prompty signed on with Arafat's Fatah. ALF or Fatah, the Popular Front for the Liberation of Palestine or the Popular Democratic Front for the Liberation of Palestine—it was still the same grenades and submachine guns, still the same bickering and rivalries, still the same waiting and frustration. But finally, when even Jordan's Hussein denounced Sadat, when Sadat in turn denounced the PLO, the rumors of a much-postponed raid began circulating in the camps. Karim, with so little seniority in Fatah, despaired of being chosen for the elite assault team. But its commander had heard that Ali was a doctor. To coax Ali onto his team, he had to agree to take Karim as well. Their mission was to land by sea near Tel Aviv and seize a luxury hotel packed with tourists who could serve as hostages for the release of Arab commandos in Israeli jails. It was a high-risk, high-visibility raid, and it was certain that not every one of the guerrillas would survive it.

Ali looked at the color photograph of himself in his splendid Russian-made uniform. Was this the image of a true revolutionary or a young man bent on suicide? He believed—yes!—in the rightness of the Palestinian cause. But was he here because of that or because there was no other way out? He expected to die tomorrow. He supposed his motives —dying for his own honor or Palestine's—wouldn't much matter after his heart stopped beating. After the raid the Revolutionary Command would release copies of his photograph to the world press. Already, in a Beirut safe house, the martyr posters were waiting in boxes to be tacked up on streetcorners as an inspiration and warning that despite Sadat, the Palestinian struggle had not yet faltered. In this photograph the line of his mouth was grim, his eyes were glittering, his posture was triumphant as he pointed the submachine gun as if the camera were imperialism itself. So would he leave his mark on the world.

Ali sighed, remembering how he had once mocked Karim for these very sentiments, and slipped the photograph into the envelope already marked with Baruch's address. He had just enough time to write the letter to accompany the picture. He had been told that if he should be martyred on the raid, a courier would deliver the packet to Baruch. He scratched on the paper slowly, the words not quite right. He had never been good with words. But it would have to do. He hesitated. Should he write to Soad as well? By now she would have given birth to their child. He didn't even know whether he would leave behind a daughter or a son. If he wrote to her, she would keep the letter forever, and it would be handed down to their child, and the child of their child. No. It was better to write nothing and so break that chain.

He untied the blue bead from around his neck, kissed it, and tucked it into the envelope. This was the closest he would allow himself to come to saying goodbye to his mother. Baruch, of course, would deliver this package to her in Karnak. Perhaps in a way she would understand. All that now seemed far enough away that Ali could even feel a kind of pity for his mother. He hoped Baruch could be a comfort to her, just as Karim had been a comfort to him.

Ali looked over at his lover laughing and talking, as always these past months, in the midst of a knot of his comrades. Karim had cast away his old moody ways when he had been chosen for the raid. His white skin was flushed with excitement, and his eyes danced as he boasted what they were about to do to the Zionists. Karim, Ali thought, had been preparing all his life for tomorrow. By now Ali knew about his miserable Gaza refugee camp, about his father shot down when he crossed the border to visit his old fields, about his brother killed in Jordan in King Hussein's Black September massacre of the Palestinians. In Cairo Karim's dark intensity, his mercurial emotions, his nervous tapping of his foot to the beat of Bob Dylan, had fascinated Ali. Karim had failed to seduce him with the delights of the *hammam* but had won him finally on that bloody night when all Egypt revolted for crusts of bread.

In violence the two of them had come together, and in violence they would end. For Ali, with Karim, passion and politics had come together. Dear Karim had all the answers: love and honor, duty and death. Yet until tonight, in a way Karim had always eluded Ali. He would allow Ali to see a little part of himself, then he would hide the rest away under the cloak of morbid romance. But here, tonight, there *were* no more secrets. Karim was surrounded by others so like himself. On the stolen summers of his youth Karim had trained with comrades like these from Iraq, Syria, Libya, Pakistan, Yemen, Egypt, and Palestine itself. All of them were consumed by their glorious commitment to fight with their blood to the end, and so wipe out the shame of their armies' defeats. These many years Karim had been preparing with fatalism, with terror, and with pride for not only a raid but a suicide mission back to his homeland.

"All men must die," the comrades assured one another too often in this camp. For them, the vindication of their own deaths was that they would take a greater number of Zionists with them. In mourning for their own dead, the Zionists would learn that the Palestinians—no matter what a certain renegade Arab leader said—would never give up the struggle. Ali knew the slogans but he could not share the certainty that was behind them. He wished he *could* believe as the others did. With envy he watched the play of a sort of ecstasy on Karim's face. His lover was willing—no, eager—to die for something that was worth more than the price of his own life. Karim was here to die for what he loved most.

And I? Ali thought, as he squared his shoulders and went to sit his fraudulent self beside Karim. I am here merely to die.

The sun was hanging low over the whipped cream of the whitecaps as the waves beat the two rubber dinghies toward the wrong beach. Already their mission had gone awry. The Lebanese merchant-ship captain had been paid a prince's ransom in Saudi riyals to deposit them, after nightfall, on a certain beach near a luxury hotel just north of Tel Aviv. But when the sea turned choppy the captain, fearing interception by Israeli patrol boats, had lost his nerve and forced them at gunpoint into these two flimsy motor-driven rafts. Worse, the captain had skimped on their fuel, and so they had run out of gas far north of their objective. For hours the guerrillas had been bickering about what to do when they finally washed ashore. They were supposed to seize tourists in the hotel, swap those hostages for a few diplomats, then demand the release of five PLO commandos held in Israeli jails. Finally they, their diplomatic hostages, and their released comrades were to fly to Damascus in a United Nations plane. The logical flaw in their mission, of course, was that never before had the Israelis negotiated with any Arab commandos. But *malesh*. If only they could do something dramatically bloody enough to seize international headlines, they would make the point that there could be no peace in the Middle East without the cooperation of the Palestinians.

As the tactical debate rose and fell around him, Ali bailed the water out of their raft. He stared at the cold gray Mediterranean. Long ago his mother had promised to take him to Alexandria for his first look at this sea. He drew his wet fingers to his mouth. At least she hadn't lied about the sea's tasting of salt. He sighed. Clearly, no matter what they did when they landed, there would be no easy escape on a plane to Damascus. There was no alternative escape plan. If he could have chosen the time and place of his death, if at least it had been Allah's will to grant him an ordinary end to an uneventful life, he would have liked to die not by this churning sea but beside his Nile. It was a Saidi custom, before death, to drink one last time from the Nile. But Saidis called the Nile *el-bahr*—they called the river the sea. He cupped his hand and drank instead from the sea. The salt water was as sweet as acid.

Karim clutched his arm. "Land! There it is! Palestine! At last I come home!"

"Sh-h-h!" Aziza, one of the two women who had been included in their raiding party for propaganda purposes, silenced them as she dipped her paddle soundlessly into the sea.

"Palestine!" Karim mouthed the word.

They beached without incident, collected the two bazookas and the boxes of grenades and explosives, and shouldered their submachine guns. But Aziza was pointing and then running toward a figure on the beach. By the time they caught up with her, she was using English to interrogate a long-haired young woman with two cameras strung around her neck. The prisoner pleaded for her life and willingly told them that just over those sand dunes lay the main coastal road. They were near the collective settlement of Maagan Michael, twenty miles north of Tel Aviv, halfway to Haifa. Aziza cocked a pistol and shot the girl in the head. Ali bent over the body, shut its eyes, and nodded to his comrades. Their missions had been baptized. Amer, their captain, raised his submachine gun. *"Allahu akbar*—God is most great!" There was vomit in Ali's mouth as he whispered the battle cry along with the rest.

They scaled the dunes and took in the lay of the tarmac highway. It was not yet four o'clock on this afternoon of the Jewish Sabbath, and nothing moved on the desolate, sand-swept road. Amer made his decision. They would not make their stand in the nearest Jewish settlement but instead would waylay and commandeer whatever came along, take every Zionist hostage, and finally, *inshallah,* proceed toward Tel Aviv for their showdown. He and five others would set an ambush on this side of the road, five others would take up positions around the bend, and Ali and Karim would wait here with the heavy guns and the explosives. They clasped hands, cheered, and separated.

Lying in the sand behind a rock, listening to the wind shaking the scrub pine, dimly they heard a burst of automatic gunfire, screams, and shouts in broken Hebrew. When Ali and Karim poked their heads cautiously above the rock, they could see a red-and-white Egged bus with bullet-ridden windows stopped on the side of the road. *Rat-tat-*

ratatatat! Their comrades were spraying their guns into the bus, and then one by one figures stumbled down the steps as if in a daze. More than forty men, women, and children stood in a frightened huddle eyeing the Arabs. From beyond the bend they heard another burst of gunfire, more cries, and finally a white Mercedes taxi with the other squad of guerrillas screeched in front of the bus. Ali and Karim carried over the armaments. As the minutes ticked by, there were howls of confusion. Ai's nervous eyes flicked from the Arabs to the Jews. Amer screamed abuse at his men because there were dead bodies but no hostages in the taxi. The Israelis began to cry, pray, and argue among themselves in Hebrew and Yiddish. A Syrian methodically shot and killed the three Israeli passengers who were wearing army uniforms. Aziza started loading the explosives onto the bus. A woman was wounded by a Libyan as she tried to crawl away toward the trees. Karim jumped aboard the bus, smashed the windshield and back windows, and took up a position at the rear in easy reach of a bazooka and a box of grenades.

At last, shooting their guns impatiently into the air, the Arabs loaded everyone onto the bus. Amer brandished a pistol to the temple of an Israeli: "Drive! Tel Aviv!" With a lurch the bus turned south. The aisles were already slick with blood. Arabs stood guard from end to end, kicking the dead bodies under the seats. A Libyan stuck the butt of his submachine gun into the side of a woman who refused to stop moaning. As they careened down the empty highway, Karim aimed his gun out at the landscape of his homeland. They whizzed past orange groves and barbed-wire fences and finally spotted another bus four miles down the road. There was a high-speed chase, random firing from the Arabs, and burning rubber when the other bus finally stopped. Four Arabs leaped to the ground, there were more shots, and finally another batch of hostages climbed onto Amer's bus. Once again the Syrian executed the three Israei men and one woman wearing soldiers' uniforms.

Ali, positioned in the center of the crowded aisle, tried to count the fifty, sixty, maybe more than seventy hostages. But he found his eyes riveted to individual faces of the wounded. A little girl's bloody head lay in her mother's lap. An old man mumbled what sounded like a prayer as he doubled over in agony. A young man with gaping holes in his chest stared sightlessly at an empty picnic basket.

As they shot their way through two makeshift roadbocks, Ali paid special attention to any Israeli who looked old enough to be his own father. As Karim took potshots at a jeep, a taxi, a truck, Ali began to scream, "Youssef al-Masri!" He strode the length of the bus crying out his father's name, not knowing what he would do if, by a trick of fate, one of the enemy answered in the affirmative. "Youssef al-Masri?" His only answer was the groans of the wounded. Amid the screaming and the gore, Ali couldn't stop himself from slinging his machine gun over his shoulder and bending to the bleeding bodies. So this, he thought as he worked ferociously but hopelessly at the wounded, so this was what Israelis looked like? They were blond, dark, thin, fat, and they were losing far too much blood. He tried to apply a tourniquet to a woman's thigh. But an old Jew who evidently thought he was about to rape the woman made a lunge for his gun. Ali batted the old man to the floor and then, in an orgy of rage, kicked him until he stopped moving. Ali seized his own head between his hands. What was wrong with him, trying to help these Zionists? He wasn't one of them! Youssef al-Masri be damned! The faces around him became blurred, until he could no longer see eyes and lips and injuries but only his duty. He checked his belt for grenades, readied his gun, and heard the whirl of helicopters in the sky.

On and on the bus swerved: ten miles, fifteen miles, unchallenged almost into Tel Aviv. Suddenly, as they dipped down a grassy hill, there were bursts of fire from all sides, and the tires of the bus were shot to bits. Ahead Ali could see helicopters, army vehicles, fire engines, ambulances. As he looked out the rear window, he saw Israelis sealing off their retreat. Ali waved hostages to the floor and waited for the voice that must come over a bullhorn to open the negotiations for the hostages' release. Instead there was a steady stream of fire coming at them from all directions. Surely, Ali thought, surely they aren't going to continue firing like this at a full busload of their own people. Surely there will be a cease-fire, a parlay, and a final lifesaving bartering.

But in the dusk the gunfire continued. A grenade landed near the driver's seat. Karim readied his bazooka, and through the smoke Amer ordered his men to be silent. In broken Hebrew and then in better English he screamed to the Israelis that they had demands. They wanted the release of five commandos. None of these hostages—men, women, children!—would be hurt if only the Israelis stopped their indiscriminate fire and promised to fetch them their imprisoned comrades. A burst of automatic gunfire was his answer. Karim fired his bazooka. Amer lobbed grenades.

Ali edged to a window and prepared to fire. It seemed they would make their stand here entirely surrounded by the Israeli army. A thought clicked like a trigger in his mind. The Israeli army! His father was probably in the Israeli army! His father could be out there. Ali stared at the trees, wondering what his father looked like. He froze, unable to shoot. The noise, the screams, the explosions of the battle continued for seconds, minutes, it seemed forever. Surely, Ali thought, surely now the Israelis will have to hold their fire. But as he looked around the bus at the wounded and dead, he began to worry that their guerrilla mission would backfire. What Fatah wanted to affirm to the world was that the righteous Palestinian cause still endured. But all a busful of dead civilians would do was call world attention to what would be branded as Palestinian terrorism. Their mission, like every other commando hijacking or raid inside Israel, might even provide the Israelis with an excuse to invade Lebanon and Syria, to bomb peaceful Arab settlements, to seize more Arab land. Through the smoke Ali stared at those who still lived on the bus. Obviously, as soon as a stray shell hit their cache of explosives, a firestorm would incinerate this bus. "Out!" Ali screamed at Karim. "Get out! They're going to blow us up!" Karim and the Syrian began herding every hostage who could move out the back door. Ali leaped to the ground. The Syrian fell at a burst of automatic fire. But under the cover of smoke Ali and Karim crawled into a ditch along with seven of the women and children. As they huddled not twenty feet away, a rain of grenades struck the bus. It exploded in a ball of fire.

Ali lay there stunned. He saw some of the hostages running to safety behind the Israeli lines. On this side of the bus, all that were left were these few here in his ditch. Karim, he noticed now, had been hit in the knee. There was no chance of trying to escape through the fields with their hostages as shields. "Hold your fire!" Ali screamed in English. "We have your women and children here. We have demands! We will trade these hostages for the release of our comrades in your jails! Hold your fire!"

"No!" Karim was screaming too. "No! Don't give up! We die as men, Ali! Don't beg!"

But it didn't matter. Even if the Israelis had heard him, there was no lull. On the contrary, as the Israelis began to pinpoint Ali's and Karim's screams, their concentrated fire became more deadly. Karim took a bullet in the neck.

Slowly, trying to think, his head abuzz with flashing images of his mother's face, a felucca on the river, Baruch's eyes, Ali pulled a grenade from his belt. He would try, *inshallah,* one more time. "Hold your fire! We don't want any more to die! We want to talk! Hold your fire! I'm going to stand up, and we will negotiate!"

"No!" Karim screamed. "Don't do it, Ali! I warn you! I'll shoot you, Ali! I'll shoot you myself if you surrender!"

Ali turned his head and stared at Karim. Would his lover kill him? He had come here for love of Karim, and was this Karim's answer?

"Jew" Karim yelled. "You're a Jew!"

"Oh, God, God, *God!*" Ali's lips moved in prayer. He had not been able to kill his mother. But here, now, at the end, he would die as an Arab and a man. Before he inched up to his knees, he pulled the pin on the grenade. Whether he would pitch it harmlessly into the burning hull of the bus or let it roll into the ditchful of women and children depended on the Israelis. At the end, he would, with his last breath, *do something.* What was that Karim had always said? "By living you learn how to die, and by dying you learn how to live." Keeping his head low, he crouched, then stood at full height. He had just enough time, in the split second when he saw the bursts of fire aimed at him by Karim and the Israelis, to decide to throw the grenade neither at the bus nor at the hostages. Instead he clutched it despairingly to his breast as he died in the crossfire. It was only seconds later, when the grenade exploded, that Karim and two of the hostages died as well.

In the weak late-afternoon light Mona played with Ali's daughter on the bank of the Nile. "She's smiling, Soad. Come see! One month old and she knows her river."

Soad went on listlessly filling the family's water jugs. She nursed the infant night and day, but it was Mona who carried the child always on her hip.

Um Mona, crouching within earshot, let loose with a mourning shriek. *"Ay-iee! Ay-iee! Ay-ieeee!"* Neither Mona nor Soad gave her a glance. In the four months since Ali had run away in the night, Um Mona had done little but shriek and cry. The notion in the village was that Um Mona had become unhinged by Muhammad's death.

Not far away boys shouted and dogs barked as if at the approach of a stranger. Mona clasped the baby closer. "Ali! He's come back. I knew he would. He's come back." She had not allowed herself to believe Baruch's story that Ali had left Egypt to join a commando unit. She had not permitted herself to speculate whether he had taken any part in last week's bloody raid on that Israeli bus.

A heavier tread than Ali's came near. Baruch, his sober face coated with dust, was trailed by a cluster of children whining for *baksheesh.* He shooed them away, greeted the women, and sat down by Mona.

"A girl," Mona said. "Soad gave us a beautiful little girl."

Baruch held out his arms for his great-grandniece. Ali's daughter was fragile and delicate. Youssef and Mona's granddaughter was pretty and pink. Um Mona's great-granddaughter, looking up at his bearded face, howled. "What's her name?"

"We're leaving that up to Ali." Mona smiled. "He'll be back soon. Her father will know. He'll decide."

The creases in Baruch's forehead deepened, and the baby cried harder. "Maybe she's hungry." Soad put down her water jug and came to nurse the child.

Mona was determined not to read what was written on Baruch's grim face. He wasn't mourning anyone. He was just tired. That train ride was always an ordeal. He must have worn that black suit because he knew the train was so dirty. Merely because of exhaustion he looked far older than he had the last time she had seen him. "The baby is beautiful, isn't she? Ali will love her. I know he will. I wonder what he'll call her. What do you think, Baruch? What do you think Ali will want to call his fine firstborn?"

Baruch let his silence speak for itself. In some part of her, surely she understood why he had come.

Mona stared at the sunset bustle on the river as if its predictable happenings were a matter of surprise and fascination. Black-robed women chattered as they collected their sun-dried laundry from the rocks. Other women rinsed out their glasses and pots in the shallows. Behind them on the road men shuffled from the fields to the village, their arms full of clover, their donkey carts piled high with their day's harvest. The patched white sail of a felucca billowed as the boat skimmed over the water toward the other side, where a line of women refilled their water jugs. For seventy centuries none of this had changed. Mona was preparing to make some comment about the river—how it was always the same, how it was a comfort that it never changed—when Baruch touched her hand.

As a doctor, he had some experience in breaking very bad news. He had found it best to tell the worst a little at a time, so the mind could have time to prepare the heart. "I've heard from Ali."

"Yes?" Mona kept her eyes on the river. Maybe the billionth barge that had plied this river since the time of the pharaohs was churning upriver to the Luxor dock.

"He wrote to me from the Lebanon."

"The Lebanon." She repeated the word as if it were a place she had heard of once in a fantastic tale the children loved. She looked over at the baby as if she would rather be telling her a story or singing her a lullaby about the Lebanon.

"I told you before that he was going there with Karim." Baruch moistened his lips. "You see, Karim was his lover. Ali, too, at the end, was a guerrila fighter for Fatah."

"At the end?" The last rays of the sun put a yellow sheen on the surface of the river.

"Yes." Baruch took her hand. "Yesterday a messenger came with two letters. One from Ali. One from the Fatah command. Karim was killed in that raid last week inside Israel."

"So." She looked at her hand in Baruch's. "So. So Ali loved Karim. He had *that*, then."

"Ali wrote to me from one of their camps along the coast. He wrote the night before they left for their mission." With his sleeve Baruch wiped the sweat from his forehead. "Or rather, he wrote just hours before they left."

"He's still there? In the Lebanon? Or is Ali in Israel with his father?"

"Mona. You must have heard on the radio about their raid. Thirty-seven Israelis died. Fatah lost thirteen guerrillas. Ali died, Mona, on March the eleventh." From the envelope he pulled the photograph of Ali in uniform.

She stared at it, then let it drop from her hand. She looked up from the river to the sky. Already it was muted from blue to rosy purple. Across the river the mountains that sheltered the Valley of the Kings glowed red. A formation of geese was flying north.

"I'll read you his letter. He wrote it to me, but I think it was meant for you." Baruch took a much-creased paper from the envelope. In that gesture he remembered reading her another letter, that first letter from her mother, in his laboratory in Alexandria. If he had been too preoccupied with his work that night to take an interest in that fragile little girl, if he had allowed her later to abandon Alexandria before it all began with Youssef . . . if, if, if. He cleared his throat and tried to believe it was God's will and not his own miscalculations that had set them on the road that led to this last letter from Ali. "Dear Uncle Baruch. We leave in a few minutes. They say it will be a lightning raid, and that I will be back in Damascus in two days. But they lie. I will not come back. What should I come back *for?* Honor is here. You told me in Cairo that I had the power to end all this. You were right about that, as you were right about so many things. This is the only honorable end. Watch over my mother. Comfort her. Protect her. Please give her my blue bead. My comrades will provide for her and for Soad and the child, if there is one. May Allah be compassionate! Ali."

Mona's head dropped to her chest. She folded her empty arms on her breasts and rocked as if she were holding a baby. She made no sound and did not seem to notice when Soad walked away, very slowly, with Ali's daughter in her arms. But then Mona stopped rocking. She turned to Baruch. "His bead?" She held out her hand. When he gave it to her, she looked down at it. She fondled it with her fingertips. She held it up to her nose and smelled it. "Ali." She kissed the bead, and then she arched her arm and threw it far out into the Nile. The hollow bead floated north with the current. Maybe, she thought, some other woman would fish the bead from the river and treasure it as a talisman against evil. But for Mona and those she loved, there could be no more magic. *"Khelas,"* she whispered. "It is finished."

But it was not over. *"Ay-iee! Ay-iee!"* Um Mona was hunched over in the posture of one weaving a basket. Her hands, however, were empty and still.

Mona's eyes hardened at the old woman. She opened her mouth and answered her mother with a mourning wail that was raw and full of fury. *"Ay-ieeeeee!"* She brought her hands to her face and scratched her own skin until she drew blood. "You! You killed my son! You!"

"Kill." Um Mona repeated the word as if it had no meaning.

"Dead!" Mona advanced on her mother. "You! You killed him!"

Baruch scrambled to his feet and tried to restrain Mona. As he kept her from striking Um Mona, she screamed, "You did it! You wanted him dead, and you killed him!"

Tears rolled in well-worn ruts down Um Mona's cheeks. "Not Ali. Not him. You. You who shamed us all. I didn't kill Ali. You did. You know you did."

Mona sized up her mother as if for the last time. "All my life I've made excuses for you, Ummie. I felt sorry for you. I tried to imagine how you felt inside. How terrible it must have been for you when your own mother died the way she did. I thought that maybe you'd change. I put up with all—"

"You feared me." The tears seemed to have washed the madness from Um Mona's eyes. "But you never loved me. I loved you. But you never loved me. You never did. You betrayed me. You were my perfect little girl. I did everything for you. I took you to Alexandria so you wouldn't die here in the village. I left you there, so that you could live, even though that meant I had to be alone. I did all that for you, Mona. And then you went bad. *Sharmoota!*" She tried to claw at her daughter's legs.

Mona contemptuously stepped back out of her reach. "You're wrong, Ummie. I *did* love you. I must have even loved you more than I loved Youssef. I came back here with you, when I should have gone off after him. And now this. Now this. Allah forgive you, Ummie. But I will not." Without another word she turned away and swept back toward the village.

Um Mona sat by the river, where the faint mourning wails for Ali drifted on the wind. Twilight moonbeams danced on the water. Like a fetus she huddled with her legs pulled up to her chest and her head to her knees.

It had all gone wrong. It wasn't supposed to have turned out this way. She had visited Sekhmet in the temple. The goddess had told her what she must do. That she must tell Ali, and that then her grandson would make it right. Mona had been evil, and Mona had to be punished. How could Ali be dead? Sekhmet had been certain that Mona was the guilty one. By killing Mona, Ali would wipe out the curse. Sekhmet had promised to look after Mona in the afterlife. After all, Mona had been dedicated to her at conception and at birth. Sekhmet would have made her pure again. When it came Um Mona's time to join them in Paradise, Mona would be as innocent as the infant she once suckled with her own milk.

Um Mona frowned. She would have to make another trip to Sekhmet. Because she was afraid Sekhmet would be angry with her, she had avoided Karnak Temple since that terrible night when Ali had run away. Um Mona sighed. Angry or not, she would have to visit Sekhmet tonight. The goddess would tell her what she must do. She hoped Sekhmet wouldn't tell her to kill Mona. Always she had feared that someday that command would come.

Um Mona rose clumsily to her feet and crept back toward the village. Under the tall date palm that stood by the new government well, she began digging in the soft earth with her bare hands. The ax was where she had buried it after her last visit to the temple. The blade had dulled, but there was no time to sharpen it. She brushed off the dirt and slipped it inside her robe. Sometimes the night watchman padlocked the door to Sekhmet's chamber, and sometimes she had to use this ax to cut to Sekhmet.

She skirted the village. While she was engaged on a sacred mission, she would talk to no one but Sekhmet.

The public entrance to the temple was deserted. In an hour or so the carriages would roll up with their loads of tourists bound for the sound-and-light show in the temple. Um Mona began to hurry. Sekhmet turned especially nasty when the tourists desecrated the temple with their loud talk and their laughter.

As fast as she could, she made her way past the main gate and slipped inside at a spot where the wall had crumbled. She looked around for the telltale watchman's lantern. The temple guards were always on the lookout for village women sneaking into the temple at night. When they had caught her here before, they had escorted her out the front gate. Always they warned her not to come back, especially at night when there were snakes and scorpions lying in wait in the darkness. Once she herself had seen a scorpion, but never a serpent. Even so, she reminded herself to be careful where she stepped.

She sidled along the main avenue of the sphinxes and into the outer temples of the sun god Amun. In the starless inky sky the three-quarter moon glimmered on the tall, thick forest of pharaonic pillars. She rested on the base of a column until she caught her breath. Even if a guard happened along, she could evade him here. But next she would have to risk the meadow path where the guards had spotted her on other nights. She would have to run that distance. She gripped the ax more tightly in her hand. By Allah, no watchman would stop her tonight!

She steeled herself for her dash through the meadow. The fields were higher than the sunken dirt path. If she kept low, no one would spy her in this black robe. Praying to Allah and Sekhmet under her breath, she ran like a beetle down the long path.

She breathed a sigh of relief when she stood at the entrance to the Temple of Ptah. Almost there. She turned to the right and scuttled down to the doors leading to Sekhmet's chamber. She was inside, she turned right again, she cursed. The door to Sekhmet's inner sanctum was padlocked. She examined the rusty metal lock. One blow with the ax should do it. She covered the lock with her shawl to muffle the sound. She brought the ax down, removed the shattered lock, and threw her ax down on the ground. She shoved hard, and the old wooden door creaked open.

She walked slowly into the morbid blackness of the room.

Sekhmet! Um Mona bowed her head and trembled. Most terrible of all goddesses—the black lion goddess of retribution—rose before her. Moonlight from the shaft in the ceiling flooded Sekhmet's cruel face. Still panting from her exertions, Um Mona prostrated herself. She waited to hear the voice of the goddess inside her head.

She heard nothing.

Perhaps she was too far away from Sekhmet. She crawled closer on her hands and knees until she was at the feet of the statue. She looked up fearfully and waited. Still the voice did not come.

Um Mona's legs ached from her long run to Sekhmet. She settled back on her haunches. But Sekhmet did not speak.

Um Mona resigned herself to speaking first. Evidently the goddess wanted her to beg. "I come to you, O Sekhmet. You told me to tell Ali the secret of his birth. You promised to take Mona as your own, and to keep her for me until I join you. I did as you asked, O Sekhmet. But what you promised did not happen. Mona still lives. Ali is dead. Why, Sekhmet, why?"

There was no answer from the goddess.

"She blames me, O Sekhmet. She blames me for that boy's death. But we know, don't we? Don't we, Sekhmet? It was not my fault. Isn't that right, Sekhmet?"

Um Mona strained to hear her answer.

"We loved her, didn't we, Sekhmet? She was ours. All ours. We loved her the best. Even when we hated her, we loved her! Didn't we?"

Um Mona shut her eyes so it would be easier to hear the voice of the goddess.

"But she said one thing to me, O Sekhmet. One thing she said to me. She said she loved me—loved me more than she loved that Jew. That's something. That's something, isn't it?"

Um Mona opened her eyes and stared up at the goddess. Maybe Sekhmet was angry with her. Maybe she blamed her for all that had gone wrong. Maybe Sekhmet was going to take vengeance on her.

"It wasn't my fault! Tell me, Sekhmet, tell me it wasn't my fault!"

As her panic rose, her breathing came in pants. The narrow room was closing in on Um Mona.

"A sign, Sekhmet! Give me a sign."

It seemed, as the moon ducked behind a cloud, that the eyes of the goddess changed. It seemed they were looking beyond Um Mona, at the ground behind her.

Um Mona turned her head to follow Sekhmet's eyes. For a moment she saw nothing in the shadows. But then there was a movement on the floor. Everything in the chamber was black, all but for the fat white thing slithering toward her. A serpent. There was a snake between her and the door.

Um Mona turned frantically back to the statue. "Don't let it get me! I'm sorry! I'm sorry! I'll make up for it! I'll kill Mona myself. I promise. Tonight. I'll bring her body here. I'll do anything you ask."

The goddess looked ahead blankly into space.

Um Mona turned her head. The serpent was closer now. Sekhmet had sent it to kill her. Sekhmet had turned against her. All her life she had served the goddess. This was her reward.

Um Mona crawled on all fours away from the snake. She crept to her feet. She was backed up against the clammy stone wall. She wished she had her ax. Why had she left it at the door? She should have had it in her hand. The long white serpent was only a few feet away. It coiled and it hissed.

Panting hard, she flattened herself against the wall. The snake was almost at her feet.

Sekhmet had abandoned her. She had better make her peace with Allah. "There is no God but Allah, and Muhammad is His Prophet!"

As the snake shot out its forked tongue to bite her, she felt a rush of blood to her head. She couldn't breathe. She gasped for air. "Allah!" She clutched at her chest and collapsed at Sekhmet's feet.

The snake slithered harmlessly over her body and into the hollow at the base of the black statue.

It was very late the next night, and Baruch was waiting for Mona on the bank of the river. Sedately, without much mourning, that afternoon they had buried Um Mona. The women had been listening to a *shaykha* chant the Koran since the sun had set. Mona had asked to talk to him privately before he left for Cairo on the morning train. He had promised to wait for her here until midnight.

He consulted his watch and yawned. It had been a gruesome day. The watchmen had brought home the remains of the old woman in the morning. After examining her unmarked body, he had tentatively concluded that she had suffered a massive heart attack. But then after the funeral, when he had found his steps turning toward Karnak Temple, he had paid a guard to show him where they had found the body. He had stood in the mysterious narrow chamber, gloomy even when the sun was high in the sky. He remembered the site very well. Mona, when she was a little girl, had burst into tears at the sight of this forbidding black statue. Since then, reading up on Sekhmet, Baruch had decided she was enough to make a grown man cry. According to the mythology, Sekhmet once, in a fit of bloodlust, threatened to devour all mankind in her ferocious lion jaws. To avert that catastrophe, the sun god made his slaves flood wide fields with a mixture of intoxicating barley and red dye. When Sekhmet mistook the fields for human blood, she drank so deeply she became too drunk to remember her plans for human extermination. Millennia ago Egyptians had feared this rampaging Sekhmet as the source of war, sickness, and pestilence. Yet at the very beginning of human history, Sekhmet had first been worshiped as the source of all love. Somewhere along the line—but how, where, when?—she had been corrupted into a spirit of darkness. Baruch had stared up at the statue's sadistic mouth and the vacant eyes. It was easy to understand how Um Mona, already half mad and highly suggestible, had died of fright in this eerie chamber.

He looked at his watch again. Almost midnight. In six hours he would be on the train to Cairo. The night was so quiet he could hear the river move. There was peace here. Again he turned his plan over in his mind. Mona was alone now. He was alone still. Why not leave his position at Kasr el-Aini and come to Karnak to work beside Mona in the village clinic? They could marry. Bliss. It would be bliss. It would be his last surrender to everything he had never understood but always yearned for in Egypt. He heard the rustle of a robe trailing through grass. "Mona? I'm over here. I'm still here."

Wearily she flung herself down beside him. She had already washed away the blue dye and mourning mud from her face. In the moonlight she seemed more composed than Baruch had expected. "I thought you weren't coming. I heard the other women leave the chanting long ago."

"I was writing a letter."

"A letter?" Idly he wondered whom she could be writing *to*. Her son and her mother were dead. He himself was here beside her.

"Youssef. I wrote to Youssef." She handed Baruch a sealed envelope. "Can you help me get it to him?"

"He's in Israel." Baruch tried to curb his jealousy. He had hoped she wanted to see him for another reason. "You know you can't mail letters from here to Israel."

"If Sadat can go to Jerusalem, then surely this letter can get there as well."

"I suppose I could send it to my niece in Switzerland. And she could forward it to him. But Mona, are you sure you really want to do this? After all this . . . time?"

"I haven't seen him for more than twenty-one years. It was twenty-one years last January. We sat on a bench near Rushdi Beach on the Corniche and planned our wedding. I told him I had finally met that fat policeman Abbas wanted me to marry. Youssef was so jealous! But he had good news. He had bribed a clerk in the municipal office. We would be married the day after my birthday. We looked out at the sea and repeated our vows. And then I had to leave because—as usual—

450

Youssef had arrived a half hour late. We were to meet there on the Corniche again the next day. 'Same time, same place!' Youssef called out to me. He was afraid I would forget. *'Jamais!'* I said, *'Jamais!'* That was twenty-one years and two months ago, Baruch. I could never forget."

Baruch shifted in discomfort. "All I meant to ask you was if you're sure you want to write to Youssef."

"I want to *see* Youssef."

"Oh. You've said as much in your letter?"

"That and other things."

"Mona, that was a long time ago. Maybe you should take a few days to think this over. I'm not so sure—"

"I am. I'm very sure. If you don't want to mail my letter, I'll find another way to get it to Youssef. Maybe the United Nations would help. Or one of the embassies. Or maybe even Sadat himself would take a personal interest. He seems to be on such good terms with the Israelis." Her lips curled with bitterness.

Baruch tried unsuccessfuly to put his arm around her. "Look, Mona. You found out yesterday that you lost your son. Today you buried your mother. I don't think you should send this letter so hastily."

"Hastily? Baruch, this letter is twenty-one years too late. I should have written it when I knew I was pregnant. But I was afraid of what could happen to Youssef if he came back. Then later I wanted to protect Ali. I didn't know how it would affect him to hear about his real father." Her face crumpled. "But now we know how Ali felt. We know. Don't we, Baruch?"

"But it's been *so long.* To write to Youssef after so many years? People change. Twenty years is longer than some people live."

"Yes. Ali was twenty."

Baruch sighed. "I just don't think this letter is very wise."

"Nothing about Youssef and me has ever been very wise. *But it was right!* Baruch, I *must* do this. I must. I must see him. When I had Ali, it was almost as if I had part of Youssef, too. But now . . . now . . ." She lowered her head and wept in her hands.

Baruch put his arm around her. Should he tell her of Youssef's marriage and divorce? From the beginning, there had been far too many secrets in this affair. Their courtship. Ali's birth. Youssef's marriage. He had known about it all and said nothing. Silently he cursed himself for making the wrong decisions. Any resolution would have been better than the chain of circumstances that had cut off Ali's life. Maybe it was too late, but he would make a clean breast of it. If the result was that she was disillusioned about Youssef, if instead of turning to Youssef for relief she turned to his own waiting arms, then maybe that would be for the best.

But Mona was wiping her eyes with the hem of her robe. "I want him to come back to Egypt. I'll see him in Alexandria. Where we used to meet, where I saw him last, along the Corniche. I've thought about this for years, Baruch. What he'd say. What I'd say. How the sea would look in the sunset."

Baruch swallowed hard. "But the danger. Sadat's trip to Jerusalem hasn't wiped away thirty years of war with Israel. Think of it, Mona. Youssef has been living in Israel for a very long time. The police here would be certain he was a spy."

"He'll come. He'll find a way. I've told him about Ali. He has to come."

"And if he doesn't? If he can't come? If, Mona, he doesn't *want* to come?"

"He'll come. Youssef *loves* me."

"He loved you twenty years ago." Now Baruch must tell her. "Knowing Youssef, I think he must still . . . care. But Mona . . . damn! Youssef took a wife."

Mona simply stared at Baruch.

"He married an Israeli girl. They had three daughters. But the marriage wasn't a happy one. They've been divorced for many years."

"Youssef married someone else?" When she squinted, even in the moonlight a network of fine lines were visible around her eyes. A deep frowning crease ran along her cheeks. "Married? But he couldn't. He was married to me. He vowed to me that we were married. That he would never marry another."

"I'm sorry, Mona. I didn't want to hurt you. But it would be worse for you, I think, if . . . Do you really want to open all this up again?"

"It was never shut. Not to me. At least, not to me."

"What do you want from him?"

Mona gave her shoulders a hopeless shrug. "To see him. I wish . . ." She would not say what it was she wished.

"You want to finish with him? Is that it?"

She wrung her hands in her lap. "I told you once it wasn't finished with Youssef and me. It still isn't." But Youssef had not been true to her. She had waited but he had not. Maybe she *should* marry Baruch. Maybe she should have married Baruch years ago. "Before I can even think of starting anything with anyone else, I must know—one way or another—what there is with Youssef."

"You mean—" Baruch was too excited to finish his sentence.

Mona gave him an enigmatic look. "You'll mail the letter?"

"Yes! Mona! I've been thinking. I could come to Karnak. Work in the clinic. You wouldn't have to leave the village."

"*Inshallah.*" She hesitated, and then spoke with uncertainty. "Baruch, I don't want you to think this is any sort of promise. I don't want another broken promise in my life."

"No. No. I understand. I've always known how you feel—felt—about Youssef."

"So," she said. "So."

They both looked back at the calm blackness of the Nile, which never changed.

26 ～～～

ALEXANDRIA, EGYPT   /   September 1978

Youssef sat on the bed in his shabby room at the Beau Rivage. The once-elegant hotel had come down in the world. The best people still knew it as the most prestigious hotel in Alexandria, but even so the Beau Rivage was seedy, third-class, Balkan. Like so much else that had been grand in prerevolutionary Egypt, the Beau Rivage was clearly past its prime. His room was large but poorly furnished. Old layers of paint had blistered on the walls. The porcelain bathtub was mottled and broken. Two light fixtures dangled with their wiring exposed. Yet the Beau Rivage retained some of its old arrogant pride. Goldfish still swam in the terrace pond while austere Nubian waiters served tea and cakes. The desk clerk still was snobbish in seven languages. The bellhops and the maids and the waiters still fussed over the guests as if this were the Georges V in a Paris of thirty years ago. There was an air of musty nostalgia in the sweep of the drafty old halls with their urns of sand and their framed prints of English flowers and birds. A sign still pointed to the *bibliothèque,* but the library shelves were dusty and bare except for some tracts from the Koran. The Beau Rivage was a period piece, but it still had at least the pretensions to class. Youssef wondered why something like the Beau Rivage was always compared to an old woman, lined now but once pretty, gracious even in her years of decline. Couldn't men, too, age gracefully? The bed creaked under him when he moved slightly to consult his watch.

It was almost time. In a half hour he would go down to the lobby, catch a taxi, and proceed to his rendezvous with Mona along the Corniche. Could this really be happening? Could he be here, in Alexandria, the city of his birth and his youth, about to be reunited with the woman who was the love of his life?

He jumped nervously to his feet, opened the French windows, and strode onto his balcony facing the sea. It was a breezy, sunny late summer's day, chill enough so that he turned up his collar against the wind. From the railing, looking out beyond the curves of the Corniche, the gray-gold skyline of Alexandria was as he remembered it. Two daring sailboats skidded over the waves, heading out to sea. Twenty-five years ago, Youssef thought, that would have been Hamid and me out there. A little wind wouldn't have kept us from our hearts' desires, whether it was a wild sail or a woman.

Hamid. For the two days Youssef had been waiting in Alexandria for Mona, he had made discreet inquiries about Hamid. Traveling under an Italian name and an Italian passport, still leery of the Egyptian police, Youssef had taken care to confide his past to no one. Under these circumstances, it had been difficult to find out about Hamid. So many of their old friends were gone from Alexandria. All the foreign boys—the Greeks, the Italians, the other Europeans, and, of course, the Jews—had left soon after he had. Greek cafés still carried the old names, but the new owners were Egyptian. The Cotton Exchange was closed. The Villa al-Masri had been converted to rented flats. Some of his friends' old mansions were shuttered shut and obviously long abandoned. Others had been turned into mysterious-sounding government agencies.

Only Victoria College was much the same. He had taken a taxi out to Victoria's back entrance. A guard wouldn't let him inside without a pass, and so he had walked the iron-gated perimeter. The gold stone buildings, the old English belltower, the skimpy royal palms were still sun-drenched and impassive. Maybe the walls of the main academic hall were layered with a little grime. Maybe the gardens were brown with neglect. But it was still Victoria, an outpost of the British Empire built to outlast the English themselves. He had stood at the rear gate and watched the students, just released from their classes, run out the gate toward the trolleys. They were wearing those same old blue-and-gray uniforms. The same ties, the same embroidered badges. But—by God!—there were little Egyptian *girls* going to school at Victoria. How the British administrators would have gagged at the idea of coeducation! How he and Hamid would have loved it! All the chubby, dark-eyed boys and girls were so gay and laughing. Had he and Hamid ever been so carefree? The students all looked Egyptian. There didn't seem to be a Bulgarian prince or a French consul's son among them. But he had imagined that two little boys, obviously plotting mischief as they giggled together behind a palm tree, were the young sons of Hamid el-Husseini.

He had finally learned about Hamid when he was getting a shave at the gossipy Cecil Hotel. Youssef remembered when the Cecil had been a hub of high society and a favorite watering hole of the colonial British. A little Arab boy used to support his entire extended family by sitting outside the Cecil with a sack of ashes and sand. Unless the boy had been bribed by *baksheesh* to keep his dirt to himself, he used to throw his ashes and sand on the tropical white suits of the British. There were no signs of the boy now, or of any colonial British. And the Cecil, with a neon "Disco!" sign defacing its grand facade, was tawdry and threadbare. Sipping a beer in the lobby lounge, he had eavesdropped for murmurs of the past. He had listened to grubby government officials, apparently here on fact-finding junkets, complain that Alexandria wasn't what it used to be. He had watched tourists leafing through dog-eared paperback copies of *The Alexandria Quartet* and looking around, puzzled, because Justine and Balthazar obviously were not about to come strolling through the door. He had smiled to himself as self-conscious Egyptians, dripping gold at their necks and on their fingers, moaned to one another about servant problems.

Youssef had thought there was nothing from the past left for him at the Cecil. But while he had waited his turn in the barber shop, glancing at the wall's tattered old portrait of Nasser and the larger and gaudier one of Sadat, his eyes had come to rest on a slew of snapshots tucked into the edge of a mirror. Faded likenesses of young men in uniform. Youssef had looked and looked again. The patent-leather hair, the droopy eyelids, the amused curve of those lips. Could that be the image of his Hamid? Cautiously, as the barber had soaped his face for the shave, speaking in French because he had not dared to speak Arabic, Youssef had begun to bemoan the price of growing old. He had said he was losing his hair and gaining a paunch. He had gestured to the snapshots. "Youth!" he had said with a dramatic sigh. Did the barber, by any chance, know the story of those young men who now rested in this place of honor at the Cecil? The barber had been delighted to linger over the past with the foreign gentleman. It was the barber's experience that the more he entertained a client, the greater was his *baksheesh*. Those eight young men on his mirror were all his former customers, all fine young Egyptian aristocrats, all now dead in the wars with the Jews. He had confided that one had died in Gaza, two on the West Bank, the rest in Sinai. Hamid had been one of those who died in '67 in the Sinai. According to the barber, Lieutenant el-Husseini had been a dashing bachelor, a terror with the ladies, one of—the barber dwelled on this point—his biggest tippers.

The barber had sighed that so many had died in the '67 war. His own duties during that war had been to shave the colonels at headquarters. The barber had remembered standing on the west bank of the Suez Canal as what was left of the Egyptian army had straggled out of the desert. Some had been wearing only their undershorts, most had been barefoot and unarmed, all had been very nearly dead. It was said that whole divisions had been stranded without food or water in the middle of the desert wasteland. It was said that treacherous Bedouins had come upon the soldiers and sold them water in exchange for their shoes and clothes and guns. The barber wasn't certain if Hamid el-Husseini had died nearly naked in the desert or in the carnage of one of the tank battles. But it was for certain—Allah keep him—that Hamid el-Husseini had not come back from the Sinai.

The barber, aware that Europeans tipped well for peaceful sentiments, had praised Sadat. "You know what we always say? 'Arabs will fight the Jews to the last drop of Egyptian blood!' Let other Arabs lose their sons if they want. We've lost enough." In honor of Hamid, Youssef had presented the barber with two pounds of *baksheesh*.

Later, wandering the downtown streets, Youssef had reflected that his old fears of killing Hamid on the battlefields had not been so far-fetched. Poor old Hamid. He would have liked to have seen old Hamid. He would have liked, here on the Nebi Daniel, to have smacked his palm on Hamid's. He would have liked to have taken him to the Sporting Club and drunk too many whiskeys with water and ice. How they could have talked! They could have shared such trivia! They would have held back their maudlin tears and instead laughed and laughed. He would have liked to have known how Hamid had turned out: the women he had loved, the battles he had fought, the jokes and the victories and the defeats that had been dealt him. He had so loved Hamid and those carefree years they had lost.

Youssef looked back at the sea. The water was a brilliant blue. Whitecaps crested near the shore. The curve of the Keit Bay promontory made a cove of the city. Youssef had seen the Mediterranean from Israel, from France, from Italy, and from Greece. But it was at its best in Alexandria. Here it was *his* sea and *his* city.

A sun haze hugged the waterfront. From this far away Alexandria was still jewel-like, with its shining minarets and mosques and steeples. It was only up close that the city was bigger and dirtier and rowdier. There was more and yet less of it. It had increased in quantity but lost in quality. He so missed the lost beauties of Alexandria. Perhaps the mass of the people suffered less here now, but he doubted it. Maybe in a generation or two there would be something to love in this new Alexandria. But for now, Youssef mourned the loss of what was. Alexandria had been glorious. It had been so easy once to believe that this had been Cleopatra's city. Walking the Corniche used to be like strolling the seaside promenades of the Riviera. But in the years of his exile, Egypt had reclaimed Alexandria. He gazed over the distant rooftops at the sunbaked bones of what remained. A film of dirt and decay glazed the colonnaded arcades and the consular centers and the sweeping stone squares. In Midan Saad Zaghloul, where long ago he stood with Batata listening to the Muslim Brotherhood's message of hate, ragged old men slept on broken marble benches while the wind riffled discarded newspapers. The flat rooftops of ornate Italian Renaissance villas were a jumble of laundry, animal pens, and the date-palm shacks in which the poor lived and died. It would have been more merciful to burn Alexandria to the ground than to let it become like this. It was almost as bad as Cairo.

That pit of a place! If Alexandria was disappointing, Cairo was shocking. He had spent only a night and a day there. At first he had tried to convince himself his own trepidations distorted what he saw. Cairo, after all, had long been the fangs of anti-Israeli venom. He himself had monitored the "Voice of Cairo" during two wars. To ride its streets, to walk its alleys, was like stalking a recurring nightmare.

He had, of course, taken every possible precaution to mask his identity from official Egypt. After Mona's letter had arrived, he had thanked God that all these years he had been prudent or wishful enough to keep renewing his old Italian passport. He had flown to Rome, consulted the Israeli embassy for advice, then legally changed his name to what it might have been if his family had never emigrated to Egypt. On his Italian passport he was not Youssef al-Masri, an Israeli Jew who was once wanted for espionage in Egypt, but a Milan-born Christian businessman by the name of Giuseppi Morenu. Knowing the reputation of the Italian bureaucracy, he had expected that all this would take time and money. But four months? An entire suitcase full of his mother's money converted to Italian lire? *Malesh*. At long last, armed with a passport and an identity that could excite no Egyptian suspicion, he had been granted his three-week tourist visa. In those months of anxious waiting, Youssef had tried to convince himself his elaborate machinations were unnecessary. The Israelis and the Egyptians seemed on the verge of finally signing a peace treaty. In the boutiques of Tel Aviv, shoppers could buy T-shirts silkscreened with Sadat's smiling face. Egypt supposedly no longer was hounding its handful of resident Jews. But still, there was that matter of his father's old involvement with Moshe's gang. Maybe Sadat was talking peace, but Youssef wasn't counting on a change of heart in every Egyptian immigration, customs, and intelligence official.

Waiting in Rome, he had tried to make contact with Baruch. His uncle had no telephone, and so he had spent days and days trying to get through to him at Kasr el-Aini Hospital. When the persistent Italian switchboard operator finally convinced Cairo to patch through to the hospital, whoever answered had said to call back another time. Two days later, when he managed to get through again, the call had been disconnected while someone tried to transfer it to Baruch's floor. After that, the Cairo operator insisted that an international call to the hospital was *mish mumkin*, not possible. Youssef could hardly believe that Baruch's world and Egypt itself were so incommunicado. Did he really want to return to a place like that? Yes. After her letter, he had to come back. Youssef had contented himself with a telegram advising Baruch that he was on his way. Prudently he had left out the exact date and time of his arrival. The Egyptians knew Baruch had once been a Jew. Perhaps they were still monitoring his mail. He had signed the telegram Giuseppi Morenu, hoped for the best, and immersed himself in spy novels in which the hero always survived.

As the Alitalia jet had finally circled Cairo for its night landing, Youssef had peered at the millions of lights spread out below him. He could smell his own fear in the sweat of his armpits. He had been glad for the human warmth of the sleeping little Arab boy he had held in his arms. Beside him a fat Egyptian matron had held two more of her young sons. The family—there were uncles and cousins and a father scattered nearby—had boarded the overbooked flight in Athens. At first Youssef had resented the discomfort and the safety risk of jamming so many bodies into these narrow seats. It wasn't *civilized*. But then after the woman pressed her cheese sandwiches and oranges and chocolates upon him, one of her boys had looked up at him with such drowsy longing that Youssef had allowed him to crawl into his lap. Had his own dead son—had Ali—been like this little boy?

Youssef had looked out at the lights of Cairo for reassurance. His mind had been a confusion of prayers and fears. Had the sloppy Italians slipped up on some detail of his passport? Please, let Mona be there! Oh, God, what if he was arrested at the airport? Would Mona think him old and balding and unworthy? What if Customs discovered the dollars he was smuggling in as a gift for his uncle?

As their plane taxied down the runway, Egyptians had popped out of their seats and begun surging toward the doors. The stewardesses had run down the aisles, shooing the Arabs back into their seats. But no sooner had one been forced down than another had jumped up. The Egyptians had laughed and joked and made a game of this, as Youssef now fondly remembered that Egyptians had made a joke of everything. They had such a gift for play. One stewardess had finally run her hands wildly through her hair and, her patience at an end, had shouted at them as a schoolteacher screams at unruly children. Youssef had laughed along with the Egyptians. He was back home. Everything was going to be all right.

As he had walked off the plane, in a rush of remembrance for the gaiety of Egypt, Youssef had puckered up his mouth and spat on the concrete runway. Hamid had always made a ritual of spitting as soon as he returned to Egyptian soil, even if he had been away only for an hour's sail on the sea. Hamid, laughing, had said it was the vulgar Egyptian equivalent of kissing the earth. Ha! Youssef had spat again for luck. Hamid!

458

His high spirits had wilted in the dirt and confusion and bewildering inefficiency of the noisy airport. The automatic baggage conveyor had been broken. He had had to climb up on a baggage cart and fight for his suitcases. A Saudi Arabian airliner had just landed, and a pushing horde of repatriated Egyptians had been struggling to claim their cardboard cartons of refrigerators, washing machines, and televisions. But—*el-hamdulillah!*—he hadn't even had to open his suitcases for inspection in Customs. Still, he was haggard when he had finaly wheeled his luggage cart out. There he had been confronted by a howling mob of Egyptians assembled to welcome their relatives back from years of toil abroad. He had recoiled and wanted to escape from all this emotion and stink and packed human flesh. He had preferred an Egypt that was happy and joking and crude only at a distance. But on the way to Baruch's, encased in the relative safety of his taxi, his eyes had darted everywhere for landmarks from his youth. As they had crept through a traffic jam, all he could wonder at was the unbelievabe chaos. Donkeys, trucks, bicycles, a camel. So many, *too* many people milling aimlessly about, overflowing from the sidewalks and streaming through the banks of stalled cars. He had heard that overpopulation was one of Egypt's most pressing problems. He had read that the population had nearly doubled over the past twenty years. And it had seemed to him that an astounding percentage of that population had been crowding these very streets. By the light of jittery neon, he had studied these Egyptians. They were short, round, and—yes!—as fat as they used to be. Maybe a little shabbier. But—*el-hamdulillah!*—they were still smiling as they surged in gabbling packs around the open doors of garishly lit shops. Baruch's neighborhood, this Sayeda Zainab, was a teeming slum. Goats roamed the streets feeding on the garbage. Youssef's thoughts had turned to the inoculations he had endured for small-pox, cholera, yellow fever, typhoid, and tetanus. He had already begun taking his malaria pills, and he had insisted that his doctor give him a shot of gamma globulin to ward off the possibility of hepatitis. But there had been no serum to counteract his shock that in this day and age human beings—and in particular his own Uncle Baruch—still had to live in this medieval way.

Youssef had at last found the tenement that was Baruch's. Uncertainly he had mounted the broken-down stairs to his uncle's room. The odor of rancid oil had drifted from the kitchens into the stairway. The slums of Jerusalem's Musrara were luxury housing compared to this. How, Youssef had thought, could Baruch live *here?*

But at the end of a hallway he had knocked on a door, and all that had mattered was that Uncle Baruch had opened it. Uncle Baruch! Youssef had fallen into his thin arms, had kissed his parchment cheeks, then had looked at his uncle's worn face. Twenty-one additional years were etched on it. Baruch had jowls, a bristly gray beard, and count-less wrinkles all around his eyes and mouth. But those eyes were nearly the same: sadder but just as gentle and brimming with compassion and concern. Yes, it was still Uncle Baruch.

Sitting at the bare wooden table, drinking the sweet black tea in the thick cheap glasses, they both had been eager to slide back into their old intimacy. But it had been hard to compress two lost decades into a few joyous hours of confidences, especially when so much of what had happened in the interval turned on death. Youssef had told the details of how his parents and Daoud had died. Baruch had faltered and wept when he told of Abbas's bloody end, and Youssef had not understood at all when Baruch had described his friend's death as his own true embrace of Islam.

It was then, wanting so much to make his uncle happy, that Youssef had opened his suitcase and pulled out great wads of American hundred-dollar bills from their hiding paces in the toes of his shoes. He had said this thirty thousand dollars was just the beginning. If Baruch wanted to leave Egypt, Youssef would see that he lived in comfort in Jerusalem or Rome or London. Baruch had shaken his head. Well, then. Youssef would open an account at the Credit Suisse and keep transferring money into it as long as Baruch lived. He could buy a decent flat or set himself up in a private medical practice or buy back the Villa al-Masri.

Hesitantly then, still not touching the crisp green bills, Baruch had begun to talk of the tragedies that had finally drawn Youssef home. He had tried to describe Mona's life in Karnak—the lies she had lived, the fears she had known, the ghastly night when Um Mona had given Ali the knife. He had talked about Ali, how they'd lived together in this very room, what Ali had said to him on the night he had left for the Lebanon. Finally, in a voice that sounded almost detached, Baruch had said that he, too, had loved Mona for many years. He had asked her to marry him many times. His dream was to go and live with her to the end of his days, *inshallah,* in Karnak village.

Later, as Youssef had lain unsleeping in the narrow bed that had been his son's, he had despaired of ever being able to make any of this right. He hadn't expected this journey to be all jasmine and romance. But neither had he been prepared for . . . all this. For Mona to have endured what she had endured! For his son's end to have been as it was! Her letter had not quite told the whole painful story. And what about this curious passion of Baruch's for Mona? If she felt the same, why had she asked him to come? Vaguely, illogically, he had imagined Mona and Baruch and all of Egypt frozen in place as he had left them. But if Baruch was so much older, what was Mona? How had living under her mother's insidious control in that backward village changed her? After all that had happened, how could anything between the two of them ever be entirely honorable? Maybe it was mad to have come here for her. But it would have been criminal not to have come.

Youssef had tossed and turned. Foreign street sounds had wafted in from the open window. Cairo's cats had howled and shrieked. In the dead of the night the donkey carts of the garbage collectors had creaked along the cobblestones. Loudspeaker calls to moonlight prayers had whined at clocklike intervals. He was a stranger to these sounds, and he was a stranger to Egypt.

The next morning, after sending a telegram to Mona, Baruch and Youssef had taken a walk through the streets of Cairo. In broad daylight, looking at the evidence of how far this city had fallen, Youssef had been embarrassed for Cairo. Everywhere there had been banks of rubble. Ragged children had played with stones and sticks. The rubber sandals of the poor had flopped along sidewalks that long ago had been tramped to bits. Drifting grains of sand had worked their way inside Youssef's custom-made shoes. The noise of the horns had given him a headache. His eyes had burned in air thick with the fumes of millions of abused cars and trucks.

Still he had found grace and beauty on the faces of the people in the streets. To a man and a woman, they had had the particular creases and crevices that could be formed only by lifetimes of suffering. Yet at the same time they had been good-natured as they smiled and joked and sauntered on their ways. Absentmindedly they had seemed not to notice that everything all around them had crumbled.

Finally, sitting with Baruch in the Fishawi café, sipping sweet and silty coffee, Youssef had asked how these people could stand it. Baruch had smiled and sighed and shrugged and said that Youssef wouldn't understand.

Yet Youssef had tried to understand. He had blamed everything— the poverty, the disease, the lack of progress—on the fatalism of Islam. Baruch had lit another of Youssef's American cigarettes, he had inhaled deeply, and yet he had not answered. Again Youssef had repeated his attack on the fatalism of Islam. He had called it both the saving grace and damnation of Egyptians. He had said the fatalism of Islam might have allowed them to accept the random blows of their lives without going mad, but hadn't it also kept them from trying to make their lives better?

Baruch had leaned back in his chair and regarded his nephew almost with amusement. Youssef, he had said, sounded just like himself ten or twenty years ago, when he had pestered Abbas with similar questions. Faith and fatalism. Baruch had said he had wanted to blame everything on faith and fatalism. Baruch had taken a sip of his coffee and said that now he knew better. He had tried to explain it all to Youssef. Religious Muslims *and* Christians *and* Jews and maybe even Buddhists always took comfort from explaining the inexplicable as part of God's mysterious will. When you couldn't see any other way out—when you couldn't do anything yourself to reverse the irreversible —there was always the answer of God's will. But Baruch had told Youssef to look around this very café. Day in and day out, he had said, men and women went about their business trying to better their lots— conniving and cheating and sometimes even being braver than anyone had any right to expect them to be. He had said Egypt was a poor country. That it was a nation of need. But he had told Youssef not to blame all the problems here on Islam.

Youssef had then reminded Baruch how Abbas's death had led him to what sounded like some sort of religious ecstasy of submission.

Baruch had sighed and praised the compassion of Allah. He had said his faith had allowed him to recover then, and that it would comfort him again if he needed to be comforted. But he had said that same faith never stopped him from thinking and acting and living like a man. He had tried to explain to Youssef that there were hidden freedoms in Allah's will. With enough confidence or cunning, any man could justify any action he took as an extension of Allah's will. After all, Baruch had said, nothing happened without Allah's will being done. Baruch had laughed, then, at Youssef's look of bewilderment. He had said, very kindly, that it was not necessary for Youssef to understand the intricacies of faith. But he wanted Youssef to know that his own faith made him not weaker but stronger. Baruch had indicated the Egyptians around him with a wave of his hand and said it was the same for all of them.

With envy Youssef had seen the faith that had always eluded him shining in Baruch's eyes. In Alexandria, Baruch had always wrestled so over the mysteries of the human condition. Had he degraded or transcended his former self when he had allowed himself to believe? Youssef had stared at the gummy residue in the bottom of his coffee cup. In the old days, *baladi* crones had said they could read the future in coffee grinds.

Oh, Egypt! Was Baruch's religious conversion just a surrender to this overload of the supernatural? Or was Baruch now, as he had always been, living several planes higher than Youssef could even comprehend? Impatiently Youssef had signaled for more coffee. Egypt was getting to him. How could any one place be so emotional? Why, here, was he finding it so hard to think logically and act decisively? What the hell was he doing, when he should be preparing to rescue Mona instead of sitting here asking himself about higher consciousness and coffee grinds and the miracles of faith? Yet, looking across the table,

Youssef had appreciated perhaps for the first time what he had here with this wise, decent, deep Uncle Baruch.

Remembering those backgammon games long ago in the al-Masri parlor, recalling Baruch giving him and Mona his blessing in the garden of the Beau Rivage, he had had an impulse to tell Baruch that maybe he *was* the one who was meant for Mona. The two of them—both good, honorable, *moral*—maybe belonged together. He himself was perhaps of another world. But the words had stuck unsaid in Youssef's craw, and he had shrugged. Despite what Baruch had told him about fatalism, it still seemed to Youssef that *inshallah* was the national sentiment. So, then, *inshallah*. She had sent for him, and he was here. Whatever was to happen between the two of them would happen. If she chose to stay here with Baruch, it would not be because he himself had abandoned her a second time.

In his room at the Beau Rivage, Youssef looked down at his chic Cartier watch again. He had bought it in a specialty shop near the Spanish Steps in Rome. The first Cartier he had ever seen was back at Victoria on the wrist of the son of the exiled king of Albania. He had wanted one as a boy, and as a man he had stood outside the jewelry store fighting his lust to have one of those absurdly expensive toys. In Israel he had grown accustomed to despising all such decadent trappings of the ruling class. But, furtively, he had finally gone inside the shop—just to look. The reptile band had coiled deliciously on his wrist. The Roman numerals on the oblong gold-rimmed face had glowed with smug sophistication. The guarantee, embossed in graceful lettering in a red leather case, had said it "sealed your alliance to the elite of the world. Throughout the five continents, the owners of Cartier watches can be recognized by their faultless taste. . . ." He had been insecure enough to buy it. As if Mona would be so *au courant* with Western fashions that she would be swayed by a Cartier watch! For good measure, his self-control totally gone, he had also purchased a gold Dunhill cigarette lighter. And then, finally admitting the real reason for coming inside this shop, he had bought two shining solid-gold wedding bands. He felt in his trouser pocket to assure himself they were still there.

He lit a cigarette. In fifteen minutes he would go to her. From his pocket he pulled out her letter and stared down at the spidery Arabic script. "I write to you after all these years because there is nothing else to be done. For more than twenty years I have kept my silence, trusting you would come to me as soon as it was possible. Sadat went to Jerusalem, Youssef! From Baruch I know only that you are still alive. The years have been. . . . We had a son, Youssef. Ali was born the autumn after you left me. Our son is dead. My mother finally told him about you, and his answer was that Fatah raid—perhaps you know of it?—in your country on March the eleventh. He was a good boy. He wanted to be a doctor, our son. Yours and mine. His body is still in Palestine—or Israel, as you must call it. Fatah wrote to me it is their practice not to ask for the return of their dead, so that they can forever remain on the soil for which they died. I beg you to have a *shaykh* read from the Koran over him. At least you are there, and so our son is not alone."

Remembering how he had followed her wishes, Youssef had a lump in his throat as he sat in his room at the Beau Rivage. Ali and the other terrorists had been buried in a Muslim cemetery in the old Arab city of Akko just north of Haifa. Youssef had accompanied the *shaykh* to the grave, he had listened to the rise and fall of the sonorous Arabic, and he had wept for the son he had never known.

He went back to Mona's letter. "I ask for one more thing. I ask you to come to me in Egypt. Perhaps I ask too much. Or perhaps I never asked enough. I know only that it is unfinished. Many things have changed—almost everything has changed—and yet *one thing*—you know *what one thing*—has not. I know that you will come. Baruch will send me a telegram when you arrive. I will meet you along the Corniche in Alexandria, where I last saw you, at two o'clock in the afternoon of the appointed day. As always—your gazelle."

Youssef folded the letter and tucked it back into his wallet. "Gazelle." Oh, God.

It was time to go. He had done as she had asked. He was here. He had come for her. He was going to ask her to marry him. They could do it in Egypt, in Israel, in Europe—anywhere she wanted. It was the only honorable response. His only condition would be that he could not possibly resettle in Egypt. He didn't trust all this talk of peace. The Egyptians would break their word. The Israelis would break their word. The other Arabs would do all they could to make sure that everyone broke his word. His old Egypt was gone, and he wasn't about to get trapped in the ruins. He was nervous even sitting in this hotel room. He would take Mona wherever she wanted. To Israel, to a reasonable Arab country like Tunisia, or even to Europe or America. Mona spoke French. Or at least Mona used to speak French. Maybe Paris or somewhere in the south of France would do. Money was no problem. He had spent little of what he had inherited from Leah.

He stood and paced, thinking of all the things that *were* a problem. Twenty years ago he had loved Mona with all that he was. He still treasured her memory. He had never loved another woman as he had Mona. But although he didn't know how he felt about her now, one thing was certain. No matter what he did, he would never be able to erase the guilt for what he had done to her. Even if he was excessively generous with himself, even if he could make himself believe he had been forced to leave her behind in Egypt, even if he had tried as hard as he could to return to her, even if no reasonable jury could hold him responsible for the death of a son he did not even know existed—still he was guilty. He had known how Arabs felt about a woman's virginity. He had known what Mona risked for him. Yet he had practically raped her that first time on the houseboat. Then later, after he had saved his own skin by leaving Egypt, the possible consequences of returning to his hostile homeland had outweighed his promises to the woman he truly loved. Was he *capable* of true love? If any one of his daughters wanted to marry a man like him, Youssef knew he would do all he could to persuade her against it.

Youssef shrugged on his jacket and walked over to the mirror on his closet door. He sucked in his stomach and looked appraisingly at the reflection of this man, pushing forty. No. He would be honest. A forty-three-year-old man with receding dark-blond hair, peppered with gray. A man fashionably, expensively turned out in this soft brown leather jacket, these well-creased black trousers, this brown cashmere turtleneck sweater that exactly matched the color of his eyes. He looked at those eyes. They weren't clear or innocent eyes. They weren't the eyes of a man who could look at himself without flinching. Could Mona love a man like this? Could she still love him after all that had happened? Would she even *want* to marry him? Youssef peered at himself in the mirror. It was an old mirror, worn away in spots, shadowed by age. Perhaps the mirror, too, was deceptive. Maybe Mona would see a different Youssef. She had always believed he was more than he was. But that wouldn't be good enough anymore. He no longer wanted his woman to love what she *thought* he could be. He shook his head at himself. There was no way out of this one. He could be happy only with a woman who loved him as he was, and yet what woman could love what he *was*? Mona would either see him realistically and have to despise him, or she would persist in thinking she loved what he had once been for her.

He smoothed down his jacket, lit another cigarette, and went out the door to meet her.

Mona shivered where she stood waiting on the seaside of the Corniche. She was a few minutes early. She pulled her long black robe around her more closely and looked down at the seven-month-old baby in her arms. Their grandchild—the living link of what had been between them—lay curled asleep against her breasts. Soad's milk had dried up when she learned of Ali's death. In the shock of all those deaths—her father's, her husband's, her aunt's—Soad had sat day after day with a transparent white veil over her face, mumbling the Holy Words of the Koran. As Mona had assumed the care of the baby herself, she had often imagined it was not her granddaughter but her son she held in her arms. She couldn't help bringing the baby to this rendezvous. It was too late to present Youssef with their son. The little girl might be all they had left to share.

She waited by Rushdi Beach where the al-Masris had always crossed on their way from the villa to the sea. This morning, trying to recapture the past, she had stood on the sidewalk outside what had been the Villa al-Masri. She had seen a clothesline full of laundry strung across what had been the silk-and-velvet drawing room. A *baladi* woman, dressed like Mona in a long black robe, had shuffled out the door with one baby in her arms and two small children trailing by her side. From an open window, from what had been Youssef's room, had drifted the shouts of a man and a woman arguing over money. She had been glad to turn away and go back to Khadiga's to wait out the hours until she was to meet Youssef. She had drunk tea and shared gossip with Khadiga. After Abbas died, Khadiga had married a tailor. Her son by Abbas was a clerk at the Customs House. She had three more sons and two daughters by the tailor. Her house was sparkling clean. Khadiga had baked her own honey cakes for Mona's visit. Khadiga, unlike herself, had dreamed small dreams and then made the best of what Allah had willed her.

It was cold on the Corniche. Surely Youssef would come soon.

Maybe, Mona thought, maybe he's been here already and didn't recognize me. Maybe I didn't recognize him. Maybe we passed each other by. Maybe he's gone away again.

She wondered how she would seem to him. This morning she had looked at herself in Khadiga's mirror and tried to see herself as Youssef would. It had been so long since she had appraised herself as a man might. She had been not quite sixteen when they had parted. Now she was thirty-seven—maybe too old, and that mattered to men. Her body, she thought, hadn't changed all that much, although no one could tell in her long black robe. She had been slim before, and she was slim still. But her face had aged. It was so dry in Karnak. Standing before the mirror, she had touched her cheek with a finger. When Youssef had seen her last, when Youssef had last touched her, her skin had been so soft. It was soft no more. Even worse than the texture were the wrinkles. There were tiny lines around her eyes and deeper laugh and frown creases on both sides of her mouth. She grinned with her lips, and her dimples were craters in her cheeks. She had considered buying cosmetics. She could use henna to coat those bristly gray hairs on the top of her head. Maybe Youssef wouldn't notice the wrinkles if she put kohl around her eyes and rouged her cheeks and lips. Finally, regretfully, thinking of Leah al-Masri, she had decided against all that. Women of her age who painted themselves were pathetic. She would face Youssef as she was. She had also thought of borrowing money from Khadiga to buy a pretty dress that showed off her figure. But what was the use? She was in mourning for Ali. A black Western dress or a black village robe wouldn't make that much difference. Youssef was coming to see *her*. It was too late for pretense. She was what she was.

Youssef was late. Mona didn't have a watch. But she knew when she had left Khadiga's, and she knew how long she had been standing on the Corniche. Youssef was late. Or maybe not. Perhaps he was sitting in one of those cars parked along the sidewalk. Maybe he hadn't said anything to her because to him she would look like just another peasant woman in black. She edged down the sidewalk. A light-skinned, light-haired man sat behind the wheel of the third car. She leaned over and tried to decide if he could be Youssef. The man dug in his pocket, slid over on the seat, and handed her ten piasters. "Take this, little mother, and may Allah's blessings be upon you."

She stared at the crumpled bill. This man thought she was a beggar woman. "Youssef?" she called, as the car pulled away from the curb. She leaned against a lamppost and shut her eyes. She shouldn't have written to Youssef. It would have been better never to have seen him again. It would have been better for him never to have seen her as she must look now. It would have been better to remember it as it once was.

Youssef scrambled out of the taxi and stood waiting to cross the street. It was not only because of the heavy traffic that he was late. Mona had told him to meet her again at their old rendezvous, but he had been up and down the Corniche trying to remember where that was. One crossroad, one worn stone bench, one overlook to the sea looked just like another. Praying that this, finally, was the right intersection, he scanned the sidewalk on the other side of the street. There were a few vendors, an old man walking with a cane, and a *baladi* woman in black. Maybe Mona was below, waiting on the beach for him.

He started across the street. The *baladi* woman was coming toward him. She held a baby in her arms. There was something familiar in the gentle sashay of her hips. He looked at her more closely as she approached. Maybe it was Mona? And the baby? Their son? Funny. He had thought for an instant that *baladi* matron was his Mona, and that she was carrying their son. The woman's face was hidden by the shawl loosely drawn over her head. He was almost upon her when she glanced up from the baby. Mona's honey amber eyes.

"Mona!" He took her arm, and she allowed herself to be steered back to the seaside of the Corniche.

They stood there for a moment looking into each other's eyes.

"Youssef?" She raised a hand as if to touch him, then uncertainly she dropped it. "Youssef?" He looked almost like Youssef. The build was right—maybe a little thicker, but just as tall. The walk was the same. But his hair was so dark. There wasn't enough of it. And his eyes. Youssef's eyes had changed. They were such weary eyes. Youssef had not had weary eyes before. Oh, Youssef. Her Youssef, too, had suffered. She had not thought he would bear the marks of suffering.

He stared back at her. The young woman who had been so like a gazelle was now, more than anything, like a statue he had admired in Rome. The statue of a woman grieving, a woman looking down at something in her arms. A mourning woman. A woman who had endured more than it was possible to endure. He did not trust himself to speak.

The baby was still asleep. "Ali's daughter." Nervously Mona gave the smile that was meant for Youssef to the baby. "Our grandchild."

He looked down at the baby. She was pretty and tiny, with skin as fair as his own.

"Our son married his cousin. Muhammad's daughter."

"What do you call her?" His voice was cracking like an adolescent's.

"Samahe. After my mother. She died, too. After Ali."

As he looked down at the baby, Youssef considered that name. *Samahe* was the Arabic for "forgiveness." From what he knew of Mona's mother, that name had been a mockery for her. But maybe Mona had chosen that name for this baby as a sign to him. "Forgiveness," he repeated. Again he looked into Mona's eyes. Before Mona had been beautiful because she had been born that way. She had been kitten-soft and so malleable he had been unable to keep his hands off her. The woman before him was different. Her face had not only weathered but had evolved into the face of another woman entirely. A deeply beautiful woman. The lines around her eyes and mouth had taken away some of her prettiness but given her the creases of character. Yet her eyes still had their clearness. In them was pain, doubt, and a puzzlement he could not quite gauge. "You named the baby after what is in your heart?" he finally asked.

The lines around Mona's eyes deepened. She had thought she would throw herself into his arms as soon as she saw him, but she had not. She had thought time would stand still and make them both young lovers again, but it had not. She tried to fight down a sudden welling anger at time, at him, at herself. "We will walk down the Corniche. It's cold standing here." Reproach crept into her voice. "I've been waiting, Youssef, for a long time."

He fell into step beside her as they headed the four miles toward the center of town. "I did as you asked. I went to the cemetery. The *shaykh* recited from the Koran over him. He's buried on a hill near the Mediterranean." They both looked out to sea. The sailboats had disappeared. The sea was calm and blue. "I'll take you to the gravesite. That is, if you want to come to Israel. We can live at Chozrim. At my kibbutz. Or I thought we might live in France. I want to marry you, Mona." Fear that she would refuse him harshened his voice. "It's the least I can do. I want to do the right thing."

Mona held the baby a little tighter. Israel? What was this talk of Israel? France? He wanted to take her to France? And he was saying he wanted to marry her because it was *the right thing to do?* Was that how he saw her? As some sort of moral obligation? She had thought he loved her.

"I come as soon as I could. It took a long while for your letter to get to me. And then I had to wait in Rome until I could get the right papers. I didn't want to take any chances."

Anger, budding deep inside her, spread to the long clipped stride of her legs. This man who walked beside her, this melancholy man who was not quite the Youssef she had remembered—what was he doing talking like this? This was not what she had expected. *Ansek!* I will never forget! Why had she sung that refrain all these lonely years for this anxious stranger? He had dishonored her, he had run away, and he had never tried to contact her. He wouldn't be here now if she hadn't written to him. *Begged him.* And he had the nerve to tell her that he didn't want to take any chances? "Once you took too many chances, Youssef."

He flushed and resolved to start again. She had a right to her anger. He tried to explain. "Mona, I'm sorry. I'm *so sorry.* I had no idea about Ali, about what your mother was doing to you. I wrote to Baruch from Israel. He told me you had gone back to Karnak with your mother. He said he thought you had married someone else in the village. He warned me not to come. He wouldn't even write to me again. I didn't want to put him in danger. I didn't want to make it any worse for you than I already had. If I had known about the baby—about our son—I swear to you that I would have come back for the two of you. I know how it looks. I know how you must feel."

"Do you, Youssef? Do you? I think not." She walked faster, and her words spilled out before she could stop them. "I waited for you, Youssef. I waited for twenty-one years for you. I thought you wouldn't forget. That you would come."

"I wanted to. God knows I wanted to. But what could I do?"

"Baruch told me what you did. How long was it, Youssef, until you married someone else? Six months, a year, two years? Three little girls. He said you had three little girls."

He wet his lips with his tongue. She knew about Rivka. But she didn't know how it had been with him and his wife. Desperately he tried to explain. "I never loved her as I loved you. The marriage was wrong from the beginning. And I'm divorced now. I'm free. I waited as long as I could Mona, before I married her. Before I gave up."

She glared at him. "You gave me up very easily, Youssef. But then maybe you didn't have it in you to do anything else. You've had a soft life, Youssef. Maybe that's the difference between you and me. *I* never gave up. *I* waited. *I* was faithful to what I promised you."

What answer, what excuse, could exonerate him? "I'm sorry," he said lamely. "I can't ask you to forgive what I can't even forgive myself. The worst was making love to you before we were married. I've had to live with that all my life. Nothing I ever do would ever make up for it. I'll never be free of that houseboat. It was wrong."

"Yes." She walked a few more paces more slowly, her rage warring with her tender memories of those fragile honeyweeks on the houseboat. After all those years dreaming of finally having him beside her, why was she fighting with him? "And yet, Youssef . . . the houseboat . . ."

"Yes?" He said it too quickly.

"Nothing." She wished she had not asked him to come. She wished she could walk away from him, sit down and compose herself, and then—maybe tomorrow, maybe after tomorrow—see him again and start all over on a new footing. There was so much to say to Youssef, and so far she had said none of it. She shifted the child in her arms.

"Let me carry her, Mona. I want to hold her. My granddaughter. And she must be heavy. We've walked a long way."

Mona's spine stiffened, and she was angry again. "I carried *our* child alone. He was heavier. I'm used to it. I'll carry this one by myself, too."

Youssef sighed deeply. She was right. He didn't deserve any more from her. If she had fallen into his arms, if she had eagerly agreed to forgive him and go with him wherever he asked, he wouldn't have had much respect for her. There was not to be a hasty grafting over of all the wrongs of the past. He would have to feel his way along with this angry new Mona. He knew so little about her. "What was it like, Mona? All those years, back in the village? You know, I never even *saw* your village. I tried to imagine it. So many times I tried to imagine you in Karnak. And I couldn't. Maybe that's why I finally married Rivka. You were gone from me. You were in a different world."

She had heard that sigh. In a way, at least a little, he must understand. The lines around her mouth softened. She would tell him how it was. "Of course, the village is by the river. The village is brown. The river is sometimes blue, sometimes green, sometimes gray, sometimes black." She glanced over at the sea. "It's never as blue as that. At first Karnak seemed a grave to me. So tight and dead. I slept and slept. Then Ali was born. It was better then. I wasn't alone." She looked down at Samahe. She was still not alone. "He was a good boy. He had dark skin like my father and dark hair like me. But he moved like you.

He had your nature. He was very brave. It was as if I had you with me."
She shut her lips firmly to stop their trembling. She must not falter
into vulnerability again. Remember, she told herself, what this man
did to you. Remember his lies. Remember his wife. But she couldn't
help wondering: If she had the father back, could it be almost like having the son as well?

"Tell me more about Ali."

"He had a quick mind. He worked hard. Everyone liked him. He
was like you in that way, too. He was training to be a doctor in Cairo.
In a few more years, he would have been back in the village with me.
We would have worked in the clinic together."

"Baruch told me that you were—no, are—a nurse."

"A *daya*. A midwife. They do me the honor of calling me Shaykha
Mona. But what do they know?" She sighed. "I thought, you know,
that if I was very good, if I helped everyone, maybe that would make
up for what I did . . . with you."

Youssef smiled eagerly. "It was like that with me, too, in a way. For
a long while I worked there in the slums with the immigrants. But at
first I hated Israel. All I thought of was getting out of there and back
to you. I had to go in the army, but—"

"I was so afraid Ali would grow up and go to war, and that you two
would kill each other. I thought it was the worst that could happen.
That's one of the reasons why I didn't marry anyone else. If I had had
more sons, Ali might have been drafted. But as it was, he was an only
son. So at least, I thought, the worst *couldn't* happen. That's funny,
isn't it? The worst did happen, but in a way I didn't imagine."

"You said that was *one* of the reasons you didn't marry. And the
others?"

She would not answer except for a hint of a smile. It was the first
time today that Youssef had seen her lips curl up in a smile. She was
radiantly beautiful when she smiled. He smiled back at her.

He looked, Mona thought, more like himself when he smiled. He
looked younger. Not as young as before, of course. She remembered,
with a tremor, how she had once thought she could never tire of looking up at him. Allah! For the first time it fully hit her that this was
Youssef.

"I told you once what the ancients called this bay. Do you remember, Mona?"

"You said it was the Harbor of Happy Return."

"I was wrong. I've found out since that I was wrong. The bay over
where the shipping docks are now was the Harbor of Happy Return.
It seems I never could get anything exactly right."

She saw the tears in his eyes, and the memories flooded back. Sitting
with Youssef and Batata at Agami, and his telling her she was as pretty
as the moon. That calèche ride when he had fingered the Evil Eye bead

471

and warned her he was bad luck. The walks through Cairo, the horseback ride at the pyramids, the houseboat. . . . She sighed.

"I was a soldier," Youssef said. "But I was an Israeli soldier who never fought. It's odd that you worried about my meeting our son on the battlefield. I didn't know about Ali. But I did know—I somehow knew—that I couldn't go to war against the people and the country I loved. I sat out the war in an office, translating speeches from the Voice of Cairo."

She raised her eyebrows. He sounded sincere. Perhaps he had not entirely forgotten her and the life they had shared.

"It was when Daoud died that everything changed for me. He died in the '67 war. In Jerusalem."

"Baruch told me. Daoud was always such a good boy. I think he must have been a good man."

"He was the best. *The best.* When he died, I had no one and nothing left from my life in Egypt. I took a long, hard look at myself. And I didn't like what I was. Maybe I never liked what I was, Mona. I made so many mistakes."

She kept silent but listened carefully to what Youssef wanted to tell her.

"I decided that it was about time I started being the man I was supposed to be. The man I could be. It was after the '67 war. I was living on a kibbutz. Everyone was so . . . smug about winning the war."

"Three boys from our village died in that war."

"Yes. Everyone on the kibbutz turned against me then. They said I was a traitor—that I was more Arab than Jew. And all I had suggested was that we bring in some boys from the Gaza refugee camps for the day. We were just a few miles from Gaza."

"Gaza. Ali loved a boy from Gaza. His name was Karim. He died with Karim on that raid."

Youssef winced. "What do you mean, our son loved a boy? Ali was a *homosexual?* You're telling me that our son was *like that?*"

"You remember love, Youssef. Ali loved Karim. It was *like that.* Or at least that's what Baruch told me. But Ali was married to his cousin Soad. He loved her, too. I like to think he had enough love for both Karim and Soad."

With an effort Youssef returned to his own past. "After all that trouble after the war, I divorced my wife and left the kibbutz. I went to Jerusalem. I took a job as a social worker. That's what Daoud used to be. My job was with the Jews who came to Israel from the Arab countries. Mostly I worked with Moroccans. They weren't exactly like Egyptians. But sometimes I pretended that I had never really left. It was the closest that I could get to home. And you know, Mona, in the back of my mind, I told myself that every time I helped somebody, every time I helped a man to get a job or a woman to take her child to a doctor, I was making up, at least a little, for all my mistakes." Youssef smiled disparagingly. "I figure that if I keep on like this, by the time I'm a very old man, maybe I'll be able to look at myself in a mirror."

Mona thought that he wasn't talking like the old Youssef. She looked at him out of the corner of her eye. "But you said you live on a kibbutz."

"After the *next* war, in '73, Rivka married again and left the kibbutz. Then some of the members invited me back. They even said that maybe I had been right when I wanted them to try to reconcile with the Arabs after the Six Day War. At least for Kibbutz Chozrim, maybe it was a good thing that Israel very nearly lost the Yom Kippur War. I suppose you can learn more from defeat sometimes than victory."

She thought he was probably referring more to themselves than to their countries.

"You know, Mona, before I left to come here, in the dining hall, in the corridors of the school, in the fields, everyone asked me to find out in Egypt if the people here want peace as much as the people of my kibbutz want peace. Not that everyone in Israel is dying for peace. The Begin government, those religious fanatics who want to annex all the occupied territories, most of our hard-line generals—I don't think they want peace. But on my kibbutz—yes!—they want it more than you can imagine. Is it the same here?"

"We're tired of war. We're tired of blood. More I cannot say." She tried to imagine the men and women of Karnak absurdly bustling about talking of war and peace instead of money and crops. She shrugged slightly. She had not summoned him to Alexandria for a summit conference. "Tell me more about your family."

"My three girls live with me on the kibbutz. The oldest is getting married this spring. I named her Ayala—the Hebrew for 'gazelle.' I named her after you, Mona."

"After me!" He had given his pet name for her to the daughter of another woman? She wanted to believe that was an act of love and not a betrayal.

"I did. And so here I am. Back in Alexandria. Walking down the Corniche with you. I was a rich young man when I was here last. And then I was poor, really poor, for many years. But when Mother died, she left me her money. So here I am again—rich, but not so young."

She felt a little sorry for Youssef. His years away from her had not been so easy after all. She wanted to take his hand in a gesture of affection and sympathy. *To touch Youssef's hand.* His hand. But she was afraid of that touch. Her composure could crack if she touched him. It was better to keep her distance.

They were approaching a casino built on pilings over the sea. "Tea? At least, Mona, you will allow me to buy you some tea?" First she politely refused. Then she allowed him to lead her out on the deck. They sat at a table facing the water.

She looked out as the outgoing tide receded on the beaches. "I haven't seen the sea for years. Not since I lived here. It's so different from the river. I sit by the river every night, watching it rush north. And this is where it ends." The baby was awake and gurgling. Mona smiled down at Samahe as their sweet black tea arrived. "She must be hungry. I'll have to go soon." She stirred the tea until the sugar danced. "So when will you be leaving? And where will you go?"

"That depends, Mona, on whether you leave with me or not." When she ignored his implied question, he sighed. "Home for me now is my kibbutz. I suppose it's about time that I try to *do* something with my time and my money. I still don't know what, exactly, but there has to be something I can at least try to do to make a difference. There's so much talk of peace now. I like to think that perhaps there's some real hope, now, of a final settlement between Arabs and Jews. It was that hate, you know, Mona, that ruined our lives. It was that hate that killed our son."

Mona sipped her tea. If Youssef wanted to blame the world for their own mistakes, she would let him.

"Tell me, Mona, do you regret what we did?"

Regret. How, she asked herself, could she regret Youssef? Years ago she had decided he was the music of her life. No, she could never regret him. As she shook her head very slightly, her shawl slipped to her shoulders.

He looked at the gray hairs mixed in with the dark. It had been such a long time ago that they had loved. But he was encouraged by her lack of regrets. And he remembered that it was an Arab custom always to refuse a first offer, whether it be of a glass of tea or the price of a copper pot or even a marriage proposal. He pulled what he hoped was their future from his pocket. He opened the red leather boxes and showed her the twin gold wedding rings. "I'd like you to come with me, Mona. I came here to ask you that. To come away and marry me. To see if we can start again. But I don't know if you could do that. If you could love me as I am. After all I've done to you. But I always knew, Mona, that I could have been happy with you for all my life. Marry me, Mona."

She looked at the gold band that she had never taken off. She was about to answer him when the baby began to cry. Mona rocked her. Samahe was so warm and soft. Mona looked down at her. This baby, not this man, would be her life.

Yes, she loved Youssef. Of course she loved Youssef. But as she had listened closely to him, it was clear to her that love wasn't enough anymore for the two of them. Where could they live together—what sort of life could they share? Memories of youth and love and passion would not be enough. It sounded as if he belonged on that kibbutz, just as she belonged in Karnak. She couldn't live in the country of Ali's death, just as Youssef could never live without fear and dread here.

But, she thought, there was another man who could be her future. Her love for Baruch was different from her love for Youssef, but it was love just the same. How right it would be to live out her years beside Baruch on the banks of the Nile. They could work and pray and dream together in the peace of Karnak. Yes, she would marry Baruch.

Mona looked down at the baby. Ali's daughter might even matter more to her than either Youssef or Baruch. Unconsciously Mona echoed her own mother's thoughts on the day of her circumcision: It will be different for Samahe. It will be better for her than it was for me, and my mother, and my mother's mother.

She would tell Youssef no.

But then she looked out at the calm steady sea. The breeze was in her face. The sun was almost to the horizon. Yes, she thought. It will be different for this baby than it was for me and my mother and my mother's mother. But it can be different for *me,* too. Perhaps.

Yet, still, she would have to forget so very much. And what guarantees were there that it would be different this time with Youssef? He wanted to take her away from Egypt. Once that might have been possible. She looked down at her black peasant's robe. She no longer believed in miracles, and it would be a miracle if she could cast off this robe and become a foreign lady walking the boulevards of Paris on Youssef's arm. That would be living a lie, and she had no more stomach for lies. Her life and Youssef's life were as different in depths and currents as the river was from the sea. Yet the Nile ran into the sea . . .

No, she loved Youssef too much to try to attempt to recapture the past with him.

They could not possibly be man and wife. But there was something they could still give to each other. There was something still unfinished.

She thought of her mother. When Ummie had been only a child and her own mother died, she had closed her heart. She had hugged her hurt to herself, she had fed upon it, and in the end she had been devoured by it. Her mother had never been able to forgive.

Mona looked over at Youssef, at this man she had loved so long, at this man she had dreamed of so much no mortal man could ever match those dreams. He was less and yet more than she had expected. She had been wrong when she had said he'd had a soft life. He had not had an easy time of it in Israel, and yet it seemed he had either found or was groping his way toward a peace of his own making. Once Youssef had needed her to make him whole. But—although it seemed that perhaps he didn't know it—Youssef no longer needed her for that. More than anything, it seemed to her that he was a decent man. He, too, had suffered much.

She cast a yearning look at Youssef. Maybe, just maybe . . .

No. They could take only one last step together, and then they would have to go their separate ways. But she could at least give him one last thing before he went on his way alone.

The baby was howling. The next time Youssef reached out to hold Samahe, Mona smiled and let him take forgiveness in his arms.

ABOUT THE AUTHOR

LAURIE DEVINE brings a distinguished career in journalism to the writing of *Nile,* a career that has encompassed regular contributions to the *Boston Sunday Globe*'s book pages, freelance reporting in Boston for *Newsweek* and in Cairo for the North American News Alliance. For five years she wrote and produced newscasts for Boston's WBZ-TV.

Of *Nile*'s genesis Laurie Devine says, "In 1979 I took a two-week holiday in Egypt, sailing down the Nile in a small primitive boat, camping out at night on islands in the river. I fell in love with Egypt and simply *had* to return to write about these people and this place." Her extensive research for the novel required that she live in Egypt for one-and-a-half years, making numerous trips to villages in Upper Egypt, at least as many forays into Alexandria, and two extended trips to Israel.

Laurie Devine is currently living near Pittsburgh, but will shortly return to the Middle East to begin research for her next book.